abled. Plaintiffs primarily used the Rehabilitation Act of 1973 (29 U.S.C.A. § 701 et seq.), the earliest law of this type. But the Rehabilitation Act has a limited scope: it applies only to federally funded workplaces and institutions, and says nothing about those that do not receive government money.

With passage of the ADA in 1990, Congress gave broad protection to people with AIDS who work in the private sector. In general, the ADA is designed to increase access for disabled persons, and it also forbids discrimination in hiring or promotion in companies with fifteen or more employees. Specifically, employers may not discriminate if the person in question is otherwise qualified for the job. Moreover, they cannot use tests to screen out disabled persons, and they must provide reasonable accommodation for disabled workers. The ADA, which took effect in 1992, has quickly emerged as the primary means for bringing AIDS-related discrimination lawsuits.

AIDS and Health Care Closely related to work is the issue of health care. In some cases, the two overlap: health insurance, Social Security, and disability benefits for AIDS victims were often hard to obtain during the 1980s. Insurance was particularly difficult because employers feared rising costs and insurance companies did not want to pay claims. To avoid the costs of AIDS, insurance companies used two traditional industry techniques: they attempted to exclude AIDS coverage from general policies, and they placed caps (limits on benefits payments) on AIDS-related coverage.

In January 1995, the settlement in a lawsuit brought by a Philadelphia construction worker with AIDS illustrated that the ADA can be used to fight caps on coverage. In 1992, the joint union-management fund for the Laborers' District Council placed a $10,000 limit on AIDS benefits, in stark contrast to the $100,000 allowed for other catastrophic illnesses. At that time, the fund said the cap on AIDS benefits was designed to curb all health care costs. In 1993, the EEOC ruled that it violated the ADA, and, backed by the AIDS Law Project of Philadelphia, the worker sued. Rather than fight an expensive lawsuit, the insurance fund settled.

AIDS and Education Issues in the field of education include the rights of HIV-positive students to attend class and of HIV-positive teachers to teach, the confidentiality of HIV records, and how best to teach young people about AIDS. A few areas have been settled in court: for instance, the right of students to attend classes was of greater concern in the early years of the epidemic, and no longer remains in dispute.

Certain students with AIDS may assert their right to public education under the Education for All Handicapped Children Act of 1975 (EAHCA), but the law is only relevant in cases involving special education programs. More commonly, students' rights are protected by the Rehabilitation Act.

Schools play a major role in the effort to educate the public on AIDS. Several states have mandated AIDS prevention instruction in their schools. But the subject is controversial: it evokes personal, political, and moral reactions to sexuality. During the 1980s, those who often criticized liberal approaches to sex education argued that AIDS materials should not be explicit, encourage sexuality, promote the use of contraceptives, or favorably portray gays and lesbians.

Civil Litigation TORT law has seen an explosion of AIDS-related suits. This area of law is used to discourage individuals from subjecting others to unreasonable risks, and to compensate those who have been injured by unreasonably risky behavior. The greatest number of AIDS-related LIABILITY lawsuits has involved the receipt of HIV-infected blood and blood products. A second group has concerned the sexual transmission of HIV. A third group involves AIDS-related psychic distress. In these cases, plaintiffs have successfully sued and recovered damages for their fear of having contracted HIV.

CROSS-REFERENCES

Disabled Persons; Discrimination; Food and Drug Administration; Gay and Lesbian Rights; Health Care; Patients' Rights; Physicians and Surgeons; Privacy.

ALLRED, GLORIA Gloria Allred, born July 3, 1941, in Philadelphia, is a flamboyant, widely recognized lawyer, feminist, activist, and radio talk show host. Though her critics dismiss her as a publicity monger and a dilettante, Allred has received praise from others who believe that she is a master at using the power of the news media to draw attention to the day-to-day struggles of ordinary people.

Born Gloria Rachel Bloom, Allred grew up in Philadelphia with her parents, Morris Bloom, a door-to-door salesman, and Stella Davidson Bloom, a homemaker. Her conventional middle-class childhood gave no hint of the outspoken activist to come. Allred graduated with honors from the University of Pennsylvania in 1963 with a bachelor's degree in English. She moved to New York to pursue a master's degree in teaching at New York University. Wh[...] interested in the CIVIL RIGHT[...] was beginning to gain mom[...] her master's degree in 19[...]

BIOGRAPHY

Gloria Allred

Annotation labels:

Cross-references at end of article

Timeline for subject of biography, including general historical events and life events

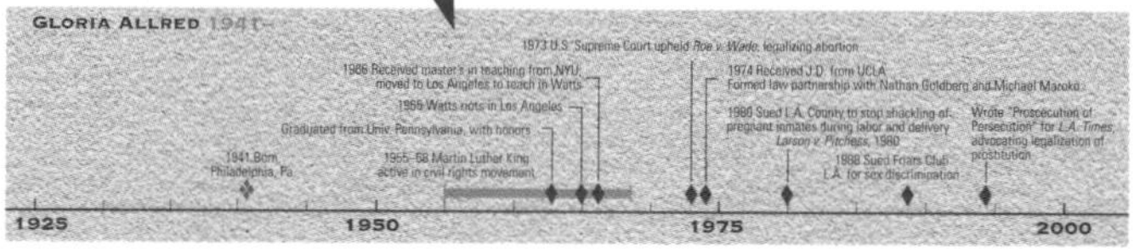

Biography of contributor to American law

Internal cross references

Quotation from subject of biography

Full cite for case

Definition enclosed in book logos with Latin translation provided

---

GLORIA ALLRED 1941–

1973 U.S. Supreme Court upheld Roe v. Wade legalizing abortion

1966 Received master's in teaching from NYU, moved to Los Angeles to teach in Watts

1974 Received J.D. from UCLA, formed law partnership with Nathan Goldberg and Michael Maroko

1965 Watts riot in Los Angeles

1986 Sued L.A. County to stop shackling of pregnant inmates during labor and delivery Lenora v. Pacheco, 1986

Wrote "Prosecution of Trespasser" for L.A. Times advocating legalization of prostitution

Graduated from Univ. Pennsylvania, with honors

1941 Born Philadelphia, Pa.

1965 Dr. Martin Luther King active in civil rights movement

1988 Sued From Club L.A. for sex discrimination

1925   1950   1975   2000

Philadelphia to teach at a high school with a predominantly black enrollment.

Allred says her interest in the struggle for equal rights arose from personal experiences. While she was in college, she married, gave birth to a daughter, and divorced. Unable to collect CHILD SUPPORT from her former husband, she was forced to return to her parents' home. She also recalls being paid less than a man for what she considered equal work. The reason given was that the man had a family to support, but at the time, Allred was the single mother of an infant.

After moving to California, Allred taught in the turbulent Watts section of Los Angeles and became the first full-time female staff member in United Teachers of Los Angeles, the union representing Los Angeles teachers. The experience stirred her interest in CIVIL RIGHTS and collective bargaining and prompted her to go to law school. She received her law degree, with honors, from Loyola Marymount University, Los Angeles, Law School in 1974. Soon after, she entered a law firm partnership with her classmates Nathan Goldberg and Michael Maroko.

Allred is probably the most flamboyant and well known member of her firm. She has achieved notoriety and name recognition through staged press conferences and demonstrations publicizing and dramatizing the cause she is championing at the time. She also accepts controversial cases that naturally attract media attention. During her years in practice, she has successfully sued Los Angeles County to stop the practice of shackling and chaining pregnant inmates during labor and delivery; put a halt on the city of El Segundo's quizzing job applicants about their sexual histories (*Thorne v. City of El Segundo*, 802 F.2d 1131 [9th Cir. 1986]); represented a client who was turned down for a job as a police officer after a six-hour lie detector exam that included questions about her sex life; and sued a dry cleaning establishment for discrimination because it charged more to launder women's shirts than men's.

Allred relishes confrontation, and her showy tactics have earned her both praise and criticism.

"THERE ARE ENOUGH HIGH HURDLES TO CLIMB, AS ONE TRAVELS THROUGH LIFE, WITHOUT HAVING TO SCALE ARTIFICIAL BARRIERS CREATED BY LAW OR SILLY REGULATIONS."

Defending what many have called self-promoting publicity stunts, Allred says she tries to use the few moments she is in the spotlight to make her point as forcefully as possible. Her detractors say that she wastes her time and energy on trivial issues that do not advance any worthwhile cause and deflect attention away from serious issues. Yet, she points out, she is often stopped on the street by people who recognize her and want to thank her for taking on the small fights that no one else wants.

Some critics say she is all show and no substance. But Allred has many supporters as well. Among them is Justice Joan Dempsey Klein, of the California Court of Appeal, who credits Allred with moving women's issues forward. Klein also points out that Allred saves her dramatics for outside the courtroom and always observes proper decorum when before the bench. According to Klein, Allred is always well-prepared and, for that reason, is quite successful.

Dressed in her trademark reds and electric blues, her striking black hair set off by deep red lipstick, Allred is a potent combination of scholarship and theatrics. Her keen intelligence and shrewd understanding of the power of the media have made her a contemporary success story in the world of law and politics.

ARBITER [*Latin, One who attends something to view it as a spectator or witness.*] Any person who is given an absolute power to judge and rule on a matter in a dispute.

WEST'S
ENCYCLOPEDIA
of
AMERICAN
LAW

WEST'S ENCYCLOPEDIA *of* AMERICAN LAW

Volume 5

WEST GROUP

This encyclopedia is the result of efforts by numerous individuals and entities from the Twin Cities and around the United States. West Group wishes to thank all who made this publication, its quality and content, a priority in their lives.

In addition to the individuals who worked on *West's Encyclopedia of American Law*, West Group recognizes Harold W. Chase (1922–1982) for his contributions to *The Guide to American Law: Everyone's Legal Encyclopedia*.

COPYRIGHT ©1998 By
    WEST GROUP
    610 Opperman Drive
    P.O. Box 64526
    St. Paul, MN 55164-0526
All rights reserved
Printed in the United States of America
05 04 03 02 01 00 99 98   8 7 6 5 4 3 2 1 0
Library of Congress Cataloging in
    Publication Data
ISBN: 0-314-20158-0 (Hard)

West's encyclopedia of American law.
        p.   cm.
    Includes bibliographical references and
    indexes.
    ISBN 0-314-20158-0 (hard   :
    alk. paper)
    1. Law—United States—Encyclopedias.
    2. Law—United States—Popular works.
    I. West Publishing Company.
KF154.W47   1997
348.73′03 —dc20
[347.30803]   96-34350
                            CIP

PRODUCTION CREDITS
Cover, interior design, and page layout:
    David J. Farr, ImageSmythe
Composition: Carlisle Communications
Proofreading: Maureen Meyer
Photo research: Elsa Peterson Ltd.
Art research: Nanette E. Bertaut
Editorial research: Pat Lewis
Artwork: Patricia Isaacs, Parrot Graphics
Indexing: Schroeder Indexing Services

This publication is designed to provide information on the subjects covered. It is sold with the understanding that the publisher is not engaged in rendering legal or other professional advice. If legal advice or other professional assistance is required, the services of a competent professional person should be sought.

WEST'S COMMITMENT TO THE ENVIRONMENT

In 1906, West Publishing Company began recycling materials left over from the production of books. This began a tradition of efficient and responsible use of resources. Today, 100 percent of our legal bound volumes are printed on acid-free, recycled paper consisting of 50 percent new paper pulp and 50 percent paper that has undergone a de-inking process. We also use vegetable-based inks to print all of our books. West recycles nearly 27,700,000 pounds of scrap paper annually—the equivalent of 229,300 trees. Since the 1960s, West has devised ways to capture and recycle waste inks, solvents, oils, and vapors created in the printing process. We also recycle plastics of all kinds, wood, glass, corrugated cardboard, and batteries, and have eliminated the use of polystyrene book packaging. We at West are proud of the longevity and the scope of our commitment to the environment.

West pocket parts and advance sheets are printed on recyclable paper and can be collected and recycled with newspapers. Staples do not have to be removed. Bound volumes can be recycled after removing the cover.

Production, printing, and binding by West Group.

PREFACE

The legal system of the United States is admired around the world for the freedoms it allows the individual and the fairness with which it attempts to treat all persons. On the surface, it may seem simple. Yet, those who have delved into it know that this system of federal and state constitutions, statutes, regulations, and common-law decisions is elaborate and complex. It derives from the English common law, but includes principles older than England, and from other lands. Many concepts are still phrased in Latin. The U.S. legal system, like many others, has a language all its own. Too often it is an unfamiliar language.

In 1983, West published *The Guide to American Law. Everyone's Legal Encyclopedia*, in response to a dearth of reference sources weaving the language of the law into the language of everyday life. *West's Encyclopedia of American Law (WEAL)*, developed with generous feedback from users of *The Guide*, replaces that set as an improved and updated legal encyclopedia. *WEAL* is a reference source devoted to the terms and concepts of U.S. law. It also covers a wide variety of persons, entities, and events that have shaped the U.S. legal system. *WEAL* contains thousands of entries, and a number of unique features and visual aids. It is the most complete reference source of its kind.

Main Features of This Set

Entries This encyclopedia contains over 4,000 entries devoted to terms, concepts, events, movements, cases, and persons significant to U.S. law. Entries on legal terms contain a definition of the term, followed by explanatory text if necessary. Entries are arranged alphabetically in standard encyclopedia format for ease of use. A wide variety of additional features, listed later in this preface, provide interesting background and supplemental information.

Definitions Every entry on a legal term is followed by a definition, which begins and ends with the symbol of an open book (📖). The appendix volume includes a glossary containing all the definitions from the *WEAL*.

Cross-References To facilitate research, *WEAL* provides two types of cross-references, within and following entries. Within the entries, terms are set in small capital letters—for example, LIEN—to indicate that they have their own entry in the encyclopedia. At the end of the entries, related entries the reader may wish to explore are listed alphabetically by title.

In Focus Pieces In Focus pieces accompany related entries and provide additional facts, details, and arguments on particularly interesting, important, or controversial issues raised by those entries. The subjects covered include hotly contested issues, such as abortion, capital punishment, and gay rights; detailed processes, such as the Food and Drug Administration's approval process for new drugs; and important historical or social issues, such as debates over the formation of the U.S. Constitution. In Focus pieces are marked by the symbol that appears in the margin.

Sidebars Sidebars provide brief highlights of some interesting facet of accompanying entries. They complement regular entries and In Focus pieces by adding informative details. Sidebar topics include the Million Man March, in Washington, D.C., and the branches of the

IN FOCUS

U.S. armed services. Sidebars appear at the top of a text page and are set in a blue box.

Biographies WEAL profiles a wide variety of interesting and influential people—including lawyers, judges, government and civic leaders, and historical and modern figures—who have played a part in creating or shaping U.S. law. Each biography includes a time line, which shows important moments in the subject's life as well as important historical events of the period. Biographies appear alphabetically by the subject's last name.

Additional Features of This Set

Milestones in the Law A special section, Milestones in the Law, appearing at the end of selected volumes, allows readers to take a close look at landmark cases in U.S. law. Readers can explore the reasoning of the judges and the arguments of the attorneys that produced major decisions on important legal and social issues. Included in the Milestones section are the opinions of the lower courts; the briefs presented by the parties to the U.S. Supreme Court; and the decision of the Supreme Court, including the majority opinion and all concurring and dissenting opinions for each case.

Enhancements Throughout WEAL, readers will find a broad array of photographs, charts, graphs, manuscripts, legal forms, and other visual aids enhancing the ideas presented in the text.

Tables and Indexes WEAL features several detailed tables and indexes at the back of each volume, as well as a cumulative index contained in a separate volume.

Appendixes An appendix volume included with WEAL contains hundreds of pages of documents, laws, manuscripts, and forms fundamental to and characteristic of U.S. law.

Citations Wherever possible, WEAL entries include citations for cases and statutes mentioned in the text. These allow readers wishing to do additional research to find the opinions and statutes cited. Two sample citations, with explanations of common citation terms, can be seen below and opposite.

Bibliography A bibliography is included at the end of each book and in the index volume.

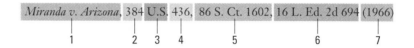

1. *Case title.* The title of the case is set in italics and indicates the names of the parties. The suit in this sample citation was between Ernesto A. Miranda and the state of Arizona.
2. *Reporter volume number.* The number preceding the reporter name indicates the reporter volume containing the case. (The volume number appears on the spine of the reporter, along with the reporter name.)
3. *Reporter name.* The reporter name is abbreviated. The suit in the sample citation is from the reporter, or series of books, called *U.S. Reports,* which contains cases from the U.S. Supreme Court. (Numerous reporters publish cases from the federal and state courts.)

4. *Reporter page.* The number following the reporter name indicates the reporter page on which the case begins.
5. *Additional reporter citation.* Many cases may be found in more than one reporter. The suit in the sample citation also appears in volume 86 of the *Supreme Court Reporter,* beginning on page 1602.
6. *Additional reporter citation.* The suit in the sample citation is also reported in volume 16 of the *Lawyer's Edition,* second series, beginning on page 694.
7. *Year of decision.* The year the court issued its decision in the case appears in parentheses at the end of the cite.

Brady Handgun Violence Prevention Act, Pub. L. No. 103-159, 107 Stat. 1536 (18 U.S.C.A. §§ 921–925A)

1   2   3   4   5   6   7   8

1. *Statute title.*
2. *Public law number.* In the sample citation, the number 103 indicates that this law was passed by the 103d Congress, and the number 159 indicates that it was the 159th law passed by that Congress.
3. *Reporter volume number.* The number preceding the reporter name indicates the reporter volume containing the statute.
4. *Reporter name.* The reporter name is abbreviated. The statute in the sample citation is from *Statutes at Large.*
5. *Reporter page.* The number following the reporter name indicates the reporter page on which the statute begins.

6. *Title number.* Federal laws are divided into major sections with specific titles. The number preceding a reference to the *U.S. Code Annotated* is the title number. Title 18 of the U.S. Code is Crimes and Criminal Procedure.
7. *Additional reporter.* The statute in the sample citation may also be found in the *U.S. Code Annotated.*
8. *Section numbers.* The section numbers following a reference to the *U.S. Code Annotated* indicate where the statute appears in that reporter.

continued

FENCES 📖 Enclosures composed of any substance that will present an adequate blockade around a field, yard, or other such expanse of land for the purpose of prohibiting intrusions from outside. 📖

A landowner is entitled to construct a fence along the BOUNDARIES of his or her property, but statutes may regulate the building and maintenance of fences. The laws of some states make provisions for the establishment of fence districts to erect and maintain fences. Fence districts are sometimes given the authority to levy taxes to absorb the costs of building and maintaining the fences.

Generally a landowner has the right to construct a partition fence on the border of the property adjoining his or her land. Owners of adjoining land may enter into agreements setting forth their rights and liabilities regarding the erection, maintenance, and repair of partition fences. State statutes sometimes govern landowners' obligations with respect to such fences. Such statutes differ from one JURISDICTION to another regarding what lands come within the scope of their regulation. Some of these statutes apply solely to agricultural lands, whereas others also control fences between urban lots. Unless otherwise provided by statute or agreement to the contrary, both parties share equally the duty to maintain the entire partition fence. Neither may allege that the other was neglectful. Various statutes permit a landowner to construct or repair the partition fence in its entirety upon a failure of an adjacent owner to build or repair his or her portion. Subsequently, the one owner may bring an action against the neighbor for a CONTRIBUTION toward the expenses incurred. Generally recovery is limited to half the expense of the fence. Some fence statutes provide that the amount recoverable from a defaulting property owner is made a LIEN on that owner's land.

Theoretically, the ideal location for a partition fence is along the boundary line between adjacent lands. Practically, substantial compliance with this requirement is adequate. An equal and reasonable amount of each owner's property may be used for construction of the structure.

A partition fence built on the boundary is deemed the joint property of adjacent landowners. For this reason, a property owner may not eliminate a partition fence without first obtaining the neighbor's consent. The laws of some states make removal of a partition fence by an owner of adjoining land contingent upon formal notice to other landowners. A landowner may bring an action for whatever damages are suffered if a fence has been improperly removed or destroyed. The standard for measuring damages for such removal or destruction is its value at the time, which is determined by replacement costs minus DEPRECIATION for age and use.

A property owner who causes injury to livestock through negligent maintenance of a fence will be held liable for resulting damages. A landowner who erects a barbed wire fence is not automatically liable to one whose livestock suffer injury. If, however, a barbed wire fence is so negligently maintained as to become a trap for passing livestock, the owner will be held liable for injuries even if the fence is entirely on his or her own property. A landowner who leaves barbed wire on the ground without protection

Although this fence may not prevent someone from walking onto the adjoining land, it shows the boundary of the owner's property.

after erecting a fence is liable to the owner of the adjacent land for injury to that owner's livestock.

If someone builds a fence on another person's land without any authority to do so, the landowner may remove or destroy such fence. An individual may not, however, remove or destroy a fence on another individual's land. A number of states impose criminal penalties on an individual who unlawfully fences the land of another.

See also ADJOINING LANDOWNERS.

FENWICK, MILLICENT VERNON HAMMOND

Millicent Vernon Hammond Fenwick, a Republican, represented New Jersey's Fifth District in Congress from 1975 to 1983 and distinguished herself as an outspoken crusader for human rights who defied conventional political labels.

Fenwick was born February 25, 1910, in Manhattan, to a wealthy and prominent family. Her father, Ogden H. Hammond, was a suc-

BIOGRAPHY

Millicent Vernon Hammond Fenwick

cessful financier. Her mother, Mary Picton Stevens Hammond, was descended from a distinguished early American family whose forebears included a colonel in the Revolutionary Army. The family was committed to public service. Fenwick's father carried out this commitment by serving two terms in the New Jersey House of Representatives and later as CALVIN COOLIDGE'S ambassador to Spain. Her mother was on a mission of mercy to establish a hospital for World War I victims in Paris when she perished in the 1915 sinking of the passenger ship *Lusitania*. At the time of her mother's death, Fenwick was five years old.

Fenwick's formal education was fragmentary. She attended the Foxcroft School, in Virginia, until age fifteen, when she left school to accompany her father to Spain. Fenwick briefly attended a convent school in Europe, and took courses at Columbia University's extension school after returning to the United States. In the late 1930s, she studied philosophy with Bertrand Russell at the New School for Social Research. Despite her lack of formal schooling, she was fluent in Spanish, French, and Italian.

Fenwick scandalized her family by falling in love with a married businessman, Hugh Fenwick. He divorced, and married Fenwick in 1934. The union did not last; and in 1938 Fenwick found herself divorced with two small children and her ex-husband's considerable debts. The Depression had devastated her family's assets, and Fenwick was forced to find a job in order to pay her creditors and support her children. She worked occasionally as a model for *Harper's Bazaar* before joining the writing staff of *Vogue* magazine, where she worked for fourteen years as a writer and editor. In 1948, she published Vogue's *Book of Etiquette*, of which a million copies were sold.

Fenwick's financial situation had improved dramatically by the time she left *Vogue* in 1952. She had always been interested in politics, and decided to expand her public service activities by running for the Bernardsville, New Jersey, Borough Council. She won a seat in 1958 and served for six years. Her concern for CIVIL

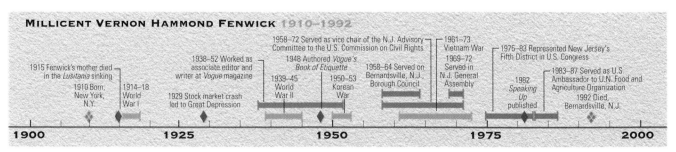

MILLICENT VERNON HAMMOND FENWICK 1910–1992

1915 Fenwick's mother died in the *Lusitania* sinking

1910 Born, New York, N.Y.

1914–18 World War I

1929 Stock market crash led to Great Depression

1938–52 Worked as associate editor and writer at *Vogue* magazine

1939–45 World War II

1948 Authored *Vogue's Book of Etiquette*

1950–53 Korean War

1958–72 Served as vice chair of the N.J. Advisory Committee to the U.S. Commission on Civil Rights

1958–64 Served on Bernardsville, N.J., Borough Council

1961–73 Vietnam War

1969–72 Served in N.J. General Assembly

1975–83 Represented New Jersey's Fifth District in U.S. Congress

1982 *Speaking Up* published

1983–87 Served as U.S. Ambassador to U.N. Food and Agriculture Organization

1992 Died, Bernardsville, N.J.

1900   1925   1950   1975   2000

RIGHTS was reflected in her decision not to run for reelection to the council. Instead, she accepted an appointment to the New Jersey Advisory Committee to the U.S. Commission on Civil Rights. She was the committee's vice chair from 1958 to 1972.

By the mid-1960s, Fenwick was also vice chair of the New Jersey Republican State Committee and was, by her own admission, longing to run for the New Jersey Legislature. However, at the time, she lacked the assertiveness to call attention to her accomplishments. Although she was anxious to be a candidate, and felt she had the qualifications and experience to win, she was reluctant to openly seek the candidacy. Instead, she hoped someone in the party would suggest that she run. She was passed over and was left to contemplate how to handle the next election. In 1969, she shed her modesty, asked for help from the Republican organization, and was elected to the general assembly. She quickly established herself as an advocate of civil rights, consumer interests, prison reform, and conservation. In the legislature, her quick wit and sharp intellect became legendary. When she proposed an equal rights amendment for women, a male colleague rose and said, "I just don't like this amendment. I've always thought of women as kissable, cuddly and smelling good." Fenwick replied, "That's the way I feel about men, too. I only hope you haven't been disappointed as often as I have."

In 1972 Fenwick resigned from the state assembly to become director of New Jersey's Division of Consumer Affairs. She embraced the job wholeheartedly, visiting supermarkets to check on the accuracy of labels on canned goods and talking with ordinary consumers about their problems and concerns. She unnerved the Bureau of Professional Boards by insisting that members of the general public be included on the boards in order to ensure impartial regulation of professional conduct.

In the spring of 1974, Fenwick left her post with the New Jersey Division of Consumer Affairs to seek the Republican nomination for the House of Representatives from the Fifth District. She carried the primary by a mere eighty-three votes but won the general election by a comfortable margin. She was sixty-four years old when she took her seat in the Ninety-Fourth Congress, but she quickly proved that she had all the vigor and commitment of any of her younger colleagues. She assumed assignments on the Committee on Banking, Currency and Housing and on the Committee on Small Business, a favorite area of interest. During her tenure in the House, she regularly worked twelve to fourteen hours a day and gained a reputation for diligence and commitment.

Fenwick earned respect in Congress through her support of equal opportunities, individual rights, and workplace safety. She worked tirelessly on behalf of poor people and advocated prison reform, strip-mining controls, reduction of military spending, urban renewal, campaign spending limits, GUN CONTROL, and restrictions on CAPITAL PUNISHMENT. Perhaps her proudest achievement was being the lead sponsor of a resolution calling for the creation of the Helsinki Commission, charged with monitoring the 1975 Helsinki human rights accords. She also served as a member of the commission.

Fenwick was a staunch feminist and strong supporter of the EQUAL RIGHTS AMENDMENT. Yet she was wary of a "women's agenda" and felt that the best way for women to advance is through achievements and accomplishments. "What after all would we think if men all got together and kept doing things that were supposed to be in the interest of men?" she once commented. She disliked women's organizations and was opposed to AFFIRMATIVE ACTION quotas. She felt that the women's movement had made a serious mistake by advancing the notion that women must pursue a career, and she defended those who chose the more traditional roles of wife and mother.

In spite of her frequent support of liberal causes, Fenwick was a loyal Republican who favored calling on the state as protector and benefactor "only as a last resort." When asked what made her a Republican and not a Democrat, she said she was a Republican because deep down she did not trust government.

Fiercely independent and outspoken, Fenwick was nonetheless charming and gracious. A former aide once described her as the Katharine Hepburn of politics. Fenwick was noted for unabashedly smoking a pipe after being told to quit smoking cigarettes. Her unconventional and idiosyncratic personality inspired the Lacey Davenport character in Garry Trudeau's *Doonesbury* cartoons. Asked what she would want on her tombstone, Fenwick replied, "I suppose the hope of furthering justice is really my main thing. That and the feeling that we're all in this together . . . and somehow we've got to try to work out a just and a peaceful society."

Fenwick died on September 16, 1992, at the age of eighty-two.

FEOFFMENT 📖 Total relinquishment and transfer of all rights of ownership in land from one individual to another. 📖

"WE MUST HAVE GOVERNMENT, BUT WE MUST WATCH THEM LIKE A HAWK."

A feoffment in old England was a transfer of PROPERTY that gave the new owner the right to sell the land as well as the right to pass it on to his HEIRS.

An essential element of feoffment was *livery of seisin*, a ceremony for transferring the possession of REAL PROPERTY from one person to another.

Feoffment is also known as ENFEOFFMENT.

FERAE NATURAE 📖 [*Latin, Of a wild nature or disposition.*] 📖

Animals that are wild by nature are called *ferae naturae*, and possession is a means of acquiring TITLE to such animals. The mere chasing of an animal *ferae naturae* does not give one party the right to title against another party who captures it through INTERVENTION. If, how-

Possession of a dove, an animal ferae naturae, *by a hunter is equal to acquiring title to it.*

ever, a wild animal is either killed or caught in a trap so that the capture is certain, the individual who traps or mortally wounds it acquires a vested right to possession and title that is not defeatable by another's intervention.

Animals *ferae naturae* differ from those that are tame or domesticated, or *domitae*, in which an individual can have an absolute property right.

FERES DOCTRINE 📖 A doctrine that bars claims against the federal government by members of the armed forces and their families for injuries arising from or in the course of activity incident to military service. 📖

The U.S. Supreme Court decided in 1950, in *Feres v. United States*, 340 U.S. 135, 71 S. Ct. 153, 95 L. Ed. 152, that the federal government could not be held liable under the statute known as the FEDERAL TORT CLAIMS ACT (28 U.S.C.A.

§§ 1291, 1346(b), (c), 1402(b), 2401(b), 2402, 2671-80) for injuries to members of the armed forces arising from activities incident to military service. The Federal Tort Claims Act allows persons intentionally or negligently wronged by a government employee to sue the government for their injuries. The Supreme Court's decision barring suits involving injuries to members of the armed forces became known as the *Feres* doctrine. The doctrine remains in force, as the Supreme Court has rejected attempts to overrule the decision.

Feres involved a suit brought by the EXECUTOR of a soldier who had died when his barracks caught fire. The executor charged that the United States had been negligent in housing the soldier in barracks whose defective heating system was known to be unsafe. First, the Supreme Court rejected the argument that such a suit could be brought under the Federal Tort Claims Act of 1946, which had waived the government's traditional IMMUNITY from claims in many circumstances. Noting that the statute said that "[t]he United States shall be liable . . . in the same manner and to the same extent as a private individual under like circumstances" (28 U.S.C.A. § 2674), the Court concluded that the relationship between the government and members of its armed forces is "distinctively federal in character." Therefore, it would be anomalous to have the government's liability depend on the law of the state where the soldier was stationed. Second, the Court observed that in several enactments, Congress had established a "no-fault" compensation plan that provides pensions to injured members of the ARMED SERVICES.

Commenting on the *Feres* doctrine in *United States v. Brown*, 348 U.S. 110, 75 S. Ct. 141, 99 L. Ed. 139 (1954), the Court emphasized that discipline and "[t]he peculiar and special relationship of the soldier to his superiors" might be affected if suits were allowed under the Tort Claims Act "for negligent orders given or negligent acts committed in the course of military duty." This view became one of the bedrock justifications for the doctrine in the years following *Brown*.

The U.S. Supreme Court has stressed that the *Feres* doctrine "cannot be reduced to a few bright-line rules," but rather "each case must be examined in light of the [Tort Claims Act] as it has been construed in *Feres* and subsequent cases" (*United States v. Shearer*, 473 U.S. 52, 105 S. Ct. 3039, 87 L. Ed. 2d 38 [1985]).

The doctrine does not bar a claim arising from an independent injury committed by the government after a soldier has been discharged

(*Brown*). In *Brown*, an injury suffered by a veteran during treatment at a VETERANS ADMINISTRATION hospital for a prior injury that he had sustained during military service was not barred by *Feres*. The Court distinguished *Brown* from *Feres* on the ground that in *Brown*, the second injury did not arise from or in the course of military service.

The doctrine did apply, however, to a suit involving the death of a soldier who was off the military base on authorized leave when he was kidnapped and murdered by a fellow soldier with a known history of violence (*Shearer*). The mother of the murdered soldier charged that the Army had been negligent in failing to warn the other soldiers that the murderer was dangerous and in failing to restrict the murderer's movements while his discharge was being processed. The Supreme Court denied her claim under the *Feres* doctrine on the ground that the suit would require a civilian court to second-guess military decisions that are directly involved in the management of the armed forces. If such suits were allowed, "commanding officers would have to stand prepared to convince a civilian court of the wisdom of a wide range of military and disciplinary decisions." As a result, military discipline would suffer the detrimental effects that the *Feres* doctrine was designed to prevent.

The doctrine also applies to third parties seeking INDEMNITY from the federal government. In *Stencel Aero Engineering Corp. v. United States*, 431 U.S. 666, 97 S. Ct. 2054, 52 L. Ed. 2d 665 (1977), an injured National Guard officer brought a suit against Stencel, the manufacturer of the ejection system in his fighter aircraft. Stencel then filed a CROSS-CLAIM against the United States for indemnity (reimbursement for damages that it might pay to the officer), alleging that any malfunction of the ejection system was due to faulty government specifications and components. The Supreme Court held that the same reasoning that prevented a member of the armed services from recovering under the Tort Claims Act would limit a third party from recovering in an indemnity action.

Members of the armed forces and their families may not sue the federal government for injuries sustained during military service.

The *Feres* doctrine was challenged in two cases decided by the Supreme Court in 1987. The doctrine had long been criticized as unfair to service members. In *United States v. Johnson*, 481 U.S. 681, 107 S. Ct. 2063, 95 L. Ed. 2d 648, the United States was sued for injuries sustained by a service member as the result of the NEGLIGENCE of air traffic controllers, who are civilian employees of the federal government. On a 5–4 decision, the Court reaffirmed the application of the *Feres* doctrine. The Court noted that civilian employees may also "play an integral role in military activities. In this circumstance, an inquiry into the civilian activities would have the same effect on military discipline as a direct inquiry into military judgments."

In *United States v. Stanley*, 483 U.S. 669, 107 S. Ct. 3054, 97 L. Ed. 2d 550 (1987), the United States was sued not only under the Federal Tort Claims Act but also directly under the Constitution. The Court rejected this attempt to circumvent *Feres*. It affirmed the lower court's decision to dismiss the lawsuit because of the principles set out in the *Feres* decision.

FERRARO, GERALDINE ANNE As the first woman candidate for VICE PRESIDENT of the United States in a major party, Geraldine Anne Ferraro expanded opportunities for women in national politics. Her place on the Democratic

BIOGRAPHY

Geraldine Anne Ferraro

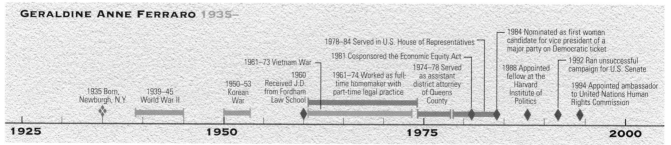

PAUL CONKLIN/PHOTOEDIT

ARTHUR GRACE/STOCK BOSTON

GERALDINE ANNE FERRARO 1935–

1935 Born, Newburgh, N.Y.

1939–45 World War II

1950–53 Korean War

1960 Received J.D. from Fordham Law School

1961–73 Vietnam War

1961–74 Worked as full-time homemaker with part-time legal practice

1974–78 Served as assistant district attorney of Queens County

1978–84 Served in U.S. House of Representatives

1981 Cosponsored the Economic Equity Act

1984 Nominated as first woman candidate for vice president of a major party on Democratic ticket

1988 Appointed fellow at the Harvard Institute of Politics

1992 Ran unsuccessful campaign for U.S. Senate

1994 Appointed ambassador to United Nations Human Rights Commission

1925 1950 1975 2000

ticket as Walter F. Mondale's running mate in 1984 broke a gender barrier that had lasted for over two hundred years. Although Mondale and Ferraro lost to RONALD REAGAN and GEORGE BUSH, Ferraro proved herself a capable and dynamic campaigner. Her selection came on the strength of a highly visible three terms in the House of Representatives, from 1978 to 1984, during which she championed liberal positions, wrote legislation aimed at establishing economic equity for women, and oversaw the drafting of the Democratic party's 1984 presidential platform. Charges that she had violated congressional rules on financial disclosure hampered her run for the vice presidency, and controversy over business investments helped sink a Senate campaign in 1992. She later headed the U.S. delegation to the United Nations Human Rights Commission.

Ferraro was born August 26, 1935, in Newburgh, New York, the fourth child of a tight-knit family enjoying prosperity. The good life did not last. When she was eight, her father, Dominick Ferraro, an Italian immigrant and successful restaurant and dime-store owner, died of a heart attack. Two of Ferraro's brothers had preceded him in death. Bad investments left her mother, Antonetta L. Corrieri, nearly broke. The three surviving family members—Ferraro, her mother, and a brother—moved into a small apartment in the Bronx. Ferraro's mother supported them by crocheting, and managed to give Ferraro an education at the exclusive Catholic school for girls, Marymount. The bright girl excelled, and a scholarship to Marymount College followed, where she earned a bachelor's degree in English in 1956. For the next four years, she taught in Queens public schools by day and took classes at Fordham University Law School by night.

The next two decades laid the groundwork for Ferraro's political future. She earned her law degree in 1960, married, and set aside her ambitions in order to raise children. Occasionally, she did part-time law work for the very successful real estate business run by her husband, developer John Zaccaro. But her main outlet for professional development was membership in local Democratic party clubs. She worked on her cousin Nicholas Ferraro's state senate campaign. When he later became district attorney for Queens County, he made her an assistant district attorney. It was 1974, and Ferraro, at the age of thirty-nine, had her first full-time job. Assigned to the Special Victims Bureau, she prosecuted cases of rape, child abuse, and domestic violence so disturbing that

she lost sleep at night. Even though she won praise for her fairness and persuasiveness in court, she was frustrated. She earned less than her male colleagues simply because she was a married woman. By 1978, more liberal in outlook than before, politics beckoned to her.

Ferraro ran for the U.S. House of Representatives. The Ninth Congressional District was a conservative, blue-collar section of Queens, and it was hardly surprising that the local Democratic machine did not support this liberal feminist. Her Republican opponent, Alfred A. DelliBovi, a three-term assemblyman, hammered at her political inexperience. But she won anyway, on a platform of law and order, support for labor and senior citizens, and neighborhood preservation, which she summed up in the campaign slogan Finally . . . a Tough Democrat. She had help—her cousin's connections, and her husband's wealth, which in time would come back to haunt her. Meanwhile, she set about making good on her promises and opened a plain storefront congressional office.

Ferraro quickly scaled Capitol Hill. In just two terms, she transformed herself from a meat-and-potatoes politician into a noticeable congressional leader. The change was accomplished by party loyalty: she voted with the Democratic party 78 percent of the time in her first term, and even more often in her successive terms. But she did not forget her own philosophy. By 1981, she cosponsored the Economic Equity Act, a bipartisan measure aimed at increasing women's economic rights that has been reintroduced in Congress several times. She took personal leadership of two sections that provided women with greater access to private pension plans and individual retirement accounts. Ferraro's personal style—tough yet compromising—won her a reputation for playing by the rules. In a short time, she came to the attention of the most powerful Democrat in Congress, Speaker of the House THOMAS P. ("Tip") O'NEILL, JR. The Speaker liked her politics and hard work, and her reward was key assignments that traditionally went to older, more seasoned leaders: an appointment to the Budget Committee in 1983; a position helping to draft rules for the Democratic National Convention; and the biggest prize of all, chair of the 1984 Democratic platform committee, drafting the party's positions in the forthcoming election. An extraordinary career leap, the chair of the platform committee meant real power and extra visibility.

The moment was ripe for even more success. Many Democrats wanted a woman nominated to the presidential ticket. Some viewed the issue

"GOVERNMENT CAN BE MORAL—AND IT MUST BE MORAL—WITHOUT ADOPTING A RELIGION. LEADERS CAN BE MORAL—AND THEY SHOULD BE MORAL—WITHOUT IMPOSING THEIR MORALITY ON OTHERS."

as one of fairness; others thought it would capture women voters. By spring 1984, as Mondale emerged as the clear favorite for the presidential nomination, party leaders began urging him to pick Ferraro. The Woman's National Democratic Club endorsed her. O'Neill followed suit. By June, members of the National Women's Political Caucus argued that an analysis of voting trends showed that a woman on the ticket would be a winner. The cover of *Time Magazine* pictured Ferraro and the other leading contender, San Francisco mayor Dianne Feinstein, under the heading "And for Vice President . . . Why Not a Woman?"

In terms of strategic advantage, Ferraro offered more than her gender. She was an Italian American Catholic from the East with working-class roots, an identity that her supporters thought would give the Democratic ticket regional and ethnic balance. But objections came from some party members who viewed her as a pork barrel politician, too brash to be widely popular and, worse, inexperienced.

The Mondale-Ferraro campaign faced a tremendous challenge in offering an alternative to an appealing incumbent. President Reagan enjoyed great popular support, buoyed by love of his personal style and the economic recovery that had begun in 1983. The Democrats stressed negatives: Reagan's economic policies were built on huge federal deficits, they charged, which would force him to cut Social Security benefits and raise taxes in a second term. Reagan responded that the United States was "standing tall" again in the eyes of the world and warned that Mondale and Ferraro would return the nation to the high inflation and unemployment that had plagued the presidency of JIMMY CARTER.

In speeches, Ferraro gave as good as she got. She blasted Reagan's penchant for tailoring facts to fit his positions, as constituting "an anecdotal presidency." Since the Democrats were reaching out for their traditional base of organized labor and the underprivileged, she seized on opportunities to present the Republicans as the party of the rich. One opportunity came after Bush made a point about taxes by asking if his audience knew what wins elections; he pulled out his wallet and said the election came down to who puts money into it and who takes money out. Ferraro told a crowd of supporters,

> That single gesture of selfishness tells us more about the true character of this Administration than all their apple pie rhetoric. There's nothing in George Bush's wallet that says we should care about the

disadvantaged. There's nothing in his wallet that tells us to search for peace. There's nothing in his wallet that says in the name of humanity let's stop the arms race.

But the voters did not respond. Democratic party polls showed that Ferraro's negative ratings increased as she attacked Reagan. Mondale, hurt by an image of weakness, was doing no better.

Reagan won by a landslide, with the greatest electoral vote margin in history, even capturing 55 percent of women voters. Ferraro's candidacy had changed history, but she had some regrets.

Ferraro's chief complaint was the Republicans' charges about her and her husband's finances. As far back as 1979, the FEDERAL ELECTION COMMISSION (FEC) had ruled that she violated the law by borrowing money from her husband for her first congressional race; she repaid it. The issue was revived in the 1984 race, along with new charges that she failed to fully disclose her family finances under the Ethics in Government Act (2 U.S.C.A. § 701). The newest accusations arose when the Washington Legal Foundation, a conservative group, filed a complaint against her with the Justice Department and the House Committee on Standards of Official Conduct. She then admitted owing back taxes amounting to $53,459, blamed them on simple errors, and paid up. Yet not until after the election did the investigations in the Justice Department, Congress, and the FEC come to an end.

Although Ferraro was cleared of any wrong doing, the inquiries hurt her political career. She later claimed that the Justice Department, under Reagan appointee Attorney General EDWIN MEESE III, bullied her into dropping plans to run for the Senate in 1986. She waited until 1992 to mount a Senate race in New York. Yet the charges of corruption resurfaced just as she was leading a three-way race for the Democratic nomination. Ferraro denied the allegations, calling them anti-Italian slurs. But her opponents exploited the charges and she lost the nomination.

In addition to being the managing partner of a New York law firm, Ferraro occasionally surfaced in national politics in the mid-1990s. She worked as a lobbyist for the American Association for Marriage and Family Therapy, arguing that family therapy should be covered under any national health care system. In 1994 President BILL CLINTON appointed her as ambassador to head the U.S. delegation at the fiftieth annual meeting of the United Nations Human Rights Commission. Among other issues, she raised concerns about the treatment of women in the former Yugoslavia.

FERRY 📖 A specially constructed vessel to bring passengers and property across rivers and other bodies of water from one shoreline to another, making contact with a thoroughfare at each terminus. The landing place for a boat. A right or privilege to maintain a vessel upon a body of water in order to transport people and their vehicles across it in exchange for payment of a reasonable TOLL. 📖

Technically a ferry is considered a continuation of a HIGHWAY from one side of the body of water that it passes over to the other.

The privilege of handling a ferry is called a FRANCHISE. A ferry franchise is a permit from the state to a specifically named individual giving that person the authority to operate a ferry. It is a general prerequisite to the lawful establishment of a public ferry. The operator of a ferry is not relieved of the duty to obtain a franchise by formation of a company, since the franchise becomes a contract between the owner and the state.

Usually the grant of a ferry franchise implicitly gives the recipient the power to collect tolls. *Ferriage* is the fare that the ferry operator may charge. The unauthorized establishment of another ferry within competing distance of an already existing one constitutes an infringement of the ferry franchise, even in the absence of physical interference.

A ferry franchise can be terminated either by expiration of its term or by revocation by the licensing authorities. It is generally subject to renewal, for which the original owner is usually given a preference.

A public ferry is for use by the public at large, whereas a private ferry is operated solely for the benefit of its proprietor.

A ferry is considered a continuation of a highway from one side of a body of water to another.

JOHN NEUBAUER/PHOTOEDIT

The state has intrinsic authority to regulate and control ferries that operate within its borders. It may exercise such power by law or by contract with the operator. The state may regulate the transportation of dangerous articles, the nature and frequency of service, and the location of terminals. In addition, it may impose a LICENSE fee or tax on the operation of ferries within its BOUNDARIES.

FETAL RIGHTS 📖 The rights of any unborn human fetus, which is generally a developing human from roughly eight weeks after conception to birth. 📖

Like other categories such as CIVIL RIGHTS and human rights, fetal rights embraces a complex variety of topics and issues involving a number of areas of the law, including criminal, employment, health care, and FAMILY LAW.

Historically, under both English COMMON LAW and U.S. law, the fetus has not been recognized as a person with full rights. Instead, legal rights have centered on the mother, with the fetus treated as a part of her. Nevertheless, U.S. law has in certain instances granted the fetus limited rights, particularly as medical science has made it increasingly possible to directly view, monitor, diagnose, and treat the fetus as a patient.

The term *fetal rights* came into wide usage following the landmark 1973 ABORTION case *Roe v. Wade*, 410 U.S. 113, 93 S. Ct. 705, 35 L. Ed. 2d 147. In that case, the Supreme Court ruled that a woman has a constitutionally guaranteed unqualified right to abortion in the first trimester of her pregnancy. She also has a right to terminate a pregnancy in the second trimester, although the state may limit that right when the procedure poses a health risk to the mother that is greater than the risk of carrying the fetus to term. In making its argument, the Court ruled that a fetus is not a person under the terms of the FOURTEENTH AMENDMENT to the U.S. Constitution. However, the Court also maintained that the state has an interest in protecting the life of a fetus after viability—that is, after the point at which the fetus is capable of living outside of the womb. As a result, states were permitted to outlaw abortion in the third trimester of pregnancy except when the procedure is necessary to preserve the life of the mother.

Roe elicited impassioned responses from those who were morally or religiously opposed to abortion, and in the years following that case, abortion became one of the most contentious issues in U.S. law. Those opposed to the procedure became a powerful political lobby in the United States. Their efforts to promote the rights of unborn humans have had a significant effect on the law.

However, the cause of fetal rights has been greeted with suspicion by those who are concerned that the state may protect fetal rights at the expense of WOMEN'S RIGHTS. For this reason, many feminists have been highly critical of claims regarding fetal rights. Such claims, they argue, can work to significantly diminish women's self-determination and bodily autonomy.

At the same time, most legal experts recognize an increasing need to clarify the legal status of the fetus, particularly as technology has made it possible to regard the fetus as a patient independent of the mother. Some scholars have even gone so far as to ask that a model fetal rights act be passed so that states—which now exhibit a wide variety of approaches to fetal rights—may develop a more coherent legislative approach to the issue of fetal rights, one that will give courts more direction in deciding relevant cases.

The specific issues in which legal claims have been made regarding the rights of the fetus usually require a careful consideration of the sometimes competing rights of the woman and the fetus.

Forced Cesarean Sections Because of improvements in fetal monitoring and surgical techniques, physicians increasingly recommend that women give birth by cesarean section, a surgical technique that involves removing the fetus through an incision in the woman's abdomen. In many cases, cesarean section improves the chance that the fetus will be delivered safely. By 1990, cesarean sections accounted for almost 23 percent of childbirths.

Some women choose not to undergo a physician-recommended cesarean section. They may do so for a variety of reasons, including a concern about their own risk of harm, including death, from the surgery; a desire to avoid repeated cesarean sections; or sincere religious, cultural, or moral beliefs. This situation has led to a number of legal questions, such as, should a woman be forced to undergo a cesarean section or other surgery in the interest of the health of the fetus? To what extent is a woman obligated to follow the advice of her physician regarding the medical care of her fetus?

The 1980s saw an increasing number of cases in which hospitals and physicians sought court orders to force women to give birth by cesarean section. From 1981 to 1986, fifteen such cases were reported, and in thirteen of them, courts decided to require cesarean section. In a 1981 case, *Jefferson v. Griffin Spalding County Hospital Authority*, 247 Ga. 86, 274 S.E.2d 457, the Georgia Supreme Court held that an expectant mother in her last weeks of pregnancy did not have the right to refuse

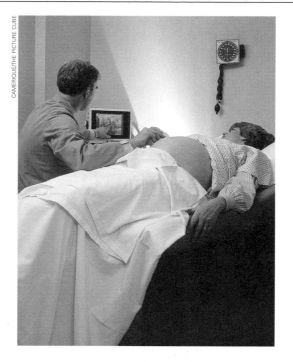

CAMERIQUE/THE PICTURE CUBE

The legal status of a fetus remains unclear, and although an unborn baby does have some rights under the law, those rights sometimes conflict with those of the mother.

surgery or other medical treatment if the life of the unborn child was at stake. As has happened in a number of other instances, the pregnant woman named in the case avoided the procedure and later delivered a healthy child by natural birth.

Later court decisions, however, increasingly recognized a pregnant woman's right to refuse medical treatment. In a 1990 case, *In re A. C.*, 573 A.2d 1235, the District of Columbia Court of Appeals ruled that a physician must honor the wishes of a competent woman regarding a cesarean section. The court's opinion was written after the woman involved in the case, Angela Carder, and her fetus died following a cesarean section forced by a lower court.

A 1994 Illinois case, *Doe v. Doe*, 260 Ill. App. 3d 392, 198 Ill. Dec. 267, 632 N.E.2d 326, involved a woman (called Doe to protect her anonymity) who was thirty-five weeks pregnant. Her doctor conducted tests that indicated her fetus was not receiving adequate oxygen. He therefore recommended that the fetus be delivered by cesarean section. Doe objected to the surgical procedure on the basis of her religious beliefs. The doctor and his hospital then contacted the Cook County state's attorney, who petitioned for a court order requiring the woman to undergo the cesarean procedure.

The case eventually reached the Illinois Appellate Court, which upheld Doe's right to refuse the cesarean section. The court held that a physician must recognize a woman's right to refuse a cesarean section. It found no statute or Illinois case to support the state's request to force a cesarean on a competent person. It also

Willow Island, West Virginia, Women Paid the Price of Fetal Protection Policies

The 1991 U.S. Supreme Court ruling that declared fetal protection policies to be a violation of civil rights laws came too late for five women from West Virginia (*International Union, UAW v. Johnson Controls, Inc.*, 499 U.S. 187, 111 S. Ct. 1196, 113 L. Ed. 2d 158 [1991]). The women worked at an American Cyanamid factory in Willow Island, a poor region where decent-paying jobs were scarce. They were all among the first women to work in American Cyanamid factories, which, before 1974, had employed only men.

In 1978 the company introduced a policy that no fertile women would be allowed to work in its lead pigments department. The company claimed that hazardous chemicals in that department might harm women's reproductive system. Fertile women under age fifty would have to be sterilized or take jobs in other areas of the company, virtually all of which paid less. Men, whose reproductive system might also be damaged by lead, were not subject to restrictions.

The seven women then employed in the lead pigments department found themselves facing an agonizing choice: whether to reduce or sacrifice their income, or undergo a surgical procedure that would render them unable to bear children. Five of the women chose sterilization.

The labor union to which the women belonged eventually took the women's case to court, claiming that the company's fetal protection policy represented a violation of federal occupational safety standards because it required an individual to be sterilized in order to be eligible for work. The union lost the case in the federal appeals court (*Oil, Chemical, & Atomic Workers International Union v. American Cyanamid Co.*, 741 F.2d 444 [D.C. Cir. 1984]).

dismissed the state's argument that *Roe's* protections of a viable fetus authorized a forced cesarean.

The court also noted the position of the American Medical Association (AMA) on the issue. The AMA has reminded physicians that their duty is to ensure that a pregnant woman is provided with the necessary and appropriate information to enable her to make an informed decision about her fetus, and that that duty does not extend to attempting to influence her decision or attempting to force a recommended procedure upon her. The court assessed the action of the physicians in the *Doe* case to be in direct opposition to the AMA's clear edict.

Shortly after the court's decision, Doe gave birth to a healthy baby boy. The Supreme Court later declined to review the case.

New types of fetal surgery now made possible by medical science promise to raise questions very similar to those found with forced cesarean sections.

Drug Use by the Mother The use of illegal drugs such as cocaine and heroin can have a devastating effect on the health of a fetus. By the early 1990s, it was estimated that 375,000 children were born annually in the United States suffering from the effects of illegal drugs taken by their mother.

As a result, some states have held women criminally liable for any use of illegal drugs that harms their fetus. Prosecutors in many states have sought to deter such behavior by charging women with a number of crimes against their fetus, including delivery of drugs, criminal CHILD ABUSE, ASSAULT with a deadly weapon, and MANSLAUGHTER. *Johnson v. State*, 578 So. 2d 419 (Fla. 1991), demonstrates the controversial aspects of such prosecutions. In this case, a Florida district court of appeal upheld a lower court's conviction of a woman for the delivery of a controlled substance by umbilical cord to two of her four children. The decision was the first appellate ruling to uphold such a conviction.

Jennifer Johnson, a twenty-three-year-old resident of Seminole County, Florida, had been arrested in 1989 after two successive instances in which a child born to her tested positive for cocaine immediately after birth. Cocaine is especially harmful to a fetus, often causing premature birth, significant deformities and ailments, and even death. After Johnson's conviction in the Seminole County Circuit Court in 1989, the AMERICAN CIVIL LIBERTIES UNION (ACLU) appealed the case with backing from an unusual alliance of medical and civil rights organizations, including the AMA, the American Public Health Association, the Florida Medical Association, and the National Abortion Rights Action League, all of which had different reasons for supporting the appeal.

The AMA stated that it opposed the use of criminal prosecutions against mothers. Imposing criminal sanctions, it said, does not prevent damage to fetal health and may violate the PRIVACY laws between doctors and women, making doctors and hospitals agents of prosecution. The ACLU echoed the AMA, arguing that prosecutions of drug-addicted women for harm to their children will greatly damage women's health, their relationship to the health care community, and their ability to control their own body. It also maintained that the policies enacted against Johnson should be made by a state legislature and not the courts, and it pointed out that many more minority women than white women are reported for child abuse after testing positive for drugs.

Other critics argued that most child abuse statutes do not specifically mention drug use by pregnant women as an offense, thereby raising the question as to whether prosecutions on charges of drug use involve a denial of DUE PROCESS. Still others said that increased funding for substance abuse treatment programs was a much better approach to the drug problem. They saw prosecutions on drug abuse charges as doing little to treat the underlying addiction and argued that such prosecutions deter at-risk women from seeking prenatal care, increasing the likelihood of harm to the fetus.

Despite these arguments, the Fifth District Court of Appeals, in Florida, upheld Johnson's conviction. It agreed with the prosecution's argument that Johnson's umbilical cord had delivered cocaine to her children after their birth but before the cord was cut, thereby violating a Florida statute against the delivery of a controlled substance to a MINOR (Fla. Stat. Ann. § 893.13(1)(c) [West 1991]).

States will continue to struggle with this issue as they seek to achieve the best balance between maternal and fetal rights. States will also have to consider whether or not to hold criminally liable women whose use of legal substances such as alcohol or tobacco harms the fetus.

Fetal Protection Policies Fetal protection policies bar fertile women from specific jobs out of fear that those jobs may cause harm to any embryos or fetuses the women might be carrying. These policies came into widespread use by many companies during the 1970s and 1980s, before a 1991 U.S. Supreme Court decision, *UAW v. Johnson Controls*, 499 U.S. 187, 111 S. Ct. 1196, 113 L. Ed. 2d 158, declared them a form of sexual discrimination that violates title VII of the CIVIL RIGHTS ACT of 1964 (42 U.S.C.A. § 2000e et seq. [1982]). Despite

the Court's decision in *Johnson Controls*, those critical of fetal protection policies feared that the policies would be continued in more subtle forms.

Johnson Controls grew out of a fetal protection policy created in 1982 by Johnson Controls, an automobile battery manufacturer. The company's policy excluded pregnant women and women capable of bearing children from battery manufacturing jobs. The company maintained that the jobs in its manufacturing plant exposed women to levels of lead that might harm any embryo or fetus they might be carrying.

In 1984, a group of Johnson Controls employees, together with their labor union, the United Automobile, Aerospace, and Agricultural Implement Workers of America (UAW), filed a CLASS ACTION suit in federal court challenging the company's policy. They charged that the policy constituted SEX DISCRIMINATION in violation of federal civil rights law.

Fetal Rights
Drug Use During Pregnancy

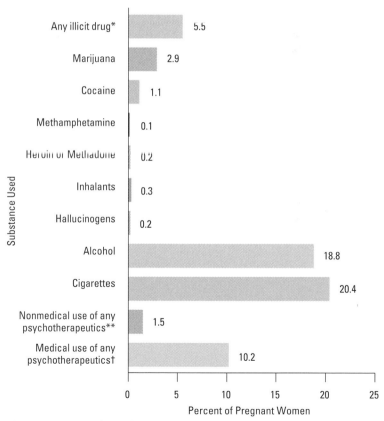

*Use of marijuana, cocaine (all forms), methamphetamine, heroin, methadone, inhalants, hallucinogens, or nonmedical use of psychotherapeutics during pregnancy.

**Nonmedical use of any prescription amphetamines, sedatives, tranquilizers or analgesics during pregnancy.

†Medical use of any prescription amphetamines, sedatives, tranquilizers or analgesics during pregnancy.

Source: National Pregnancy and Health Survey, National Institute on Drug Abuse (a division of NIH), 1992. This survey collected data from a representative sample of the 4 million women who delivered babies in 1992.

In the final ruling on the case, the U.S. Supreme Court held that fetal protection policies unfairly discriminate against women because they do not demand that men make a similar choice regarding the preservation of their reproductive health in a potentially hazardous workplace.

Companies that have created fetal protection policies argue that they are necessary to protect their employees. Critics of fetal protection policies maintain that they effectively exclude all women aged fifteen to fifty from well-paying jobs unless the women can prove they have been sterilized. They also contend that such policies raise privacy questions because they often require women to provide proof that they cannot have children in order to take specific jobs. Critics also point to instances in which women have undergone sterilization procedures because they faced the loss of high-paying jobs. Other critics argue that male reproductive organs may also be affected by hazardous substances in such a way that a fetus might be harmed. Nevertheless, no companies have created similar policies for men.

CROSS-REFERENCES

Drugs and Narcotics; Fetal Tissue Research; Parent and Child; Physicians and Surgeons; *Roe v. Wade.*

FETAL TISSUE RESEARCH Scientific experimentation performed upon or using tissue taken from human fetuses.

Although fetal tissue research has led to medical advances, including the development of the polio and rubella vaccines in the 1950s, it has also generated controversy because of its use of fetuses from elective abortions. Fetal tissue research has been subject to strict government regulation and periodic moratoriums on federal funding. The National Institutes of Health (NIH) Revitalization Act of 1993 (Pub. L. No. 103-43 [42 U.S.C.A. §§ 289g-1, -2]) regulates many aspects of fetal tissue research.

History Fetal tissue research has been conducted in the United States since the middle of the twentieth century. Its practice became more common as the amount of biomedical research increased and as restrictions on the availability of abortion decreased. Research on fetal tissue led to significant advances in the scientific understanding of fetal development and in the diagnosis and treatment of fetal diseases and defects, including the development of amniocentesis as a diagnostic tool. It also played a role in advancing the scientific understanding of cancer, immunology, and transplantation.

Because fetal tissue grows more rapidly and is more flexible than other human tissue, and is

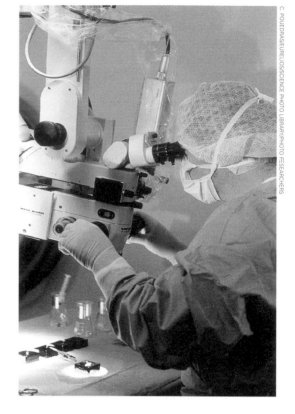

A scientist removes mesencephalon brain tissue from human fetuses. Fetal brain tissue is sometimes implanted in the brains of patients with Parkinson's disease.

less likely to be rejected by the immune system, it has also been used to treat diseases through transplantation. Fetal tissue transplantation usually involves the injection of fetal cells into a diseased organ such as the brain or pancreas. Many scientists believe that fetal tissue transplantation will lead to significant new developments in medical science. Researchers have already had limited success in using fetal tissue transplants to treat patients with Parkinson's disease, diabetes, Alzheimer's disease, and other illnesses. Although most medical ethicists agree that these new procedures hold great promise, they warn that the use of fetal tissue must be strictly regulated in order to avoid ethical abuses.

Law Fetal tissue research became a subject of controversy in U.S. law following the 1973 U.S. Supreme Court decision in *Roe v. Wade,* 410 U.S. 113, 93 S. Ct. 705, 35 L. Ed. 2d 147, which protects the right of a woman to have an ABORTION in the first and second trimesters of pregnancy. After *Roe,* research performed on fetuses obtained from elective abortions came under close scrutiny.

In 1974, the National Research Act (Pub. L. No. 93-348) created a national commission to oversee research involving fetuses. This body released research guidelines and also placed restrictions on what types of fetal research might be allowed to receive federal funding.

In 1988, NIH scientists requested approval from the Department of Health and Human Services (HHS) to begin transplantation experiments using fetal brain tissue. Because the administration of President RONALD REAGAN was concerned about the link between fetal tissue research and abortion, the HHS imposed a temporary moratorium on federal funds for research in fetal tissue transplantation. Although a twenty-one-member NIH panel later approved the use of human fetal tissue for transplantation and disagreed with the contention that such research would cause more abortions, the moratorium was extended indefinitely by Secretary Louis W. Sullivan, of the HHS, in 1989.

In subsequent years, legislation to overturn the moratorium repeatedly failed in Congress. Then, shortly after taking office in 1993, President BILL CLINTON ordered the end of the moratorium (58 Fed. Reg. 7457). Later in 1993, Congress passed the NIH Revitalization Act, which permits the tissue from any type of abortion to be used for fetal tissue research. The law includes elaborate consent and documentation requirements that attempt to separate the mother's decision to abort from the decision to donate fetal remains. It also criminalizes the sale or purchase of fetal tissue and the designation of the recipient of fetal tissue.

The Debate Those opposed to fetal tissue research have made a number of arguments against the use of fetuses from elective abortions. Morally opposed to abortion itself, they argue that the fetal tissue researcher is complicit in the destruction of the fetus and that fetal tissue research will create incentives for more abortions. Moreover, they maintain that a woman who has an abortion cannot legally authorize research on the aborted fetus because she has abandoned her parental responsibility through the act of abortion. They also argue that fetal tissue research can and should be restricted to fetuses from spontaneous abortions and ectopic pregnancies.

Those who favor fetal tissue research contend that it has already led to significant medical gains that have saved and improved many lives, and will continue to do so. They argue that researchers have an ethical duty to relieve suffering and cure diseases and that fetal tissue research contributes greatly to this cause. They also contend that researchers must continue to have access to ethically obtained fetuses. They hold that the tissue of fetuses from elective abortions has far fewer defects and is much easier to obtain than that of fetuses from non-elective abortions or ectopic pregnancies.

FEUDALISM 📖 A series of contractual relationships between the upper classes, designed to maintain control over land. 📖

Feudalism flourished between the tenth and thirteenth centuries in western Europe. At its core, it was an agreement between a lord and a vassal. A person became a vassal by pledging political allegiance and providing military, political, and financial service to a lord. A lord possessed complete SOVEREIGNTY over land, or acted in the service of another sovereign, usually a king. If a lord acted in the service of a king, the lord was considered a vassal of the king.

As part of the feudal agreement, the lord promised to protect the vassal and provided the vassal with a plot of land. This land could be passed on to the vassal's HEIRS, giving the vassal TENURE over the land. The vassal was also vested with the power to lease the land to others for profit, a practice known as subinfeudation. The entire agreement was called a fief, and a lord's collection of fiefs was called a fiefdom.

The feudal bond was thus a combination of two key elements: fealty, or an oath of allegiance and pledge of service to the lord, and homage, or an acknowledgment by the lord of the vassal's tenure. The arrangement was not forced on the vassal; it was profitable for the vassal and made on mutual consent, and it fostered the allegiance necessary for royal control of distant lands.

The bond between a lord and a vassal was made in a ceremony that served to solemnize the fief. The vassal knelt before the lord and placed his hands between those of the lord as a sign of subordination. Immediately afterward, the lord raised the vassal to his feet and kissed him on the mouth to symbolize their social equality. The vassal then recited a predetermined oath of fealty, and the lord conveyed a plot of land to the vassal.

In the seventeenth century, more than three centuries after the death of this particular social practice, English scholars began to use the term *feudalism* to describe it. The word was derived by English scholars from *foedum*, the Latin form of *fief*. The meaning of feudalism has expanded since the seventeenth century, and it now commonly describes servitude and hierarchical oppression. However, feudalism is best understood as an initial stage in a social progression leading to private ownership of land and the creation of different ESTATES, or interests in land.

Before feudalism, the European population consisted only of wealthy nobility and poor peasants. Little incentive existed for personal loyalty to sovereign rulers. Land was owned outright by nobility, and those who held land for lords held it purely at the lords' will. Nevertheless, the feudal framework was preceded by similar systems, so its exact origin is disputed by scholars. Ancient Romans, and Germanic tribes in the eighth century, gave land to warriors, but unlike land grants under feudalism, these were not hereditary.

In the early ninth century, control of Europe was largely under the rule of one man, Emperor Charlemagne (771–814). After Charlemagne's death, his descendants warred over land ownership, and Europe fell apart into thousands of *seigniories*, or kingdoms run by a sovereign lord. Men in the military service of lords began to press for support in the late ninth century, especially in France. Lords acquiesced, realizing the importance of a faithful military.

Military men, or knights, began to receive land, along with peasants for farmwork. Eventually, knights demanded that their estates be hereditary. Other persons in the professional service of royalty also began to demand and receive hereditary fiefs, and thus began the reign of feudalism.

In 1066, William the Conqueror invaded England from France and spread the feudal framework across the land. The feudal relationship between lord and vassal became the linchpin of English society. To become a vassal was no disgrace. Vassals held an overall status superior to that of peasants and were considered equal to lords in social status. They took leadership positions in their locality and also served as advisers for lords in feudal courts.

The price of a vassal's power was allegiance to the lord, or fealty. Fealty carried with it an obligation of service, the most common form being knight service. A vassal under knight service was obliged to defend the fief from invasion and fight for a specified number of days in an offensive war. In wartime, knight service also called for guard duty at the lord's castle for a specified period of time. In lieu of military service, some vassals were given *socage*, or tenure in exchange for the performance of a variety of duties. These duties were usually agricultural, but they could take on other forms, such as personal attendance to the lord. Other vassals were given *scutage*, in which the vassal agreed to pay money in lieu of military service. Priests received still other forms of tenure in exchange for their religious services.

A lord also enjoyed incidental benefits and rights in connection with a fief. For example, when a vassal died, the lord was entitled to a large sum of money from the vassal's heirs. If the heir was a MINOR, the lord could sell or give away custody of the land and enjoy its profits until the heir came of age. A lord also had the right to reject the marriage of an heiress to a fief if he did not want the husband as his vassal. This kind of family involvement by the lord made the feudal relationship intimate and complex.

The relationship between a lord and a vassal depended on mutual respect. If the vassal refused to perform services or somehow impaired the lord's interests, the lord could file suit against the vassal in feudal court to deprive him of his fief. At the same time, the lord was expected to treat the vassal with dignity, and to refrain from making unjust demands on the vassal. If the lord abused the vassal, the vassal could break faith with the lord and offer his services to another lord, preferably one who could protect the vassal against the wrath of the defied lord.

Predictably, the relationship between lord and vassal became a struggle for a reduction in the services required by the fief. Lords, as vassals of the king, joined their own vassals in revolt against the high cost of the feudal arrangement. In England, this struggle culminated in the MAGNA CHARTA, a constitutional document sealed by King John in 1215 that signaled the beginning of the end for feudalism. The Magna Charta, forced on King John by his lords, contained thirty-eight chapters outlining demands for liberty from the Crown, including

This illustrated manuscript from the fifteenth century depicts an eighth-century battle between Charlemagne and his forces and Neapolitan forces. After Charlemagne's death, Europe was no longer ruled by one leader and fell apart into thousands of small kingdoms, which was the start of feudalism.

THE GRANGER COLLECTION, NEW YORK

limitations on the rights of the Crown over land.

Other circumstances also contributed to the decline of feudalism. As time passed, the power of organized religion increased, and religious leaders pressed for freedom from their service to lords and kings. At the same time, the development of an economic wealth apart from land led to the rise of a bourgeoisie, or middle class. The middle class established independent cities in Europe, which funded their military with taxes, not land-based feudal bonds. Royal sovereigns and cities began to establish parliamentary governments that made laws to replace the various rules attached to the feudal bond, and feudal courts lost jurisdiction to royal or municipal courts. By the fourteenth century, the peculiar arrangement known as feudalism was obsolete.

Feudalism is often confused with manorialism, but the two should be kept separate. Manorialism was another system of land use practiced in medieval Europe. Under it, peasants worked and lived on a lord's land, called a manor. The peasants could not inherit the land, and the lord owed them nothing beyond protection and maintenance.

Feudalism should also be distinguished from the general brutality and oppression of medieval Europe. The popular understanding of feudalism often equates the bloody conquests of the medieval period (500–1500) with feudalism because feudalism was a predominant social framework for much of the period. However, feudalism was a relatively civil arrangement in an especially vicious time and place in history. The relationship of a vassal to a lord was servile, but it was also based on mutual respect, and feudalism stands as the first systematic, voluntary sale of inheritable land.

The remains of feudalism can be found in contemporary law regarding land. For example, a rental agreement is made between a landlord and a tenant, whose business relationship echoes that of a lord and a vassal. State property taxes on landowners resemble the services required of a vassal, and like the old feudal lords, state governments may take possession of land when a landowner dies with no will or heirs.

FIAT 📖 [*Latin, Let it be done.*] In old English practice, a short order or WARRANT of a judge or magistrate directing some act to be done; an authority issuing from some competent source for the doing of some legal act.

One of the proceedings in the English bankruptcy practice: a power, signed by the lord CHANCELLOR and addressed to the court of bankruptcy, authorizing the petitioning creditor to prosecute his complaint before that court. By the statute 12 & 13 Vict., c. 116, fiats were abolished.

Arbitrary or authoritative order or decision. 📖

F.I.C.A. 📖 An abbreviation for the Federal Insurance Contributions Act (26 U.S.C.A. § 3101 et seq. [1954]), which established the SOCIAL SECURITY tax on income received in the form of wages from employment. 📖

FICTION 📖 An ASSUMPTION made by a court and embodied in various legal doctrines that a fact or concept is true when in actuality it is not true, or when it is likely to be equally false and true. 📖

A legal fiction is created for the purpose of promoting the ends of justice. A COMMON-LAW action, for example, allowed a father to bring suit against his daughter's seducer, based on the legal fiction of the loss of her services. Similarly, the law of TORTS encompasses the legal fiction of the rule of VICARIOUS LIABILITY, which renders an employer responsible for the civil wrongs of his or her employees that are committed during their COURSE OF EMPLOYMENT. Even though the employer generally is uninvolved in the actual act constituting the tort, the law holds the employer responsible since, through a legal fiction, he or she is deemed to be in direct control of the employee's actions. A seller of real estate might, for example, be liable in an action for FRAUD committed by his or her AGENT in the course of a sale.

FICTITIOUS 📖 Based upon a fabrication or pretense. 📖

A fictitious name is an assumed name that differs from an individual's actual name. A *fictitious* ACTION is a lawsuit brought not for the adjudication of an actual controversy between the parties but merely for the purpose of obtaining the opinion of the court on a particular point of law.

FIDELITY BOND 📖 An INSURANCE device in the form of a personal GUARANTY that protects against loss resulting from disreputable or disloyal employees or other individuals who possess positions of confidence. 📖

A bank might, for example, insure itself against losses deliberately or negligently caused by their officers and staff through the execution of a fidelity BOND. If such losses occur, the amount of the bond is forfeited to reimburse the losses.

FIDELITY INSURANCE 📖 An agreement whereby, for a designated sum of money, one party agrees to guarantee the loyalty and honesty of an AGENT, officer, or employee of an employer by promising to compensate the employer for losses incurred as a result of the disloyalty or dishonesty of such individuals. 📖

FIDUCIARY 📖 An individual in whom another has placed the utmost trust and confidence to manage and protect PROPERTY or money. The relationship wherein one person has an obligation to act for another's benefit. 📖

A fiduciary relationship encompasses the idea of faith and confidence and is generally established only when the confidence given by one person is actually accepted by the other person. Mere respect for another individual's judgment or general trust in his or her character is ordinarily insufficient for the creation of a fiduciary relationship. The duties of a fiduciary include loyalty and reasonable care of the assets within custody. All of the fiduciary's actions are performed for the advantage of the beneficiary.

Courts have neither defined the particular circumstances of fiduciary relationships nor set any limitations on circumstances from which such an alliance may arise. Certain relationships are, however, universally regarded as fiduciary. The term embraces legal relationships such as those between ATTORNEY and CLIENT, BROKER and PRINCIPAL, principal and AGENT, TRUSTEE and BENEFICIARY, and EXECUTORS or ADMINISTRATORS and the HEIRS of a decedent's ESTATE.

A fiduciary relationship extends to every possible case in which one side places confidence in the other and such confidence is accepted; this causes dependence by the one individual and

A financial advisor is a fiduciary because she has been entrusted with the property or money of her clients.

influence by the other. Blood relation alone does not automatically bring about a fiduciary relationship. A fiduciary relationship does not necessarily arise between parents and children or brothers and sisters.

The courts stringently examine transactions between people involved in fiduciary relationships toward one another. Particular scrutiny is placed upon any transaction by which a dominant individual obtains any advantage or profit at the expense of the party under his or her influence. Such transaction, in which undue influence of the fiduciary can be established, is void.

FIELD, DAVID DUDLEY David Dudley Field secured a place in the nineteenth century as a commanding legal reformer. The primary achievements of the New York lawyer include his CODIFICATION of the United States' COMMON LAWS. In addition, Field was among the most successful commercial and constitutional lawyers in New York. The cases he took on most likely anticipated those of the modern, made-for-hire corporate lawyer. He consistently represented a range of interests, sometimes including his own. Field also made contributions to the national political scene. In different capacities, both before and after the Civil War, he managed to represent the constitutional interests of both the Democratic and Republican parties. As a Northern opponent of SLAVERY, still sympathetic to the rights of Southerners, he pursued a fight for justice for the common person on legal and moral grounds. At the same time, his somewhat radical belief in the need to streamline law incited considerable resistance. During and after his life, lawyers and others remembered him as a champion for the progress of procedural law throughout the United States. His lifelong goal of extending justice to the common person left a lasting impression on the U.S. legal system and, to some degree, on the rest of the world.

Field was born February 13, 1805, in Haddam, Connecticut, into a remarkable, aristocratic family. Nearly all the Fields of that era achieved a degree of success. Field's grandfather Captain Timothy Field, of Guilford, Con-

BIOGRAPHY

David Dudley Field

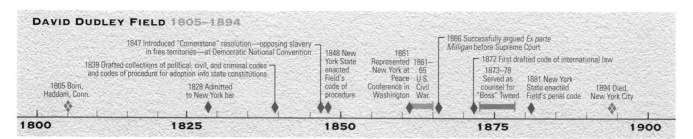

DAVID DUDLEY FIELD 1805–1894

1847 Introduced "Cornerstone" resolution—opposing slavery in free territories—at Democratic National Convention

1839 Drafted collections of political, civil, and criminal codes and codes of procedure for adoption into state constitutions

1805 Born, Haddam, Conn.

1828 Admitted to New York bar

1848 New York State enacted Field's code of procedure

1861 Represented New York at Peace Conference in Washington

1861–65 U.S. Civil War

1866 Successfully argued *Ex parte Milligan* before Supreme Court

1872 First drafted code of international law

1873–78 Served as counsel for "Boss" Tweed

1881 New York State enacted Field's penal code

1894 Died, New York City

| 1800 | 1825 | 1850 | 1875 | 1900 |

necticut, set the standard by fighting in the Revolutionary War. Field's father, the Reverend Dr. David Dudley Field, was educated at Yale College, became a minister, and received his doctorate at the prestigious Williams College. Field's three brothers also obtained influence; in particular, STEPHEN J. FIELD became a justice of the U.S. Supreme Court.

Field followed his father's lead by also studying at Williams. He left the school in 1825 and began the study of law in the office of Hermanus Bleecker of Albany, New York. In 1828, he was admitted to the bar as an attorney, and in 1830 he was appointed a counselor. He went on to practice law with his former teachers from Williams, Henry Sedgwick and Robert Sedgwick.

The tasks Field took on as a lawyer indicated a daring side. JEREMY BENTHAM, an economic and legal philosopher and contemporary of Field's, characterized the legal system of the day when he quipped, "Do you know how judges make the common law?—Just as a man makes laws for his dog." Before Field's initiatives, the only way for persons to know the state of the law was to look through collections of court opinions. Field, Bentham, and others found this recourse unsatisfactory.

With his goal "to bring justice within the reach of all men," Field set out to put the rules of law into a single book, through which persons could determine their rights. His proposals for procedural CODES rested on four basic principles: One, PLEADINGS are meant to state facts truthfully and to then prove those facts by trial. Two, equitable defenses and COUNTERCLAIMS are available in all trial proceedings. Three, the court holds the power (formerly held by the CHANCELLOR) to compel parties to testify and to produce EVIDENCE. Four, evidence at the trial that varies from the pleading is a ground for the DISMISSAL of the ACTION. The development of these principles introduced a new set of procedural standards that he hoped the legal system would follow.

In 1839, Field drafted a collection of codes intended for adoption into state constitutions. The codes comprised 371 sections, filling fewer than seventy pages. The groupings of legal principles under a code of procedure, a political code, a civil code, a code of CRIMINAL PROCEDURE, and a penal code treated law in the essential terms of CIVIL RIGHTS and due remedies.

Ironically, Field's codes faced their strongest resistance in New York. Lawyers throughout the East feared that the codes would interfere with the progress of law as they knew it. Nevertheless, New York enacted Field's code of procedure in 1848. In 1881, the state also passed his penal code. The rest of Field's codes, although passed by both houses of the New York Legislature, were never signed into law. The codes did better elsewhere, particularly in the West. There and throughout the country, twenty-four states enacted them. California enacted the civil code in 1872, aided by the lobbying efforts of Field's brother Stephen, then a practicing lawyer in the state.

Meanwhile, Field did even more to establish his reputation as a controversial figure. He had been a Democrat through much of his early life. Starting in the 1840s, however, he broke sharply with party lines over the annexation of Texas. Democrats sought to expand slavery by permitting it in that state. Field objected and instead supported antislavery Republicans. In fact, some politicians credited Field with contributing a key influence in the nomination of ABRAHAM LINCOLN as the Republican presidential candidate in 1860.

However, labels could not stick to Field. Even as an opponent of slavery, he defended the rights of Southerners after the Civil War by challenging certain Republican Reconstruction laws. In *Ex parte Milligan*, 71 U.S. (4 Wall.) 2, 18 L. Ed. 281 (1866), Field argued successfully that a Reconstruction military commission could not constitutionally convict a Southern civilian, Lamdin B. Milligan, of previous actions as a Confederate. And in *Cummings v. Missouri*, 71 U.S. (4 Wall.) 277, 18 L. Ed. 356 (1867), he helped dismiss a device in the Missouri Constitution that would have prevented former Confederates from holding office.

In addition to legal reform, Field established himself as a representative of other unpopular causes. He continued in this role while representing James Fisk and Jay Gould. His clients faced accusations of manipulating the Erie Railroad system for illegal profit. The case drew considerable attention in the late 1860s from Field's critics around the nation. Fisk and Gould had already become notorious from charges of corruption thrown at them. Field's record of serving in heated cases added to his detractors' ire. In successfully defending the two, he faced criticisms of implementing his own legal codes for personal gain. Newspapers charged him with unethical abuse of the legal system. A group of lawyers even threatened Field with punitive action. However, only the formation of the Association of the Bar of the City of New York ensued. The association, the first of its kind, sought to raise the professional standards of lawyers because the founding members believed Field had demeaned the profession.

"NEVER IS IT SAFE TO ENTRUST ANY MAN OR SET OF MEN WITH THE ABSOLUTE GOVERNMENT OF OTHER MEN."

Field's influence extended beyond the United States. Traveling extensively throughout his life, Field also created a code of international law, first drafted in 1872. Great Britain received the code with the most welcome. The country adopted substantial aspects of Field's American Code of Procedure. Other sets of codes went on to influence countries throughout Europe and the rest of the world. In fact, Field was surprised to discover, during a trip to Asia in 1874, that the Indian legal system had implemented his procedural doctrine.

CROSS-REFERENCES

Code Pleading; Field Code of New York; *Milligan, Ex Parte.*

FIELD, STEPHEN JOHNSON Stephen Johnson Field served as associate justice of the U.S. Supreme Court from 1863 to 1897, making him the second longest serving justice in the history of the Court. Field was a conservative who consistently upheld the interests of business. He became the prime advocate of the theory of "substantive due process," which favored private property rights over attempts by state and federal government to regulate the economy. Conservatives on the Court used substantive DUE PROCESS to strike down regulatory legislation until the 1930s.

Field was born in Haddam, Connecticut, on November 4, 1816. His family moved to Stockbridge, Massachusetts, when he was a young child. At thirteen he was sent to Turkey to live with his sister and her missionary husband. They later moved to Athens, Greece, where Field remained until entering Williams College in 1833. After graduating in 1837 he read the law with his older brother, DAVID DUDLEY FIELD, who had emerged as a prominent New York City attorney and legal reformer.

In 1849 Field left New York City for the Gold Rush in northern California. He speculated in land, developed a thriving legal practice involving property and mineral rights, and organized the town of Marysville. He became Marysville's mayor and judge. In 1850 he was elected to the state legislature. He was instrumental in organizing standards of procedure for civil and criminal law and he also drafted mining laws. He ran for the state senate in 1851 but was defeated.

Field was elected to the California Supreme Court in 1857. He became chief justice in 1859 and served until 1863. He concentrated his efforts on cases dealing with titles to land and mineral rights. In 1863 President ABRAHAM LINCOLN, a Republican, appointed Field to the U.S. Supreme Court. Though Field was a Democrat, he was a loyal Unionist during the Civil War and a well-respected state judge.

Field established his opposition to government interference with business in the *Slaughter-House Cases*, 83 U.S. (16 Wall) 36, 21 L. Ed. 394 (1873). The case involved a Louisiana state law that allowed one meat company the exclusive right to slaughter livestock in New Orleans. Other packing companies were required to pay a fee for using the slaughterhouses. These companies filed suit, claiming that the law violated the Privileges and Immunities Clause of the FOURTEENTH AMENDMENT.

The Court upheld the Louisiana monopoly law, ruling that the Privileges and Immunities Clause had limited effect as it only reached PRIVILEGES AND IMMUNITIES guaranteed by U.S. citizenship, not state citizenship. Field wrote a dissent, maintaining that "the privileges and immunities designated are those which of right belong to the citizens of all free governments." He saw the clause as a powerful tool to keep state government out of the affairs of business and the economy.

Field saw an opportunity to use the Fourteenth Amendment's Due Process Clause to curtail government interference with business. He first articulated the idea of substantive due process in his dissent in *Munn v. Illinois*, 94 U.S. 113, 24 L. Ed. 77 (1876). The majority upheld the Illinois legislature's right to fix maximum storage rates charged by grain elevators and public warehouses and to require LICENSES to operate these facilities.

Field contended that the regulations violated due process and that under the U.S. system of government the legislature lacked the power "to fix the price which anyone shall receive for

BIOGRAPHY

ARTIST ALBERT ROSENTHAL, COLLECTION OF THE SUPREME COURT OF THE UNITED STATES

Stephen Johnson Field

"THE PRESENT ASSAULT UPON CAPITAL IS BUT THE BEGINNING. IT WILL BE BUT THE STEPPING-STONE TO OTHERS, LARGER AND MORE SWEEPING, 'TIL OUR POLITICAL CONTESTS WILL BECOME A WAR OF THE POOR AGAINST THE RICH; A WAR CONSTANTLY GROWING IN INTENSITY AND BITTERNESS."

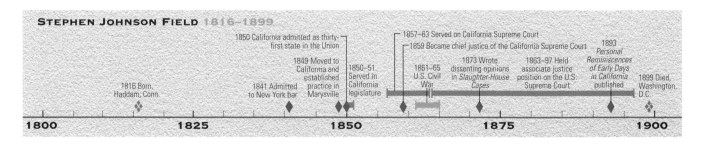

STEPHEN JOHNSON FIELD 1816–1899

- 1816 Born, Haddam, Conn.
- 1841 Admitted to New York bar
- 1849 Moved to California and established practice in Marysville
- 1850 California admitted as thirty-first state in the Union
- 1850–51 Served in California legislature
- 1857–63 Served on California Supreme Court
- 1859 Became chief justice of the California Supreme Court
- 1861–65 U.S. Civil War
- 1863–97 Held associate justice position on the U.S. Supreme Court
- 1873 Wrote dissenting opinions in *Slaughter-House Cases*
- 1893 *Personal Reminiscences of Early Days in California* published
- 1899 Died, Washington, D.C.

1800   1825   1850   1875   1900

his property of any kind." By 1890 he had convinced the majority of the Court that his view of the Due Process Clause was correct and had extended its reach to the FIFTH AMENDMENT's Due Process Clause, using it to invalidate federal legislation that regulated business. Until the 1930s the Court overturned a succession of state and federal laws that attempted to regulate business and labor.

Field voted to strike down a federal INCOME TAX in *Pollock v. Farmers' Loan and Trust Co.*, 157 U.S. 429, 15 S. Ct. 673, 39 L. Ed. 759 (1895), seeing the tax as a plot against capitalism. In his concurring opinion, Field warned, "The persistent assault upon capital is but the beginning. It will be a stepping stone to others larger and more sweeping till our political contests will become a war of the poor against the rich, a war constantly growing in intensity and bitterness."

Field entertained political ambitions while on the Court. In 1880 he sought the Democratic party presidential nomination but did poorly at the nominating convention. He became increasingly infirm during the 1890s and did little work. He was determined, however, to break JOHN MARSHALL's record of thirty-three years on the Court. He achieved that record in 1896 (later to be surpassed by WILLIAM O. DOUGLAS) and retired in 1897. He died in Washington, D.C., on April 9, 1899.

CROSS-REFERENCES

Pollock v. Farmers' Loan & Trust Co.; Slaughter-House Cases.

FIELD AUDIT  A systematic investigation by the INTERNAL REVENUE SERVICE of a taxpayer's financial records and his or her tax return that is conducted at the taxpayer's place of business or at the office of the individual who prepared the return.

A field audit differs from a CORRESPONDENCE AUDIT and an OFFICE AUDIT in the location where it occurs. See also INCOME TAX.

FIELD CODE OF NEW YORK The first code of CIVIL PROCEDURE that established simplified rules for PLEADING an ACTION before a court, which was proposed by DAVID DUDLEY FIELD in 1848 for the state of New York and enacted by the state legislature.

The Field Code served as the prototype for other states in codifying and revising the rules of civil practice in their respective courts. Prior to the code, no uniform rules existed for the commencement of an action. Each common-law FORM OF ACTION and each EQUITY action had its own rigid procedural requirements to be satisfied and the language of such pleadings was highly formalized and verbose. A plaintiff's al-

legation rarely was stated in simple, clear language.

The Field Code was a radical departure from the procedures of the past. As a result of its merger of law and equity actions into one action, the code provided a uniform set of rules of pleading to be used in each type of case. The pleadings were to be in simple, concise language that set forth only the facts of the dispute between the two parties.

This clarification of procedure was a significant factor in bringing about a more efficient system of justice. Within twenty-five years of the enactment of the Field Code, about one-half of the states enacted comparable codes. The Field Code was also influential in English law, its principles drafted into the JUDICATURE ACTS of 1873 and 1875.

The term CODE PLEADING is derived from the Field Code, although code pleading can refer to compliance with the requirements of either a legislative enactment or a rule of the court.

FIERI FACIAS [*Latin, Cause (it) to be done.*] The name of a WRIT of EXECUTION that directs a sheriff to seize and sell the GOODS and CHATTELS of a JUDGMENT DEBTOR in order to satisfy the judgment against the debtor.

In its original form, the writ directed the seizure and sale of goods and chattels only, but eventually was enlarged to permit levy on REAL PROPERTY, too; largely synonymous with a modern writ of execution.

FIFO An abbreviation for first-in, first-out, a method employed in accounting for the identification and valuation of the INVENTORY of a business.

FIFO assumes that the first GOODS purchased are the first sold. As a consequence, the items that remain in the inventory at the end of the year are assumed to be those purchased last. See also LIFO.

First-in, first-out is a method of inventory control that means that inventory bought first is sold first.

FIFTEENTH AMENDMENT The Fifteenth Amendment to the U.S. Constitution reads:

Section 1. The right of citizens of the United States to vote shall not be denied or abridged by the United States or by any State on account of race, color, or previous condition of servitude.

Section 2. The Congress shall have power to enforce this article by appropriate legislation.

The Fifteenth Amendment was ratified by the states in 1870 and also gave Congress the power to enforce such rights against governments that sought to undermine this guarantee through the enactment of appropriate legislation. Enforcement was, however, difficult as states employed GRANDFATHER CLAUSES and other eligibility requirements to maintain racial discrimination in the electoral process. See also ELECTIONS; VOTING RIGHTS.

FIFTH AMENDMENT The Fifth Amendment to the U.S. Constitution reads:

No person shall be held to answer for a capital, or otherwise infamous crime, unless on a presentment or indictment of a Grand Jury, except in cases arising in the land or naval forces, or in the Militia, when in actual service in time of War or public danger; nor shall any person be subject for the same offence to be twice put in jeopardy of life or limb; nor shall be compelled in any criminal case to be a witness against himself, nor be deprived of life, liberty, or property, without due process of law; nor shall private property be taken for public use, without just compensation.

The BILL OF RIGHTS, which consists of the first ten amendments to the U.S. Constitution,

The judiciary may declare unconstitutional laws that infringe on the Bill of Rights, the first ten amendments to the U.S. Constitution.

SPENCER GRANT/THE PICTURE CUBE

B. TAM NOMOTO
JUDGE

enumerates certain basic personal liberties. Laws passed by elected officials that infringe on these liberties are invalidated by the judiciary as unconstitutional. The Fifth Amendment to the Constitution, ratified in 1791, represents five distinct liberties the Framers attempted to safeguard from majoritarian impulses: (1) the right to be indicted by an impartial GRAND JURY before being tried for a federal criminal offense, (2) the right to be free from multiple prosecutions or punishments for a single criminal offense, (3) the right to remain silent when prosecuted for a criminal offense, (4) the right to have personal liberties protected by DUE PROCESS OF LAW, and (5) the right to receive JUST COMPENSATION when the government takes private property for public use.

The Framers of the Fifth Amendment intended that its provisions would apply only to the actions of the federal government. However, after the FOURTEENTH AMENDMENT was ratified, most of the Fifth Amendment's protections were made applicable to the states. Under the doctrine of incorporation, most of the liberties set forth in the Bill of Rights were made applicable to state governments through the Supreme Court's interpretation of the Due Process and Equal Protection Clauses of the Fourteenth Amendment. As a result, all states must provide protection against DOUBLE JEOPARDY, SELF-INCRIMINATION, deprivation of due process, and government taking of private property without just compensation. The Grand Jury Clause of the Fifth Amendment has not been made applicable to state governments. See also INCORPORATION DOCTRINE.

Double Jeopardy Clause The Double Jeopardy Clause of the Fifth Amendment prohibits state and federal governments from re-prosecuting for the same offense a defendant who has already been acquitted or convicted. It also prevents state and federal governments from imposing more than one punishment for the same offense.

For more than a century, courts have wrestled with the question of what constitutes an ACQUITTAL such that a person has already been placed in jeopardy for a particular offense. However, all courts agree that the Double Jeopardy Clause applies only to legal proceedings brought by state and federal governments in criminal court. It does not apply to legal proceedings instituted by purely private individuals in civil court.

The U.S. legal system has two primary divisions, criminal and civil. Criminal actions are designed to punish individuals for wrongdoing. CIVIL ACTIONS are designed to compensate victims with money DAMAGES for injuries suffered at the hands of another. Thus, an individual who has been acquitted in criminal court of murder can, without violating the Double Jeopardy Clause, be required in civil court to pay money damages to the family of a victim. Thus, the successive criminal and civil trials of O. J. Simpson, regarding the deaths of Nicole Brown Simpson and Ronald Goldman, did not violate double jeopardy.

The Fifth Amendment's prohibition against double jeopardy is rooted in Anglo-Saxon jurisprudence. Yet the right against double jeopardy in England was sometimes ignored by the Crown. In certain important cases where an acquittal undermined royal interests, the defendant was tried again in a different manner or by a different court. The protection against double jeopardy was also extremely narrow under English law. It applied only to capital crimes, in which the defendant would be subject to the death penalty if convicted. It did not apply to lesser offenses such as noncapital FELONIES and MISDEMEANORS.

Massachusetts was the first colony that recognized a right against double jeopardy. Its colonial charter provided, "No man shall be twise sentenced by Civil Justice for one and the same Crime, offence, or Trespasse" (as quoted in *United States v. Halper*, 490 U.S. 435, 109 S. Ct. 1892, 104 L. Ed. 2d 487 [1989]). This charter, which served as a model for several other colonies, expanded the protection against double jeopardy to all crimes and offenses, not just capital felonies. Nonetheless, at the time the Bill of Rights was ratified in 1791, the constitutions of only two states expressly afforded double jeopardy protection. Thus, when JAMES MADISON submitted his proposal for the Fifth Amendment to Congress, he wanted to make sure that the right against double jeopardy would not be abused by the government, as it had been in England, or altogether forgotten, as it had been in the constitutions of eleven states.

Although Congress and the state ratifying conventions said very little about the Fifth Amendment's Double Jeopardy Clause, the Supreme Court has identified several concerns the Framers were trying to address when they drafted it: (1) preventing the government from employing its superior resources to wear down and erroneously convict innocent persons; (2) protecting individuals from the financial, emotional, and social consequences of successive prosecutions; (3) preserving the finality and integrity of criminal proceedings, which would be compromised were the state allowed to arbitrarily ignore unsatisfactory outcomes; (4) restricting prosecutorial discretion over the charging process; and (5) eliminating judicial discretion to impose cumulative punishments not authorized by the legislature.

Self-Incrimination Clause   The Fifth Amendment's right against self-incrimination permits an individual to refuse to disclose information that could be used against her or him in a criminal prosecution. The purpose of this right is to inhibit the government from compelling a CONFESSION through force, coercion, or deception. The Self-Incrimination Clause applies to any state or federal legal proceeding, whether it is civil, criminal, administrative, or judicial in nature. This privilege is frequently invoked during the trial phase of legal proceedings, where individuals are placed under OATH and asked questions on the witness stand.

The privilege is also asserted with some frequency during the pretrial phase of legal proceedings. In the pretrial phase of criminal cases, it is usually asserted in response to pointed questions asked by law enforcement agents, PROSECUTORS, and other government officials who are seeking to determine the persons responsible for a particular crime. During the pretrial phase of civil cases, parties may assert the right against self-incrimination when potentially damaging questions are posed in DEPOSITIONS and INTERROGATORIES.

The right against self-incrimination largely took hold in English law with the seventeenth-

A witness may refuse to disclose information that would incriminate him and lead to his own prosecution.

century trial of John Lilburne. Lilburne was a Puritan agitator who opposed British attempts to impose Anglican religious uniformity across England. In 1637 Lilburne was prosecuted for attempting to smuggle several thousand Puritan pamphlets into England. Before the STAR CHAMBER (an English court with JURISDICTION to extinguish nonconformity in the realm), Lilburne refused to take an oath requiring him to answer truthfully any question asked of him. He said he could see that the court was trying to ensnare him, and he claimed that the law of God and the law of the land supported his right against self-accusation. Lilburne was whipped and pilloried for refusing to take the oath. Parliament later declared his punishment illegal, abolished the Star Chamber, and ultimately recognized the right against self-incrimination.

The American colonists, particularly the Puritans in Massachusetts, were familiar with the plight of Lilburne. Nonetheless, the Massachusetts Body of Liberties, a collection of rules of conduct for the Puritan colonists taken nearly verbatim from the Bible, permitted the use of torture to extract confessions from defendants accused of capital crimes. Many other colonies subjected political and religious dissenters to inquisitorial judicial proceedings not unlike those employed in England. In many of these proceedings, the accused persons were not entitled to remain silent but were often asked to provide EVIDENCE of their innocence. Even after the Revolution, the constitutions of four states offered no protections against self-incrimination. As Madison drafted the original version of the Fifth Amendment, the lessons of English and colonial history were firmly in his mind.

The Supreme Court has interpreted the Self-Incrimination Clause more broadly than many of the Framers probably would have. *Miranda v. Arizona*, 384 U.S. 436, 86 S. Ct. 1602, 16 L. Ed. 2d 694 (1966), illustrates this point. In *Miranda* the Supreme Court held that any statements made by defendants while in police custody before trial will be inadmissible during prosecution unless the police first warn the defendants that they have (1) the right to remain silent, (2) the right to consult an attorney before being questioned by the police, (3) the right to have an attorney present during police questioning, (4) the right to a court appointed attorney if they cannot afford one, and (5) the right to be informed that any statements they do make can and will be used in their prosecution. Although the *Miranda* warnings are not in the Fifth Amendment's Self-Incrimination Clause, the Supreme Court has ruled that they constitute an essential part of a judicially created buffer zone that is necessary to protect rights that *are* specifically set forth in the Constitution.

Due Process Clause The Fifth Amendment's Due Process Clause has two aspects: procedural and substantive. Procedural due process is concerned with the process by which legal proceedings are conducted. It requires that all persons who will be materially affected by a legal proceeding receive notice of its time, place, and subject matter so that they have an adequate opportunity to prepare. It also requires that legal proceedings be conducted in a fair manner by an IMPARTIAL judge who will allow the interested parties to present fully their complaints, grievances, and defenses. The Due Process Clause governs civil, criminal, and administrative proceedings from the pretrial stage through final appeal, and proceedings that produce arbitrary or capricious results will be overturned as unconstitutional.

Substantive due process is concerned with the content of particular laws applied during legal proceedings. Before World War II, the Supreme Court relied on substantive due process to overturn legislation that infringed on a variety of property interests, including the right of employers to determine the wages their employees would be paid and the number of hours they could work. Since World War II, the Supreme Court has relied on substantive due process to protect PRIVACY and autonomy interests of adults, including the right to use contraception and the right to have an ABORTION.

The line separating procedure from substance is not always clear. For example, procedural due process guarantees criminal defendants the right to a fair trial, and substantive due process specifies that twelve jurors must return a unanimous guilty VERDICT before the death penalty can be imposed. The concepts of substantive and procedural due process trace back to English law. The MAGNA CHARTA provided, "No free man shall be seized, or imprisoned, or disseised, or outlawed, or exiled, or injured in any way . . . except by the lawful judgment of his peers, or by the law of the land" (art. 39). According to eminent English jurist SIR EDWARD COKE, *law of the land* and *due process of law* were interchangeable terms possessing both procedural and substantive meaning.

The American colonists followed the English tradition of attributing substantive and procedural qualities to the concepts of due process and LAW OF THE LAND. Maryland and Massachusetts, for example, equated the two concepts with colonial COMMON LAW and legislation regardless of their procedural content. On the other hand, Virginia, Pennsylvania, and Vermont all passed constitutional provisions identifying *law of the land* with specific procedural safeguards, including the right against self-incrimination. Thus, when the Due Process Clause was submitted to the state conventions for ratification, it was popularly understood to place both procedural requirements on legal proceedings and substantive limitations on the law applied in those proceedings.

Eminent Domain Clause When the government takes someone's PERSONAL PROPERTY for public use, the law calls it a taking and protects it under the Eminent Domain Clause of the Fifth Amendment. The Eminent Domain Clause permits the government to appropriate private property, both REAL ESTATE and personal belongings, for a public purpose so long as the owner receives just compensation, which is normally equated with the FAIR MARKET VALUE of the property. The Fifth Amendment attempts to strike a balance between the needs of the public and the PROPERTY RIGHTS of the owner.

The government may take the personal property of an individual for public use, such as the construction of a railroad, under the Eminent Domain Clause of the Fifth Amendment.

CLAUDIA DHIMITRI/THE PICTURE CUBE

The power of EMINENT DOMAIN was first recognized in England in 1215. Article 39 of the Magna Charta (the Great Charter of English liberties) read, "no free man shall be . . . disseised [deprived] of his freehold . . . except by the lawful judgment of his peers, or by the law of the land." No compensation was awarded to owners whose property was taken by the government for public use. Instead, English law merely required that the government obtain ownership of private property through existing legal channels, such as parliamentary legislation. This principle was followed in England for several centuries, and was later adopted by the American colonies.

Uncompensated takings of private property by colonial governments generally involved unimproved land (land that had not been built on). Colonial governments often appropriated private land to build roads and bridges to develop America's frontiers. During the American Revolution, the power of eminent domain was used to seize the land of colonists loyal to Great Britain, and to obtain various goods for military consumption. Compensation was rarely given to individual owners deprived of their property by colonial governments because making personal sacrifices for the common good, including forfeiting personal property, was considered an essential duty of every colonist.

Not everyone in the colonies believed that personal property interests should always be sacrificed for the greater good of society. Many colonists expressed distress over legislatures that were abusing their power of eminent domain. New York, for example, regularly failed to recognize TITLES to real estate in its colony held by residents of Vermont. Other colonies also discriminated in favor of their own residents, and against persons whose patriotism was questionable during the Revolution. It was in this context that the Eminent Domain Clause of the Fifth Amendment was drafted.

During the twentieth century, the Supreme Court has enlarged the protection against uncompensated takings of private property by state and federal governments. The Eminent Domain Clause has been interpreted to protect not only owners whose property is physically taken by the government, but also owners whose property value is diminished as a result of government activity. Thus, compensable takings under the Fifth Amendment result from ZONING ordinances that deny property owners an economically viable use of their land (*Agins v. City of Tiburon*, 447 U.S. 255, 100 S. Ct. 2138, 65 L. Ed. 2d 106 [1980]), environmental regulations that require the government to occupy an owner's land in order to monitor groundwater wells (*Hendler v. United States*, 952 F.2d 1364 [Fed. Cir. 1991], land-use regulations that curtail mining operations (*Pennsylvania Coal Co. v. Mahon*, 260 U.S. 393, 43 S. Ct. 158, 67 L. Ed. 322 [1992]), and government owned airports that lower property values in adjacent neighborhoods (*United States v. Causby*, 328 U.S. 256, 66 S. Ct. 1062, 90 L. Ed. 1206 [1946]).

Grand Jury Clause A grand jury is a group of citizens summoned to criminal court by the SHERIFF to consider accusations and complaints leveled against persons suspected of engaging in criminal conduct. Grand juries do not determine guilt or innocence. Instead, they determine whether PROBABLE CAUSE exists to believe that the ACCUSED has committed a crime, and return an INDICTMENT (a formal charge against the accused) if they do find probable cause. At common law a grand jury consisted of not less than twelve or more than twenty-three men. Today grand juries impaneled before a federal district court must consist of not less than sixteen or more than twenty-three men and women.

Potential jurors are usually drawn from lists of qualified residents. Persons who are below the AGE OF MAJORITY, have been convicted of certain crimes, or are biased toward the accused are ineligible to serve as grand jurors.

The Fifth Amendment's Grand Jury Clause has not been made applicable to state governments through the doctrine of incorporation. In place of grand juries, most states use a document known as an INFORMATION, which is drafted by the prosecutor, to tell accused persons about the charges against them.

The grand jury originated in England during the reign of HENRY II (1154–89). In 1166 a statute called the Assize of Clarendon was enacted. The ASSIZE provided that no person could be prosecuted unless four men from each township and twelve men from each hundred appeared before the county court to accuse the individual of a specific crime. This compulsory process, called a presenting jury, foreshadowed the grand jury as an accusatory body that identified individuals for prosecution but made no finding as to guilt or innocence.

As the grand jury system developed in England and colonial America, it protected innocent persons facing unfounded charges initiated by political, religious, and personal adversaries. The impartiality of grand juries is essential. This is a significant reason the proceedings are convened in secrecy; otherwise, public scrutiny and similar prejudicial influences could affect their decision-making process. Although grand juries must be impartial, accused persons have no constitutional right to present evidence on their behalf or cross-examine witnesses, and HEARSAY evidence may be introduced against them.

CROSS-REFERENCES

Criminal Law; Criminal Procedure; Custodial Interrogation; *Miranda v. Arizona.*

FILE A record of the court. A paper is said to be filed when it is delivered to the proper officer to be kept on file as a matter of record and reference. But in general the terms *file* and *the files* are used loosely to denote the official custody of the court or the place in the offices of a court where the records and papers are kept. The file in a case includes the original COMPLAINT and all PLEADINGS and papers belonging thereto.

A clerk files a document by endorsing it on the date it is received and retaining it in his or her office for inspection by the parties that it might concern.

FILIATION PROCEEDING A process whereby a court determines the paternity of an illegitimate child in order to establish the father's duty to provide support for the child.

A filiation proceeding is also referred to as a bastardy proceeding or an AFFILIATION PROCEEDING.

See also ILLEGITIMACY.

FILIBUSTER A tactic used by a LEGISLATIVE representative to hinder and delay consideration of and action to be taken on a proposed

Senator Gonzalo Barrientos filibustered a bill in the Texas Senate in order to delay its discussion and decision.

bill through prolonged, irrelevant, and procrastinating speeches on the floor of the House, Senate, or other legislative body. 📖

A filibuster is stopped by CLOTURE, a legislative procedure that enables a vote to be taken on the proposed measure.

FILIUS NULLIUS 📖 [*Latin, A son of nobody.*] An illegitimate child who had few legal rights under the COMMON LAW. 📖

Laws have broadened the legal rights of illegitimate children who, in the language of some statutes, are referred to as nonmarital children. See also ILLEGITIMACY.

FILLMORE, MILLARD Millard Fillmore was a Whig, a member of the New York Assembly, a member of the U.S. Congress, vice president of the United States under ZACHARY TAYLOR, and the thirteenth president of the United States. Despite a personal dislike of SLAVERY, he signed into law the FUGITIVE SLAVE ACT OF 1850, among other bills that originated in the COMPROMISE OF 1850. His administration supported trade with foreign countries, forging one of the first trade agreements with Japan, but Fillmore was opposed to expansionism and refused to support an attempted annexation of Cuba in 1851.

Fillmore was born June 7, 1800, in Locke, New York. His father, Nathaniel Fillmore, was a farmer who wanted Fillmore to escape a life of poverty. Fillmore left school at an early age to become apprenticed, but a judge recognized his talents and ambition and persuaded him to study law. He was admitted to the bar at the age of twenty-four and soon became a leading lawyer in the state of New York.

In 1828, Fillmore was elected to the New York Assembly, and in 1832, he was elected to Congress, where he served three terms. In 1844, he ran unsuccessfully for governor of New York State. In 1848, the Whig party nominated him for vice president to run with the Mexican War hero Taylor. Fillmore and Taylor won the election by appeasing both northern and southern voters, taking the position that although slavery was evil, it was a problem that had to be solved by the states.

Fillmore was disappointed with his lack of power and voice as vice president. The country was facing a crisis over the issues of slavery and

BIOGRAPHY

Millard Fillmore

"LET US REMEMBER THAT REVOLUTIONS DO NOT ALWAYS ESTABLISH FREEDOM. OUR OWN FREE INSTITUTIONS WERE NOT THE OFFSPRING OF OUR REVOLUTION. THEY EXISTED BEFORE."

the admittance of Texas, California, and New Mexico into the Union. The Compromise of 1850, written by Senator HENRY CLAY, was an omnibus that recommended that California be admitted to the Union as a free state, the rest of Mexican cession be formed without restrictions on slavery, Texas end its boundary dispute with New Mexico, and a new fugitive slave law be passed. As president of the Senate, Fillmore was involved in the debate over the compromise but found himself unable to influence its course.

President Taylor was seen as the greatest obstacle to the compromise because he refused to sign it as one comprehensive piece of legislation, wanting to consider separately the issue of California's admission into the Union as a free state. The South feared that if California was admitted as a free state, other western territories would eventually become free states, thereby giving the antislavery movement a more powerful voice in Congress. In the summer of 1850, Taylor became even more hostile to the South when he threatened to lead the U.S. Army against the Texas militia, which was trying to spread slavery westward by threatening Texas's boundary with the territory of New Mexico. This never transpired because on July 9, 1850, Taylor died suddenly and Fillmore was sworn in as president.

Fillmore supported the compromise, but he too wanted the legislation divided into separate bills. With the departure from the Senate of the compromise's strongest supporters—Clay, DANIEL WEBSTER, and JOHN C. CALHOUN—and the maneuvering of new leaders such as STEPHEN A. DOUGLAS, Jefferson Davis, and William H. Seward, the bill was split up. Only three months after Taylor's death, all the separate bills were passed by Congress and signed into law by Fillmore.

Fillmore was opposed to slavery and had difficulty signing one of those bills, the Fugitive Slave Act of 1850. The act forbade both government and individuals to help slaves escape from their master. It also made the federal government responsible for recovering and returning runaway slaves. Fillmore believed it was his constitutional responsibility to enforce the

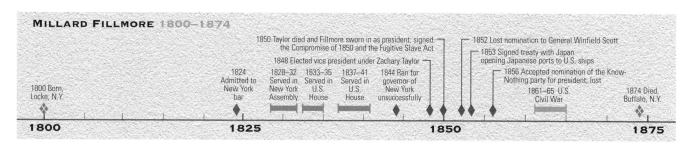

MILLARD FILLMORE 1800–1874

1800 Born, Locke, N.Y.

1824 Admitted to New York bar

1828–32 Served in New York Assembly

1833–35 Served in U.S. House

1837–41 Served in U.S. House

1844 Ran for governor of New York unsuccessfully

1848 Elected vice president under Zachary Taylor

1850 Taylor died and Fillmore sworn in as president; signed the Compromise of 1850 and the Fugitive Slave Act

1852 Lost nomination to General Winfield Scott

1853 Signed treaty with Japan opening Japanese ports to U.S. ships

1856 Accepted nomination of the Know-Nothing party for president; lost

1861–65 U.S. Civil War

1874 Died, Buffalo, N.Y.

1800   1825   1850   1875

law even though he disagreed with it. In a letter to Webster, he wrote,

> God knows I detest slavery, but it is an existing evil, for which we are not responsible, and we must endure it and give it such protection as is guaranteed by the constitution, till we get rid of it without destroying the last hope of free government in the world.

In the area of foreign policy, the Fillmore administration achieved one of the first trade agreements ever reached between the empire of Japan and a foreign country. This agreement opened up new sources of coal to power the United States' seagoing steamers, and it helped establish a Pacific trade route between the United States and Asia. Fillmore opposed the popular nineteenth-century philosophy of Manifest Destiny, which regarded U.S. expansion into the Pacific as inevitable. He thought seizing another nation's land was dishonorable. In August 1851, he refused to give military support to an attempted annexation of Cuba by four hundred U.S. citizens, mostly veterans of the Mexican War. The invasion of the Spanish colony failed, and most of the invaders, including their leader, Narciso Lopez, were captured and executed.

Early in his presidency, Fillmore had determined that he would not seek reelection, but in the months leading up to the 1852 election, it became clear that the southern Whigs would support only Fillmore. Even though he did not desire his party's nomination, Fillmore left his name on the convention ballot to prevent the nomination of General Winfield Scott. Fillmore knew the general would be a hopeless candidate in the South because of his connections with abolitionists like Seward. But on the fifty-third ballot, Scott was nominated. As Fillmore predicted, Scott lost the general election to Democrat Franklin Pierce.

Fillmore's last venture into politics came in 1856 when he accepted the presidential nomination of the Know-Nothing party. This political party was formed as a result of a division in the Whig party between those who favored national expansion and those who were against slavery. The Know-Nothings, created by the national Whigs, used their opposition to mass immigration from Europe to unite northern and southern voters. U.S. citizens never took the party seriously, and Fillmore lost the election to southern Democrat James Buchanan.

After the election, Fillmore settled down in Buffalo, New York, and became the city's leading citizen. He participated in many committees and supported institutions such as the University of Buffalo and the Orphan Asylum. When the nation fell into civil war in 1861, he pledged his support to the Union cause and worked to enlist Buffalo men in the war effort. His support dwindled as the war raged on, and in 1863, he publicly denounced Abraham Lincoln's administration's handling of the conflict and supported George B. McClellan in the 1864 presidential election.

Fillmore died March 8, 1874.

FINAL DECISION ⬚ The resolution of a controversy by a court or series of courts from which no APPEAL may be taken and that precludes further action. The last act by a lower court that is required for the completion of a lawsuit, such as the handing down of a final judgment upon which an appeal to a higher court may be brought. ⬚

FINANCE CHARGE ⬚ The amount owed to a lender by a purchaser-debtor to be allowed to pay for goods purchased over a series of installments, as opposed to one lump sum at the time of the sale or billing. ⬚

A finance charge, sometimes called the cost of CREDIT, is expressed as an annual interest rate levied upon the purchase price. It does not include any amounts that the lender might require for insurance premiums, delinquency charges, attorney's fees, court costs, collection expenses, or official fees that might be incurred should the debtor default in the repayment of the debt.

Federal and state "truth-in-lending" laws mandate that the complete cost of finance charges be fully disclosed on credit agreements and billing statements. See also Consumer Credit Protection Act.

FINANCIAL RESPONSIBILITY ACTS ⬚ State statutes that require owners of motor vehicles to produce proof of financial accountability as a condition to acquiring a LICENSE and registration so that judgments rendered against them arising out of the operation of the vehicles may be satisfied. ⬚

See also AUTOMOBILES.

FINANCIAL STATEMENT ⬚ Any report summarizing the financial condition or financial results of a person or an organization on any date or for any period. Financial statements include the BALANCE SHEET and the income statement and sometimes the statement of changes in financial position. ⬚

FINDER ⬚ An intermediary who contracts to find, introduce, and bring together parties to a business opportunity, leaving ultimate negotiations and consummation of business transaction to the principals. With respect to a securities issue, refers to one who brings together an issuer and an underwriter; in connection with mergers, refers to one who brings two companies together. May also refer to one who secures MORTGAGE financing for a borrower, locates a particular type of executive or professional for a corporation, or locates a particular type of business acquisition for a corporation. 📖

FINDING 📖 The result of the deliberations of a JURY or a court. A decision upon a question of fact reached as the result of a judicial examination or investigation by a court, jury, referee, coroner, etc. A recital of the facts as found. The word commonly applies to the result reached by a judge or jury. 📖

FINDING LOST GOODS 📖 The discovery of PERSONAL PROPERTY that has been unintentionally removed from its owner's POSSESSION through his or her neglect or inadvertence. 📖

The fact that an owner has involuntarily parted with the property and that he or she is ignorant of its location sufficiently establishes that the property is lost. *Mislaid property* is property that an owner intentionally places somewhere so that it can eventually be found again, but he or she subsequently forgets where it was placed. The right to possess the property rests in the issue of whether the property is to be considered lost or mislaid. This issue must be determined upon examination of the particular facts and circumstances of any given case.

Abandoned property is property to which the owner has purposefully relinquished all rights as an owner thereto. Since such property is ownerless, it can be owned by the first person who takes it with the intent to claim it as his or her property.

The place where the property is discovered is an important factor in determining whether it is lost or mislaid.

When property is in someone's possession, it cannot be found within the meaning of lost property. An article in the possession and protection of the owner of the place where it is found is not legally considered lost. Similarly, an owner of land is considered to have possession of all articles on the land even though he or she may be unaware of their presence. If the finder of lost property is an employee of the owner of the land, the owner's right to custody of the property is superior to that of the employee.

Property found in a public or semipublic place—where the public is ordinarily invited and expected to be—may be considered lost, since the owner or manager of the location does not represent its owner.

Treasure trove is any gold or silver in coin, plate, or bullion hidden in the earth or other private place by an unknown owner for a long time. The property is not treasure trove unless the identity of the owner is unascertainable. Ordinarily, the treasure must be in the form of coin or bullion, but it may also include paper currency—particularly when such currency is discovered with both these precious metals.

An individual who finds lost property does not acquire absolute ownership of the property. In order to obtain title to, or rights in, the lost property, the finder must intentionally take possession and control over it.

The individual who acquires possession of a lost or mislaid article has superior rights to the item over anyone except the true owner. This person is only the apparent owner. The finder's TITLE to the property may be forfeited upon discovery of the true owner, whose title in it is unaffected by the fact that the article has been lost. A finder's title is CONTINGENT upon the potential discovery of the true owner. He or she may not, therefore, transfer title to another individual.

If the true owner of lost property dies before his or her identity is discovered, the title and right to the lost article passes to the EXECUTOR or ADMINISTRATOR of the owner's ESTATE for distribution to his or her heirs pursuant to the terms of his or her WILL or the laws of DESCENT AND DISTRIBUTION.

As between the finder of treasure trove and its true owner, the true owner prevails. It has been held, however, that the finder of treasure trove has greater rights to it than the heirs of the individual who concealed it.

The true owner of lost property is responsible for paying all reasonable expenses incurred by a finder in the discovery and preservation of lost property. The finder may also be entitled to a small compensation for his or her time and effort; however, the finding party does not acquire a LIEN against the property. The finder cannot receive reimbursement for his or her

Treasure trove, such as these shipwrecked gold coins, ingots, and bars dating from the 18th century, is the property of the person who takes possession of it.

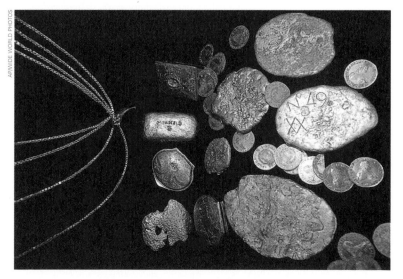

AP/WIDE WORLD PHOTOS

expenses and time with use of the property, nor is the individual entitled to a REWARD for finding it unless one has been offered.

Some state statutes provide that a finder of lost goods is entitled to recover expenses that were necessary to preserve the property and to a reward for holding it. These statutes are consistent with statutes providing that the finder must return the property to its true owner and that a finder who is aware of the identity of the true owner is guilty of LARCENY if he or she keeps the goods. Such statutes are enacted in order to aid the finding of lost property.

An individual who finds and takes possession of lost property ordinarily has the right to possess it over everyone but the true owner. Some statutes provide that if the true owner neglects to appear and claim the property within a certain time period after the finding of the article has been published in a local newspaper, the finder is entitled to retain part of the property or part of its value while the remaining portion passes to the state, or one of its departments or agencies.

The finder of treasure trove, under early COMMON LAW, took title to it over everyone except the true owner. This doctrine was changed in England by a statute that granted title to the crown, subject to the claims of the true owner. In the United States, the law regarding treasure trove has largely been combined into the law governing lost property. Some cases still hold, however, that the old treasure trove law is not merged into the statutory law relating to lost property. The common law of early England has also been held to apply in the absence of a statute governing treasure trove.

In either instance, the title to treasure trove belongs to the finder over all other people except the true owner, unless otherwise provided by statute. If there is a conflict as to ownership between the true owner and the state, the owner is entitled to treasure trove.

FINES ▣ Monetary charges imposed upon individuals who have been convicted of a CRIME or a lesser offense. ▣

A fine is a criminal sanction. A civil sanction, by contrast, is called a PENALTY. The term *fine* is sometimes used to describe a penalty, but the terms *fine* and *penalty* should be kept separate because the consequences are different: nonpayment of a criminal fine can result in incarceration, whereas nonpayment of a civil penalty cannot.

Federal and state criminal statutes authorize fines for certain offenses. Depending on the crime, a fine may be imposed in addition to INCARCERATION, RESTITUTION, community service, or PROBATION. The amount of a fine varies with the severity of the offense. State and federal criminal codes generally break down felonies and misdemeanors into classes or degrees. In Kentucky, for example, the fine for a violation or a class B MISDEMEANOR may not exceed $250. For a class A misdemeanor, the fine may not exceed $500. For a FELONY conviction, Kentucky courts are bound by statute to fine the defendant not less than $1,000, and not more than $10,000 or double the gain from the commission of the offense, whichever is greater (Ky. Rev. Stat. Ann. § 534.030 [Baldwin]). Two or more felonies committed through a single act may be fined separately in Kentucky, but the aggregate may not exceed $10,000 or double the amount of the illicit gain, whichever is greater. The maximum amount for fines seems to bear little relation to the cost of living. For example, in New York, where the cost of living is quite high, the fine for a violation may not exceed $250, the same as in Kentucky, where the cost of living is much lower.

In federal court, a felony is subject to a fine of not more than $250,000. A fine of $250,000 is also authorized for a misdemeanor resulting in death. Fines for class A misdemeanors not resulting in death may reach $100,000, and similar class B and C misdemeanors may result in a fine of up to $5,000 (18 U.S.C.A. § 3571). Federal law also allows a court to fine a defendant who has financially benefited from a crime, an amount twice that illicitly gained.

Federal and state laws authorize fines of similarly scaled amounts for organizations. The maximum fine for organizations is much higher than that for individuals. For instance, under 18 U.S.C.A. § 3571, an organization guilty of a felony may be fined as much as $500,000. Kentucky also doubles the fine limit for organizations. For example, an organization in Kentucky that commits a felony may be fined $20,000, up from $10,000 for an individual (Ky. Rev. Stat. Ann. § 534.050 [Baldwin]).

States also authorize fines for specific crimes. In Kentucky, for example, a fine of not more than $250 and not less than $100 is required for the illegal sale of tobacco to a minor (§ 438.13 [Baldwin]). Statutes fix the maximum fine for a given offense, and statutes can be changed, so fine amounts can change.

In state courts, sentencing is usually left to the discretion of the judge. If a defendant is found by a court to be indigent, the court generally will not impose a fine (see, e.g., Ky. Rev. Stat. Ann. §§ 534.030, 534.040 [Baldwin]).

A determination of indigence generally involves an examination of several factors, including income, earning capacity, financial resources, the burden the fine may impose on persons dependent on the defendant, and the need to deprive the defendant of any illegally obtained gains. Where an indigent defendant is convicted of an offense that calls for incarceration, the court generally will not impose a fine in addition to the incarceration.

Federal courts must sometimes follow prison sentences mandated by federal statute, but the decision of whether to impose a fine in addition to any SENTENCE is generally within the judge's discretion. Both state and federal courts may later reduce the amount of a fine. The statutory repayment period of a fine may be extended upon request of the court, and payments may be allowed in installments.

The U.S. Supreme Court has placed limits on incarceration for nonpayment of fines. In *Williams v. Illinois*, 399 U.S. 235, 90 S. Ct. 2018, 26 L. Ed. 2d 586 (1970), the defendant, Willie E. Williams, was convicted of petty theft and sentenced to one year in prison and a $500 fine, the maximum sentence allowed under the applicable statute. When Williams was unable to pay the fine upon completing his year in jail, he was kept incarcerated to "work off" the fine at a rate of $5 a day. Williams appealed, and the U.S. Supreme Court ruled that, under the Equal Protection Clause of the FOURTEENTH AMENDMENT, no state may increase the sentence of a defendant beyond the maximum period specified by statute for failure to pay a fine.

Shortly after the *Williams* case, the Supreme Court ruled that a state may not convert a fine into incarceration if the conviction warrants only a fine. In *Tate v. Short*, 401 U.S. 395, 91 S. Ct. 668, 28 L. Ed. 2d 130 (1971), the defendant, Preston A. Tate, was unable to pay $425 in fines for traffic offenses and was committed to prison to work off his fine at a rate of $5 a day. The Supreme Court ruled that a state may not "impos[e] a fine as a sentence and then automatically conver[t] it into a jail term solely because the defendant is indigent and cannot forthwith pay the fine in full."

Neither the *Williams* ruling nor the *Tate* ruling prevents a court from imprisoning a defendant who is able, but refuses, to pay a fine. The court may do so after finding that the defendant was somehow responsible for the failure to pay and that alternative forms of punishment would be inadequate to meet the state's interest in punishment and deterrence (*Bearden v. Georgia*, 461 U.S. 660, 103 S. Ct. 2064, 76 L. Ed. 2d 221 [1983]).

In a case of willful nonpayment, the court may order incarceration for a period of time specified under statute. In Kentucky, a prison term of up to six months may be imposed if the unpaid fine was imposed for the conviction of a felony. Nonpayment of a misdemeanor fine may result in a prison term of up to one-third the maximum authorized term for the offense committed. For a violation, the maximum term is ten days. This amount can be cumulative. For example, if a person refuses to pay the fines for ten violations, that person can be incarcerated for one hundred days (Ky. Rev. Stat. Ann. § 534.060 [Baldwin]).

Fines are often used to pay for incarceration and other sentencing costs. In 1984, Congress passed the Comprehensive Crime Control Act (codified in scattered sections of 5, 8, 29, 41, 42, and 50 App. U.S.C.A.), which established the U.S. Sentencing Guidelines Commission. According to section 5E1.2 of the act, a federal court shall impose a fine that is at least sufficient to pay the costs of imprisonment, probation, or supervised release order. Many states have followed suit, and fines are increasingly used to defray the costs of punishment.

FINGERPRINTS Impressions or reproductions of the distinctive pattern of lines and grooves on the skin of human fingertips.

Fingerprints are reproduced by pressing a person's fingertips into ink and then onto a piece of paper. Fingerprints left on surfaces can be obtained and examined through a dusting process and other processes conducted by forensics experts.

The lines and grooves in fingertips are unique personal characteristics, and thus no two persons have identical fingerprints. Although various scientists had earlier observed the intricate and varying patterns of fingerprints, their

If a store violates the law by selling alcohol to a person younger than age twenty-one, both the store and the offender may be fined.

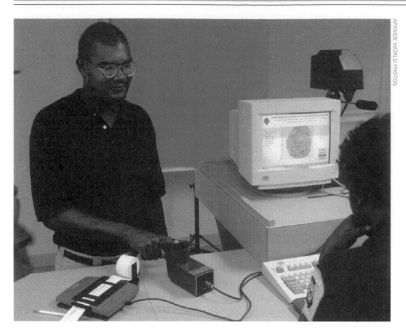

Some states are using fingerprints as a form of identification for people renewing their drivers' licenses.

use as evidence in trials is undocumented in Anglo-American law before the nineteenth century. In 1880 Henry Faulds, a Scottish physician, suggested in a letter to the British journal *Nature* that fingerprints could be used for identification purposes in a criminal investigation. Courts in the United States began to accept fingerprints as identification evidence in legal cases in the early twentieth century.

Fingerprints may be used in both civil and criminal courts when they are relevant to a case. They are most common in criminal prosecutions, where they may be used to identify the defendant and connect the defendant to the crime. In a murder prosecution, for example, the defendant's fingerprints on the murder weapon may be offered as EVIDENCE tending to show that the defendant committed the crime.

The taking of fingerprints from a criminal defendant raises no FIFTH AMENDMENT concerns. Under the Fifth Amendment to the U.S. Constitution, no person may be compelled to be a compulsory witness against himself or herself. However, this provision generally applies only to involuntary CONFESSIONS and forced TESTIMONY. A person suspected of a crime does not have the right to be free from the taking of fingerprints. Criminal suspects may also be required to surrender other personal information, such as physical appearance and measurements, handwriting and voice samples, teeth bites, normal walking gait, and normal standing posture. Unlike most of these characteristics, fingerprints cannot be easily changed.

Fingerprints are also used outside of court for a variety of purposes. Federal, state, and local lawmakers use them to help manage government resources. For instance, many states fingerprint the recipients of public assistance to ensure that only qualified recipients receive assistance. In many JURISDICTIONS a set of fingerprints or a thumbprint is taken from a person who is arrested and then released before her or his court date. This gives law enforcement authorities an identifying characteristic to use in apprehending the defendant in case the defendant does not appear in court for the prosecution.

In Georgia, liquor manufacturers, distributors, wholesalers, and retailers must send a set of fingerprints to the Georgia Bureau of Investigation when they apply for a LICENSE to conduct business in the state. The fingerprints are checked against those of convicted criminals as part of a background check on the applicant (Ga. Code Ann. § 3-3-2 [1996]).

Fingerprint information is easily accessible to police departments across the United States. Under 28 U.S.C.A. § 531 (1996), Congress appropriates funds for the creation and maintenance of a national computer database containing the fingerprints of convicted criminals and former criminal suspects. The database is called the Integrated Automated Fingerprint Identification System. Any state that requires persons convicted of sex offenses to submit DNA samples qualifies for the funding and federal support needed to implement the system.

DNA fingerprinting, or profiling, identifies the chemical pattern in an individual's genetic material. It is a very complex analysis. Nevertheless, it is widely accepted by courts in the United States and generally is considered to yield results that are as accurate as those of regular fingerprinting.

See also DNA EVIDENCE; FORENSIC SCIENCE.

FIRE 📖 The primary result of combustion. The juridical meaning does not differ from the vernacular meaning. 📖

It is a CRIME to burn certain types of PROPERTY under particular circumstances, both under the COMMON LAW and a number of state statutes. Some of these crimes are regarded as ARSON, but ordinarily, arson relates specifically to buildings and their contents.

The act of willfully and maliciously setting fire to property belonging to another person—such as stacks of hay or grain, grasses, fences, or wood—is ordinarily punishable as a MISDEMEANOR. Some JURISDICTIONS grade the offense as a FELONY.

Statutes relating to fires ordinarily define the acts required for conviction. Under these statutes, *willfully* is defined as meaning with an evil or MALICIOUS intent or malevolent motive.

An individual who willfully or negligently sets fire to his or her own woods, prairie land, or other specified areas might be guilty of a misdemeanor. In addition, it is a misdemeanor to burn such areas without first giving proper notice to adjacent landowners or for an individual to allow a fire kindled on his or her wood or prairie to escape and burn adjoining property.

Some statutes relate to burning cultivated ground. Such legislation exists to prevent disastrous fires, and they do not apply to ordinary acts of agriculture that are properly conducted, such as the setting of fire to an area of land to prepare for planting.

Under some statutes that prohibit or regulate the setting of fires, a monetary penalty is imposed on people who violate their provisions. Frequently an agency—such as a state board of forest park preservation commissioners—is named specifically in the statute to bring an action to collect the penalty. Some statutes impose liability on an individual who allows fire to escape from his or her own property even though such escape is not willful, while other statutes provide that a landowner who sets a fire as a result of necessity—such as a back fire used to subdue another fire—will not be held liable.

An individual is usually free from liability when he or she is lawfully burning something on his or her own farm and the fire accidentally spreads to an adjacent farm or woods.

There is civil LIABILITY for DAMAGES at common law imposed upon anyone who willfully and intentionally sets a fire. Some statutes under which criminal liability is imposed for setting certain types of fires also make express provisions that the individual whose property is damaged by the fire may initiate a CIVIL ACTION to recover any loss. Generally, the limit of damages is the loss actually incurred by the fire. Some statutes, however, provide for the recovery of double or treble damages.

FIRE STATUTE In ADMIRALTY law, a federal law that exempts the owner of a vessel from liability to any person for loss of, or damage to, merchandise shipped, taken in, or put on board such vessel as a result of a fire, unless the fire was intentionally or negligently caused by the owner.

FIRM OFFER A definite and binding proposal, in writing, to enter into a contractual agreement.

A firm offer generally states that it will remain open for a certain set time period during which it is incapable of being revoked.

According to legend the Chicago fire was started by a cow kicking over a lantern. This contemporary lithograph by Currier & Ives is titled The Great Fire at Chicago, October 8th 1871.

Firm offers are frequently made by merchants who wish to buy or sell goods and are governed by the UNIFORM COMMERCIAL CODE.

FIRST AMENDMENT The First Amendment to the U.S. Constitution reads:

Congress shall make no law respecting an establishment of religion, or prohibiting the free exercise thereof; or abridging the freedom of speech, or of the press; or the right of the people peaceably to assemble, and to petition the Government for a redress of grievances.

At first glance, the First Amendment appears to be written in clear, unequivocal, and facile terms: "Congress shall make *no* law" (emphasis added) in contravention of certain religious and political principles. After a closer reading and upon further reflection, the amendment's underlying complexities rise to the surface in the form of persistent questions that have nagged the legal system over the last two centuries.

For example, what kind of law "respect[s] the establishment of religion"? Does the First Amendment include here only laws that would establish an official national RELIGION as the Anglican Church was established in England prior to the American Revolution? Or does it also include laws that recognize or endorse religious activities such as the celebration of Christmas? More important, can people agree on what is meant by the word *religion* so that judges may know when religion is being "established" or when the right to its "free exercise" has been infringed?

In the area of free speech, does the right to speak your mind include the right to use offensive language that could start a fight or incite a riot? Is FREEDOM OF SPEECH synonymous with freedom of expression, such that the right to condemn the U.S. government extends to offensive symbolic actions involving no written or spoken words, like burning the U.S. flag? Does FREEDOM OF THE PRESS protect the right to publish scurrilous, defamatory, and libelous material? If not, can the government prohibit the publication of such material before it goes to print?

The Supreme Court has confronted most of these questions. Its answers have not always produced unanimous, or even widespread, agreement around the United States. But the Court's decisions have provided a prism through which U.S. citizens have examined the appropriate limitations society may place on the freedoms protected by the First Amendment, and have sparked colorful and spirited discussions among friends and family members, as well as politicians and their constituents.

Demonstrators protest what they see as a restriction of first amendment rights by the government in the form of lack of funding for certain kinds of art.

Freedom of Speech The Founding Fathers were intimately familiar with government suppression of political speech. Prior to the American Revolution, the Crown imprisoned, pilloried, mutilated, exiled, and even killed men and women belonging to minority political parties in England in order to extinguish dissenting views. Many of these dissenters left England searching for more freedom in the New World, where they instead found colonial governments that stifled political dissidence with similar fervor. Maryland, for example, passed a law prohibiting "all speeches, practices and attempts relating to [the British Crown], that shall be thought mutinous and seditious," and provided punishments that included whipping, branding, fines, imprisonment, banishment, and death. The Free Speech Clause of the Constitution was drafted to protect such political dissenters from a similar fate in the newly founded United States.

In light of this background, the U.S. Supreme Court has afforded dissident political speech unparalleled constitutional protection. However, all speech is not equal under the First Amendment. The Supreme Court has identified five areas of expression that the government may legitimately restrict under certain circumstances. These areas are speech that incites illegal activity and subversive speech, fighting words, obscenity and pornography, commercial speech, and symbolic expression.

Speech that Incites Illegal Activity and Subversive Speech Some speakers intend to arouse their listeners to take constructive steps to alter the political landscape. Every day in the United States, people hand out leaflets imploring neighbors to write Congress about a particular subject, vote in a certain fashion on a referendum, or contribute financially to political campaigns and civic organizations. For other speakers, existing political channels provide insufficient means to effectuate the type of change desired. These speakers may encourage others to take illegal and subversive measures to change the status quo. Such measures include resisting the draft during wartime, threatening public officials, and joining political organizations aimed at overthrowing the U.S. government.

The Supreme Court has held that the government may not prohibit speech that advocates illegal or subversive activity unless "such advocacy is directed to inciting or producing imminent lawless action and is likely to incite or produce such action" (*Brandenburg v. Ohio*, 395 U.S. 444, 89 S. Ct. 1827, 23 L. Ed. 2d 430 [1969]). Applying the *Brandenburg* test, the Supreme Court ruled that the government could not punish an antiwar protester who yelled, "[W]e'll take the fucking street later," because such speech "amounted to nothing more than advocacy of illegal action at some indefinite future time" (*Hess v. Indiana*, 414 U.S. 105, 94 S. Ct. 326, 38 L. Ed. 2d 303 [1973]). Nor could the government punish someone who, in opposition to the draft during the Vietnam War, proclaimed, "[I]f they ever make me carry a rifle the first man I want in my sights is [the president of the United States] L.B.J." (*Watts v. United States*, 394 U.S. 705, 89 S. Ct. 1399, 22 L. Ed. 2d 664 [1969]). Such politically charged rhetoric, the Supreme Court held, was mere hyperbole and not a threat intended to be acted on at a definite point in time.

Fighting Words Fighting words are words that "by their very utterance inflict injury or tend to incite an immediate breach of the peace" or have a "direct tendency to cause acts of violence by the person to whom, individually, the remark is addressed" (*Chaplinsky v. New Hampshire*, 315 U.S. 568, 62 S. Ct. 766, 86 L. Ed. 1031 [1942]). Whereas subversive advocacy exhorts large numbers of people to engage in lawless conduct, fighting words are directed at provoking a specific individual. Generally, only the most inflammatory and derisive epithets will be characterized as fighting words.

Fighting words should also be distinguished from speech that is merely offensive. Crude or insensitive language may be heard in a variety of contexts—at work, on television, even at home. The Supreme Court has ruled that speech that merely offends, or hurts the feelings of, another person—without eliciting a more dramatic response—is protected by the First Amendment. The Supreme Court has also underscored the responsibility of receivers to ignore offensive speech. Receivers can move away or divert their eyes from an offensive speaker,

program, image, or message. In one case, the Court ruled that a young man had the right to wear, in a state courthouse, a jacket with the aphorism Fuck the Draft emblazoned across the back, because persons at the courthouse could avert their eyes if offended (*Cohen v. California*, 403 U.S. 15, 91 S. Ct. 1780, 29 L. Ed. 2d 284 [1971]). "One man's vulgarity," the Court said, "is another's lyric," and the words chosen in this case conveyed a stronger message than would a sublimated variation such as Resist the Draft.

Obscenity and Pornography State and federal laws attempt to enforce societal norms by encouraging acceptable depictions of human sexuality and eliding unacceptable portrayals. Over the years, libidinous books such as *Lady Chatterly's Lover* (1951–1975) and adult movies such as *Deep Throat* (1972) have rankled communities, which have struggled to determine whether such works should be censored as immoral or protected as art.

The Supreme Court has always had difficulty distinguishing OBSCENE material, which is not protected by the First Amendment, from material that is merely salacious or titillating. Justice POTTER STEWART admitted that he could not define OBSCENITY, but quipped, "I know it when I see it." Nonetheless, the Supreme Court has articulated a three-part test to determine when sexually oriented material is obscene. Material will not be declared obscene unless (1) the average person, applying contemporary community standards, would find that its predominant theme appeals to a "prurient" interest; (2) it depicts or describes sexual activity in a "patently offensive" manner; and (3) it lacks, when taken as a whole, serious literary, artistic, political, or scientific value (*Miller v. California*, 413 U.S. 15 93 S. Ct. 2607, 37 L. Ed. 2d 419 [1973]).

Although the Supreme Court has failed to adequately define words like *prurient*, *patently offensive*, and *serious artistic value*, literary works that deal with sexually related material are strongly protected by the First Amendment, as are magazines like *Playboy* and *Penthouse*. More difficult questions are presented in the area of adult cinema. Courts generally distinguish hard-core PORNOGRAPHY, which graphically depicts copulation and oral sex, from soft-core pornography, which displays nudity and human sexuality short of these ultimate sex acts. In close cases falling somewhere in the gray areas of pornography, the outcome may turn on the community standards applied by a JURY in a particular locale. Thus, pornography that could be prohibited as obscene in a small rural community might receive First Amendment protection in Times Square.

Commercial Speech Commercial speech, such as advertising, receives more First Amendment protection than fighting words and obscenity, but less protection than political oratory. Advertising deserves more protection than the first three categories of expression because of the consumer's interest in the free flow of market information (*Virginia State Board of Pharmacy v. Virginia Citizens Consumer Council*, 425 U.S. 748, 96 S. Ct. 1817, 48 L. Ed. 2d 346 [1976]). In a free enterprise economy, consumers depend on information regarding the quality, quantity, and price of various goods and services. Society is not similarly served by the free exchange of obscenity.

At the same time, commercial speech deserves less protection than political orations because society has a greater interest in receiving accurate commercial information and may be less savvy in flushing out false and deceptive rhetoric. The average citizen is more prone, the Supreme Court has suggested, to discount the words of a politician than to discount the words of a Fortune 500 company. The average citizen may be more vulnerable to misleading advertising as well. Even during an election year, most people view more commercial advertisements than political advertisements, and rely on those advertisements when purchasing the clothes they wear, the food they eat, and the automobiles they drive. Thus, the Supreme Court permits government regulation of commercial speech that is intended to prevent misleading and deceptive advertising.

Symbolic Expression Not all forms of expression involve words. The nod of a head, the wave of a hand, and the wink of an eye all communicate something without language. The television image of a defenseless Chinese student facing down a line of tanks during protests in support of democracy near Tiananmen Square in 1989 will be forever seared into the minds of viewers.

Not all symbolic conduct is considered speech for First Amendment purposes. If an individual uses a symbolic expression with the intent to communicate a specific message and under circumstances in which the audience is likely to understand its meaning, the government may not regulate that expression unless the regulation serves a significant societal interest unrelated to the suppression of ideas (*Spence v. Washington*, 418 U.S. 405, 94 S. Ct. 2727, 41 L. Ed. 2d 842 [1974]; *United States v. O'Brien*, 391 U.S. 367, 88 S. Ct. 1673, 20 L. Ed. 2d 672 [1968]). Applying this standard, the Supreme Court overturned the conviction of a person who burned the U.S. flag in protest over the policies of President RONALD REAGAN (*Texas v. Johnson*, 491 U.S. 397, 109 S. Ct. 2533, 105 L. Ed. 2d 342 [1989]), and reversed the suspension of a high school student for wearing a black armband in protest of the Vietnam War (*Tinker v. Des Moines Independent School District*, 393 U.S. 503, 89 S. Ct. 733, 21 L. Ed. 2d 731 [1969]), but upheld federal legislation that prohibited the burning of draft cards (*O'Brien*). Of the government interests asserted in these three cases, maintaining the integrity of the Selective Service System was the only interest of sufficient weight to overcome the First Amendment right to engage in symbolic expression.

Freedom of the Press The American Revolution was a revolution of literature as well as politics. The colonists published a profusion of newspaper articles, books, essays, and pamphlets in opposition to various forms of British tyranny. THOMAS PAINE's *Common Sense* (1776) and THOMAS JEFFERSON's DECLARATION OF INDEPENDENCE (1776) are two well-known and influential examples of Revolutionary literature published in the colonies. A free press, the Founding Fathers believed, was an essential check against despotism, and integral to advancing human understanding of the sciences, arts, and humanities.

However, the Founding Fathers did not agree on how best to protect the press from arbitrary government action. A majority of the Founding Fathers adhered to the English common-law view that equated a free press with the doctrine of no PRIOR RESTRAINT. This doctrine provided that no publication could be suppressed by the government before it is released to the public, and that the publication of something could not be conditioned upon judicial approval before its release. On the other hand, the English COMMON LAW permitted prosecution for libelous and seditious material after publication. Thus, the law protected vituperative political publications only insofar as the author was prepared to serve time in jail or pay a fine for wrongful published attacks.

A minority of Founding Fathers adhered to the view articulated by JAMES MADISON: "The security of the freedom of the press requires that it should be exempt, not only from previous restraint of the executive, as in Great Britain; but from legislative restraint also; and this exemption, not only from the previous inspection of licensers, but from the subsequent penalty of laws." Madison was concerned that authors would be deterred from writing articles assailing government activity if the government

*Burning a U.S. flag
to protest
government policies
is protected as
symbolic expression
under the First
Amendment.*

were permitted to prosecute them following release of their works to the public.

Before 1964, the Madisonian concept of a free press found very little support among the fifty states. Not only was subsequent punishment permitted for seditious and libelous publications, but in many states, truth was not a defense to allegations of DEFAMATION. If a story tended to discredit the reputation of a public official, the publisher could be held liable for money damages even if the story was accurate. In states where truth was allowed as a defense, the publisher often carried the burden of demonstrating its veracity. Newspapers and other media outlets soon flooded the courts with lawsuits alleging that these LIBEL laws violated their First Amendment rights by "chilling" the pen of writers with the specter of civil liability for money damages.

In the seminal case *New York Times v. Sullivan*, 376 U.S. 254, 84 S. Ct. 710, 11 L. Ed. 2d 686 (1964), the Supreme Court extended First Amendment protection for print and electronic media far beyond the protection envisioned by the English common law. Before money damages can be assessed against a member of the media for a libelous or defamatory statement, the Supreme Court held, the injured party, not the publisher, must demonstrate by "clear and convincing" evidence that the statement not only was false but was published with "actual malice." Actual malice may be established only by proof that the media member recklessly published a statement without regard to its veracity or had actual knowledge of its falsity. In arriving at this standard, the Court balanced society's need for an uninhibited flow of information about public figures, particularly elected officials, against an individual's right to protect the integrity and value of his or her reputation.

The twentieth century has also seen the Supreme Court strengthen the doctrine of no prior restraint. In *Near v. Minnesota*, 283 U.S. 697, 51 S. Ct. 625, 75 L. Ed. 1357 (1931), the Court ruled that there is a constitutional presumption against prior restraint that may not be overcome unless the government can demonstrate that CENSORSHIP is necessary to prevent a "clear and present danger" of a national security breach. In *New York Times v. United States*, 403 U.S. 713, 91 S. Ct. 2140, 29 L. Ed. 2d 822 (1971), the Court applied this presumption against the U.S. Department of Justice, which had sought an INJUNCTION to prevent the publication of classified material revealing the secrecy and deception behind the U.S. involvement in the Vietnam War. If this classified material, also known as the Pentagon Papers, had threatened U.S. troops by disclosing their location or movement, the Court said, publication would not have been permitted.

Freedom of Religion

Establishment Clause Prior to the American Revolution, the English designated the Anglican Church as the official church of their country. The church was supported by taxation, and all English people were required to attend its services. No marriage or baptism was sanctioned outside the church. Members of religious minorities who failed to abide by the strictures of the church were forced to endure civil and criminal penalties, including banishment and death. Some American colonies were also ruled by persecutorial theocrats, such as the Puritans in Massachusetts.

These English and colonial experiences influenced the Founding Fathers, including Jefferson and Madison. Jefferson supported a high wall of separation between church and state. Furthermore, Jefferson, a student of the Enlightenment (an eighteenth-century philosophical movement whose members rejected traditional values and embraced rationalism), opposed religious influence on the business of government. In turn, Madison, a champion of religious minorities, opposed government interference with religion. For Madison, the establishment of a national church differed from the Spanish Inquisition "only in degree," and he vociferously attacked any legislation that would have led the colonies down that path. For example, Madison led the fight against a Virginia bill that would have levied taxes to subsidize Christianity.

Yet the thoughts and intentions of Madison have been the subject of rancorous discord among the Supreme Court justices who have attempted to interpret the Establishment Clause in a variety of contexts. Some justices, for example, cite Madison's opposition to the Virginia bill as evidence that he opposed only discriminatory government assistance to particular religious denominations, but favored nonpreferential aid to cultivate a diversity in faiths. Thus, the Framers of the First Amendment left posterity with three considerations regarding religious establishments: (1) a wall of separation that protects government from religion and religion from government; (2) a separation of church and state that permits nondiscriminatory government assistance to religious groups; and (3) government assistance that preserves and promotes a diversity of religious beliefs.

The Supreme Court attempted to incorporate these three considerations under a single test in *Lemon v. Kurtzman*, 403 U.S. 602, 91 S. Ct. 2105, 29 L. Ed. 2d 745 (1971). In *Lemon*, the Court held that state and federal governments may enact legislation that concerns religion or religious organizations so long as the legislation has a secular purpose, and a primary effect that neither advances nor inhibits religion nor otherwise fosters an excessive entanglement between church and state. Under this test, the federal court of appeals for the fifth circuit invalidated a Mississippi statute that permitted public school students to initiate nonsectarian prayers at various compulsory and noncompulsory school events (*Ingebretsen v. Jackson Public School District*, 88 F.3d 274 [1996]). In contrast, the Court permits state legislatures to open their sessions with a short prayer—because, the Court says, history and tradition have secularized this otherwise religious act (*Marsh v. Chambers*, 463 U.S. 783, 103 S. Ct. 3330, 77 L. Ed. 2d 1019 [1983]).

The Court has made seemingly inconsistent rulings in other areas as well. For instance, it permitted a municipality to include a Nativity scene in its annual Christmas display (*Lynch v. Donnelly*, 465 U.S. 668, 104 S. Ct. 1355, 79 L. Ed. 2d 604 [1984]), whereas it prohibited a county courthouse from placing a crèche on its staircase during the holiday season (*Allegheny v. ACLU*, 492 U.S. 573, 109 S. Ct. 3086, 106 L. Ed. 2d 472 [1989]). In *Allegheny*, the Court said that nothing in the county courthouse indicated that the crèche was anything other than a religious display, whereas in *Lynch*, the Nativity scene was part of a wider celebration of the winter holidays. Such inconsistencies will continue to plague the Supreme Court as the justices attempt to reconcile the language of the Establishment Clause with the different considerations of the Founding Fathers.

Free Exercise Clause The Establishment Clause and the Free Exercise Clause represent flip sides of the same coin. Whereas the Establishment Clause focuses on government action that would create, support, or endorse an official national religion, the Free Exercise Clause focuses on the pernicious effects government action may have on an individual's religious beliefs or practices. Like the Establishment Clause, the Free Exercise Clause was drafted in response to the Framers' desire to protect members of religious minorities from persecution.

The Framers' understanding of the Free Exercise Clause is illustrated by the NEW YORK CONSTITUTION OF 1777, which stated,

[T]he free exercise and enjoyment of religious . . . worship, without discrimination or preference, shall forever . . . be allowed . . . to all mankind: *Provided*, that the liberty of conscience, hereby granted, shall not be so construed as to excuse acts of licentiousness, or justify practices inconsistent with the peace or safety of this State. (N.Y. Const. Art. 1 § 3)

The New Hampshire Constitution of 1784 similarly provided that "[e]very individual has a natural and unalienable right to worship God according to the dictates of his own conscience, and reason; and no subject shall be hurt . . . in his person, liberty or estate for worshipping God" in a manner "most agreeable" to those dictates, "provided he doth not disturb the public peace" (N.H. Const. Pt. 1, Art. 5).

These state constitutional provisions not only provide insight into the Founding Fathers' original understanding of the First Amendment, they embody the fundamental tenets of modern free exercise jurisprudence. The Supreme Court has identified three principles underlying the Free Exercise Clause: (1) no individual may be compelled by law to accept any particular religion or form of worship; (2) all individuals are constitutionally permitted to choose a religion freely in accordance with their conscience and spirituality, and the government may not inhibit their religious practices; and (3) the government may enforce its criminal norms against persons whose religious practices would thwart a compelling societal interest.

Rarely is a law that infringes upon someone's religious beliefs or practices supported by a compelling state interest. The Supreme Court has held that no compelling societal interest would be served by actions that conflict with

The Supreme Court has interpreted the Free Exercise Clause of the First Amendment to mean that only a compelling state interest may override the religious beliefs of individuals. Amish children do not have to follow laws that require attendance at state schools until the age of sixteen.

deeply held religious beliefs: coercing members of the Jehovah's Witnesses to salute the U.S. FLAG in public schools (*West Virginia State Board of Education v. Barnette*, 319 U.S. 624, 63 S. Ct. 1178, 87 L. Ed. 1628 [1943]), denying unemployment benefits to Seventh-Day Adventists who refuse to work on Saturdays (*Sherbert v. Verner*, 374 U.S. 398, 83 S. Ct. 1790, 10 L. Ed. 2d 965 [1963]), or requiring Amish families to keep their children in state schools until the age of sixteen (*Wisconsin v. Yoder*, 406 U.S. 205, 92 S. Ct. 1526, 32 L. Ed. 2d 15 [1972]). However, a compelling government interest is served by the federal revenue system, so no member of any religious sect can claim exemption from taxation (*United States v. Lee*, 455 U.S. 252, 102 S. Ct. 1051, 71 L. Ed. 2d 127 [1982]).

A different question is presented when the government disputes whether a particular belief or practice is religious in nature. This typically happens when CONSCIENTIOUS OBJECTORS resist the government's attempt to conscript them during wartime. Some draft resisters object to war on moral or ethical grounds unrelated to orthodox or doctrinal religions. If a conscientious objector admits to being atheistic or agnostic, the government asks, how can that objector avoid conscription by relying on the First Amendment, which protects the free exercise of religion?

In an effort to answer this question, the Supreme Court explained that the government cannot "aid all religions against non-believers," any more than it can aid one religion over another (*Torasco v. Watkins*, 367 U.S. 488, 81 S. Ct. 1680, 6 L. Ed. 2d 982 [1961]). Thus, as long as a person "deeply and sincerely holds beliefs which are purely ethical or moral in source and content but that nevertheless impose upon him a duty of conscience to refrain from participating in any war at any time, those beliefs" are protected by the First Amendment (*Welsh v. United States*, 398 U.S. 333, 90 S. Ct. 1792, 26 L. Ed. 2d 308 [1970]). A belief—religious, moral, or ethical—that manifests itself in a person's selective opposition to only certain wars or military conflicts is not protected by the Free Exercise Clause.

CROSS REFERENCES

Abington School District v. Schempp; Engel v. Vitale; New York Times v. Sullivan; New York Times v. United States; School Prayer.

FIRST IMPRESSION 📖 The initial presentation to, or examination by, a court of a particular QUESTION OF LAW. 📖

A case is labeled *of the first impression* when it sets forth a completely original issue of law for

VANESSA VICK/PHOTO RESEARCHERS

decision by the court. Such a case cannot be decided by reliance on any existing PRECEDENT, law formulated in a prior case decided on a comparable question of law, or similar facts.

FIRST INSTANCE 📖 The initial trial court where an action is brought. 📖

A court of first instance is distinguishable from an APPELLATE COURT, which is a court of last instance. In the FEDERAL COURT system, a federal district court is a court of *first instance*, whereas the Supreme Court is the court of *last instance*.

FISCAL 📖 Relating to finance or financial matters, such as money, taxes, or public or private revenues. 📖

A *fiscal agent* is a bank engaged in the business of collecting and disbursing money. Such a bank also serves as a place for the deposit of private and public funds on behalf of others.

A *fiscal year* is a period of twelve months that does not necessarily correspond with the traditional calendar year. During this time period, appropriations are made and expenditures are authorized. At the end of the year, accounts are composed and the books are balanced. It is an accounting year frequently used by a state or large business, the first day of which is usually April, July, or October 1.

Fiscal officers are those individuals whose role it is to collect and distribute public money, such as state revenues or the revenues of a county or MUNICIPAL CORPORATION. The title is also used to describe officers in a private CORPORATION who have the duty to oversee financial transactions. Fiscal officers of a corporation include a treasurer and a COMPTROLLER.

FISH AND FISHING From earliest times, fish and fishing have played a crucial role in the life of the people of North America. Native Americans of all tribes depended heavily on fish to eat and to trade, and fishing also held an important place in native cultural practices and religious rites. Beginning in the sixteenth century, and possibly even earlier, European adventurers were drawn to the rich fishing grounds off the coast of New England, and the settlers who followed them eagerly harvested the tremendous stocks of fish they found in America's lakes, rivers, and coastal areas. Fish were considered to be an inexhaustible resource, a common property available to all in endless quantities.

As early as the late eighteenth century, however, it became clear that the rush to exploit fish and other species of wildlife was jeopardizing the continued survival of several species. Eventually, state governments passed laws regulating hunting and fishing practices, and established fish and GAME agencies to enforce those laws. Because these state laws met with very limited success, the federal government soon stepped in and passed legislation designed to strengthen them and make them more enforceable. Over time, the federal government's role in managing and protecting fish and wildlife grew, occasionally conflicting with state authority. The question of wildlife jurisdiction was ultimately resolved by the Supreme Court, which found the federal government to be the ultimate authority in the area of fish and wildlife management.

Though states must ultimately defer to federal authority, state governments continue to play the primary role in fish and wildlife management, determining details such as harvesting seasons, methods, and limits. The federal government plays a broader role in protecting and managing wildlife, including funding state wildlife programs, regulating the commercial harvesting of fish, managing national forests and wildlife refuges, and negotiating international treaties involving ocean fisheries. Finally, the federal government has played a principal role in adjudicating the fishing rights of Native American tribes, determining what rights are guaranteed by the TREATIES signed between the tribes and the federal government, and working to ensure that those rights are protected.

The Evolution of U.S. Wildlife Law
The evolution of U.S. laws applying to the management of fish and fishing is complex. The different types of fishing practiced in the United States—commercial and recreational, for example—have required different types of laws and regulations. In addition, many of the general provisions of wildlife law, such as those addressing the question of state versus federal authority, apply not only to fish but also to birds and fur-bearing animals, whereas other provisions, such as those regulating ocean fisheries, apply only to fish and fishing.

In general, the objective of wildlife law has been to regulate the taking of fish and other wildlife species in order to ensure their continued survival. Early attempts by the states to regulate fish and wildlife were based on the state ownership doctrine. This doctrine declared that the authority over wildlife rested with each state, which held the resource as a public trust.

Despite states' efforts, state wildlife laws often provided too little protection too late. Over the last part of the nineteenth century, it became clear that the states were unable to enforce effectively the laws they had passed, and migrations and movements of fish and animals

Recreational fishing is regulated differently from commercial fishing but both sets of laws attempt to ensure the continued survival of many species.

across state lines made it difficult for states to regulate harvests in any rational way. Wildlife populations dwindled, and recreational fishers and hunters began to pressure the federal government to take action. George Grinnell, a prominent sportsman and editor of *Forest and Stream* magazine, led the way, establishing interest groups to lobby Congress on behalf of wildlife. In 1886, Grinnell founded the National Audubon Society, and in 1888, he founded the Boone and Crockett Club, both of which were instrumental in securing passage of the Lacey Act of 1900 (ch. 553, 31 Stat. 187 [current, amended version at 16 U.S.C.A. §§ 701, 3371–3378, and 18 U.S.C.A. § 42 (1985)]), which was the first federal wildlife statute.

The Lacey Act prohibited the interstate shipment of wildlife taken in violation of state law. This provision did not ban the taking of wildlife, but used Congress's power to regulate interstate commerce as a way to enforce state

game laws. It effectively put market hunters—hunters who took great numbers of game for commercial purposes—out of business. In addition, the act gave real authority to the U.S. Biological Survey, which was a predecessor to the U.S. Fish and Wildlife Service (FWS). The original purpose of the Survey, established in 1885, was to carry out a national biological survey as well as various bird studies. The Lacey Act gave greater powers to the agency, charging it with administering and implementing the act's provisions, thus marking the beginning of an active role for the federal government in protecting and managing wildlife resources.

As passed, the Lacey Act referred to "wild animals and birds," which were construed to include only fur-bearing animals and game birds. In the 1920s, Congress became concerned about the nation's fish—particularly the smallmouth and largemouth bass, whose numbers had dwindled after years of overfishing throughout the country. State bag limits had failed to prevent excessive catches, and commercial restrictions were ineffective in preventing the illegal interstate transport of mismarked or concealed fish. To prevent the extinction of these species, Congress passed the Black Bass Act of 1926 (16 U.S.C.A. §§ 851–856). This act was fashioned after the Lacey Act in that it sought to enforce state wildlife laws by prohibiting certain interstate shipments of bass. The Black Bass Act was amended several times in the following years: in 1947, to apply to all game fish, as each state defined them; in 1952, to apply to all fish; and in 1969, to apply to fish taken in violation of the law of a foreign country. The Black Bass Act was repealed in 1981, and its provisions were consolidated into the Lacey Act amendments of that year (Pub. L. No. 97-79, 95 Stat. 1073). In general, these amendments significantly broadened and strengthened the Lacey Act and the provisions of the former Black Bass Act.

Throughout the twentieth century, federal authority over fish and wildlife has expanded, while state authority has become much more limited. The doctrine of state ownership was progressively invalidated as the federal government established provisions to protect various fish and wildlife species, asserting that such species were the property of the federal government, and not the states.

Though the states no longer retain ultimate legal authority over wildlife, they continue to play the primary role in managing and regulating local wildlife populations, even on federal lands. The states set hunting seasons and bag limits, specify harvest methods, and regulate the size and gender of game that can be taken. The states also have important wildlife management programs designed to ensure that sufficient numbers of animals, birds, and fish are available for recreational and subsistence hunting and fishing. Though state laws are ultimately subject to constitutional limits, the federal government has exercised its preemption authority very sparingly. The assumption is that state law is in force until preempted by federal law.

The Federal Government's Role in the Conservation of Fish and Wildlife

The federal government has played an extensive role in working to conserve the habitats of fish and wildlife. Conservation became an important theme in the late nineteenth century, when people began to believe that wildlife and wild places should be protected not only for utilitarian reasons but because they had their own intrinsic value and were important national resources. Influenced by the writings of HENRY DAVID THOREAU and following the lead of wildlife advocates such as John Muir, the federal government began to establish national parks, forests, and wildlife refuges. One of the first wildlife refuges was created by President BENJAMIN HARRISON in 1892 when he reserved Afognak Island, in Alaska, for the protection and preservation of "salmon and other fish and sea animals and other animals and birds" (Proclamation No. 39, 27 Stat. 1052). Though most

In the late nineteenth century many people realized the value of protecting wildlife and wild places not just to preserve fish and animals but also for the value of recreation and natural beauty.

DAVID J SAMS/STOCK BOSTON

of the refuges established were specifically designed for waterfowl and fur-bearing species, the need to protect fish habitats was recognized in 1972 when Congress passed the Marine Protection, Research, and Sanctuaries Act (16 U.S.C.A. §§ 1431–1445). This act authorizes the secretary of commerce, with the approval of the president, to designate as marine sanctuaries areas of the Great Lakes and the oceans, extending out to the edge of the continental shelf, when the secretary determines that that action is necessary for the purpose of preserving or restoring such areas for their conservation, recreational, ecological, or esthetic values. Fish and wildlife refuges are administered by the Fish and Wildlife Service, which is housed in the Department of Interior.

In addition to establishing wildlife refuges and sanctuaries, the federal government provides states with financial assistance to fund projects pertaining to fish. This funding was created by the Federal Aid in Fish Restoration Act (16 U.S.C.A. § 777-777k), more commonly known as the Dingell-Johnson Act, which was passed in 1950. This act directs that funds derived from the federal excise tax on fishing rods, creels, reels, and artificial lures, baits, and flies be annually apportioned among the states, 40 percent on the basis of geographic area and 60 percent on the basis of the number of persons holding paid fishing licenses. These funds can be used by the states for "fish restoration and management projects" or, since 1970, for "comprehensive fish and wildlife resource management plans." The Dingell-Johnson Act specifies that its provisions are to apply only to "fish which have material value in connection with sport or recreation in the marine and/or fresh waters of the United States." With the Fish and Wildlife Conservation Act of 1980 (16 U.S.C.A. §§ 2901–2911), commonly referred to as the Nongame Act, a similar funding program was provided for the protection of nongame fish and wildlife. The FWS is responsible for maintaining and administering these trust funds.

The most extensive federal efforts to protect endangered fish and wildlife species have been generated through the ENDANGERED SPECIES ACT of 1973 (16 U.S.C.A. §§ 1531–1543). The Endangered Species Act provides much broader coverage than has previous wildlife legislation, defining the fish or wildlife to be protected as including "any member of the animal kingdom," and expressing the goal of preserving plant life as well. The Endangered Species Act also differs from previous wildlife laws in that it is founded on not a primarily utilitarian view of wildlife but the philosophy that wildlife has intrinsic value for the nation and its citizens. The act declares, for example, that endangered wildlife "are of esthetic, ecological, educational, historical, recreational, and scientific value to the Nation and its people."

Ocean Fisheries Law With over one hundred thousand miles of linear coastline bordering some of the richest marine fisheries in the world, the United States has always been heavily involved in the ocean fishing industry. Marine fishing is an important contributor to the U.S. economy. In 1990, for example, commercial fisheries contributed $16.6 billion to the U.S. gross national product. Ocean fisheries in the United States are officially managed by the secretary of commerce, though actual fisheries management responsibilities have been delegated first to the administrator of the National Oceanic and Atmospheric Administration (NOAA), and within NOAA to the National Marine Fisheries Service (NMFS), which is primarily responsible for federal fisheries management. The NMFS, which is made up largely of biologists and fishery managers, has a staff of about twenty-two hundred, which is divided among its headquarters in Washington, D.C., and its five major regional offices.

Traditionally, marine fishers operated independently and fishing businesses were small, family owned, and locally operated. The great range of fish species and harvesting practices in the United States encouraged this independence and small scale, as diverse practices, conditions, and locales kept fishers from organizing themselves or combining their efforts.

These traditions dominated the U.S. industry until well into the 1970s. In many areas, fishing businesses continue to operate as they always have. However, some aspects of the U.S. marine fishing industry have changed tremendously since the 1970s, primarily owing to the activities of foreign fishing fleets off U.S. coasts and to international treaties and agreements the United States has entered into regarding ocean fishing.

Historically, the right of all nations to fish on the high seas has been recognized as a fundamental principle of INTERNATIONAL LAW. Even so, disputes have frequently arisen over whether specific areas are part of the high seas or part of a particular nation's territorial sea. Until relatively recently, such disputes were generally handled by the parties involved.

Within the United States, the years prior to World War II were marked by a predominance of state controls over ocean fisheries. Though the federal government had broad management

authority to regulate these resources, its involvement was very limited, and individual states exercised much of the responsibility for fisheries management, particularly within the territorial sea. On the high seas, state authority was recognized when the state had a legitimate enforcement or conservation interest, and when the state had a sufficient basis for asserting PERSONAL JURISDICTION over the fisher, based on the landing of fish at a state port, the state citizenship of the fisher, or a minimum level of contact between the state and the fisher. State controls were limited to the extent that they could not unduly burden interstate commerce, discriminate against noncitizens in favor of citizens, or override federal laws to the contrary.

After the end of World War II, the traditional freedom to fish anywhere on the high seas began to be limited by international agreements. The first development in this area was what came to be known as the Truman Proclamation of 1945 (Proclamation No. 2667, 10 Fed. Reg. 12,303, *reprinted in* 59 Stat. 84). In this proclamation, President HARRY TRUMAN declared that the United States would move

> to establish conservation zones in those areas of the high seas contiguous to the coast of the United States wherein fishing activities have been or in the future may be developed and maintained on a substantial scale . . . and all fishing activities in such zones shall be subject to regulations and control.

This statement did not establish a conservation zone, but instead announced that the United States would seek to negotiate agreements with foreign countries fishing in nearby waters. Even so, many countries interpreted this proclamation to mean that the United States recognized

In the 1960s the United States reached agreements with other nations concerning the harvesting of tuna off its western coast.

the right of a coastal nation to establish unilaterally a special "conservation zone" between its TERRITORIAL WATERS and the high seas, in which it would regulate all fishing activities. Chile was one such country, immediately responding to Truman's proclamation by declaring its own two-hundred-mile conservation zone.

At the 1958 Convention on Fishing and Conservation of the Living Resources of the High Sea, the Truman Proclamation was ratified internationally, with delegates declaring that "[a] coastal State has a special interest in the maintenance of the productivity of the living resources in any area of the high seas adjacent to its territorial sea" (art. 6, § 1 [17 U.S.T. 138, T.I.A.S. No. 5969]). The convention encouraged nations to negotiate agreements concerning the use of their adjacent waters, adding that countries could take unilateral conservation measures if such negotiations were unsuccessful. The convention did not specify the size of the area in which such unilateral measures could be taken, nor did it define the limits of the territorial sea.

Following the convention, the United States entered into a series of agreements with other nations concerning the fishery resources off its coasts, including agreements over tuna, New England groundfish, halibut, herring, and salmon. In addition, in 1964, Congress passed the Bartlett Act (Pub. L. No. 88-308, 78 Stat. 194), which excluded foreign vessels from fishing within the United States' territorial sea, defined as all ocean waters within three miles from the coast. Two years later, Congress passed the Contiguous Fisheries Zone Act (Pub. L. No. 89-658, 80 Stat. 908), which created a nine-mile contiguous zone extending out from the three-mile limit, from which foreign fishing vessels would be excluded.

These acts and treaties failed to protect U.S. fisheries as they were intended to. The Bartlett Act provided no authority for federal management measures, limiting the federal government's role to data collection and law enforcement against foreign fishers. Other nations also found their fisheries to be suffering, as most treaties provided no means of enforcement against nations who had not chosen to enter into an agreement. As a result, several countries moved to extend the area of their marine jurisdiction. By 1975, of the parties involved in ongoing law-of-the-sea negotiations, sixty nations including the United States, favored a twelve-mile territorial sea and a two-hundred-mile resource conservation zone.

In the United States, government officials and fishing industry representatives had been considering just such an extension in marine jurisdiction. From 1950 on, foreign fishing near U.S. waters had expanded dramatically, as integrated harvesting and processing vessels, called factory trawlers, came from areas such as the Soviet Union, Eastern Europe, and Japan to take advantage of the rich groundfish fisheries off the New England and Alaska coasts. Because these vessels had stayed outside the United States' territorial sea, they had been beyond the reach of U.S. authority.

Alarmed by the effect of these foreign fishing fleets on the U.S. fishing industry, Congress in 1976 passed the Fishery Conservation and Management Act (U.S.C.A. §§ 1801–1882), otherwise known as the Magnuson Act for its author, Senator Warren Magnuson of Washington. This act declared a new, two-hundred-mile U.S. fishery conservation zone (FCZ), thereby terminating the freedom of foreign fishing fleets to operate off U.S. shores. Within the FCZ, the act asserts for the United States exclusive management authority over not only fish but also "all other forms of marine animal and plant life other than marine mammals, birds, and highly migratory species." Soon after the Magnuson Act became effective on March 1, 1977, the great foreign factory trawler fleets largely disappeared from the fishing grounds off New England. In other areas, it took longer for foreign vessels to vacate U.S. waters. However, as the U.S. factory trawler fleet grew, it displaced its foreign competitors, and the last foreign trawlers left U.S. fishing areas in 1991.

The Magnuson Act requires that the various fish and other marine species within the FCZ be managed in accordance with comprehensive plans drawn up by regional fishery management councils, composed of both state and federal officials. Whereas general responsibility for implementing the Magnuson Act is vested in the secretary of commerce, acting through NOAA and the NMFS, planning decisions are entrusted to these regional councils. Eight such councils were created, each having authority over the fisheries seaward of the states represented on the council. The voting members of each council include the principal official with marine fishery management responsibility from each state in the region, the regional director of the NMFS for the area, and four to twelve persons appointed by the secretary of commerce from lists of qualified people submitted to him or her by the state governors in the region.

Each council is responsible for creating a management plan for each fishery within its jurisdiction. In preparing their plans, the coun-

The Magnuson Act required the establishment of regional fishery management councils, each of which creates a management plan for each fishery within its jurisdiction. The plan is designed to prevent overfishing and ensure an optimum yield from each fishery.

cils are required to hold public hearings. When complete, the plans are submitted to the secretary of commerce, who must approve them or return them to the councils for modification. The plans are expected to meet seven national conservation and management measures, the most important being that they prevent overfishing and ensure an optimum yield from each fishery. The act defines optimum yield very broadly, describing it as the amount of fish that "will provide the greatest overall benefit to the Nation" and that is based on the "maximum sustainable yield" from each fishery.

The Magnuson Act generally applies only beyond waters under state jurisdiction, which in most places extends to three miles from the coast. The act specifically preserves the rights of states to regulate all fishing within their boundaries, and even specifies that management plans created for fisheries within the FCZ may incorporate "the relevant fishery conservation and management measures of the coastal States nearest to the fishery." In only rare instances may the secretary of commerce preempt a state's authority to regulate fishing in its waters.

In general, the Magnuson Act marked a new era in U.S. fisheries. A principal goal of Magnuson was Americanization, which means the development and promotion of the U.S. fishing industry. A second goal was full domestic utilization, which means the elimination of foreign fishing operations within U.S. jurisdiction. Since the act was passed in 1976, it has been amended several times to try to increase the levels of Americanization and full domestic utilization. The federal government and the ocean fishing industry have increasingly recognized, however, that laws encouraging these priorities alone are not enough to secure productive fisheries. Rather, effective conservation requires international cooperation, as many important species are highly migratory or are found in fisheries that straddle national boundaries.

Native American Fishing Rights Just as the United States has entered into treaties with foreign countries specifying certain fishing rights and privileges, so also has it entered into treaty agreements with many Native American tribes concerning fishing and hunting rights. In theory, U.S. treaties with foreign countries and with sovereign Indian nations are the same, as both represent negotiated agreements with independent nations that the parties are bound to honor. In reality, however, treaties involving Native American fishing and hunting rights are much more controversial and complicated, as their provisions often conflict with state and federal wildlife efforts as well as with the interests of non-Indian fishers and hunters. Though many legal developments in the area of Native American fishing rights have broad application, treaty rights pertaining to fishing often vary from tribe to tribe, and depend on the language and historical context of the treaties involved.

Historically, fishing has always been an important activity for Native American tribes. Fish constituted a major portion of most Indians' diets, and dried fish were traded in large

PAUL CONKLIN/PHOTOEDIT

Ice fishing is a traditional activity for Native Americans. Native American fishing rights are often unclear because conditions have changed since the signing of treaties written in the mid–nineteenth century.

quantities. Religious rites were performed to ensure the return of local fish species each year, and tribes planned their own movements around the annual migrations of fish populations.

When Indian tribes signed treaties with the U.S. government to relinquish their lands—as nearly all did at some point—they often received assurance, either in the treaties or in statutes, that they could continue to hunt, fish, and gather food on their reservation and often in traditional locations off the reservation as well. In the mid–nineteenth century, when most of these treaties were signed, government officials willingly included such provisions because few non-Indians lived in frontier lands and because fish were thought to be an inexhaustible resource. Since then, the demand for fish has come to outstrip the supply, leading to battles over how to interpret and enforce treaty provisions guaranteeing Native Americans certain fishing rights.

Many of the treaties by which Indian tribes relinquished land to the United States expressly guaranteed the tribes' fishing and hunting rights. Even when treaties did not specifically mention fishing and hunting, those rights are considered to be retained. As the Supreme Court explained in the 1905 case *United States v. Winans*, 198 U.S. 371, 25 S. Ct. 662, 49 L. Ed. 1089, a treaty is not a grant of rights to the Indians but a taking of rights from them, and any right not specifically removed by a treaty is assumed to remain with the tribe. Though Congress has the power to extinguish Indian hunting and fishing rights, it must do so clearly and explicitly; rights cannot be considered ex-

tinguished based on ambiguous language or assumptions. Even when a tribe is officially "terminated" by Congress, its rights are retained unless Congress explicitly declares that it is terminating them. In *Menominee Tribe v. United States*, 391 U.S. 404, 88 S. Ct. 1705, 20 L. Ed. 2d 697 (1968), for example, Congress had terminated the Menominee tribe, but the Supreme Court ruled that the tribe's hunting and fishing rights were not affected because the termination statute did not explicitly mention those rights.

In many cases, Indian tribes have also retained the right to fish at locations off the reservation. In the Pacific Northwest, for example, many Indian tribes signed treaties guaranteeing them the right to take fish at their traditional fishing locations, whether those locations were on or off the newly created reservations. This right was upheld by the Supreme Court in *Winans*, in which the Court ruled that tribal members were entitled to "tak[e] fish at all usual and accustomed places," even though those places might be on privately owned land.

Though the fishing rights cases from the Pacific Northwest apply to specific parties and situations, they have had a broad effect on Indian fishing rights cases in other parts of the country. Today, case law in states such as Wisconsin, Minnesota, and Michigan are consistent with these cases in terms of Indian off-reservation fishing rights, the allocation of fish between Indians and non-Indians, and the relationship between tribal and state regulatory schemes. Rather than rely on the court system to resolve disputes, tribes and states now frequently attempt to reach negotiated settlements.

CROSS-REFERENCES

Environmental Law; Interior Department (Fish and Wildlife Service); Native American Rights.

FISHING TRIP 📖 Using the courts to find out information beyond the fair scope of the lawsuit. The loose, vague, unfocused questioning of a WITNESS or the overly broad use of the DISCOVERY process. Discovery sought on general, loose, and vague allegations, or on suspicion, surmise, or vague guesses. The scope of discovery may be restricted by protective orders as provided for by the Federal Rules of CIVIL PROCEDURE. 📖

FISHING VESSELS Customary international law provides that coastal fishing boats and small boats engaged in trade, as distinguished from seagoing fishing boats and large traders, are immune from attack and seizure

during war. This IMMUNITY is lost if fishing vessels take part in the hostilities. To prevent such involvement many nations have agreed not to take advantage of the peaceful character of such vessels in their war effort.

FIXED ASSET 📖 Property, such as machinery or buildings, utilized in a business that will not be used or liquidated during the current fiscal period. 📖

FIXED CHARGES 📖 Costs that do not vary with changes in output and would continue even if a firm produced no output at all, such as most management expenses, interests on bonded debt, DEPRECIATION, property taxes, and other irreducible overhead. 📖

FIXTURE 📖 An article in the nature of PERSONAL PROPERTY which has been so annexed to the realty that it is regarded as a part of the REAL PROPERTY. That which is fixed or attached to something permanently as an appendage and is not removable.

A thing is deemed to be affixed to real property when it is attached to it by roots, imbedded in it, permanently resting upon it, or permanently attached to what is thus permanent, as by means of cement, plaster, nails, bolts, or screws.

GOODS are fixtures when they become so related to particular REAL ESTATE that an interest in them arises under real estate law, e.g. a furnace affixed to a house or other building, counters permanently affixed to the floor of a store, or a sprinkler system installed in a building.

Fixtures possess the attributes of both real and personal property. 📖

Types Fixtures are generally classified as agricultural, domestic, ornamental, or trade. Agricultural fixtures are articles that are an-

Fishing vessels, such as these two boats in the Wrangell Narrows near Petersburg, Alaska, are immune from attack and seizure during war unless they are participating in the hostilities.

nexed for the purpose of farming. Domestic and ornamental fixtures are objects that a tenant may attach to a unit in order to render it more habitable. Stoves, shelves, and lighting equipment are types of domestic fixtures. Ornamental fixtures include curtains, chimney grates, blinds, and beds fastened to walls.

Trade fixtures are articles affixed to rented buildings by merchants, in order to pursue the business for which the premises are occupied. They encompass those items that merchants annex to the premises to facilitate the storage, handling, and display of their stock for sale to the public—such as booths, bars, display cases and lights—that are usually removable without material damage to the premises. The objective of this rule is to promote trade and industry. A TENANT, however, has no right to disengage a trade fixture if its detachment would cause substantial damage to the premises.

Requirements The article must be physically annexed to the realty or something appurtenant thereto in order for it to become a fixture. ANNEXATION to land occurs when the object is permanently affixed to the property through the application of plaster, cement, bolts, screws, nuts, or nails.

The attached article must also be adapted to the intended use or purpose of the realty so that it effectively becomes inseparable from the land itself.

The intention of the person who attaches the article determines whether or not the article is a fixture. The individual is not required to verbalize the intent, although the courts will evaluate such expressions. The courts consider the tenant's intent, which is inferred from all of the facts and circumstances concerning the actual annexation of the object, such as the nature of the article affixed, the method of annexation, and the extent to which the object has been integrated into the real estate.

Agreement of the Parties The parties may enter into an agreement in regard to the nature of an item to be utilized with realty. Statutes confer this right in some jurisdictions, and these agreements are enforceable whenever the rights of third persons are not violated.

The terms of a lease often define the rights of a LANDLORD AND TENANT in regard to fixtures. If the LEASE unequivocally stipulates that the tenant has the right to remove particular articles, the fact that the removal will damage the rented premises is immaterial.

Fixtures are usually attached to rented premises for the tenant's benefit without any intention of increasing the value of the landlord's

Fixtures such as ovens, stoves, and cabinets are considered part of the real property and not personal property once they have been installed.

property. Generally when no agreement exists between the parties, articles annexed by the tenant may be detached by the tenant, during the term of the tenancy, provided such can be done without damaging the premises.

The law favors the tenant's position that certain articles should be regarded as personal property rather than as part of the realty. Such improvements are those made to the rented premises by a tenant for personal enjoyment and use and, therefore, should retain their character as personal property.

Time of Removal If a trade fixture is not removed from the premises within the period specified in the lease, it becomes part of the realty and the landlord acquires title to it. A tenant's failure to remove domestic fixtures within the proper period will usually have the same result. The tenant is presumed to have abandoned the fixtures by failing to remove them.

The amount of time allotted to the tenant to remove the fixtures varies. In some JURISDICTIONS, the objects must be removed during the term of the tenancy. The right to remove the articles terminates with tenancy, in some states; whereas, in others, the tenant may remove the articles within a reasonable time after the expiration of the tenancy. The facts and circumstances of each case determine what period constitutes a "reasonable time."

The landlord can expressly consent to the tenant's removal of the fixtures even after the conclusion of the lease term or the surrender of possession. If the owner persuades the tenant to leave fixtures on the premises for some particular objective, he or she cannot acquire TITLE to the fixtures because the tenant has postponed their removal.

In most states, if a tenant accepts a new lease that contains no provisions concerning articles attached during tenancy under the prior lease, the tenant will lose the right to remove them. At the expiration of the initial lease, the fixtures become part of the realty. By accepting the new lease, the tenant acquires a temporary interest in both the fixtures and the land.

Generally, an extension of the original lease does not deprive the tenant of the right to remove fixtures. The tenant's right of removal is lost, however, if he or she merely stays or holds over without extending the current lease.

If the landlord prevents the tenant from detaching fixtures to which he or she is entitled, the time for removal is extended until it can be accomplished. If the landlord wrongfully ends the tenancy and the tenant is ousted, the tenant has a reasonable time in which to remove his or her fixtures.

After the tenancy expires, a landlord can order the tenant to unfasten unwanted fixtures. If the tenant fails to do so, the landlord can have the fixtures removed and charge the tenant for expenses incurred in their removal.

FLAG 📖 The official banner of a state or nation, often decorated with emblems or images that symbolize that state or nation. 📖

On the U.S. flag, thirteen horizontal stripes (in red and white) represent the original thirteen colonies. The union is represented by fifty white stars, for the fifty states, arrayed on a field of blue. The U.S. flag is sometimes called the Stars and Stripes, Old Glory, or the Red, White, and Blue.

Titles 4 and 36 of the U.S. Code govern when, where, and how a flag may be displayed; how a flag may be used; and the proper means of disposing of a worn or soiled flag.

The Stars and Stripes became a popular and revered symbol of the United States during and after the Civil War. The Union's victory over the Confederacy and the return to a united country engendered patriotic fervor that was embodied in this symbol. When large numbers of immigrants entered the United States during the late nineteenth and early twentieth centuries, the flag was appropriated as a symbol of nationalism and patriotism by groups that felt that the cultures and customs of the new citizens threatened national unity and security. During the same period, as the advertising industry grew along with rapid industrialization, the flag was commonly used for commercial purposes. Flags or images of flags were used to promote everything from toilet paper to chewing gum. The flag was also appropriated for political gain. In 1896, Republican presidential candidate WILLIAM MCKINLEY's campaign manager distributed millions of flags for use at McKinley's rallies. The McKinley campaign also distributed buttons bearing the likeness of a flag, as symbols of support for the candidate.

The turn of the century saw the beginnings of a movement to protect and honor the flag. In the early part of the twentieth century, schools commonly required students to salute the flag each morning. Some students refused to participate in the salute, mainly on religious grounds. By 1940, at least two hundred public school students had been expelled in sixteen states for refusing to salute the flag. Many of them were Jehovah's Witnesses, who maintained that any salute to the national flag constituted an act of idolatry and thus violated their religious beliefs. The expulsion of two Jehovah's Witnesses was challenged in *Minersville School District v. Gobitis*, 310 U.S. 586, 60 S. Ct. 1010, 84 L. Ed. 1375 (1940). In *Gobitis*, a father sued to enjoin the school district from prohibiting his children's attendance at school after they refused to salute the flag. The U.S. district court granted the INJUNCTION allowing the children to return to school, and the U.S. Court of Appeals for the Third Circuit affirmed the district court. On appeal, the Supreme Court reversed the lower courts, holding that the school district's requirement that students salute the flag did not unconstitutionally infringe their religious freedoms. Writing for the 8–1 majority, Justice

FELIX FRANKFURTER said the salute requirement was constitutional as long as the students' "right to believe as they please, to win others to their way of belief, and their right to assemble in their chosen places of worship for the devotional ceremonies of their faith, are fully respected."

A few years later, the Court reversed its position, in *West Virginia State Board of Education v. Barnette*, 319 U.S. 624, 63 S. Ct. 1178, 87 L. Ed. 1628 (1943), another challenge to mandatory flag salutes brought by members of Jehovah's Witnesses. In *Barnette*, the Court held that the school board could not require public school teachers and students to salute the flag. The Court said freedom of the press, of assembly, and of worship may be restricted "only to prevent grave and immediate danger to interests which the state may lawfully protect." In a companion case, *Taylor v. Mississippi*, 319 U.S. 583, 63 S. Ct. 1200, 87 L. Ed. 1600 (1943), the Court overturned the convictions of two people found guilty under a state statute that forbade the dissemination of information advocating refusal to salute, honor, or respect the flag. The Court held that the statute infringed FREEDOM OF SPEECH and FREEDOM OF THE PRESS. The *Barnette* and *Taylor* decisions signaled the Court's emerging support for the notion that freedom of speech extends to symbolic as well as oral and written speech.

Also during the early 1900s, numerous state laws were passed prohibiting the desecration of

The U.S. flag is a powerful symbol used to express patriotism and protest.

the flag or the use of the flag in advertising. Some of these laws were struck down by state courts, but in 1905, the U.S. Supreme Court upheld their validity when it affirmed a lower court that had refused to strike down a Nebraska statute prohibiting the use of the flag in advertising (*Halter v. Nebraska*, 205 U.S. 34, 27 S. Ct. 419, 51 L. Ed. 696 [1907]). The Court said the flag, as an emblem of national authority and an object of patriotic fervor, should not be associated with personal or commercial interests. It held that the Nebraska statute did not infringe PERSONAL PROPERTY rights or individual freedom.

For eighty years, *Halter* was cited as PRECEDENT in cases upholding flag desecration statutes, and these laws stood solidly intact through most of the twentieth century. The laws were invoked frequently to prosecute demonstrators who burned flags to protest U.S. involvement in the Vietnam War. Between 1965 and the end of the war in 1973, as many as one thousand arrests were made under various state laws prohibiting the desecration of the flag.

The Supreme Court addressed the constitutionality of flag desecration laws again in *Texas v. Johnson*, 491 U.S. 397, 109 S. Ct. 2533, 105 L. Ed. 2d 342 (1989). During the 1984 Republican National Convention, in Dallas, the defendant, Gregory Lee Johnson and one hundred others staged a protest outside the convention hall. During the demonstration, Johnson burned a U.S. flag. He was later arrested for violating the Texas Venerated Objects Law (Tex. Penal Code Ann. § 42.09(a)(3) [Vernon 1974]), which outlawed intentionally or knowingly desecrating a flag in a way that some observer might find seriously offensive. Johnson was convicted, but his conviction was overturned by the Texas Court of Criminal Appeals (*Johnson*, 755 S.W.2d 92 [Tex. Crim. App. 1988]). The state appealed to the U.S. Supreme Court. In a 5–4 decision, the Court affirmed the court of criminal appeals, holding that Johnson's conduct was expressive communication, a form of speech that requires FIRST AMENDMENT protection. Addressing Texas's claim that it had a legitimate interest in preventing a BREACH OF THE PEACE, the Court observed that no disturbance of the peace occurred or was threatened by Johnson's burning of the flag. The Court also held that the venerated objects statute was subject to the strictest constitutional scrutiny because it restricted Johnson's freedom of expression based on the content of the message he sought to convey. The Court concluded, "We do not consecrate the flag by punishing its desecration, for in doing so we dilute the freedom that this cherished emblem represents."

Many people were outraged by the *Johnson* decision. President GEORGE BUSH denounced flag burning and proposed a constitutional amendment to overturn *Johnson*. The Senate and the House of Representatives passed numerous resolutions calling for a CONSTITUTIONAL AMENDMENT outlawing flag burning. When it became clear that a constitutional amendment was probably not feasible, Congress instead passed the Flag Protection Act of 1989 (Pub. L. No. 101-131, 103 Stat. 777 [amending 18 U.S.C.A. § 700]), which made it a criminal offense to mutilate, deface, or burn a flag; place a flag on the floor or ground; or walk on a flag. The act did not mention the motive of the actor or the effect on observers of the act. With these omissions, the statute was designed to be content neutral and to pass the most stringent constitutional scrutiny.

The Flag Protection Act was tested in *United States v. Eichman*, 496 U.S. 310, 110 S. Ct. 2404, 110 L. Ed. 2d 287 (1990). In *Eichman*, the defendants were arrested for burning a flag in a protest. They moved to dismiss the charges on the ground that the Flag Protection Act violated the First Amendment. The district court dismissed the charges, and the government appealed directly to the Supreme Court. Affirming the district court's findings, the Court reasserted its position that flag burning is expressive conduct protected by the First Amendment. The Court conceded that the federal act differed from the Texas statute in *Johnson* because it did not appear to regulate the content of the message conveyed by the prohibited acts. Nonetheless, the Court held that the government's interest in preserving the flag as a national symbol was implicated under the act only when a person's treatment of the flag communicated a message that opposed the government's ideals. In effect, the act did regulate the content of protected speech. The Court concluded that the government may not prohibit the expression of an idea, no matter how disagreeable or offensive that idea may be.

The *Eichman* decision prompted President Bush to renew his efforts to gain passage of a constitutional amendment banning flag desecration. The measure came to a vote in June 1990. By then, public and political interest in the issue had dissipated, and many members of Congress who had voted for the Flag Preservation Act were unwilling to support a change to the Constitution. The proposed amendment failed by a vote of 254–177 in the House of Representatives and 58–42 in the Senate.

See also RELIGION.

FLAGRANTE DELICTO [*Latin, In the act of perpetrating the crime.*]

FLETCHER v. PECK An 1810 decision by the U.S. Supreme Court, *Fletcher v. Peck*, 10 U.S. (6 Cranch) 87, 3 L. Ed. 162, that held that public grants were contractual obligations that could not be abrogated without fair compensation even though the state legislature that made the grant had been corrupted and a subsequent legislature had passed an act nullifying the original grant.

The plaintiff, Robert Fletcher, brought suit against John Peck for breach of COVENANT on land that Fletcher had purchased in 1803. This land was part of a tract of 35 million acres in the area of the Yazoo River (Mississippi and Alabama) that the state of Georgia had taken from the Indians and then sold in 1795 to four land companies for a modest sum ($500,000) for so much land. The land companies then broke up the tract and resold parcels for enormous profits.

When a new Georgia legislature learned in 1796 that some of the legislators who had voted to sell the land had been stockholders in the companies that purchased the tract and that many of the legislators who had authorized the sale had received bribes from the land speculators, it RESCINDED the original sale on the grounds that it had been attended by FRAUD and corruption.

The property in question had passed through several hands before Peck purchased it in 1800. Three years later, he sold the land to Fletcher with a DEED stating that all the previous sales had been legal. Fletcher, however, contended that the original sale to the land companies was void and that Peck was guilty of breach of covenant because the land was not legally his to sell. After a circuit court found in favor of Peck, the case came before the U.S. Supreme Court on a WRIT of error.

Speaking for the Court, Chief Justice JOHN MARSHALL deplored the corruption that had found its way into the state legislature but found that the validity of a law cannot depend on the motives of its framers. Nor can private individuals be expected to conduct an inquiry into the probity of a legislature before they enter into a private contract on the basis of a statute enacted by that legislature.

Marshall then turned to the question of whether the statute enacted in 1796 could nullify rights and claims established under the bill that had authorized the land sale in 1795. Although he agreed that as a general principle "one legislature is competent to repeal any act which a former legislature was competent to pass," Marshall held that actions taken under a law cannot be undone by a subsequent legislature. If the law in question is a CONTRACT, he reasoned, repeal of the law cannot divest rights that have vested under the contract. To hold otherwise would be tantamount to seizing with-

Fletcher v. Peck concerned the sale of land that the State of Georgia had taken from Native American tribes. The sale was rescinded by a later Georgia Legislature because of corruption surrounding the sale, but the rescinding act was found unconstitutional.

CORBIS-BETTMANN

out compensation property that an individual had acquired fairly and honestly.

In addition to basing his argument on such general considerations, Marshall found that the original grant was a contract within the meaning of the Contract Clause of the U.S. Constitution, which provides that "[n]o State shall . . . pass any Bill of Attainder, ex post facto Law, or Law impairing the Obligation of Contracts . . ." (Art. I, § 10, clause 1). Reasoning that the Constitution did not distinguish between contracts between individuals and contracts to which a state was a party, Marshall held that the Framers of the Constitution intended the clause to apply to both. The purpose of the clause, he explained, was to restrain the power of the state legislatures over the lives and property of individuals.

Under the act rescinding the bill of 1795, however, Fletcher would forfeit the property "for a crime not committed by himself, but by those from whom he purchased." Thus the rescinding act "would have the effect of an *ex post facto* law" and would therefore be unconstitutional. Accordingly Marshall concluded that in spite of the profits reaped by the dishonesty of the land speculators, both general principles and the U.S. Constitution prevented a state legislature from rendering a contract null and void.

Fletcher v. Peck was the first case in which the Supreme Court invalidated a state law as contrary to the Constitution. It also exemplified the protective approach of the Marshall court toward business and commercial interests. In *Fletcher* and later in the *Dartmouth College* case (*Trustees of Dartmouth College v. Woodward*, 17 U.S. [4 Wheat.], 518, 4 L. Ed. 629 [1819]), the Court expanded the scope of the term *contract* and limited the degree to which the states could encroach upon property rights and contractual obligations.

FLOATING CAPITAL 📖 Funds retained for the purpose of paying current expenses as opposed to fixed ASSETS. 📖

Floating capital is also known as circulating capital. It encompasses (1) the raw materials con-

sumed in each phase of manufacturing; (2) money designated for wages; and (3) products stored in the warehouses of manufacturers or merchants.

FLOATING LIEN 📖 A security interest retained in COLLATERAL even when the collateral changes in character, classification, or location. An inventory loan in which the lender receives a security interest or general claim on all of a company's INVENTORY. A security interest under which the borrower pledges security for present and future advances. 📖

FLOTSAM 📖 A name for the goods that float upon the sea when cast overboard for the safety of the ship or when a ship is sunk. Distinguished from JETSAM (goods deliberately thrown over to lighten ship) and LIGAN (goods cast into the sea attached to a buoy). 📖

F.O.B. 📖 An abbreviation for free on board, which means that a vendor or consignor will deliver goods on a railroad car, truck, vessel, or other conveyance without any expense to the purchaser or consignee. 📖

FOLLOW 📖 To conform to, comply with, or be fixed or determined by; as in the expression "costs follow the event of the suit." To go, proceed, or come after. To seek to obtain; to accept as authority, as in adhering to PRECEDENT. 📖

BIOGRAPHY

UPI/CORBIS-BETTMANN

Clara Shortridge Foltz

FOLTZ, CLARA SHORTRIDGE Clara Shortridge Foltz has been called California's First Woman. The first woman on the Pacific Coast to pass the bar, she did so after successfully lobbying the legislature to change a law that denied women the right to become lawyers. She was the first woman to serve as clerk of the judiciary committee of the state assembly, to be selected as a trustee of the State Normal School, to serve on the California State Board of Charities and Corrections, to serve as a deputy district attorney in Los Angeles, and to run for governor. She was the first woman to argue a motion in the New York City courts. And, in 1893, she was the first person to propose a model PUBLIC DEFENDER bill—the blueprint for the system that remains in place today. Her efforts resulted in the passage of the bill in more than thirty states.

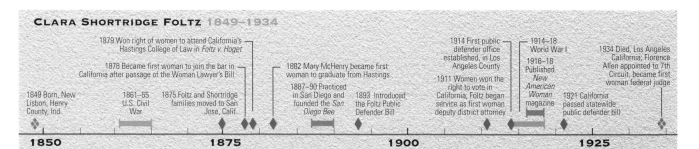

CLARA SHORTRIDGE FOLTZ 1849–1934

1879 Won right of women to attend California's Hastings College of Law in *Foltz v. Hoget*

1878 Became first woman to join the bar in California after passage of the Woman Lawyer's Bill

1882 Mary McHenry became first woman to graduate from Hastings

1914 First public defender office established, in Los Angeles County

1914–18 World War I

1916–18 Published *New American Woman* magazine

1934 Died, Los Angeles California; Florence Allen appointed to 7th Circuit, became first woman federal judge

1849 Born, New Lisbon, Henry County, Ind.

1861–65 U.S. Civil War

1875 Foltz and Shortridge families moved to San Jose, Calif.

1887–90 Practiced in San Diego and founded the *San Diego Bee*

1893 Introduced the Foltz Public Defender Bill

1911 Women won the right to vote in California; Foltz began service as first woman deputy district attorney

1921 California passed statewide public defender bill

1850 1875 1900 1925

Foltz was born July 16, 1849, in New Lisbon, Henry County, Indiana, the second of five children, and the only girl, to Elias Willets Shortridge and Telitha Cumi Harwood Shortridge, both of Indiana. Her father was at times a druggist, a lawyer, and a preacher in the Campbellite Church.

The Shortridges moved to Dalton Township, Wayne County, Indiana, the next year. By the time Clara was eleven years old, the family was living in Mount Pleasant, Iowa. There, she received her only formal education, at Howe's Academy, a progressive school whose mission and purposes were coeducation, WOMEN'S RIGHTS, and the abolition of SLAVERY. She earned honors in Latin, philosophy, history, and rhetoric. At age fourteen, she accepted a teaching post near Keithsburg, Illinois, which she held for only one term because, at age fifteen, on December 30, 1864, she eloped with a Union soldier, Jeremiah Richard Foltz.

The Foltzes lived on a farm in Iowa, where they had the first three of their five children. In 1871, Foltz's husband moved to Oregon; in 1872, Foltz and their four children (the youngest being nine weeks old) followed. She found him working as a clerk for miniscule pay. To support her family, she went to work as a dressmaker and took in boarders.

In 1875, Foltz and her family moved to San Jose, California. Although her marriage ended there in 1877, her public life began. Foltz became involved in the SUFFRAGE movement, attending, and then giving, lectures. Foltz also began her legal career in San Jose. She attempted to study with the preeminent member of the legal community Francis Spencer, but he refused her request. Foltz then turned to C. C. Stephens, who was a friend, an occasional legal partner, and a fellow silver prospector of her father's. Stephens accepted her as a student at his firm, Black and Stephens.

In 1877, California law allowed only white males over twenty-one years of age and of good moral character to become lawyers. Foltz wrote a proposed amendment to section 275 of the Code of Civil Procedure, changing "white male" to "person." Foltz and her sister suffragist Laura deForce Gordon lobbied throughout the twenty-second session of the California Legislature for the Woman Lawyer's Bill. It easily passed the senate but met strong opposition in the assembly. Foltz's ally, the senate sponsor of the bill, Grove L. Johnson, switched his aye vote to nay in order to move for reconsideration of the defeated bill. After a heated debate at the very end of the legislative session, the Woman Lawyer's Bill passed the assembly. The bill nearly died until Foltz managed a last-minute audience with Governor William Irwin. In the waning hours of the session, on the last possible day, March 29, 1878, the governor signed the bill.

Foltz and Gordon divided their responsibilities the summer of 1878. Foltz studied and was the first woman to take advantage of their recent legislative success, taking the BAR EXAMINATION. Gordon, although she was not a delegate, attended the first California constitutional convention as a member of the press, and successfully lobbied for the inclusion of two clauses that she and Foltz had a hand in drafting. The first clause prohibited restrictions to any business, vocation, or profession based on sex; the second prohibited sex discrimination in college faculty hiring. Foltz passed the bar examination and became California's first female lawyer on September 5, 1878.

In January 1879, Foltz and Gordon registered for classes at Hastings, California's first law school. However, after only a few days of classes, Foltz received a letter from the Hastings Law School Board, informing her that the directors had resolved not to admit women. Foltz and Gordon filed suit to compel the college, as a state institution, to admit women. The district court judge, who reportedly did not believe in women lawyers, nevertheless found these women lawyers to be correct in the law, and ordered Hastings to admit them. Hastings appealed, and the case went to the California Supreme Court (*Foltz v. Hoge*, 54 Cal. 28 [1879]). Although Foltz and Gordon were victorious again, the time for Foltz to attend law school had passed. She went to Sacramento to serve as clerk, or counsel, to the judiciary committee of the state assembly. Foltz nevertheless considered the Hastings victory to be her finest moment.

Foltz had a long and successful career as an attorney, first in San Francisco and then in Los Angeles. She practiced probate, criminal, family, and corporate law. Some of her very first cases, in 1878, heard in justice court, involved reclaiming the property of young women put in vulnerable circumstances by desertion, illness, or an ex-employer.

Throughout her career, in addition to conducting a thriving practice, she worked for suffrage and women's rights. She actively encouraged the participation of women in the legal profession. In 1893, she organized the Portia Law Club in San Francisco. She taught women the law at her offices in San Francisco and in Los Angeles, where she relocated in 1906. In 1918, she helped found the Women

"THEY CALLED ME THE LADY LAWYER . . . A DAINTY SOBRIQUET THAT ENABLED ME TO MAINTAIN A DAINTY MANNER AS I BROWBEAT MY WAY THROUGH THE MARSHES OF IGNORANCE AND PREJUDICE."

Lawyers' Club in Los Angeles. She was responsible for California laws allowing qualified women to act as ADMINISTRATORS, EXECUTORS, and NOTARIES PUBLIC.

Foltz was a primary force behind improving the criminal defense system. In 1893, she represented the California bar at the National Congress of Jurisprudence and Law Reform, held in conjunction with the Chicago World's Fair. It was there that she first introduced the Foltz Public Defender Bill. This proposal was subsequently adopted, owing in large part to her lobbying, in over thirty states.

The Foltz Public Defender Bill proposed a defender system in which salaried lawyers would devote all or a substantial part of their time to the specialized practice of representing indigent defendants, as opposed to the existing system, in which the court appointed lawyers on an ad hoc basis from the bar at large. The model bill proposed that public defenders meet certain qualifications, receive a salary, have clearly defined job responsibilities, and serve for a term of office. A public defender would be a county officer who would defend, without expense to them, all persons who were not financially able to employ counsel and who were charged with the commission of any CONTEMPT, MISDEMEANOR, FELONY, or other offense.

Nearly two decades passed before the first public defender office was actually established in Los Angeles County in 1914, where Foltz was then living. In fact, she had already served as the first woman deputy district attorney, in 1911. It was 1921 before California passed a statewide public defender bill.

Foltz was also an active writer and publisher. She founded the weekly newspaper *The San Diego Bee*. She also published a feminist weekly, *The Mecca*, during a brief stay in Colorado, and a magazine, *The New American Woman*. She also contributed articles to other papers and magazines throughout her life.

Foltz died in Los Angeles on September 4, 1934. The pallbearers for her funeral included the governor and several prominent federal and state judges.

FOOD AND DRUG ADMINISTRATION

One of the oldest U.S. CONSUMER PROTECTION agencies, the Food and Drug Administration (FDA) protects the public from unsafe foods, drugs, medical devices, cosmetics, and other potential hazards. Part of the Department of Health and Human Services, the FDA regulates over $1 trillion worth of products, which account for one-fourth of all consumer spending in the United States. It also protects the rights and safety of patients in clinical trials of new medical products, monitors the promotional activities of drug and device manufacturers, regulates the labeling of all packaged foods, and monitors the safety of the nation's blood supply.

To ensure compliance with its regulations, the FDA employs over one thousand investigators and inspectors who visit over fifteen thousand food processing, drug manufacturing, and other facilities each year. If violations of law are found, the FDA first encourages the company to voluntarily correct the problem or recall the faulty product from the market. If the firm does not voluntarily comply with the law, the FDA may take it to court and seek criminal penalties against it. Each year, the FDA declares about three thousand products and thirty thousand import shipments to be unacceptable.

The FDA employs over two thousand scientists—including nine hundred chemists and three hundred microbiologists—who provide the scientific evidence to back up its regulatory and inspection duties. These scientists analyze samples of products for purity and review test results of new products. The FDA does not itself do research for a new medical product. Instead, it evaluates the results of studies undertaken by the manufacturer.

History Food production in the United States has been regulated since the late eighteenth century. Colonies and later states passed laws banning impurities from selected foods. In 1848, the United States began regulating imported drugs, under the Drug Importation Act (Ch. LXX, 9 Stat. 237). The enforcement of food and drug laws was first assigned to the Chemical Division of the new U.S. Department of Agriculture in 1862 (12 Stat. 387).

The need for laws to regulate food and drug purity became increasingly urgent in the late nineteenth century, when substances such as opium, cocaine, and heroin were commonly added to medicinal elixirs and tonics. On June 30, 1906, Congress, with the support of President THEODORE ROOSEVELT, passed two landmark pieces of Progressive Era legislation that strengthened the government's ability to protect consumers: the Food and Drug Act (34 Stat. 768 [21 U.S.C.A. § 1–15]) and the Meat Inspection Act (21 U.S.C.A. § 601 et seq.). The former prohibited interstate commerce in misbranded and adulterated foods, drinks, and drugs, and the latter addressed the unsanitary conditions and use of poisonous preservatives and dyes in the meatpacking industry.

In 1927, Congress authorized the creation of the Food, Drug, and Insecticide Administration within the U.S. Department of Agriculture. In 1930, the agency's name was changed to the

HOW THE FDA APPROVES NEW DRUGS

The process by which the Food and Drug Administration (FDA) approves drugs as safe and effective is generally long and complicated, though it may vary according to the type of drug and the nature of the illness for which it is being developed. The FDA refers to drugs under development as investigational new drugs, or INDs.

The evaluation of new drugs requires the skills of many different FDA scientists and professionals performing a wide variety of tasks. Biochemists and molecular biologists evaluate the basic chemistry and biology of new chemical compounds and molecular structures. Toxicologists assess the potential harm of proposed drugs, and pharmacologists study how these drugs affect the body and are broken down and absorbed by it. Computer scientists create electronic models that aid in the understanding of new chemicals. Physicians evaluate the results of clinical trials, assessing both the beneficial and adverse effects of the drugs. And statisticians evaluate the design and results of controlled studies.

It is an expensive and time consuming process, particularly for the company developing the drug, called a drug sponsor. A sponsor spends an average of $359 million for each new drug brought to market. Typically, the process takes eight and a half years and may be divided into roughly three stages: preclinical trials, involving animal and other laboratory tests (lasting one and a half years on average); clinical trials, involving tests on humans (five years); and FDA review (two years).

Preclinical Trials

Once a sponsor has developed a drug, it must test the drug on animals in the laboratory. In doing so, the drug sponsor must follow FDA guidelines and regulations. These tests, also called preclinical trials, are usually done on more than one species of animals. FDA guidelines call for the inspection of animal laboratories every two years to ensure that they are being operated according to the administration's regulations.

After short-term lab testing has been performed and the sponsor has deemed its results adequate, the sponsor submits test data and plans for future clinical trials to the FDA. FDA scientists, together with a local institutional review board composed of scientists, ethicists, and nonscientists, then conduct a thirty-day safety review to decide whether to allow testing on humans.

The vast majority of new drugs tested in the laboratory are rejected by either the sponsor or the FDA because they are unsafe or ineffective.

If the FDA indicates approval, the drug sponsor may begin clinical testing on humans. Even if a drug is approved for clinical trials, the sponsor continues animal testing of the drug in order to better understand the drug's long-term effects.

Clinical Trials

Clinical trials are scientifically controlled studies in which the drug being tested is given to one group of patients, while another treatment, often a placebo (an inactive substance that looks like the drug being tested), is given to another group. Ideally, neither group of patients knows which is receiving the new drug and which is receiving the placebo.

The clinical trials, like the animal tests, examine what happens to the drug in the body, including whether it is changed, or metabolized, in the body, how much of it is absorbed into the blood, and how long it remains in the body. If human tests produce unexpected results, researchers may conduct further animal tests to better understand the drug.

Clinical trials proceed in three phases:

- Phase 1 involves testing primarily for safety and dosage level. Twenty to one hundred healthy patients are assessed over several months. If the results are within FDA safety guidelines, the trials proceed to phase 2.
- Phase 2 involves a greater number of patients—up to several hundred—who have the condition that the drug is intended to treat. During this stage, which lasts from several months to two years, researchers attempt to determine the drug's effectiveness in achieving its stated purpose, as well as its safety. At the end of this phase, sponsors meet with FDA officials to discuss the best way to conduct the next phase of testing.
- In phase 3, the most crucial stage of testing, the number of patients is expanded still further, to several hundred to several thousand, and the length of the study is increased to one to four years. This phase establishes the correct dosage of the drug and how it will be labeled, and provides further evidence regarding its safety and effectiveness.

Of one hundred drugs submitted for testing in humans, an average of seventy will pass phase 1. Of these seventy, on average, only thirty-three will remain after phase 2 testing, and twenty-five to thirty after phase 3. Finally, an average of only twenty will actually receive FDA approval.

Once the drug sponsor has completed clinical trials, it submits a new drug application (NDA) to the FDA, requesting approval to market the drug. This application consists of documentation detailing the chemical composition of the drug, the design of the trials, the results of the trials, and the means by which the drug is made and packaged.

FDA Review

In assessing an NDA, the FDA undertakes its closest scrutiny of all during the drug approval process. Its principal goal during review is to determine

HOW THE FDA APPROVES NEW DRUGS
(CONTINUED)

whether the benefits of the new drug outweigh the risks. To reach this determination, the FDA examines the documentation provided by the sponsor and looks at samples of the drug.

If inadequacies are discovered in the NDA, the FDA may require additional information, further testing, or modified labeling. In cases where it is difficult to establish clearly whether the benefits of the drug outweigh the risks, a panel of outside experts is often consulted.

If the FDA approves the drug, the sponsor may begin manufacturing and marketing the drug immediately.

The FDA does not stop monitoring a drug once it has been marketed. It continues to evaluate the drug's safety and effectiveness through its program of postmarket surveillance. This program consists of surveys, the testing of product samples, and the analysis of reported adverse reactions.

Speeding Drugs to Those Who Need Them

The FDA has long-standing policies allowing what it calls the compassionate use of new drugs for those in desperate need. Innovative cancer treatments, for example, have been made available to patients since the 1970s through the National Cancer Institute.

However, during the 1980s, the FDA came under increasing fire for its slow approval of new drugs. Particularly with the emergence of AIDS during the 1980s, the public outcry for fast delivery of innovative new drugs strengthened. As science produces ever more pharmaceuticals, the FDA is called on to review drug applications as quickly as is reasonably possible.

In response to the growing demand for speedy drug evaluation, the FDA has made significant changes in its re-

view protocols. In 1987, for example, the agency adopted "expanded access" regulations, which permit certain drugs to be designated as treatment INDs. A treatment IND may be administered to patients even while it is still undergoing clinical trials. This program allows patients with no other alternatives to undergo a treatment that may benefit their health. By August 1994, twenty-nine agents had been designated treatment INDs, and by 1995, more than seventy-five thousand patients had received access to new therapies through this program. New drugs used to treat patients with AIDS are made available through a similar process known as the parallel track approach.

Identifying priorities is another method the FDA uses to provide more rapid access to promising new treatments. AIDS drugs, drugs that treat life-threatening or severely debilitating illnesses, and drugs that appear to offer significant improvements over existing therapies are classified as priority drugs and receive faster review than those classified as standard drugs. With priority drugs, the FDA typically becomes involved earlier in the development process, and is thereby able to more quickly review the relevant applications.

Drugs are also classified as to chemical type, so that those closely similar in structure to existing drugs will receive less intensive review than those with a molecular structure that has never been marketed before.

Accelerated approval is another mechanism for faster review of promising new drugs. Under this program, created in 1991, a product may be approved for limited use if it has been shown in trials to achieve particular results—such as lowering blood pressure or cholesterol. Drugs approved under this program include didanosine

for AIDS, interferon beta-1B for multiple sclerosis, and DNase for cystic fibrosis.

The Prescription Drug User Fee Act of 1992 (Pub. L. 102-571, Title 1, Oct. 29, 1992, 106 Stat. 4491 to 4500) has also enabled the FDA to speed drug review. Under this law, fees paid by drug manufacturers are used by the agency to hire hundreds of additional review staff and buy improved equipment, including computers that make review more efficient.

The FDA is also attempting to streamline red tape and bureaucracy. In 1995, President Bill Clinton and Vice President Albert Gore, Jr., announced that twenty-one separate product license applications used by the FDA would be consolidated into one simplified form. This form would also be available in an electronic format, making it easier to distribute, prepare, and review.

Results indicate that these changes have led to faster approval of important new drugs. One signal success of FDA reform was the prompt approval of taxol, a treatment for advanced ovarian cancer that was approved in December 1992 after a record 5 months. By 1994, all new drugs were being approved by the FDA in a median time of 19 months, and priority drugs with important therapeutic uses were approved in an average of 10.4 months. In the late 1980s, by comparison, the FDA took an average of 27 months to approve new drugs.

In 1995, President Clinton established even more ambitious new goals for FDA approval. These goals, to be met by 1997, require the FDA to approve priority drugs within 6 months and standard drugs within 12 months.

AZT: An Agent of Change for the FDA

The AIDS drug AZT, or azidothymidine, is a celebrated example of speedy FDA approval of a new drug. The unusually swift approval of AZT during the early years of the AIDS epidemic led to the creation of a new FDA category, treatment investigational new drug (treatment IND), that established new procedures for more rapid and flexible drug approval.

The pharmaceutical company Burroughs Wellcome first presented AZT as a new drug to the FDA in June 1985. Public fear of AIDS had increased dramatically during the previous few years, as had protests by AIDS activists who complained of slow FDA movement with regard to promising new treatments. Keenly aware of the need for swift decision making in the face of the deadly AIDS disease, the FDA approved phase 1 clinical trials of the drug within one week of the initial application.

Phase 1 testing of AZT, between July and December 1985, was promising, and phase 2, involving three hundred patients in placebo-controlled trials, began in February 1986. After six months, 19 of the 137 patients in the group taking the placebo had died, whereas only 1 of 145 in the group taking AZT had died. The results were encouraging enough for the FDA to forgo further testing. The group taking the placebo was switched to AZT, and phase 3 testing, traditionally the most important step in clinical trials, was deemed unnecessary.

In September 1986, the FDA authorized the treatment of patients who wanted access to AZT, even before it had given approval to the drug. By the time approval for general public use came in March 1987, four thousand patients had already been treated with AZT, and thus the drug was already potentially extending the lives of hundreds of people.

Taking an example from its handling of AZT, the FDA in May 1987 created the treatment IND classification to facilitate faster approval and wider distribution of promising new therapies for life-threatening diseases. The rapid approval of AZT also proved greatly encouraging to the pharmaceutical industry, which could now hope to bring AIDS drugs to market much more rapidly and at lower cost.

---

current one, Food and Drug Administration (Agriculture Appropriation Act, 46 Stat. 976).

In 1937, 107 people died after taking the elixir sulfanilamide, a supposedly healing tonic. This tragedy prompted the passage of the next major reform of food and drug law, the Federal Food, Drug, and Cosmetic Act of 1938 (21 U.S.C.A. § 301 et seq.). The FDA was now entrusted with the regulation of cosmetics and therapeutic devices and was authorized to do factory inspections. Even more important, the act required new drugs to be tested on animals and humans for safety before being marketed. In 1957, the Food Additives Amendment (Pub. L. 85-250, Aug. 31, 1957, Stat. 567) required the evaluation of food additives to establish safety, and in the following year, the Delaney Clause (Pub. L. 85-929, Sept. 6, 1958, 72 Stat. 1784) forbade the use in food of substances found to cause cancer in laboratory animals.

In 1962, the Kefauver-Harris Drug Amendments (Pub. L. 87-781, Oct. 10, 1962, 76 Stat. 780) were passed. These laws required drug manufacturers not only to show that their drugs were safe but also to prove that their drugs achieved the effects claimed for them. That same year, FDA regulations were shown to be effective after the drug thalidomide, for which the FDA had delayed approval, caused thousands of birth defects in Western Europe.

In 1979, the FDA was made part of the Department of Health and Human Services (96 Stat. 668, 695). Other laws with major implications for the FDA's activities include the 1990 Nutrition Labeling and Education Act (Pub. L. 101-535, Nov. 8, 1990, 104 Stat. 2353), which requires all packaged foods to carry labels with nutrition information, and the Prescription Drug User Fee Act of 1992 (Pub. L. 102-571, Title 1, Oct. 29, 1992, 106 Stat. 4491 to 4500), which requires drug and biologics manufacturers to pay fees that support FDA assessment of their products.

Organization The FDA carries out its activities through a number of subdivisions. The Center for Drug Evaluation and Research regulates the safety, effectiveness, and labeling of all prescription and over-the-counter drugs intended for human use. It also monitors drug advertising for accuracy, ensures the safety and rights of patients in drug studies, and distributes information on drug products to the medical community and the public.

The Center for Biologics Evaluation and Research regulates biological products, which include blood, vaccines, human tissues, and drugs derived from living organisms. It coordinates an AIDS program, which works to develop an AIDS vaccine and AIDS diagnostic tests. It also conducts research on the safety of blood and blood products and inspects manufacturing plants to ensure compliance with FDA standards. See also ACQUIRED IMMUNE DEFICIENCY SYNDROME.

The Center for Food Safety and Applied Nutrition develops regulations related to food, food additives and colorings, and cosmetics. The Center for Devices and Radiological Health seeks to ensure the safe use of potentially hazardous radiation such as that produced by X rays. It conducts research into the effects of exposure to radiation-producing medical devices and develops manufacturing standards for such devices.

The Center for Veterinary Medicine evaluates the safety of drugs and devices used on animals. The National Center for Toxicological Research assesses the biological effects of toxic chemical substances.

Other offices of the FDA include the Office of Policy, the Office of External Affairs, Office of Management and Systems, Office of AIDS Coordination, Office of Orphan Products Development, and Office of Biotechnology. The administration operates six field offices, twenty-one district offices, and 135 resident inspection posts throughout the United States and Puerto Rico.

FOOTNOTE 4 Footnote 4 is a footnote to *United States v. Carolene Products Co.*, 304 U.S. 144, 58 S. Ct. 778, 82 L. Ed. 1234 (1938), in which the U S. Supreme Court upheld the constitutionality of the Filled Milk Act, 42 Stat. 1486, which Congress passed in 1923 to regulate certain dairy products. Written by Justice Harlan F. Stone, footnote 4 symbolizes the end of one era of constitutional jurisprudence and the dawning of another.

In upholding the constitutionality of the Filled Milk Act, the Supreme Court drew a distinction between legislation that regulates ordinary economic activities and legislation that curtails important personal liberties. The constitutional authority of state and federal legislatures over economic matters is plenary, the Court said, and laws passed to regulate such matters are entitled to a presumption of constitutionality when reviewed by the judicial branch of government.

Courts must pay great deference to legislation that is principally aimed at economic affairs, the Court continued, and judges should refrain from questioning the wisdom or policy judgments underlying such legislation. Although some commercial laws may seem undesirable or unnecessary to a particular judge, the Court cautioned, the judicial branch may not overturn them unless they fail to serve a rational or legitimate purpose.

This deferential posture toward the legislative branch represents the crux of judicial self-restraint, a judicial philosophy that advocates a narrow role for courts in U.S. constitutional democracy. Because state and federal legislatures are constitutionally authorized to make the law, proponents of judicial self-restraint argue, courts must limit their role to interpreting and applying the law, except in the rare instance where a piece of legislation clearly and unequivocally violates a constitutional provision, in which case they may strike it down.

In footnote 4 the Supreme Court indicated that this presumption of constitutionality might not apply to certain categories of noneconomic legislation. Legislation that restricts political processes, discriminates against minorities, or contravenes a specifically enumerated constitutional liberty, the Court said, may be subject to "more searching judicial scrutiny."

Legislation that limits the right to assemble peaceably, the freedom to associate, or the liberty to express dissenting viewpoints, the Court suggested, tends to obstruct ordinary political channels that average citizens traditionally rely on to participate in the democratic process. By the same token, the Court suggested that legislation discriminating against racial, religious, and ethnic minorities tends to marginalize groups that are already politically weak and vulnerable.

The Court also reasoned that legislation contravening a specifically enumerated constitutional right should be given less deference by the judiciary than legislation that purportedly contravenes an unenumerated right. This passage in the Court's opinion alluded to its decision in an earlier case, *Lochner v. New York*, 198 U.S. 45, 25 S. Ct. 539, 49 L. Ed. 937 (1905), which has been maligned throughout the twentieth century.

In *Lochner* the Supreme Court recognized an unenumerated freedom of contract that is loosely derived from the Fifth and Fourteenth Amendments to the U.S. Constitution. Based on this freedom, the Court struck down a New York law (N.Y. Laws 1897, chap. 415, art. 8, § 110) that regulated the number of hours employees could work each week in the baking industry. The Court said employers and employees enjoy an unwritten constitutional right to determine their wages, hours, and working conditions without government interference.

Over the next thirty-two years, state and federal courts relied on *Lochner* to invalidate scores of statutes that attempted to regulate employment relations, business affairs, and various property interests. At the same time, the Supreme Court was upholding legislation that restricted specifically enumerated constitutional liberties, such as the FREEDOM OF SPEECH. For example, in *Schenck v. United States*, 249 U.S. 47, 39 S. Ct. 247, 63 L. Ed. 470 (1919), the Supreme Court upheld the Espionage Act of 1917, 40 Stat. 217, which prohibited the circulation of printed material that encouraged resistance to the military draft during World War I.

The reasoning of footnote 4 helped bring an end to the *Lochner* era and a reversal of the judicial standards of review for economic and noneconomic legislation. Before *Carolene Products*, legislation that in any way touched upon an economic interest was subject to judicial scrutiny. During the same period, state and federal courts gave leeway to legislation touching upon noneconomic freedoms, even the personal freedoms expressly contained in the BILL OF RIGHTS.

Since *Carolene Products*, state and federal legislatures have been given wide latitude to regulate the workplace, commercial interests, and other economic matters. Conversely, laws that have hindered access to political processes, discriminated against minorities, or impinged on fundamental freedoms contained in the Bill of Rights, as made applicable to the states through the FOURTEENTH AMENDMENT, have been deemed suspect, and subject to strict judicial scrutiny. Such laws are typically invalidated by the judiciary unless the government can demonstrate that they serve a compelling interest.

The legacy of footnote 4 can be observed in cases where the Supreme Court has expanded the class of minorities who are protected by heightened judicial scrutiny. In addition to the racial, ethnic, and religious minorities referenced in footnote 4, women, illegitimate children, and other "discrete and insular" minorities have received increased constitutional protection by the Supreme Court since 1938.

CROSS-REFERENCES

Judicial Review; *Lochner v. New York*; Schenck v. United States; Strict Scrutiny.

FORBEARANCE 📖 Refraining from doing something that one has a legal right to do. Giving of further time for repayment of an obligation or agreement; not to enforce claim at its due date. A delay in enforcing a legal right. Act by which CREDITOR waits for payment of DEBT due by a DEBTOR after it becomes due.

Within USURY law, the contractual obligation of a lender or creditor to refrain, during a given period of time, from requiring the borrower or debtor to repay the loan or debt then due and payable. 📖

FORCE 📖 Power, violence, compulsion, or constraint exerted upon or against a person or thing. Power dynamically considered, that is, in motion or in action; constraining power, com-

pulsion; strength directed to an end. Commonly the word occurs in such connections as to show that unlawful or wrongful action is meant, e.g., forcible entry.

Power statically considered, that is, at rest, or latent, but capable of being called into activity upon occasion for its exercise. Efficacy; legal validity. This is the meaning when we say that a statute or a contract is *in force*. 📖

Reasonable force is that degree of force that is appropriate and not inordinate in defending one's person or property. A person who employs such force is justified in doing so and is neither criminally liable nor civilly liable in TORT for the conduct.

DEADLY FORCE is utilized when a person intends to cause death or serious bodily harm or when he or she recognizes personal involvement in the creation of a substantial risk that death or bodily harm will occur.

FORCED SALE 📖 An involuntary transaction that occurs in the form and at the time specified by law for the purpose of applying the proceeds to satisfy DEBTS, such as a MORTGAGE or a tax lien, incurred by the owner of the property. 📖

A forced sale results from the EXECUTION of a JUDGMENT previously rendered by a court.

FORCE MAJEURE 📖 [*French, A superior or irresistible power.*] An event that is a result of the elements of nature, as opposed to one caused by human behavior. 📖

The term *force majeure* relates to the law of INSURANCE and is frequently used in construction

A force majeure, like an act of God, is an event that is the result of the elements of nature. Hurricane damage in Massachusetts set this house at a precarious angle.

JAMES LEMASS/THE PICTURE CUBE

CONTRACTS to protect the parties in the event that a segment of the contract cannot be performed due to causes that are outside the control of the parties, such as natural disasters, that could not be evaded through the exercise of due CARE.

FORCIBLE DETAINER 📖 A summary and expeditious statutory REMEDY used by a party entitled to actual POSSESSION of premises to secure its possession, where the occupant initially in lawful possession of it refuses to relinquish it when his or her right to possession ends. 📖 See also FORCIBLE ENTRY AND DETAINER.

FORCIBLE ENTRY AND DETAINER

📖 A SUMMARY PROCEEDING to recover POSSESSION of land that is instituted by one who has been wrongfully ousted from, or deprived of, possession. 📖

Forcible entry and detainer, one aspect of which is known as UNLAWFUL DETAINER, alludes to two separate misdeeds and two divergent remedies of statutory origin.

The forcible intrusion into another person's peaceable possession constitutes one type of infraction. Even if it is unlawful, peaceable possession cannot be terminated by violence. In many JURISDICTIONS, even the rightful owner is held liable for DAMAGES, which as provided by statutes are often multiple in nature, if he or she employs excessive force in ousting one in peaceful possession. In such instances, the offense involved is the force itself and not the actual dispossession.

The second form of misdeed entails the initiation of legal proceedings by the rightful owner against a SQUATTER without TITLE or a TENANT who declines to depart. Force in such instances might be inconsequential, figurative, or nonexistent. Damages are avoidable, but the restoration of the lawful owner to possession of the property by EVICTION of the defendant is also within the purview of the remedy. This remedy, which awards both damages and possession, resembles EJECTMENT, which also entails the recoupment of possession of property by the person entitled to it, but significant differences exist.

In addition to historical dissimilarities, the summary nature of the forcible entry and detainer action is unlike the nature of an ejectment action. The trial and eviction can be accomplished within a few days after service of process. Statutes frequently provide, however, that the decision in forcible entry or unlawful detainer is not binding as to title. If title is seriously disputed, a second and more comprehensive suit in ejectment or TRESPASS is warranted.

The forcible entry or unlawful detainer action is restricted to cases in which the plaintiff's right to possession is unequivocal, since summary proceedings would not be justified under any other circumstances. A minority of jurisdictions, however, limit the action to the eviction of those who have actually entered by force.

A forcible entry suit, although burdensome in nature, functions not merely as a method of prompt relief but also affects a subsequent ejectment action. Since the burden of proof is imposed upon the plaintiff who has been dispossessed in the ejectment suit, in regard to his or her own paramount title, the issue of possession determined in the forcible entry suit affects the ultimate burden of proof. It would be inequitable to permit this to be manipulated by those who forcibly enter, or perhaps even by holdover tenants. The forcible entry action, in dispossessing the occupant where his or her title is patently invalid, influences the ejectment action by its principle that the plaintiff never prevails on the basis of the possessor's defective title, but must instead recover on the validity of his or her own title.

The supposition that unlawful detainer involves possession and not title, whereas ejectment entails title, is somewhat inaccurate. Both ejectment and unlawful detainer actions are possessory in nature, and title is nearly always the basis of possessory rights. The differences in the two actions reside in the summary character of forcible entry, the restricted class of person against whom it can be instituted, and its lack of RES JUDICATA effect on title issues.

These forcible entry and detainer, or summary eviction, statutes are primarily utilized by LANDLORDS attempting to regain possession of premises from recalcitrant tenants. The Supreme Court has upheld the validity of such

The city of New York boarded up an old building after evicting squatters from it. Squatters are guilty of forcible entry even if they did not have to use force to get into the abandoned buildings.

CINDY REIMAN/IMPACT VISUALS

statutes, regardless of the limited number of issues triable and the brief period between summons and trial.

FORD, GERALD RUDOLPH Without winning a single vote in a presidential election, Gerald Rudolph Ford became chief executive of the United States on August 9, 1974. The sixty-year-old Ford was the first person in the nation's history to be appointed to the presidency.

Ford's ascent to the White House began on October 12, 1973, when he was appointed by President RICHARD M. NIXON to succeed Vice President Spiro T. Agnew. Agnew left office on October 10, 1973, after pleading NOLO CONTENDERE (I will not contest it) to felonious TAX EVASION. Ford was a popular Republican congressman from Grand Rapids, Michigan, and the minority leader of the U.S. House of Representatives. The Nixon administration was on the brink of collapse as evidence mounted of its criminal involvement in the WATERGATE break-in and cover-up. The scandal ultimately destroyed the Nixon White House, forcing the president to resign from office to avoid IMPEACHMENT. As a result, on August 9, 1974, Ford was sworn in as the nation's thirty-eighth president—and the first chief executive to be appointed to office.

Named Leslie Lynch King, Jr., when born July 14, 1913, in Omaha, Ford spent most of his childhood in Grand Rapids, where his mother settled in 1914 after divorcing his father. When Ford was three years old, his mother remarried, and the future president was adopted by and renamed after his stepfather, Gerald Ford, Sr.

Ford was a gifted athlete in high school and a college all-star on championship football teams at the University of Michigan. After graduating from Michigan in 1935, he turned down offers to play professional football and instead coached football and boxing at Yale University for five years. Ford attended Yale Law School during this time, and graduated in 1941 in the top third of his class.

After briefly practicing law in Grand Rapids, he enlisted in 1942 for a four-year tour with the Navy during World War II. When the war

BIOGRAPHY

Gerald Rudolph Ford

"TRUTH IS THE GLUE THAT HOLDS OUR GOVERNMENT TOGETHER . . . OUR LONG NATIONAL NIGHTMARE IS OVER. OUR CONSTITUTION WORKS."

ended, Ford returned to Grand Rapids and reestablished his law practice. He married Elizabeth ("Betty") Bloomer Warren in 1948, and by 1957, the couple had four children.

Ford was first elected to the U.S. House of Representatives from Michigan's Fifth Congressional District in 1948. He served in the House for twenty-five years, consistently winning reelection in his home district by 60 percent or more of the vote. A domestic affairs moderate and a fiscal conservative, Ford was assigned to the Public Works Committee during his first term in Congress. In 1951, he managed to transfer committees, and subsequently served on the influential House Appropriations Committee until 1965. Ford supported large defense budgets and a strong foreign policy, and opposed federal spending for several domestic social programs.

After the 1963 ASSASSINATION of President JOHN F. KENNEDY, Ford was selected to serve on the Warren Commission, a bipartisan task force set up to investigate Kennedy's murder. Later, Ford coauthored a book supporting the WARREN COMMISSION's report that Kennedy was killed by lone gunman Lee Harvey Oswald.

In 1963, Ford became chair of the House Republican Conference, and in 1964, he was named minority leader of the House of Representatives. At this stage in Ford's political career, his greatest ambition was to become Speaker of the House. However, because Congress was controlled by a majority of Democrats, Ford's goal was unattainable.

Ford was a GOP loyalist who campaigned tirelessly for other Republican candidates. An accomplished fund-raiser, he was given credit for helping elect forty-seven new Republicans to the House of Representatives in 1966. In addition to campaigning and performing his congressional duties, Ford served as permanent chair of both the 1968 and 1972 Republican National Conventions. After the GOP's victory in the 1968 presidential election, Ford could be counted on to support vigorously Nixon's foreign and domestic programs in Congress.

When it became clear in 1973 that Vice President Agnew's legal and ethical problems

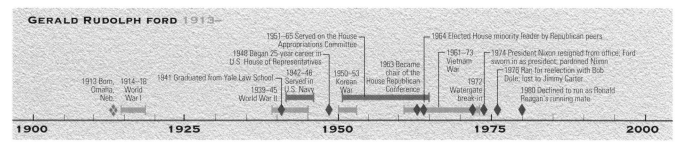

GERALD RUDOLPH FORD 1913–

1913 Born, Omaha, Neb.

1914–18 World War I

1941 Graduated from Yale Law School

1948 Began 25-year career in U.S. House of Representatives

1942–46 Served in U.S. Navy

1939–45 World War II

1951–65 Served on the House Appropriations Committee

1950–53 Korean War

1963 Became chair of the House Republican Conference

1964 Elected House minority leader by Republican peers

1961–73 Vietnam War

1972 Watergate break-in

1974 President Nixon resigned from office; Ford sworn in as president; pardoned Nixon

1976 Ran for reelection with Bob Dole; lost to Jimmy Carter

1980 Declined to run as Ronald Reagan's running mate

1900   1925   1950   1975   2000

would force him out of the Nixon White House, the president turned to Ford as a logical replacement. The TWENTY-FIFTH AMENDMENT to the U.S. Constitution allows the president to nominate a VICE PRESIDENT in the event of a vacancy. Ford was a plausible choice because of his solid track record in the House, his popularity with Congress and the public, and his loyalty to Nixon. After Agnew's resignation, Ford publicly accepted Nixon's offer and was confirmed by a majority vote of both houses of the U.S. Congress. He was sworn in during a joint session of Congress on December 6, 1973.

Ford knew that he was joining a doomed, scandal-plagued administration and that in all likelihood he would become president. For eight months, he performed his vice presidential duties and waited as the Watergate investigators closed in on Nixon. With Nixon's resignation inevitable, Ford prepared what he hoped would be a reassuring speech to his weary country. On August 9, 1974, the day Nixon resigned and Ford was sworn in, Ford spoke to the nation on television, telling citizens that the U.S. system worked and that "our long national nightmare is over."

At the beginning of Ford's term as president, members of Nixon's cabinet, including Secretary of State Henry Kissinger, agreed to stay on in the interest of continuity. Ford appointed Nelson A. Rockefeller, former governor of New York, to serve as his vice president. As the transition from Nixon to Ford was made, key Nixon appointees departed, and the Ford administration floundered.

The nation's economy was a pressing problem, with both inflation and unemployment running high. To combat inflation, Ford proposed a voluntary program, Whip Inflation Now (WIN), which was neither an economic nor a popular success. Without mandatory controls to keep prices and wages in check, the program was ineffective. Although other measures introduced by Ford eventually helped stabilize the economy, unemployment remained high, reaching more than nine percent in May 1975.

Clearly the most damaging event during Ford's two-and-a-half years in office occurred about a month after he was sworn in. On September 8, 1974, Ford granted Nixon a full PARDON for any possible crimes committed during the Watergate cover-up. Although Ford pardoned Nixon out of compassion and a desire to move the nation from its Watergate paralysis, he suffered tremendously in the public opinion polls for his action. Many U.S. citizens opposed special treatment for Nixon, believing that the former president should be fully prosecuted for the crimes that toppled his administration. Some historians believe that Ford's unconditional pardon of Nixon cost him the 1976 presidential election.

Another misstep was Ford's AMNESTY proposal for young men who had dodged the draft during the Vietnam War. Although the program did not offer automatic reentry into U.S. society—it did require two years of public service—it was unpopular with conservative groups and with the very men it was supposed to help. The amnesty program received applications from only 20 percent of eligible U.S. citizens and was discontinued after two years.

In foreign affairs, Ford continued Nixon's policies of détente with the Soviet Union and negotiations for a Middle East peace accord. Perhaps the most newsworthy event of international importance during Ford's term was the *Mayaguez* incident. When the U.S. merchant ship *Mayaguez* was seized off the coast of Cambodia in 1975, Ford sent in U.S. troops to retrieve the crew and ship. The operation was an unmitigated success for Ford because bloodshed was avoided and his leadership qualities were demonstrated in the international arena.

During his brief term, Ford made one U.S. Supreme Court appointment, nominating Justice JOHN PAUL STEVENS, a moderate, to replace retiring Justice WILLIAM O. DOUGLAS in 1975. Ford became the first U.S. president to travel to Japan on an official visit, in 1974, and the first chief executive to survive two assassination attempts.

Initially, Ford considered himself an interim president. As he grew accustomed to the White House, he changed his mind and decided to run for his party's presidential nomination in 1976. Although Ford was opposed at the Republican convention by California governor RONALD REAGAN, he managed to win the nomination on the first ballot. He selected Senator BOB DOLE, of Kansas, as his running mate.

JIMMY CARTER, governor of Georgia and the 1976 Democratic presidential nominee, made personal integrity and honesty in government the central themes of his campaign. Carter criticized Ford's association with the tainted Nixon administration and stressed his own reputation for moral rectitude. In a tight race, Carter and running mate Walter F. Mondale, from Minnesota, won the election, receiving half the popular votes and 297 ELECTORAL COLLEGE votes.

After his defeat, Ford retired from public service. In 1980, he was asked to run as Reagan's vice presidential candidate; he declined.

FORECLOSURE

FORECLOSURE 📖 A procedure by which the holder of a MORTGAGE—an interest in land providing security for the performance of a duty or the payment of a DEBT—sells the property upon the failure of the DEBTOR to pay the mortgage debt and, thereby, terminates his or her rights in the property. 📖

Statutory foreclosure is foreclosure by performance of a POWER OF SALE clause in the mortgage without need for court action, since the foreclosure must be done in accordance with the statutory provisions governing such sales.

STRICT FORECLOSURE refers to the procedure pursuant to which the court ascertains the amount due under the mortgage; orders its payment within a certain limited time; and

A sample order for a mortgage foreclosure

At a Special Term, Part _____ of the Supreme Court of the State of New York, held in and for the County of _____, at the County Courthouse, located at _____, on the_____ day of _____, 19_____.

Present: Hon. _____, Justice.

Order

Index No. _____

The plaintiff, _____ Savings Bank, by its attorneys, _____, _____ & _____, Esqs. having duly moved for an order pursuant to CPLR 3212 striking out the defendants' answer and directing the entry of summary judgment in his favor and against the defendants for the relief demanded in the complaint, upon the ground that there is no defense to the cause of action alleged in the complaint, and said motion having regularly come on to be heard,

NOW, upon reading and filing the notice of motion dated _____, 19_____, the affidavits of _____ and _____, in support of the motion, both sworn to on the _____ day of _____, 19_____, the summons, complaint and answers of the defendants, _____; _____, _____, _____, and _____, and upon the affidavit of _____ sworn to on the _____ day of _____, 19_____ and the affirmation of _____, Esq., dated the _____ day of _____, 19_____, both on behalf of the defendants, _____, _____, _____ and _____, and the affidavit of _____, Esq., sworn to on the _____ day of _____, 19_____ on behalf of the defendant, _____; and the affidavits of _____ and _____, Esq., both sworn to on the _____ day of _____, 19_____ on behalf of the defendant, _____, all in opposition thereto, and upon the reply affidavits of _____ on behalf of the plaintiff, sworn to the _____ day of _____, 19_____, and after hearing _____, _____ & _____, Esqs. _____, Esq., of counsel, for the plaintiff in support of said motion, and _____, Esq., of counsel for the defendant, _____, in opposition thereto, and after due deliberation having been held thereon, and the Court having rendered its decision in writing on the _____ day of _____, 19_____,

NOW, upon motion of _____, _____ & _____, attorneys for plaintiff, _____ Savings Bank, it is

ORDERED, that the motion be and the same is hereby in all respects granted, and that the answers herein be and the same are hereby stricken out, and it is further

ORDERED, that the plaintiff have judgment of foreclosure and sale against all defendants and the sum due plaintiff shall be determined by a Referee who shall compute the amount due plaintiff upon notice to defendants. Plaintiff is awarded the sum of _____ Dollars costs of this motion.

Enter,

_____

J.S.C.

prescribes that in DEFAULT of such payment a debtor will permanently lose his or her EQUITY OF REDEMPTION, the right to recover the property upon payment of the debt, INTEREST, and COSTS. The TITLE of the property is conveyed absolutely to the CREDITOR, on default in payment, without any sale of the property.

FOREIGN 📖 That which belongs to, or operates in accordance with, another nation, territory, state, or JURISDICTION, as in the case of nonresident trustees, corporations, or persons. 📖

FOREIGN AFFAIRS POWER Under international law a state has the right to enter into relations with other states. This power to conduct foreign affairs is one of the rights a state gains by attaining independence. The division of authority within a government to exercise its foreign affairs power varies from state to state. In the United States that power is vested primarily in the president, although the Congress retains important express and implied powers over international affairs.

FORENSIC 📖 Belonging to courts of justice. 📖

FORENSIC ACCOUNTING Forensic accounting, sometimes called investigative accounting, involves the application of ACCOUNTING concepts and techniques to legal problems. Forensic accountants investigate and document financial FRAUD and white-collar crimes such as EMBEZZLEMENT. They also provide litigation support to attorneys and law enforcement agencies investigating financial wrongdoing.

Many different organizations consult forensic accountants. Corporations hire forensic accountants to investigate allegations of fraud on the part of their employees, suppliers, or customers. Attorneys consult forensic accountants to obtain estimates of losses, damages, and assets related to specific legal cases in many areas of the law, including PRODUCT LIABILITY, shareholder disputes, and breaches of contract. In criminal investigations, forensic accountants analyze complex financial transactions such as those in stock market manipulations and price fixing schemes. They also help governments achieve compliance with various forms of regulation.

Forensic accountants typically become involved in financial investigations after fraud auditors have discovered evidence of deceptive financial transactions. After conducting an investigation, they write and submit a report of their findings. When a case goes to trial, they are likely to testify as expert witnesses.

FORENSIC SCIENCE 📖 The application of scientific knowledge and methodology to legal problems and criminal investigations. 📖

Sometimes called simply forensics, forensic science encompasses many different fields of science, including anthropology, biology, chemistry, engineering, genetics, medicine, pathology, phonetics, psychiatry, and toxicology.

The related term *criminalistics* refers more specifically to the scientific collection and analysis of physical evidence in criminal cases. This includes the analysis of many kinds of materials, including blood, fibers, bullets, and FINGERPRINTS. Many law enforcement agencies operate crime labs that perform scientific studies of evidence. The largest of these labs is run by the FEDERAL BUREAU OF INVESTIGATION.

Forensic scientists often present expert TESTIMONY to courts, as in the case of pathologists who testify on causes of death and engineers who testify on causes of damage from equipment failure, fires, or explosions.

Modern forensic science originated in the late nineteenth century, when European criminal investigators began to use fingerprinting and other identification techniques to solve crimes. As the field of science expanded in scope throughout the twentieth century, its application to legal issues became more and more common. Because nearly every area of science has a potential bearing on the law, the list of areas within forensic science is long.

Forensic Medicine and Psychology
Forensic medicine is one of the largest and

A forensic scientist removes a fragment of material from a bloodstained garment recovered from a crime scene. The fabric will be used to extract a blood sample for DNA testing.

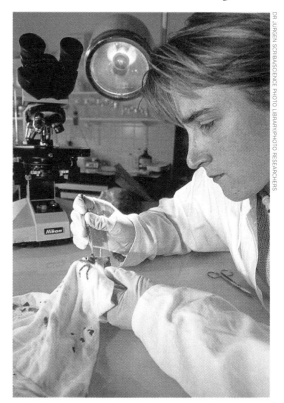

DR. JÜRGEN SCRIBA/SCIENCE PHOTO LIBRARY/PHOTO RESEARCHERS

Forensic Science in the Federal Bureau of Investigation

Since its establishment in 1932, the FBI Laboratory has been a world leader in the scientific analysis of physical evidence related to crime. From its location in the J. Edgar Hoover FBI Building, in Washington, D.C., the laboratory provides a wide range of free forensic services to U.S. law enforcement agencies. The laboratory is divided into several major departments: the Document Section, Scientific Analysis Section, Special Projects Section, Latent Fingerprint Section, and Forensic Science Research and Training Center.

The laboratory's Document Section examines paper documents, ink, shoe and tire tread designs, and other forms of evidence related to a wide variety of crimes, including forgery and money laundering. It performs linguistic analysis of documents to determine authorship. It also evaluates the validity and danger of written threats. Its Computer Analysis and Response Team recovers evidence, including encrypted information, from computer systems—evidence that is crucial to the prosecution of white-collar crime. The Document Section also maintains files of bank robbery notes, anonymous extortion letters, and office equipment specifications.

The Scientific Analysis Section has seven divisions: Chemistry Toxicology, DNA Analysis/Serology, Elemental and Metals Analysis, Explosives, Firearms-Toolmarks, Hairs and Fibers, and Materials Analysis. This section's analysis of blood, semen, and saliva assists the investigation of violent crimes such as murder, rape, assault, and hit-and-run driving. Its research also provides insight into many other crimes, including bombings, arson, drug tampering, and poisoning.

The services provided by the Special Projects Section include composite sketches of suspects, crime scene drawings and maps, videotape and audiotape analysis and enhancement, and analysis of electronic devices such as wiretaps and listening devices.

The Latent Fingerprint Section examines evidence for hidden fingerprints, palm prints, footprints, and lip prints.

The Forensic Science Research and Training Center offers classes to law enforcement officials from the United States and other countries. These classes cover DNA analysis, the detection and recovery of human remains, arson and bomb blast investigation, and many other topics.

To better perform its research, the laboratory maintains files on many kinds of physical evidence, including adhesives, ammunition, paint, and office equipment. The laboratory also provides experts who will furnish testimony on the nature of the evidence.

The laboratory publishes the *Handbook of Forensic Science* to explain its forensic services to law enforcement agencies. The handbook outlines procedures for safely and effectively gathering evidence from crime scenes and shipping it to the laboratory for analysis.

---

most important areas of forensic science. Also called legal medicine or medical jurisprudence, it applies medical knowledge to criminal and civil law. Areas of medicine that are commonly involved in forensic medicine are anatomy, pathology, and psychiatry.

Many law enforcement agencies employ a forensic pathologist, sometimes called a medical examiner, who determines the causes of sudden or unexpected death. Forensic toxicologists, who study the presence of poisons or drugs in the deceased, often help forensic pathologists. Forensic odontologists, or dentists, analyze dental evidence to identify human remains and the origin of bite marks.

Forensic medicine is often used in civil cases. The cause of death or injury is considered in settling insurance claims or medical MALPRACTICE suits, and blood tests often contribute to a court's decision in cases attempting to determine the paternity of a child.

Mental health and psychology professionals have contributed a great deal to the legal understanding of issues such as the reliability of eyewitness testimony, responsibility for criminal behavior, and the process of decision making in juries. These professionals include those with a medical degree, such as psychiatrists, neurologists, and neuropsychologists, as well as individuals without a medical degree, such as psychologists.

Mental health professionals are frequently consulted in civil and criminal cases to help determine an individual's state of mind with regard to a crime, the validity of testimony before a court, or an individual's competence to stand trial or make a legal decision. Their input may also be vital to legal procedures for deciding whether to commit a person to an institution because of mental illness, or to allow a person to leave an institution for those who are mentally ill.

Forensic neuropsychology is a specialized area of forensic medicine that applies the functioning of the nervous system and brain to legal issues involving mind and behavior. Equipped with an improved understanding of how the brain works and influences behavior, neuropsychologists have increasingly been asked to provide testimony to courts attempting to determine whether a criminal act is a result of a nervous system dysfunction. They also testify as to the reliability of witness testimony given by victims of crime, the competency of individuals to stand trial, the likelihood that a condition of mental retardation or brain injury predisposed an individual to commit a crime, the possibility that an individual has verifiable memory loss, and various aspects of dementias and other brain disorders caused by AIDS, head injuries, and drugs, alcohol, and other chemicals.

In civil cases, the work of neuropsychologists has been used to determine whether a defendant's wrongdoing caused a plaintiff's injury. In family courts, neuropsychologists assess brain damage in children who have been physically abused.

Forensic psychologists provide expert testimony that touches on many of the same areas as that given by forensic psychiatrists and neuropsychologists. In addition, psychologists consult with the legal system on issues such as correctional procedures and crime prevention. In 1962, a U.S. court of appeals issued an influential decision that established the ability of a psychologist to testify as an expert witness in a federal court of law (*Jenkins v. United States*, 113 U.S. App. D.C. 300, 307 F.2d 637 [D.C. Cir. 1962]). Before that time, expert testimony on mental health was largely restricted to physicians.

Other Areas of Forensic Science Forensic engineers provide courts with expertise in areas such as the design and construction of buildings, vehicles, electronics, and other items. Forensic linguists determine the authorship of written documents through analyses of handwriting, syntax, word usage, and grammar. Forensic anthropologists identify and date human remains such as bones. Forensic geneticists analyze human genetic material, or DNA, to provide evidence that is often used by juries to determine the guilt or innocence of criminal suspects. Forensic phoneticians deal with issues such as the validity of tape-recorded messages, the identification of speakers on recorded messages, the enhancement of recorded messages, the use of voiceprints, and other aspects of ELECTRONIC SURVEILLANCE.

See also DNA EVIDENCE.

FORESEEABILITY The facility to perceive, know in advance, or reasonably anticipate that damage or injury will probably ensue from acts or omissions.

In the law of NEGLIGENCE, the foreseeability aspect of PROXIMATE CAUSE—the event which is the primary cause of the injury—is established by proof that the actor, as a person of ordinary intelligence and circumspection, should reasonably have foreseen that his or her negligent act would imperil others, whether by the event that transpired or some similar occurrence, and regardless of what the actor surmised would happen in regard to the actual event or the manner of causation of injuries.

FORFEIT To lose to another person or to the state some privilege, right, or property due to the commission of an error, an offense, or a CRIME, a breach of CONTRACT, or a neglect of DUTY; to subject property to CONFISCATION; or to become liable for the payment of a PENALTY, as the result of a particular act. To lose a FRANCHISE, ESTATE, or other property, as provided by the applicable law, due to NEGLIGENCE, MISFEASANCE, or omission.

This nonconsensual deprivation transfers the property to another person or restores it to the original GRANTOR.

FORFEITURE The involuntary relinquishment of money or property without compensation as a consequence of a breach or nonperformance of some legal obligation or the commission of a crime. The loss of a corporate CHARTER or FRANCHISE as a result of illegality, MALFEASANCE, or NONFEASANCE. The surrender by an owner of her or his entire interest in real property mandated by law as a punishment for illegal conduct or NEGLIGENCE. In old English law, the release of land by a tenant to the tenant's lord due to some breach of conduct, or the loss of GOODS or CHATTELS (articles of personal property) assessed as a penalty against the perpetrator of some crime or offense and as a recompense to the injured party.

Forfeiture is a broad term that can be used to describe any loss of property without compensation. A forfeiture may be privately arranged. For example, in a contractual relationship, one party may be required to forfeit specified property if the party fails to fulfill its contractual obligations. Courts are often called on to resolve disputes regarding a forfeiture of property pursuant to a private CONTRACT. Such cases may be examined by the courts to see if they are fair and not the result of DURESS, deception, or other nefarious tactics.

The forfeitures that inspire the most discussion in U.S. society are those exercised by the government. Congress and state legislatures maintain statutes allowing law enforcement to seize property on suspicion of certain criminal activity. The property may thereafter be forfeited to the government upon conviction. In many cases, forfeiture to the government occurs without criminal prosecution.

The general concept of forfeiture in the United States can be traced to the English COMMON LAW, or court decisions. Three types of forfeitures were recognized by English courts: ESCHEAT upon ATTAINDER, deodand, and statutory forfeiture. Under the doctrine of escheat upon attainder, a person's property reverted to the government upon that person's conviction for a FELONY or TREASON. This doctrine was premised on the theory that the sovereign government possessed an interest in property superior to all other interests in property.

The doctrine of deodand, or guilty property, allowed English courts to strip a person of property if the property was involved in a certain offense. This doctrine allowed a court to seize property regardless of the owner's culpability. For example, if a person's horse caused the death of another person, the owner of the horse would lose the horse, even if the owner was completely blameless.

Statutory forfeiture, or forfeiture based on written laws, was the only kind of English forfeiture recognized in the American colonies. In other words, the colonies did not order the forfeiture of property unless it was required pursuant to a law passed by the legislature. However, the written laws in the colonies sustained the concept of deodand, and this concept survives to the present day.

Although forfeiture laws have existed in the United States since the colonial period, they have not always been favored. Early cases of forfeiture usually involved extraordinary circumstances, such as the seizure of pirate ships or warring ships. After the Civil War, forfeitures were used for tax revenue violations, but generally, government-imposed forfeiture was a rarity.

In 1970, Congress enacted the Comprehensive Drug Abuse Prevention and Control Act (21 U.S.C.A. § 881), also known as the Forfeiture Act. The Forfeiture Act authorized federal prosecutors to bring civil forfeiture actions against certain properties owned by persons convicted in federal court of dealing drugs. This act was seldom used because it limited forfeiture to the property of persons convicted of participating in continuing criminal enterprises.

In 1978, Congress amended the Forfeiture Act to allow the forfeiture of anything of value used or intended to be used by a person to purchase illegal drugs (Psychotropic Substances Act of 1978 [Pub. L. No. 95-633, tit. III, § 301(a), 92 Stat. 3768, 3777 (codified as amended at 21 U.S.C.A. § 8821(a)(6))]). This expanded the Forfeiture Act to allow the forfeiture of all proceeds and property traceable to the purchase of an illegal drug. Under the 1978 amendments, the federal government was authorized to proceed IN REM against property. In rem forfeiture actions are taken against the property, not the owner of the property. In such proceedings, the guilt or innocence of the property owner regarding any criminal activity is irrelevant. Thus, under the Forfeiture Act, the government may remove property from persons suspected of a crime without ever charging them with a crime. The reason for this kind of forfeiture is traced back to the deodand doctrine of the English common law.

The Forfeiture Act was again amended in 1984, when the Comprehensive Crime Control Act (Pub. L. No. 98-473, § 306, 98 Stat. 1837, 2050 [codified as amended at 21 U.S.C.A. § 881(a)(7)]) expanded it to authorize the in rem forfeiture of REAL PROPERTY, or land and buildings. Under the 1984 act, federal authorities may seize any real property purchased, used, or intended to be used to facilitate narcotics trafficking. Although the LEGISLATIVE HISTORY of the 1984 act suggests that Congress intended real property forfeiture to apply only to drug manufacturing or storage facilities, courts have construed the act to allow the seizure of any real property, including fraternity houses, hotels,

STEVE STARR/STOCK BOSTON

The Forfeiture Act allows law enforcement officials to seize property used in or derived from illegal activities such as purchasing or selling drugs. This Florida warehouse is filled with sports cars forfeited by drug dealers.

ranches, and private residences. Furthermore, courts have allowed real property forfeiture regardless of whether the property was used to store or manufacture drugs.

Forfeiture under the Forfeiture Act begins with the CONSTRUCTIVE or actual seizure of property after a WARRANT has been issued by a district court. This warrant must be based on a reasonable belief that the property was used in a crime subject to forfeiture, but this reasonable belief can be based entirely on HEARSAY and CIRCUMSTANTIAL EVIDENCE. After the property is seized, it is held by the court until the case is resolved.

Forfeiture proceedings may be either criminal or civil. If the forfeiture is sought pursuant to criminal charges, the government must establish the defendant's guilt beyond a reasonable doubt. If the defendant is acquitted, the defendant is entitled to retrieve the seized property.

To initiate a civil forfeiture proceeding, the government need only show reasonable grounds to believe that the property was used, or was derived from, certain prohibited activities. If the defendant fails to REBUT the showing of PROBABLE CAUSE with sufficient evidence, the government is allowed to keep the property. At trial, the government's standard of proof in a civil forfeiture is by a PREPONDERANCE OF THE EVIDENCE, a lesser burden of proof than the criminal standard of BEYOND A REASONABLE DOUBT.

The Forfeiture Act also allows law enforcement agencies to receive a portion of the proceeds from property forfeiture. Many legal scholars claim that this is a perversion of the police function because it detracts from the more compelling, traditional police function of fighting violent crime. These critics also argue that law enforcement agencies may become financially dependent on the very drug activity they are supposed to curtail. Proponents of this budgetary scheme argue that drug activity is the source of much violent crime. They further note that the proceeds benefit community programs and increase the capacity to fight violent crime.

The RACKETEER INFLUENCED AND CORRUPT ORGANIZATIONS ACT (RICO) (18 U.S.C.A. § 1961 et seq.) is another vehicle for forfeiture in federal court. Enacted as title IX of the Organized Crime Control Act of 1970 (U.S. Pub. L. 91-452, 84 Stat. 922), RICO allows federal authorities to seize the property of persons engaged in a pattern of racketeering. This means that persons who commit murder, kidnapping, perjury, extortion, arson, robbery, bribery, gambling, or narcotics offenses two or more times within a ten-year period may be forced to forfeit all property traceable to the crimes. In a 1984 amendment, Congress added the violation of federal and state obscenity laws to the list of racketeering offenses.

The case against Ferris Alexander illustrates the way in which federal authorities exercise the forfeiture provisions of RICO (*Alexander v. United States*, 509 U.S. 544, 113 S. Ct. 2766, 125 L. Ed. 2d 441 [1993]). Alexander, the owner of more than a dozen adult stores and theaters offering sexually explicit materials in Minneapolis, was charged in 1989 with operating a racketeering enterprise in violation of RICO. Alexander was convicted based on the jury's determination that four magazines and three videotapes from his enterprises were OBSCENE. The trial court sentenced Alexander to six years in prison, fined him $100,000, and ordered him to pay the cost of his prosecution, incarceration, and supervised release.

After the conviction, federal authorities sought the forfeiture of all ASSETS related to Alexander's businesses. The jury made FINDINGS to identify precisely what was owned by Alexander. Based on these findings, the trial court ordered Alexander to forfeit $8.9 million in cash and inventory, ten bookstores valued at a total of $2 million, his interest in eighteen other businesses, and proceeds from fifteen other businesses. The merchandise from Alexander's businesses was later burned by law enforcement officers.

Alexander appealed to the Eighth Circuit Court of Appeals, which affirmed. On appeal to the U.S. Supreme Court, Alexander argued, in part, that the forfeiture was excessive. Alexander also argued that the forfeiture was a form of prior restraint, in violation of his free speech rights. According to the Court, the forfeiture did not violate Alexander's free speech rights because it did not prevent him from publishing nonobscene material in the future. However, the Court also held that the amount of the forfeiture should have been examined to see if it violated the EIGHTH AMENDMENT's prohibition of excessive FINES.

The Supreme Court remanded the case to the appeals court for review on the excessive fines issue. The appeals court sent the case to the trial court. In March 1996, the district court affirmed the original forfeiture of approximately $8.9 million in property.

To many scholars, the *Alexander* case stands as a serious threat to FREEDOM-OF-SPEECH rights. Although Alexander's businesses dealt specifically in PORNOGRAPHY, the *Alexander* decision nevertheless puts artists who create material with a sexual content in danger of losing their property. Many legal analysts also maintain that the forfeiture was excessive compared with the offenses for which Alexander was convicted. Proponents maintain that the forfeiture helped create cleaner, safer city neighborhoods.

Most states maintain statutes allowing forfeiture upon conviction of certain crimes. For example, volume 15 of the Maine Revised Statutes Annotated, section 5821, authorizes the forfeiture of prohibited drugs; materials related to prohibited drugs; property used to contain, defend, protect, guard, or secure prohibited drugs; firearms; and vehicles used in the violation of litter laws. Real property used in connection with illegal drugs is also subject to forfeiture under section 5821, with the exception of real property connected to marijuana offenses.

Maine does not provide for the forfeiture of property used for PROSTITUTION or the solicitation of prostitution, but many states do. For example, section 600.3801 of the Michigan Compiled Laws Annotated authorizes state law enforcement to seize property used to support or solicit prostitution. In the 1990s, the application of this statute inspired a challenge that went all the way to the Supreme Court (*Bennis v. Michigan*, __U.S. __, 116 S. Ct. 994, 134 L. Ed. 2d 68 [1996]).

In *Bennis v. Michigan*, Tina B. Bennis brought suit against the state of Michigan after it seized the 1977 Pontiac she owned jointly with her husband, John Bennis. Her husband had been arrested and convicted in Michigan state court of gross indecency in connection with his encounter with a prostitute. The county prosecutor filed a complaint alleging that the Pontiac was a public NUISANCE and subject to ABATEMENT, or forfeiture. An order of abatement was entered by the trial court. On appeal by Bennis, the appeals court reversed. On subsequent appeal by the state of Michigan, the Michigan Supreme Court also reversed. Bennis appealed to the U.S. Supreme Court.

The Supreme Court affirmed the decision of the Michigan Supreme Court. Bennis argued that the forfeiture was a violation of the Due Process Clause of the FOURTEENTH AMENDMENT because she had not known that the Pontiac would be used for prostitution. The Court cited a long line of cases supporting the proposition that a person may be deprived of property if it has been put to criminal use, regardless of the owner's knowledge or participation.

The Court also dismissed Bennis's argument that the forfeiture violated the Fifth Amendment's Takings Clause, which generally re-

quires compensation for property seized by the government. According to the Court, the government is under no obligation to reimburse a person for property it has seized pursuant to government authority other than the power of EMINENT DOMAIN. Ultimately, Bennis lost her ownership of the Pontiac, despite being innocent of any wrongdoing. In a strong dissent, Justice JOHN PAUL STEVENS argued that "neither logic nor history supports the Court's apparent assumption that [a person's] complete innocence imposes no constitutional impediment to the seizure of their property simply because it provided the locus for a criminal transaction."

Defendants have cultivated several defenses to forfeiture, and some have been successful. If the initial seizure is not preceded by notice and a HEARING before a court, a defendant may argue that a forfeiture violates the Due Process Clause of the Fifth and Fourteenth Amendments. Despite the decision in the *Alexander* case, if a massive, estate-depleting forfeiture is disproportionate to the offense that gave rise to it, it may be found to violate the Excessive Fines Clause of the Eighth Amendment.

In addition, Congress has enacted an "innocent owner" defense in civil drug forfeitures (21 U.S.C.A. § 881(a)(6) [1988]). These are cases in which forfeiture is sought without prosecution of the owner. A defendant in a civil forfeiture case may invoke this defense if the property was connected with the illegal drugs without the owner's knowledge or consent.

Supporters of forfeiture laws cite the laws' effectiveness in fighting crime and stripping criminals of their resources. Many legal observers argue that the increasing use of government forfeiture is a flagrant violation of several constitutional rights. The state of forfeiture in contemporary law has been compared to "an

Most states provide for the forfeiture of prohibited drugs. Federal officials guard this supply of cocaine that was seized in a raid.

Orwellian nightmare" (Aznavoorian 1995, 553), creating a climate that has "turned police agencies into bounty hunters, who, in their quest for cash, have harmed innocent citizens or those guilty of only minor offenses" (Henry 1994, 52). In 1992 alone, the federal government seized $531 million in cash and property under the Forfeiture Act, and 80 percent of the owners of the seized goods were never charged with a crime.

See also DRUGS AND NARCOTICS.

FORGERY 📖 The creation of a false written document or alteration of a genuine one, with the intent to DEFRAUD. 📖

Forgery consists of filling in blanks on a document containing a genuine SIGNATURE, or materially altering or erasing an existing instrument. An underlying intent to defraud, based on knowledge of the false nature of the instrument, must accompany the act. Instruments of forgery may include BILLS OF EXCHANGE, BILLS OF LADING, PROMISSORY NOTES, CHECKS, BONDS, receipts, orders for money or goods, MORTGAGES, discharges of mortgages, deeds, public records, account books, and certain kinds of tickets or passes for transportation or events. Statutes define forgery as a FELONY. Punishment generally consists of a fine or imprisonment, or both. Methods of forgery include handwriting, printing, engraving, and typewriting. The related crime of uttering a forged document occurs when an inauthentic writing is intentionally offered as genuine. Some modern statutes include this crime with forgery.

Perhaps the most famous case of forgery in the twentieth century took place in 1983 with the "discovery" of the Hitler diaries. The dia-

ries supposedly contained passages written by German dictator Adolf Hitler between 1932 and 1945. Gerd Heidemann, a German reporter for *Stern* magazine, had claimed the writings as genuine and sold them. He had obtained them from Konrad Kujau, a Stuttgart dealer in military memorabilia and documents. The magazines *Newsweek* and *Paris Match*, along with other media, paid more than $5 million for the documents. Major news sources around the world quickly published major stories detailing the historical information that the diaries allegedly contained. Investigative experts from around the world later conducted forensic examinations on the diaries and found the documents to be fake. Kujau then admitted forging the diaries, and news sources immediately retracted their coverage. Both Kujau and Heidemann were sentenced to four and a half years in a German prison—but not before Kujau embarrassed the media even further by forging Hitler autographs for spectators at his circuslike trial.

In the United States, the Mormon Bible forgeries resulted in more extreme consequences. Beginning in the early 1980s, Mark Hofmann, a disillusioned Salt Lake City Mormon and part-time dealer in historical documents, forged documents of major importance to Mormon history. He sold most of the creations to the Mormon Church and to others interested in Mormon religious history. Hofmann reaped hundreds of thousands of dollars from his fraud. His boldest forgery, the White Salamander letter, cast doubt on the credibility of the Mormon Church's founder, Joseph Smith. In this letter, Hofmann portrayed Smith as a dabbler in folk magic and the occult, which greatly distressed the Mormon community. When individuals within Hofmann's ring of buyers raised doubts about the authenticity of one of his later creations, Hofmann murdered one buyer and the spouse of another before their suspicions became public.

Hofmann was charged with murder and fraud. Prosecutors relied on expert testimony regarding the authenticity of the documents. When the experts declared that the documents were worthless, Hofmann's attorneys offered to plea bargain on the counts of forgery and second-degree murder. The prosecution agreed to negotiate the charges to avoid an embarrassing trial for the Mormon Church. Hofmann pleaded guilty to murder. In January 1988, the Utah Board of Pardons sentenced Hofmann to life in prison without parole.

Most forgeries are less sensational than those in the Hitler diaries and Mormon Bible cases.

Gerd Heidemann, a reporter for a German magazine, claimed that writings he bought from Konrad Kujau were diaries written by Adolf Hitler between 1932 and 1945. When experts determined that they were fake, Kujau admitted to having forged the diaries.

AP/WIDE WORLD PHOTOS

Common forgery usually involves manufacturing or tampering with documents for economic gain. The intent to defraud remains essential.

COUNTERFEITING, often associated with forgery, is a separate category of fraud involving the manufacture, alteration, or distribution of a product that is of lesser value than the genuine product.

FORM 📖 A prototype of an instrument to be employed in a legal transaction or a judicial proceeding that includes the primary essential matters, the appropriate technical phrases or terms, and any additional material required to render it officially accurate, arranged in suitable and systematic order, and conducive to adaptation to the circumstances of the particular case. 📖

The expression *form of the statute* signifies the language or structure of a statute, and, therefore, the restriction or command that it might include, as used in the phrase in criminal pleading "against the form of statute in that case made and provided."

A *matter of form*, as distinguished from a *matter of substance*—with respect to PLEADINGS, AFFIDAVITS, INDICTMENTS, and other legal instruments—entails the method, style, or form of relating the applicable facts; the selection or arrangement of terms; and other such matters without influencing the essential sufficiency or validity of the instrument, or without reaching the merits.

FORMAL PARTY 📖 A person who has no interest in the dispute between the immediate litigants but has an interest in the subject matter that can be expeditiously settled in the current proceedings and thereby prevent additional litigation. 📖

The rules of CIVIL PROCEDURE of the various states determine who constitutes a formal party and define the rights and obligations of other categories of PARTIES.

FORMED DESIGN 📖 In criminal law, and especially in regard to HOMICIDE, the killing of one human being by the instigation, act, or omission of another, who has a deliberate and fixed intention to kill, whether or not directed against a certain person. 📖

FORMS OF ACTION 📖 The old common-law patterns for different kinds of lawsuits. 📖

A plaintiff could start an ACTION only if it was possible to state the claim in words that followed one of the forms. The forms of action governed all COMMON-LAW PLEADING.

Origin of the Forms of Action The common-law forms of action were not planned and enacted like a statute, but they developed over hundreds of years out of the struggle to centralize justice in England. They were the

first WRITS by which the king's courts took notice of a dispute and asserted its authority to resolve it. When William the Conqueror first established the English throne in 1066 there were already local courts that handled most legal disputes. The king's courts began to hear cases involving the assertion of royal rights and disputes between high noblemen.

In time, dissatisfied litigants from the community courts appealed to the king's courts for review of the decisions. The king's courts became one of his tools for consolidating his power, and the scope of the authority of the court reflected political struggles through the centuries.

A person who thought he had been wronged had to serve notice on the defendant, but something more was needed to engage the legal process that led to judgment. A court would examine the substance of the claim only if it were cast in the correct form. As courts were organized beyond the local level in medieval England, writs were designed to give recognition to the sort of disputes that were most important to the king. The possibility of obtaining relief, then, depended on the plaintiff's ability to fit his grievance into one of the available writs.

During the middle ages a plaintiff could start an action only if it fit one of the established forms of action. Disputes that arose between noblemen, such as the one shown here, were heard in the king's courts.

Real Actions Royal power was first and most vigorously asserted in disputes involving land because all of society was organized under the land tenure system of the feudal law. The foundation of this system was the principle that no one should be deprived of his interest in REAL PROPERTY without a fair judgment against him, and no one should be made to answer a challenge to his rights without the king's command in a writ. The protection of these individual rights was so important to the stability of the society that the procedures for resolving land disputes became very formal. The forms for these lawsuits, called REAL ACTIONS, determined the way facts could be presented to constitute a legal cause of action, the defenses to such claims, and the remedies available for a successful plaintiff.

Personal Actions By the early part of the thirteenth century, PERSONAL ACTIONS were allowed. A litigant could sue for money due on an account, make a demand for a certain sum of money, or demand a specific item of PERSONAL PROPERTY. The action of REPLEVIN appeared for the recovery of personal goods wrongfully taken or withheld from the plaintiff. The action of COVENANT covered disputes arising from agreements under SEAL, originally covering LEASES of land but eventually contributing to the development of all contract law.

The most important form of action, the action of TRESPASS, appeared later in the thirteenth century. The great legal scholar FREDERIC WILLIAM MAITLAND once called trespass "that fertile mother of actions." It might have had its roots in the criminal law, a sort of appeal to redress the harm caused by the defendant's violence. The action of trespass became very popular because a form allowing the claim that force had been wrongfully used could cover a wide variety of injuries.

By the fourteenth century, forms were firmly established for trespass *vi et armis* ("with force and arms") for injuries to the plaintiff or his property, trespass *de bonis asportatis* ("for goods carried away"), and trespass *quare clausum fregit* ("whereby he broke the close") for an unlawful entry on the premises. The JURISDICTION of the courts was thus enlarged and the chance of finding legal relief substantially increased.

The justification for extending the authority of the royal courts to cover personal actions for private wrongs was the claim that the trespass was committed *vi et armis et contra pacem Domini Regis* ("with force and arms and against the peace of the Lord King"). During the fifteenth century, this principle supported an additional form of action for cases where the plaintiff's injury was a more indirect result of the defendant's conduct. This action was called trespass on the case, action on the case, a trampling on the plaintiff's legal rights, or his case. Sometimes the action was simply called "case," and different forms were used for special circumstances, for deceit and for defamation, for example. This form gave birth to our entire modern system of NEGLIGENCE law.

The next important innovation was the action of TROVER, by which the ownership of personal property could be challenged. Originally, the claim was good only when the plaintiff had lost his goods and the defendant had found them, but later the action required no more than a claim that the defendant refused to turn over personal property that belonged to the plaintiff.

By the sixteenth century the action of ASSUMPSIT took over as the dominant form of action for recovering DAMAGES for a broken contract that was not under seal. Special assumpsit was an action brought on an express contract or promise, and general assumpsit allowed monetary damages for the failure to perform an obligation that arose out of the facts of the situation and was implied by the law. Our modern law of CONTRACTS developed from the old action of assumpsit.

Forms of Action in the United States American colonies under English rule were less restrained by complicated distinctions among the various forms of action, probably because legal systems in the United States were less formal until a time when dissatisfaction with the technicalities of the forms was beginning to peak. For example, there were lawsuits where both trespass and case were used for the recovery of real property and for specific items of personal property. Trover and assumpsit frequently were used interchangeably.

As a result of the Federal Rules of Civil Procedure applicable in FEDERAL COURTS and adopted to a large degree by many state courts, there is only one form of action, a CIVIL ACTION.

See also CASE, ACTION ON THE; CIVIL PROCEDURE; FEUDALISM.

FORNICATION Sexual intercourse between a man and a woman who are not married to each other.

Under the COMMON LAW, the crime of fornication consisted of unlawful sexual intercourse between an unmarried woman and a man, regardless of his marital status. If the woman was married, the crime was ADULTERY.

Today, statutes in a number of states declare that fornication is an offense, but such statutes are rarely enforced. On the theory that fornication is a victimless crime, many states do not prosecute persons accused of the offense.

Under modern-day legislation, if one of the two persons who engage in sexual intercourse is married to another person, he (or she) is guilty of adultery. Statutes in some states declare that if the woman is married, the sexual act constitutes adultery on the part of both persons, regardless of the man's marital status.

Fornication is an element of a number of sex offenses such as RAPE, INCEST, and SEDUCTION.

Although penalties are seldom enforced, they usually consist of a fine, imprisonment, or both. In November of 1996 an Idaho prosecutor brought fornication charges against a teenage couple in an effort to curb teen pregnancy.

FORSWEAR In criminal law, to make OATH to that which the DEPONENT knows to be untrue. This term is wider in its scope than PERJURY, for the latter, as a technical term, includes the idea of the oath being taken before a competent court or officer and relating to a material issue, which is not implied by the word *forswear.*

FORTAS, ABE Abe Fortas served as a justice of the U.S. Supreme Court from 1965 to 1969. A renowned and powerful Washington, D.C., attorney before he joined the Court, Fortas resigned from the bench in disgrace after allegations of unethical behavior led to calls for his IMPEACHMENT.

Fortas was born June 19, 1910, in Memphis, to English immigrant Jews. He graduated from Southwestern College, in Memphis, in 1930 and received a law degree from Yale Law School in 1933. An outstanding student at Yale, Fortas became a protégé of WILLIAM O. DOUGLAS, a member of the school's faculty and a future Supreme Court justice. Following graduation Fortas divided his time between Yale and Washington, D.C., serving as an assistant professor at the school and working in several federal government agencies.

Fortas's arrival in Washington, D.C., coincided with President FRANKLIN D. ROOSEVELT'S New Deal administration. Under Roosevelt the federal government greatly expanded as it assumed more regulatory power over the national economy. Fortas severed his connections with

BIOGRAPHY

ARTIST: GEORGE AUGUSTA. COLLECTION OF THE SUPREME COURT OF THE UNITED STATES.

Abe Fortas

Yale in 1937 and went to work full-time for the SECURITIES AND EXCHANGE COMMISSION, which was chaired by Douglas.

Fortas proved to be an effective administrator. He joined the Department of the Interior in 1939 and soon became a confidant of Secretary of the Interior Harold L. Ickes. Ickes, a powerful member of the Roosevelt administration, named Fortas undersecretary in 1942. Fortas served in that position until 1946, when he left government to start a private law firm.

Fortas and Thurman W. Arnold, a former law professor and chief of the Antitrust Division of the Department of Justice, created the firm of Arnold and Porter to help corporations and other powerful interest groups deal with the new federal bureaucracy. Fortas knew his way around the halls of power and became an influential lobbyist and interpreter of government regulations in post–World War II Washington, D.C.

His path to the Supreme Court began in 1948, when he led the legal team that fought to place LYNDON B. JOHNSON'S name on the Texas election ballot for U.S. senator. Johnson, a Texas congressman in the 1940s, got to know Fortas while Fortas was at the Department of the Interior. The 1948 Texas Democratic primary election gave Johnson an eighty-seven-vote margin of victory, but his opponent, Coke R. Stevenson, alleged that Johnson's supporters had stuffed the ballot box with phony ballots. After Stevenson filed suit in federal court, a judge removed Johnson's name from the final election ballot, pending an investigation into the alleged election irregularities. Fortas convinced Justice HUGO L. BLACK, of the Supreme Court, to order the restoration of Johnson's name, pursuant to Black's judicial power to review the actions of the federal courts in Texas. Johnson was elected to the Senate and became majority leader in 1955. He was elected vice president of the United States in 1960 and became president November 22, 1963, following the ASSASSINATION of President JOHN F. KENNEDY.

Though Fortas served the powerful, he also provided pro bono (unpaid) legal services to

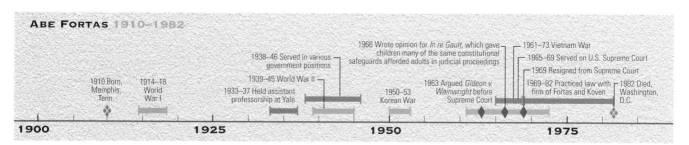

ABE FORTAS 1910–1982

1910 Born, Memphis, Tenn.

1914–18 World War I

1933–37 Held assistant professorship at Yale

1938–46 Served in various government positions

1939–45 World War II

1950–53 Korean War

1963 Argued *Gideon v. Wainwright* before Supreme Court

1966 Wrote opinion for *In re Gault,* which gave children many of the same constitutional safeguards afforded adults in judicial proceedings

1961–73 Vietnam War

1965–69 Served on U.S. Supreme Court

1969 Resigned from Supreme Court

1969–82 Practiced law with firm of Fortas and Koven

1982 Died, Washington, D.C.

1900   1925   1950   1975

those with pressing legal issues. His most famous pro bono case was *Gideon v. Wainwright*, 372 U.S. 335, 83 S. Ct. 792, 9 L. Ed. 2d 799 (1963). A Florida court had convicted Clarence Gideon, a drifter and small-time gambler, of breaking into a poolroom and removing the change from a vending machine. Gideon could not afford an attorney and the court would not appoint one. Gideon prepared his own APPEAL to the U.S. Supreme Court, arguing that denial of legal counsel because a person could not afford an attorney was unconstitutional. The Court accepted his appeal and appointed Fortas to serve as his attorney.

Fortas convinced the Court to overrule its PRECEDENT in *Betts v. Brady*, 316 U.S. 455, 62 S. Ct. 1252, 86 L. Ed. 1595 (1942), in which it held that an ordinary person charged with a FELONY could do an adequate job of personal defense and was not entitled to the appointment of an attorney. In his majority opinion for *Gideon*, Justice Black ruled that an indigent defendant in a criminal trial had a constitutional right to a court-appointed attorney. In so ruling, the Court incorporated through the FOURTEENTH AMENDMENT the SIXTH AMENDMENT's right to counsel, thus making that right applicable to state as well as federal criminal proceedings.

When Johnson assumed the presidency, he looked to Fortas as a confidential adviser. Johnson wished to appoint Fortas to the Supreme Court, but there were no vacancies. He convinced Justice ARTHUR J. GOLDBERG to resign from the Court in 1965 to become U.S. ambassador to the United Nations. Goldberg left the Court reluctantly, and Johnson nominated Fortas to fill its so-called Jewish seat. The "Jewish seat" began with the 1939 appointment of Felix Frankfurter, who was Jewish, to succeed Justice Benjamin Cardozo, also Jewish. It was assumed that for political reasons, Democratic presidents would appoint a Jewish person to that vacancy. This tradition ended with the appointment of Fortas.

Fortas fit in well with the liberal Court, then headed by Chief Justice EARL WARREN. Concerned with policy more than precedent, Fortas was a strong defender of CIVIL RIGHTS and civil liberties. His two most significant opinions dealt with the rights of children. The 1967 landmark case *In re Gault*, 387 U.S. 1, 87 S. Ct. 1428, 18 L. Ed. 2d 527, changed the nature of the JUVENILE LAW system. Fortas and the Court essentially made the juvenile courts adhere to standards of DUE PROCESS, applying most of the procedural safeguards enjoyed by adults

accused of crimes. Under *Gault* juvenile courts were to respect the RIGHT TO COUNSEL, the right to freedom from compulsory SELF-INCRIMINATION, and the right to confront hostile witnesses.

Tinker v. Des Moines Independent Community School District, 393 U.S. 503, 89 S. Ct. 733, 21 L. Ed. 2d 731 (1969), accorded juveniles FIRST AMENDMENT rights. Des Moines high school officials had suspended students for wearing black armbands to school to protest U.S. involvement in the Vietnam War. On appeal Fortas rejected the idea that the school's response was reasonable because it was based on the fear that a disturbance would result from the wearing of armbands. Fortas ruled that the wearing of armbands was "closely akin to 'pure speech' which . . . is entitled to comprehensive protection under the First Amendment." He added that public school officials could not ban expression out of the "mere desire to avoid discomfort and unpleasantness that always accompany an unpopular viewpoint."

In June 1968 Chief Justice Warren announced that he would retire. President Johnson nominated Fortas to succeed Warren, but the political mood of the Senate was hostile to the nomination. It had been an open secret in Washington, D.C., that Fortas continued to advise the president after joining the Court. Fortas was a key participant in Vietnam War policymaking. Some senators were troubled by his breach of the SEPARATION OF POWERS; others, especially conservatives, attacked his liberal voting record on the Court. Republicans hoped to derail the nomination so as to give RICHARD M. NIXON, then running for the presidency, the opportunity to appoint a more conservative chief justice. Johnson, who had already announced he would not run for reelection, was a lame duck and could do nothing to help Fortas. Opponents conducted a filibuster when the appointment was brought to the Senate floor. In October Fortas, sensing defeat, asked that his name be withdrawn from consideration. Warren remained on the Court until 1969, when President Nixon appointed WARREN E. BURGER chief justice.

Matters worsened for Fortas in 1969 when *Life* magazine reported that he had accepted a $20,000 fee from a foundation established by the family of Louis Wolfson, a financier under federal investigation for securities violations. The fee was the first of a series of annual payments that were to be made to Fortas for the duration of his life, and thereafter to his widow until her death, in exchange for Fortas's guid-

"FOR A JUSTICE OF THIS ULTIMATE TRIBUNAL [THE U.S. SUPREME COURT], THE OPPORTUNITY FOR SELF-DISCOVERY AND THE OCCASION FOR SELF-REVELATION IS GREAT."

ance of the foundation's programs. The arrangement was terminated in 1966 when Fortas returned the money upon Wolfson's indictment.

Despite Fortas's ultimate return of the money, his initial acceptance of it troubled many senators. It was alleged that Fortas had done more than foundation work, giving Wolfson legal advice. The *Life* article noted that Wolfson had used Fortas's name in the hope of helping himself. Fortas issued an ambiguous statement that did not resolve the situation. The Nixon administration and Republican senators hinted that Fortas should be impeached for his actions, which were contrary to the ethical provision that judges must be free of the appearance of impropriety. Fortas ended the controversy by resigning from the Court May 14, 1969, though he contended he had done nothing wrong. This was the first time in U.S. history that a justice resigned under the threat of impeachment.

Following his resignation Fortas sought to return to his old law firm. When the firm refused to take him back, he set up his own law practice, Fortas and Koven. He resumed advising corporate clients on how to do business in Washington, D.C., and he continued his pro bono work.

Fortas died April 6, 1982, in Washington, D.C.

CROSS-REFERENCES
Children's Rights; *In re Gault*; *Gideon v. Wainwright*.

FORTHWITH 📖 Immediately; promptly; without delay; directly; within a reasonable time under the circumstances of the case. 📖

44 LIQUORMART v. RHODE ISLAND
See LIQUORMART V. RHODE ISLAND.

FORUM 📖 A court of justice where disputes are heard and decided; a judicial tribune that hears and decides disputes; a place of JURISDICTION where remedies afforded by the law are pursued. 📖

The appropriate forum for a lawsuit depends upon which court has jurisdiction over the PARTIES and the subject matter of the case, a matter governed mostly by statutes and court rules. For example, rules of procedure provide that disputes involving a certain dollar amount or disputes between citizens of different states may be heard in a particular court. When a CONTRACT is the subject of the litigation, the parties may have included in the contract a forum selection clause that designates the court where any disputes arising from the contract may be heard. A forum selection clause will generally be upheld by a court unless the party resisting it can show that enforcement of the clause would be unfair or unreasonable under the circumstances of the particular case.

When more than one court is the appropriate forum to hear a dispute, the PLAINTIFF may engage in forum shopping. In this situation, the plaintiff seeks to have a dispute heard in the court that the plaintiff believes will render the most favorable VERDICT or JUDGMENT, regardless of whether that forum imposes hardship or inconvenience on the opposing party. The DEFENDANT may even be unable to appear in the forum selected by the plaintiff, thus permitting the plaintiff to win the action by DEFAULT.

Forum shopping is frowned upon by the courts. Many federal and state procedural rules, as well as federal and state statutes, discourage this practice by limiting a plaintiff's choice of forum to locations reasonably convenient to both parties. The Uniform Child Custody Jurisdiction Act, for example, limits the exercise of jurisdiction over child custody decrees to the home state of the child.

A court that has jurisdiction may decline to exercise it when the parties and the interests of justice would benefit if the action were heard in another court that also has jurisdiction over the matter. This is called the doctrine of *forum non conveniens* (Latin for "forum not convenient"). A defendant seeking to invoke the doctrine of forum non conveniens must make a motion to have the action dismissed even though the original forum has jurisdiction to hear the action. The court, in its discretion, will consider a number of factors in deciding whether to grant or deny the motion, including whether the necessary witnesses can be compelled to attend the proceedings and the cost of obtaining their

The Denver Federal Courthouse is a forum for the resolution of disputes over which it has jurisdiction and disputes that have been transferred to that court for other reasons.

KARL GEHRING/THE GAMMA LIAISON NETWORK

attendance; ease of access to evidence pertinent to the dispute, including the distance from the site of the events that resulted in the litigation; and any other practical factors that would facilitate the trial of the lawsuit. For instance, if a lawsuit is brought in Alaska but all the witnesses live in Washington State, and the property that is the subject of the dispute is also in Washington, then the court may conclude that it is more convenient to litigate the case in Washington than in Alaska. In some states, however, the court will rarely dismiss an ACTION on the grounds of forum non conveniens when the plaintiff is a resident of the forum state. In addition, to protect the plaintiff's interests, a court will permit dismissal of the action only if the plaintiff consents to the trial of the lawsuit in the more convenient forum.

In the FEDERAL COURT system and within many states, statutes have been enacted to allow a court to transfer a case to another court that operates within the same system or state and where the case might have been brought in the first place. Thus, the court to which the case is transferred must also have jurisdiction over the matter. Unlike a forum non conveniens MOTION, a transfer request may be made by either party and does not require that the action be dismissed and then reinstituted in the new court. In addition, to obtain a transfer, the requesting party needs to show a lesser degree of inconvenience than that required before a court will grant a forum non conveniens motion. For example, federal law provides that a case may be transferred from one federal forum to another "[f]or the convenience of parties and witnesses" and "in the interest of justice" (28 U.S.C.A. § 1404(a) (West Supp. 1995)). But, since transfers are limited to courts within the same system or state, a defendant who wants to change from a federal forum to a state court, or to a court in another country, or from a state court of one state to a state court of another state, must still bring a motion to dismiss the action based on forum non conveniens.

FORWARDING FEE 📖 A payment of money made by one ATTORNEY who receives a client to another attorney who referred the client. 📖

The Code of Professional Responsibility, which has been established by the AMERICAN BAR ASSOCIATION to regulate the professional conduct of attorneys, proscribes the payment of forwarding fees—sometimes called referral fees—to an attorney who has merely secured the employment of another attorney without rendering any services or assuming any responsibility to the client in the matter. An apportionment of reasonable fees between attorneys is proper only when the client is cognizant of, and consents to, this arrangement, and when the allocation is in proportion to the services rendered and the responsibility assumed by each attorney.

The Code of Professional Responsibility has been adopted by many state bar associations. If an attorney accepts a forwarding fee without providing any services, or undertaking any responsibility, the bar association may institute disciplinary proceedings against the individual for his or her unethical behavior.

FOUNDATION 📖 A permanent fund established and maintained by contributions for charitable, educational, religious, research, or other benevolent purposes. An institution or association given to rendering financial aid to colleges, schools, hospitals, and CHARITIES and generally supported by gifts for such purposes.

The founding or building of a college or hospital. The incorporation or ENDOWMENT of a college or hospital is the foundation, and those who endow it with land or other property are the founders.

Preliminary questions to a WITNESS to establish admissibility of evidence. *Laying a foundation* is a prerequisite to the admission of evidence at trial. It is established by TESTIMONY that identifies the evidence sought to be admitted and connects it with the issue in question. 📖

FOUR CORNERS 📖 The document itself; the face of a written instrument. 📖

The term is ordinarily included in the phrase *within the four corners of the document*, which denotes that in ascertaining the legal significance and consequences of the document, the parties and the court can only examine its language and all matters encompassed within it. Extraneous information concerning the document that does not appear in it—*within its four corners*—cannot be evaluated.

FOURTEENTH AMENDMENT The Fourteenth Amendment to the U. S. Constitution reads:

Section 1. All persons born or naturalized in the United States, and subject to the jurisdiction thereof, are citizens of the United States and of the State wherein they reside. No State shall make or enforce any law which shall abridge the privileges or immunities of citizens of the United States; nor shall any State deprive any person of life, liberty, or property, without due process of law; nor deny to any person within its jurisdiction the equal protection of the laws.

Section 2. Representatives shall be apportioned among the several States according to their respective numbers, counting the whole number of persons in each State, excluding Indians not taxed. But when the right to vote at any election for the choice of electors for President and Vice President of the United States, Representatives in Congress, the Executive and Judicial officers of a State, or the members of the Legislature thereof, is denied to any of the male inhabitants of such State, being twenty-one years of age, and citizens of the United States, or in any way abridged, except for participation in rebellion, or other crime, the basis of representation therein shall be reduced in the proportion which the number of such male citizens shall bear to the whole number of male citizens twenty-one years of age in such State.

Section 3. No person shall be a Senator or Representative in Congress, or elector of President and Vice President, or hold any office, civil or military, under the United States, or under any State, who, having previously taken an oath, as a member of Congress, or as an officer of the United States, or as a member of any State legislature, or as an executive or judicial officer of any State, to support the Constitution of the United States, shall have engaged in insurrection or rebellion against the same, or given aid or comfort to the enemies thereof. But Congress may by a vote of two-thirds of each House, remove such disability.

Section 4. The validity of the public debt of the United States, authorized by law, including debts incurred for payment of pensions and bounties for services in suppressing insurrection or rebellion, shall not be questioned. But neither the United States nor any State shall assume or pay any debt or obligation incurred in aid of insurrection or rebellion against the United States, or any claim for the loss or emancipation of any slave; but all such debts, obligations and claims shall be held illegal and void.

Section 5. The Congress shall have power to enforce, by appropriate legislation, the provisions of this article.

The Fourteenth Amendment, ratified in 1868, has generated more lawsuits than any other provision of the U.S. Constitution. Section 1 of the amendment has been the center-piece of most of this litigation. It makes "[a]ll persons born or naturalized in the United States" CITIZENS of the United States and citizens of the state in which they reside. This section also prohibits state governments from denying persons within their jurisdiction the "privileges or immunities" of U.S. citizenship, and guarantees to every such person "due process" and "equal protection of the laws." The Supreme Court has ruled that any state law that abridges FREEDOM OF SPEECH, freedom of RELIGION, the right to trial by JURY, the RIGHT TO COUNSEL, the right against SELF-INCRIMINATION, the right against unreasonable SEARCHES AND SEIZURES, or the right against CRUEL AND UNUSUAL PUNISHMENTS will be invalidated under section 1 of the Fourteenth Amendment. This holding is called the INCORPORATION DOCTRINE.

Sections 2 to 5 have been the subject of far fewer lawsuits. Some of these sections seem anachronistic today because they reflect the immediate concerns of the Union's political leadership following the North's victory over the South in the Civil War (1861–65). Section 2, for example, penalized any state that attempted to abridge the VOTING RIGHTS of its black male residents by reducing the state's representation in Congress (no female resident of any race was afforded the constitutional right to vote in the United States until 1920). Section 3 prohibited from holding state or federal office any person who engaged in "insurrection or rebellion" or otherwise gave "aid or comfort to the enemies" during the Civil War. Section 4 reaffirmed the United States' commitment to pay its Civil War debt, while declaring all debts and obligations incurred by the Confederate government "illegal and void." Section 5 enabled, and continues to enable, Congress to pass "appropriate legislation" to enforce the provisions of the Fourteenth Amendment.

The Fourteenth Amendment was drafted to alleviate several concerns harbored by many U.S. citizens prior to its ratification. The most obvious concern related to the status of the recently freed slaves. Five years before hostilities commenced in the Civil War, the Supreme Court declared that people of African descent living in the United States were not "citizens" of the United States, but merely members of a "subordinate and inferior class of human beings" deserving no constitutional protection whatsoever (*Dred Scott v. Sandford*, 60 U.S. [19 How.] 393, 15 L. Ed. 691 [1856]). The Fourteenth Amendment vitiated the Supreme Court's holding in *Dred Scott* by making all blacks "born or naturalized in the United

Black residents of Washington, D.C., celebrated the abolition of slavery April 19, 1866. Two years later the Fourteenth Amendment made all blacks full-fledged citizens and afforded them the same constitutional rights and protections as other citizens.

CELEBRATION OF THE ABOLITION OF SLAVERY IN THE DISTRICT OF COLUMBIA BY THE COLORED PEOPLE, IN WASHINGTON, April 19, 1866.—[Sketched by F. Dielman.]

States" full-fledged citizens entitled to the same constitutional rights provided for every other U.S. citizen.

The racist attitudes expressed in *Dred Scott* also manifested themselves after the Civil War. In 1865, the southern states began enacting the Black Codes, which deprived African Americans of many basic rights afforded to white Americans, including the right to travel, bear arms, own property, make contracts, peaceably assemble, and testify in court. The Black Codes also authorized more severe punishments for African Americans than would be imposed on white persons for committing the same criminal offense. The Fourteenth Amendment offered an antidote to these discriminatory laws by guaranteeing to members of all races "due process of law," which requires the legal system to provide fundamentally fair trial procedures, and "equal protection of the laws," which requires the government to treat all persons with equal concern and respect.

Dred Scott was not the only Supreme Court decision that influenced the framers of the Fourteenth Amendment. *Barron v. City of Baltimore*, 32 U.S. (7 Pet.) 243, 8 L. Ed. 672 (1833), also played a significant role. This case involved a Maryland wharf owner who brought a lawsuit against the city of Baltimore for violating the Fifth Amendment's EMINENT DOMAIN Clause,

which prohibits the government from taking private property without "just compensation." Baltimore defended against the wharf owner's lawsuit by arguing that the FIFTH AMENDMENT only provides relief against action taken by the federal government, and offers no protection against state governments or their political subdivisions. The Supreme Court agreed with Baltimore.

Writing for the Court, Chief Justice JOHN MARSHALL asserted that the Constitution created the federal government, and the provisions of the Constitution were designed to regulate the activity of the federal government. The people of each state enacted their own constitution, Marshall contended, to regulate the activities of their state and local governments. Thus, Marshall reasoned that the U.S. Constitution operates only as a limitation on the powers of the federal government, unless one of its provisions expressly restricts the powers of state governments, as does Article I, Section 10.

Article I, Section 10, provides that "[n]o State shall enter into any Treaty, Alliance, or Confederation," or "pass any Bill of Attainder, ex post facto Law, or Law impairing the Obligation of Contracts." This wording, Marshall maintained, demonstrates that the Framers understood the type of clear and unequivocal language that must be used to make a provision of the federal Constitution binding on the states. Because neither the Fifth Amendment nor any of the other first eight amendments to the Constitution contain any similar language restricting the powers of state governments, Marshall concluded that the BILL OF RIGHTS was inapplicable to the states.

The Supreme Court's decision in *Barron* weighed heavily on the mind of JOHN BINGHAM, the Republican representative from Ohio who was the primary architect of Section 1 of the Fourteenth Amendment. Bingham said he "noted ... certain words in the opinion of Marshall" when he was "reexamining that case of *Barron*." The chief justice, Bingham stressed, denied the wharf owner's claim because the Framers of the Bill of Rights, unlike the Framers of Article I, Section 10, had not chosen the type of explicit language that would clearly make the Bill of Rights applicable to state governments. "Acting upon" Marshall's "suggestion" in *Barron*, Bingham said, he "imitated" the Framers of Article I, Section 10: "As [these Framers had written] 'no state shall . . . pass any Bill of Attainder . . . ' I prepared the provision of the first section of the fourteenth amendment."

Bingham's remarks shed light on the Supreme Court's decision to make most of the provisions contained in the Bill of Rights applicable to state governments through the doctrine of incorporation. Under this doctrine, the Supreme Court has ruled that every protection contained in the Bill of Rights—except for the right to bear arms, the right to INDICTMENT by GRAND JURY, the right to trial by jury in civil cases, and the right against quartering soldiers—must be protected by state governments under the Equal Protection and Due Process Clauses of the Fourteenth Amendment.

The Supreme Court has explained that each of these incorporated rights is "deeply rooted in the nation's history" and "fundamental" to the concept of "ordered liberty" represented by the Due Process Clause (*Palko v. Connecticut*, 302 U.S. 319, 58 S. Ct. 149, 82 L. Ed. 288 [1937]). Any state that denies one of these rights is violating its duty to provide the "equal protection of the laws" guaranteed to the residents of every state by the Fourteenth Amendment.

Although a state may provide more constitutional protection to its residents than is conferred by the Bill of Rights, the Fourteenth Amendment prohibits any state from providing less protection. For example, the Supreme Court upheld the constitutionality of sobriety checkpoints, which authorize police officers to stop motor vehicles to determine if the driver

has been consuming ALCOHOL, regardless of whether the stop was based on PROBABLE CAUSE or made pursuant to a SEARCH WARRANT as required by the Fourth Amendment (*Michigan v. Sitz*, 496 U.S. 444, 110 S. Ct. 2481, 110 L. Ed. 2d 412 [1990]). The Minnesota Supreme Court reached the opposite conclusion, invalidating arrests made during traffic stops at sobriety checkpoints because they did not comport with the state's constitutional provisions prohibiting unreasonable searches and seizures (*Ascher v. Commissioner of Public Safety*, 519 N.W.2d 183 [Minn. 1993]).

Whereas the Due Process and Equal Protection Clauses have given rise to a panorama of legal claims such as the sobriety checkpoint cases, the Privileges and Immunities Clause has produced only a few lawsuits since the end of the 1800s. Like most other legal terms in the Bill of Rights, the phrase *privileges or immunities* is not defined in the Constitution. Nor does the phrase possess a meaning that is self-evident. However, some insight into the meaning of the Privileges and Immunities Clause may be gleaned from statements made by the man who drafted it, Congressman Bingham.

Bingham said the "privileges and immunities of citizens of the United States . . . are chiefly defined in the first eight amendments to the Constitution of the United States. . . . These eight articles . . . never were limitations upon the power of the states until made so by the Fourteenth Amendment" (quoted in *Adamson v. California*, 332 U.S. 46, 67 S. Ct. 1672, 91 L. Ed. 1903 [1947] [Murphy, J., dissenting]). Senator Jacob Howard echoed these thoughts, stating that "these privileges and immunities, whatever they may be—for they are not and cannot be fully defined in their entire extent and precise nature—[include] . . . personal rights . . .

Although the U.S. Supreme Court upheld the constitutionality of sobriety checkpoints, the Minnesota Supreme Court ruled that checkpoints constitute unreasonable searches and seizures. The Fourteenth Amendment prohibits states from providing less protection to citizens than the Bill of Rights, but providing more protection is allowed.

such as the freedom of speech and of the press, [and] the right of the people to peaceably assemble and petition the government for redress of grievances." Similarly, Representative James Wilson made it clear that the "privileges and immunities of the citizens of the United States" include "[f]reedom of religious opinion" and "freedom of speech and press."

Notwithstanding the statements made by these congressmen, the Supreme Court has limited the application of the Fourteenth Amendment's Privileges and Immunities Clause to provide only negligible protection against the state and federal governments. In the *Slaughter-House* cases, 83 U.S. (16 Wall.) 16, 21 L. Ed. 268 (1873), a group of New Orleans butchers brought a lawsuit to invalidate a Louisiana law that granted a MONOPOLY to a local slaughterhouse. The butchers alleged that the state-chartered monopoly violated their "privileges and immunities" to pursue gainful employment free from unlawful restraints.

In an extremely narrow reading of the Fourteenth Amendment, the Supreme Court rejected the butchers' argument. The Court held that the Privileges and Immunities Clause protects only rights derived from U.S. citizenship, such as the right to HABEAS CORPUS and interstate travel, and not rights derived from state law, such as the COMMON-LAW rights of TORT and PROPERTY asserted by the New Orleans butchers. The Supreme Court has neither overruled its decision in the *Slaughter-House* cases nor expanded its narrow interpretation of the Privileges and Immunities Clause. Most constitutional scholars have since pronounced this clause a dead letter.

If the Supreme Court has provided a more conservative interpretation of the Privileges and Immunities Clause than envisioned by the Framers of the Fourteenth Amendment, it has provided a more liberal interpretation of the Equal Protection Clause. In *Brown v. Board of Education*, 347 U.S. 483, 74 S. Ct. 686, 98 L. Ed. 873 (1954), the Supreme Court ruled that the doctrine of "separate but equal," in which the black and white races were segregated in public schools and other places of public accommodation, was "inherently unequal" and denied African Americans "equal protection of the laws." The ambit of the Equal Protection Clause was later enlarged by the Supreme Court beyond racial segregation to cover an assortment of gender discrimination claims asserted by women.

The Court made these rulings in spite of evidence that racial segregation was prevalent at the time the Fourteenth Amendment was adopted and that women were treated like second-class citizens during most of the nineteenth century. In 1868, for example, racial segregation of public schools was permitted throughout the South and in eight northern states. The gallery of the U.S. Senate was itself segregated by race during the debate of the Equal Protection Clause. During the first half of the nineteenth century, every state proscribed married women from devising a WILL, owning or inheriting property, entering into a contract, or exercising almost any other basic CIVIL RIGHT afforded to women in the modern United States. Indeed, the common law recognized no existence for married women independent from their husband. By marriage, the husband and wife became one person in law, and that person was the husband.

Thus, the Framers' original understanding of the Fourteenth Amendment has not provided a useful yardstick to measure the Supreme Court's interpretation of the Due Process and Equal Protection Clauses. Since the mid-1940s, the Supreme Court has strayed further from the Framers' original understanding, recognizing controversial PRIVACY rights to use contraceptives (*Griswold v. Connecticut*, 381 U.S. 479, 85 S. Ct. 1678, 14 L. Ed. 2d 510 [1965]), obtain ABORTIONS prior to the third trimester of pregnancy (*Roe v. Wade*, 410 U.S. 113, 93 S. Ct. 705, 35 L. Ed. 2d 147 [1973]), and view OBSCENE pornographic material in the privacy of one's own home (*Stanley v. Georgia*, 394 U.S. 557, 89 S. Ct. 1243, 22 L. Ed. 2d 542 [1969]). In 1996 the Supreme Court held that the Equal Protection Clause had been violated by an amendment to the Colorado constitution prohibiting legislative, judicial, or executive action at the state or local level from protecting homosexual persons from discrimination in *Romer v. Evans*, __U.S. __, 116 S. Ct. 1620, 134 L. Ed. 2d 855 (1996).

CROSS-REFERENCES

Brown v. Board of Education of Topeka, Kansas; *Dred Scott v. Sandford*; Due Process of Law; Equal Protection; Gay and Lesbian Rights; *Griswold v. Connecticut*; Privileges and Immunitites; *Roe v. Wade*; *Slaughter-House Cases*.

FOURTH AMENDMENT   The Fourth Amendment to the U.S. Constitution reads:

> The right of the people to be secure in their persons, houses, papers, and effects, against unreasonable searches and seizures, shall not be violated, and no Warrants shall issue, but upon probable cause, supported by Oath or affirmation, and particularly describing the place to be searched, and the persons or things to be seized.

The American Revolution was fought in part to create a system of government in which the

RULE OF LAW would reign supreme. The rule of law is often identified with the axiom that the United States is a nation of laws and not of men and women. Under the rule of law, the actions of government officials are prescribed by the principles and laws that make up the U.S. legal system, and do not reflect the arbitrary whim and caprice of the government officials themselves.

A distinction is sometimes drawn between power and authority. Law enforcement officers are entrusted with the power to conduct investigations, make arrests, and occasionally use lethal force in the line of duty. But this power must be exercised within the parameters authorized by the law. Power exercised outside these legal parameters transforms law enforcers into lawbreakers, as happened when Laurence Powell was convicted for using excessive force against RODNEY KING, who had been stopped for speeding in Los Angeles. Powell repeatedly struck King with his nightstick even though King was in a submissive position lying prone on the ground.

The Fourth Amendment was intended to create a constitutional buffer between U.S. citizens and the intimidating power of law enforcement. It has three components. First, it establishes a PRIVACY interest by recognizing the right of U.S. citizens to be "secure in their persons, houses, papers, and effects." Second, it protects this privacy interest by prohibiting SEARCHES AND SEIZURES that are "unreasonable" or are not authorized by a "warrant" based upon "probable cause." Third, it states that no WARRANT may be issued to a law enforcement officer unless that warrant describes with particularity "the place to be searched, and the persons or things to be seized."

The Framers drafted the Fourth Amendment in response to their colonial experience with British officials whose discretion in collecting revenues for the Crown often went unchecked. Upon a mere suspicion held by British tax collectors or their informants, colonial magistrates were compelled to issue general warrants, which permitted blanket door-to-door searches of entire neighborhoods without limitation as to person or place. The law did not require MAGISTRATES to question British officials regarding the source of their suspicion or to make other credibility determinations.

The WRIT of assistance was a particularly loathsome form of general warrant. The name of this writ derived from the power of British authorities to enlist local peace officers and colonial residents who might "assist" in executing a particular search. A writ of assistance lasted for the life of the king or queen under whom it was issued, and applied to every officer and subject in the British Empire. In essence, such a writ "constituted a long-term hunting license for customs officers on the lookout for smugglers and articles imported in violation" of the law (Levy 1988, 227).

Colonial opposition to general warrants was pervasive and kinetic. In Paxton's case, 1 Quincy 51 (Mass. 1761), JAMES OTIS, appearing on behalf of colonists who opposed the issuance of another writ of assistance, denounced general

Law enforcement officers may search individuals if the officers have reason to believe, or probable cause, that those being searched have committed a crime.

warrants as instruments of "slavery," "villainy," and "arbitrary power." These writs, Otis continued, were "the most destructive of English liberty" because they placed the freedom of every person "in the hands of a petty officer" (as quoted in *O'Rourke v. City of Norman*, 875 F.2d 1465 [10th Cir. 1989]). To be valid, Otis railed, a warrant must be "directed to specific officers, and to search certain houses" for particular goods, and may only be granted "upon oath made" by a government official "that he suspects such goods to be concealed in those very places he desires to search" (as quoted in *Illinois v. Krull*, 480 U.S. 340, 107 S. Ct. 1160, 94 L. Ed. 2d 364 [1987]).

Although Otis lost the case, his arguments fueled angry colonial crowds that subsequently interfered with British customs and revenue agents who attempted to seize miscellaneous goods pursuant to general warrants. Some provincial courts began declining to issue writs of assistance, and other courts issued writs with greater specificity. Colonial newspapers complained that British officers were ransacking the colonists' houses, violating the sanctity of their bedrooms, and plundering their privacy under the auspices of general warrants. On the night before the DECLARATION OF INDEPENDENCE was published, JOHN ADAMS cited the "argument concerning the Writs of Assistance . . . as the commencement of the controversy between Great Britain and America."

The American Revolution answered the questions surrounding writs of assistance, but the Fourth Amendment raised other questions in the newly founded republic. If a police officer's suspicion is no longer sufficient to obtain a search warrant, as it was in colonial America, where should the line be drawn separating SUSPICION from PROBABLE CAUSE? Although general warrants are now clearly prohibited, how detailed must warrants be to pass constitutional muster? The Fourth Amendment expressly forbids "unreasonable" searches and seizures, but what criteria should be considered in evaluating the reasonableness of a search? The Fourth Amendment also leaves open the question of who should review warrant applications—the judiciary or some other branch of government. The answers to these questions were fleshed out in criminal litigation over the next two centuries.

Fourth Amendment questions arise during criminal litigation in the context of a suppression hearing. This hearing is prompted by a defendant who asks the court to review the method by which the police obtained EVIDENCE against her or him, and to determine whether that evidence survives constitutional scrutiny. If the evidence was obtained in violation of the Fourth Amendment, it is usually excluded from trial, which means the prosecution is unable to present it to the jury. The legal doctrine under which illegally obtained evidence is suppressed is known as the EXCLUSIONARY RULE, and its purpose is to deter police misconduct and protect defendants from rogue cops.

The exclusionary rule requires the suppression of not only evidence that was the direct product of illegal police work but also any evidence derived from a tainted source. The suppression of tainted derivative evidence, also known as FRUIT OF THE POISONOUS TREE, typically occurs when the police obtain a CONFESSION after an illegal arrest or pursuant to an unconstitutional search. Although the manner in which the confession itself was obtained may have been perfectly constitutional, the confession is still suppressed because the law does not permit the government, which the prosecution represents at a criminal trial, to benefit from its own misconduct.

Before a court may exclude any evidence, it must first determine whether the Fourth Amendment even applies to the case under consideration. Two requirements must be met before a particular search or seizure will give rise to Fourth Amendment protection. First, the search or seizure must have been conducted by a government agent or pursuant to government direction. Thus, the actions of state and federal law enforcement officers or private persons working with law enforcement officers will be subject to the strictures of the Fourth Amendment. Bugging, WIRE TAPPING, and other related snooping activities performed by purely private citizens, such as private investigators, will not receive Fourth Amendment protection.

Second, a defendant must be able to demonstrate that he or she had a "reasonable expectation of privacy" in the place that was searched or the thing that was seized (*Katz v. United States*, 389 U.S. 347, 88 S. Ct. 507, 19 L. Ed. 576 [1967]). In *Katz*, the Supreme Court explained that "[w]hat a person knowingly exposes to the public, even in his own home or office, is not a subject of Fourth Amendment protection. . . . But what he seeks to preserve as private, even in an area accessible to the public, may be constitutionally protected."

Applying this principle, the Supreme Court has ruled that U.S. citizens maintain a reasonable expectation of privacy in the "CURTILAGE" immediately surrounding their home, but not in the "open fields" and "wooded areas" extending beyond this area (*Hester v. United States*, 265

Items in a boat that are in "plain view" from outside the vehicle, as with an automobile, would probably not be private and could be seized by law enforcement officials.

U.S. 57, 44 S. Ct. 445, 68 L. Ed. 898 [1924]). A person may have a reasonable expectation of privacy in the AUTOMOBILE she or he is driving, but not in items that are in "plain view" from outside the vehicle (*Coolidge v. New Hampshire*, 403 U.S. 443, 91 S. Ct. 2022, 29 L. Ed. 564 [1971]). Nor do people have reasonable expectations of privacy in personal characteristics (*United States v. Dionisio*, 410 U.S. 1, 93 S. Ct. 764, 35 L. Ed. 2d 67 [1973]). Thus, the police may require individuals to give handwriting and voice exemplars as well as fingerprint samples, without complying with the Fourth Amendment's warrant or reasonableness requirements.

Once a court has determined that the Fourth Amendment is an issue in a particular case, it must next decide whether law enforcement complied with the amendment's requirements. When making this decision, a court begins with the premise that the Constitution expresses a preference for searches made pursuant to a warrant (*Mincey v. Arizona*, 437 U.S. 385, 98 S. Ct. 2408, 57 L. Ed. 2d 290 [1978]). Searches performed without a warrant are presumptively invalid, and evidence seized during a warrantless search is suppressed unless the search was reasonable under the circumstances.

The Supreme Court has ruled that warrantless searches may be deemed reasonable in certain situations. First, no warrant is required for searches incident to a lawful arrest (*United States v. Watson*, 423 U.S. 411, 96 S. Ct. 820, 46 L. Ed. 2d 598 [1976]). If a police officer has probable cause to believe a crime has occurred, the Fourth Amendment permits the officer to arrest the suspect and conduct a search of the suspect's person and clothing and of all areas within the suspect's immediate reach. Second, a police officer who possesses an "articulable" and "reasonable" suspicion that an automobile has violated a state or local traffic law may stop the driver and conduct a search of the vehicle's interior, including the glove compartment (*Delaware v. Prouse*, 440 U.S. 648, 99 S. Ct. 1391, 59 L. Ed. 2d 660 [1979]). The trunk of a

vehicle cannot be searched unless an officer has probable cause to believe that it contains CONTRABAND or the instrumentalities of criminal activity.

Third, an officer who reasonably believes "that criminal activity may be afoot" in a public place may stop an individual suspected of wrongdoing and "conduct a carefully limited search of [the suspect's] outer clothing" for weapons that may be used against the officer (*Terry v. Ohio*, 392 U.S. 1, 88 S. Ct. 1868, 21 L. Ed. 889 [1968]). Fourth, officers who are in "HOT PURSUIT" of "fleeing felons" or are gathering "evanescent" evidence (evidence that could readily disappear—e.g. blood samples from drunken drivers) are also permitted to act without first obtaining a SEARCH WARRANT.

These four exceptions to the warrant requirement are based on the need to facilitate law enforcement during unforeseen or emergency circumstances in which criminal activity is strongly suspected but police officers lack sufficient time to complete an application for a search warrant and testify before a magistrate. These exceptions also reflect a need to protect police officers from hidden weapons and to preserve evidence that could easily be destroyed or compromised.

When law enforcement does obtain a warrant before conducting a search, the warrant must comply with the Fourth Amendment before evidence from the search will be admissible in court. A warrant may be defective if it is not

When a search warrant has been obtained by law enforcement officers, they may thoroughly search the premises. If the warrant is defective, evidence obtained during the search will not be admissible in court.

supported by probable cause established by a detailed sworn statement made by a law enforcement officer appearing before a magistrate.

No definition of *probable cause* has ever satisfied both prosecutors and defense attorneys. But the Supreme Court has said that probable cause exists where "the facts and circumstances within [the police officer's] knowledge" are of a "reasonably trustworthy" basis to "warrant a man of reasonable caution" to believe that an offense has been or is about to be committed (*Carroll v. United States*, 267 U.S. 132, 45 S. Ct. 280, 69 L. Ed. 543 [1925]). Probable cause can be established by out-of-court statements of reliable police informants even though the credibility of those statements cannot be tested by a magistrate (*Illinois v. Gates*, 462 U.S. 213, 103 S. Ct. 2317, 76 L. Ed. 2d 527 [1983]). However, probable cause will not be found where the only evidence of criminal activity is an officer's "good information" or "belief" (*Aguilar v. Texas*, 378 U.S. 108, 84 S. Ct. 1509, 12 L. Ed. 2d 723 [1964]).

The Fourth Amendment requires not only that search warrants be supported by probable cause but also that they "particularly" describe the person or place to be searched. A warrant must provide enough detail so that an "officer with the search warrant can, with reasonable effort, ascertain and identify the place [or person] intended" (*Steele v. United States*, 267 U.S. 498, 45 S. Ct. 414, 69 L. Ed. 757 [1925]). For most residences, a street address usually satisfies the particularity requirement. However, if a warrant designates an apartment complex, hotel, or other multiple-unit building, the warrant must describe the specific subunit that will be searched. When a warrant designates that a person will be searched, it must include a description that provides enough detail so that the suspect's identity can be ascertained with reasonable certainty.

Probable cause must be established by TESTIMONY made under OATH by a law enforcement officer appearing before a magistrate. The testimony can be oral or written, and cannot contain any "knowingly" or "intentionally" false statements, or statements made in "reckless disregard for the truth" (*Franks v. Delaware*, 438 U.S. 154, 98 S. Ct. 2674, 57 L. Ed. 2d 667 [1978]). Inaccuracies due to negligence or innocent omission do not jeopardize a warrant's validity.

The magistrate before whom an officer applies for a warrant must be "neutral and detached" (*Coolidge v. New Hampshire*, 403 U.S. 443, 91 S. Ct. 2022, 29 L. Ed. 2d 564 [1971]). This means the magistrate must be impartial and not a member of the "competitive enterprise" of law enforcement (*California v. Acevedo*, 500 U.S. 565, 111 S. Ct. 1982, 114 L. Ed. 2d 619 [1991]). Thus, police officers, prosecutors, and attorneys general are disqualified from the role of magistrate. However, judges, lawyers, and court clerks all potentially qualify as "neutral and detached," and therefore may become magistrates. The requirements that states set for becoming a magistrate vary widely, from having an attorney's license to having a high school diploma to simply being literate.

If a search is performed pursuant to a defective warrant, any evidence obtained as a result of the search is usually suppressed. An exception to this rule arises when an officer has obtained evidence pursuant to a defective warrant that the officer relied on in "good faith" (*United States v. Leon*, 468 U.S. 897, 104 S. Ct. 3430, 82 L. Ed. 2d 677 [1984]). For this exception to apply, the warrant must have been issued by a magistrate and then later ruled defective for a valid reason, and the defect must not have been the result of willful police deception. If these two requirements are satisfied, law enforcement was entitled to rely on the warrant in conducting the search, and any evidence obtained during the search is ADMISSIBLE against the defendant.

This exception was created to ensure that police officers would not be punished for blunders made by magistrates when issuing search warrants. Again, the primary reason courts sup-

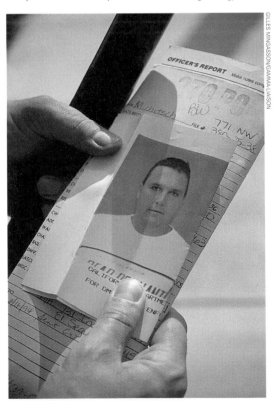

A search warrant such as this one that authorizes the search of a person must describe the individual clearly enough that he can be identified by the officer carrying the warrant.

GILLES MINGASSON/GAMMA-LIAISON

press illegally obtained evidence is to deter future police misconduct. No deterrent value is served by excluding evidence obtained by an honest police officer who acted pursuant to an ostensibly valid warrant that was later ruled defective owing to an error by the magistrate.

CROSS-REFERENCES

Criminal Law; Criminal Procedure; *Mapp v. Ohio;* Stop and Frisk; *Terry v. Ohio.*

FRANCHISE A special PRIVILEGE to do certain things that is conferred by government on an individual or a CORPORATION and which does not belong to citizens generally of common right, e.g., a right granted to offer CABLE TELEVISION service.

A privilege granted or sold, such as to use a name or to sell products or services. In its simplest terms, a franchise is a LICENSE from the owner of a TRADEMARK or TRADE NAME permitting another to sell a product or service under that name or mark. More broadly stated, a *franchise* has evolved into an elaborate agreement under which the franchisee undertakes to conduct a business or sell a product or service in accordance with methods and procedures prescribed by the franchisor, and the franchisor undertakes to assist the franchisee through advertising, promotion, and other advisory services.

The right of SUFFRAGE; the right or privilege of voting in public elections. Such right is guaranteed by the FIFTEENTH, NINETEENTH, and TWENTY-FOURTH AMENDMENTS to the U.S. Constitution.

As granted by a professional sports association, *franchise* is a privilege to field a team in a given geographic area under the auspices of the league that issues it. It is merely an incorporeal right.

Government Franchises

The CONSIDERATION to be given by a person or corporation in order to receive a franchise from the government can be an agreement to pay money, to bear some burden, or to perform a public duty. The primary objective of all grants of franchises is to benefit the public; the rights or interests of the grantee, the franchisee, are secondary. A corporation is a franchise, and the various powers conferred on it are also franchises, such as the power of an insurance corporation to issue an insurance policy. Various types of business—such as water companies, gas and electric companies, bridge and tunnel authorities, taxi companies, along with all types of corporations—operate under franchises.

The CHARTER of a corporation is also called its general franchise. A franchise tax is a tax imposed by the state on the right and privilege of conducting business as a corporation for the

DAVID YOUNG-WOLFF/PHOTOEDIT

purposes for which it was created and in the conditions that surround it.

Power to Grant The power to grant franchises is vested in the legislative department of the government, subject to limitations imposed by the state constitution. A franchise can be derived indirectly from the state through the agency that has been duly designated for that purpose, such as the local transportation agency that can grant a franchise for bus routes. Franchises are usually conferred on corporations, but natural persons can also acquire them. The grant of a franchise frequently contains express conditions and STIPULATIONS that the GRANTEE, or holder, of the franchise must perform.

Not every privilege granted by a governmental authority is a franchise. A franchise differs from a license, which is merely a personal privilege or temporary permission to do something; it can be revoked and can be derived from a source other than the legislature or state agencies. A franchise differs from a LEASE, which is a CONTRACT for the possession and profits of property in exchange for the payment of rent.

Regulation Once a franchise is granted, its exercise is usually subject to regulation by the state or some duly authorized body. In the exercise of POLICE POWER—which is the authority of the state to legislate to protect the health, safety, welfare, and morals of its citizens—local authorities or the political subdivisions of the state can regulate the grant or exercise of franchises.

Right to Compete While a franchise can be EXCLUSIVE, exclusiveness is not a necessary element of it. Nonexclusive franchises—including those to function or operate as a PUBLIC UTILITY—do not include the right to be free of competition. The grant of such a franchise does not prevent the grant of a similar one to another, or lawful competition on the part of

The Fifteenth, Nineteenth, and Twenty-fourth Amendments to the Constitution guarantee the rights of franchise to all U.S. citizens.

Chrysler Corporation
Jeep®
SALES AND SERVICE AGREEMENT

_____
(DEALER Firm Name and D/B/A, if applicable)

located at _____
(STREET)   (CITY)   (STATE)

a(n) _____ hereinafter called DEALER, and Chrysler Corporation, a
(INDIVIDUAL, CORPORATION OR PARTNERSHIP)

Delaware corporation, hereinafter sometimes referred to as "CC", have entered into this Chrysler Corporation Jeep
Sales and Service Agreement, hereinafter referred to as "Agreement", the terms of which are as follows:

INTRODUCTION

The purpose of the relationship established by this
Agreement is to provide a means for the sale and service of specified Jeep vehicles and the sale of CC vehicle parts and accessories in a manner that will maximize customer satisfaction and be of benefit to
DEALER and CC.

While the following provisions, each of which is material, set forth the undertakings of this relationship, the
success of those undertakings rests on a recognition of
the mutuality of interests of DEALER and CC, and a
spirit of understanding and cooperation by both parties
in the day to day performance of their respective functions. As a result of such considerations, CC has entered into this Agreement in reliance upon and has
placed its trust in the personal abilities, expertise,
knowledge and integrity of DEALER's principal owners and management personnel, which CC anticipates
will enable DEALER to perform the personal services
contemplated by this Agreement.

It is the mutual goal of this relationship to promote
the sale and service of specified CC products by maintaining and advancing their excellence and reputation
by earning, holding and furthering the public regard
for CC and all CC dealers.

1 PRODUCTS COVERED

DEALER has the right to order and purchase from
CC and to sell at retail only those specific models of
CC vehicles, sometimes referred to as "specified CC
vehicles," listed on the Motor Vehicle Addendum, attached hereto and incorporated herein by reference.
CC may change the models of CC vehicles listed on
the Motor Vehicle Addendum by furnishing DEALER
a superseding Motor Vehicle Addendum. Such a superseding Motor Vehicle Addendum will not be deemed
or construed to be an amendment to this Agreement.

2 DEALER'S MANAGEMENT

CC has entered into this Agreement relying on the active, substantial and continuing personal participation in the
management of DEALER's organization by:

NAME   POSITION

_____   _____

_____   _____

DEALER represents and warrants that at least one of the above named individuals will be physically present at
DEALER's facility (sometimes referred to as "Dealership Facilities") during most of its operating hours and will
manage all of DEALER's business relating to the sale and service of CC products. DEALER shall not change the
personnel holding the above described position(s) or the nature and extent of his/her/their management participation
without the prior written approval of CC.

3 DEALER'S CAPITAL STOCK OR PARTNERSHIP INTEREST

If DEALER is a corporation or partnership, DEALER represents and agrees that the persons named below own beneficially the capital stock or partnership interest of DEALER in the percentages indicated below. DEALER warrants there will be no change affecting more than 50% of the ownership interest of DEALER, nor will there be any other change in the ownership interest of DEALER which may affect the managerial control of DEALER without CC's prior written approval.

Name	Voting Stock	Non-Voting Stock	Partnership Interest	Active Yes/No
_____	_____%	_____%	_____%	_____
_____	_____%	_____%	_____%	_____
_____	_____%	_____%	_____%	_____
_____	_____%	_____%	_____%	_____
_____	_____%	_____%	_____%	_____
Total	_____%	_____%	_____%	

4 SALES LOCALITY

DEALER shall have the non-exclusive right, subject to the provisions of this Agreement, to purchase from CC those new specified CC vehicles, vehicle parts, accessories and other CC products for resale at the DEALER's facilities and location described in the Dealership Facilities and Location Addendum, attached hereto and incorporated herein by reference. DEALER will actively and effectively sell and promote the retail sale of CC vehicles, vehicle parts and accessories in DEALER's Sales Locality. As used herein, "Sales Locality" shall mean the area designated in writing to DEALER by CC from time to time as the territory of DEALER's responsibility for the sale of CC vehicles, vehicle parts and accessories, although DEALER is free to sell said products to customers wherever they may be located. Said Sales Locality may be shared with other CC dealers of the same line-make as CC determines to be appropriate.

5 ADDITIONAL TERMS AND PROVISIONS

The additional terms and provisions set forth in the document entitled "Chrysler Corporation Sales and Service Agreement Additional Terms and Provisions" marked "Form 91 (J-E)," as may hereafter be amended from time to time, constitute a part of this Agreement with the same force and effect as if set forth at length herein, and the term "this Agreement" includes said additional terms and provisions.

6 FORMER AGREEMENTS, REPRESENTATIONS OR STATEMENTS

This Chrysler Corporation Jeep Sales and Service Agreement and other documents, (or their successors as specifically provided for herein) which are specifically incorporated herein by reference constitute the entire agreement between the parties relating to the purchase by DEALER of those new specified CC vehicles, parts and accessories from CC for resale; and it cancels and supersedes all earlier agreements, written or oral, between CC and DEALER relating to the purchase by DEALER of Jeep vehicles, parts and accessories, except for (a) amounts owing by CC to DEALER, such as payments for warranty service performed and incentive programs, or (b) amounts owing or which may be determined to be owed, as a result of an audit or investigation, by DEALER to CC due to DEALER's purchase from CC of vehicles, parts, accessories and other goods or services, or (c) amounts DEALER owes to CC as a result of other extensions of credit by CC to DEALER. No representations or statements, other than those expressly set forth herein or those set forth in the applications for this Agreement submitted to CC by DEALER or DEALER's representatives, are made or relied upon by any party hereto in entering into this Agreement.

7 WAIVER AND MODIFICATION

No waiver, modification or change of any of the terms of this Agreement or change or erasure of any printed part of this Agreement or addition to it (except the filling in of blank spaces and lines) will be valid or binding on CC unless approved in writing by the President or a Vice President or the National Dealer Placement Manager of Chrysler Corporation.

8 AMENDMENT

DEALER and CC recognize that this Agreement does not have an expiration date and will continue in effect unless terminated under the limited circumstances set forth in Paragraph 28. DEALER and CC further recognize that the passage of time, changes in the industry, ways of doing business and other unforeseen circumstances may cause CC to determine that it should amend all Chrysler Corporation Jeep Sales and Service Agreements. Therefore, CC will have the right to amend this Agreement to the extent that CC deems advisable, provided that CC makes the same amendment in Chrysler Corporation Jeep Sales and Service Agreements generally. Each such amendment will be issued in a notice sent by certified mail or delivered in person to DEALER and signed by the President or a Vice President or the National Dealer Placement Manager of Chrysler Corporation. Thirty-five (35) days after mailing or delivery of such notice to DEALER, this Agreement will be deemed amended in the manner and to the extent set forth in the notice.

9   ARBITRATION

Any and all disputes arising out of or in connection with the interpretation, performance or non-performance of this Agreement or any and all disputes arising out of or in connection with transactions in any way related to this Agreement (including, but not limited to, the validity, scope and enforceability of this arbitration provision, or disputes under rights granted pursuant to the statutes of the state in which DEALER is licensed) shall be finally and completely resolved by arbitration pursuant to the arbitration laws of the United States of America as codified in Title 9 of the United States Code, §§ 1-14, under the Rules of Commercial Arbitration of the American Arbitration Association (hereinafter referred to as the "Rules") by a majority vote of a panel of three arbitrators. One arbitrator will be selected by DEALER (DEALER's arbitrator). One arbitrator will be selected by CC (CC's arbitrator). These arbitrators must be selected by the respective parties within ten (10) business days after receipt by either DEALER or CC of a written notification from the other party of a decision to arbitrate a dispute pursuant to this Agreement. Should either CC or DEALER fail to select an arbitrator within said ten-day period, the party who so fails to select an arbitrator will have its arbitrator selected by the American Arbitration Association upon the application of the other party. The third arbitrator must be an individual who is familiar with business transactions and be a licensed attorney admitted to the practice of law within the United States of America, or a judge. The third arbitrator will be selected by DEALER's and CC's arbitrators. If said arbitrators cannot agree on a third arbitrator within thirty (30) days from the date of the appointment of the last selected arbitrator, then either DEALER's or CC's arbitrator may apply to the American Arbitration Association to appoint said third arbitrator pursuant to the criteria set forth above. The arbitration panel shall conduct the proceedings pursuant to the then existing Rules.

Notwithstanding the foregoing, to the extent any provision of the Rules conflict with any provision of this Paragraph 9, the provisions of this Paragraph 9 will be controlling.

CC and DEALER agree to facilitate the arbitration by: (a) each party paying to the American Arbitration Association one-half (1/2) of the required deposit before the proceedings commence; (b) making available to one another and to the arbitration panel, for inspection and photocopying all documents, books and records, if determined by the arbitrator to be relevant to the dispute; (c) making available to one another and to the arbitration panel personnel directly or indirectly under their control, for testimony during hearings and prehearing proceedings if determined by the arbitration panel to be relevant to the dispute; (d) conducting arbitration hearings to the greatest extent possible on consecutive business days; and (e) strictly observing the time periods established by the Rules or by the arbitration panel for the submission of evidence and of briefs.

Unless otherwise agreed to by CC and DEALER, a stenographic record of the arbitration shall be made and a transcript thereof shall be ordered for each party, with each party paying one-half (1/2) of the total cost of such recording and transcription. The stenographer shall be state-certified, if certification is made by the state, and the party to whom it is most convenient shall be responsible for securing and notifying such stenographer of the time and place of the arbitration hearing(s).

If the arbitration provision is invoked when the dispute between the parties is either the legality of terminating this Agreement or of adding a new CC dealer of the same line-make or relocating an existing CC dealer of the same line-make, CC will stay the implementation of the decision to terminate this Agreement or add such new CC dealer or approve the relocation of an existing CC dealer of the same line-make until the decision of the arbitrator has been announced, providing DEALER does not in any way attempt to avoid the obligations of this Paragraph 9, in which case the decision at issue will be immediately implemented.

Except as limited hereby, the arbitration panel shall have all powers of law and equity, which it can lawfully assume, necessary to resolve the issues in dispute including, without limiting the generality of the foregoing, making awards of compensatory damages, issuing both prohibitory and mandatory orders in the nature of injunctions and compelling the production of documents and witnesses for pre-arbitration discovery and/or presentation at the arbitration hearing on the merits of the case. The arbitration panel shall not have legal or equitable authority to issue a mandatory or prohibitory order which: (a) extends or has effect beyond the subject matter of this Agreement, or (b) will govern the activities of either party for a period of more than two years; nor shall the arbitration panel have authority to award punitive, consequential or any damages whatsoever beyond or in addition to the compensatory damages allowed to be awarded under this Agreement.

The decision of the arbitration panel shall be in written form and shall include findings of fact and conclusions of law.

It is the intent and desire of DEALER and CC to hereby and forever renounce and reject any and all recourse to litigation before any judicial or administrative forum and to accept the award of the arbitration panel as final and binding, subject to no judicial or administrative review, except on those grounds set forth in 9 USC § 10 and § 11. Judgment on the award and/or orders may be entered in any court having jurisdiction over the parties or their assets. In the final award and/or order, the arbitration panel shall divide all costs (other than attorney fees, which shall be borne by the party incurring such fees and other costs specifically provided for herein) incurred in conducting the arbitration in accordance with what the arbitration panel deems just and equitable under the circumstances. The fees of DEALER's arbitrator shall be paid by DEALER. The fees of CC's arbitrator shall be paid by CC.

10 SIGNATURE

This Agreement becomes valid only when signed by the President or a Vice President or the National Dealer Placement Manager of Chrysler Corporation and by a duly authorized officer or executive of DEALER if a corporation; or by one of the general partners of DEALER if a partnership; or by DEALER if an individual.

IN WITNESS WHEREOF, the parties hereto have signed this Agreement which is finally executed at

_____, Michigan, in

triplicate, on _____

_____

(DEALER Firm Name and D/B/A, if applicable)

By _____

(Individual Duly Authorized to Sign)

_____

(Title)

CHRYSLER CORPORATION

By _____

(Title)

---

public authorities. The holder of a nonexclusive franchise is legally entitled to be free from the competition of one not having a valid franchise to compete. One can institute a proceeding for an INJUNCTION—a court order that commands or prohibits a certain act—and monetary DAMAGES for the unlawful invasion of the franchise. Although the franchise is not exclusive, one is entitled to protection against competition from persons operating without a franchise.

Duration The legislature can prescribe the duration of a franchise. The powers of local authorities or political subdivisions of the state depend upon the statute that confers the power to make grants and upon any constitutional limitation.

A franchise can be terminated by the mutual agreement of the state that is the franchisor, and the grantee or the franchisee. It can be lost by ABANDONMENT, such as when a corporation dissolves because of its fiscal problems. A mere change in the government organization of a political subdivision of a state does not divest franchise rights that have been previously acquired with the consent of local authorities. A franchise cannot be revoked arbitrarily unless that power has been reserved by the legislature or proper agency.

Forfeiture A franchise can be subject to FORFEITURE due to nonuse. Misuse or failure to provide adequate services under the franchise can also result in its loss. The REMEDY for nonuse or misuse lies with the state. Persons other than the state or public authorities cannot challenge the validity of the exercise of a franchise unless they can demonstrate that they have a peculiar interest in the matter distinct from that of the general public.

Invasion of the Franchise A person or corporation holding a valid franchise can obtain an injunction to prevent the unlawful invasion of the franchise rights and can sue for monetary damages if there has been financial loss as a result of the INFRINGEMENT.

Transfer of Franchises Subject to applicable constitutional or statutory limitation, franchises can be sold or transferred. Where the franchises involve public service, they cannot be sold or transferred unless there is authorization by the state. The person or corporation purchasing the franchise in an authorized sale takes it subject to its restrictions.

Private Franchises Certain written contractual agreements are sometimes loosely referred to as franchises, although they lack the essential elements in that they are not conferred by any SOVEREIGNTY. The franchise system or method of operation, which is of comparatively recent development, has had a phenomenal growth in particular consumer product industries, such as automobile sales, fast foods, and ice cream. The use of a franchise in this manner has enabled individuals with minimal capital to invest to become successful members of the business community.

Under the most common method of operation, the cornerstone of a franchise system must be a trademark or trade name of a product. A franchise is a license from an owner of a trademark or trade name permitting another to sell a product or service under the name or mark. A franchisee agrees to pay a FEE to the franchisor in exchange for permission to operate a business or sell a product or service according to the methods and procedures prescribed by the franchisor as well as under the trade name or trademark of the franchisor. The franchisee is usually granted an exclusive territory in which he or she is the only DISTRIBUTOR of the particular goods or services in that area. The franchisor is usually obligated by CONTRACT to assist the franchisee through advertising, promotion, research and development, quantity purchasing, training and education, and other specialized management resources.

Before 1979 fewer than twenty state legislatures had enacted laws to protect prospective franchisees from being deceived by the falsehoods of dishonest franchisors. These laws, known as financial disclosure laws, mandated that anyone offering franchises for sale in the state had to disclose material facts—such as the true costs of operating a franchise, any recurring expenses, and substantiated reports of profit earned—that would be instrumental in the making of an informed decision to purchase a franchise.

In states that did not have such legislation, the unsophisticated investor was at the mercy of the franchisor's statements. A victimized franchisee could sue a franchisor for breach of contract, but this was an expensive proposition for someone who typically had invested virtually all of his or her financial resources in an unprofitable franchise. Franchisors confronted with numerous lawsuits often would declare BANKRUPTCY so that the franchisees had little possibility of recouping any of their investments.

The Federal Trade Commission received numerous complaints about inequitable and dishonest practices in the sale of such franchises. In late 1978 it issued regulations, effective October 21, 1979, that require franchisors and their representatives to disclose material facts necessary to make an informed decision about the proposed purchase of a franchise and that establish certain practices to be observed in the franchisor-franchisee relationship.

A franchisor must disclose the background of the company—including the business experience of its high-level executives—for the previous five years; and whether any of its executives, within the last seven years, have been convicted of a FELONY, have pleaded NOLO CONTENDERE to FRAUD, have been held liable in a CIVIL ACTION for fraud, are subject to any currently effective court order or ADMINISTRATIVE AGENCY ruling concerning the franchise business or fraud, or have been involved in any proceedings for bankruptcy or corporate REORGANIZATION for INSOLVENCY during the previous seven years.

In addition, there must be a factual description of the franchise as well as an unequivocal statement of the total funds to be paid, such as initial franchise fees, deposits, down payments, prepaid rent on the location, and equipment and INVENTORY purchases. The conditions and time limits to obtain a refund, as well as its amount, must be clear as well as the amount of recurring costs, such as ROYALTIES, rents, advertising fees, and sign rental fees. Any restrictions imposed—such as on the amount of goods or services to be sold, the types of customers with which the franchisee can deal—the geographical area, and whether the franchisee is entitled to protection of his or her territory by the franchisor must be discussed. The duration of the franchise, in addition to reasons why the franchise can be terminated or the franchisee's license not renewed when it expires, also must be explained. The number of franchises voluntarily terminated or terminated by the franchisor must be reported. The franchisor must disclose the number of franchises that were operating at the end of the previous year, as well as the number of company-owned outlets. The franchisee must also be supplied with the names, addresses, and telephone numbers of the franchisees of the ten outlets nearest the prospective franchisee's location, so that the prospective franchisee can contact them to obtain a realistic perspective of the daily operations of a franchise.

If the franchisor makes any claims about the actual or projected sales of its franchises or their actual or potential profits, facts must be presented to substantiate such statements.

All of these facts—embodied in an accurately, clearly, and concisely written document—must be given to the prospective franchisee at the first personal meeting or at least ten days before any contractual relationship is entered or deposit made, whichever date is first. The purpose of this disclosure statement is to provide the potential investor with a realistic view of the business venture upon which he or she is about to embark. Failure to comply with the FTC regulation could result in a fine of up to $10,000 a day for each violation.

Some states have also enacted laws that prohibit a franchisor from terminating a franchise without GOOD CAUSE, which usually means that the franchisee has breached the contract. In such a case, the franchisor is entitled to reacquire the outlet—usually by repurchasing the franchisee's assets, such as inventory and equipment.

In states without "good cause" laws, franchisees claim that they are being victimized by franchisors who want to reclaim outlets that have been proved to be highly profitable. They allege that the franchisor imposes impossible or ridiculous demands that cannot be met to harass the franchisee into selling the store back to

the franchisor at a fraction of its value. Company-owned outlets yield a greater profit to the franchisor than the royalty payments received from the franchisee. Other franchisees claim that their licenses have been revoked or not renewed upon expiration because they complained to various state and federal agencies of the ways in which the franchisors operate. Such controversies usually are resolved in the courtroom.

BIOGRAPHY

Jerome N. Frank

"THE EFFORTS OF MEN PLANNING TO ACHIEVE A CERTAIN GOAL HAVE FREQUENTLY HAD RESULTS WHICH THOSE MEN DID NOT INTEND, WHICH INDEED WERE THE VERY OPPOSITE OF THEIR INTENTIONS."

FRANK, JEROME N. Jerome Frank had a distinguished career as a judge but won perhaps even more renown as a legal philosopher and author.

Frank was born September 10, 1889, in New York City. He received a Ph.B. from the University of Chicago in 1909 and a law degree from the University of Chicago Law School in 1912. His next twenty years were spent in private practice where he specialized in the reorganization of corporations.

During the 1930s, Frank became involved in several of the agencies established as part of President FRANKLIN D. ROOSEVELT's New Deal. In 1933 FELIX FRANKFURTER, then a law professor at Harvard, recommended Frank for the position of general counsel to the Agricultural Adjustment Administration (AAA) and the Federal Surplus Relief Corporation. In 1935, however, Frank and several of his staff were fired because they insisted that benefits provided to cotton growers under AAA contracts should be shared with sharecroppers. Almost immediately, Roosevelt appointed Frank as special counsel to the Reconstruction Finance Corporation. From there Frank went to the Public Works Administration (PWA) where he took an active part in the litigation that surrounded Roosevelt's public power program. In his most notable case for the PWA, Frank prepared the government's case in a suit that involved federal construction of electricity distribution systems. The Supreme Court upheld the government's position in *Alabama Power Co. v. Ickes*, 302 U.S. 464, 58 S. Ct. 300, 82 L. Ed. 374 (1938).

After a brief return to private practice, Frank reentered public service in 1937 when

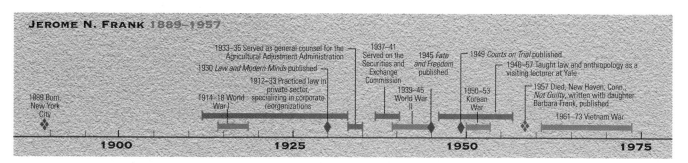

JEROME N. FRANK 1889–1957

1889 Born, New York City

1900

1912–33 Practiced law in private sector, specializing in corporate reorganizations

1914–18 World War I

1925

1930 *Law and Modern Minds* published

1933–35 Served as general counsel for the Agricultural Adjustment Administration

1937–41 Served on the Securities and Exchange Commission

1939–45 World War II

1945 *Fate and Freedom* published

1950

1950–53 Korean War

1949 *Courts on Trial* published

1946–57 Taught law and anthropology as a visiting lecturer at Yale

1957 Died, New Haven, Conn., *Not Guilty*, written with daughter Barbara Frank, published

1961–73 Vietnam War

1975

Roosevelt appointed him to the SECURITIES AND EXCHANGE COMMISSION (SEC) at the request of the commission's chairman, WILLIAM O. DOUGLAS. After Douglas's appointment to the Supreme Court in 1939, Frank succeeded him as chairman of the SEC. Two years later in 1941, Frank was appointed to the U.S. Court of Appeals for the Second Circuit, a position that he held until his death.

Frank's opinions were praised for their literary quality as well as for their legal analysis. Characteristically, they drew from a wide range of subjects—history, philosophy, art and literature, sociology, and psychology, to name but a few—as well as from the more standard legal sources. In his concurring opinion in *United States v. Roth*, 237 F.2d 796 (1956), an OBSCENITY case, Frank cited scientific, psychological, and economic evidence to support his conclusions.

Another theme that runs through Frank's opinions was his concern for persons who are weak and lacking in influence. In *United States ex rel. Caminito v. Murphy*, 222 F.2d 698, 706 (1955); *cert. denied*, 350 U.S. 896, 76 S. Ct. 155, 100 L. Ed. 788, he wrote that the "test of the moral quality of a civilization is its treatment of the weak and powerless." In his dissent in *United States v. Johnson*, 238 F.2d 565, 568 (1956), he argued that a defendant with a meritorious case should not suffer a penalty "because he is guilty of the crime of being poor." On appeal, the Supreme Court accepted Frank's position and reversed the appeals court's decision (352 U.S. 565, 77 S. Ct. 550, 1 L. Ed. 2d 593 [1957]).

Frank's reputation as a jurist was equaled, if not exceeded, by his fame as a legal philosopher. In 1930 he published *Law and the Modern Mind*. Through this book and his later publications, Frank became known as one of the leading exponents of LEGAL REALISM, a movement that flourished during the 1920s and 1930s.

Legal realism began as a reaction against analytical positivism with its formalism and emphasis on logic that had dominated legal thought at the turn of the century. In contrast to the positivists who claimed that judges could apply known rules to the available facts and arrive with certainty at their decisions, Frank stressed the uncertainty of the decision-making process. He argued that psychological forces, including personal biases buried so deep in the unconscious that the judge was unaware of their existence, might influence the decision.

Frank was also troubled by the difficulty of determining what was fact and what was not. He observed that courts receive their information months or even years after events occurred from witnesses who may be biased or may simply lack complete knowledge of the events they recount. The possibility that an innocent person might be convicted worried Frank and led him to suggest reforms in the methods for ascertaining certain facts. His last book *Not Guilty*, in which his daughter collaborated, dealt with cases in which innocent people had been convicted.

Frank also played a role in LEGAL EDUCATION, most notably at the Yale Law School. In 1932 he became a research associate at the Yale Law School and held the position of visiting lecturer at Yale from 1946 until his death. In addition, in 1931 and in 1946–47 he was a visiting lecturer in law and anthropology at the New School for Social Research in New York City. At Yale Frank advocated changes in legal education including adding more social studies to the curriculum. He also argued that legal education had strayed too far from law as it was actually practiced.

In addition to the works mentioned earlier, Frank's books included *Save America First* (1938); *If Men Were Angels* (1942); *Fate and Freedom* (1945); and *Courts on Trial* (1949), a major discussion—and criticism—of the U.S. trial system. Frank died January 13, 1957, in New Haven, Connecticut.

See also JURISPRUDENCE.

BIOGRAPHY

Felix Frankfurter

FRANKFURTER, FELIX   Felix Frankfurter served as a government attorney in the early nineteenth century and then taught law at Harvard Law School. In the 1920s and 1930s, he supported a number of liberal causes, including President FRANKLIN D. ROOSEVELT's New Deal.

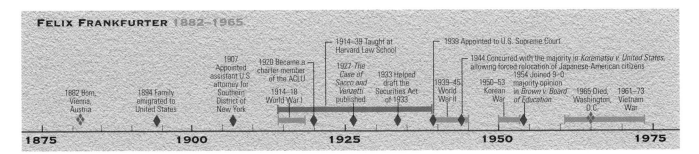

FELIX FRANKFURTER 1882–1965

1882 Born, Vienna, Austria

1894 Family emigrated to United States

1907 Appointed assistant U.S. attorney for Southern District of New York

1914–18 World War I

1920 Became a charter member of the ACLU

1914–39 Taught at Harvard Law School

1927 *The Case of Sacco and Venzetti* published

1933 Helped draft the Securities Act of 1933

1939 Appointed to U.S. Supreme Court

1939–45 World War II

1944 Concurred with the majority in *Korematsu v. United States*, allowing forced relocation of Japanese-American citizens

1950–53 Korean War

1954 Joined 9–0 majority opinion in *Brown v. Board of Education*

1965 Died, Washington, D.C.

1961–73 Vietnam War

1875   1900   1925   1950   1975

In 1939, he was appointed to the U.S. Supreme Court as an associate justice. Throughout his twenty-three years on the Court, he was known for consistently applying the theory of judicial self-restraint.

Frankfurter was born November 15, 1882, in Vienna. At the age of twelve, he emigrated from Vienna to the United States with his parents and four siblings. The Frankfurters, like many other Jews in Vienna, had lived in Leopoldstadt, the center of the Jewish Ghetto, where they faced an undercurrent of hostility and a future of economic uncertainty. Along with 18 million other Europeans who immigrated to the United States between 1890 and 1920, the family sought a fresh start.

Upon his arrival in the Lower East Side of Manhattan in 1894, Frankfurter could not speak a word of English. Yet, twelve years later, after earning his undergraduate degree from City College, in New York, Frankfurter graduated first in his class from Harvard Law School. Following a short stint with a private law firm on Wall Street, where he represented corporate interests, Frankfurter was appointed to serve for the next four years as assistant U.S. attorney in the Southern District of New York, prosecuting white-collar criminals. In 1911, he was named solicitor to the federal Bureau of Insular Affairs.

Frankfurter enjoyed working as an attorney for the government much more than representing corporations in private practice. He stressed that "the American lawyer should regard himself as a potential officer of his government and a defender of its laws and Constitution." He predicted that "if the time should ever come when this tradition ha[s] faded out and the members of the bar ... become merely the servants of business, the future of our liberties would be gloomy indeed."

In 1914, Frankfurter returned to his alma mater Harvard Law School, as professor of law. Frankfurter's tenure as professor was marked by his intellectual honesty and rigor. Teaching only students of high academic standing, he tirelessly explored the law's complexities and reveled in its nuances, helping his classes see both the gray areas and the bright lines. He also took a personal interest in his students, helping many of them obtain a clerkship with one of the United States' leading judges, including OLIVER WENDELL HOLMES, JR., LOUIS D. BRANDEIS, and LEARNED HAND.

Brandeis, a Supreme Court justice from 1916 to 1939, was one of Frankfurter's closest friends. The two met after a lecture Brandeis gave before the Harvard Ethical Society during Frankfurter's days as a law student. Brandeis, who never had a son of his own, acted as a father and mentor to Frankfurter, who was twenty-six years his junior. During the 1930s, acting as an informal adviser to President Roosevelt, Frankfurter cajoled the president into supporting liberal causes espoused by Brandeis.

Although Frankfurter claimed that he was not a member of any political party, he supported many liberal causes. In 1920, he became a charter member of the newly founded AMERICAN CIVIL LIBERTIES UNION, an organization created to protect the constitutional rights of members of ethnic, religious, and racial minorities. During the 1930s, Frankfurter served as an adviser to the NATIONAL ASSOCIATION FOR THE ADVANCEMENT OF COLORED PEOPLE. Frankfurter also helped develop many aspects of President Roosevelt's New Deal programs. For example, he brought together the legislative engineers who drafted the Securities Act of 1933 (15 U.S.C.A. § 77a to 77z, 77aa), which today remains a prominent piece of federal law regulating the trading of stocks and bonds.

Frankfurter's contribution to the case of Nicola Sacco and Bartolomeo Vanzetti identified him as an activist for liberal causes in the mind of many U.S. citizens. Sacco and Vanzetti, two Italian immigrants who spoke only broken English, were indicted for killing a guard and a paymaster from a shoe company in Massachusetts in 1920. The physical evidence presented against Sacco and Vanzetti was tenuous. For the jurors who heard the case, the most incriminating information may have been the defendants' radical political beliefs: both were known anarchists who opposed the military draft. Sacco and Vanzetti were convicted and executed for the two murders.

Writing an article for the *Atlantic Monthly*, a venerable national publication with a wide readership, Frankfurter accused the prosecuting attorney and trial judge of appealing to the jurors' prejudice against the defendants' political activities and immigrant status. Frankfurter also accused the prosecutor of conspiring with the government's ballistics expert to mislead the jury. Finally, Frankfurter suggested that the court-appointed interpreter nefariously misrepresented the defendants' testimony in order to enhance the prosecution's case. Frankfurter supported each accusation with passages from the trial record. His article was later published as a book titled *The Case of Sacco and Vanzetti* (1927). The article and the book have served as a starting point for subsequent generations examining the role that passion, prejudice, and politics played in the trial of Sacco and Vanzetti,

"THE HISTORY OF LIBERTY HAS LARGELY BEEN THE HISTORY OF THE OBSERVANCE OF PROCEDURAL SAFEGUARDS."

as well as in the trials of members of other unpopular minorities in the United States.

In light of Frankfurter's unyielding support for CIVIL RIGHTS and individual liberties, as a lawyer and professor of law, many liberals rejoiced when President Roosevelt appointed him to serve as an associate justice on the U.S. Supreme Court in 1939. However, by the time Frankfurter retired twenty-three years later, many of these same liberals were disappointed by his failure to embrace every religious and political minority that presented a claim before the Supreme Court. In retrospect, Frankfurter's actions as a Supreme Court justice cannot adequately be characterized as liberal or conservative but are most accurately described as exhibiting a consistent pattern of judicial self-restraint.

Judicial self-restraint is a theory by which a judge decides cases according to the express legal rules contained in constitutional and statutory provisions as well as common-law PRECEDENT, independent of the judge's own personal predilections. According to this theory, state and federal legislatures are the only legitimate government bodies empowered to make laws under the U.S. Constitution, which separates the powers delegated to each branch of government.

The role of the judiciary in this system of checks and balances is simply to interpret and apply the laws passed by legislatures, and decide cases based on politically neutral principles regardless of how insensitive the outcome may seem. Advocates of judicial self-restraint believe that judges, many of whom are appointed to the bench for life and are therefore not accountable to the electorate, upset the democratic authority of the people when they overturn laws passed by elected officials in order to achieve politically palatable results.

Many observers point to the two *Flag Salute* cases—*Minersville School District v. Gobitis*, 310 U.S. 586, 60 S. Ct. 1010, 84 L. Ed. 1375 (1940), and *West Virginia State Board of Education v. Barnette*, 319 U.S. 624, 63 S. Ct. 1178, 87 L. Ed. 1628 (1943)—as evidence that Frankfurter was a steadfast adherent to the philosophy of judicial self-restraint. Separated by only three years, the two cases presented the same issue: whether the government could compel schoolchildren who were Jehovah's Witnesses to salute the U.S. FLAG in violation of their religious beliefs, which prohibited them from engaging in any form of idolatry other than worshiping the Almighty. In both cases, Frankfurter resolved the issue in favor of the government. In the first case, only one justice dissented from Frankfurter's majority opinion, which upheld the expulsion of students who had refused to salute the flag. In the second case, Frankfurter was one of three justices dissenting from the Supreme Court's invalidation of a state law requiring all schoolchildren to salute the flag.

Writing for the majority in *Gobitis*, Frankfurter recognized the FIRST AMENDMENT right of members of religious minorities to exercise their religious beliefs free from government intimidation or coercion. But "the mere possession of religious convictions," Frankfurter cautioned, "does not relieve the citizen from discharge of political responsibilities." He reasoned, "National unity is the basis of national security," and exempting some schoolchildren from their duty to salute the flag "might introduce elements of difficulty into the school discipline . . . [and] cast doubts into the minds of other children." Because he saw no indication that the Framers of the First Amendment explicitly intended to protect the Jehovah's Witness children in these circumstances, Frankfurter concluded that the legislature, not the judiciary, must be permitted to select the "appropriate means" to establish "the binding tie of cohesive sentiment" that forms the "ultimate foundation of a free society."

In *Barnette*, the Supreme Court overruled *Gobitis* and held that the First Amendment prohibits the government from compelling schoolchildren to salute the U.S. flag when such activity violates their religious beliefs. Many observers attribute the shift in the Court's opinion to a decrease in the perceived need for patriotic obeisance: the outcome of World War II, which was in doubt when *Gobitis* was decided in 1940, was clearer when *Barnette* was decided in 1943, as the Allied powers moved closer to victory.

Yet Frankfurter, who had been excoriated in the newspapers and by his former colleagues in academia for his decision in *Gobitis*, remained unwavering in his commitment to judicial self-restraint. In a vituperative dissenting opinion to *Barnette*, Frankfurter wrote,

> One who belongs to the most vilified and persecuted minority in history is not likely to be insensible to the freedoms guaranteed by our Constitution. Were my purely personal attitude relevant I should wholeheartedly associate myself with the general libertarian views in the Court's opinion, representing as they do the thought and action of a lifetime. But as judges we are neither Jew nor Gentile, neither Catholic

nor agnostic. We owe equal attachment to the Constitution and are equally bound by our judicial obligations whether we derive our citizenship from the earliest or the latest immigrants to these shores. As a member of this Court I am not justified in writing my private notions of policy into the Constitution, no matter how deeply I may cherish them or how mischievous I may deem their disregard. . . . In the light of all the circumstances, including the history of this question in this Court, it would require more daring than I possess to deny that reasonable legislators could have taken the action which is before us for review.

Frankfurter was again assailed for his failure to protect political minorities, in *Korematsu v. United States*, 323 U.S. 214, 65 S. Ct. 193, 89 L. Ed. 194 (1944), where he concurred with the Court's majority opinion permitting the U.S. government to confine over one hundred thousand U.S. citizens of Japanese descent to "relocation centers" (essentially concentration camps) across the United States during World War II. These relocation centers were authorized pursuant to joint presidential and congressional action initiated as part of an effort to tighten internal security in the United States following the December 7, 1941, Japanese attack on Pearl Harbor. The Court's determination that these centers represented a "reasonably expedient" exercise of the government's power "to wage war successfully," Frankfurter wrote, "d[id] not carry with it [the justices] approval of that which Congress and the Executive did" because "[t]hat is their business, not ours."

Frankfurter retired from the Supreme Court in 1962, and died three years later on February 22, 1965, in Washington, D.C. His legal career spanned over 50 years. Perceived as an advocate of liberal causes at the beginning of his career, Frankfurter is now remembered as much for his conservative judicial style. Regardless of political labels, Frankfurter remains one of the most respected Supreme Court justices in U.S. history.

BIOGRAPHY

Benjamin Franklin

CROSS-REFERENCES

Brown v. Board of Education of Topeka Kansas; Japanese American Evacuation Cases; Judicial Review; *Korematsu v. United States;* Sacco (Nicola) and Vanzetti (Bartolomeo).

FRANKLIN, BENJAMIN As the only person to have signed the three most significant founding documents of the United States—the DECLARATION OF INDEPENDENCE (1776), the TREATY OF PARIS (1783), and the U.S. Constitution (1787)—Benjamin Franklin holds a revered place in the history of U.S. law. Through his great success as a newspaper publisher, journalist, writer, civic leader, scientist, politician, and diplomat, and as an inventor, Franklin became an international celebrity in his day and an icon of the American character to later generations.

Franklin's varied career had a lasting effect on U.S. law and politics. As a leading local figure, he established and shaped many of the fundamental institutions of Philadelphia and colonial Pennsylvania. Before the Revolutionary War (1775–83), Franklin served as envoy to Great Britain for several colonies. Though he first advocated reconciliation with Britain, he eventually supported the cause of American independence. He was assigned the task of securing an alliance with France during the war, and his political skill and prestige helped gain vital support for his young country as it fought the world's greatest military power. After the war, Franklin used his diplomatic ingenuity to negotiate a successful peace treaty with Britain. Franklin also helped persuade the Constitutional Convention of 1787 to reach important compromises on the particulars of the Constitution, and his support of that document greatly improved its chances of ratification.

Franklin was born January 17, 1706, in Boston, into a devout Puritan household. His only formal education consisted of two years of grammar school, after which he began work for his father, who was a tallow chandler, or candle maker. At age twelve, he was apprenticed to his half-brother, James Franklin, a printer and the founder of the *New England Courant*, the fourth newspaper established in the British colonies.

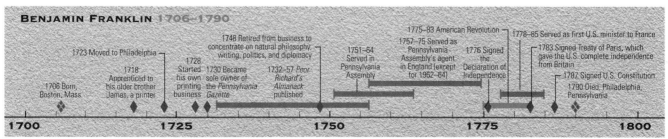

BENJAMIN FRANKLIN 1706–1790

1723 Moved to Philadelphia

1718 Apprenticed to his older brother James, a printer

1728 Started his own printing business

1730 Became sole owner of the *Pennsylvania Gazette*

1732–57 *Poor Richard's Almanack* published

1748 Retired from business to concentrate on natural philosophy, writing, politics, and diplomacy

1751–64 Served in Pennsylvania Assembly

1757–75 Served as Pennsylvania Assembly's agent in England (except for 1962–64)

1775–83 American Revolution

1776 Signed the Declaration of Independence

1778–85 Served as first U.S. minister to France

1783 Signed Treaty of Paris, which gave the U.S. complete independence from Britain

1787 Signed U.S. Constitution

1706 Born, Boston, Mass.

1790 Died, Philadelphia, Pennsylvania

1700   1725   1750   1775   1800

In his teenage years, Franklin began to improve himself by reading on his own, including the works of such authors as John Bunyan, Plutarch, Daniel Defoe, Cotton Mather, Joseph Addison, and JOHN LOCKE. Franklin employed his literary talents early, and wrote for the *Courant* articles satirizing Boston life and politics. He became a manager of the newspaper, but then abruptly moved to Philadelphia in 1723 after disagreements with his brother.

Franklin arrived in Philadelphia at age seventeen with only one Dutch dollar and a copper shilling in his pocket. He found work in a print shop and prospered enough to start his own printing business in 1728. In 1730, Franklin became sole owner of the *Pennsylvania Gazette*, which he transformed from a failing enterprise into a very influential newspaper. He also had success in other publishing ventures, including *Poor Richard's Almanack* (1732–57), an annual that presented practical information, satire, proverbs, and aphorisms. In 1730, Franklin married Deborah Read, with whom he had two children. He also had two illegitimate children, one of whom, William Franklin, later became governor of New Jersey.

In 1727, still a rising young businessman, Franklin formed a club of tradesmen called the Junto, which met each week for discussion. This group became highly influential in the life of Philadelphia and Pennsylvania. Under his leadership, it founded a circulating library, the first of its kind in the colonies, in Philadelphia in 1731; the American Philosophical Society in 1743; a city hospital in 1751; and an academy that developed into the University of Pennsylvania. Franklin led the group in making many other civic improvements as well.

In 1748, now wealthy from his printing and publishing interests, Franklin retired from business. He devoted the rest of his life to natural philosophy, writing, politics, and diplomacy. In the area of natural philosophy, or science, Franklin's ingenuity and curiosity gained him world renown as both an inventor and a theoretician. He designed an improved stove, later dubbed the Franklin stove, that was widely used, as well as bifocal glasses and a new type of clock. He began to study electricity in 1746. His ideas and experiments on this subject—including the famous experiment that involved a kite with a metal key attached to it—identified the electrical nature of lightning. His work with electricity gained him many honorary degrees, including membership in the Royal Society in 1756 and in the French Academy of Sciences in 1772. He also developed a theory of heat ab-

sorption and was among the first to describe the Gulf Stream ocean current.

Franklin's study of natural philosophy was interrupted by an involvement in politics and diplomacy that ultimately dominated the last part of his life. In Pennsylvania, he was a member of the Quaker party, which sought to democratize the colony's politics and wrest power from its original founders, the Penn family. He served as a representative to the Pennsylvania Assembly from 1751 to 1764. In 1754, he represented Pennsylvania at the Albany Congress, which had been called to unite the colonies in a war against the French and Indians. There, he unsuccessfully presented the Plan of Union, which would have established partial self-government for the colonies. The British did not approve of Franklin's plan because they felt it gave too much power to the colonies, and the colonial assemblies rejected it because they felt it gave the British monarch too much power. Franklin also shared with another person the office of deputy postmaster for the colonies, from 1753 to 1774. In this office, he did a great deal to increase the frequency and efficiency of mail delivery.

Franklin began a long and successful diplomatic career when he went to England in 1757 as the agent of the Pennsylvania Assembly. He remained in Britain through 1762 and met many leading figures of British society, including the philosopher DAVID HUME and the author Dr. Samuel Johnson. After spending two more years in Pennsylvania, he returned to England in 1764 to serve again as the Pennsylvania Assembly's agent, and remained in Britain as an agent for various colonies in turn, until 1775. During his years abroad, he witnessed firsthand the growing rift between Britain and the colonies.

In the controversy over the 1765 STAMP ACT, Franklin emerged as the American colonies' chief spokesperson and defender. The act imposed a tax on publications and papers and provoked an outrage in the colonies. As the first of a series of major disputes between the colonies and Britain, the Stamp Act catalyzed the American colonies' desire for independence and united them in opposition to Britain. Franklin opposed the Stamp Act before Britain's House of Commons. His articulate answers before Parliament were published widely and earned him much admiration in America and abroad. Franklin also opposed such controversial acts of Parliament as the TOWNSHEND ACTS (1767) and the Tea Act (1773). Although he originally worked for reconciliation with Britain, Franklin

"THOSE WHO WOULD GIVE UP ESSENTIAL LIBERTY, TO PURCHASE A LITTLE TEMPORARY SAFETY, DESERVE NEITHER LIBERTY OR SAFETY."

left for America in March 1775 convinced of the need for American independence.

Immediately upon his return to Philadelphia, Franklin was chosen to be a member of the Second Continental Congress. He again sketched a plan of union for the colonies. He also was one of a committee of five, including JOHN ADAMS and THOMAS JEFFERSON, appointed in 1776 to draft the Declaration of Independence, the document that formally announced the colonies' break from Britain. Franklin signed the document, thereby becoming a revolutionary at age seventy. Soon after, the CONTINENTAL CONGRESS sent Franklin and two others to negotiate a critical treaty with France. Before he left, the wealthy Franklin also loaned the struggling Congress several thousand pounds.

Franklin was greeted as a hero in France, where translations of his scientific and literary works had gained him much admiration. He was treated by all classes of society as a great oracle, and his image was reproduced widely in prints, medallions, jewelry, and snuffboxes. "His reputation in Europe," Adams commented, "was more universal than that of Leibnitz or Newton, Frederick or Voltaire, and his character more beloved and esteemed than any or all of them."

During the first years of the Revolutionary War, Franklin worked in France to secure war supplies and build credibility with the French, who were reluctant at first to cast their lot with an untested new country. France and the United States finally signed an alliance in 1778, after which Franklin became the first U.S. minister to France. Fulfilling the myriad duties of that office with great diplomatic skill, he continued to gain crucial supplies and money for the U.S. cause. In 1781, after defeat at the Battle of Yorktown had persuaded the British to give up the war, Franklin participated in delicate peace talks with Britain. He had much to do with the favorable terms of peace set forth in the Treaty of Paris, which finally gave the United States complete independence from Britain.

Franklin returned to the United States in 1785. After serving three years as president of the Executive Council of Pennsylvania, he was chosen as a member of the Constitutional Convention, which met in Philadelphia in 1787. Now eighty-one, he attended the convention regularly for over four months and served as unofficial host to the delegates. Although Franklin's calls for a single national legislative chamber and for an executive board (as opposed to a president) were not honored, his arguments helped the convention reach the important compromises that were necessary to secure agreement on the document. In particular, Franklin called for mutual compromise on the sticky issue of the number of representatives to be allotted to each state in the national legislature. Of this disagreement, which pitted small states against large states, Franklin commented,

> If a property representation takes place, the small states contend that their liberties will be in danger. If an equality of votes is to be put in its place, the large states say their money will be in danger. When a broad table is to be made, and the edges of the planks do not fit, the artist takes a little from both, and makes a good joint.

Later, Franklin urged other members of the convention to approve the final version of the Constitution. "I consent, Sir, to this Constitution," he declared to the convention, "because I expect no better, and because I am not sure that it is not the best. The Opinions I have had of its Errors, I sacrifice to the Public Good." In the following battle for ratification of the Constitution, Franklin used his considerable reputation to promote its success.

For the last few years of his life, Franklin retired to Philadelphia. In his last public act, he signed a memorial to Congress for the abolition of SLAVERY. He died in Philadelphia on April 17, 1790, at the age of eighty-four. Among his many lasting literary works is his autobiography.

See also CONSTITUTION OF THE UNITED STATES.

FRAUD 📖 A false representation of a matter of fact—whether by words or by conduct, by false or misleading ALLEGATIONS, or by concealment of what should have been disclosed—that deceives and is intended to deceive another so that the individual will act upon it to her or his legal injury. 📖

Fraud is commonly understood as dishonesty calculated for advantage. A person who is dishonest may be called a fraud. In the U.S. legal system, fraud is a specific offense with certain features.

Fraud is most common in the buying or selling of property, including REAL ESTATE, PERSONAL PROPERTY, and intangible property, such as STOCKS, BONDS, and COPYRIGHTS. State and federal statutes criminalize fraud, but not all cases rise to the level of criminality. PROSECUTORS have discretion in determining which cases to pursue. Victims may also seek redress in civil court.

Fraud must be proved by showing that the defendant's actions involved five separate elements: (1) a false statement of a MATERIAL fact,

(2) knowledge on the part of the defendant that the statement is untrue, (3) intent on the part of the defendant to deceive the alleged victim, (4) justifiable reliance by the alleged victim on the statement, and (5) injury to the alleged victim as a result.

These elements contain nuances that are not all easily proved. First, not all false statements are fraudulent. To be fraudulent, a false statement must relate to a material fact. It should also substantially affect a person's decision to enter into a contract or pursue a certain course of action. A false statement of fact that does not bear on the disputed transaction will not be considered fraudulent.

Second, the defendant must know that the statement is untrue. A statement of fact that is simply mistaken is not fraudulent. To be fraudulent, a false statement must be made with an intent to deceive the victim. This is perhaps the easiest element to prove, once falsity and materiality are proved, because most material false statements are designed to mislead.

Third, the false statement must be made with the intent to deprive the victim of some legal right.

Fourth, the victim's reliance on the false statement must be REASONABLE. Reliance on a patently absurd false statement generally will not give rise to fraud; however, people who are especially gullible, superstitious, or ignorant or who are illiterate may recover damages for fraud if the defendant knew and took advantage of their condition.

Finally, the false statement must cause the victim some injury that leaves her or him in a worse position than she or he was in before the fraud.

A statement of belief is not a statement of fact and thus is not fraudulent. PUFFING, or the expression of a glowing opinion by a seller, is likewise not fraudulent. For example, a car dealer may represent that a particular vehicle is "the finest in the lot." Although the statement may not be true, it is not a statement of fact, and a reasonable buyer would not be justified in relying on it.

The relationship between parties can make a difference in determining whether a statement is fraudulent. A misleading statement is more likely to be fraudulent when one party has superior knowledge in a transaction, and knows that the other is relying on that knowledge, than when the two parties possess equal knowledge. For example, if the seller of a car with a bad engine tells the buyer the car is in excellent running condition, a court is more likely to find fraud if the seller is an auto mechanic as opposed to a sales trainee. Misleading statements are most likely to be fraudulent where one party exploits a position of trust and confidence, or a FIDUCIARY relationship. Fiduciary relationships include those between ATTORNEYS and clients, PHYSICIANS and patients, stockbrokers and clients, and the officers and partners of a CORPORATION and its stockholders.

A statement need not be affirmative to be fraudulent. When a person has a duty to speak, silence may be treated as a false statement. This can arise if a party who has knowledge of a fact fails to disclose it to another party who is justified in assuming its nonexistence. For example, if a real estate agent fails to disclose that a home is built on a toxic waste dump, the omission may be regarded as a fraudulent statement. Even if the agent does not know of the dump, the omission may be considered fraudulent. This is constructive fraud, and it is usually inferred when a party is a fiduciary and has a duty to know of, and disclose, particular facts.

Fraud is an independent criminal offense, but it also appears in different contexts as the means used to gain a legal advantage or accomplish a specific crime. For example, it is fraud for a person to make a false statement on a LICENSE application in order to engage in the regulated activity. A person who did so would not be convicted of fraud. Rather, fraud would simply describe the method used to break the law or regulation requiring the license.

Fraud resembles THEFT in that both involve some form of illegal taking, but the two should not be confused. Fraud requires an additional element of FALSE PRETENSES created to induce a victim to turn over property, services, or money. Theft, by contrast, requires only the unauthorized taking of another's property with the intent to permanently deprive the other of the

Dan Rostenkowski, a representative of Illinois in the U.S. House, was indicated on counts of mail and wire fraud in 1994.

property. Because fraud involves more planning than does theft, it is punished more severely.

Federal and state criminal statutes provide for the punishment of persons convicted of fraudulent activity. Interstate fraud and fraud on the federal government are singled out for federal prosecution. The most common federal fraud charges are for mail and wire fraud. Mail and wire fraud statutes criminalize the use of the mails or interstate wires to create or further a scheme to defraud (18 U.S.C.A. §§ 1341, 1342).

Tax fraud against the federal government consists of the willful attempt to evade or defeat the payment of taxes due and owing (I.R.C. § 7201). Depending on the defendant's intent, tax fraud results in either civil penalties or criminal punishment. Civil penalties can reach an amount equal to 75 percent of the underpayment. Criminal punishment includes fines and imprisonment. The degree of intent necessary to maintain criminal charges for tax fraud is determined on a case-by-case basis by the Internal Revenue Service and federal prosecutors.

There are other federal fraud laws. For example, the fraudulent registration of ALIENS is punishable as a MISDEMEANOR under federal law (8 U.S.C.A. § 1306). The "victim" in such a fraud is the U.S. government. Fraud violations of securities laws are also subject to federal prosecution (15 U.S.C.A. § 78(u)), as are fraudulent bank transactions (18 U.S.C.A. §§ 104 et seq.).

The Federal Sentencing Guidelines recommend consideration of the intended victims of fraud in the sentencing of fraud defendants. The guidelines urge an upward departure from standard sentences if the intended victims are especially vulnerable. For example, if a defendant markets an ineffective cancer cure, that scheme, if found to be fraudulent, would warrant more punishment than a scheme that targets persons generally and coincidentally happens to injure a vulnerable person. Federal courts may require persons convicted of fraud to give notice and an explanation of the conviction to the victims of the fraud (18 U.S.C.A. § 3555).

All states maintain a general criminal statute designed to punish fraud. In Arizona, the statute is called the fraudulent scheme and artifice statute. It reads, in pertinent part, that "[a]ny person who, pursuant to a scheme or artifice to defraud, knowingly obtains any benefit by means of false or fraudulent pretenses, representations, promises or material omissions" is guilty of a felony (Ariz. Rev. Stat. Ann. § 13-2310(A)).

States further criminalize fraud in a variety of settings, including trade and commerce, securities, taxes, real estate, gambling, insurance, government benefits, and credit. In Hawaii, for example, fraud on a state tax return is a FELONY warranting a fine of up to $100,000 or three years of imprisonment, or both, and a fraudulent corporate tax return is punished with a fine of $500,000 (Haw. Rev. Stat. § 231-36). Other fraud felonies include fraud in the manufacture or distribution of a controlled substance (§ 329-42) and fraud in government ELECTIONS (§ 19-4). Fraud in the application for and receipt of public assistance benefits is punished according to the illegal gain: fraud in obtaining over $20,000 in food coupons is a class B felony; fraud in obtaining over $300 in food coupons is a class C felony; and all other public assistance fraud is a misdemeanor (§ 346-34). Alteration of a measurement device is fraud and is punished as a misdemeanor (§ 486-136).

In civil court, the remedy for fraud can vary. In most states, a plaintiff may recover "the benefit of the bargain." This is a measure of the difference between the represented value and the actual value of the transaction. In some states, a plaintiff may recover as actual DAMAGES only the value of the property lost in the fraudulent transaction. All states allow a plaintiff to seek PUNITIVE DAMAGES in addition to actual damages. This right is exercised most commonly in cases where the fraud is extremely dangerous or costly. Where the fraud is contractual, a plaintiff may choose to cancel, or rescind, the contract. A court order of RESCISSION returns all property and restores the parties to their precontract status.

Fraud is also penalized by ADMINISTRATIVE AGENCIES and professional organizations that seek to regulate certain activities. Under state statutes, a professional may lose a license to work if the license was obtained with a false statement.

FRAUDULENT 📖 The description of a willful act commenced with the specific intent to deceive or cheat, in order to cause some financial detriment to another and to engender personal financial gain. 📖

FRAUDULENT CONVEYANCE 📖 A TRANSFER of PROPERTY that is made to swindle, hinder, or delay a CREDITOR, or to put such property beyond his or her reach. 📖

For example, a man transfers his bank account to a relative by putting the account in the relative's name. He informs the relative that he has not relinquished ownership of the funds, but merely wants to isolate the money from the reach of his creditors. This is a fraudulent conveyance that can be set aside by the court at the request of the defrauded creditor.

Every kind of property that can be used for the payment of debts can be the subject of a fraudulent conveyance and reclaimed by the creditors in a proper case. By statute many states exempt personal items—such as clothing, kitchen appliances, and household furniture—from being reached by creditors to satisfy DEBTS.

Any creditor who can establish that he or she has been harmed by the fraudulent conveyance can attack it. The DEBTOR must have owed the creditor a valid and enforceable debt at the time the conveyance was made. A creditor who seeks to set aside a fraudulent conveyance must comply with the requirements in his or her JURISDIC-TION. Generally, the individual must acquire a LIEN—a right or claim—or a JUDGMENT—a court decision—against the property. A judgment is usually required to show with certainty the existence of a valid and enforceable debt, but it can be dispensed with, depending upon the particular circumstances of the case. In many jurisdictions, a court will not set aside the conveyance if the debtor owns property, other than that which has been fraudulently con-veyed, that is sufficient to pay the debt.

Fraudulent Intent Whether a transac-tion constitutes a fraudulent conveyance de-pends upon the existence of the intent to de-fraud that must exist at the time that the challenged transfer was made. The mere fact that a person is in debt does not make a conveyance of his or her property for a valuable CONSIDERATION fraudulent unless it is made with an intent to cheat the person's creditors. Suspi-cious circumstances surrounding the transfer of property by a debtor can justify an inference of fraud. If a debtor transfers his or her property to another for a grossly inadequate consider-ation in anticipation of, or during, the course of a lawsuit by creditors to enforce the payment of debts, the transfer can be set aside by the court. If the conduct of a sale or transfer of a debtor's property is done in the usual manner of doing business, the court can scrutinize the transac-tion to determine whether it was made with an intent to defraud. The failure to record a con-veyance, such as a DEED to land, indicates the existence of FRAUD, which when coupled with other suspicious circumstances can justify a determination that the conveyance was fraudu-lent. If a debtor retains possession of personal property after it has been sold to another, this is evidence of fraud, which can lead to the sale being set aside as a fraudulent conveyance.

Consideration A valuable consideration is necessary to support a conveyance made by a debtor against the challenge of his or her credi-tors. The payment of money or the surrender of a legal right, such as relinquishing a right to institute a lawsuit to enforce a court order, is usually regarded as valuable consideration. Where a person pays a valuable consideration for a transfer of a debtor's property without knowledge of the debtor's fraudulent intent, the creditors cannot have that transfer set aside.

Where a debtor is insolvent—his or her debts exceed assets—at the time he or she makes a voluntary conveyance to someone without re-ceiving anything in return, this is usually treated as a fraudulent conveyance. If a volun-tary conveyance renders a debtor insolvent or leaves the debtor without the means of paying the debts existing at the time of the conveyance, it is fraudulent and without any legal effect, regardless of the intent of the parties.

Family Relationships A conveyance by one spouse to the other based upon a fictitious or nominal consideration is generally treated as fraudulent if it is made to defeat the spouse's creditor's claims. However, if the one spouse pays the other the MARKET VALUE of the property, the transfer is valid and will not be set aside as a fraudulent conveyance. Where a conveyance between spouses is made in consideration of love and affection, it is voluntary and fraudulent if it renders the debtor spouse unable to pay existing personal debts.

Property purchased in the name of one spouse, for example the wife, but paid for with the funds of the other, the husband, can be challenged by the husband's existing creditors. A BONA FIDE debt due by one spouse to the other, which can be established by showing that the spouses dealt with each other as debtor and creditor, is sufficient consideration to support a conveyance of property in payment of a debt as long as the debt bears a reasonable proportion to the value of the property conveyed.

Creditors will lose their attack upon a con-veyance by a parent to his or her child, or between any family members, for valuable con-sideration unless the transfer is for a grossly inadequate consideration and is surrounded by other circumstances that establish fraud.

Preferences A debtor, although insolvent or in failing financial circumstances, can prefer one or more of his or her creditors in the payment of debts by paying these persons first, provided no fraudulent intent exists to cheat the other creditors. The debtor's motives for a PREFERENCE among the creditors are immaterial unless they establish the fraudulent intent of the debtor. The property transferred must not un-reasonably exceed the amount of the claim, and the transaction must not provide for special benefits to the creditor. A debtor can give a preference to his or her creditors because as absolute owner of his or her PERSONAL PROPERTY, the debtor can do with it as he or she pleases, so long as the law is not violated. (By law certain debts—such as those owed to the United States, which are given preference by statute, or debts created by SECURED TRANSACTIONS—must be satisfied before any preferred creditors.) The existence of a family relationship, such as husband and wife, between the debtor and preferred creditor does not in itself affect the validity of a preference. The relationship between the parties is just one factor to be considered, along with other circumstances, and is given commensurate weight in determining the GOOD FAITH of the transaction. A transaction involving a family relationship, however, will be more closely examined than if it had taken place between strangers.

Remedies Once a conveyance is declared VOID in fraud of creditors, the court can do full justice by ordering a sale of the property under its own direction. The proceeds are used to pay off the COSTS of the lawsuit and the complaining creditors who brought their claims before the court. A debtor who has fraudulently transferred property to cheat his or her creditors might also be subject to statutory penalties and criminal prosecution, depending upon the law in the debtor's home state.

Bankruptcy In the context of BANKRUPTCY law, a fraudulent conveyance can be the basis for an objection to DISCHARGE. Federal law denies a discharge to a debtor who transfers property with intent to hinder, delay, or defraud within the twelve months immediately prior to the filing of the bankruptcy petition or after the filing of bankruptcy petition.

FREEDOM OF ASSOCIATION

The right to associate with others for the purpose of engaging in constitutionally protected activities.

The right to associate is not an independent constitutional right but is derived from and dependent on the FIRST AMENDMENT guarantees of FREEDOM OF SPEECH and expression. It is protected only to the extent that it is asserted in conjunction with a First Amendment right. However, some legal scholars maintain that freedom of association is more fundamental than the rights enumerated in the Constitution because without it those other rights have little meaning.

One early case to recognize freedom of association was *NAACP v. Alabama ex rel. Patterson*, 357 U.S. 449, 78 S. Ct. 1163, 2 L. Ed. 2d 1488 (1958). In *Patterson*, the Supreme Court held that a lower court's order compelling the NAACP to disclose records containing the names and addresses of its Alabama members violated the group's right to associate freely. The Court recognized freedom of association as an adjunct to the NAACP's free speech rights and held that the freedom to associate for the advancement of beliefs and ideas is inseparable from the freedom of speech.

General types of association unrelated to First Amendment rights are not protected by the Constitution. For instance, in *City of Dallas v. Stanglin*, 490 U.S. 19, 109 S. Ct. 1591, 104 L. Ed. 2d 18 (1989), the Court held that a city ordinance limiting adult entrance into teenage dance halls did not violate the associational rights of either the adults or the MINORS. The association of adults and minors in a social setting does not fall within the purview of any rights protected by the First Amendment and therefore is not a constitutionally protected activity.

The activities of groups organized to pursue economic activity are sometimes protected if the individuals have come together to advance beliefs or ideas. Generally, the Court's decisions in this area depend on whether the economic activities are found to be sufficiently expressive to invoke First Amendment protection. In *NAACP v. Claiborne Hardware Co.*, 458 U.S. 886, 102 S. Ct. 3409, 73 L. Ed. 2d 1215 (1982), the NAACP was held not liable for economic damage suffered by merchants in a boycott it had sponsored. The BOYCOTT was a legal, nonviolent action against white merchants to pressure them to comply with CIVIL RIGHTS laws. The Court found that though clearly an economic activity, it was primarily designed to advance the NAACP's political beliefs in civil rights. This added purpose gave the boycott an expressive character sufficient to warrant First Amendment protection. On the other hand, an economic boycott that is not intended to express political ideas or beliefs is not protected under the First Amendment. In *FTC v. Superior Court Trial Lawyers Ass'n*, 493 U.S. 411, 110 S. Ct. 768, 107 L. Ed. 2d 851 (1990), the Court found that a boycott organized by trial lawyers in an effort to secure increased compensation for their representation of indigent clients was a fundamentally economic activity that did not rise to the level of expressive conduct contemplated by the First Amendment.

During the 1940s and 1950s, a number of cases tested the constitutionality of the Alien Registration Act (also known as the SMITH ACT) (18 U.S.C.A. § 2385), which makes it a crime to conspire to overthrow the government or promote doctrines that advocate sedition. The act was sometimes used to prosecute individuals merely for their membership in organizations suspected of promoting insurrection. The general principle that evolved from these cases is that an individual cannot be punished for membership in an organization that is committed to illegal conduct, unless he or she is an active member with knowledge of the organization's illegal objectives and specific intent to further those objectives. (See *Noto v. United States*, 367 U.S. 290, 81 S. Ct. 1517, 6 L. Ed. 2d 836 [1961]; *Scales v. United States*, 367 U.S. 203, 81 S. Ct. 1469, 6 L. Ed. 2d 782 [1961]). This principle has also been applied to invalidate blanket prohibitions on government employment or membership in organizations such as a state bar because of an individual's past associations. The government may inquire into past associations, but must limit the inquiry to the person's actual knowledge of illegal activity and intent to further it. (See *Schware v. Board of Bar Examiners*, 353 U.S. 232, 77 S. Ct. 752, 1 L. Ed. 2d 796 [1957]; *United States v. Robel*, 389 U.S. 258, 88 S. Ct. 419, 19 L. Ed. 2d 508 [1967]).

The outcome of cases challenging indirect government regulation of freedom of association has been somewhat inconsistent. In general, the Court has balanced the individual's associational interests against the state's interests. In the early twentieth century, the Supreme Court held that a Ku Klux Klan membership list had to be disclosed because the members' freedom of association was subordinate to the state's interest in controlling the Klan's illegal activities (*New York ex rel. Bryant v. Zimmerman*, 278 U.S. 63, 49 S. Ct. 61, 73 L. Ed. 184 [1928]). Similarly, in 1961 the Court upheld a forced disclosure of the Communist party's membership because of the perceived dangers posed by the party's activities (*Communist Party of the United States v. Subversive Activities Control Board*, 367 U.S. 1, 81 S. Ct. 1357, 6 L. Ed. 2d 625 [1961]). Conversely, in 1958, in *Patterson*, the Court had struck down the state's order that the NAACP disclose its membership, distinguishing *Bryant* on the grounds that the Klan was involved in illegal activities, whereas the NAACP was not. A similar rationale was applied in *Communist Party*. In the late twentieth century, the Court moved away from the balancing approach toward a STRICT SCRUTINY standard that made it more difficult for the government to impinge indirectly on freedom of association.

In general, freedom of association includes the right to be free from compelled association. In *Wooley v. Maynard*, 430 U.S. 705, 97 S. Ct. 1428, 51 L. Ed. 2d 752 (1977), and *Abood v. Detroit Board of Education*, 431 U.S. 209, 97 S. Ct. 1782, 52 L. Ed. 2d 261 (1977), the Court held that freedom of association is unconstitutionally burdened where the state requires an individual to support or espouse ideals or beliefs with which he or she disagrees. Similarly, in *Keller v. State Bar*, 496 U.S. 1, 110 S. Ct. 2228, 110 L. Ed. 2d 1 (1990), the Court held that mandatory state bar membership dues could not be used to further ideological causes with which some members might disagree, unless the state could show that the expenditures were incurred for the purpose of regulating the legal profession or improving the quality of legal service.

When the right to be free from compelled association is exercised on the basis of race, gender, religion, or sexual orientation, competing constitutional rights clash. Such was the dilemma faced by the Court in *Roberts v. United States Jaycees*, 468 U.S. 609, 104 S. Ct. 3244, 82 L. Ed. 2d 462 (1984). The Jaycees is a national organization whose bylaws limited full membership to men age eighteen to thirty-five. When a group of women challenged their exclusion, this policy was held unconstitutional. The Court found that the state's interest in eliminating gender discrimination outweighed the male Jaycees' interest in freedom from compelled association. Although the Court reiterated its position that freedom of association is fundamental, it also stated that such freedom is not absolute: "Infringements on that right may be justified by regulations adopted to serve compelling state interests, unrelated to the suppression of ideas, that cannot be achieved through means significantly less restrictive of associational freedoms."

The Court has also recognized a constitutional right to freedom of intimate association, the fundamental human right to create and maintain intimate human relationships. Freedom of intimate association is generally included within the right of PRIVACY as enunciated in cases such as *Griswold v. Connecticut*, 381 U.S. 479, 85 S. Ct. 1678, 14 L. Ed. 2d 510 (1965), invalidating a state statute forbidding use of contraception; *Roe v. Wade*, 410 U.S. 113, 93 S. Ct. 705, 35 L. Ed. 2d 147 (1973), holding a Texas law criminalizing abortion unconstitutional; and *Carey v. Population Services International*, 431 U.S. 678, 97 S. Ct. 2010, 52 L. Ed. 2d 675 (1977), holding limits on distribution of contraceptives and contraceptive information unconstitutional.

FREEDOM OF INFORMATION ACT 📖 A

federal law (5 U.S.C.A. § 552 et seq.) providing for the disclosure of information held by ADMIN- ISTRATIVE AGENCIES to the public, unless the documents requested fall into one of the specific exemptions set forth in the statute. 📖

The Freedom of Information Act (FOIA) was implemented to prevent federal agencies from abusing their discretionary powers by forcing them to make certain information about their work available to the public. The law was

A letter requesting information under the Freedom of Information Act (FOIA) should be directed to the head of the agency that maintains the documents you want or to the agency's FOIA officer. The agency's address can be found in *The United States Government Manual* or the *Congressional Directory*. Write "Freedom of Information Request" on the bottom left-hand corner of the envelope.

Identify the records you want as accurately as possible. Although you are not required to specify a document by name or title, your request must "reasonably describe" the information sought. The more specific and limited the request, the greater the likelihood that it will be processed expeditiously. You are not required to demonstrate a need or even a reason for wanting to see the information, but in some instances the probability of obtaining the documents you desire may be enhanced by explaining your reasons for requesting them.

Agency Head or FOIA Officer
Title
Name of Agency
Address of Agency
City, State, zip

Re: Freedom of Information Act Request.

Dear _____:

Under the provisions of the Freedom of Information Act, 5 U.S.C. 552, I am requesting access to (identify the records as clearly and specifically as possible).

If there are any fees for searching for, or copying, the records I have requested, please inform me before you fill the request. (Or: . . . please supply the records without informing me if the fees do not exceed $_____.)

[Optional] I am requesting this information (state the reason for your request if you think it will assist you in obtaining the information.)

[Optional] As you know, the act permits you to reduce or waive fees when the release of the information is considered as "primarily benefiting the public." I believe that this request fits that category and I therefore ask that you waive any fees.

If all or any part of this request is denied, please cite the specific exemption(s) that you think justifies your refusal to release the information, and inform me of the appeal procedures available to me under the law.

I would appreciate your handling this request as quickly as possible, and I look forward to hearing from you within 10 days, as the law stipulates.

Sincerely,

Signature
Name
Address
City, State, zip

[*continued on page 102*]

Source: U.S. Congress. House. Committee on Government Operations. *A Citizen's Guide on How to Use the Freedom of Information Act and the Privacy Act Requesting Government Documents,* 95th Congress, 1st sess. (1977).

A sample letter requesting information under the Freedom of Information Act

regarded as a great milestone because it guarantees the right of people to learn about the internal workings of their government. Almost all agencies of the EXECUTIVE BRANCH of the federal government have issued REGULATIONS implementing the FOIA. These regulations inform the public where certain types of information are kept, how the information may be obtained on request, and what appeals are available if a member of the public is denied requested information.

A person requesting information under the FOIA must generally send a letter to the head of the agency maintaining the documents that are sought, identifying the records as clearly as possible. If the request for information is denied, a letter of appeal may be filed, citing, if possible, court rulings explaining why the agency's decision to withhold the information is inappropriate. If the agency denies the appeal, the individual may seek judicial review of the agency's action.

Exemptions to the FOIA are designed to allow an agency to withhold records in situations where disclosure would cause harm to an important government function or private in-

A sample letter appealing a denial of a request for information under the Freedom of Information Act (continued)

If your request for information is denied, you should send a letter of appeal to the person or office specified in the agency's reply. Include a copy of the rejection letter along with a copy of your original request.

Although it is not necessary, it will strengthen your appeal if you are able to cite court rulings concerning why the agency's use of a particular exemption to withhold information is inappropriate. Depending upon your need for the information, you might want to consult a lawyer to help you with this.

Most agency regulations require that appeals be made within thirty days after the individual has been notified that his or her request has been denied. The agency is required to respond to an appeal within twenty working days after receiving it. However, if the initial request was answered within a ten-day time period, an extension of up to ten working days may be granted.

If the agency denies your appeal in whole or in part, it must inform you of your right to seek judicial review. If you have not received a reply after twenty working days from the time of the agency's receipt of your appeal, you may take your case to court.

Name of Agency Official
Title
Name of Agency
Address of Agency
City, State, zip
Re: Freedom of Information Act Appeal.

Dear _____:
    This is to appeal the denial of my request for information pursuant to the Freedom of Information Act, 5 U.S.C. 522.
    On _____ (date), I received a letter from _____ (individual's name) of your agency denying my request for access to _____ (description of the information sought). I am enclosing a copy of this denial along with a copy of my original request. I trust that upon examination of these communications you will conclude that the information I am seeking should be disclosed.
    As provided for in the Act, I will expect to receive a reply within 20 working days.
    [Optional] If you decide not to release the requested information, I plan to take this matter to court.

                                                    Sincerely,

                                                    Signature
                                                    Name
                                                    Address
                                                    City, State, zip

terest. The FOIA explicitly exempts from disclosure a variety of different types of information, including materials that have been classified as secret in the interest of national defense or foreign policy; information related solely to the internal personnel rules and practices of an agency; TRADE SECRETS and commercial or financial information; and personnel and medical files and similar files for which disclosure would constitute an unwarranted invasion of personal PRIVACY (5 U.S.C.A. § 552(b)). Although the exemptions appear to run counter to the public interest in gaining access to information, they serve certain important national policy interests, including those of national defense, foreign policy, civilian cooperation with law enforcement, and the efficient operation of government agencies. Courts have held that, consistent with the purpose of the FOIA, these exemptions must be narrowly construed.

Most litigation under the FOIA has occurred when an agency refuses to release government information, citing one or more of the exemptions set forth in the statute. In *United States Department of Justice v. Landano*, 508 U.S. 165, 113 S. Ct. 2014, 124 L. Ed. 2d 84 (1993), for example, the U.S. Supreme Court held that the FEDERAL BUREAU OF INVESTIGATION (FBI) does not have a blanket exemption under the FOIA from disclosing the identity of FBI informants. Instead, the Court ruled, the bureau must justify, on a case-by-case basis, why informants' identities must not be disclosed. Thus, the Court performed the difficult task of reconciling two important but opposing interests: the FOIA policy of favoring the fullest disclosure possible, versus the interest of law enforcement agencies in protecting their cooperative sources. Writing for the Court, Justice SANDRA DAY O'CONNOR stated, "Although we recognize that confidentiality often will be important to the FBI's investigative efforts, we cannot say that the government's sweeping presumption comports with common sense and probability." Instead, she maintained, the agency must be able to demonstrate that it was reasonable to infer under the circumstances that the information had been provided with an expectation of confidentiality.

Since the FOIA was enacted in 1966, over a half million requests for information have been filed with government agencies. Although initially envisioned as a means to make the federal government more accessible to citizens, the FOIA has been used extensively by reporters and news-gathering agencies, corporations, and even foreign governments.

When the act was first passed, most government data were stored primarily on paper, microfilm, and microfiche. With the advent of the computer age, more information is available to more people than ever before, creating the need for new guidelines in disseminating government information. In particular, computer technology raises questions about what constitutes a reasonable request for information under the act and about how information should be disclosed. The act does not mention computerized records, but the Computer Security Act of 1987 (Act of Jan. 8, 1988, Pub. L. No. 100-235, 101 Stat. 1724 [1988]) prohibits agencies from withholding computerized records from the public if the records would be available under the FOIA as paper documents. Nevertheless, some groups seeking government information have been concerned that government agencies may release large volumes of paper records when more manageable and convenient computer records may be available.

FREEDOM OF SPEECH 📖 The right, guaranteed by the FIRST AMENDMENT to the U.S. Constitution, to express beliefs and ideas without unwarranted government restriction. 📖

Democracies have long grappled with the issue of what limits, if any, to place on the expression of ideas and beliefs. The dilemma dates back at least to ancient Greece, when the Athenians, who cherished individual freedom, nevertheless prosecuted Socrates for his teachings, claiming they corrupted young people and insulted the gods.

The Framers of the Constitution guaranteed freedom of speech and expression to the citizens of the United States with the First Amendment, which reads, in part, "Congress shall make no law ... abridging the freedom of speech." Almost since the adoption of the Bill of Rights, however, the judiciary has struggled to define speech and expression and the extent to which freedom of speech should be protected. Some, like Justice HUGO L. BLACK, have believed that freedom of speech is absolute. But most jurists, along with most U.S. citizens, agree with Justice OLIVER WENDELL HOLMES, JR., who felt that the Constitution allows some restrictions on speech under certain circumstances. To illustrate this point, Holmes wrote, "The most stringent protection of free speech would not protect a man in falsely shouting fire in a theater and causing a panic" (*Schenck v. United States*, 249 U.S. 47, 39 S. Ct. 247, 63 L. Ed. 470 [1919]).

During the two centuries since the adoption of the First Amendment, the Supreme Court has held that some types of speech or expression may be regulated. At the same time, the

Court has granted protection to some areas of expression that were clearly not contemplated by the Framers.

Public Forum Regulation When the government attempts to regulate the exercise of speech rights in traditional public forums, such as parks or public sidewalks, the Court examines whether the regulation restricts the content of the speech or merely regulates the time, place, and manner in which the speech is delivered.

If the law regulates the content of the expression, it must serve a compelling state interest and must be narrowly written to achieve that interest (*Perry Education Ass'n v. Perry Local Educators' Ass'n*, 460 U.S. 37, 103 S. Ct. 948, 74 L. Ed. 2d 794 [1983]). Restrictions on speech in a public forum may also be upheld if the expressive activity being regulated is a type that is not entitled to full First Amendment protection, such as OBSCENITY.

Laws that regulate the time, place, and manner, but not content, of speech in a public forum receive less scrutiny by the Court than do laws that restrict the content of expression. These so-called content-neutral laws are permissible if they serve a significant government interest and allow ample alternative channels of communication (see *Perry*). It is not necessary that a content-neutral law be the least restrictive alternative, only that the government's interest would be achieved less effectively without it (*Ward v. Rock against Racism*, 491 U.S. 781, 109 S. Ct. 2746, 105 L. Ed. 2d 661 [1989]).

An important distinction is drawn between public premises that serve as traditional public forums and public premises that constitute limited public forums. For example, state fair grounds are public premises that have not traditionally served as public forums. The govern-

ment may impose more restrictions on free speech in limited public forums than in traditional public forums. In *Heffron v. International Society for Krishna Consciousness*, 452 U.S. 640, 101 S. Ct. 2559, 69 L. Ed. 2d 298 (1981), the Court upheld regulations limiting the sale or distribution of religious materials to fixed locations on state fair grounds.

Although it seems reasonable to assume that public premises owned and operated by the government are public forums, some are not. In *Adderley v. Florida*, 385 U.S. 39, 87 S. Ct. 242, 17 L. Ed. 2d 149 (1966), the Court upheld the trespass conviction of students who demonstrated on the grounds of a jail. Although jailhouse grounds are public property, they have not traditionally been used as public forums: "The State, no less than a private owner of property, has the power to preserve the property under its control for the use to which it is lawfully dedicated." Later cases challenging restricted access to public premises focused on whether the government, in creating the premises, intended to create a public forum. In *United States v. Kokinda*, 497 U.S. 720, 110 S. Ct. 3115, 111 L. Ed. 2d 571 (1990), the Court upheld a postal service regulation that bars the solicitation of contributions on a post office sidewalk, because that sidewalk lacked the characteristics of a general public sidewalk. Similarly, it declared an airport terminal to be a nonpublic forum because "the tradition of airport activity does not demonstrate that airports have historically been made available for speech activity" (*International Society for Krishna Consciousness v. Lee*, 505 U.S. 672, 112 S. Ct. 2701, 120 L. Ed. 2d 541 [1992]).

When private PROPERTY RIGHTS conflict with the public forum doctrine, the Court examines whether the regulation in question is narrowly tailored to serve a significant government interest. A law may not prohibit all canvassing or solicitation of, or distribution of handbills to, homeowners in a residential neighborhood, because a public street is a traditional public forum. However, it may limit specific types of speech activity that target particular individuals. In *Frisby v. Schultz*, 487 U.S. 474, 108 S. Ct. 2495, 101 L. Ed. 2d 420 (1988), the Court upheld an ordinance that prohibited the PICKETING of individual residences. The law was narrowly drawn to serve the government's interest in precluding the picketing of captive householders, and allowed picketers ample alternative means of expression.

Inciting, Provocative, or Offensive Speech Laws that limit inciting or provocative speech, often called fighting words, or offensive expressions such as PORNOGRAPHY, are

Freedom of speech is protected in public premises that are traditional public forums. A park is considered a public forum although an airport terminal is not.

FRANK SITEMAN/THE PICTURE CUBE

subject to STRICT SCRUTINY. It is well established that the government may impose content regulations on certain categories of expression that do not merit First Amendment protection. To illustrate this point, the Court stated in *Chaplinsky v. New Hampshire*, 315 U.S. 568, 62 S. Ct. 766, 86 L. Ed. 1031 (1942), "There are certain well-defined and narrowly limited classes of speech, the prevention and punishment of which have never been thought to raise constitutional problems."

The Court has also upheld laws that regulate speech activity if those laws do not limit the content of speech and impose only an indirect burden on freedom of speech. In such cases, the Court applies a less stringent test and balances the individual's free speech interests against the government's interest furthered by the law. In *O'Brien v. United States*, 393 U.S. 900, 89 S. Ct. 63, 21 L. Ed. 2d 188 (1968), the Court held that a statute prohibiting the destruction of draft cards did not violate the First Amendment, because the government's interest in maintaining a viable selective service pool outweighed the statute's incidental infringement of free expression.

During the 1980s and 1990s, a number of laws were passed that attempted to regulate or ban "hate speech," defined as utterances, displays, or expressions of racial, religious, or sexual bias. The Court has generally invalidated such laws on the ground that they infringe First Amendment rights. In *R.A.V. v. City of St. Paul*, 505 U.S. 377, 112 S. Ct. 2538, 120 L. Ed. 2d 305 (1992), the Court invalidated the city of St. Paul's hate-crime ordinance, saying that it unconstitutionally infringed free speech. The defendant had been prosecuted for burning a cross on the lawn of an African American family's residence.

Like fighting words, materials judged obscene are not protected by the First Amendment. The three-part *Miller* test stands as the yardstick for differentiating material that is merely offensive and therefore protected by the First Amendment, from that which is legally obscene and therefore subject to restriction (*Miller v. California*, 413 U.S. 15, 93 S. Ct. 2607, 37 L. Ed. 2d 419 [1973]). This text determines that material is obscene if (1) the average person, applying contemporary community standards, would find that it appeals to shameful or morbid sexual interests; (2) it depicts or describes patently offensive sexual conduct; and (3) it lacks serious literary, artistic, political, or scientific value.

Prior Restraint The Court uses a stringent standard when it evaluates statutes that impose a PRIOR RESTRAINT on speech. The test

ROBERT GINN/THE PICTURE CUBE

Freedom of speech is guaranteed to groups that many people may find offensive.

most frequently employed asks whether the prohibited activity poses a clear and present danger of resulting in damage to a legitimate government interest. Most often, the CLEAR AND PRESENT DANGER doctrine has applied to prior restraints on the publication of materials thought to threaten national security. This test was first expressed by Justice Holmes in the *Schenck* case. Charles T. Schenck was charged with violating the Espionage Act (Tit. 1, §§ 3, 4 [Comp. St. 1918, §§ 10212c, 10212d]) by distributing pamphlets urging insubordination among members of the military. The Court held that his activities created "a clear and present danger that they will bring about the substantive evils that Congress has a right to prevent." The government's interest in maintaining national security and preventing dissension among the troops outweighed Schenck's interest in free speech.

The clear-and-present-danger test was extended during the 1950s, when widespread fear of COMMUNISM led to the passage of the SMITH ACT, 18 U.S.C.A. § 2385, which prohibited advocating the overthrow of the government. The act was challenged as a prior restraint on speech. It was upheld by the Court, which stated that the clear-and-present-danger test does not require the government to prove that a threat is imminent or that a plot would probably be successful (*Dennis v. United States*, 341 U.S. 494, 71 S. Ct. 857, 95 L. Ed. 1137 [1951]).

The *Dennis* decision was criticized as weakening the clear-and-present-danger test and allowing the government too much freedom to restrict speech. These results were remedied somewhat in *Brandenburg v. Ohio*, 395 U.S. 444, 89 S. Ct. 1827, 23 L. Ed. 2d 430 (1969), in which the Court invalidated a statute that punished the advocacy of violence in industrial disputes. The Court held that the government cannot forbid the advocacy of the use of force unless that advocacy is directed to inciting imminent illegal activity and is likely to succeed.

Expressive Conduct In *West Virginia State Board of Education v. Barnette*, 319 U.S. 624, 63 S. Ct. 1178, 87 L. Ed. 1628 (1943), Justice ROBERT H. JACKSON said that symbols are "a short cut from mind to mind." Expressive conduct or symbolic speech involves communicative conduct that is the behavioral equivalent of speech. The conduct itself is the idea or message. Some expressive conduct is the equivalent of speech and is protected by the First Amendment.

In *Tinker v. Des Moines Independent Community School District*, 393 U.S. 503, 89 S. Ct. 733, 21 L. Ed. 2d 731 (1969), the Court held that it was unconstitutional to suspend high school students for wearing black armbands to protest the Vietnam War, because their conduct was "akin to pure speech" and did not interfere with the work of the school or the rights of other students.

Statutes that prohibit the desecration of the U.S. FLAG have been found to unconstitutionally restrict free expression. In *Texas v. Johnson*, 491 U.S. 397, 109 S. Ct. 2533, 105 L. Ed. 2d 342 (1989), the Court overturned Gregory L. Johnson's conviction for burning a U.S. flag during a demonstration. Johnson's actions were communicative conduct that warranted First Amendment protection, even though they were repugnant to many people. Similarly, in *United States v. Eichman*, 496 U.S. 310, 110 S. Ct. 2404, 110 L. Ed. 2d 287 (1990), the Court struck down the federal Flag Protection Act of 1989, 103 Stat. 777, 18 U.S.C.A. § 700, stating that the government's interest in passing the act was a desire to suppress free expression and the content of the message conveyed by the act of flag burning.

Prohibitions on nudity and other erotic but nonobscene expressive conduct have generally been struck down by the Court. However, in *Barnes v. Glen Theatre*, 501 U.S. 560, 111 S. Ct. 2456, 115 L. Ed. 2d 504 (1991), the Court upheld a ban on totally nude dancing, on the ground that it was part of a general ban on public nudity. While recognizing that nude dancing has generally been considered protected expressive conduct, the justices pointed out that such activity is only marginally within the perimeters of First Amendment protection.

Commercial Speech Commercial speech, usually in the form of advertising, enjoys some First Amendment protection, but not to the same degree as that given to noncommercial forms of expression. Generally, commercial speech that is not false or misleading and does not advertise illegal or harmful activity is protected by the First Amendment. Commercial speech may be restricted only to further a substantial government interest and only if the restriction actually furthers that interest. In *Central Hudson Gas & Electric Co. v. Public Service Commission*, 447 U.S. 557, 100 S. Ct. 2343, 65 L. Ed. 2d 341 (1980), the Court held that a statute banning promotional advertising by PUBLIC UTILITIES was unconstitutional.

Defamation and Privacy In *New York Times v. Sullivan*, 376 U.S. 254, 84 S. Ct. 710, 11 L. Ed. 2d 686 (1964), the Supreme Court declared that the First Amendment protects open and robust debate on public issues even when such debate includes "vehement, caustic, unpleasantly sharp attacks on government and public officials." In *Sullivan*, a public official claimed that allegations about him that appeared in the *New York Times* were false, and sued the newspaper for LIBEL. The Court balanced the plaintiff's interest in preserving his reputation against the public's interest in freedom of expression, particularly in the area of political debate. The Court decided that to recover damages, a public official must prove actual malice, meaning knowledge that the statements were false or were made with reckless disregard of whether they were false.

Where the plaintiff in a DEFAMATION action is a private citizen not in the public eye, the law extends a lesser degree of constitutional protection to the statements at issue. Public figures voluntarily place themselves in positions that invite close scrutiny, whereas private citizens have a greater interest in protecting their reputation. A private citizen's reputational and privacy interests tend to outweigh free speech considerations, and therefore deserve greater protection from the courts (see *Gertz v. Robert Welch, Inc.*, 418 U.S. 323, 94 S. Ct. 2997, 41 L. Ed. 2d 789 [1974]).

CROSS-REFERENCES

Broadcasting; Censorship; *Dennis v. United States;* E-mail; Fairness Doctrine; Freedom of the Press; Hate Crimes; Movie Ratings; *New York Times v. Sullivan;* Overbreadth Doctrine; Privacy; *Roth v. United States; Schenck v. United States;* Symbolic Speech; X or XXX Rating.

FREEDOM OF THE PRESS 📖 The right, guaranteed by the FIRST AMENDMENT to the U.S. Constitution, to gather, publish, and distribute information and ideas without government restriction; this right encompasses freedom from PRIOR RESTRAINTS on publication and freedom from CENSORSHIP. 📖

The First Amendment to the U.S. Constitution reads, in part, "Congress shall make no law . . . abridging the freedom of speech, or of the press." The courts have long struggled to determine whether the Framers of the Constitution intended to differentiate press freedom from speech freedom. Most have concluded that freedom of the press derives from FREEDOM OF SPEECH. Although some cases and some legal scholars, including Justice POTTER STEWART, of the U.S. Supreme Court, advocate special press protections distinct from those accorded to speech, most justices believe that the Freedom of the Press Clause has no significance independent of the Freedom of Speech Clause.

The Court explained its reasoning in *First National Bank of Boston v. Bellotti*, 435 U.S. 765, 98 S. Ct. 1407, 55 L. Ed. 2d 707 (1978). According to Chief Justice WARREN E. BURGER, conferring special status on the press requires that the courts or the government determine who or what the press is and what activities fall under its special protection. Burger concluded that the free speech guarantees of the First Amendment adequately ensure freedom of the press, and that there is no need to distinguish between the two rights:

> Because the First Amendment was meant to guarantee freedom to express and communicate ideas, I can see no difference between the right of those who seek to disseminate ideas by way of a newspaper and those who give lectures or speeches and seek to enlarge the audience by publication and wide dissemination.

The Court has generally rejected requests to extend to the press PRIVILEGES AND IMMUNITIES beyond those available to ordinary citizens. In *Branzburg v. Hayes*, 408 U.S. 665, 92 S. Ct. 2646, 33 L. Ed. 2d 626 (1972), it held that a journalist's privilege to refuse to disclose information such as the names of informants is no broader than that enjoyed by any citizen. As long as an inquiry is conducted in GOOD FAITH, with relevant questions and no harassment, a journalist must cooperate.

Justice Stewart's dissent in *Branzburg* urged the Court to find that a qualified journalistic privilege exists unless the government is able to show three things: (1) probable cause to believe

that the journalist possesses information that is clearly relevant, (2) an inability to obtain the material by less intrusive means, and (3) a compelling interest that overrides First Amendment interests. In an unusual break with tradition, several circuit courts have applied Stewart's test and ruled in favor of journalists seeking special First Amendment protection. Nonetheless, the Supreme Court has steadfastly held to its decision in *Branzburg*, and shows no sign of retreating from its position that the First Amendment confers no special privileges on journalists.

Laws that affect the ability of the press to gather and publish news are suspect, but not automatically unconstitutional. In *Cohen v. Cowles Media Co.*, 501 U.S. 663, 111 S. Ct. 2513, 115 L. Ed. 2d 586 (1991), reporters for two Twin Cities newspapers were sued for breach of contract when they published the name of their source after promising confidentiality. The reporters claimed that the law infringed their First Amendment freedom to gather news unencumbered by state law. The Court held that the law did not unconstitutionally impinge their rights because its enforcement imposed only an incidental burden on their ability to gather and report information. Writing for the majority, Justice BYRON R. WHITE said that laws that apply to the general public and do not target the press do not violate the First Amendment simply because their enforcement against members of the press has an incidental burden on their ability to gather and report the news: "[E]nforcement of such general laws against the press is not subject to stricter scrutiny than would be applied to enforcement against other persons or organizations." The *Cohen* decision indicates the Court's

The guarantee of freedom of the press includes the right to publish stories that are scandalous.

continued unwillingness to extend special First Amendment protection to journalists.

Generally, the First Amendment prohibits prior restraint, that is, restraint on a publication before it is published. In a landmark decision in *Near v. Minnesota*, 283 U.S. 697, 51 S. Ct. 625, 75 L. Ed. 1357 (1931), the Court held that the government could not prohibit the publication of a newspaper for carrying stories that were scandalous or scurrilous. The Court identified three types of publications against which a prior restraint might be valid: those that pose a threat to national security, those that contain OBSCENE materials, and those that advocate violence or the overthrow of the government.

The government argued that publication of certain material posed a threat to national security in the so-called *Pentagon Papers* case, *New York Times Co. v. United States*, 403 U.S. 713, 91 S. Ct. 2140, 29 L. Ed. 2d 822 (1971). Here, the government sought an INJUNCTION against newspapers planning to publish classified material concerning U.S. policy in Vietnam. The Court found that the government had not proved an overriding government interest, or an extreme danger to national security if the material were published. The justices reiterated their position that a request for a prior restraint must overcome a heavy presumption of unconstitutionality.

The Court is steadfast in its holding that prior restraints are among the most serious infringements on First Amendment freedoms and that attempts to impose them must be strictly scrutinized. In *Nebraska Press Ass'n v. Stuart*, 427 U.S. 539, 96 S. Ct. 2791, 49 L. Ed. 2d 683 (1976), the Court overturned a state court's attempt to ban the press from a criminal trial. The Court held that GAG ORDERS, although not PER SE invalid, are allowable only when there is a CLEAR AND PRESENT DANGER to the administration of justice.

Freedom of the press, like freedom of speech, is not absolute. Notwithstanding the limitations placed on it, the press exercises enormous power and influence, and is burdened with commensurate responsibility. Because journalists have access to more information than the average individual, they serve as the eyes, ears, and voice of the public. Some legal scholars even argue that the press is an important force in the democratic system of checks and balances.

CROSS-REFERENCES

Broadcasting; Cameras in Court; Evidence *In Focus: Journalists' Privilege*; Fairness Doctrine; Federal Communications Commission; Libel and Slander; Mass Communications Law; *New York Times v. Sullivan; New York Times v. United States;* Pretrial Publicity; Sheppard, Sam; Shield Laws; Trial.

FREE EXERCISE CLAUSE See RELIGION.

FREEHOLD A LIFE ESTATE, an interest in land the duration of which is restricted to the life or lives of a particular person or persons holding it, or an ESTATE in FEE, an interest in PROPERTY that is unconditional and represents the broadest ownership interest recognized by law.

In order to be categorized as a freehold, an estate must possess the characteristics of (1) immobility—in the sense that the property must be either land, or some interest derived from or affixed to land—and (2) indeterminate duration.

Determinable freeholds are life estates created by language that provides that the estate is to terminate automatically upon the occurrence of a specified event.

FREIGHT The price or compensation paid for the transportation of GOODS by a carrier. *Freight* is also applied to the goods transported by such CARRIERS.

The LIABILITY of a carrier for freight damaged, lost, or destroyed during shipment is determined by contract, statute, or TORT law.

The responsibility for the payment of freight is a subject of a term of a sales contract between the buyer and seller of the goods to be shipped. When a contract contains a C.F. & I. provision, the buyer accepts liability for paying the cost of freight in addition to the costs of the goods and insurance on them.

FREIGHT FORWARDER An individual who, as a regular business, assembles and combines small shipments into one lot and takes the responsibility for the transportation of such property from the place of receipt to the place of destination.

The role of a freight forwarder is to collect and consolidate shipments that are less than a carload or truckload and obtain COMMON CARRIER transportation for the long-haul transport of the property, which is owned by individual carload or truckload shippers. Such a forwarder ordinarily has the same LIABILITY for loss as a common carrier.

See also SHIPPING LAW.

FREUND, ERNST Ernst Freund was a brilliant legal scholar who oversaw the development of U.S. administrative law at the turn of the twentieth century. A social reformer, Freund was an early proponent of social research as a means of shaping the content of U.S. law. As a political progressive, he also was an articulate supporter of free speech rights under the FIRST AMENDMENT of the U.S. Constitution.

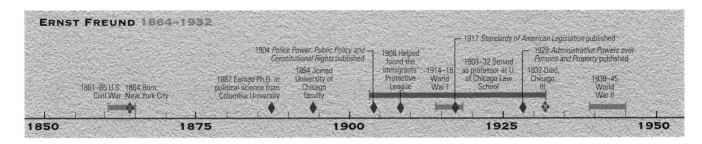

ERNST FREUND 1864–1932

1861–65 U.S. Civil War · 1864 Born, New York City

1887 Earned Ph.D. in political science from Columbia University

1904 *Police Power: Public Policy and Constitutional Rights* published

1894 Joined University of Chicago faculty

1908 Helped found the Immigrants' Protective League

1914–18 World War I

1903–32 Served as professor at U. of Chicago Law School

1917 *Standards of American Legislation* published

1928 *Administrative Powers over Persons and Property* published

1932 Died, Chicago, Ill.

1939–45 World War II

1850 · 1875 · 1900 · 1925 · 1950

Freund was born in New York City on January 30, 1864, to German American parents. He attended the University of Berlin and the University of Heidelberg, receiving a law degree from the latter in 1884. After practicing law in New York City from 1886 to 1894, Freund earned a doctor's degree in political science from Columbia University, in 1897. He also received an honorary doctor of laws degree from the University of Michigan, in 1931.

Freund entered academe in 1892 when he became professor of administrative law and municipal corporations at Columbia University. In 1894, he began a long association with the University of Chicago, accepting a position in the political science department as a professor of Roman law and jurisprudence. In 1903, he joined the faculty of the university's newly opened law school. Freund taught courses in social legislation and proposed a new field, the "science of legislation," to underscore the connection between political science and law.

Freund became a prominent figure at the law school and served as the John P. Wilson Professor of Law from 1929 to 1932. Among his many achievements was the establishment of the University of Chicago's highly regarded graduate-level social services program, the first such program in the nation. Involved in several professional organizations, Freund served as president of the American Political Science Association in 1915.

Freund's renown in legal circles grew as a result of his cogent writing on the function and parameters of ADMINISTRATIVE LAW (the body of statutes, regulatory rules and regulations, and court decisions implemented by administrative and government agencies). Freund's most famous publication on the subject was *Police Power: Public Policy and Constitutional Rights*, published in 1904. Freund analyzed the limitations imposed on legislative power by the FOURTEENTH AMENDMENT of the U.S. Constitution. He advocated a system of legal regulations that balanced individual rights against business and property rights.

Freund's interest in statutory drafting led to a position on the Commission on Uniform

BIOGRAPHY

UNIVERSITY OF CHICAGO LIBRARY

Ernst Freund

"THE STATE TAKES PROPERTY BY EMINENT DOMAIN BECAUSE IT IS USEFUL TO THE PUBLIC, AND UNDER POLICE POWER BECAUSE IT IS HARMFUL."

State Laws in 1908. Freund created model statutes to bolster the civil rights of married women, as well as commentary on divorce, guardianship, illegitimacy, labor law, and child labor. He also produced a handbook on legislative drafting in 1921 and offered drafting instructions to the American Bar Association.

In 1928, Freund published *Administrative Powers over Persons and Property*, a treatise on the distinctions between the power held by government, individuals, and property. In other works, Freund wrote about the necessity of protecting what he termed the dependent class, the less privileged members of society who were vulnerable to exploitation. A man of action, he helped organize the Immigrants' Protective League in 1908 and served as president of that organization for several terms.

A staunch supporter of free speech, Freund published articles on the specific rights guaranteed by the First Amendment of the U.S. Constitution. He believed that the open discussion of public affairs was a crucial underpinning of U.S. society.

Freund married Harriet Walton on May 13, 1916. The couple had two children, Nancy Freund and Emma Louise Freund. Freund died in Chicago at age sixty-eight, on October 20, 1932.

FRIEDAN, BETTY NAOMI GOLDSTEIN

In 1963, author Betty Naomi Goldstein Friedan's first book, *The Feminine Mystique*, launched the feminist movement, which eventually expanded the lifestyle choices for U.S. women. By the 1990s, she had also become a spokesperson for older people and economically disadvantaged people and was recognized and honored by women outside the United States for her global leadership and influence on women's issues.

Born February 4, 1921, in New York, Friedan grew up in Peoria, Illinois. She entered Smith College in 1939, majored in psychology, and served as editor of the college newspaper. After graduating summa cum laude in 1942, she interviewed for the only type of job available to women journalists at the time: researcher for a major U.S. news magazine. But the position of

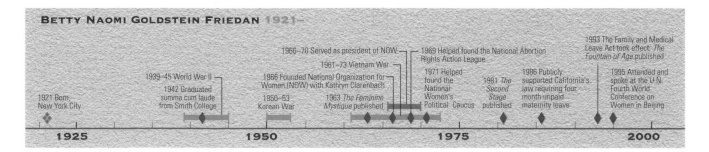

BETTY NAOMI GOLDSTEIN FRIEDAN 1921–

1921 Born, New York City

1939–45 World War II

1942 Graduated summa cum laude from Smith College

1950–53 Korean War

1966 Founded National Organization for Women (NOW) with Kathryn Clarenbach

1963 *The Feminine Mystique* published

1961–73 Vietnam War

1966–70 Served as president of NOW

1969 Helped found the National Abortion Rights Action League

1971 Helped found the National Women's Political Caucus

1981 *The Second Stage* published

1986 Publicly supported California's law requiring four month unpaid maternity leave

1993 The Family and Medical Leave Act took effect; *The Fountain of Age* published

1995 Attended and spoke at the U.N. Fourth World Conference on Women in Beijing

1925   1950   1975   2000

researcher amounted to doing all the work while someone else received the byline, and Friedan was not interested in that. Instead, she wrote for a Greenwich Village news agency, covering the labor movement.

When World War II ended, Friedan lost her job to a returning veteran. (Returning veterans were guaranteed their prewar jobs.) Friedan then thought of going to medical school, a choice very few women could pursue. But instead, she followed the traditional path, marrying returning veteran Carl Friedan in 1947 and starting a family. After her first child was born, she worked for another newspaper, but was fired when she became pregnant with her second child. She protested to the newspaper guild, as no one had ever questioned her ability to perform her job, but was told that losing her job was "her fault" because she was pregnant. At that time, the term *sex discrimination* did not exist.

While she was a mother and housewife living in suburban New York, Friedan wrote articles for women's magazines such as *McCall's* and *Ladies' Home Journal* on a freelance basis. Tapped by *McCall's* to report on the state of the alumnae of the Smith class of 1942 as they returned for their fifteenth reunion in 1957, Friedan visited the campus and was struck by the students' lack of interest in careers after graduation. This disinterest in intellectual pursuits contrasted greatly with Friedan's perception of her Smith classmates of the 1930s and 1940s.

Extensive research over the next several years brought Friedan to the conclusion that women's magazines were at fault because they defined women solely in relationship to their husbands and children. This had not always been the case; the magazines had evolved in the postwar years from promoters of women's independence into paeans to consumerism, bent on keeping U.S. housewives in the home by selling them more and more household products.

Not surprisingly, Friedan was unable to get her work on this issue published in an acceptable format by the women's magazines she was

BIOGRAPHY

Betty Naomi Goldstein Friedan

criticizing. Her report was published in book form in 1963 as *The Feminine Mystique*, in which she chronicled the dissatisfaction of suburban housewives, dubbing it "the problem with no name." The book struck a common chord among U.S. women, who recognized themselves in the women she described in its pages. For the first time since the women's suffrage movement ended successfully with the passage of the NINETEENTH AMENDMENT granting women the right to vote, women gathered together on a large scale to work for equal rights with men, a concept that at the time was nothing less than revolutionary.

In 1966, with Kathryn Clarenbach, Friedan cofounded the National Organization for Women (NOW). NOW's original statement of purpose was written by Friedan: "Women want feminism to take the actions needed to bring women into the mainstream of American society, now; full equality for women, in fully equal partnership with men." Friedan served as NOW's president until 1970. Under her leadership, NOW propelled the women's movement from middle-class suburbia to nationwide activism. Friedan also helped organize the National Abortion Rights Action League in 1969, and the National Women's Political Caucus in 1971. All three organizations were still active participants in U.S. politics and culture into the 1990s.

On August 26, 1970, the fiftieth anniversary of the ratification of the Nineteenth Amendment, the Women's Strike for Equality took place. Friedan's brainchild, this WOMEN'S RIGHTS demonstration was the largest that had ever occurred in the United States. Thousands of U.S. women marched in the streets for a day rather than working as housewives, secretaries, and waitresses, to show how poorly society would fare without women's labor and to demand three things for women: equal opportunity in employment and education, twenty-four-hour child care centers, and legalized ABORTION. Although the media at the time portrayed the strike as frivolous or a result of female hysteria, their compulsion to pay the event any attention at all was a step forward for the women's movement.

By the 1980s, it was apparent that Friedan's feminism differed from that of other U.S. feminists such as GLORIA STEINEM and KATE MILLETT. When other feminist leaders were saying women could "have it all," meaning a successful career, fulfilling marriage, and happy children, Friedan, who had been divorced from her husband since 1969, wrote articles such as "Being 'Superwoman' Is Not the Way to Go" (*Woman's Day*, Oct. 1981) and "Feminism's Next Step" (*New York Times Magazine*, July 1981). Rather than focusing on sexual violence and abortion rights, Friedan's writings emphasized the necessity of working with other groups to improve the plight of children, members of minorities, and economically disadvantaged people. In her 1981 book *The Second Stage*, Friedan called for an open discussion of traditional feminism's denial of the importance of family and of women's needs to nurture and be nurtured. She predicted that the women's movement would die out if feminists did not take the issues of children and men more seriously. It was not surprising that this position was roundly criticized as antifeminist by many of Friedan's contemporaries. Another position that was at odds with NOW surfaced in 1986 when she declared her support for a California law requiring employers to grant up to four months of unpaid leave for women who were disabled by pregnancy or childbirth. The 1980 law (West's Ann. Cal. Gov. Code § 12945) was the subject of a U.S. Supreme Court case, *California Federal Savings and Loan Ass'n v. Guerra*, 479 U.S. 272, 107 S. Ct. 683, 93 L. Ed. 2d 613 (1987). NOW opposed the law as a dangerous singling out of women for special treatment; Friedan called it outrageous that feminists would side with employers who were trying to evade offering women important and needed benefits. These opinions, among other things, caused Friedan to lose support within the women's movement as well as an audience in the media.

Another reason for Friedan's fall from media attention was her style, which, like her philosophy, also differed from that of other feminist spokespersons, most notably Steinem. Whereas Steinem was a favorite of the media and actively courted their attention, Friedan did not seek out media attention and often railed against what she saw as the stereotyping of women. Her stormy relationship with the media contributed to an image of her as old, unattractive, and out of touch with modern feminism.

By 1990, although Friedan was moving away from what was considered mainstream feminism, she had earned a permanent place in history. That year, *Life* magazine named her one of the one hundred most important people of the twentieth century.

In September 1995, a new generation of journalists seemed surprised at Friedan's extensive international influence, which was demonstrated at the Non-Governmental Organization Forum on Women, an unofficial gathering at the U.N. Fourth World Conference on Women. Friedan attended the forum as one of only a few women who had participated in all four U.N. women's conferences since the first one in Mexico City in 1975. Women of all nationalities and ages sought her out, listened to her speeches, and attended her workshops. Her focus was to move the women's movement away from conflict with men and toward economic policies that benefited both sexes, such as shorter workweeks and higher MINIMUM WAGES. As she saw it, policies that were pro-women alone were portrayed in the media and by opponents as antifamily and antimen. Poor economic conditions and shrinking job opportunities often resulted in the treatment of women's developing economic power as a scapegoat for difficulties suffered by men or families. In Friedan's opinion, this unnecessary tension between men and women diverted attention from the issues that really threatened the well-being of women and families: poverty, unemployment, lack of education and health care, and crime. To combat these problems, she supported a proposal put forth by distinguished academics and public policy researchers that would provide low-income parents, not just women on welfare, with health insurance and child care.

Friedan's focus on more gender-neutral policies was an outgrowth of her research into gerontology and the issues facing aging people. The 1993 publication of *The Fountain of Age* had put Friedan back in the media spotlight as the spokesperson of her generation, an advocate for freeing older people from damaging stereotypes, just as she had previously done for women. Friedan brought to her advocacy for older people her philosophy of cooperation, developed during her decades of work in the women's movement. A delegate to the Fourth White House Conference on Aging in 1995, she fought against the polarization of young and older U.S. citizens that some politicians encouraged in order to increase their political power. She eschewed the idea of forced retirement, instead arguing for older workers to voluntarily and gradually cut down their work schedules and to explore job sharing and con-

"MEN WEREN'T REALLY THE ENEMY—THEY WERE FELLOW VICTIMS SUFFERING FROM AN OUTMODED MASCULINE MYSTIQUE THAT MADE THEM FEEL UNNECESSARILY INADEQUATE WHEN THERE WERE NO BEARS TO KILL."

sultant work. At the same time, Friedan vowed to save programs such as Social Security, Medicare, and Medicaid, which were under attack by fiscal conservatives. With that full plate of issues, it was clear that Friedan was not ready to stop her advocacy work.

CROSS-REFERENCES

Age Discrimination; Ireland, Patricia; Sex Discrimination.

FRIENDLY, HENRY J. Henry J. Friendly served for twenty-seven years on the U.S. Court of Appeals for the Second Circuit where he won a wide reputation for his scholarly, well-crafted opinions.

Friendly was born July 3, 1903, in Elmira, New York. He graduated from Harvard College in 1923 and from Harvard Law School in 1927. In law school he studied under Professor Felix Frankfurter, later a U.S. Supreme Court justice, who recommended Friendly for a clerkship with Supreme Court Justice LOUIS D. BRANDEIS. After his clerkship Friendly entered private practice where he specialized in railroad reorganizations and corporate law. He later became a vice president and general counsel for Pan American World Airways.

In 1959 President DWIGHT D. EISENHOWER appointed Friendly to the U.S. Court of Appeals for the Second Circuit where he remained until his death. Although Friendly was a semi-retired senior judge during his last years on the court, he remained an active participant and was involved in more than one hundred cases each year. He served as chief judge of the court from 1971 to 1973. In 1974 Friendly took on the additional duties of the presiding judge of a Special Railroad Court, which was established to deal with the reorganization of rail service in the Northeast and the Midwest that resulted from the bankruptcy of the Penn Central Railroad and the formation of Conrail.

Friendly wrote nearly a thousand judicial opinions as well as a number of notes and articles on a wide range of issues, but he is probably best known for his work in the areas of diversity jurisdiction, criminal procedure, and securities law. Diversity jurisdiction refers to

BIOGRAPHY

Henry J. Friendly

"THE QUESTION OF HOW JUDGES GO ABOUT THE BUSINESS OF JUDGING CONTINUES TO HOLD INTEREST— ALTHOUGH APPARENTLY MORE FOR LAWYERS AND LAW PROFESSORS THAN FOR JUDGES."

the JURISDICTION that federal courts have over lawsuits in which the plaintiff and the defendant are residents of different states. Friendly first became interested in the subject when he was in law school, and one of his first articles was "The Historic Basis of Diversity Jurisdiction," 41 *Harvard Law Review* (1928). Later, after the U.S. Supreme Court had established a new precedent for cases involving diversity jurisdiction (*Erie Railroad Co. v. Tompkins*, 304 U.S. 64, 58 S. Ct. 817, 82 L. Ed. 1188 [1938]), Friendly wrote "In Praise of *Erie*—and of the New Federal Common Law," 39 *New York University Law Review* (1964). A few years later he provided an overview of federal jurisdiction in *Federal Jurisdiction: A General View* (1973).

During the 1960s Friendly became involved in the debate over the changes in CRIMINAL PROCEDURE that were occurring as the U.S. Supreme Court, in a series of decisions, held that many of the rights guaranteed in the Bill of Rights applied to the states. In "The Bill of Rights as a Code of Criminal Procedure," *Benchmarks* (1967), Friendly expressed doubts about some of the Court's decisions and worried that they would cut off debate in Congress and the state legislatures that might have proved fruitful in developing new solutions to the problems of criminal procedure. He also criticized the decision in *Miranda v. Arizona*, 384 U.S. 436, 86 S. Ct. 1602, 16 L. Ed. 2d 694 (1966), on the ground that it was predicated on the unfounded assumption that all CUSTODIAL INTERROGATIONS are inherently coercive.

In the area of SECURITIES law, Friendly wrote more than one hundred opinions, several of them in the relatively new field of transnational law, which deals with corporations that have activities in several countries. He was also notably unsympathetic toward white-collar criminals who perpetrated financial frauds; in *United States v. Benjamin*, 328 F.2d 854 (1964), he observed that "[i]n our complex society the accountant's certificate and the lawyer's opinion can be instruments for inflicting pecuniary loss more potent than the chisel or the crowbar."

Friendly's colleagues respected him for his scholarship, his reasoning, and his self-restraint.

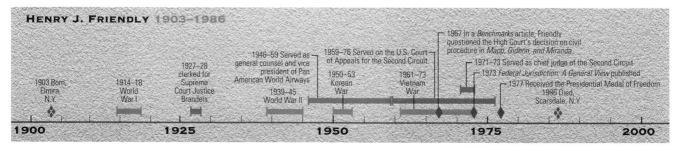

HENRY J. FRIENDLY 1903–1986

1903 Born, Elmira, N.Y.

1914–18 World War I

1927–28 clerked for Supreme Court Justice Brandeis

1946–59 Served as general counsel and vice president of Pan American World Airways

1939–45 World War II

1959–76 Served on the U.S. Court of Appeals for the Second Circuit

1950–53 Korean War

1961–73 Vietnam War

1967 In a *Benchmarks* article, Friendly questioned the High Court's decision on civil procedure in *Mapp, Gideon, and Miranda*

1971–73 Served as chief judge of the Second Circuit

1973 *Federal Jurisdiction: A General View* published

1977 Received the Presidential Medal of Freedom

1986 Died, Scarsdale, N.Y.

1900   1925   1950   1975   2000

As another federal jurist, JOHN MINOR WISDOM put it, Friendly was "unsurpassed as a judge—in the power of his reasoning, the depth of his knowledge of the law, and his balanced judgment in decision-making."

FRIENDLY FIRE Fire burning in a place where it was intended to burn, although damages may result. In a military conflict, the discharge of weapons against one's own troops.

A fire burning in a fireplace is regarded as a friendly fire, in spite of the fact that extensive smoke damage might result therefrom. Ordinarily, when an individual purchases fire INSURANCE, the coverage does not extend to damages resulting from a friendly fire but only to loss resulting from an uncontrollable HOSTILE FIRE.

FRIENDLY SUIT A lawsuit brought by an EXECUTOR or administrator of the estate of a deceased person in the name of a CREDITOR as if that creditor had initiated the action. The executor or administrator brings the suit against himself or herself in order to compel the creditors to take an equal distribution of the assets of the estate. An action brought by parties who agree to submit some doubtful question to the court in order to obtain an opinion on that issue.

FRIEND OF THE COURT A person who has a strong interest in a matter that is the subject of a lawsuit in which he or she is not a party.

A friend of the court may be given permission by the court to file a written statement of his or her views on the subject, ostensibly to bolster the case of one party but even more to persuade the court to adopt the party's views. The Latin translation, AMICUS CURIAE, is used most often for a friend of the court; the written argument that he or she files may be called an amicus curiae BRIEF.

FRIES'S REBELLION John Fries was an auctioneer from rural Pennsylvania who led a small group of tax protesters in what came to be known as Fries's Rebellion. He was tried and convicted of TREASON but was eventually pardoned.

Fries served as a captain in the Continental Army during the Whiskey Rebellion of 1794. He then returned to Pennsylvania to resume his life there. In 1798, Congress authorized the collection of property taxes to replenish funds depleted by the Whiskey Rebellion and to finance an anticipated war with France. Revenue officers were sent to all parts of the United States to assess the value of homes, land, and slaves for taxation. The tax assessment was well publicized and understood in urban areas, where most residents paid little attention to the

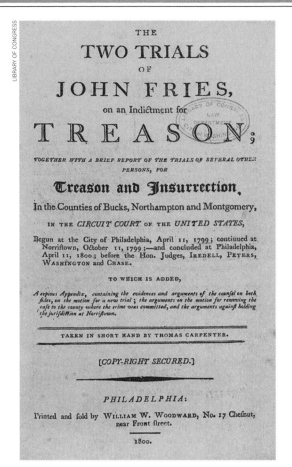

THE
TWO TRIALS
OF
JOHN FRIES,
on an Indictment for
TREASON;
TOGETHER WITH A BRIEF REPORT OF THE TRIALS OF SEVERAL OTHER PERSONS, FOR

Treason and Insurrection,

In the Counties of Bucks, Northampton and Montgomery,

IN THE *CIRCUIT COURT* OF THE *UNITED STATES,*

Begun at the City of Philadelphia, April 11, 1799; continued at Norristown, October 11, 1799;—and concluded at Philadelphia, April 11, 1800; before the Hon. Judges, IREDELL, PETERS, WASHINGTON and CHASE.

TO WHICH IS ADDED,

A copious Appendix, containing the evidences and arguments of the counsel on both sides, on the motion for a new trial ; the arguments on the motion for removing the cause to the county where the crime was committed, and the arguments against holding the jurisdiction at Norristown.

TAKEN IN SHORT HAND BY THOMAS CARPENTER.

[COPY-RIGHT SECURED.]

PHILADELPHIA:

Printed and sold by WILLIAM W. WOODWARD, No. 17 Chesnut, near Front street.

1800.

In 1800 a publisher in Philadelphia used shorthand notes taken by Thomas Carpenter to produce a report of John Fries's two trials for treason. Fries had led several hundred residents of eastern Pennsylvania in a protest against a federal tax on houses.

assessors' activities. However, in the rural regions of northeastern Pennsylvania, where many residents spoke and read only German, many people were unaware of Congress's action and were resentful and fearful of the inquisitive assessors. They responded by attacking the revenue officers, both verbally and physically. Their treatment of the assessors was dubbed the Hot Water War, after an incident in which a woman dumped a bucket of hot water on a revenue agent.

The Pennsylvanians' protests escalated until a group of residents took several revenue officers captive and held them until they had satisfactorily explained their actions. Upon their release, the officers arrested twenty-three men for insurrection. Fries and a group of men who believed that the property tax was a deprivation of liberty took up arms and liberated their detained comrades. When the group resisted orders from President JOHN ADAMS to disperse and to allow the federal officers to carry out their duties, Fries and its other leaders were arrested for treason.

Fries was brought to trial in 1799, before Judge Richard Peters, of the Pennsylvania District Court, and Justice JAMES IREDELL, of the Supreme Court. Fries's defense counsel argued that their client's offense was a simple protest that perhaps could be characterized as SEDITION, but certainly did not rise to the level of treason, a capital crime. They contended that, in a free republic, the treason charge should be reserved for the most extreme cases of armed attempt to overthrow the government.

Defense counsel's pleas for freedom of expression of political sentiment did not convince members of the jury, who were probably influenced by Iredell's and Peters's instructions. In those instructions, Peters equated opposing or preventing the implementation of a law with treason, and Iredell agreed with him. Fries was found guilty, but was granted a new trial when the court learned that before the trial began, one juror had expressed a belief in his guilt.

Fries's second trial took place in April 1800, before Justice SAMUEL CHASE, of the Supreme Court, and Judge Peters. Determined to expedite the second trial, Chase took the unprecedented step of preparing an opinion on the law of the case. Before the trial began, he distributed copies of his summary to the defense attorneys, the district attorney, and the jury. Chase made it clear that his opinion represented the court's view of the law of treason and that the defense would not be permitted to present lengthy arguments to the contrary, as it had in the first trial.

Outraged that the court had prejudged their client's case, Fries's attorneys withdrew from the case. Fries chose to proceed to trial without benefit of legal representation. He was again found guilty and sentenced to death by hanging. However, after studying the case, President Adams pardoned him and the other insurgents. Soon after his PARDON, Fries was promoted from captain to lieutenant colonel in the Montgomery County, Pennsylvania, militia.

Justice Chase's conduct in Fries's second trial was harshly criticized as indirectly depriving Fries of counsel. The justice's actions were used against him in 1805, in an unsuccessful IMPEACHMENT proceeding.

See also WHISKEY REBELLION.

FRISK A term used in CRIMINAL LAW to refer to the superficial running of the hands over the body of an individual by a law enforcement agent or official in order to determine whether such individual is holding an illegal object, such as a weapon or narcotics.

A frisk is distinguishable from a SEARCH, which is a more extensive examination of an individual.

FRIVOLOUS Of minimal importance; legally worthless.

A *frivolous suit* is one without any legal merit. In some cases, such an action might be brought in BAD FAITH for the purpose of harrassing the defendant. In such a case, the individual bringing the frivolous suit might be liable for DAMAGES for MALICIOUS PROSECUTION.

A *frivolous appeal* is one that is completely lacking merit, since no reviewable question has been raised therein.

FROLIC Activities performed by an employee during working hours that are not considered to be in the course of his or her employment, since they are for the employee's personal purposes only.

The doctrine of RESPONDEAT SUPERIOR makes a principal liable for the TORTS of his or her AGENT occurring during the course of employment. This is based on the concept that a principal has control over his or her agent's behavior. If an agent was hired to drive from point A to point B, and, through reckless driving, hit a pedestrian along the way, the principal would ordinarily be held liable. If, however, the agent was engaged in frolic, the principal would not be liable. This might occur, for example, if an employee were hired to transport goods from point A to point B and made several detours along the way for personal reasons. If the employee became involved in an accident while on a frolic, the employer would not be liable unless it could be established that he or she was negligent in the hiring or supervision of the employee.

FRUIT OF THE POISONOUS TREE The principle that proscribes the use of EVIDENCE directly derived from an illegal SEARCH AND SEIZURE.

The "fruit of the poisonous tree" doctrine is an offspring of the EXCLUSIONARY RULE. The exclusionary rule mandates that evidence obtained from an illegal arrest, unreasonable search, or coercive interrogation must be excluded from trial. Under the fruit of the poisonous tree doctrine, evidence is also excluded from trial if it was gained through evidence uncovered in an illegal arrest, unreasonable search, or coercive interrogation. Like the exclusionary rule, the fruit of the poisonous tree doctrine was established primarily to deter law enforcement from violating rights against unreasonable searches and seizures.

The name *fruit of the poisonous tree* is thus a metaphor: The poisonous tree is evidence seized in an illegal arrest, search, or interrogation by law enforcement. The fruit of this poisonous tree is evidence later discovered because of knowledge gained from the first illegal search, arrest, or interrogation. The poisonous tree and the fruit are both excluded from a criminal trial.

Assume that a police officer searches the AUTOMOBILE of a person stopped for a minor traffic violation. This violation is the only reason the officer conducts the search; nothing indicates that the driver is impaired by DRUGS or ALCOHOL, and no other circumstances would lead a reasonable officer to believe that the car contains evidence of a crime. This is an unreasonable search under the FOURTH AMENDMENT to the U.S. Constitution.

Assume further that the officer finds a small amount of marijuana in the vehicle. The driver is subsequently charged with possession of a controlled substance and chooses to go to trial. The marijuana evidence culled from this search is excluded from trial under the exclusionary rule, and the criminal charges are dropped for lack of evidence.

Also suppose that before the original charges are dismissed, the police officers ask a magistrate or judge for a WARRANT to search the home of the driver. The only evidence used as a basis, or PROBABLE CAUSE, for the warrant is the small amount of marijuana found in the vehicle search. The magistrate, unaware that the marijuana was uncovered in an illegal search, approves the warrant for the home search.

The officers search the driver's home and find a lawn mower stolen from a local park facility. Under the fruit of the poisonous tree doctrine, the lawn mower must be excluded from any trial on theft charges because the search of the house was based on evidence gathered in a previous illegal search.

The Supreme Court first hinted at the fruit of the poisonous tree doctrine in *Silverthorne Lumber Co. v. United States*, 251 U.S. 385, 40 S. Ct. 182, 64 L. Ed. 319 (1920). In *Silverthorne*, defendant Frederick W. Silverthorne was arrested on suspicion of federal violations in connection with his lumber business. Government agents then conducted a warrantless, illegal search of the Silverthorne offices. Based on the evidence discovered in the search, the prosecution requested more documents, and the court ordered Silverthorne to produce the documents. Silverthorne refused and was jailed for CONTEMPT of court.

On appeal, the Supreme Court reversed the contempt judgment. In its argument to the High Court, the government conceded that the search was illegal and that the prosecution was not entitled to keep the documents obtained in it. However, the government held that it was

U.S. customs officers sometimes use dogs to search vehicles for drugs. If the customs officer does not have a valid reason to search this truck, any evidence found will be considered fruit of the poisonous tree.

entitled to copy the documents and use knowledge gained from the documents for future prosecution. The Court rejected this argument. According to the Court, "[T]he essence of forbidding the acquisition of evidence in a certain way is that . . . it shall not be used at all." *Silverthorne* concerned only evidence gained in the first illegal search or seizure, but the wording of the opinion paved the way for the exclusion of evidence gained in subsequent searches and seizures.

The term *fruit of the poisonous tree* was first used in *Nardone v. United States*, 308 U.S. 338, 60 S. Ct. 266, 84 L. Ed. 307 (1939). In *Nardone*, Frank C. Nardone appealed his convictions for SMUGGLING and concealing alcohol and for CONSPIRACY to do the same. In an earlier decision, the High Court had ruled that an interception of Nardone's telephone conversations by government agents violated the Communications Act of 1934 (47 U.S.C.A. § 605). The issue before the Court was whether the trial court erred in refusing to allow Nardone's lawyer to question the prosecution on whether, and in what way, it had used information obtained in the illegal WIRE TAPPING.

In reversing Nardone's convictions, the Court stated that once a defendant has established that evidence was illegally seized, the trial court "must give opportunity, however closely confined, to the accused to prove that a substantial portion of the case against him was a fruit of the poisonous tree." The *Nardone* opinion established that evidence obtained in violation of a statute was subject to exclusion if it was obtained in violation of a statutory right.

The fruit of the poisonous tree doctrine was first held applicable to Fourth Amendment violations in the landmark case *Wong Sun v. United States*, 371 U.S. 471, 83 S. Ct. 407, 9 L. Ed. 2d 441 (1963). The Court in *Wong Sun* also set forth the test for determining how closely DE-RIVATIVE EVIDENCE must be related to illegally obtained evidence to warrant exclusion.

In *Wong Sun*, a number of federal narcotics agents had arrested Hom Way in San Francisco at 2:00 A.M. on June 4, 1959, on suspicion of narcotics activity. Although the agents had been watching Way for six weeks, they did not have a warrant for his arrest. Way was searched, and the agents found heroin in his possession. After his arrest, Way stated that he had bought an ounce of heroin the night before from Blackie Toy, the proprietor of a laundry on Leaven-worth Street.

Though Way had never been an informant for the police, the agents cruised Leavenworth Street. At 6:00 A.M., they stopped at Oye's Laundry on Leavenworth. The rest of the agents remained out of sight while Agent Alton Wong rang the bell. When James Wah Toy answered the door, Wong said he was there for laundry and dry cleaning. Toy answered that he did not open until 8:00 A.M. and started to close the door. Wong then identified himself as a federal narcotics agent. Toy slammed the door and began to run down the hallway, through the laundry, and to his bedroom, where his wife and child were sleeping. Again without a warrant, Wong and the other agents broke open the

door, followed Toy, and arrested him. A search of the premises uncovered no illegal drugs.

While Toy was in handcuffs, one of the agents told him that Way had said Toy sold Way narcotics. Toy denied selling narcotics, but then said he knew someone who had. When asked who, Toy answered that he knew the man only as Johnny. Toy told the officers that Johnny lived on Eleventh Avenue, and then he described the house. Toy also volunteered that Johnny kept about an ounce of heroin in his bedroom, and that he and Johnny had smoked some heroin the night before.

The agents left and located the house on Eleventh Avenue. Without a search or an arrest warrant, they entered the home, went to the bedroom, and found Johnny Yee. After a "discussion" with the agents, Yee surrendered a little less than one ounce of heroin.

The same morning, Yee and Toy were taken to the office of the Bureau of Narcotics. While in custody there, Yee stated that he had gotten the heroin about four days earlier from Toy and another person he knew as Sea Dog. The agents then asked Toy about Sea Dog, and Toy identified Sea Dog as Wong Sun. Some of the agents took Toy to Sun's neighborhood, where Toy pointed out Sun's house. The agents walked past Sun's wife and arrested Sun, who had been sleeping in his bedroom. A search of the premises turned up no illegal drugs.

Toy and Yee were arraigned in federal court on June 4, 1959, and Sun was arraigned the next day. All were released without BAIL. A few days later, Toy, Yee, and Sun were interrogated separately at the Narcotics Bureau by Agent William Wong. Sun and Toy made written statements but refused to sign them.

Sun and Toy were tried jointly on charges of transporting and concealing narcotics in violation of 21 U.S.C.A. § 174. Way did not testify at the trial. The government offered Yee as its principal WITNESS, but Yee recanted his statement to Agent William Wong and invoked his FIFTH AMENDMENT right against SELF-INCRIMINA-TION. With only four items in evidence, Sun and Toy were convicted by the court in a BENCH TRIAL. The Court of Appeals for the Ninth Circuit affirmed the convictions (*Wong Sun*, 288 F.2d 366 (9th Cir. 1961)). Sun and Toy appealed to the U.S. Supreme Court.

The Supreme Court accepted the case and reversed the convictions. The Court began its analysis by noting that the court of appeals had held that the arrests of both Sun and Toy were illegal. The question was whether the four items in evidence against Sun and Toy were

Wong Sun was the first case that held the fruit of the poisonous tree doctrine applicable to Fourth Amendment violations. In deciding to make a search, law enforcement officers must rely on legally obtained evidence and not the statements of suspects.

CHRIS BROWNSTOCK BOSTON

ADMISSIBLE despite the illegality of the arrests. The four pieces of evidence were the oral statements made by Toy in his bedroom at the time of his arrest, the heroin surrendered to the agents by Yee, Toy's unsigned statement to Agent William Wong, and Sun's unsigned statement to Agent William Wong.

The government submitted several theories to support the proposition that the statements made by Toy in his bedroom were properly admitted at trial. The Court rejected all the arguments. According to the Court, the arrest was illegal because the agents had no evidence supporting it other than the word of Way, an arrestee who had never been an informer for law enforcement. The officers did not even know whether Toy was the person they were looking for. Furthermore, Toy's flight did not give the officers probable cause to arrest Toy: Agent Alton Wong had first posed as a customer, and this made Toy's flight ambiguous and not necessarily the product of a guilty mind. Thus, under the exclusionary rule, the oral statements made by Toy in his bedroom should not have been allowed at trial.

The Court then turned to the actual drug evidence seized from Yee. The Court, in deference to *Nardone*, stated, "We need not hold that all evidence is 'fruit of the poisonous tree.'" Instead, the question in such a situation was "'whether, granting establishment of the primary illegality, the evidence . . . has been come at by exploitation of that illegality or instead by means sufficiently distinguishable to be purged of the primary taint.'"

According to the Court, the narcotics in *Wong Sun* were indeed "come at" by use of Toy's statements. Toy's statements were, in fact, the only evidence used to justify entrance to Yee's bedroom. Since the statements by Toy were INADMISSIBLE, the narcotics in Yee's possession were also inadmissible, as fruit of the poisonous tree. The Court went on to hold that Sun's written statements about Toy should also have been excluded as HEARSAY, and the Court ultimately overturned Toy's conviction.

The Court did not reverse Sun's conviction. The heroin in Yee's possession was admissible at trial, as was Sun's own statement. According to the Court, "The exclusion of narcotics as to Toy was required solely by their tainted relationship to information unlawfully obtained from Toy, and not by any official impropriety connected with their surrender by Yee." The Court did, however, grant Sun a new trial, because it was unable to conclude that Toy's statements, erroneously admitted at trial as evi-

dence against Sun, had not affected the VERDICT. The Court advised that on REMAND and in similar cases, "particular care ought to be taken . . . when the crucial element of the accused's possession is proved solely by his own admissions."

In determining whether evidence is fruit of a poisonous tree, the trial court judge must examine all the facts surrounding the initial seizure of evidence and the subsequent gathering of evidence. This determination is usually made by the judge in a suppression hearing held before trial. In this hearing, the judge must first determine that an illegal search or seizure occurred and then decide whether the evidence was obtained as a result of the illegal search or seizure.

The Supreme Court found such a causal connection lacking in *United States v. Ceccolini*, 435 U.S. 268, 98 S. Ct. 1054, 55 L. Ed. 2d 268 (1978). In *Ceccolini*, Ralph Ceccolini was found guilty of PERJURY by a district court in New York. However, the court set aside the verdict after it threw out TESTIMONY by Lois Hennessey against Ceccolini. According to the district court, Hennessey's testimony was tied to an illegal search conducted a year earlier. The government appealed to the U.S. Court of Appeals for the Second Circuit. The appeals court affirmed, and the government appealed to the U.S. Supreme Court.

According to the High Court, the exclusion of Hennessey's testimony was an error because sufficient time had elapsed to separate the illegal search from the testimony. Furthermore, Hennessey's testimony was not coerced by law enforcement officials as a result of the illegal search. An officer had questioned Hennessey four months after the search without specifically referring to the illegal search, and Hennessey volunteered the incriminating evidence against Ceccolini. The Court reversed, reasoning that the exclusion of testimony such as Hennessey's would not have a deterrent effect on misconduct by law enforcement officers.

See also CRIMINAL LAW; CRIMINAL PROCEDURE.

FRUSTRATION 📖 In the law of CONTRACTS, the destruction of the value of the PERFORMANCE that has been bargained for by the promisor as a result of a supervening event. 📖

Frustration of purpose has the effect of discharging the promisor from his or her obligation to perform, in spite of the fact that performance by the promisee is possible, since the purpose for which the contract was entered into has been destroyed. For example, an individual reserves a hall for a wedding. In the event that the wedding is called off, the value of the agreement would be destroyed. Even though the promisee could still literally perform the obligation by reserving and providing the hall for the wedding, the purpose for which the contract was entered into was defeated. Apart from a nonrefundable deposit fee, the promisor is ordinarily discharged from any contractual duty to rent the hall.

In order for frustration to be used as a defense for nonperformance, the value of the anticipated counterperformance must have been substantially destroyed and the frustrating occurrence must have been beyond the contemplation of the parties at the time the agreement was made.

FUGITIVE FROM JUSTICE An individual who, after having committed a criminal offense, leaves the JURISDICTION of the court where such CRIME has taken place or hides within such jurisdiction to escape prosecution.

A fugitive from justice who flees from one state to another may be subjected to EXTRADITION in the state to which he or she has fled.

FUGITIVE SLAVE ACT OF 1850 Federal legislation enacted by Congress that mandated that states to which escaped slaves fled were obligated to return them to their masters upon their discovery and subjected persons who helped runaway slaves to criminal sanctions.

The first Fugitive Slave Act was enacted by Congress in 1793 but as the northern states abolished SLAVERY, the act was rarely enforced. The southern states bitterly resented the northern attitude toward slavery, which was ultimately demonstrated by the existence of the Underground Railroad, an arrangement by which abolitionists helped runaway slaves obtain freedom.

To placate the South, the Fugitive Slave Act of 1850 (9 Stat. 462) was enacted by Congress as part of the COMPROMISE OF 1850. It imposed a duty on all citizens to assist federal marshals to enforce the law or be prosecuted for their failure to do so. The act also required that when a slave was captured, he or she was to be brought before a federal court or commissioner, but the slave would not be tried by a jury nor would his or her testimony be given much weight. The statements of the slave's alleged owner were the main evidence, and the alleged owner was not even required to appear in court.

Northern reaction against the Fugitive Slave Act was strong, and many states enacted laws that nullified its effect, making it worthless. In cases where the law was enforced, threats or acts of mob violence often required the dispatch

CAUTION!!
COLORED PEOPLE
OF BOSTON, ONE & ALL,
You are hereby respectfully CAUTIONED and advised, to avoid conversing with the
Watchmen and Police Officers of Boston,
For since the recent ORDER OF THE MAYOR & ALDERMEN, they are empowered to act as
KIDNAPPERS
AND
Slave Catchers,
And they have already been actually employed in KIDNAPPING, CATCHING, AND KEEPING SLAVES. Therefore, if you value your LIBERTY, and the *Welfare of the Fugitives* among you, *Shun* them in every possible manner, as so many *HOUNDS* on the track of the most unfortunate of your race.
Keep a Sharp Look Out for KIDNAPPERS, and have TOP EYE open.
APRIL 24, 1851.

The Compromise of 1850 included the Fugitive Slave Act, which mandated that citizens assist in the capture of runaway slaves or be punished for failure to provide assistance. The act pointed to the differences that later divided the North and South in the U.S. Civil War.

of federal troops. Persons convicted of violating the act were often heavily fined, imprisoned, or both. The refusal of northern states to enforce the Fugitive Slave Act was alleged by South Carolina as one reason for its SECESSION from the Union prior to the onset of the Civil War.

The acts of 1793 and 1850 remained legally operative until their repeal by Congress on June 28, 1864 (13 Stat. 200).

FULBRIGHT, JAMES WILLIAM James William Fulbright served as a U.S. senator from Arkansas from 1945 to 1974. Fulbright played an important role in shaping U.S. foreign policy as chairman of the Senate Foreign Relations Committee. His opposition to the VIETNAM WAR and to unbridled PRESIDENTIAL POWER in foreign affairs contributed to major shifts in the conduct of U.S. foreign relations.

Fulbright was born in Sumner, Missouri, on April 9, 1905, the son of a prosperous Arkansas businessman. He entered the University of Arkansas at the age of sixteen, and graduated in 1925. From 1925 to 1928, Fulbright attended Oxford University, in England, as a Rhodes scholar. This educational experience deepened his intellectual interests and provided a strong

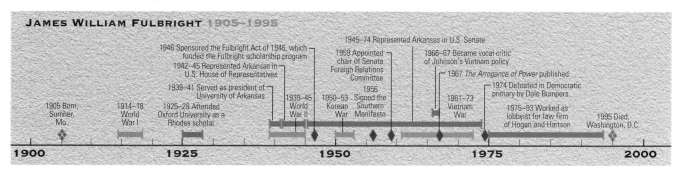

JAMES WILLIAM FULBRIGHT 1905–1995

1905 Born, Sumner, Mo.

1914–18 World War I

1925–28 Attended Oxford University as a Rhodes scholar

1939–41 Served as president of University of Arkansas

1942–45 Represented Arkansas in U.S. House of Representatives

1946 Sponsored the Fulbright Act of 1946, which funded the Fulbright scholarship program

1939–45 World War II

1945–74 Represented Arkansas in U.S. Senate

1950–53 Korean War

1956 Signed the Southern Manifesto

1959 Appointed chair of Senate Foreign Relations Committee

1961–73 Vietnam War

1966–67 Became vocal critic of Johnson's Vietnam policy

1967 The Arrogance of Power published

1974 Defeated in Democratic primary by Dale Bumpers

1975–93 Worked as lobbyist for law firm of Hogan and Hartson

1995 Died, Washington, D.C.

1900   1925   1950   1975   2000

background for public life. He graduated from George Washington University Law School in 1934, and then taught at that school for two years. In 1936 he accepted a teaching position at the University of Arkansas. In 1939 he was appointed president of the University of Arkansas. At age thirty-four, he was the youngest college president in the United States. His tenure was short, however, as a new governor dismissed him in 1941.

Fulbright then turned his focus to politics. As a Democrat he was elected to the U.S. House of Representatives in 1942. In 1945 he was elected to the U.S. Senate. His previous time as a Rhodes scholar led him to sponsor the Fulbright Act of 1946, 22 U.S.C.A. § 245 et seq., which awards scholarships to U.S. citizens for study and research abroad and to citizens from other nations for study in the United States. The establishment of the Fulbright Scholarship exchange program has proved to be an enduring legacy.

Fulbright, although personally a moderate on matters of race, believed in the 1950s that he needed to move to the right on race issues to protect his political future in Arkansas. This led him to sign the Southern Manifesto, a 1956 document signed by Southern senators and representatives that expressed their displeasure at the Supreme Court's decision in *Brown v. Board of Education (Brown I)*, 347 U.S. 483, 74 S. Ct. 686, 98 L. Ed. 873 (1954), which struck down state-sponsored racially segregated public school systems, and *Brown v. Board of Education (Brown II)*, 349 U.S. 294, 75 S. Ct. 753, 99 L. Ed. 1083 (1955), in which the Court directed that schools be desegregated with "all deliberate speed." The manifesto condemned these decisions as abuses of judicial power and approved of Southern resistance, by all legal means, to the demand for desegregation. Fulbright doomed his national political prospects by signing the manifesto.

In the 1950s Fulbright became a close friend and colleague of Senate Majority Leader LYNDON B. JOHNSON, a Democrat from Texas. In 1959 Johnson engineered Fulbright's elevation

BIOGRAPHY

LIBRARY OF CONGRESS

James William Fulbright

"POWER TENDS TO CONFUSE ITSELF WITH VIRTUE AND A GREAT NATION IS PECULIARLY SUSCEPTIBLE TO THE IDEA THAT ITS POWER IS A SIGN OF GOD'S FAVOR."

to chairman of the Senate Foreign Relations Committee. Following the election of JOHN F. KENNEDY as president in 1960, Johnson, now vice president, urged Kennedy to appoint Fulbright secretary of state. Johnson's efforts failed, in large part because Fulbright had supported the Southern Manifesto and racial segregation.

During the Kennedy administration, Fulbright opposed the United States' indirect involvement in the 1961 Bay of Pigs invasion, in which Cuban exiles made a futile attempt to overthrow the premier of Cuba, Fidel Castro. When the Vietnam War escalated under President Johnson, Fulbright became a consistent critic of presidential foreign policy. Fulbright had supported Johnson's Vietnam policy in the early part of the conflict, sponsoring the Gulf of Tonkin Resolution in 1964, Pub. L. No. 88-408, 78 Stat. 384, which allowed Johnson to wage war without seeking a congressional declaration. Within a year, however, Fulbright had become convinced that Johnson had misled him about events that had brought about the 1964 resolution. See also CUBAN MISSILE CRISIS.

Fulbright used the Foreign Relations Committee as a platform to criticize Vietnam policy. In January 1966 he held televised hearings on Vietnam. Leading opponents of the war testified that the conflict was going badly and that the United States did not have a legitimate role to play in Vietnam. Fulbright called Secretary of State Dean Rusk to appear three times during the hearings, repeatedly asking hard questions about U.S.-Asian policy. These hearings and additional ones in 1967 gave credibility to the antiwar movement and damaged the Johnson administration's credibility.

Skeptical about U.S. foreign policy and the attitudes of those who conduct it, Fulbright criticized policy makers in his books, *Old Myths and New Realities* (1964) and *The Arrogance of Power* (1967). His opposition continued during the Nixon administration.

In 1974 Fulbright was defeated by Dale L. Bumpers in the Democratic primary election. He served as a Washington lobbyist following his defeat, and remained active in the Fulbright Scholarship program.

Fulbright died in Washington, D.C., on February 9, 1995.

FULLER, MELVILLE WESTON

Melville Weston Fuller served as chief justice of the U.S. Supreme Court from 1888 to 1910. Fuller's term as chief justice was marked by many decisions that protected big business from federal laws that sought to regulate interstate commerce. In addition, the Fuller Court's restrictive reading of the FOURTEENTH AMENDMENT led it to render the infamous "separate-but-equal" racial segregation decision in *Plessy v. Ferguson*, 163 U.S. 537, 16 S. Ct. 1138, 41 L. Ed. 256 (1896).

Fuller was born February 11, 1833, in Augusta, Maine, into an old English family. He grew up in the household of his maternal grandfather, the chief justice of the Maine Supreme Judicial Court. Following his graduation from Bowdoin College in 1853, he apprenticed in his uncles' law offices and briefly attended Harvard Law School. Even though he did not receive a law degree, he was the first chief justice of the Supreme Court to serve with significant academic legal preparation. Fuller moved to Chicago in 1856 and set up a law practice. An active member of the Democratic party, he served in the Illinois Constitutional Convention of 1861 and for one term (1862–64) in the state house of representatives. He attended as a delegate every national Democratic convention between 1864 and 1880.

Fuller withdrew from day-to-day politics after he married Mary Ellen Coolbaugh, the daughter of a prominent Chicago banker, in 1866. His law practice thrived because of this family connection, and with his new wealth, he invested in real estate. Fuller specialized in appellate practice, appearing before the U.S. Supreme Court many times.

Fuller's appointment to the Supreme Court in 1888 was driven by presidential politics and his long service to the Democratic party. President GROVER CLEVELAND, a Democrat, believing it essential to win the state of Illinois as part of his reelection bid, nominated Fuller as chief

ARTIST ALBERT ROSENTHAL, COLLECTION OF THE SUPREME COURT OF THE UNITED STATES

Melville Weston Fuller

"IF THE PROVISIONS OF THE CONSTITUTION CAN BE SET ASIDE BY AN ACT OF CONGRESS, WHERE IS THE COURSE OF USURPATION TO END?"

justice to replace MORRISON R. WAITE, who died in March 1888. Fuller and Cleveland were friends and political colleagues. At the time the press described Fuller as "the most obscure man ever appointed Chief Justice" (Baker 1991, 360). Others were more unkind, dubbing him "the fifth best lawyer from the City of Chicago" (review of *The Chief Justiceship of Melville W. Fuller* 1996, 109).

Fuller's twenty-two-year term as chief justice was distinguished by his skillful handling of often contentious Court conferences. Justice OLIVER WENDELL HOLMES, JR., thought highly of Fuller's ability to maintain collegiality. At the end of his own legal career, Holmes ranked Fuller as the best chief justice under whom he had served. Fuller was an energetic jurist who also served on the Permanent Court of Arbitration, at The Hague, Netherlands. This international organization, comprising jurists from various countries, ruled on world disputes. In 1899 Fuller arbitrated a boundary dispute between Venezuela and British Guiana.

Fuller was chief justice when the U.S. economy was growing rapidly. This situation led to the concentration of economic power in certain industries by a small number of individuals and corporations. The federal government's efforts to regulate interstate commerce and curtail the power of monopolies and trusts met fierce opposition from both the affected businesses and those who believed in a restricted role for the national government. Opponents of national power argued for continued adherence to the doctrine of FEDERALISM. This doctrine has many facets, including a fundamental assumption that the national government must not intrude on the power of the states to handle their affairs.

Fuller believed in federalism and demonstrated this belief in his votes with the conservative majority on the Court. Writing for the majority in *United States v. E. C. Knight Co.*, 156 U.S. 1, 15 S. Ct. 249, 39 L. Ed. 325 (1895), Fuller took the teeth out of the SHERMAN ANTI-TRUST ACT of July 2, 1890, which declared illegal "every contract, combination in the form of a trust, or conspiracy in restraint of trade and

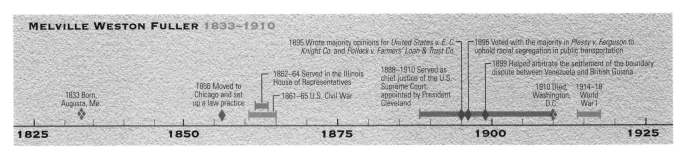

MELVILLE WESTON FULLER 1833–1910

1833 Born, Augusta, Me.

1856 Moved to Chicago and set up a law practice

1862–64 Served in the Illinois House of Representatives

1861–65 U.S. Civil War

1888–1910 Served as chief justice of the U.S. Supreme Court, appointed by President Cleveland

1895 Wrote majority opinions for *United States v. E. C. Knight Co.* and *Pollock v. Farmers' Loan & Trust Co.*

1896 Voted with the majority in *Plessy v. Ferguson* to uphold racial segregation in public transportation

1899 Helped arbitrate the settlement of the boundary dispute between Venezuela and British Guiana

1910 Died, Washington, D.C.

1914–18 World War I

1825   1850   1875   1900   1925

commerce among the several states" (26 Stat. 209, c. 647). Finding in favor of the Sugar Trust, a CORPORATION that controlled virtually all sugar refining, Fuller held that a MONOPOLY of manufacturing was not a monopoly of trade or commerce prohibited by the Sherman Act, as the manufacture of a product for sale is not commerce. It was up to each state, not the federal government, to protect its citizens from monopolistic business practices. The mere fact that goods were transported in interstate commerce was not sufficient to give Congress, under the COMMERCE CLAUSE, the authority to regulate business. The holding in *Knight* survived until the New Deal era of the 1930s, when power shifted to the federal government.

Fuller's belief in a limited role for the federal government was also demonstrated in *Pollock v. Farmers' Loan & Trust Co.*, 157 U.S. 429, 15 S. Ct. 673, 39 L. Ed. 759 (1895). In *Pollock*, Fuller ruled invalid a federal law that imposed a two percent tax on incomes of more than $4,000. Article I of the Constitution requires that "direct taxes shall be apportioned among the several states . . . according to their respective numbers." In a 5–4 vote, Fuller's Court held that the new INCOME TAX was a DIRECT TAX insofar as it was based on incomes derived from land and, as such, had to be apportioned among the states. Since the law did not provide for apportionment, it was unconstitutional.

Decisions such as *Knight* and *Pollock* led critics to call Fuller and the conservative members of the Supreme Court tools of business interests and protectors of wealth. In response to *Pollock*, the SIXTEENTH AMENDMENT was ratified by the states in 1913, authorizing the collection of a federal income tax.

Fuller's most dubious distinction is that he voted with the majority in *Plessy* to uphold racial segregation in public transportation. At issue in *Plessy* was an 1890 Louisiana law requiring passenger trains operating within the state to provide "equal but separate" accommodations for the "white and colored races." By a 7–1 vote, with one judge abstaining, the Supreme Court rejected the idea that the Fourteenth Amendment, enacted after the Civil War to preserve the CIVIL RIGHTS of newly freed slaves, "could have been intended to abolish distinctions based upon color, or to enforce social, as distinguished from political, equality, or a commingling of the two races upon terms unsatisfactory to either."

With its focus on a limited national government and support of legally enforced racial segregation, the twenty-two-year period of the Fuller Court has, in the words of legal historian

Richard A. Epstein, "often been regarded as a black hole of American Constitutional law." But with the conservative political and legal renaissance of the 1980s and 1990s, Fuller has come back into favor. He is now regarded by some legal scholars as a jurist committed to economic development, market institutions, and limited government.

CROSS-REFERENCES

Plessy v. Ferguson; Pollock v. Farmers' Loan & Trust Co.; Separate but Equal.

FULL FAITH AND CREDIT CLAUSE

The clause of the U.S. Constitution that provides that the various states must recognize legislative acts, public records, and judicial decisions of the other states within the United States.

The Full Faith and Credit Clause—Article IV, Section 1, of the U.S. Constitution—provides, "Full Faith and Credit shall be given in each State to the public Acts, Records, and judicial Proceedings of every other State." The statute that implements the clause, 28 U.S.C.A. § 1738, further specifies that "a state's preclusion rules should control matters originally litigated in that state." The Full Faith and Credit Clause ensures that judicial decisions rendered by the courts in one state are recognized and honored in every other state. It also prevents PARTIES from moving to another state to escape enforcement of a JUDGMENT or to relitigate a controversy already decided elsewhere, a practice known as FORUM shopping.

In drafting the Full Faith and Credit Clause, the Framers of the Constitution were motivated by a desire to unify their new country while preserving the autonomy of the states. To that end, they sought to guarantee that judgments rendered by the courts of one state would not be ignored by the courts of other states. The Supreme Court reiterated the Framers' intent when it held that the Full Faith and Credit Clause precluded any further litigation of a question previously decided by an Illinois court in *Milwaukee County v. M. E. White Co.*, 296 U.S. 268, 56 S. Ct. 229, 80 L. Ed. 220 (1935). The Court held that by including the clause in the Constitution, the Framers intended to make the states "integral parts of a single nation throughout which a remedy upon a just obligation might be demanded as of right, irrespective of the state of its origin."

The Full Faith and Credit Clause is invoked primarily to enforce judgments. When a valid judgment is rendered by a court that has JURISDICTION over the parties, and the parties receive proper notice of the action and a reasonable

The Full Faith and Credit Clause has been invoked to recognize the validity of same-sex marriages but the Defense of Marriage Act grants states the right to refuse to recognize a same-sex marriage performed in another state.

opportunity to be heard, the Full Faith and Credit Clause requires that the judgment receive the same effect in other states as in the state where it is entered. A party who obtains a judgment in one state may petition the court in another state to enforce the judgment. When this is done, the parties do not relitigate the issues, and the court in the second state is obliged to fully recognize and honor the judgment of the first court in determining the enforceability of the judgment and the procedure for its execution.

The Full Faith and Credit Clause has also been invoked to recognize the validity of a MARRIAGE. Traditionally, every state honored a marriage legally contracted in any other state. However, in 1993, the Hawaii Supreme Court held that Hawaii's statute restricting legal marriage to parties of the opposite sex establishes a sex-based classification, which is subject to STRICT SCRUTINY if challenged on EQUAL PROTECTION grounds (*Baehr v. Lewin*, 852 P.2d 44, 74 Haw. 530). Although the court did not recognize a constitutional right to same-sex marriage, it raised the possibility that a successful equal protection challenge to the state's marriage laws could eventually lead to state-sanctioned same-sex marriages. In response to the *Baehr* case, Congress in 1996 passed the Defense of Marriage Act (110 Stat. § 2419), which defines marriage as a union of a man and a woman for federal purposes and expressly grants states the right to refuse to recognize a same-sex marriage performed in another state.

During the 1980s and 1990s, the Full Faith and Credit Clause was applied to new matters. CHILD CUSTODY determinations had historically fallen under the jurisdiction of state courts, and before the 1970s, other states did not accord them full faith and credit enforcement. As a

result, a divorced parent who was unhappy with one state's custody decision could sometimes obtain a more favorable ruling from another state. This was an incentive for a dissatisfied parent to KIDNAP a child and move to another state in order to petition for custody. In response to this situation, the Uniform Child Custody Jurisdiction Act (UCCJA) was adopted by the National Conference of Commissioners on Uniform State Laws in 1968. By 1984, every state had adopted a version of the UCCJA. In 1980, Congress passed the Parental Kidnapping Prevention Act (28 U.S.C.A. § 1738A), which aids enforcement and promotes finality in child custody decisions by providing that valid custody decrees are entitled to full faith and credit enforcement in other states. The Violence against Women Act of 1994 (Pub. L. No. 103-322 [codified in scattered sections of 8 U.S.C.A., 18 U.S.C.A., 42 U.S.C.A.]) extends full faith and credit to the enforcement of PROTECTIVE ORDERS, which previously were not enforced except in the state where they were rendered. This gave a new measure of protection to victims who moved to a different state after obtaining a protective order in one state.

FUND 📖 A comprehensive term for any money that is set aside for a particular purpose or that is accessible for the satisfaction of debts or claims. 📖

The term *public funds* is a colloquial label for the revenue of a government, state, or MUNICIPAL CORPORATION.

FUNDAMENTAL LAW 📖 The CONSTITUTION of a state or nation; the basic law and principles contained in federal and state constitutions that direct and regulate the manner in which government is exercised. 📖

FUNGIBLE 📖 A description applied to items of which each unit is identical to every other unit, such as in the case of grain, oil, or flour. 📖

Fungible goods are those that can readily be estimated and replaced according to weight, measure, and amount.

FURMAN v. GEORGIA In *Furman v. Georgia*, 408 U.S. 238, 92 S. Ct. 2726, 33 L. Ed. 2d 346 (1972), the U.S. Supreme Court struck down three death sentences, finding that they constituted CRUEL AND UNUSUAL PUNISHMENT in violation of the Eighth and Fourteenth Amendments to the U.S. Constitution. At the time hailed as a victory for opponents of the death penalty, *Furman* actually helped states rewrite their death penalty laws to pass constitutional muster.

The death penalty was in widespread use at the time the Constitution was adopted. The

Due Process Clauses of the Fifth and Fourteenth Amendments recognize the death penalty in phrases stating the government shall not deprive any person of "*life*, liberty, or property without due process of law" (emphasis added). Yet the EIGHTH AMENDMENT prohibits "cruel and unusual punishments." The path to *Furman* was opened in the 1962 case *Robinson v. California*, 370 U.S. 660, 82 S. Ct. 1417, 8 L. Ed. 2d 758, where the U.S. Supreme Court ruled that the Cruel and Unusual Punishments Clause could be applied to the states through the FOURTEENTH AMENDMENT. Opponents of the death penalty now had the opportunity to litigate in federal court the constitutionality of state death penalty cases. See also INCORPORATION DOCTRINE.

Ironically, the use of the death penalty declined in the 1960s. Only two persons were executed in the United States between 1967 and the date of the *Furman* decision in 1972. Public opinion polls showed that a majority of U.S. citizens were opposed to CAPITAL PUNISHMENT.

Furman arose out of the convictions and death sentences of three African American men. William Henry Furman was convicted in Georgia for murder, Lucious Jackson was convicted in Georgia for rape, and Elmer Branch was convicted in Texas for rape. The juries in these cases were not mandated by law to vote for the death penalty, nor were they given specific criteria to evaluate in making their penalty decisions.

The U.S. Supreme Court typically issues its decisions with a majority opinion written and signed by one the justices. On rare occasions the Court will issue a PER CURIAM decision, which takes the form of a brief, unsigned opinion. A per curiam decision does not have as much precedential value as a signed opinion, as it signifies that the Court was deeply divided over the reasons that went into its ultimate decision to either affirm or reverse the lower court.

Furman was issued as a per curiam decision, on a 5–4 vote to reverse the death sentences. All nine justices wrote a separate opinion to articulate their reasoning. Though five justices voted to reverse the death sentences, their concurring opinions revealed that it was a shaky coalition. Justices WILLIAM O. DOUGLAS, WILLIAM J. BRENNAN, JR., and THURGOOD MARSHALL doubted that any application of the death penalty could avoid being a cruel and unusual punishment.

Justice Douglas concluded that the death penalty was disproportionately applied to people who were poor and socially disadvantaged. This disproportion suggested that the Equal Protection Clause of the Fourteenth Amendment must be applied to strike down the death penalty because any inequality of application was cruel and unusual punishment. Douglas's opinion raised the possibility that proportionate application would make capital punishment constitutional.

Justices Brennan and Marshall staked out an absolutist position, finding the death penalty PER SE cruel and unusual punishment, given the "evolving standards of decency" they saw in contemporary U.S. society. This meant that no matter the fact situation, no matter the proper application of DUE PROCESS and EQUAL PROTECTION, capital punishment was inherently unconstitutional.

The most influential opinion came from Justice POTTER STEWART:

> The penalty of death differs from all other forms of criminal punishment, not in degree but in kind. It is unique in its rejection of rehabilitation of the convict as a basic purpose of criminal justice. And it is unique, finally, in its absolute renunciation

Elmer Branch, one of the plaintiffs in Furman v. Georgia, holds out a newspaper to another death row inmate after the Supreme Court held that the death penalty constituted cruel and unusual punishment.

APWIDE WORLD PHOTOS

of all that is embodied in our concept of humanity.

Stewart held that because death was different from any other punishment, it had to be administered rationally and fairly. He rejected the absolutist position of Brennan and Marshall, yet still voted to reverse the penalties of Furman, Jackson, and Branch because he believed their death sentences were imposed capriciously.

Stewart looked at the circumstances surrounding the imposition of the three death sentences. The juries in these cases had been given unbridled discretion to do what they wished in deciding whether to impose capital punishment. The result, in Stewart's view, was that the death penalty was "wantonly and . . . freakishly imposed." These death sentences were "cruel and unusual in the same way that being struck by lightning is cruel and unusual."

Justice BYRON R. WHITE took a slightly different tack, concluding that the infrequency of execution prevented the penalty from serving as an effective deterrent and from consistently meeting legitimate social needs for retribution.

Chief Justice WARREN E. BURGER dissented, as did Justices HARRY A. BLACKMUN, LEWIS F. POWELL, JR., and WILLIAM H. REHNQUIST. The dissenters argued that the Court was straying into an area properly delegated to the judgment of state legislatures. The private opinions of justices about the morality of capital punishment, they opined, should not be presented as PUBLIC POLICY in a court of law. They also pointed out that recent polls showed that public opinion now supported the death penalty.

The *Furman* decision stopped all executions then pending in the thirty-nine states that authorized the death penalty. More than six hundred persons were awaiting execution at the time. Faced with a splintered Supreme Court decision, states had three options: develop mandatory death sentences for crimes that were carefully defined by statute, develop JURY guidelines to reduce juror discretion, or abolish capital punishment.

The state of Georgia chose to develop guidelines for jurors. Once a person is convicted in a capital trial, the jury must determine, in the penalty phase, whether any unique aggravating and MITIGATING CIRCUMSTANCES should be considered before the court decides whether to impose a death sentence. In 1976 the U.S. Supreme Court upheld these jury guidelines in *Gregg v. Georgia,* 428 U.S. 153, 96 S. Ct. 2909, 49 L. Ed. 2d 859. With the *Gregg* decision, the four-year moratorium on the death penalty ended.

FUTURE   ACQUIRED   PROPERTY

📖 Property that is received or obtained by a borrower subsequent to the date that he or she executes a loan agreement which offers property currently owned as COLLATERAL. 📖

Future acquired property, which is also known as after-acquired property, encompasses both PERSONAL PROPERTY and REAL PROPERTY and provides additional collateral to ensure that a loan will be satisfied. There must, however, be a provision in the loan agreement between the borrower and the lender that gives the lender a right to the specific property of the borrower that he or she acquires subsequent to the execution of the agreement.

SECURED TRANSACTIONS frequently involve the treatment of personal property as future acquired property. For example, a DEBTOR who owns a retail store might accept a future acquired property provision in a security agreement with a CREDITOR in order to obtain funds to buy additional inventory. The purchase of new inventory constitutes additional collateral that ensures the satisfaction of the loan. Language commonly used to phrase a future acquired property term in a contract is "any or all obligations covered by the security agreement are to be secured by all inventory now or hereafter acquired by the debtor."

MORTGAGES, particularly those affecting commercial properties, involve the treatment of real property as future acquired property. The mortgagee (who is the lender) will include in the mortgage an AFTER-ACQUIRED PROPERTY CLAUSE which provides that the mortgagee will have an equitable LIEN, which is a right to have property used to repay a debt, in all the real property that the mortgagor (who is the borrower) obtains after the mortgage is executed.

If a mortgage contains a future acquired property clause, the lender can obtain a lien on property subsequently acquired by the borrower, such as real estate in the form of an apartment building.

JOHN BERRY/THE IMAGE WORKS

For example, ABC Co. owns BLACKACRE and borrows funds from XYZ Bank. ABC executes a note and mortgage on Blackacre to XYZ, which XYZ records. The mortgage also contains an after-acquired property clause. When ABC subsequently purchases Whiteacre to serve as its warehouse, XYZ automatically obtains an equitable lien in Whiteacre. Since a mortgage with an after-acquired property clause cannot be traced through an examination of the CHAIN OF TITLE of the after-acquired property, anyone who subsequently buys or has a lien against the mortgagor's property has no notice of the equitable lien of the mortgagee. Such purchasers or lienors might, therefore, have greater rights to the property than the mortgagee if they took the property in GOOD FAITH and without notice. The mortgagee must take additional steps to protect the priority of his or her lien in future acquired property. It is a common practice for mortgage lenders to require that the mortgagor execute a recordable AMENDMENT to his or her mortgage describing in detail the future acquired property immediately after its acquisition.

The treatment of future acquired property varies, however, from JURISDICTION to jurisdiction.

FUTURE EARNINGS ◫ Earnings that, if it had not been for an injury, could have been made in the future, but which were lost as result of the injury. ◫

FUTURES ◫ Contracts that promise to purchase or sell standard COMMODITIES at a forthcoming date and at a fixed price. ◫

This type of contract is an extremely speculative transaction and ordinarily involves such standard goods as rice or soybeans. Profit and loss are based upon promises to deliver—as opposed to possession of—the actual commodities.

GAG ORDER 📖 A court order to gag or bind an unruly defendant or remove her or him from the courtroom in order to prevent further interruptions in a trial. In a trial with a great deal of notoriety, a court order directed to attorneys and witnesses not to discuss the case with the media—such order being felt necessary to assure the defendant of a fair trial. A court order, directed to the media, not to report certain aspects of a crime or criminal investigation prior to trial. 📖

Unruly defendants who disrupt trials are very rarely literally gagged in modern courts. However, the U.S. Supreme Court has upheld the constitutionality of the practice in cases where a defendant is particularly disruptive. In *Illinois v. Allen*, 397 U.S. 337, 90 S. Ct. 1057, 25 L. Ed. 2d 353 (1970), the Court affirmed that gagging or binding the defendant, or removing him or her from the courtroom, does not violate the Confrontation Clause of the SIXTH AMENDMENT to the U.S. Constitution, which holds, "In all criminal prosecutions, the accused shall enjoy the right . . . to be confronted with the witnesses against him." According to Associate Justice HUGO L. BLACK, who wrote the Court's opinion,

> [A] defendant can lose his right to be present at trial if, after he has been warned by the judge that he will be removed if he continues his disruptive behavior, he nevertheless insists on conducting himself in a manner so disorderly, disruptive, and disrespectful of the court that his trial cannot be carried on with him in the courtroom. Once lost, the right to be present can, of course, be reclaimed as soon as the defendant is willing to conduct himself consistently with the decorum and respect inherent in the concept of courts and judicial proceedings.

Of the three methods that the Court found available to a judge when faced with a disruptive defendant—gag and shackles, citation for CONTEMPT of court, and physical removal—the Court held that a gag and shackles should be considered the option of last resort. According to the Court,

> Not only is it possible that the sight of shackles and gags might have a significant effect on the jury's feelings about the defendant, but the use of this technique is itself something of an affront to the very dignity and decorum of judicial proceedings that the judge is seeking to uphold.

One of the few modern instances of literal gagging occurred in the 1968 CHICAGO EIGHT trial (sometimes called the Chicago Seven trial because one defendant was removed). In that trial, federal judge Julius J. Hoffman ordered BLACK PANTHERS leader BOBBY SEALE bound and gagged after Seale and Hoffman engaged in vociferous argument during the trial. Seale still managed to disrupt the proceedings. He was then removed from the trial and tried separately.

Courts may attempt to control prejudicial publicity by restricting the information that trial participants can give to the press both before and during a trial. This remains the type of gag order most frequently used by courts.

Another type of gag order was for a while used by courts to restrict the press from reporting certain facts regarding a TRIAL. This gag order became more common after the Supreme Court's 1966 decision in *Sheppard v. Maxwell,* 384 U.S. 333, 86 S. Ct. 1507, 16 L. Ed. 2d 600, in which it reversed a criminal conviction on the grounds that PRETRIAL PUBLICITY had unfairly prejudiced the JURY against the defendant and denied him his Sixth Amendment right to a fair trial. However, in a 1976 decision, *Nebraska Press Ass'n v. Stuart,* 427 U.S. 539, 96 S. Ct. 2791, 49 L. Ed. 2d 683, the Court held that pretrial gag orders on the press are unconstitutional. It ruled that such orders represent an unconstitutional PRIOR RESTRAINT and violate the First Amendment, which guarantees the FREEDOM OF THE PRESS.

See also SHEPPARD, SAM.

GAG RULE 📖 A rule, regulation, or law that prohibits debate or discussion of a particular issue. 📖

Between 1836 and 1844, the U.S. House of Representatives adopted a series of RESOLUTIONS and rules that banned PETITIONS calling for the abolition of SLAVERY. Known as gag rules, these measures effectively tabled antislavery petitions without submitting them to usual House procedures. Public outcry over the gag rules ultimately aided the antislavery cause, and the fierce House debate concerning their future anticipated later conflicts over slavery.

The submission of petitions to Congress has been a feature of the U.S. political system ever since its inception. The FIRST AMENDMENT to the U.S. Constitution guarantees "the right of the people . . . to petition the Government for a redress of grievances." First used in England, petitions have been considered an important means for the people to communicate grievances to their representatives or other public officials.

When the first gag rule was instituted in 1836, House protocol required that the first thirty days of each session of Congress be devoted to the reading of petitions from constituents. After those thirty days, petitions were read in the House every other Monday. Each petition was read aloud, printed, and assigned to an appropriate committee, which could choose to address or ignore it. This traditional procedure had been interrupted in 1835, when the House began to receive a large number of petitions advocating the abolition of slavery. Many of the petitions were organized by the American Anti-Slavery Society, which had formed in 1833.

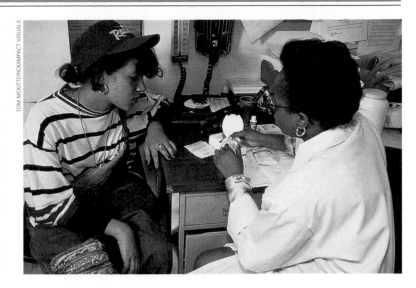

Southern representatives, many of whom were slave owners and entertained no thoughts of abolishing slavery, were outraged by the antislavery petitions. In December 1835, southerners, uniting with northern Democrats, won a vote to table a petition that called for the abolition of slavery in the District of Columbia. Breaking established precedent, the pro-slavery faction also won a vote to deny the petition its usual discussion, printing, and referral to committee.

This procedure for the "gagging" of abolition petitions was made into a formal resolution by the House on May 26, 1836: "All petitions, memorials, resolutions, propositions, or papers, relating in any way, or to any extent whatsoever, to the subject of slavery or the abolition of slavery, shall, without being either printed or referred, be laid on the table and . . . no further action whatever shall be had thereon." The resolution incited strong opposition from many northerners, who perceived it as a violation of their time-honored CIVIL RIGHTS. JOHN QUINCY ADAMS, a former president and now a representative from Massachusetts, emerged as the leader of an effort to revoke the new resolution. JOHN C. CALHOUN (D-S.C.), although a member of the Senate rather than the House, orchestrated the battle to preserve it.

The pro-slavery faction succeeded in renewing the gag resolution, which expired at the end of each session of Congress, in both sessions of the Twenty-fifth Congress (1837–39). On January 28, 1840, it succeeded again when it won a vote to turn the resolution into House Rule 21 (in later versions, Rules 23 and 25):

No petition, memorial, resolution, or other paper praying the abolition of slavery in the

Family planning clinics that received federal funding were under a gag rule from 1988 to 1993 when they were prevented from discussing abortion with clients.

District of Columbia, or any State or Territory, or the slave trade between the States or Territories of the United States, in which it now exists, shall be received by this House, or entertained in any way whatever.

As a formal House rule rather than a resolution, the gag rule was now a permanent part of House procedure and did not have to be renewed by vote each session.

This new gag rule provoked even stronger opposition. Whereas the previous gag resolution tabled antislavery petitions after they were received, the new gag rule did not allow petitions to be received. It was also more extreme than the Senate's approach, which was to receive such petitions but answer them in the negative. As a result of these changes, northerners who had previously supported the gag now joined Adams in opposing it. Several years later, on December 3, 1844, those opposed to the gag rule finally succeeded in rescinding it.

The term *gag rule* was also applied to regulations issued by the administration of President RONALD REAGAN in 1988. These regulations (53 Fed. Reg. 2923–2924) banned all ABORTION counseling by employees of the four thousand family planning clinics funded by the federal Title X Program of the Public Health Service Act (42 U.S.C.A. §§ 300–300a-6). The regulations also prohibited referrals to clinics that perform abortions. In one of his first acts as president, BILL CLINTON revoked the gag rule by EXECUTIVE ORDER on January 22, 1993 (58 Fed. Reg. 7455, 1993 WL 2406 [Pres.]), allowing clinics to counsel pregnant women on all family planning options, including abortion.

See also CONGRESS OF THE UNITED STATES.

GAME 📖 Wild birds and beasts. The word includes all game birds and game animals. 📖

The state, in its sovereign power, owns game for the benefit of the general public. The only manner in which a private individual can acquire ownership in game is by possessing it lawfully such as by hunting and killing it under a LICENSE.

Generally, every individual has the right to hunt and take game in any public place where his or her presence is lawful, so long as the person neither violates statutory regulations nor injures or infringes upon the rights of others. A hunter does not acquire an absolute right to a wild animal by mere pursuit alone, and the individual forfeits any potential ownership by abandoning the chase prior to capture. The exclusive right to hunt or take game on privately owned property vests in the owner or his or her GRANTEES. This PROPERTY RIGHT of the owner is limited by the right of the state to regulate and preserve the game for public use. A suit for TRESPASS may be brought against one who interferes with another's right to hunt.

A statute that proscribes the hunting of game without a license, and that requires the payment of a fee for such license, constitutes a proper exercise of the POLICE POWER of the state.

Game laws govern the killing or taking of birds and beasts. Game wardens ordinarily can arrest violators, seize illegally taken game, bring actions for trespass, or institute prosecutions for violations of the game laws.

Under a number of game laws, it is a penal offense to kill or take certain types of game in certain seasons of the year or without a license. A hunter is required to exhibit a license when properly called on to do so, and it constitutes a legal violation if the person cannot do so.

In a situation where an individual has lawfully obtained possession of game—enclosing and caring for them as DOMESTIC animals—the person can kill one or more of them if necessary for care and management or for humane purposes. In addition, an individual might be justified in killing game in violation of the law if it were necessary for the protection of persons or property. It sometimes constitutes an offense to export game beyond the limits of the nation or state in which it was killed or captured, to ship it for sale in a certain manner, or to absent certain information upon the package.

The United States has entered into treaties with other countries, including Great Britain and Mexico, for the protection and preservation of migratory birds and game animals. It constitutes an offense to violate statutes that were enacted to implement such treaties. For ex-

A hunter must obtain a license and obey state and federal game laws. This woman used a rifle to shoot an antelope in Wyoming.

ample, a regulatory statute might limit the number of birds that can be killed by any individual each day, and it would be an offense to exceed such limit.

The federal government, subject to the consent of the state, can establish a game refuge for the protection of game and migratory birds and proscribe all hunting in the vicinity. The U.S. Fish and Wildlife Service is administered by the Department of the Interior, to conserve and preserve fish and game in wildlife refuges and game ranges.

See also ENDANGERED SPECIES ACT; FISH AND FISHING.

GAMING 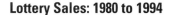 The act or practice of gambling; an agreement between two or more individuals to play collectively at a game of chance for a stake or wager, which will become the property of the winner and to which all involved make a contribution.

Since the early 1990s, gaming laws have been in a constant state of flux. Regulation of gaming is generally reserved to the states, but the U.S. Congress became involved in it in 1988 with the passage of the Indian Gaming Regulatory Act (Gaming Act) (Pub. Law. No. 100-497, 102 Stat. 2467 [25 U.S.C.A. § 2701 ct seq.] [Oct. 17, 1988]), which brought tribal gaming under the regulation of state and federal governments.

Before the 1990s, most gaming was illegal in a majority of states. Since the passage of the Gaming Act, many state legislatures have approved gaming in a variety of forms. Some states still outlaw all but charitable gambling, but most have expanded their definition of legal gaming operations to promote economic development.

The legal history of gambling in the United States is marked by dramatic swings between prohibition and popularity. In colonial times, games of chance were generally illegal except for state and private lotteries. Other gaming was considered a sin and not fit for discussion in polite society. In the early nineteenth century, the popular concept changed from gaming's being a sin to its being a vice. Gamblers were no longer considered fallen in the eyes of God, but were now seen as simply victims of their own weaknesses.

Gaming came under renewed attack during the presidency of ANDREW JACKSON (1829–37). Part of the "Jacksonian morality" of the period revived the view of gambling as sinful. By 1862, gaming was illegal in all states except Missouri and Kentucky, both of which retained state lotteries.

After the Civil War, legal gaming experienced a brief renaissance, only to fall out of

Lottery Sales: 1980 to 1994

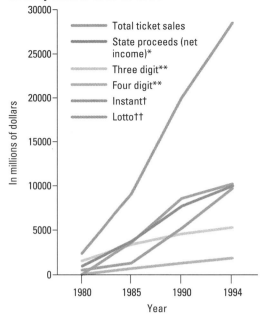

* Net income equals total sales minus a lottery's payouts and direct costs and expenses.
** Players choose and bet on three or four digits, depending on game, with various payoffs for different straight order or mixed combination bets.
† Player scratches a latex section on ticket which reveals instantly whether ticket is a winner.
†† Players typically select six digits out of a large field of numbers. Varying prizes are offered for matching three through six numbers drawn by lottery.

Source: TLF Publications, Inc., Boyds, MD, *1995 World Lottery Almanac,* annual; *La Fleur's Fiscal 1994 Lottery Special Report.*

favor again in the 1890s. At this point, it was outlawed even in the western territories, where card games such as poker and blackjack had become a regular diversion in frontier life. By 1910, the United States was again virtually free of legalized gaming. Only Maryland and Kentucky allowed gambling, in the sole form of horse race betting.

In 1931, Nevada re-legalized casino gaming. Many states followed this lead in the 1930s by legalizing pari-mutuel betting, wherein all bets are pooled and then paid, less a management fee, to the holders of winning tickets. In 1963, New Hampshire formed the first state lottery since the 1910s. By the 1990s, gaming was the largest and fastest growing segment of the U.S. entertainment industry. In 1992, for example, U.S. citizens spent approximately four times more on gaming than on movies. Gaming is still illegal in some states, but most states have at least one form of legal gambling, most commonly a state-run lottery. In fact, instead of prohibiting gaming, many states now actively promote it by sponsoring lotteries and other games of chance.

Gaming laws vary from state to state. Idaho, for example, declares that "gambling is contrary to public policy and is strictly prohibited except for" pari-mutuel betting, bingo and raffle games for charity, and a state lottery (Idaho Const. art. III, § 20). Like lotteries in other states, the purpose of the one in Idaho is to generate revenue for the state. The lottery is run by the Idaho State Lottery Commission, which oversees all aspects of the game, including expenses and advertising.

Alabama is one of the few states that prohibit all gambling except for charitable gaming. Alabama maintains no state lottery and punishes gambling through criminal statutes. Under the Code of Alabama, sections 13A-12-24 and 13A-12-25 (1975), the possession of gambling records is a class A MISDEMEANOR, which carries a penalty of not more than one year in jail or a $2,000 fine, or both.

Nevada is the most permissive state for gambling. The public policy of gaming here holds that "[t]he gaming industry is vitally important to the economy of the state and the general welfare of the inhabitants" (Nev. Rev. Stat. § 463.0129). Nevada statutes allow the broadest range of gaming activities, including pari-mutuel betting, betting on sports competitions and other events, and the full panoply of casino games. Gambling is heavily regulated by the Nevada Gaming Commission, and a wide range of criminal statutes are designed to ensure cooperation with the regulations of the commission.

New Jersey is another active promoter of gaming. In 1976, New Jersey voters passed a REFERENDUM approving casino gaming, and that decision was codified in the Casino Control Act (N.J. Stat. Ann. § 5:12-1 et seq.). Gaming is limited to Atlantic City, and it does not include betting on sports events other than horse and dog races. However, like Nevada, New Jersey offers the full array of casino games.

The Gaming Act divides all gambling into three classes. Class I includes all traditional Indian games performed as a part of, or in connection with, tribal ceremonies or celebrations. Class II is limited to bingo, pull tabs, and card games not explicitly prohibited by the laws of the state. Class III encompasses all other forms of gambling, such as slot machines, poker, blackjack, dice games, off-track betting (where bets may be placed by persons not at the race track) and pari-mutuel betting on horses and dogs, and lotteries.

An Indian tribe may operate a class I game without restrictions. It may offer class II games with the oversight of the National Indian Gaming Commission, and class III games only if it reaches an agreement with the state in which it resides.

The Gaming Act provides that Native American tribes may operate high-stakes casinos only if they reach an agreement with the state in which they reside. Under the act, a state is required to enter into GOOD FAITH negotiations with a federally recognized tribe to allow class III gaming that was legal in the state before the negotiations began. For example, if a state has legalized blackjack but not poker, blackjack is available for negotiations but not poker. Furthermore, when a state approves a new form of gambling, the state must make the new game available in negotiations with native tribes.

Native American groups have criticized the Gaming Act as interfering with tribal SOVEREIGNTY. Indeed, a primary purpose of the act was to reconcile state interests in gaming with those of the tribes. Before the act, some Native American tribes ran sizable gambling operations on their land without regulation by the federal or state governments.

The Gaming Act has also created opposition in some states that seek to minimize gambling within their boundaries. Maine, for example, refused to give the Passamaquoddy tribe a license to conduct class III gaming operations on tribal land in Calais, near the Canadian border. The tribe sued the state for the right to conduct the high-stakes gaming. However, several years earlier, Maine had given the tribe land in exchange for the tribe's agreement to submit to state jurisdiction. In *Passamaquoddy Tribe v. Maine*, 1996 WL 44707, 75 F. 3d 784 (1st Cir. 1996), the First Circuit Court of Appeals ruled against the tribe. The court noted that Congress had been aware of Maine's agreement with the tribe, and that Congress could have added to the Gaming Act, but chose not to, language making the act applicable to the state of Maine. According to the court, the gaming statute did not erase the 1980 agreement between the tribe and the state, and Maine had the right to refuse the tribe's request.

See also NATIVE AMERICAN RIGHTS; STATE LOTTERY.

GAOL The old English word for jail.

GARFIELD, JAMES ABRAM James Abram Garfield was a soldier and congressman who became the twentieth president of the United States. His inability to perform the duties of office following an ASSASSINATION attempt on July 2, 1881, raised, for the second time in U.S. history, the question of presidential succession.

Garfield was born November 19, 1831, in a log cabin near the town of Orange in Cuyahoga County, Ohio. He was the fourth and final child of Abram Garfield and Eliza Ballou Garfield. Garfield's father's ancestors were among the

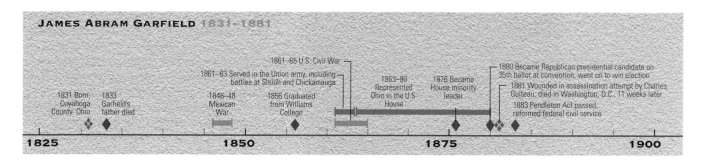

JAMES ABRAM GARFIELD 1831–1881

1861–65 U.S. Civil War

1861–63 Served in the Union army, including
battles at Shiloh and Chickamauga

1880 Became Republican presidential candidate on
35th ballot at convention; went on to win election

1831 Born,
Cuyahoga
County, Ohio

1833
Garfield's
father died

1846–48
Mexican
War

1856 Graduated
from Williams
College

1863–80
Represented
Ohio in the U.S.
House

1876 Became
House minority
leader

1881 Wounded in assassination attempt by Charles
Guiteau; died in Washington, D.C., 11 weeks later

1883 Pendleton Act passed,
reformed federal civil service

1825   1850   1875   1900

original settlers of the Massachusetts Bay Colony. In 1827 the father carried their pioneering spirit to Ohio, where he worked on an Ohio Canal construction crew. By the time Garfield was born, his father was a struggling farmer and a founding member of the local Disciples of Christ church. In 1833, when Garfield was just two years old, his father died suddenly, leaving the family in poverty.

Garfield's mother, a descendant of an old Rhode Island family, was a remarkable woman. After her husband's death, she ran the small family farm on her own and saw to it that Garfield and his siblings worked hard, attended church, and finished school.

After completing his studies at the local school in Orange, Garfield enrolled at the Western Reserve Eclectic Institute (later Hiram College), at Hiram, Ohio. He eventually went on to Williams College, in Massachusetts. After graduating from Williams with the class of 1856, he returned to the institute at Hiram and assumed the duties of teacher and later principal. On November 11, 1858, he married Lucretia Rudolph, his childhood friend, fellow student, and pupil.

In addition to teaching and tending to the administration of the institute, Garfield frequently served as a lay speaker in Disciples of Christ churches throughout northern Ohio. Like many members of his church, Garfield advocated free-soil principles and was a firm supporter of the newly organized Republican party. (Free-Soilers were opposed to the expansion of SLAVERY in the western states and territories.)

With his natural speaking ability, Garfield soon found himself in the political arena. In 1859 he was elected to the Ohio state senate. As the United States neared civil war, Garfield put his speaking abilities to work for the Union, recruiting men and raising troops for battle.

In the summer of 1861, he followed his own advice and recruited a group of volunteers from his former school. He assembled the Forty-second Ohio Volunteer Infantry, and served as the unit's lieutenant colonel and later colonel. Though he had no military experience, Garfield

BIOGRAPHY

James Abram Garfield

did have a voracious appetite for knowledge and access to books that could guide his command. He and his men fought at the Battle of Shiloh, in western Tennessee. Garfield left the field when he became ill. After recovering he returned as chief of staff under Major General William S. Rosencrans, with whom he fought at Chickamauga, Georgia.

After Chickamauga, Garfield was promoted to brigadier general of volunteers, and he was elected, in absentia, to a seat in the U.S. House of Representatives. It has been suggested that Garfield was reluctant to surrender his command and take the seat, but he acquiesced when President ABRAHAM LINCOLN pointed out that brigadier generals were in far greater supply than administration Republicans.

In December 1863 Garfield took his seat in the Thirty-eighth Congress as the Republican representative from the nineteenth congressional district of Ohio. When the Republicans became the minority party in the House after the election of 1864, Garfield and Congressman James G. Blaine, of Maine, emerged as minority party leaders. Garfield distinguished himself as chairman of the committee on appropriations, and he established himself as an expert on the budget. He also focused his attention on legislation related to Reconstruction policies in the South, protective TARIFF issues, and the maintenance of a sound currency. When Blaine was elected to the Senate in 1876, Garfield became the House minority leader—a position he held for the remainder of his congressional service.

Garfield held his House office for eighteen years, for the most part easily winning the nomination of his party and the vote of the electorate as each term concluded. Only once during his time in the House was his reelection in question. In the early 1870s, the Republican party was discredited by allegations of scandal in the administration of President ULYSSES S. GRANT—including the CRÉDIT MOBILIER SCANDAL. Crédit Mobilier of America was a construction company established to build the Union Pacific Railroad. It became known that Garfield was among a group of congressmen who had accepted stock in Crédit Mobilier, in exchange for legislative consideration. Garfield ultimately refused the stock, but it took him two years to do so. His critics maintained that he decided not to take the stock only because the issue had placed him in political hot water.

During the same period, Garfield accepted a RETAINER for legal services from a Washington, D.C., company seeking to supply paving materials in the nation's capital. He argued that because he had no direct connection to city government, there was no CONFLICT OF INTEREST. Not everyone shared his opinion.

Though many public servants of the day conducted personal business while in office, Garfield found it increasingly difficult to distinguish clients who wanted his legal advice from those who wanted his political influence. Garfield was reelected in 1874, despite the controversy, but to avoid future problems, he ceased taking outside legal clients. The incident also fueled Garfield's desire to eliminate political patronage in the CIVIL SERVICE system.

Garfield took an active role in the 1876 presidential election of RUTHERFORD B. HAYES. When Senator JOHN SHERMAN, of Ohio, was named to the Hayes CABINET, Garfield expressed an interest in filling his vacant Senate seat. Needing Garfield in the House, Hayes discouraged him from pursuing the matter. Near the close of Hayes's term, there was talk that Sherman would seek to regain his Senate seat, but he chose instead to seek his party's nomination for the presidency. It was widely presumed that Sherman supported Garfield's election to the Senate in exchange for Garfield's support at the Republican convention, but no such deal was struck.

In due course the Ohio legislature elected Garfield to the U.S. Senate for a six-year term to begin in 1881, and he attended the 1880 Republican National Convention in Chicago as head of the Ohio delegation. Because of home state support for Sherman, Garfield reluctantly agreed to act as Sherman's floor manager and to canvass for delegates on his behalf—even though Senator Blaine, Garfield's old friend and colleague, was also seeking the party's nomination.

Garfield was a formidable and well-known figure at the convention. His persuasive skill on the floor did not go unnoticed. He kept Sherman's chances alive by fighting for the delegates' freedom to vote their choice, and by opposing a unit rule that forced delegations to cast all their votes for the candidate holding the majority of votes within a state delegation. Former president Grant, who was also running for nomination, and his supporters, called the

Stalwarts, supported the unit rule because Grant held the majority in many delegations.

Garfield managed to block the nominations of Blaine and Grant, but he could not secure a majority for Sherman. With the convention deadlocked, twenty Wisconsin delegates made a bold move on the thirty-fifth ballot and, in protest, cast twenty votes for Garfield.

On the next ballot, Garfield found himself the unanimous choice of the convention and the unwitting beneficiary of his own floor maneuvering. CHESTER A. ARTHUR was named his running mate. Blaine followers supported the ticket, and most Sherman followers were willing to overlook the manner in which the nomination had been secured, but Grant's forces never forgave Garfield for his opposition.

Garfield pacified unhappy Sherman supporters by surrendering his new Senate seat, enabling Sherman to return to his old post. Throughout the summer of 1880, Garfield attempted to meet with the national committee and with Grant supporters, but he was never given an audience. In November Garfield returned to his farm in Mentor, Ohio, to wait them out.

Finally, on the eve of the election, Grant was persuaded to recognize Garfield as the party's choice. Grant and his followers were invited to the Garfield farm for a historic meeting, often called the Mentor Summit. What was said at the meeting—and what was promised—has been the subject of much debate. Grant thought he had extracted a personal promise from Garfield that, in exchange for Grant's support, the Stalwarts would be named to influential posts in the new administration.

With the help of Grant's supporters, Garfield won the election by a narrow margin over Democrat Winfield Scott Hancock. Between the election and the inauguration, Garfield busied himself with the selection of his cabinet. All factions of the party called on the president-elect to lobby for their preferred nominees, but Grant Stalwarts remained assured that Garfield would bow to their influence. Garfield's first known appointment, making Blaine secretary of state, caused an uproar among the Grant faction and was viewed as a breach of the promises made at Mentor. Garfield nevertheless remained committed to building a conciliation cabinet that would balance everyone's interests and eliminate political patronage jobs—and kept the rest of his choices well guarded until inauguration day, March 4, 1881.

The first months of his term continued to be plagued with appointment and confirmation

"ALL FREE GOVERNMENTS ARE MANAGED BY THE COMBINED WISDOM AND FOLLY OF THE PEOPLE."

battles. Grant supporters continued to believe that he should have been the party's presidential nominee and that in an election deal Garfield had agreed to consult Grant about appointments. Those in the Senate who supported Grant rallied to systematically reject undesirable appointments, but Garfield was equally stubborn. Of the Stalwarts' attempt to derail his nomination for collector of customs for the port of New York City, Garfield said, "They may take him out of the Senate head first or feet first, but I will never withdraw him."

Though confirmation battles consumed a majority of Garfield's time, he also carried out other presidential duties and commitments. On July 2, 1881, he was en route to a speaking engagement at his alma mater Williams College, when lawyer Charles J. Guiteau shot him at a Washington, D.C., railroad station. Described as an erratic character, Guiteau shouted to a crowd at the railroad station that he was a Stalwart.

Garfield lingered for eleven weeks. Daily reports from physicians showed that he was unable to carry out his responsibilities. By August the question of Garfield's succession was being discussed in the press and debated by constitutional scholars. It was agreed that the VICE PRESIDENT was constitutionally allowed to assume the president's powers and duties, but it was not clear whether he should serve as acting president until Garfield recovered, or assume the office itself and displace Garfield altogether. The pertinent provision of the Constitution—Article II, Section 1, Clause 6—was ambiguous, and expert opinion was still divided over the precedent set by JOHN TYLER, who had taken the oath of office in 1841 after the death of President WILLIAM H. HARRISON, rather than merely assuming Harrison's duties until the next election.

Because Congress was not in session, the issue could not be debated there, but it was addressed by Garfield's cabinet members on September 2, 1881. They agreed that it was time for the vice president to assume Garfield's duties, but they too were divided as to the

permanence of the vice president's role. The problem was never resolved because Garfield died September 19, 1881, before any action was taken by the cabinet or the vice president. Following the precedent set by Tyler, Arthur took the oath of office and assumed the presidency, following Garfield's death.

Garfield's unexpected nomination, bitter election, and tragic death often overshadow his previous accomplishments and his presidential agenda. His efforts to build a conciliation cabinet and to purge administrative agencies of old patronage jobs made him a strong advocate of civil service reforms. Ironically, the appointment battles preceding his murder probably caused Congress to pass civil service reforms in 1883 that were far broader in reach and scope than anything Garfield had envisioned.

GARLAND, AUGUSTUS HILL   Augustus Hill Garland served as attorney general of the United States from 1885 to 1889 under President GROVER CLEVELAND.

Garland was born June 11, 1832, in Tipton County, Tennessee. His parents, Rufus K. Garland and Barbara Hill Garland, settled in Hempstead County, Arkansas, when he was an infant. Garland was educated at local schools in Hempstead County, and at St. Joseph's College, in Bardstown, Kentucky. He graduated from St. Joseph's in 1851 and was admitted to the bar in 1853. Garland's first practice was established in Washington, Arkansas. He eventually moved to Little Rock, Arkansas, where he earned a reputation as one of the best lawyers in the South. He married Sarah Virginia Sanders in Little Rock. She died early in their marriage, and Garland's mother ran his household for most of his life.

At the outbreak of the Civil War, Garland opposed the SECESSION of Arkansas, but he eventually supported his state when the ordinance of secession was passed. He was elected to the Confederate provisional congress, in Montgomery, Alabama, and to the first and second Confederate congresses, in Richmond.

In an effort to unify the North and South after the war, President ANDREW JOHNSON

BIOGRAPHY

Augustus Hill Garland

"WE, AS ATTORNEYS, GET LITERALLY WRAPPED UP IN OUR CLIENT'S CAUSE . . . AND SEE NOTHING BUT HIS SIDE OF THE CASE . . . AND DECLARE THAT THE COURT CAN DECIDE IT ONLY OUR WAY."

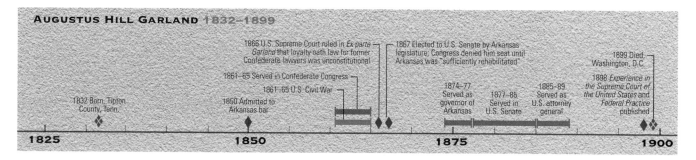

AUGUSTUS HILL GARLAND 1832–1899

1832 Born, Tipton County, Tenn.

1850 Admitted to Arkansas bar

1861–65 U.S. Civil War

1861–65 Served in Confederate Congress

1866 U.S. Supreme Court ruled in *Ex parte Garland* that loyalty oath law for former Confederate lawyers was unconstitutional

1867 Elected to U.S. Senate by Arkansas legislature; Congress denied him seat until Arkansas was "sufficiently rehabilitated"

1874–77 Served as governor of Arkansas

1877–85 Served in U.S. Senate

1885–89 Served as U.S. attorney general

1898 *Experience in the Supreme Court of the United States and Federal Practice* published

1899 Died, Washington, D.C.

1825   1850   1875   1900

granted a full PARDON to Garland (and others) for wartime service to the Confederacy. The president's actions were not widely supported; Congress enacted a number of laws that continued to punish the pardoned Southerners for their wartime allegiances by restricting their ability to participate in their former businesses or professions. Two restrictions, enacted in 1865, required attorneys to swear a test (loyalty) oath affirming that they had not participated in the rebellion, as a condition for appearing before the U.S. Supreme Court, the district and circuit courts, and the Court of Claims (13 Stat. 424). Attorneys who could not take the oath were denied the right to appear before the high courts—and thereby prevented from practicing law.

Garland challenged the law in 1867. He argued that the law was unconstitutional, and that even if the law were constitutional, he would be released from compliance with its provisions by his presidential pardon. The Supreme Court found the law to be unconstitutional because it violated the president's power to pardon. "When a pardon is full," the majority opinion said, "it releases the punishment, and blots out of existence the guilt" (*Ex parte Garland*, 71 U.S. (4 Wall.) 333, 18 L. Ed. 366 [1866]). The case restored Garland's right to practice law before the nation's high courts and established him as a nationally recognized constitutional lawyer. It also reestablished him as a political force in the South.

In 1867, Garland was elected to the U.S. Senate by the legislature of Arkansas, only to be denied a seat because Congress found that his state had not been sufficiently rehabilitated. For the next few years, he used his abilities to return his state to favor. By 1874, he was elected governor of the state; his administration is credited with bringing order out of the chaos that permeated Arkansas during the Reconstruction era. In 1877, Garland was finally allowed to take his seat in the U.S. Senate. He was reelected in 1883 and became a ranking member of the Senate's Judiciary Committee.

Garland resigned his Senate seat on March 4, 1885, to accept the position of attorney general in President Cleveland's cabinet. As attorney general, he was frequently consulted on issues of constitutional law. He was known as an advocate who insisted on the enforcement of constitutional freedoms for all citizens.

He also worked to earn the trust of those who condemned him for his Confederate service. As a U.S. senator and cabinet officer, Garland was wary of both individuals and institutions who sought to influence his opinions and actions. It is said that he steadfastly avoided society events and that he refused to read daily newspapers. Even so, he was once called back from a holiday by an angry President Cleveland to explain his ownership of stock in a company that would have been helped by a Justice Department lawsuit. (The lawsuit was eventually withdrawn.)

In 1889 Garland returned to the practice of law, and he maintained an active caseload until the end of his life. He also began to record his life's work for publication. His *Experience in the Supreme Court of the United States* and *Federal Practice* were published in 1898.

Having fought so hard to retain his right to appear before the nation's high courts, Garland's final hour was fitting: he died while arguing a case before the Supreme Court of the United States on January 26, 1899.

GARNISHEE An individual who holds money or property that belongs to a DEBTOR subject to an ATTACHMENT proceeding by a CREDITOR.

For example, when an individual owes money but has for a source of income only a salary, a creditor might initiate GARNISHMENT proceedings. If the creditor is successful, a certain portion of the debtor's salary will be automatically sent to the creditor from each paycheck. In such case, the debtor's employer is the garnishee.

GARNISHMENT A legal procedure by which a CREDITOR can collect what a DEBTOR owes by reaching the debtor's property when it is in the hands of someone other than the debtor.

Garnishment is a drastic measure for collecting a debt. A court order of garnishment allows a creditor to take the property of a debtor when the debtor does not possess the property. A garnishment action is taken against the debtor as defendant and the property holder as garnishee. Garnishment is regulated by statutes, and is usually reserved for the creditor who has obtained a JUDGMENT, or court order, against the debtor.

A debtor's property may be garnished before it ever reaches the debtor. For example, if a debtor's work earnings are garnished, a portion of the wages owed by the employer go directly to the judgment creditor and is never seen by the debtor.

Some property is exempt from garnishment. Exemptions are created by statutes to avoid leaving a debtor with no means of support. For example, only a certain amount of work income may be garnished. Under 15 U.S.C.A. § 1673, a garnishment sought in federal court may not exceed 25 percent of the debtor's disposable earnings each week, or the amount by which the debtor's disposable earnings for the week exceed thirty times the federal minimum hourly wage in effect at the time the earnings are payable. In Alaska, exemptions include a burial plot; health aids necessary for work or health; benefits paid or payable for medical, surgical, or hospital care; awards to victims of violent crime; and assets received from a retirement plan (Alaska Stat. § 09.38.015, .017).

Because garnishment involves the taking of property, the procedure is subject to DUE PROCESS requirements. In *Sniadatch v. Family Finance Corp. of Bay View*, 395 U.S. 337, 89 S. Ct. 1820, 23 L. Ed. 2d 349 (1969), the U.S. Supreme Court struck down a Wisconsin statute that allowed pretrial garnishment of wages without an opportunity to be heard or to submit a defense. According to the Court, garnishment without prior notice and a prior hearing violated fundamental principles of due process.

Garnishment may be used as a provisional remedy. This means that property may be garnished before a judgment against the debtor is entered. This serves to protect the creditor's interest in the debtor's property. Prejudgment garnishment is usually ordered by a court only when the creditor can show that the debtor is likely to lose or dispose of the property before the case is resolved. Property that is garnished before any judgment is rendered is held by the third party, and is not given to the creditor until the creditor prevails in the suit against the debtor.

Garnishment is similar to LIEN and to ATTACHMENT. Liens and attachments are court orders that give a creditor an interest in the property of the debtor. Garnishment is a continuing lien against nonexempt property of the debtor. Garnishment is not, however, an attachment. Attachment is the process of seizing property of the debtor that is in the debtor's possession, whereas garnishment is the process of seizing property of the debtor that is in the possession of a third party.

GAS Various legal issues arise concerning the use and distribution of gas.

Supply A MUNICIPAL CORPORATION does not have the duty to supply gas to its population. In the event that a city assumes the performance of such function, it is acting merely as a business CORPORATION.

The CHARTER of a gas company is a FRANCHISE granted by the state. The manufacture of distribution of gas for light, fuel, or power is a business of a public character, and, therefore, a gas company is ordinarily considered to be a

public or quasi-public corporation or a BUSINESS AFFECTED WITH A PUBLIC INTEREST. A state may regulate gas companies for the protection of the public and may delegate its regulatory powers to municipal corporations in which gas companies operate. In a number of states, gas companies are subject to a public service commission or other such agency. The JURISDICTION of the commission ordinarily includes the power to establish rates and to set forth rules and regulations affecting the service, operation, management, and conduct of the business.

Consumer Supply Upon obtaining a franchise to supply gas to a particular geographic area, a gas company is bound to fulfill its obligation; it cannot withdraw its service from an area merely because it is dissatisfied with the rates permitted there. Once the franchise of a company has expired, it may withdraw the service. A court may, in certain instances, ENJOIN the discontinuance of service for a reasonable period—to circumvent undue hardship and inconvenience to the residents of the area.

A gas company has the duty to serve all those who are within the franchise area who desire service and subscribe to the reasonable rules that it may set forth. A municipality or corporation supplying gas may make reasonable rules and regulations to secure the payment of bills, such as eliminating service to the consumer. If there is a genuine controversy about the

U.S. Production, Import, and Consumption of Natural Gas: 1960 to 1995

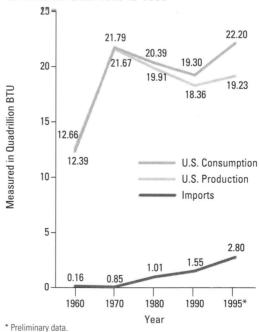

* Preliminary data.

Source: Energy Information Administration, U.S. Department of Energy, *Annual Energy Review 1995.*

amount owed, a company is not permitted to discontinue service. A gas company may not require the owner or occupant of a building to pay overdue and unpaid bills by a former owner or occupant before it continues service to the building. Some statutes require that gas companies install a meter on the premises, in order to register the consumption of gas by each customer; and where a customer tampers with the meter and uses a significant amount of unmetered gas, the company can discontinue service and refuse to restore it until the customer pays the amount due for the unmetered gas taken.

A gas company that wrongfully refuses to supply a customer with gas is liable for DAMAGES. There are also statutory penalties in some states for such wrongful refusal.

Injuries A gas company is under the obligation to exercise ordinary care in the construction of its works and the conduct of its business in order to protect life and property.

Gas has a highly dangerous and volatile character and tends to escape. A gas company must, therefore, exercise care to avoid harm to others and is liable for its NEGLIGENCE that results in injury to others by reason of the escape or explosion of gas. It must exercise reasonable care in the inspection of its pipes to ensure that leaks may be discovered promptly; and if leaks or defects in the pipes of the company occur due to faulty construction or maintenance, the company is liable for resulting injuries, even though it did not know about the leak.

In the event that the company has taken due care in the inspection of its pipes and a defect or a break occurs through natural causes or by the act of a third person, the gas company must be given notice of the defect and reasonable time to repair it before liability accrues. A gas company subject to notice that gas is escaping is under an obligation to shut off the gas supply until the necessary repairs have been made.

A gas company has a PROPERTY RIGHT in the mains and pipes and other appliances, and where there is unauthorized interference with, or damage to, this property, the company is entitled to recover damages and an INJUNCTION if the circumstances so warrant.

Rates A gas company has a legal obligation to charge reasonable rates. One of the main purposes of the regulation of gas companies is to prescribe fair and reasonable rates for the selling of gas to the public. Rate increases are permitted only following an impartial and complete investigation—with the object of doing justice to the gas company as well as the public. Relief can be sought in the courts if gas rates

are unreasonable—to determine whether the rate making body acted beyond the scope of its power or against the weight of the EVIDENCE. The courts, however, cannot decide what rates are reasonable, nor can they put those rates into effect.

See also PUBLIC UTILITIES.

IN RE GAULT Originally, juvenile court was a place for the informal resolution of a broad range of matters concerning children. The hearings were not adversarial. Instead, they focused on the juvenile's best interests. A juvenile was brought to the juvenile court, the prosecution presented EVIDENCE, the juvenile and other WITNESSES gave TESTIMONY, and the juvenile court judge made a decision based on the perceived best interests of the juvenile.

In the same spirit of informality, juvenile courts provided fewer procedural protections than did adult courts. Juveniles did not have the right to a court-appointed attorney or to NOTICE of charges of criminal behavior. They did not have the right to confront accusers and cross-examine witnesses. They did not have the right to a written record of the proceedings or to appeal the juvenile court judgment.

The problem with this lack of procedural protections was that a juvenile risked losing his or her liberty for several years. The best interests of the child usually involved placement in a secure reformatory or some other secure facility until the age of eighteen or, in some states, twenty-one. This amounted to a deprivation of liberty similar to that resulting from a prison sentence.

In 1967 the U.S. Supreme Court issued a decision that would change dramatically the character of juvenile courts. In *In re Gault*, 387 U.S. 1, 87 S. Ct. 1428, 18 L. Ed. 2d 527, fifteen-year-old Gerald Gault was committed to a reform school until age twenty-one for allegedly making an OBSCENE phone call to a neighbor. Gault had been found delinquent without receiving notice of the charges or the assistance of an attorney. In addition, Gault had been interviewed by a probation officer without having an attorney present, and the statements made in this interview were submitted as proof that Gault had made the obscene phone call.

The U.S. Supreme Court ruled that Gault's commitment to the reformatory constituted a deprivation of liberty. This meant that Gault should have been provided with most of the procedural protections afforded to adults in criminal prosecutions. According to the Court in *Gault*, "[U]nbridled discretion, however benevolently motivated, is frequently a poor substitute for principle and procedure."

The purpose of the *Gault* decision was to make juvenile proceedings more fair to the juvenile. The decision accomplished this, but it also made juvenile proceedings more adversarial. With the increased procedural protections, juveniles became more capable of resisting commitment to secure reformatories, and it became more difficult for the juvenile courts summarily to obtain control over juveniles.

The adversarial tenor in contemporary juvenile courts is thus an unfortunate by-product of the decision in *Gault*. Prosecutors must now work harder to persuade the juvenile court to find in favor of the state so that the system may take control of the juvenile. They must shift the focus of juvenile court proceedings away from the needs of the juvenile and onto the offense. This shifted focus is similar to the focus of proceedings in adult criminal court, and it amounts to a reversal of the traditional emphasis in juvenile court.

CROSS-REFERENCES

Adversary System; Children's Rights; Criminal Procedure; Juvenile Law.

GAY AND LESBIAN RIGHTS The goal of full legal and social equality for gay men and lesbians sought by the gay movement in the United States and other Western countries.

The term *gay* originally derived from slang, but it has gained wide acceptance in recent years, and many people who are sexually attracted to others of the same sex prefer it to the older and more clinical term *homosexual*. The drive for legal and social equality represents one aspect of a broader gay and lesbian movement that, since the late 1960s, has worked to change attitudes toward homosexuality, develop gay community institutions, and improve the self-image of gay men and lesbians.

Although homosexuality has been recorded in every historical period and culture, the gay and lesbian rights movement developed only with the emergence of a self-conscious, gay-identified subculture that was willing to openly assert its demands for equality. Until the 1960s, virtually all lesbians and gay men were secretive about their sexual orientation and frequently shared the attitude of the general society that homosexuality was sick, sinful, or both. The phrase "in the closet" refers to gay men and lesbians who hide their sexual orientation.

The first national gay organizations in the United States were the Mattachine Society (1951) and the Daughters of Bilitis (1956). The emergence of the CIVIL RIGHTS MOVEMENT of the 1960s energized gay and lesbian groups, and the development of the women's movement of the late 1960s made explicit the link between political activities and personal identity.

The watershed moment for gay men and lesbians occurred in 1969 when the patrons of the Stonewall Inn, a gay bar in New York City's Greenwich Village, forcefully resisted arrest by city police officers who had raided the bar. Stonewall became a symbol for a new set of attitudes on the part of younger gay men and lesbians who resisted DISCRIMINATION and negative stereotyping. As gay men and lesbians became more open and decided to "come out of the closet," U.S. society was challenged to question assumptions about homosexuality.

Though most gay and lesbian rights activity remains local, national organizations such as the National Gay Task Force, the Lambda Defense and Education Fund, and the Human Rights Campaign have played a significant role in challenging discriminatory treatment. For example, in 1974, the National Gay Task Force successfully lobbied the American Psychiatric Association to remove homosexuality from its list of mental disorders.

The recognition of gay and lesbian rights has been accomplished through both court challenges and legislative action. The ability of gay and lesbian organizations to make significant financial contributions to political candidates has helped lead to more sympathetic hearings in the legislative arena.

Criminal Prohibitions on Sexual Activity Most gay men and lesbians remained in the closet until the modern movement for equality because homosexual behavior has been a crime throughout U.S. history. Homosexual activity includes anal sex and oral sex, which have been labeled SODOMY. Criminal laws against sodomy date from the colonial period, when a conviction for a "crime against nature" could lead to a death sentence. Although few if any people have ever been executed for sodomy, the penalties for this crime have remained heavy, and the act is now classified a FELONY in states that have sodomy statutes.

Advocates of gay and lesbian rights have made the repeal of sodomy statutes a leading goal. Twenty-seven states have repealed these statutes, usually as part of a general revision of the criminal code and with the recognition that heterosexuals as well as homosexuals engage in oral and anal sex.

The Supreme Court has found that state laws prohibiting homosexual sodomy are not unconstitutional. In *Bowers v. Hardwick*, 478 U.S. 186, 106 S. Ct. 2841, 92 L. Ed. 2d 140 (1986), the Court upheld the Georgia sodomy statute (Ga. Code Ann. § 16-6-2 [1984]).

Gay men and lesbians face discrimination from many groups in U.S. society.

Michael Hardwick was arrested and charged with committing sodomy with a consenting male adult in the PRIVACY of his home. Although the state prosecutor declined to prosecute the case, Hardwick brought suit in federal court, seeking a declaration that the statute was unconstitutional.

Writing for the majority, Justice BYRON R. WHITE rejected the argument that previous decisions such as the Court's rulings on ABORTION and contraception had created a right of privacy that extends to homosexual activity. Instead, the Court drew a sharp distinction between the previous cases, which involved "family, marriage, or procreation," and homosexual activity.

The Court also rejected the argument that a fundamental right to engage in homosexual activity can be found in the DUE PROCESS Clauses of the Fifth and Fourteenth Amendments. Justice White observed that the rights protected under those clauses have been characterized as fundamental liberties implicit in the concept of ordered liberty and as liberties that are deeply rooted in tradition. In contrast, prohibitions against sodomy have appeared in the laws of most states since the nation's founding.

To the argument that homosexual activity should be protected when it occurs in the privacy of a home, Justice White said that "otherwise illegal conduct is not always immunized whenever it occurs in the home." For example, the possession of drugs or stolen goods is not protected because it occurs at home.

Hardwick was a setback to the gay and lesbian rights movement, as it allowed opponents to argue that it was absurd to grant CIVIL RIGHTS to persons who engage in criminal acts.

Antidiscrimination Laws Advocates of gay and lesbian rights have sought the passage of legislation that prohibits discrimination in employment, housing, public accommodations, or public service on the basis of sexual orientation. Many U.S. cities have passed gay rights ordinances that accomplish these objectives. In 1982, Wisconsin became the first state to pass gay rights legislation.

At the national level, gay men and lesbians have fought legal battles in the 1980s and 1990s to allow them to serve in the ARMED SERVICES. A series of lawsuits were filed that sought to overturn military regulations that mandated discharge for disclosing a homosexual orientation.

In *Meinhold v. United States Department of Defense,* 34 F.3d 1469 (9th Cir. 1994), a three-judge panel ruled that Petty Officer Keith Meinhold, of the U.S. Navy, could not be discharged for stating on a national television broadcast that he was gay. In the discharge proceedings, the Navy had taken the position that Meinhold should be discharged even though the Navy had not proved that Meinhold had committed any act of homosexual conduct.

The Ninth Circuit Court of Appeals concluded that a Navy policy against homosexual conduct was constitutional, as it was based on the Navy's professional judgment that homosexual conduct "seriously impairs the accomplishment of the military mission." However, the court of appeals ruled that Meinhold's statement that he was gay was not grounds for discharge. In the court's view, Meinhold had not demonstrated "a concrete, expressed desire to commit homosexual acts." Thus, the focus for the armed services must be on prohibited conduct and persons who are likely to engage in prohibited conduct.

The issue moved into the political arena following President BILL CLINTON's election in November 1992. Clinton promised to honor his campaign pledge to exercise his authority as commander in chief of the armed forces, and remove the military ban against gays. But the Joint Chiefs of Staff, headed by General Colin L. Powell, and many other senior Pentagon officers strenuously objected to Clinton's plan, claiming that ending the ban would interfere with military order, discipline, and morale. Led by Senator Sam Nunn (D-Ga.), chairman of the

SAME-SEX MARRIAGE:
A CIVIL RIGHT OR A MORAL WRONG?

Since the birth of the U.S. gay and lesbian rights movement in the late 1960s, members of the movement have sought to attain civil rights already granted to racial and ethnic minorities. These attempts at legal change have met with some success, yet a fundamental issue for gay and lesbian couples, that of same-sex marriage, has found strong resistance, even from supporters of gay rights.

Same-sex marriage is controversial not only because it would require legal change but also because it raises a host of issues surrounding the definitions of marriage and family. The issue is packed with social and cultural beliefs and symbols that force parties to the debate to examine basic assumptions about how social life should be ordered. Though the overwhelming majority of opposition comes from heterosexuals, there are gays and lesbians who have doubts about the wisdom of same-sex marriage.

Advocates of same-sex marriage argue that many same-sex couples consider themselves married for all intents and purposes. The only thing lacking is legal recognition by the government—in this case, the state government—that such marriages exist. The denial of legal recognition constitutes sexual discrimination, resulting in the loss of the legal rights and benefits afforded heterosexual marriages. Thus, unless a surviving member of a same-sex couple has been named in the deceased partner's will, the survivor has no legal right to any portion of the deceased's probate estate—whereas in heterosexual marriages, a surviving spouse has a legal right to such assets. In addition, same-sex couples lose out on health care benefits extended to heterosexual married couples.

The legal arguments for same-sex marriage are grounded in the constitutional concepts of equal protection and due process. Proponents of same-sex marriage point to the U.S. Supreme Court's decision in *Loving v. Virginia*,

388 U.S. 1, 87 S. Ct. 1817, 18 L. Ed. 2d 1010 (1967), which ruled that state laws that prohibited interracial marriages (antimiscegenation laws) were unconstitutional. The case established that it is a denial of due process of law to forbid marriages on the basis of race, and that the creation of such classifications denied couples equal protection of the law because the classifications had "no legitimate purpose independent of invidious racial discrimination."

IN FOCUS

For advocates of same-sex marriage, *Loving* was an example of the proper modern legal response to irrational racial prejudice. The Hawaii Supreme Court's decision in *Baehr v. Lewin*, 74 Haw. 530, 852 P.2d 44 (1993), that the state must have a compelling state interest in order to ban same-sex marriage, used *Loving* as a controlling legal precedent.

Opponents of same-sex marriage make three main arguments against it: the definition-of-marriage argument, the moral tradition argument, and the pragmatism argument.

The definition-of-marriage argument goes to basic social and cultural assumptions. Opponents claim that marriage is necessarily based on heterosexual couples and therefore cannot include same-sex couples. Thus, any statute that describes marriage could have only contemplated heterosexual couples, even if the statute does not use the specific terms *husband* and *wife*. In *Jones v. Hallahan*, 501 S.W.2d 588 (1973), the Kentucky Court of Appeals used this line of reasoning to prohibit same-sex marriage, noting that "marriage has always been considered as the union of a man and a woman and we have been presented with no authority to the contrary."

Proponents of same-sex marriage argue that courts have not been presented with "authority to the contrary" because gays and lesbians have been ignored by historians. Major research on gay and lesbian history and anthropology has

led some historians and legal scholars to conclude that Western and non-Western cultures have recognized same-sex relationships. In European history, stigmatizing and closeting of gays and lesbians started at the end of the medieval period and the beginning of the growth of nation-states. Thus, the North American continent was colonized at a time when same-sex relationships had lost their cultural and legal protection.

Opponents of same-sex marriage who make the moral tradition argument state that defining marriage to include only heterosexual couples is justified to preserve family values and traditional ethical notions. They point to passages in the Bible that either affirm heterosexual marriages (Adam and Eve) or denounce homosexual practices (Sodom and Gomorrah). The Judeo-Christian moral tradition formed the basis of English law; thus, it must be assumed that religious teachings against homosexual relationships informed the law. The U.S. Supreme Court echoed the moral tradition argument in its ruling that criminal sodomy laws are not unconstitutional, suggesting that "millennia of moral teaching" supported a state's right to forbid homosexual acts (*Bowers v. Hardwick*, 478 U.S. 186, 106 S. Ct. 2841, 92 L. Ed. 2d 140 [1986]).

Another argument often raised with moral tradition is that heterosexual marriage is based on the need to procreate, something that same-sex couples cannot do. Proponents of same-sex marriage point out that heterosexual couples who cannot procreate are not denied a marriage license. Elderly, disabled, and infertile individuals may choose to marry for reasons other than procreation. In addition, both heterosexual and homosexual couples have taken advantage of advances in technologies such as artificial insemination and in vitro fertilization to overcome physical limitations on procreation. Critics of the moral tradition argument contend that it is based on misguided

(continued on next page)

SAME-SEX MARRIAGE: A CIVIL RIGHT OR A MORAL WRONG?
(CONTINUED)

readings of the Bible and history. They note that many religious leaders support same-sex marriage, and that many same-sex couples solemnize their relationship in a religious ceremony performed by a minister or rabbi.

The pragmatism argument against same-sex marriage is typically made by those who support gay and lesbian rights generally but stop short of endorsing same-sex marriage. The call for marriage, they maintain, will create a backlash against the entire gay and lesbian rights movement. In addition, permitting same-sex marriage would be interpreted as legitimizing homosexuality. The pragmatic position is that gays and lesbians should be tolerated and protected; it does not extend to support the recognition of an alternative life-style or the expansion of the traditional concept of marriage.

Along with homosexual opponents who advance these arguments, some gays and lesbians are less than enthused with the prospect of same-sex marriage. This group believes that heterosexual marriage is not a good model for gays and lesbians, as it has traditionally established a hierarchical relationship that has produced the subordination of women. The structure of marriage has fostered domestic abuse, economic disempowerment, and other forms of social dysfunction.

Another argument against same-sex marriage is that it will assimilate gays and lesbians into the dominant culture and drain off the radicalism implicit in the gay and lesbian lifestyle. In lobbying for same-sex marriage, gay and lesbian leaders will put forward couples who most resemble their mainstream, heterosexual counterparts. This argument has been met with skepticism as romanticizing the movement. All gays and lesbians cannot be grouped as radicals, and it is to be expected that many gays and lesbians would enjoy the legal protection that same-sex marriage would bring.

The debate over same-sex marriage becomes heated because of the fundamental issues at stake. Proponents see marriage as socially constructed and therefore open to changes that society wishes to make. Opponents see less flexibility, citing tradition, morality, and the integrity of the family.

---

powerful Armed Services Committee, Congress demanded an opportunity to comment on the policy.

Faced with increasing pressure at the beginning of his administration, Clinton agreed to a six-month delay in lifting the ban. He agreed to establish a temporary policy developed by Nunn, and issued a directive ordering the military to stop asking new recruits about their sexual orientation; stop investigations to ferret out gays in uniform; and suspend current cases seeking to discharge gays, as long as those cases were based solely on homosexual status rather than on improper conduct. This policy, dubbed "don't ask, don't tell," became permanent when Congress wrote it into law in September 1993 (Pub. L. No. 103-160, 1993 H.R. 2401 § 571(a)). With this policy, gay men and lesbians were directed to keep their sexuality hidden if they intended to pursue a military career.

Legal Recognition of Gay and Lesbian Relationships Gay and lesbian activists have pressed for legal recognition of homosexual relationships. Under current law, a gay couple is treated differently than a married heterosexual couple. Thus, the benefits of PROBATE and tax law are denied same-sex couples. For example, if a partner in a same-sex relationship dies, under law, the surviving partner is not entitled to any of the deceased's property, unless the deceased provided for such an entitlement in a WILL.

With the appearance of AIDS, health benefits became particularly important to gay couples. Unless a company or government unit makes specific provisions for same-sex couples, an employee's same-sex partner who is not employed by the organization will not be allowed to join the employee's health plan.

Faced with these disparities, gay and lesbian activists first focused their attention on "domestic partnership" laws that would allow unmarried couples to register their relationship with a municipality. Attempts to implement domestic partnership failed in several cities, but New York City, New York; Madison, Wisconsin; Takoma Park, Maryland; and Berkeley, San Francisco, Santa Cruz, and West Hollywood, California, have enacted this type of ordinance.

A more radical attempt to redefine the family and domestic relationships occurred in Hawaii, where gay and lesbian couples filed a lawsuit when they were refused a MARRIAGE license. The issue of same-sex marriage reached the Hawaii Supreme Court in *Baehr v. Lewin*, 74 Haw. 530, 852 P.2d 44 (1993). The court ruled that the state must have a compelling state interest in order to ban same-sex marriages. Though the court did not make a final ruling on the issue, it sent the case back to the lower court with instructions to apply the highest level of constitutional scrutiny to Hawaii's marriage law, Hawaii Revised Statutes, section 572-1. Many legal commentators believe the state will not be able to show a compelling state interest.

This decision triggered a national debate, raising the ire of groups such as the Family Research Council and the Roman Catholic Church. Even some gay rights advocates argued that assimilationist goals such as those reflected by the plaintiffs in *Baehr* were an affront to their movement and a means of subverting an alternative lifestyle.

The issue of same-sex marriage is of national interest because states traditionally accord full faith and credit (full legal recognition) to marriages performed in other states. Faced with the prospect of gay and lesbian couples flying to Hawaii and then demanding legal recognition of their union, several state legislatures passed laws that forbid recognition. Congress responded in 1996 with the introduction of the Defense of Marriage Act (H.R. 3396, 104th Cong., 2d Sess.). The bill denies certain federal benefits and entitlements to same-sex marriage partners by defining marriage as a union between a man and a woman. It also allows states to ban same-sex marriages within their borders and to not recognize such marriages performed in other states. Critics of the bill argued that Republicans were pushing it for political purposes, yet Democratic President Clinton indicated he would sign the bill into law if it reached his desk.

In contrast to the national focus on issues such as same-sex marriage, local gay and lesbian groups have spent their energies helping defend lesbian mothers and gay fathers faced with the loss of their children in custody cases. In the Virginia case of *Bottoms v. Bottoms*, 18 Va. App. 481, 444 S.E.2d 276 (1994), a trial judge awarded custody of Sharon Bottoms's son to her mother, solely because Bottoms is a lesbian. The Virginia Court of Appeals reversed the decision as an abuse of the court's discretion and returned custody to the mother. This case indicates the problems gay men and lesbians have in court. The National Center for Lesbian Rights believes that only approximately one hundred homosexuals gained parental rights through the courts between 1985 and 1994.

Backlash As the same-sex marriage issue demonstrates, the efforts of gay men and lesbians to achieve social and legal equality have generated a backlash from those who oppose their agenda. Domestic partnership acts and gay rights ordinances have been rejected by voters in a number of cities and municipalities, including Irvine and Concord, California. At the state level, the voters of Oregon in 1988 approved a REFERENDUM that repealed an executive order by former governor Neil Goldschmidt that had prohibited state agencies from discriminating based on sexual orientation. Measure 8, as the referendum was labeled, never went into effect, as the Oregon Court of Appeals ruled it unconstitutional (*Merrick v. Board of Higher Education*, 116 Or. App. 258, 841 P.2d 646 [1992]).

Undaunted by this court decision, the antigay Oregon Citizens Alliance placed a referendum on the 1992 Oregon ballot called Measure 9. Measure 9 was a strongly worded initiative that would have prohibited civil rights protection based on sexual orientation and required state and local governments and school districts to discourage homosexuality. Proponents of the initiative believed that homosexuality was abnormal and perverse. The referendum was rejected on November 3, 1992, by a margin of 57 to 42 percent.

In contrast, voters in Colorado signaled a distinct displeasure with gay and lesbian rights. In November 1992, Colorado took the unprecedented step of amending the state constitution to prohibit state and local governments from enacting any law, regulation, or policy that would, in effect, protect the civil rights of gays, lesbians, and bisexuals. The amendment, known as Amendment 2, did not go into effect, as a lawsuit was filed challenging the constitutionality of the new provision.

This lawsuit—*Romer v. Evans*, __U.S.__, 116 S. Ct. 1620, 134 L. Ed. 2d 855 (1996)—reached the U.S. Supreme Court. In a landmark and controversial decision, the Supreme Court struck down the amendment as unconstitutional. Justice ANTHONY M. KENNEDY, writing for the majority, declared that the Colorado provision violated the Equal Protection Clause of the FOURTEENTH AMENDMENT. The Court found that the amendment did more than repeal state and municipal gay rights laws. The amendment prohibited "all legislative, executive or judicial action at any level of state or local government designed to protect . . . gays and lesbians." Under this provision, the only way gay men and lesbians could secure their civil rights was through amendment of the state constitution. This approach was too limited. Kennedy concluded that "[i]t is not within our constitutional tradition to enact laws of this sort." The Colorado amendment classified gay men and lesbians "not to further a proper legislative end but to make them unequal to everyone else. This Colorado cannot do."

The *Romer* decision was a major advance for gay and lesbian rights, as in it, the Supreme Court made clear that states cannot use a broad brush to limit civil rights. The political process cannot be changed to prevent gay men and lesbians from using the political and legal tools afforded all other citizens. The decision did suggest, however, that it is not unconstitutional to repeal specific legislation that favors gay rights.

The quest by gay men and lesbians for legal and social equality has both empowered a historically stigmatized subculture and enraged conservative groups in U.S. society. Issues of morality, sexuality, and family always generate social friction. The U.S. legal system is likely to see many more challenges involving gay and lesbian rights.

CROSS-REFERENCES

Acquired Immune Deficiency Syndrome; Child Custody; Equal Protection; Ettelbrick, Paula Louise; Full Faith and Credit Clause.

GENERAL ACCOUNTING OFFICE   The

General Accounting Office (GAO), created by the Budget and Accounting Act, 1921 (31 U.S.C.A. 41), was vested with all powers and duties of the six auditors and the comptroller of the Treasury, as stated in the act of July 31, 1894 (28 Stat. 162), and other statutes extending back to the original Treasury Act of 1789 (1 Stat. 65). The 1921 act broadened the AUDIT activities of the government and established new responsibilities for reporting to Congress.

The scope of the activities of the GAO was further extended by the Government Corporation Control Act (31 U.S.C.A. 841 [1945]), the Legislative Reorganization Act of 1946 (31 U.S.C.A. 60), the Accounting and Auditing Act of 1950 (31 U.S.C.A. 65), the Legislative Reorganization Act of 1970 (31 U.S.C.A. 1151), the Congressional Budget and Impoundment Control Act of 1974 (31 U.S.C.A. 1301), the General Accounting Office Act of 1974 (31 U.S.C.A. 52c), and other legislation.

The GAO is under the control and direction of the comptroller general of the United States and the deputy comptroller general of the United States, appointed by the president with the advice and consent of the Senate for terms of fifteen years.

The GAO has the following basic purposes: to assist Congress, its committees, and its members in carrying out their legislative and oversight responsibilities, consistent with its role as an independent nonpolitical agency in the legislative branch; to carry out legal, ACCOUNTING, auditing, and claims settlement functions with respect to federal government programs and operations as assigned by Congress; and to make recommendations designed to provide for more efficient and effective government operations.

Direct Assistance to Congress The GAO directly assists Congress and its committees, members, and officers on request. This assistance can be in any of the forms described in the following paragraphs.

Legislation may be enacted directing the GAO to examine a specific matter; special audits, surveys, and reviews may be performed for the committees, members, or officers of Congress; professional staff members may be assigned to assist committees in conducting studies and investigations; the comptroller general or his or her representatives may testify before committees on matters considered to be within the special competence of the GAO; and committees or members may request comments on or assistance in drafting proposed legislation or other advice in legal and legislative matters.

Further, the GAO responds to numerous requests from congressional sources for information relating to or resulting from its work and provides advice on congressional, administrative, and financial operations.

The Congressional Budget and Impoundment Control Act of 1974 specified numerous additional ways in which the GAO is to assist Congress: (1) provide information, services, facilities, and personnel (as mutually agreed) to the Congressional Budget Office; (2) assist congressional committees in developing statements of legislative objectives and goals and methods for assessing and reporting actual program performance; (3) assist such committees in analyzing and assessing federal agency program reviews and evaluation studies; (4) develop and recommend methods for review and evaluation of government programs; (5) conduct a continuing program to identify needs of committees and members of Congress for fiscal, budgetary, and program-related information; (6) assist congressional committees in developing their information needs; (7) monitor recurring reporting requirements of the Congress; (8) develop, in cooperation with the CONGRESSIONAL BUDGET OFFICE, the Treasury, and the Office of Management and Budget, an up-to-date inventory and directory of sources and information systems for fiscal, budgetary, and program-related information; (9) assist committees and members to obtain information from such sources and to appraise and analyze it; (10) develop, with the Congressional Budget Office, a central file of data and information to meet recurring requirements of Congress for fiscal, budgetary, and program-related information; (11) review and report to Congress on deferrals and rescissions of budget authority proposed by the president; and (12) bring suit, where necessary, to assure the availability for obligation of budget authority.

Auditing In general, the audit authority of the GAO extends to all departments and agencies of the federal government. Exceptions to this audit authority relate principally to funds relating to certain intelligence activities.

Where audit authority exists, the GAO has the right of access to, and examination of, any books, documents, papers, or records of the departments and agencies. The law provides that departments and agencies furnish to the comptroller general such information as he or she may require, including that related to their powers, duties, activities, organization, financial transactions, and methods of business.

The GAO has statutory authority to investigate all matters relating to the receipt, disbursement, and application of public funds. Additionally, the audit authority of the GAO covers wholly and partially owned government corporations and certain nonappropriated fund activities. By law, it is authorized and directed to make expenditure analyses of executive agencies to enable Congress to determine whether public funds are efficiently and economically administered and expended, and to review and evaluate the results of existing government programs and activities.

The scope of the audit work of the GAO extends not only to the programs and activities that the federal government itself conducts but also to the activities of state and local governments, quasi-governmental bodies, and private organizations in their capacity as recipients under, or administrators for, federal aid programs financed by loans, advances, grants, and contributions. The interest of the GAO also extends to certain activities of those having negotiated contracts with the government.

The audit activities of the GAO also include examining and settling accounts of the certification, disbursement, and collection officers of the federal government, including determinations involving accountability for improper or illegal expenditures of public funds. Balances

certified by the comptroller general are binding on the EXECUTIVE BRANCH; however, any settled account can be reviewed on motion by the comptroller general or other interested party.

In its audit work the GAO makes recommendations for greater economy and efficiency in government operations and for improving the effectiveness of government programs. Within this audit authority is a responsibility to report significant matters to Congress for information and use in carrying out its legislative and executive branch surveillance functions.

Accounting The comptroller general has the following statutory responsibilities with respect to the accounting systems of federal agencies:

- Prescribe the accounting principles, standards, and related requirements to be followed by the agencies
- Cooperate with federal agencies in developing their accounting systems
- Approve AGENCY accounting systems when they are deemed adequate and meet prescribed principles, standards, and related requirements
- Review from time to time agency accounting systems in operation
- Conduct—jointly with the Office of Management and Budget, the Department of the Treasury, and the Office of Personnel Management—a continuous program to improve accounting and financial reporting in the federal government

By law, the comptroller general cooperates with the secretary of the Treasury and the director of the Office of Management and Budget in developing for use by all federal agencies standardized information and data processing

The General Accounting Office assists Congress in carrying out its responsibilities, performs audits when necessary, and makes recommendations for efficient operations.

systems and also standard terminology, definitions, classifications, and codes for federal fiscal, budgetary, and program-related data and information.

Legal Services and Decisions The legal work of the GAO is centered at the headquarters office in its Office of the General Counsel.

The comptroller general makes final determinations as to the legality of actions taken by federal departments and agencies with regard to accountability for the use of public funds. These determinations are made in connection with actions already taken and on an advance basis upon request by certain responsible officers of the government. Decisions of the comptroller general concerning the legality of payments may arise from the audit work of the GAO or may be applied for by the heads of departments or agencies or by certifying and disbursing officers with regard to payments to be made or as a result of congressional inquiries.

The comptroller general also considers questions that arise in connection with the award of government contracts and certain contracts under government grants. Statutory and regulatory procedures precisely define the manner in which these government awards are to be made, and those competing for such awards who believe that requirements have not been met in any particular instance may apply to the comptroller general for a determination.

The legal work of the GAO also covers a wide range of advisory services—to Congress, its committees, and members with respect to the legal effect of statutory provisions and implications of proposed legislation as well as assistance in drafting legislation; to the Department of Justice primarily in the form of litigation reports on court cases generated by or related to the work of the GAO; and to the courts in connection with cases involving the award of government contracts. In addition there is daily coordination between the staff of the Office of the General Counsel and the audit and operating staffs with regard to the legal consequences of issues raised in the course of reviews of government activities.

Claims Settlement and Debt Collection The GAO settles claims by and against the United States as required by law. Claims may involve individuals; business entities; or foreign, state, and municipal governments as claimant or debtor. Settlement of these claims by the GAO is binding upon executive branch agencies. However, the comptroller general may review any settled claim on his or her own initiative or at the request of an interested party. Claimants and debtors have further recourse to the Congress or to the courts.

Where an ADMINISTRATIVE AGENCY has been unable to collect a debt due the government, the debt is certified to the GAO as uncollectible. After determining the amount due the United States, the GAO superintends its recovery, and ultimately makes final settlement and adjustment.

Energy Data Verification Under the Energy Policy and Conservation Act (42 U.S.C.A. 6201), approved December 22, 1975, the comptroller general is empowered to conduct verification examinations of energy-related information developed by private business concerns under certain circumstances delineated in the act. For the purpose of carrying out this authority, the comptroller general may issue SUBPOENAS, require written answers to INTERROGATORIES, administer oaths, inspect business premises, and inspect and copy specified books and records. Certain enforcement powers are provided, including for some types of noncompliance the power to assess civil penalties and to collect such penalties through civil action.

Rules, Regulations, and Decisions The comptroller general makes such rules and regulations as deemed necessary for carrying on the work of the GAO, including those for the admission of attorneys to practice before it. Under the seal of the office, he or she furnishes copies of records from books and proceedings thereof, for use as evidence in accordance with the act of June 25, 1948 (62 Stat. 946; 28 U.S.C.A. 1733).

The GAO Personnel Act of 1980, approved February 15, 1980 (94 Stat. 27; 31 U.S.C.A. 52–1), requires the comptroller general to establish an independent personnel management system for employees of the GAO. The system would not be subject to regulation or oversight of executive branch agencies. Employee rights, such as appeals from adverse actions, are protected by creation of a GAO Personnel Appeals Board.

The GAO "Policy and Procedures Manual for Guidance of Federal Agencies" is the official medium through which the comptroller general promulgates principles, standards, and related requirements for accounting to be observed by the federal departments and agencies; uniform procedures for use by the federal agencies; and regulations governing the relationships of the GAO with other federal agencies and with individuals and private concerns doing business with the government.

General Accounting Office

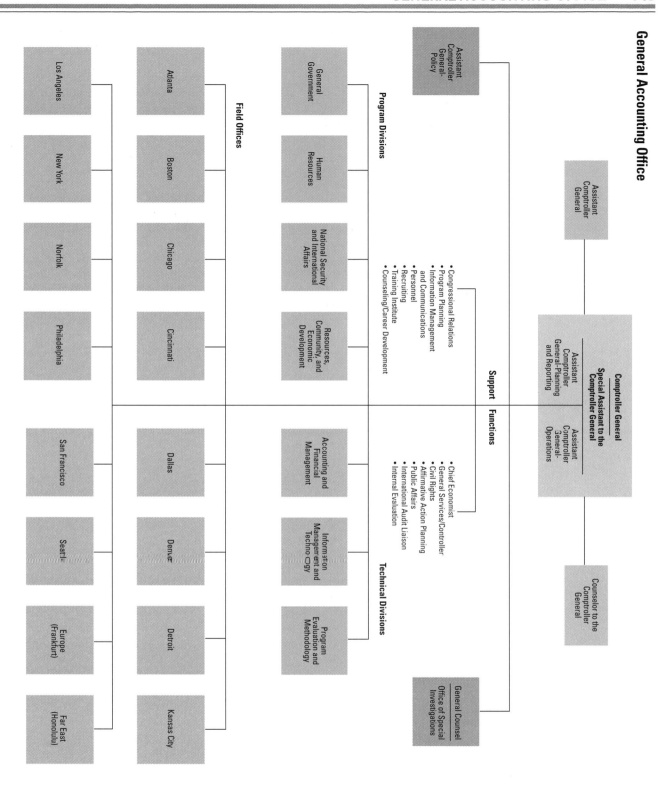

Comptroller General
Special Assistant to the
Comptroller General

Assistant Comptroller General

Counselor to the Comptroller General

General Counsel
Office of Special Investigations

Assistant Comptroller General-Policy

Assistant Comptroller General-Planning and Reporting

Assistant Comptroller General-Operations

Program Divisions

General Government

Human Resources

National Security and International Affairs

Resources, Community, and Economic Development

Accounting and Financial Management

Information Management and Technology

Program Evaluation and Methodology

Technical Divisions

Support Functions

- Congressional Relations
- Program Planning
- Information Management and Communications
- Personnel
- Recruiting
- Training Institute
- Counseling/Career Development

- Chief Economist
- General Services/Controller
- Civil Rights
- Affirmative Action Planning
- Public Affairs
- International Audit Liaison
- Internal Evaluation

Field Offices

Los Angeles

New York

Norfolk

Philadelphia

Atlanta

Boston

Chicago

Cincinnati

San Francisco

Seattle

Europe (Frankfurt)

Far East (Honolulu)

Dallas

Denver

Detroit

Kansas City

All decisions of the comptroller general of general import are published in monthly pamphlets and in annual volumes.

GAO Reports As required by law a list of GAO reports issued or released during the previous month is furnished monthly to Congress, its committees, and its members.

Copies of GAO reports are provided without charge to members of Congress and congressional committee staff members; officials of federal, state, local, and foreign governments; members of the press; college libraries, faculty members, and students; and nonprofit organizations.

CROSS-REFERENCES

Congress of the United States; Federal Budget; Office of Management and Budget; Treasury Department.

GENERAL AGREEMENT ON TARIFFS AND TRADE (GATT)

The General Agreement on Tariffs and Trade (GATT) originated with a meeting of twenty-two nations meeting in 1947 in Geneva, Switzerland. The detailed commitments by each country to limit TARIFFS on particular items by the amount negotiated and specified in its tariff schedule is the central core of the GATT system of international obligation.

The obligations relating to the tariff schedules are contained in Article II of GATT. For each COMMODITY listed on the schedule of a country, that country agrees to charge a tariff that will not exceed an amount specified in the schedule. It can, if it wishes, charge a lower tariff.

GENERAL APPEARANCE

The act by which a defendant completely consents to the JURISDICTION of the court by appearing before it either in person or through an authorized representative thereby waiving any jurisdictional defects that might be raised except for that of the competency of the court.

A general appearance differs from a SPECIAL APPEARANCE in which a defendant agrees to submit to the jurisdiction of the court for a restricted purpose, such as to test whether the SERVICE OF PROCESS made upon him or her was legally sufficient.

GENERAL CREDITOR

An individual to whom money is due from a DEBTOR, but whose debt is not secured by property of the debtor. One to whom property has not been PLEDGED to satisfy a debt in the event of nonpayment by the individual owing the money.

GENERAL EXECUTION

A court order commanding a public official, such as a SHERIFF, to take the PERSONAL PROPERTY of a defendant to satisfy the amount of a JUDGMENT awarded against such defendant.

When such officer is given the authority to seize only particular property or types of property, the WRIT or order is sometimes known as a *special execution.*

GENERAL INTENT

In CRIMINAL LAW and TORT law, a mental plan to do that which is forbidden by the law.

Unlike offenses that require a SPECIFIC INTENT, it is not necessary that the accused intend the precise harm or result. It is sufficient if the person meant to do the act that caused the harm or result. For example, BATTERY is a general intent offense. If a defendant commits a battery that results in harm to the victim, it does not matter if the defendant did not intend the harm.

GENERAL JURISDICTION

The legal authority of a COURT to entertain whatever type of case comes up within the geographical area over which its power extends.

General JURISDICTION differs from special or limited jurisdiction, which is the power of a court to hear only certain types of cases, or those in which the amount in controversy is below a certain sum or that is subject to exceptions.

GENERAL LEGACY

A monetary gift, payable out of the collective ASSETS of the estate of a testator—one who makes a WILL —and not from a designated source.

Unlike a SPECIFIC LEGACY, a general legacy is not subject to ADEMPTION, extinction that results when a testator revokes his or her intention to leave designated property to another either by altering the property or removing it from the estate.

GENERAL SERVICES ADMINISTRATION

The General Services Administration (GSA) was established by section 101 of the Federal Property and Administrative Services Act of 1949 (40 U.S.C.A. § 751). The GSA sets policy for and manages government property and records. More specifically, the GSA's duties include the construction and operation of buildings; procurement and distribution of supplies; utilization and disposal of property; management of transportation, traffic, and communications; and management of the government's automatic data processing resources program. Like a large business conglomerate, the GSA conducts business in many different areas and operates on different levels of organization: the central Washington, D.C., office, eleven regional offices, and field activities.

First Level of Hierarchy The first level of hierarchy in the GSA consists of the Office of Ethics, administrator, deputy administrator, chief of staff, Board of Contract Appeals, and Office of the Inspector General.

The Office of Ethics governs the standards of ethical conduct for the agency's employees.

The Board of Contract Appeals resolves disputes concerning contracts with the GSA and other independent agencies, such as the Department of the Treasury. It operates as an independent tribunal within the AGENCY.

The Office of the Inspector General audits and investigates the agency and its various offices. This office informs Congress of problems and mismanagement in the agency and recommends changes. The office also maintains a toll-free telephone number for complaints concerning fraud, waste, and mismanagement in agency programs.

Second Level of Hierarchy The second level of the GSA hierarchy comprises the Federal Supply Service, Information Technology Service, Public Buildings Service, and Office of Federal Telecommunications System 2000.

Federal Supply Service The Federal Supply Service (FSS) provides low-price, quality goods and services to federal departments and agencies. Its services include governmentwide programs for the management of transportation, mail, and travel; audits of transportation; management of a federal fleet; and management of aircraft owned or operated by civilian agencies in support of government missions.

The FSS provides over $8 billion annually in common-use goods and services to federal agencies. It emphasizes purchasing environmentally safe products and services and supplies over three thousand environmentally oriented products to the federal government, such as retread tires, shipping boxes made with recycled materials, and water-saving devices.

The service also coordinates a worldwide program for the management of government property, through the Office of Property Disposal, which is responsible for allocating excess PERSONAL PROPERTY among the agencies and donating or disposing of property through public sales.

The FSS Interagency Fleet Management Program controls approximately 145,000 vehicles, including over 10,000 alternative fuel vehicles. The FSS also acts as the government's civilian freight manager by providing rating and routing services to customer agencies and overnight delivery of small packages at reduced rates, and managing the postpayment audit of freight and passenger transportation bills.

Information Technology Service The Information Technology Service (ITS) directs governmentwide programs for automated data processing and local TELECOMMUNICATIONS equipment and services, coordinates programs for federal records and information management practices, and provides information to the public through the Federal Information Center.

The ITS helps federal agencies manage information resources through the Office of Information Technology Integration (ITI). The ITI provides assistance through three programs: the Federal Systems Integration and Management System, Federal Computer Acquisition Center, and Federal Information System Support Program. The ITS also procures automatic data processing and telecommunications hardware, software, and services involving information resources of governmentwide agencies.

In addition to technical assistance, the service provides various management assistance programs and policies to governmentwide agencies concerning information-related functions and activities. It is in charge of the GSA's governmentwide telecommunications service and assists with the interagency Information Resources Management infrastructure. It also provides internal information systems management for the GSA.

The ITS's Office of Information Security supports all government activities conducting sensitive and classified national security, diplomatic, and Department of Defense missions.

Another program overseen by ITS is the Federal Information Center Program, which is a clearinghouse for information about the federal government. The center answers questions regarding government programs and refers people to the appropriate agency. Depending upon their geographic location, residents may be able to access the center through a toll-free telephone number. Another resource, the Federal Domestic Assistance Catalog Program, provides information on federally operated programs that offer domestic assistance, such as loans, grants, and insurance, to interested persons.

The ITS also offers the Federal Information Relay Service to help hearing-impaired and speech-impaired individuals communicate with the government.

The service manages numerous programs that maintain information on equipment, goods, and services bought by the government. The information is available to the public.

Also within the ITS is the Office of Emerging Technology. It plans, manages, and directs activities that promote the identification, development, and use of current and emerging technologies in the federal government.

Public Buildings Service The Public Buildings Service (PBS) designs, builds, leases, repairs, and maintains approximately seventy-three hundred federally controlled buildings in

General Services Administration

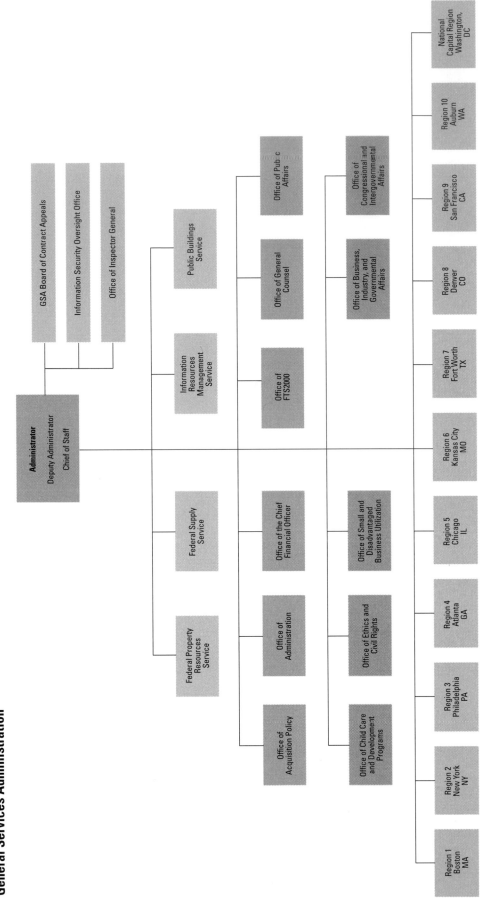

the United States. The service is also responsible for property management information systems throughout the government and for the maintenance of PUBLIC UTILITIES and their costs.

The Office of the Commercial Broker and its eleven regional offices and various facility support centers work with real estate professionals to acquire and lease space for federal agencies. The Office of Property Management manages all aspects of the properties and ensures that the properties adhere to energy conservation, handicapped-accessibility, and historic preservation requirements. The Office of Business Development directs the national strategic plans and programs for REAL PROPERTY and also manages the long-term strategic and business direction of the PBS.

The Office of the Fee Developer represents the fee developer in agency dealings of national scope with representatives of the other executive branches and with representatives of other government and private-sector interests.

The Office of the Federal Protective Service supplies law enforcement and security devices and services, such as bomb threat investigations, to properties under the agency's control. It provides standards for the operation of a uniformed force and investigates criminal offenses not involving GSA employees. It provides these services through regional centers.

The Office of Property Disposal utilizes and disposes of the government's surplus real property. The property is disposed of by reallocation; transfer to a local public body for an authorized public use, such as for operation as a homeless shelter; or sale through negotiated or public competitive sales.

Office of Federal Telecommunications System 2000 The Office of Federal Telecommunications System 2000 (FTS2000) provides common-user, long-distance telecommunications services through contracts from private companies. It manages the government program involving data processing and local telecommunications equipment and services.

Third Level of Hierarchy The third level of hierarchy at the GSA consists of several offices that support all GSA services: the Offices of Acquisition Policy, the Chief Financial Officer, Enterprise Development, Portfolio Management, Governmentwide Real Property Policy, Equal Employment Opportunity Program, General Counsel, Congressional and Intergovernmental Affairs, Public Affairs, and Management and Human Resources.

The Office of Portfolio Management manages all aspects of the portfolio management business line at the national level.

The Office of Acquisition Policy directs and coordinates the agency's acquisitions policy program. It develops and administers guiding principles that are applicable to all federal agencies. This office also coordinates the Federal Procurement Data System and manages training and recruitment for employees involved with acquisition.

The Office of the Chief Financial Officer is in charge of the overall financial management within the GSA, including developing and maintaining agency accounting systems; developing policies and procedures; and reviewing fees, royalties, rents, and other charges imposed by the agency for its goods and services. Other responsibilities include the commercial activities program and the executive information system.

The Office of Enterprise Development plans, implements, and evaluates preference programs for agency procurement, including but not limited to the Small Business Program, Minority Business Enterprise Program, and Subcontracting Program. The office carries out many of its main duties through five regional business centers.

The Office of Government-wide Real Property Policy provides overall direction in governmentwide policy and related activities regarding real property.

GENERAL TERM 📖 A sitting of the court EN BANC, with the participation of the entire membership of the court rather than the regular QUORUM. A phrase used in some JURISDICTIONS to signify the ordinary session of a court during which the trial determination of actions occur. 📖

General term is distinguishable from SPECIAL TERM, in that the latter entails the hearing of MOTIONS, which are applications for court orders, arguments, the disposition of various types of formal business, or the trial of a special list or class of cases.

GENERAL VERDICT 📖 A decision by a JURY that determines which side in a particular controversy wins, and in some cases, the amount of money in DAMAGES to be awarded. 📖

GENERAL WARRANTY DEED Another name for a WARRANTY DEED.

GENERAL WELFARE 📖 The concern of the government for the health, peace, morality, and safety of its citizens. 📖

Providing for the welfare of the general public is a basic goal of government. The preamble to the U.S. Constitution cites promotion of the general welfare as a primary reason for the creation of the Constitution. Promotion of the general welfare is also a stated purpose in state constitutions and statutes. The concept has sparked controversy only as a result of its inclusion in the body of the U.S. Constitution.

The first clause of Article I, Section 8, reads, "The Congress shall have Power To lay and collect Taxes, Duties, Imposts and Excises, to pay the Debts and provide for the common Defence and general Welfare of the United States." This clause, called the General Welfare Clause or the Spending Power Clause, does not grant Congress the power to legislate for the general welfare of the country; that is a power reserved to the states through the TENTH AMENDMENT. Rather, it merely allows Congress to spend federal money for the general welfare. The principle underlying this distinction—the limitation of federal power—eventually inspired the only important disagreement over the meaning of the clause.

According to JAMES MADISON, the clause authorized Congress to spend money, but only to carry out the powers and duties specifically enumerated in the subsequent clauses of Article I, Section 8, and elsewhere in the Constitution, not to meet the seemingly infinite needs of the general welfare. ALEXANDER HAMILTON maintained that the clause granted Congress the power to spend without limitation for the general welfare of the nation. The winner of this debate was not declared for 150 years.

In *United States v. Butler*, 56 S. Ct. 312, 297 U.S. 1, 80 L. Ed. 477 (1936), the U.S. Supreme Court invalidated a federal agricultural spending program because a specific congressional power over agricultural production appeared nowhere in the Constitution. According to the Court in *Butler*, the spending program invaded a right reserved to the states by the Tenth Amendment.

Though the Court decided that *Butler* was consistent with Madison's philosophy of limited federal government, it adopted Hamilton's interpretation of the General Welfare Clause, which gave Congress broad powers to spend federal money. It also established that determination of the general welfare would be left to the discretion of Congress. In its opinion, the Court warned that to challenge a federal expense on the ground that it did not promote the general welfare would "naturally require a showing that by no reasonable possibility can the challenged legislation fall within the wide range of discretion permitted to the Congress." The Court then obliquely confided, "[H]ow great is the extent of that range . . . we need hardly remark." "[D]espite the breadth of the legislative discretion," the Court continued,

"our duty to hear and to render judgment remains." The Court then rendered the federal agricultural spending program at issue invalid under the Tenth Amendment.

With *Butler* as precedent, the Supreme Court's interest in determining whether congressional spending promotes the general welfare has withered. In *South Dakota v. Dole*, 483 U.S. 203, 107 S. Ct. 2793, 97 L. Ed. 2d 171 (1987), the Court reviewed legislation allowing the secretary of transportation to withhold a percentage of federal highway funds from states that did not raise their legal drinking age to twenty-one. In holding that the statute was a valid use of congressional spending power, the Court in *Dole* questioned "whether 'general welfare' is a judicially enforceable restriction at all."

Congress appropriates money for a seemingly endless number of national interests, ranging from federal courts, policing, imprisonment, and national security to social programs, environmental protection, and education. No federal court has struck down a spending program on the ground that it failed to promote the general welfare. However, federal spending programs have been struck down on other constitutional grounds.

CROSS-REFERENCES

Congress of the United States; Constitution of the United States; Federal Budget; Federalism.

GENETIC ENGINEERING   The human manipulation of the genetic material of a cell.

Genetic engineering involves isolating individual DNA fragments, coupling them with other genetic material, and causing the genes to replicate themselves. Introducing this created complex to a host cell causes it to multiply and produce clones that can later be harvested and used for a variety of purposes. Current applications of the technology include medical investigations of gene structure for the control of genetic disease, particularly through antenatal diagnosis. The synthesis of hormones and other proteins (e.g., growth hormone and insulin), which are otherwise obtainable only in their natural state, is also of interest to scientists. Applications for genetic engineering include disease control, hormone and protein synthesis, and animal research.

International Codes and Ethical Issues for Society   An international code of ethics for genetic research was first established in the World Medical Association's Declaration of Helsinki in 1964. The guide prohibited outright most forms of genetic engineering and was accepted by numerous U.S. professional medical societies, including the American Medical Association (AMA).

In 1969 the AMA promulgated its own ethical guidelines for clinical investigation, key provisions of which conflicted with the Helsinki Declaration. For example, the AMA guidelines proposed that when mentally competent adults were found to be unsuitable subjects for genetic engineering studies, minors or mentally incompetent subjects could be used instead. The Helsinki Declaration did not condone testing on humans.

The growth of genetic engineering in the 1970s aroused international concern, but only limited measures were taken by governments and medical societies to control it. Concern focused on the production of dangerous bacterial mutants that could be used for harmful eugenics tools or weapons. The Genetic Manipulation Advisory Group was established in England based on the recommendations of a prominent medical group, the Williams Committee. Scientists were required to consult this group before carrying out any activity involving genetic manipulation in England. Additional measures required scientific laboratories throughout the world to include physical containment labs to prevent manipulated genes from escaping and surviving in natural conditions. These policies were subsequently adopted in the United States.

The Breakdown of Regulation: Genetic Inventions and Patents in the United States   In 1980 the Supreme Court created an economic incentive for companies to develop genetically engineered products by holding that such products could be patented. In *Diamond v. Chakrabarty*, 447 U.S. 303, 100 S. Ct. 2204, 65 L. Ed. 2d 144, the Court held that a patent could be issued for a novel strain of bacteria that could be used in the cleanup of oil spills. In 1986, the U.S. Department of Agriculture approved the sale of the first living genetically altered organism. The virus was used as a pseudorabies vaccine, from which a single gene had been cut. Within the next year, the U.S. Patent and Trademark Office announced that nonnaturally occurring, nonhuman, multicellular living organisms, including animals, were patentable under the Patent Act of 1952 (35 U.S.C.A. § 101).

The Department of Agriculture formally became involved in genetic engineering in April of 1988, when the Patent and Trademark Office issued the first animal patent, granted on a genetically engineered mouse used in cancer research. U.S. scientists began experiments with

the genetic engineering of farm animals, such as creating cows that would give more milk, chickens that would lay more eggs, and pigs that would produce leaner meat. These developments only raised more objections from critics who believed that genetic experimentation on animals violated religious, moral, and ethical principles. In spite of the controversy, the U.S. House of Representatives approved the Transgenic Animal Patent Reform bill on September 13, 1988. The bill would have allowed exempted farmers to reproduce, use, or sell patented animals, although it prohibited them from selling germ cells, semen, or embryos derived from animals. However, the Senate did not vote on the act and so it did not become law.

Significant State Laws   Certain states have passed laws restricting genetic engineering. By the early 1990s, six states had enacted laws designed to curb or prohibit the spread of genetically engineered products in the marketplace (see Ill. Ann. Stat. ch. 430, § 95/1 [Smith-Hurd 1995]; Me. Rev. Stat. Ann. tit. 7, § 231 et seq. [West 1995]; Minn. Stat. Ann. § 116C.91 et seq. [West 1995]; N.C. Gen. Stat. § 106-765-780 [Supp. 1991]; Okla. Stat. Ann. tit. 2, §§ 2011–2018 [West 1996]; Wis. Stat. Ann. § 146.60 [West 1996]). North Carolina's law sets the most comprehensive restrictions on genetic engineering. Resembling the earlier measures proposed by organizations such as England's Genetic Manipulation Advisory Group, it requires scientists to hold a permit for any release of a genetically engineered product outside of a closed-containment enclosure. The North Carolina statute has been cited as a possible model for advocates of comprehensive federal regulations.

One application of genetic engineering is in the creation of colored cotton. A French research center has bred colored cotton from a plant traditionally used to produce white cotton by changing one of the genes.

Recent Developments In the mid 1990s the international guidelines established by the Declaration of Helsinki were modified to allow certain forms of cell manipulation in order to develop germ cells for therapeutic purposes. Scientists are also exploring genetic engineering as a means of combating the HIV virus.

In 1997 the cloning of an adult sheep by Scottish scientist, Ian Wilmut, brought new urgency to the cloning issue. This breakthrough (prior cloning had been successful only with immature cells, not those from an adult animal) raised the prospect of human cloning and prompted what is likely to be a continuing ethical and legal debate on how to regulate cloning.

See also GENETIC SCREENING.

GENETIC SCREENING 📖
The scientific procedure of examining genetic makeup to determine if an individual possesses genetic traits that indicate a tendency toward acquiring or carrying certain diseases. 📖

Genetic testing of humans may allow the discovery and treatment of genetic defects, both before and after birth. CIVIL RIGHTS proponents, employers, and those who suffer from genetic diseases have debated genetic screening because the procedure poses practical and theoretical legal, economic, and ethical problems. Some theorists, for example, have suggested that genetic screening could improve society if it were

The examination of genetic material to determine an individual's propensity to acquire or carry a disease is the subject of legal and ethical debate.

made mandatory before hiring or marriage. Others say that this practice would be unconstitutional. A specific form of genetic screening known as amniocentesis has already raised constitutional issues. Genetic screening is a practice over which scientific, legal, and ethical interests differ.

Federal and State Legislation in the 1970s Most national and state legislation concerning genetic screening was enacted in the 1970s. The legislation focused on voluntary genetic testing. The laws generally protect the interests of those who suffer from genetic disease, offer federal and state subsidies for counseling, and support research in genetic diseases.

Congress enacted in 1976 the National Sickle Cell Anemia, Cooley's Anemia, Tay-Sachs, and Genetic Diseases Act (42 U.S.C.A. § 300b-1 et seq.), which permitted the use of public funds for voluntary genetic screening and counseling programs. State legislatures passed measures, with certain exceptions, requiring genetic screening of school-age children for sickle cell anemia. New York enacted a law that provides for premarital testing to identify carriers of the defective sickle cell gene (N.Y. Dom. Rel. Law §13-aa [McKinney 1977]). Other states provided for voluntary premarital testing for the sickle cell disease (e.g., Cal. Health & Safety Code § 325-331 [West 1978]); Ga. Code Ann. § 19-3-40 [1974]). Such legislation often included provisions for voluntary, funded counseling (see Va. Code Ann. § 32.1-68 [Michie]).

The Constitution, Civil Rights, and Scientific Theory In 1981, Congress held hearings to identify potential problems of widespread genetic screening. Subsequent legal and medical discussion has focused on the ethics of certain practices such as eugenics, a form of GENETIC ENGINEERING that involves the systematic programming of genes to create a specific life-form.

One potential problem with genetic screening arises in its use by employers. Although an employer considering hiring an individual with a genetic disease often relies primarily on economic issues, the practice of screening prospective employees and eliminating those with defective genes may be discriminatory, because some genetic diseases afflict certain ethnic and racial groups more often than others. G-6-PD deficiency, for example, occurs most frequently in blacks and persons of Mediterranean descent. If screening excludes persons with G-6-PD deficiency, it will have a stronger effect on those groups. This practice could violate title VII of the Civil Rights Act of 1964 (42 U.S.C.A. §§ 2000e et seq.). However, genetic screening has not been challenged in the courts.

Nevertheless, some legal scholars maintain that compulsory genetic screening programs violate the Constitution. They assert, for example, that taking a child's blood sample constitutes a physical invasion of the body in violation of the FOURTH AMENDMENT. Compulsory counseling programs for parents, they say, interfere with the fundamental rights to marry and procreate. The critics of screening propose that less intrusive voluntary programs together with education could accomplish the same objectives.

Even though genetic screening involves at least a minor intrusion into an individual's body and may involve a search within the meaning of the Fourth Amendment, proponents of genetic science maintain that such searches are not unreasonable if executed in a proper manner and justified by a legitimate state interest (see *Schmerber v. California*, 384 U.S. 757, 86 S. Ct. 1826, 16 L. Ed. 2d 908 [1966] [holding that a compulsory blood test to determine intoxication of an automobile driver is not an unreasonable search]). Proponents of mandatory screening and counseling agree that these practices could interfere with the right to procreate. However, they suggest that the state's interests in improving the quality of a population's genetic pool in order to minimize physical suffering, and reducing the number of economically dependent persons, justifies the infringement on the civil liberties of individuals.

Amniocentesis and the Abortion Debate Advancements in the early 1990s in amniocentesis have raised constitutional issues. Amniocentesis consists of inserting a needle through the abdominal wall of a pregnant woman into the amniotic sac containing the fetus, withdrawing a sample of the sac fluid, analyzing it for genetic characteristics, and determining whether the fetus has certain genetic defects. If amniocentesis reveals a genetically defective fetus, the parents may choose to abort it or carry it to term. Children born with genetic defects have brought legal claims against their parents for the TORT of wrongful life, or WRONGFUL BIRTH.

Before the advent of amniocentesis, wrongful life actions generally failed (*Pinkney v. Pinkney*, 198 So. 2d 52, [Fla. App. 1967] [refusing to recognize tort of wrongful life for extramarital child plaintiff against father]; *Zepeda v. Zepeda*, 41 Ill. App. 2d 240, 190 N.E.2d 849 [1963], *cert. denied*, 379 U.S. 945, 85 S. Ct. 444,

13 L. Ed. 2d 545 [1964]). The development of procedures such as amniocentesis, coupled with a shift in societal attitudes toward ABORTION, has led to successful claims for wrongful life. For example, in *Haymon v. Wilkerson*, 535 A.2d 880 (D.C. App. 1987), a mother brought a wrongful birth action against a physician after her child was born with Down's syndrome. The court of appeals held that the mother was entitled to recover extraordinary medical and health care expenses incurred as a result of the child's mental and physical abnormalities. As a result of cases such as *Haymon*, doctors have increased their use of genetic counseling and prenatal testing.

The Future of Genetic Screening In 1993, the Nobel Prize for chemistry was awarded to Kary Mullis for his development of a technique known as polymerase chain reaction, a method for rapidly isolating and copying any DNA sequence out of a sample that may contain thousands of other genes. The success of such work in the field of genetics ensures that the use of genetic screening will continue.

CROSS-REFERENCES

Employment Law; Fetal Rights; Privacy; Searches and Seizures.

GENEVA (RED CROSS) CONVENTIONS, 1949 The horrors of World War II led nations to recognize that existing rules governing the conduct of warfare were inadequate to cover a prolonged and expanded conflict. The resulting efforts to codify new restrictions on belligerent conflict led to the four conventions concluded at Geneva, Switzerland, in 1949. These four treaties related to (1) the treatment of prisoners of war; (2) the alleviation of the suffering of wounded and sick combatants in the field; (3) the alleviation of the suffering of the wounded, sick, and shipwrecked members of the armed forces at sea; and (4) the protection of civilian persons during WAR.

The International Committee of the Red Cross was active in organizing the conferences and preparing draft treaties that resulted in the final conventions. In addition, the International Red Cross assumed responsibility under portions of the conventions to serve as a neutral party to observe compliance with the conventions and to perform humanitarian tasks.

GENOCIDE The crime of destroying or conspiring to destroy a national, ethnic, racial, or religious group.

Genocide can be committed in a number of ways, including killing members of a group or causing them serious mental or bodily harm, deliberately inflicting conditions that will bring about a group's physical destruction, imposing measures on a group to prevent births, and forcefully transferring children from one group to another.

Genocide's archetype was the World War II Holocaust, in which German Nazis starved, tortured, and executed an estimated 6 million European Jews as part of an effort to develop a master Aryan race. Immediately upon coming to power in Germany in 1933, the Nazis began a systematic effort to eliminate Jews from economic life. The Nazis defined persons with three or four Jewish grandparents as being Jewish, regardless of their religious beliefs or affiliation with the Jewish community. Those with one or two Jewish grandparents were known as Mischlinge, or half-breeds. As non-Aryans, Jews and Mischlinge lost their jobs and their Aryan clients, and were forced to liquidate or sell their businesses.

With the onset of World War II in 1939, the Germans occupied the western half of Poland, forcing nearly 2 million Jews to move into crowded captive ghettos. Many of these Jews died of starvation and disease. In 1941 Germany invaded the Soviet Union. The Nazis dispatched three thousand troops to kill Soviet Jews on the spot, most often by shooting them in ditches or ravines on the outskirts of cities and towns. Meanwhile, the Nazis began to organize what they termed a final solution to the Jewish question in Europe. German Jews were required to wear a yellow star stitched on their clothing and were deported to ghettos in Poland and the Soviet Union. Death camps equipped with massive gas chambers were constructed at several sites in occupied Poland, and large crematories were built to incinerate the bodies. Ultimately, the Nazis transported millions of Jews to concentration camps, in crowded freight trains. Many did not survive the journey. Once at the death camps, many more died from starvation, disease, shooting, or routine gassings, before Allied forces liberated the survivors and forced the Nazis to surrender in 1945.

Following the exterminations of World War II, the UNITED NATIONS passed a resolution in an effort to prevent such atrocities in the future. Known as the Convention on the Prevention and Punishment of the Crime of Genocide (78 U.N.T.S. 278 [Dec. 9, 1948]), the resolution recognized genocide as an international crime and provided for its punishment. The convention also criminalized CONSPIRACY to commit genocide, direct and public incitement to commit genocide, attempted genocide, and com-plicity in genocide. Its definition of genocide specified that a person must intend to destroy a national, ethnic, racial, or religious group. Thus, casualties of war are not necessarily victims of genocide, even if they are all of the same national, ethnic, racial, or religious group. The convention requires signatory nations to enact laws to punish those found guilty of genocide, and allows any signatory state to ask the United Nations to help prevent and suppress acts of genocide.

The convention was, by itself, ineffective. Article XI of the convention requires the United Nations' member countries to ratify the document, which many did not do for nearly fifty years. The United States did not ratify the convention until 1988. Before doing so, it conditioned its obligations on certain understandings: (1) that the phrase *intent to destroy* in the convention's definition of genocide means "a specific intent to destroy"; (2) that the term *mental harm* used in the convention as an example of a genocidal tactic, means "permanent impairment of mental faculties through drugs or torture"; (3) that an agreement to grant EXTRADITION, which is part of the convention, extends only to acts recognized as criminal under both the country requesting extradition and the country to which the request is made; and (4) that acts in the course of armed conflict or war do not constitute genocide unless they are performed with the specific intent to destroy a group of people.

On November 4, 1988, the United States passed the Genocide Implementation Act of 1987 (18 U.S.C.A. § 1091 [1994]). This act created "a new federal offense that prohibits the commission of acts with the specific intent to destroy, in whole or in substantial part, a national, ethnic, racial or religious group; and to provide adequate penalties for such acts" (S. Rep. No. 333, 100th Cong., 2d Sess. 1 [1988], *reprinted in* 1988 U.S.C.C.A.N. 4156).

In 1990 the U.S. Congress passed the Immigration and Nationality Act (INA) (8 U.S.C.A. § 1182), a comprehensive reform of immigration laws. As part of this reform, Congress mandated that ALIENS guilty of genocide are excluded from entry into the United States, or deported when discovered. However, the INA lacks a clear definition of genocide, referring only to the U.N. convention drafted more than forty years earlier.

The unclear definition of genocide makes its prevention and punishment difficult. Whether massive, and often barbaric, loss of life within ethnic, national, religious, or racial groups rises to the crime of genocide—or is simply an unpleasant by-product of WAR—is open to debate. The Holocaust of Nazi Germany is the only example recognized throughout the international community as genocide.

Apart from the Holocaust, there have been a number of other events that at least some commentators have described as genocide. These include the devastation of numerous Native American tribes through battles with European settlers and exposure to their diseases; the killing of some 1.5 million Armenians by the Turks during and after World War I; the deaths of more than twenty thousand Christian Orthodox Serbs, Muslims, and Roman Catholic Croats in "ethnic cleansing" arising out of the civil war in Croatia and Bosnia-Herzegovina in the early 1990s; and the deaths of more than a million Rwandan civilians in ethnic clashes between the Hutu and Tutsi peoples, also in the early 1990s.

Humanitarians, politicians, and international legal scholars are struggling to find an effective way to prevent and punish genocide. Many have called for revising the genocide convention to better meet the needs of the current political, social, and economic environment, by creating a broader definition of genocide and establishing procedural guidelines.

See also HITLER, ADOLF; NUREMBERG TRIALS.

GENTLEMEN'S AGREEMENT Although agreements between individuals often create legally binding commitments, instances may arise in which mutual promises yield no legally enforceable AGREEMENT. Sometimes called "gentlemen's agreements," parties may honor them because moral obligations compel observance or because future relations will be more difficult if the present arrangement is broken. International organizations likewise may depend on such informal arrangements so as to maintain COMITY among members.

Occasionally the enabling treaties that create an international organization will leave some procedural or voting matter unresolved. Rather than amend the formal document, which is usually a difficult task, an informal working agreement will develop to resolve a particular problem. As long as the consensus holds to honor the informal agreement, there is no need to embody it into a legal document.

GERRYMANDER The process of dividing a particular state or territory into election districts in such a manner as to accomplish an unlawful purpose, such as to give one party a greater advantage.

State constitutions or amendments to those constitutions empower state legislatures, and sometimes state or federal courts, to apportion and reapportion election districts. This generally means that states may draw and redraw the lines around election districts for offices ranging from local to congressional. It can also mean that states may calculate and recalculate the numbers of representatives in election districts. Any form of unfair APPORTIONMENT may be called gerrymandering, but generally, a gerrymander is understood to be invalid redistricting.

Redistricting is usually used to adjust the populations of election districts to achieve equality in representation among those districts. Sometimes, however, it is used for unlawful ulterior motives. Then it crosses the line to become gerrymandering.

The classic example of a gerrymander is a legislative redistricting scheme designed to benefit the party in power. Assume that a state legislature has redrawn its voting districts to divide and fold all communities that vote predominantly Democratic into larger communities that vote Republican. This is a political gerrymander. Such redistricting decreases the likelihood of Democratic representation in the state legislature because the Democratic vote in each new district is diluted by the predominant Republican vote.

The term *gerrymander* was inspired by an 1812 Massachusetts redistricting scheme that favored the party of Governor Elbridge Gerry. Portraitist Gilbert C. Stuart noted that one new election district had the shape of a salamander. Stuart drew an outline of the district, put a salamander's head on one end, and called the creature a Gerry-mander.

The gerrymander has been used by state legislatures ever since. It thrived all the way through the 1950s, when many southeastern states reapportioned in an effort to weaken the voting power of African Americans. This usually involved the drawing of complex, irregularly shaped election districts. A legislature could divide and fold predominantly African American communities into surrounding districts with large blocs of white voters. Such schemes diluted the vote of African Americans, placed their representation in faraway communities, and effectively prevented African Americans from expressing their collective will in elections.

In 1960, the U.S. Supreme Court struck down the first gerrymander scheme it reviewed, in *Gomillion v. Lightfoot*, 364 U.S. 339, 81 S. Ct. 125, 5 L. Ed. 2d 110 (1960). In *Gomillion*, the Alabama Legislature altered the city limits of Tuskegee to remove all but four of the city's four hundred African American voters. It changed the city limits of Tuskegee, for election purposes, from a square to, according to the Court, "an uncouth twenty-eight-sided figure." According to the Court, the redistricting discriminated against African Americans and violated the Equal Protection Clause of the FOURTEENTH AMENDMENT.

Gomillion did not establish that the drawing of election districts was always a proper matter for the courts. Before *Gomillion*, the Court had refused to review gerrymandering claims, holding that the issue of reapportionment was political and beyond the reach of the courts. The Court heard *Gomillion* only because the issue of racial discrimination lifted the controversy out of the arena traditionally beyond the power of the courts.

In 1962, the U.S. Supreme Court took the first step in establishing its right to review all districting, with its decision in *Baker v. Carr*, 369 U.S. 186, 82 S. Ct. 691, 7 L. Ed. 2d 663. At issue in *Baker* was a decades-old Tennessee apportionment. According to urban Tennessee voters, the outdated apportionment was a "silent gerrymander" or a "malapportionment." Although the population in urban election districts had increased, Tennessee had made no changes to reflect this population shift; thus, sparsely populated rural districts had the same representation in the state legislature as did densely populated urban districts. The Court in *Baker* did not reach a decision on the validity of the Tennessee districting; *Baker* established only that the issue of districting was JUSTICIABLE and not merely a POLITICAL QUESTION.

The Court next established the "ONE PERSON, ONE VOTE" requirement for federal ELECTIONS, in *Wesberry v. Sanders*, 376 U.S. 1, 84 S. Ct. 526, 11 L. Ed. 2d 481 (1964). This requirement, which held that voting districts should be roughly equal in population, was extended to the states in *Reynolds v. Sims*, 377 U.S. 533, 84 S. Ct. 1362, 12 L. Ed. 2d 506 (1964). In *Wesberry*, the Court struck down a Georgia redistricting statute (Ga. Code § 34-2301) because its voting districts were unequal in population. Georgia's Fifth Congressional District, largely populated by African Americans, was two to three times the size of other districts in the state. As a result, the African Americans in the Fifth District received less representation in Congress than persons in the other districts. According to the Court, this violated Article I, Section 2 of the U.S. Constitution, which stated that U.S. Representatives were to be "apportioned among the several States . . . according to their respective Numbers" (*Wesberry*).

Since these seminal cases, courts have become intimately involved in the review of apportionment, reapportionment, and redistricting. In their review of districting schemes, courts use CENSUS figures to compare election district populations for equality of representation. Courts also examine census figures for racial populations and compare overall percentages with percentages in election districts.

Courts have developed redistricting principles that favor compact, contiguous election districts that respect already existing municipal boundaries. Gerrymanders may be easy to recognize because they usually produce election districts that are irregularly shaped. However, not all irregularly shaped election districts are the result of gerrymanders. Indeed, Congress has encouraged the creation of "majority-minority" voting districts, which often call for an inventive drawing of election districts. Majority-minority districts are those in which racial minorities constitute the majority of votes.

Under section 4(b) of the Voting Rights Act (79 Stat. 438, *as amended* [42 U.S.C.A. § 1973b(b)]), some states, or specified counties in some states, may need to preclear redistricting plans with the attorney general or the U.S. District Court for the District of Columbia. The states subject to preclearance are those that have historically used constraints such as POLL

The term gerrymander originated from a political cartoon in which the shape of an election district of Massachusetts Governor Elbridge Gerry was compared to that of a salamander.

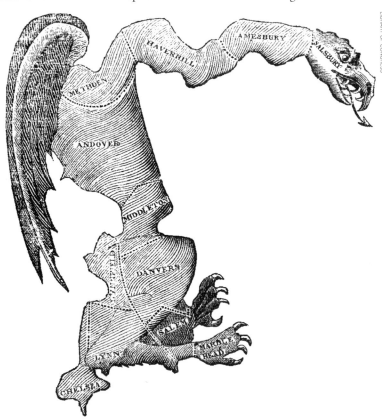

TAXES and literacy tests in an effort to exclude minority voters.

Section 4(b) of the Voting Rights Act presses the issue of redistricting based on race. The Supreme Court has responded by questioning the constitutionality of the provision. In *Shaw v. Reno*, 509 U.S. 630, 113 S. Ct. 2816, 125 L. Ed. 2d 511 (1993), a group of white North Carolina voters challenged the creation of two North Carolina majority-minority districts, which had the approval of the attorney general. One of the districts at issue had the shape of a "bug splattered on a windshield" (*Shaw*). The other district was so thin in parts that one legislator remarked, "If you drove down the interstate with both car doors open, you'd kill most of the people in the district" (*Shaw*). According to the Court, the redistricting was a racial gerrymander because it could not be explained by anything other than race. The holding of the Court emphasized that redistricting based entirely on race, with no respect for other redistricting principles, was a violation of the Equal Protection Clause and therefore invalid.

The Supreme Court reaffirmed and extended the *Shaw* holding in *Miller v. Johnson*, 515 U.S. 900, 115 S. Ct. 2475, 132 L. Ed. 2d 762 (1995). In *Miller*, the state of Georgia had complied with the redistricting provisions of the Voting Rights Act, but still found its redistricting scheme struck down by the U.S. Supreme Court as a racial gerrymander. As a designated state under the act, Georgia reapportioned three times before the attorney general accepted a plan. In its first two plans, Georgia drew two districts in which the majority of the voting population was African American. The scheme eventually accepted by the attorney general contained three congressional districts in which the majority of the voting population was African American. According to the Court, the redistricting was a racial gerrymander because its guiding principle was racial division, even though the new election districts were not bizarrely shaped.

CROSS-REFERENCES

Baker v. Carr; Equal Protection; *Reynolds v. Sims*; Voting Rights.

GIBBONS v. OGDEN

Gibbons v. Ogden, 22 U.S. (9 Wheat.) 1, 6 L. Ed. 23, was a landmark decision of the Supreme Court that defined the scope of power given to Congress pursuant to the COMMERCE CLAUSE of the Constitution.

In 1800, the state of New York enacted a statute that gave ROBERT LIVINGSTON and Robert Fulton a MONOPOLY—an exclusive right—to have their steamboats operate on the state waterways. Aaron Ogden owned a steamboat company and had received a LICENSE from Livingston and Fulton to conduct a business between ports in New York City and New Jersey. Ogden had formerly been in business with Thomas Gibbons, who started his own steamship company that operated between New York and New Jersey, in direct competition with Ogden.

Ogden brought an action to ENJOIN Gibbons from continuing to run his steamships, which were licensed in the coastal trade under a 1793 act of Congress. The state courts granted Ogden the INJUNCTION, and the case was brought on appeal to the Supreme Court.

DANIEL WEBSTER, the attorney for Gibbons, argued that the issuance of the injunction was wrongful since the laws that authorized the monopoly were enacted in violation of the Commerce Clause of the Constitution. This clause gave Congress, not the states, the power to regulate commerce among the states. The term *commerce* included not only buying and selling but also navigation necessary to bring about such transactions.

In the majority opinion drafted by Chief Justice JOHN MARSHALL, the Court agreed with this definition of commerce and then reasoned that since Congress was vested with the power to regulate commerce, there could be no infringement of this power other than that specified in the Constitution. States cannot act in this area without express permission of Congress. The actions of New York State were an unauthorized interference with the power of Congress to regulate commerce, and therefore, the Court reversed the decree of the state court and dismissed the injunction against Gibbons.

GI BILL

Federal legislation that created a comprehensive package of benefits, including financial assistance for higher education, for veterans of U.S. military service.

The benefits of the GI Bill are intended to help veterans readjust to civilian life following service to their country, and to encourage bright, motivated men and women to volunteer for military duty. This legislation came in two parts: the Servicemen's Readjustment Act of 1944 and the Montgomery GI Bill.

Servicemen's Readjustment Act of 1944

The first GI Bill was proposed and drafted by the American Legion, led by former Illinois governor John Stelle, during World War II. The public remembered a post–World War I recession, when millions of veterans returned to face unemployment and homelessness. Twice as many veterans would return from World War II, and widespread economic hardship was a real concern. A healthy postwar economy, it seemed, would depend on providing soldiers with a means to support themselves once they were back home.

Newspaper tycoon William Randolph Hearst became the bill's most ardent and vocal supporter. Hearst and his nationwide string of newspapers lobbied the public and members of Congress to support those who served their country, and his effort was a success. The bill unanimously passed both chambers of Congress in the spring of 1944. President FRANKLIN D. ROOSEVELT signed the bill into law on June 22, 1944, just days after the D day invasion of Normandy (Servicemen's Readjustment Act of 1944, ch. 268, 58 Stat. 284).

The original GI Bill offered veterans up to $500 a year for college tuition and other educational costs—ample funding at the time. An unmarried veteran also received a $50-a-month allowance for each month spent in uniform; a married veteran received slightly more. Other benefits included mortgage subsidies, enabling veterans to purchase homes with relative ease.

Despite initial misgivings over its success, the GI Bill proved to be enormously effective. Prior to its passage, detractors feared that paying the education expenses of veterans would lead to overcrowding at colleges, which before World War II were accessible predominantly to members of society's upper class. Critics were concerned that veterans would wreak havoc on educational standards and overburden campuses with their lack of preparation for the rigors of higher learning.

College campuses did become grossly overcrowded in the postwar years: approximately 7.8 million World War II veterans received benefits under the original GI Bill, and 2.2 million of those used the program for higher education. By 1947 half of all college students were veterans. Prefabricated buildings and Quonset huts were used as classrooms, and military barracks were often converted into dormitories. However, having spent a large part of their youth engaged in battle, World War II veterans were highly motivated. GIs in their late twenties and early thirties returned to the United States in droves, anxious to catch up with their nonmilitary peers, marry, settle down, and support a family. The benefits provided by the GI Bill facilitated these goals.

Veterans were not the only beneficiaries of the GI Bill. Colleges, with increased enrollments, received years of financial security following its enactment. Veterans demanded more practical college course work, and this led to a changed concept of higher education, with more emphasis on degree programs like business and engineering. The lines of race, class, and religion blurred as higher education became attainable for all veterans. No longer was a college degree—and the higher paying jobs that normally follow it—limited to members of the upper class. Federal income increased as the average income of taxpayers in the United States increased, and as the veterans graduated from colleges, women and members of minorities enrolled to fill the gaps they left. The GI Bill's mortgage subsidies led to an escalated demand for housing and the development of suburbs. One-fifth of all single-family homes built in the twenty years following World War

The original GI bill provided up to $500 a year for tuition, books, and supplies to veterans who attended college after leaving the armed services following World War II.

UPI/CORBIS-BETTMANN

II were financed with help from the GI Bill's loan guarantee program, symbolizing the emergence of a new middle class.

Montgomery GI Bill   Following the United States' involvement in the Vietnam War and the end of the military draft in 1973, the number of qualified young adults willing to voluntarily serve in the military declined. In 1984 Representative G. V. ("Sonny") Montgomery (D-Miss.), chairman of the House Veterans' Affairs Committee, proposed a new GI Bill to encourage military service, even in times of peace. That year President RONALD REAGAN signed into law the Montgomery GI Bill (38 U.S.C.A. § 1401), which continues to provide optional benefits for qualified U.S. veterans.

The Montgomery GI Bill is a voluntary plan that requires a contribution from the soldier who chooses to take part. Upon entry into the ARMED SERVICES, including the National Guard and military reserves, participants may elect to have their military pay reduced by $100 each month of the first twelve months of service. This sacrifice makes them eligible to receive up to $400 a month for thirty-six months toward tuition and other educational expenses. To receive these benefits, soldiers must receive an honorable discharge, earn a high school diploma or its equivalent, and serve in active duty for the length of their enlistment. The federal government supplies funding but does not set standards or administer the plan; the VETERANS ADMINISTRATION determines whether a veteran is eligible, and the colleges and universities (including religious and vocational schools) make admissions policies and keep track of expenditures.

Effects of the GI Bill   The GI Bill, in both its versions, is widely regarded as a success. Senator Daniel K. Inouye (D-Haw.) has called it the most significant legislation passed by Congress in the twentieth century. Over the years the program has cost $70 billion; Senator Dale Bumpers (D-Ark.) considers it to be the best single investment the federal government has ever made. Military recruiters routinely promote its benefits as a way to attract and enlist the best and brightest young adults: in 1996, 95 percent of new armed services recruits were high school graduates, and in 1995, 95 percent of eligible recruits chose to enroll in the education program. And the GI Bill more than pays for itself: a 1986 Congressional Research Office study indicated that for every dollar invested in the GI Bill, the country recoups between $5.00 and $12.50, the result of increased taxes paid by veterans who have achieved higher incomes made possible by a college education.

Earned Degrees Conferred in United States: 1930 to 1970

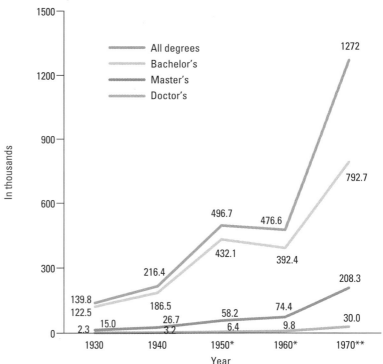

* First-professional degrees are included with bachelor's degrees for 1950 and 1960.

** "All degrees" totals for 1965 to 1970 include associates and first professional degrees, which have not been listed separately in this graph.

Source: U.S. National Center for Education Statistics, *Digest of Education Statistics*, annual.

Beneficiaries of the GI Bill include Presidents GEORGE BUSH and GERALD R. FORD; Vice President Albert Gore, Jr.; Chief Justice WILLIAM H. REHNQUIST and Justice JOHN PAUL STEVENS, both of the Supreme Court; Secretary of State Warren M. Christopher; journalists David Brinkley and John Chancellor; actors Clint Eastwood, Paul Newman, and Jason Robards, Jr.; and former Dallas Cowboys football coach Tom Landry.

GIDEON v. WAINWRIGHT   *Gideon v. Wainwright*, 372 U.S. 335, 83 S. Ct. 792, 9 L. Ed. 2d 799, is a 1963 U.S. Supreme Court decision that established an indigent criminal defendant's right, under the SIXTH AMENDMENT of the U.S. Constitution, to COUNSEL in state criminal trials.

In 1961, Clarence Earl Gideon was charged in a Florida state court with breaking into and entering a poolroom with intent to commit a MISDEMEANOR, a combination of offenses that constituted a FELONY under Florida law. He could not afford a lawyer, and he requested to have one appointed by the court. Nearly twenty years earlier, the U.S. Supreme Court had held in *Betts v. Brady*, 316 U.S. 455, 62 S. Ct. 1252, 86 L. Ed. 1595 (1942), that an ordinary person could do an adequate job of defending himself or herself. A court-appointed lawyer was required only if the defendant had mental or physical deficiencies, the case was unusually complicated, or the case involved "special circumstances." None of these exceptions applied to Gideon, the Florida trial court ruled, and thus his request for counsel was denied.

Gideon conducted his own defense and was found guilty of the charges. He then filed a handwritten petition with the Supreme Court of Florida, seeking to overturn his conviction on the ground that the trial court's refusal to appoint an attorney for him denied him the rights "guaranteed by the Constitution and the Bill of Rights by the United States Government." The state supreme court denied Gideon's PETITION.

While in prison, Gideon, using law books available to him, drafted a petition for writ of CERTIORARI to the U.S. Supreme Court. (The petition is the legal document in which a person requests the Supreme Court to hear an APPEAL. The Court has the discretion to accept or decline the appeal.) According to Anthony Lewis's acclaimed book on the case, *Gideon's Trumpet* (1964), in the handwritten petition Gideon stated that it "just was not fair" that he had no lawyer at his trial. The petition was granted, and ABE FORTAS, who would later serve as an associate justice on the Court, was appointed to argue Gideon's case.

In a unanimous decision, the Supreme Court overruled *Betts*, holding the guarantee of counsel to be a fundamental right under the U.S. Constitution. The Court ruled that the Due Process Clause of the FOURTEENTH AMENDMENT required that the Sixth Amendment, which guarantees indigent defendants the RIGHT TO COUNSEL in federal criminal proceedings, be interpreted to include indigent defendants in state criminal trials. In his majority opinion, Justice HUGO L. BLACK wrote, "[R]eason and reflection require us to recognize that in our . . . system of criminal justice, any person hailed into court, who is too poor to hire a lawyer, cannot be assured a fair trial unless counsel is provided." Black further pointed out that the government hires attorneys to prosecute defendants, and individuals charged with crimes who are financially able hire attorneys to defend them, both "strong indications . . . that lawyers in criminal courts are necessities, not luxuries."

Gideon was later retried with a court-appointed lawyer representing him and was found not guilty.

Following *Gideon*, it was unclear whether the decision applied only to indigent defendants facing felony convictions and not to individuals charged with lesser crimes. Nine years later, that issue was clarified in *Argersinger v. Hamlin*, 407 U.S. 25, 92 S. Ct. 2006, 32 L. Ed. 2d 530 (1972). In *Argersinger*, the Supreme Court expanded its holding in *Gideon*, ruling that the Sixth Amendment right to appointed counsel extended to misdemeanor cases in which the person charged may face imprisonment, unless the defendant makes a "knowing and intelligent waiver" of her or his right to counsel. The Court concluded that an accused in a misdemeanor trial likewise has a strong need for representation and that *Gideon* should apply "to any criminal trial, where an accused is deprived of his liberty."

Argersinger was limited a few years later by *Scott v. Illinois*, 440 U.S. 367, 99 S. Ct. 1158, 59 L. Ed. 2d 383 (1979). In *Scott*, the Supreme Court held that the Sixth Amendment right to counsel extends only to cases where "actual imprisonment" is imposed, and not to cases where the "mere threat of imprisonment" exists (where the crime charged authorizes a possible jail sentence).

See also CRIMINAL PROCEDURE; DUE PROCESS OF LAW; PUBLIC DEFENDER.

GIFT 📖 A present voluntary transfer of PROPERTY or of a property interest from one individual to another, made gratuitously to the recipient. 📖

The individual who makes the gift is known as the DONOR, and the individual to whom the gift is made is called the DONEE.

If a GRATUITOUS transfer of property is to be effective at some future date, it constitutes a mere PROMISE to make a gift that is unenforceable due to lack of CONSIDERATION. A present gift of a future interest is, however, valid. Special rules are applied to determine whether or not a legal gift has been made. Three elements are essential to the making of a valid gift: *delivery*, *donative intent*, and *acceptance* by the donee.

DELIVERY of a gift is complete when it is made directly to the donee, or to a third party on the donee's behalf. In the event that the third person is the donor's AGENT, BAILEE, or TRUSTEE, delivery is complete only when such person actually hands the property over to the donee.

A delivery may be actual, implied, or symbolic, provided some affirmative act takes place. If, for example, a man wishes to give his grandson a horse, an actual delivery might take place when the donor hires someone to bring the horse to the grandson's farm. Similarly, the symbolic delivery of a car as a gift can take place when the donor hands the keys over to the donee.

Delivery can only occur when the donor surrenders control of the property. For example, an individual who expresses the desire to make a gift of a car to another but continues to drive the car whenever he or she wishes has not surrendered control of the car.

A majority of states are practical about the requirement of a delivery. Where the donor and the donee reside in the same house, it ordinarily is not required that the gift be removed from the house to establish a delivery. If the donee has possession of the property at the time that the donor also gives the person ownership, there is no need to pass the property back and forth in order to make a legal delivery. Proof that the donor relinquished all claim to the gift and recognized the donee's right to exercise control over it is generally adequate to indicate that a gift was made.

In instances where delivery cannot be made to the donee, as when the person is out of the country at the time, delivery can be made to someone else who agrees to accept the property for the donee. If the individual accepting delivery is employed by the donor, however, the court will make the assumption that the donor has not rendered control of the property and that delivery has not actually been made. The individual accepting delivery must be holding the property for the donee and not for the donor.

In situations where the donee does not have legal CAPACITY to accept delivery, such delivery can be made to an individual who will hold it for him or her. This might, for example, occur in the case of an INFANT or an insane person.

Donative intent to make a gift is essentially determined by the donor's words, but the courts also consider the surrounding circumstances, the relationship of the parties, the size

of the gift in relation to the amount of the donor's property as a whole, and the behavior of the donor toward the property subsequent to the purported gift.

The donor must have the legal capacity to make a gift. For example, infants or senile persons who are unable to attend to their own affairs have a legal disability to make a gift.

In addition, an intent to make a gift must actually exist. For example, a landlord who rents a house to a tenant does not have the intent to give such premises to the tenant, even though the tenant takes possession for an extended period of time. Similarly, a gift to the wrong person will not take effect. If an individual mistakenly gives gold jewelry to an imposter who is believed to be a niece, the gift is invalid because there was no intention to benefit anyone but the niece.

The intent must be present at the time the gift is made. For example, if one person promises to give a house to an artist "someday," the promise is unenforceable because there is no intent to make an effective gift at the time the promise is made. The mere expectation that something will someday be given is not legally adequate to create a gift.

The final requirement for a valid gift is ACCEPTANCE, which means that the donee unconditionally agrees to take the gift. It is necessary for the donee to agree at the same time the delivery is made. The gift can, however, be revoked at any time prior to acceptance.

A court ordinarily makes the assumption that a gift has been accepted if the gift is beneficial, or unless some event has occurred to indicate that it is not.

The two principal categories of gifts are INTER VIVOS gifts and CAUSA MORTIS gifts.

Inter vivos gifts *Inter vivos* is Latin for "between the living" or "from one living person to another." A gift *inter vivos* is one that is perfected and takes effect during the lifetime of the donor and donee and that is irrevocable when made. It is a voluntary transfer of property, at no cost to the donee, during the normal course of the donor's life.

A gift *inter vivos* differs from a SALE, a loan, or BARTER since something is given in exchange for the benefit in each of such transfers. Whether the value given is a money price, a percentage interest or an equivalent item of property, or a promise to repay, the element of exchange makes such transfers something other than a gift.

When an employee is given a bonus, it does not constitute a gift but a form of additional compensation for services that have already been rendered.

A gift is the voluntary transfer of property from one person to another.

TOM MCCARTHY/THE PICTURE CUBE

A gift of a car is not complete unless the recipient is named as the owner on the title to the car.

Property can be placed into a TRUST for the benefit of the donee, and in many aspects a trust is similar to a gift. The main distinguishing characteristic is that the donee may hold and use a gift, but only has equitable TITLE to the property in trust.

Any legal interest in, or ownership of, real or personal property can be transferred by gift. For example, a woman who has the right to take money held in trust when her mother dies can write out a DEED giving that same right to someone else. One partner can give to another partner all the interest in a mutually held business, and this will transfer legal rights in addition to physical possessions.

The law favors enforcing gifts since every individual has the right to dispose of PERSONAL PROPERTY as he or she chooses.

Gifts are frequently made in an informal manner without the presence of disinterested witnesses who could later describe the transaction. Courts ordinarily require proof of intent, delivery, and acceptance. Even when such elements are present, however, they will set aside an otherwise valid gift if the circumstances suggest that the donor was, in actuality, defrauded by the donee, coerced to make the gift, or strongly influenced in an unfair manner.

A donor can limit an *inter vivos* gift in certain ways. For example, he or she might give someone a LIFE ESTATE in his or her property. When the donee dies, the property reverts to the donor.

In the event that property offered as a gift is subject to ENCUMBRANCES, such as a LIEN or MORTGAGE, the donee takes the debt along with the property.

A donor cannot place other restrictions on a gift if the restrictions would operate to make the gift invalid. If, for example, the donor reserves the power to revoke a gift, there is no

gift at all. A gift that is to take effect only after a future event is void, because a gift must go into effect precisely when it is made.

There are a number of special types of *inter vivos* gifts. Forgiveness of a DEBT is a gift of the amount of money owed, and delivery can be accomplished by destroying the PROMISSORY NOTE signed by the debtor and handing it over to him or her. A share of STOCK in a CORPORATION may ordinarily be given to someone else by having ownership transferred to the person on the books of the corporation or by having a new stock certificate issued in the person's name. A life INSURANCE policy can generally be given to someone by delivering the policy, but it is more expedient to express in writing that all interest in the policy is assigned, or transferred, to the donee and to notify the insurance company to that effect. Certain states require these formalities since insurance is strictly regulated by state law. Gifts of land can only be made by written transfer.

Causa Mortis Gifts A gift *causa mortis* (Latin for "in contemplation of approaching death") is one that is made in anticipation of imminent death. This type of gift takes effect upon the death of the donor from the expected disease or illness. A *causa mortis* gift may be revoked until the donor's death. In the event that the donor recovers from the peril, the gift is automatically revoked.

Gifts *causa mortis* only apply to personal property.

The difference between a gift *causa mortis* and a *testamentary gift* made by WILL is that a will operates to transfer ownership only subsequent to the death of the donor, but a gift *causa mortis* takes effect immediately. The donee becomes owner of the gift as soon as it is given, subject only to the condition that the gift must be returned if the donor does not actually die.

The requirements of a *causa mortis* gift are essentially the same as a gift *inter vivos*. In addition, such a gift must be made with a view toward the donor's death, the donor must die of the ailment, and there must be a delivery of the gift.

Gifts *causa mortis* are usually made in a very informal manner and are frequently made because dying people want to be certain that their dearest possessions go to someone they choose.

A donor who is approaching death might make a gift by putting his or her intention in writing. This procedure is likely to be followed, when, for example, the donee is in another state, and personal delivery is thereby impractical. The courts only permit the donee to keep the gift if the donor clearly intended the gift to take effect at the time it was made. If the gift is made in writing in a will and is intended to become effective only after the donor dies, the gift is a TESTAMENTARY one. The law in each JURISDICTION is very strict about the features that make a will valid. One requirement, for example, is that the will must be signed by witnesses. If the donor writes down that he or she is making a gift, but the writing is neither an immediate gift nor a witnessed will, the donee cannot keep the gift.

The delivery requirement is frequently relaxed when a *causa mortis* gift is involved, since a donor is less likely to be able to make an actual delivery as his or her death approaches. A symbolic delivery is frequently sufficient to show that a gift was made, provided at least some effort to make a delivery is exercised. The overt act aids a court in its determination as to whether a delivery has been made.

A gift *causa mortis* is only effective if the donor actually dies. It is not necessary that the donor die immediately, but the person must die of a condition or danger that existed when the gift was made and without an intervening recovery. The donee becomes legal owner of the property in most states from the time the gift is made. The person must, however, later return the gift if the donor does not actually die. If the donor changes his or her mind and revokes the gift, or recovers from the particular illness or physical injury, the gift is invalid. A donor also has the right to require that debts or funeral expenses be paid out of the value of the gift.

GIFTS TO MINORS ACT 📖 A law that has been enacted in every state (with only minor variations) that facilitates the management of money given to INFANTS. 📖

Initially, in 1955 and 1956, thirteen states enacted a law called an *Act Concerning Gifts of Securities to Minors*. The New York Stock Exchange and the Association of Stock Exchange Firms sponsored the development of the law, to make it possible to donate shares of STOCK to children without the creation of a formal TRUST. The scope of the law was subsequently expanded to encompass all gifts to MINORS.

The law allows the individual giving the property to choose an adult in whom he or she has confidence to serve as custodian of the property for the infant. The custodian has authority to collect, hold, manage, invest, and reinvest the property.

The custodian may pay out some of the money for the child's support, if necessary, and must manage the funds reasonably. The custodian must maintain accurate records of transactions and pay over the property when the child reaches majority. A custodian is not permitted to use any of the money personally or for anyone else except the child, nor can the person commingle the property with his or her own.

A professional custodian, such as a trust company or an attorney serving as GUARDIAN of the property for the minor, can be remunerated out of the child's property. Such a custodian is, however, held to a higher standard of care in management of the property. Other business people who deal with the custodian in management of the property are not responsible for ascertaining that the custodian has authority to act.

When a custodian resigns, dies, or is removed from the position by court order, another custodian can be appointed as a successor. Before dying, a custodian can designate who his or her successor will be, or a court may appoint one. A PETITION to appoint a new custodian can be filed in court by the individual who initially made the gift, by an adult member of the child's family, by a guardian, or generally by the child if the child is over fourteen years of age.

The AGE OF MAJORITY varies from one state to another. Within some states, the age of majority is not the same for all purposes, so it is necessary to check the Gifts to Minors Act in the state in which the child resides.

GIGNOUX, EDWARD THAXTER
In his thirty-year career in the federal courts, Edward Thaxter Gignoux developed a reputation as an articulate, compassionate, and competent trial judge. He was also a leader in the fields of judicial ethics, court administration, and trial practice and techniques. He showcased his skills in a number of high-profile cases—including the contempt trial of Abbie Hoffman and other defendants known as the Chicago Seven (*In re*

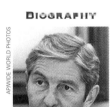

BIOGRAPHY

Edward Thaxter Gignoux

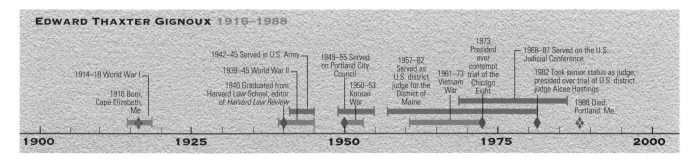

EDWARD THAXTER GIGNOUX 1916–1988

1914–18 World War I

1916 Born, Cape Elizabeth, Me.

1939–45 World War II

1940 Graduated from Harvard Law School, editor of *Harvard Law Review*

1942–45 Served in U.S. Army

1949–55 Served on Portland City Council

1950–53 Korean War

1957–82 Served as U.S. district judge for the District of Maine

1961–73 Vietnam War

1973 Presided over contempt trial of the Chicago Eight

1968–87 Served on the U.S. Judicial Conference

1982 Took senior status as judge; presided over trial of U.S. district judge Alcee Hastings

1988 Died, Portland, Me.

1900   1925   1950   1975   2000

Dellinger, 370 F. Supp. 1304, N.D. Ill., E.D. [1973]).

Gignoux was born in Cape Elizabeth, Maine, on June 28, 1916. He graduated cum laude from Harvard College in 1937, and went on to Harvard Law School, where he was editor of the *Harvard Law Review*. He graduated magna cum laude from the law school in 1940, and began his legal career with the firm of Slee, O'Brian, Hellings, and Ulsh, in Buffalo. After a year in Buffalo, he joined the Washington, D.C., firm of Covington, Burling, Rublee, Acheson, and Shorb.

World War II interrupted Gignoux's Washington, D.C., career after just a few months. In 1942, Gignoux joined the U.S. Army. During his three-year tour of duty with the First Cavalry Division in the Southwest Pacific, he rose to the rank of major and was awarded the Legion of Merit and the Bronze Star.

After the war, Gignoux returned to Covington, Burling, in Washington, D.C., to resume the practice of law, but a bout with malaria, contracted during his years in service, forced a return to his native Maine for convalescence. As his health returned, Gignoux joined the Portland, Maine, law firm of Verrill, Dana, Walker, Philbrick, and Whitehouse, and he married Hildegard Schuyler.

Gignoux and his wife had two children as they settled into life in Portland. In addition to practicing law, Gignoux was named assistant corporation counsel for the city of Portland, and he was twice elected to a three-year term on the Portland City Council, serving from 1949 to 1955.

By 1957, Gignoux was well-known and respected in Maine legal and political circles, and he was a logical choice to fill a vacancy on the federal bench. He was appointed U.S. district judge for the District of Maine in August 1957 by President DWIGHT D. EISENHOWER, and he served as Maine's only federal court judge for the next twenty years.

One of the first cases he heard as a federal judge was an ANTITRUST action brought by the government against the Maine Lobstermen's Association—an important group in a very visible industry (*United States v. Maine Lobstermen's Ass'n*, 160 F. Supp. 115 [D. Me. 1957]). A jury found the lobstermen guilty, but Gignoux, showing both wisdom and compassion early on, managed to satisfy both parties when he imposed only a small fine on the guilty defendants. Gignoux was also a central figure in Indian settlement claims in his native state, and he was instrumental in establishing that several Native American groups in Maine were "federal"

rather than "colonial" Indians, making them eligible for millions of dollars a year in federal benefits for housing, education, and health care (*Joint Tribal Council v. Morton*, 528 F.2d 370 [1st Cir. 1975]). Prior to the Gignoux decision, Maine Indians were considered "colonial" Indians and not the Indians of the frontier that Congress meant to protect in the Nonintercourse Act. Gignoux ruled in 1975 that the Act did apply, making some previous land transactions illegal and making the Maine tribes "federal" Indians.

His reputation as a trial judge spread quickly. According to one of his former law clerks, lawyers and judges from other courtrooms packed his court during their spare time to witness Gignoux's performance.

Gignoux was serious about the fair and equitable administration of justice. Throughout the 1960s and 1970s, he served the U.S. Judicial Conference with distinction. The JUDICIAL CONFERENCE is the principal machinery through which the FEDERAL COURT system operates. This important group establishes the standards and shapes the policies governing the federal judiciary. Gignoux's commitment to the Judicial Conference included working on the Advisory Committee on Bankruptcy Rules (1960–72), Committee on Trial Practice and Technique (1965–67), Committee on the Operation of the Jury System (1966–68), Committee on Court Administration (1969–80), Review Committee (1975–78), Joint Committee on the Code of Judicial Conduct (1975–85), and Judicial Ethics Committee (1978–85). He was chairman of the Subcommittee on Supporting Personnel (1968–70), chairman of the Subcommittee of Federal Jurisdiction (1975–80), and chairman of the Judicial Conference Committee on Rules of Practice and Procedure (1980).

Gignoux's work with the Judicial Conference brought him national recognition, and in 1970, he was considered for a nomination to the U.S. Supreme Court. Though he was not appointed, he did make an impression on future Supreme Court justice DAVID H. SOUTER. When Souter filled out a questionnaire in preparation for his confirmation hearing twenty years later, he noted a voting rights case he had argued in 1970 before Gignoux. He said, "It was one of the most gratifying events of my life, for the argument included a genuinely dialectical exchange between the great jurist and me."

As Gignoux's reputation grew, Chief Justice WARREN E. BURGER called on him to preside over some very political, and potentially explosive, cases. In 1973, Warren appointed him to preside over the CONTEMPT trial of Abbie Hoff-

"TRIALS WHICH PROCEED IN ACCORDANCE WITH THE LAW, THE RULES OF EVIDENCE AND THE STANDARDS OF DEMEANOR NOT ONLY REAFFIRM THE INTEGRITY AND VIABILITY OF THE JUDICIAL PROCESS, BUT ALSO SERVE TO INSURE THE ABILITY OF EACH ONE OF US TO PROTECT THE RIGHTS AND LIBERTIES WE ENJOY AS CITIZENS."

man, BOBBY SEALE, Jerry Rubin, Tom Hayden, David Dellinger, Rennie Davis, Lee Weiner, and John Froines. These 1960s radicals known as the Chicago Seven (even though there were eight of them) had already been tried and convicted for their participation in violent demonstrations at the 1968 Democratic National Convention, in Chicago. Following their trial, contempt charges were filed against the individuals and their lawyer, WILLIAM M. KUNSTLER, for their behavior in court. (Contempt is a willful disregard or disobedience of a public authority.) Gignoux found three of the eight—Hoffman, Rubin, and Dellinger—and their lawyer to be in contempt, but he did not impose additional sentences on the parties involved, saying that their conviction and their previous time served were punishment enough.

In 1982, after twenty-five years on the federal bench, Gignoux took senior (or semiretired) status, but he continued to hear cases around the country and to serve on the Temporary Emergency Court of Appeals. Gignoux's ability to uphold both the letter and the spirit of the law, against overwhelming political and social pressures, was still very much in evidence when he was asked to preside over the trial of U.S. district judge Alcee L. Hastings during his first year of "retirement." Hastings, who was later acquitted of conspiracy to solicit a bribe and obstruction of justice, was the United States' first sitting judge to be brought up on criminal charges. Though pressured to drop the charges throughout the trial, Gignoux said, "[T]he court is entirely persuaded that the government has submitted evidence that is sufficient to sustain a finding by the jury of guilty." Also during the *Hastings* trial, Gignoux rejected one of the first serious efforts to open a federal court trial to television coverage; Gignoux felt he was prohibited by federal law from permitting cameras in the courtroom.

On February 11, 1987, Gignoux was chosen to receive the Devitt Distinguished Service to Justice Award, which is administered by the American Judicature Society. This award—named for Edward J. Devitt, former chief U.S.

district judge for Minnesota—acknowledges the dedication and contributions to justice made by all federal judges, by recognizing the specific achievements of one judge who has contributed significantly to the profession. Gignoux was acknowledged for improving the administration of the federal courts through his work with the Judicial Conference of the United States and its committees.

Gignoux died on November 4, 1988, in Portland, Maine. Shortly before his death, the city renamed the federal courthouse there in his honor. He was acknowledged by friend and circuit judge Frank M. Coffin as an "inspiration" and as a jurist who served honorably and well "in the most demanding and delicate of trial situations."

See also CHICAGO EIGHT.

BIOGRAPHY

Cass Gilbert

"LET US PAY OUR ARCHITECTURAL DEBTS TO THE CREATORS OF THE PLAN OF WASHINGTON."

GILBERT, CASS Cass Gilbert was the U.S. architect responsible for the traditional style and regal proportions seen in many of the nation's finest public buildings—including the Supreme Court Building, in Washington, D.C. His remarkable body of work included federal, state, municipal, educational, and religious structures as well as facilities designed for commercial, industrial, and private use. Gilbert believed strongly that architecture should serve the established political and social order; much of his work continues to serve its public purpose decades after its conception and completion.

Gilbert was born November 24, 1859, in Zanesville, Ohio, where his grandfather, Charles Champion Gilbert, was the first mayor. He attended school in Zanesville until the death of his father, Samuel Augustus Gilbert, in 1868. At that time, his mother, Elizabeth Fulton Wheeler, apprenticed him to an architectural firm in St. Paul, Minnesota. There, he completed his education and trained as a surveyor. In 1878, Gilbert enrolled at the Massachusetts Institute of Technology, where he studied architecture for one year.

Income from occasional surveying work allowed Gilbert to embark, in 1879, on the customary grand tour of Europe, undertaken by many young men of his social standing and

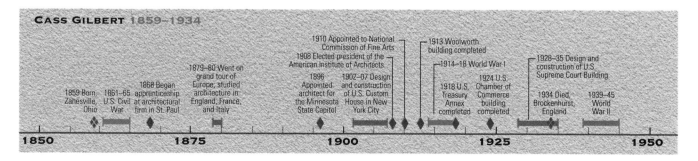

CASS GILBERT 1859–1934

1859 Born Zanesville, Ohio

1861–65 U.S. Civil War

1868 Began apprenticeship at architectural firm in St. Paul

1879–80 Went on grand tour of Europe, studied architecture in England, France, and Italy

1896 Appointed architect for the Minnesota State Capitol

1902–07 Design and construction of U.S. Custom House in New York City

1908 Elected president of the American Institute of Architects

1910 Appointed to National Commission of Fine Arts

1913 Woolworth building completed

1914–18 World War I

1918 U.S. Treasury Annex completed

1924 U.S. Chamber of Commerce building completed

1928–35 Design and construction of U.S. Supreme Court Building

1934 Died, Brockenhurst, England

1939–45 World War II

1850   1875   1900   1925   1950

economic means. He traveled in England, France, and Italy and was exposed to many of the classic architectural styles that would later dominate his work.

Upon his return to the United States, Gilbert was employed as a draftsman by the New York architectural firm of McKim, Mead, and White, where he was influenced by name partner and noted architect Stanford White. His association with this firm gave him an opportunity to hone his skills and to learn the business side of running an architectural enterprise. Seeing his promise, the firm sent him to St. Paul in 1881 to oversee a building project.

By December 1882, Gilbert had severed ties with McKim, Mead and formed a partnership with St. Paul architect James Knox Taylor. Together, Gilbert and Taylor pursued both institutional and residential work, but they were unable to succeed financially. The business partnership dissolved. Well organized and efficient, Gilbert found that he preferred to work alone; he did not form another professional partnership during his career. His architectural work from this period included the Dayton Avenue Church, St. Paul (1888); St. Martin's by the Lake, Minneapolis (1888); and the Lightner House, St. Paul (1893).

Gilbert did establish a personal partnership, on November 29, 1887, when he married Julia T. Finch. Their growing family—which ultimately included Emily, Elizabeth Wheeler, Julia Swift, and Cass, Jr.—added to the financial burdens of the struggling architect. To supplement his income from design work, Gilbert sold watercolors. He had begun painting during his European travels, and he was known locally as a talented artist.

In 1896, Gilbert landed the job that would launch him to national prominence: he was appointed architect for the Minnesota State Capitol Building, in St. Paul. The majestic domed structure that he created was immensely popular. Both its scale and detail were considered appropriate for its public purpose. His success convinced Gilbert that he was ready to compete in New York.

Shortly after moving to New York, Gilbert was among those invited to submit plans for the U.S. Custom House. He won the competition, but not without controversy. Other firms involved in the competition thought Taylor, then architect of the Treasury Building, in Washington, D.C., had unfairly influenced the choice of his former partner. Despite the controversy, Gilbert was eventually awarded other commissions, including the Union Club and the West Street Building, in New York, and the Essex County Courthouse, in Newark, New Jersey.

He also began to play a role in organizations associated with his profession, being elected president of the American Institute of Architects in 1908. At various points in his career, he was an active member of the Architectural League of New York, Academy of Design, National Institute of Arts and Letters, Academy of Arts and Letters, Royal Institute of British Architects, Royal Institute of Canada, Architectural Society of Liverpool, Royal Academy of Arts, and French Legion of Honor.

Although Gilbert entered, and won, a number of competitions during his career, most of his work came from his professional associations and his power of persuasion. His pursuit of the contract for the Woolworth Building, in New York, is just one example of his tenacious nature. Hearing that Frank W. Woolworth was going abroad before naming an architect for his new building, Gilbert booked passage on the same boat; he had a signed contract in hand before the boat docked.

The Woolworth Building, with its tremendous height and inventive use of terra-cotta, was a huge success. It was the tallest building in the world and it towered over the New York skyline for almost twenty years. The building made Gilbert a celebrity and substantially increased the demand for his professional services. The Scott Memorial Fountain, Detroit (1914); Detroit Public Library (1917); Brooklyn Army Terminal (1918); St. Louis Public Library (1921); and a host of other schools, banks, libraries, museums, and municipal structures were commissioned in the years following his completion of the Woolworth Building in 1913.

In 1910, Gilbert was appointed to the National Commission of Fine Arts by President WILLIAM HOWARD TAFT. He was reappointed for another term by President WOODROW WILSON in 1914. Through this association, Gilbert secured some of his most prestigious work, including the U.S. Treasury Annex (1918), Chamber of Commerce (1924), and, finally, the Supreme Court Building.

In 1928, Chief Justice and former president William Howard Taft became chairman of the Supreme Court Building Commission, created by Congress to build a permanent home for the nation's High Court. Taft remembered Gilbert's work on the National Commission of Fine Arts and selected him to design the new Court building.

The structure envisioned by Gilbert was a monumental temple of justice—one that evoked the power, authority, and solemnity of the Court. His design, which filled the square-block site, featured a neo-classical white marble structure with an enormous central hall housing the courtroom. Two symmetrical wings on either side of the central hall contained offices, libraries, and other Court functions. The focus of the Court chamber was an elevated bench, which looked out on seating for more than three hundred spectators.

The interior layout of the building separated the justices' private areas from the public areas, and was designed to facilitate grand entrances into the courtroom. The building's private areas contained three-room office suites, a robing room, underground parking and entrances, temperature- and humidity-controlled library and document storage facilities, and press-rooms.

Gilbert's architectural sketches were approved by the commission in 1929, and construction began in 1931. The building was not completed until after Gilbert's death in 1934; Gilbert's son, Cass, Jr., supervised the final stages of the project.

The Supreme Court Building opened its doors to the public on Monday, October 7, 1935. Initially, the building was criticized for both its size and its exterior embellishment. To a large extent, the size was dictated by the site: Gilbert strove to complement the scale of the adjacent LIBRARY OF CONGRESS and of other buildings in the Capitol complex. Charges of wasted space in the halls and corridors, and excessive seating in the courtroom, have diminished with time. The building's exterior embellishment featured prominent legal figures and themes and was executed by some of the finest artists and sculptors of the day. It is said that one of the toga-clad figures depicted on the building bears the likeness of the architect himself.

As a space designed for hearing arguments and holding public discussion, the large courtroom was also criticized for its poor acoustics. Time and improved sound technology have diminished this criticism. Today, the Supreme Court Building is considered the pinnacle of Gilbert's work and is one of the nation's finest public buildings.

While developing the Supreme Court Building, Gilbert also continued to work in New York and across the country. During this period, he designed the New York Life Insurance Building, the U.S. Courthouse in New York City, the George Washington Memorial Bridge, and the state capitol buildings in Arkansas and West Virginia.

Biographer Egerton Swartwout described Gilbert as "purposely impressive in manner and rather pompous at times." This description could as easily be applied to the public buildings Gilbert designed. Gilbert's work stayed true to the traditional themes that inspired him as a young man traveling in Europe. Though his Woolworth Building and other commercial structures contributed to the evolution of the modern skyscraper, Gilbert was not a fan of the modern functional architecture that emerged in the 1920s. The turmoil of World War I and the economic difficulties of the 1920s were said to have solidified Gilbert's commitment to classic traditional style.

Still much in demand by those who shared his architectural vision, Gilbert died suddenly May 17, 1934, on a golf holiday at Brockenhurst, England, at age seventy-five. He is buried in New York City. His personal and professional papers are housed at the Library of Congress—across the street from his Supreme Court Building.

BIOGRAPHY

Emma Millinda Gillett

NEW YORK PUBLIC LIBRARY

GILLETT, EMMA MILLINDA Emma Millinda Gillett was a remarkable attorney who helped establish one of the first coeducational law schools in the United States. In 1896, Gillett and a colleague, ELLEN SPENCER MUSSEY, sponsored a series of lectures in Washington, D.C., for local women interested in law. Despite social pressures against women in the legal profession, Gillett and Mussey held the lectures for two years. They expanded their curriculum and created Washington College of Law, a coeducational institution that later became part of American University.

Gillett was born July 30, 1852, in Princeton, Wisconsin. After her father, Richard J. Gillett, died in 1854, Gillett moved to Girard, Pennsylvania, with her mother, Sarah Ann Gillett, and family. Like Mussey, Gillett attended Lake Erie Seminary in Painesville, Ohio. Upon gradua-

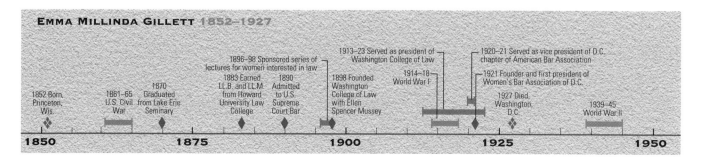

EMMA MILLINDA GILLETT 1852–1927

1852 Born, Princeton, Wis.

1861–65 U.S. Civil War

1870 Graduated from Lake Erie Seminary

1883 Earned LL.B. and LL.M. from Howard University Law College

1890 Admitted to U.S. Supreme Court Bar

1896–98 Sponsored series of lectures for women interested in law

1898 Founded Washington College of Law with Ellen Spencer Mussey

1913–23 Served as president of Washington College of Law

1914–18 World War I

1920–21 Served as vice president of D.C. chapter of American Bar Association

1921 Founder and first president of Women's Bar Association of D.C.

1927 Died, Washington, D.C.

1939–45 World War II

1850　　　1875　　　1900　　　1925　　　1950

tion in 1870, Gillett became a public school teacher.

After ten years of teaching, she decided to move to Washington, D.C., to pursue a LEGAL EDUCATION and career. Her plans were thwarted by the refusal of most district law schools to admit women. Gillett overcame the obstacle by enrolling at Howard University Law College, a well-known, predominantly African American institution that did accept female students. Gillett earned a law degree from Howard in 1882 and a master of law degree in 1883. She began a successful law practice in Washington, D.C., and became vice president of the D.C. region of the previously all-male AMERICAN BAR ASSOCIATION. She also was elected president of the Women's Bar Association of the District of Columbia.

When Gillett teamed up with Mussey to establish Washington College of Law, they struck a blow against SEX DISCRIMINATION in higher education. The law school was a fitting testament to Gillett's commitment to the profession and to WOMEN'S RIGHTS. Gillett became president of Washington College of Law in 1913, succeeding Mussey. She headed the institution for ten years.

Gillett died January 23, 1927, in Washington, D.C., at the age of seventy-four.

GILPIN, HENRY DILWORTH

Henry Dilworth Gilpin served as attorney general of the United States from 1840 to 1841 under President MARTIN VAN BUREN.

Gilpin was born April 14, 1801, in Lancaster, England. He and his parents, Joshua Gilpin and Mary Dilworth Gilpin, boarded a ship for the United States in 1802. The Gilpins were aristocratic and socially prominent, not a struggling immigrant family. Gilpin's grandfather Thomas Gilpin was a manufacturer and businessman who had been shipping goods to U.S. harbors since colonial days. He was among those who helped to plan and execute the construction of the Chesapeake and Delaware Canal (which connects the head of Chesapeake Bay with the Delaware River estuary and thereby shortens sea routes to Baltimore from the north and

"THE MAJORITY OF THE [WOMEN] PRACTITIONERS WHO ARE STICKING TO THEIR WORK AND PLODDING ON [THEIR] WAY TO SUCCESS ARE UNMARRIED."

BIOGRAPHY

LIBRARY OF CONGRESS

Henry Dilworth Gilpin

from Europe). Gilpin's father, an author and poet with published works in both England and the United States, dabbled in a number of artistic and business ventures in the United States. He eventually settled in Pennsylvania, where he ran a successful papermaking business.

Gilpin was brought up near Philadelphia and was educated at the University of Pennsylvania. He graduated, valedictorian of his class, in 1819 and began to study law with a local attorney. In 1822 he was admitted to the bar but he did not establish a practice. Instead, he went to work as an agent for the Chesapeake and Delaware Canal Company. The position allowed him to travel and to pursue the literary interests encouraged by his father. From 1826 to 1832 he wrote detailed accounts of his visits to Harper's Ferry, the Shenandoah Valley, Weyer's Cave, Natural Bridge, Lexington, Charlottesville, Fredericksburg, Washington, D.C., and other locations in the Atlantic and southern states. His writings were collected by his father and later published in a seven-volume work called *Atlantic Souvenirs* (1826–1832).

Gilpin's pedigree and business interests permitted him to mix with prominent citizens wherever he traveled. During this early period of travel, he met and married Eliza Johnson, of New Orleans. In 1826, he attended—and wrote a famous account of—President JOHN QUINCY ADAMS's inaugural ball and public reception. On subsequent trips to the nation's capital, he developed an interest in politics by writing profiles of men like HENRY CLAY, DANIEL WEBSTER, and ANDREW JACKSON.

Gilpin was a great admirer of Jackson and was active in Jackson's successful bid for the presidency in 1828. In appreciation for Gilpin's support, Jackson named him to the board of directors of the Second National BANK OF THE UNITED STATES. The Second National Bank, located in Gilpin's hometown of Philadelphia, was established as the nation's central bank in 1816 during the financial crisis after the War of 1812. The First National Bank of the United States had opened in 1791 and closed in 1811

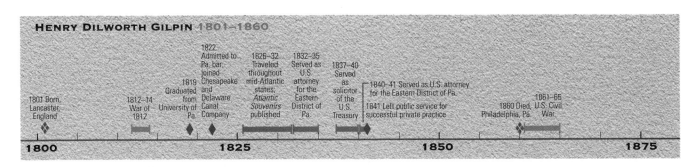

HENRY DILWORTH GILPIN 1801–1860

1801 Born, Lancaster, England

1812–14 War of 1812

1819 Graduated from University of Pa.

1822 Admitted to Pa. bar; joined Chesapeake and Delaware Canal Company

1826–32 Traveled throughout mid-Atlantic states; *Atlantic Souvenirs* published

1832–35 Served as U.S. attorney for the Eastern District of Pa.

1837–40 Served as solicitor of the U.S. Treasury

1840–41 Served as U.S. attorney for the Eastern District of Pa.

1841 Left public service for successful private practice

1860 Died, Philadelphia, Pa.

1861–65 U.S. Civil War

1800　1825　1850　1875

after its renewal charter was successfully challenged by agricultural interests who were not served by the bank's commercial focus.

Like its predecessor, the Second National Bank had strong opposition. Jackson believed it had become too powerful and wanted to diminish its influence by withdrawing federal funds and depositing the money in selected state banks. The Bank War, as the debate over the bank's role in the federal economy came to be called, was a central issue in Jackson's second presidential campaign. His reelection, along with the presence of his ally Gilpin on the board, ensured the bank's demise. Gilpin successfully pressed Jackson's arguments against the institution, and the renewal of the bank's charter was rejected. The bank closed in 1836 when its charter expired.

Gilpin's willingness to act as Jackson's chief spokesman at the height of the Bank War resulted in his removal from the board in the bank's final years. To fill the void left by his removal, Gilpin renewed his interest in the practice of law, and from 1832 to 1835 he served as U.S. attorney for the Eastern District of Pennsylvania. He also pursued a number of land investment and business opportunities in the Michigan Territory.

Jackson named Gilpin territorial governor of Michigan in 1835, but the president's opponents in Congress blocked the confirmation. It was not until President Van Buren was elected a year later that Gilpin returned to a role in the federal government.

Van Buren named Gilpin solicitor of the U.S. Treasury in 1837, and elevated him to attorney general of the United States from 1840 to 1841. As in his early years, Gilpin continued to chronicle his experiences. The *Gilpin Reports*, published in 1837, and the *Opinions of Attorneys-General of the United States*, published in 1840, record his service to the Van Buren administration.

Gilpin's term as attorney general increased the demand for his legal services, and after leaving the cabinet, he devoted the last twenty years of his life to the practice of law. He also

"I KNOW FEW THINGS MORE STRIKING IN THE HISTORY OF HUMANKIND THAN THAT KINDLING ENTHUSIASM WHICH, SPRINGING FROM ONE INDIVIDUAL . . . SWAYS THE CONDUCT OF IMMENSE BODIES OF MEN."

BIOGRAPHY

STEPHEN JAFFE/THE IMAGE WORKS

Newton Leroy Gingrich

continued to oversee development of the Chesapeake and Delaware Canal Company, where he rose to the positions of secretary and director.

He retained a lifelong interest in politics and the Democratic party, and served as a delegate to the party's national convention in 1844. Gilpin tutored his younger brother, William, in the study of the law, and was instrumental in launching his political career. His brother went on to become governor of Colorado.

Throughout his life, Gilpin—no doubt influenced and encouraged by his artistic father—supported the growth of the fine arts in the United States. He wrote and lectured on a wide variety of related subjects, and he was an active member of a number of organizations promoting the fine arts. Gilpin was a member of the American Philosophical Society, a director of Girard College of Arts, and an associate member of the Massachusetts Historical Society. He was also president of the Pennsylvania Academy of Fine Arts, and vice president and trustee of the Pennsylvania Historical Society.

Gilpin's family and business papers are housed at the Historical Society of Delaware.

GINGRICH, NEWTON LEROY With his election as Speaker of the U.S. House of Representatives in January 1995, Newton Leroy Gingrich (R-Ga.) became a powerful politician. Assuming control of the first Republican majority in the House since 1952, Gingrich ruled that body during his first year with an authority unseen since the nineteenth century. The veteran congressman from Georgia used his new position to proclaim the arrival of an era in which his conservative agenda—including lower taxes, decentralized government, and deep cuts in social programs—would fundamentally alter the fabric of U.S. society.

Since his arrival on the Washington, D.C., scene in 1979 as a brash and combative new member of Congress, Gingrich has shaped and guided Republican efforts on Capitol Hill. With an affinity for both intellectual debate and backroom deal making, this white-haired former professor provided the vision, verve, and

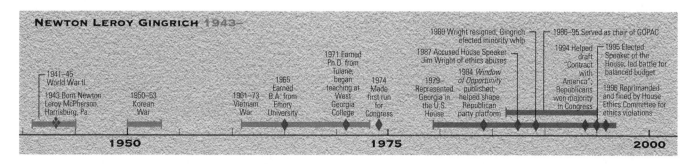

NEWTON LEROY GINGRICH 1943–

1941–45 World War II.

1943 Born Newton Leroy McPherson, Harrisburg, Pa.

1950–53 Korean War

1961–73 Vietnam War

1965 Earned B.A. from Emory University

1971 Earned Ph.D. from Tulane; began teaching at West Georgia College

1974 Made first run for Congress

1979– Represented Georgia in the U.S. House

1984 *Window of Opportunity* published; helped shape Republican party platform

1987 Accused House Speaker Jim Wright of ethics abuses

1989 Wright resigned; Gingrich elected minority whip

1986–95 Served as chair of GOPAC

1994 Helped draft "Contract with America"; Republicans won majority in Congress

1995 Elected Speaker of the House; led battle for balanced budget

1996 Reprimanded and fined by House Ethics Committee for ethics violations

1950   1975   2000

ideas that built a Republican majority. His opponents, however, accuse him of a lack of concern for poor and disadvantaged persons as well as an overly optimistic view of technology and the free market. Observers have described his actions in Congress as alternately brilliant and petty, leaving many to wonder whether he will be a passing footnote or a pivotal chapter in U.S. political history.

Gingrich was born June 17, 1943, in Harrisburg, Pennsylvania. His parents, Newton C. McPherson and Kathleen Daugherty McPherson, were separated after only three days of marriage. Gingrich's mother remarried three years after his birth, and her new husband, Robert Bruce Gingrich, adopted Gingrich. Gingrich's adoptive father was a career Army officer, and the family moved frequently, living in Kansas, France, Germany, and Fort Benning, Georgia.

In 1958, the fifteen-year-old Gingrich accompanied his family on a trip to Verdun, France, site of the bloodiest battle of World War I. Deeply moved by the story and scene of the battle, along with a visit to rooms filled with bones of the dead, Gingrich experienced an epiphany that he later described as "the driving force which pushed me into history and politics, and molded my life." The day after this visit, he told his family that he would run for Congress because politicians could prevent such senseless bloodshed. Later, as both a student and a young professor, he would tell others of his desire to become Speaker of the House.

At age nineteen, Gingrich, who was then an undergraduate at Emory University, married his former high school math teacher, Jackie Battley. The couple had two daughters, Linda Kathleen and Jacqueline Sue. Gingrich completed his bachelor of arts degree at Emory in 1965 and a doctor of philosophy degree in modern history at Tulane University in 1971. A liberal, reform-minded Republican in these years, Gingrich worked for Nelson A. Rockefeller's 1968 presidential campaign in Louisiana.

Gingrich took his first college teaching job at West Georgia College, in Carrollton, Georgia, with one eye toward an eventual seat in Congress. He nevertheless became a popular teacher at West Georgia, and founded environmental studies and future studies programs.

In 1974 and 1976, Gingrich ran for a seat in the U.S. House from Georgia's Sixth District, a rural and suburban region on the northern outskirts of Atlanta. Still voicing moderate and even liberal positions, he was endorsed in 1974 by the liberal newspaper the *Atlanta Constitution*. He narrowly lost both ELECTIONS.

In a move that some have called a calculated ploy to gain political office, Gingrich cast himself as a conservative for the 1978 election. In his platform, he called for lower taxes and opposed the Panama Canal Treaty. He beat the Democratic contender by seventy-six hundred votes, earning a seat in the Ninety-sixth Congress.

Shortly after his election, Gingrich and his wife separated. He married Marianne Ginther in 1981.

In Washington, D.C., Gingrich joined a number of Republican first-year Congress members eager to leave their mark on the political landscape. Unafraid of making enemies, he vigorously attacked Democrats and sometimes his own party, criticizing it for a complacent acceptance of its minority status in Congress. He called instead for an aggressive effort to build a Republican majority, a feat he would orchestrate sixteen years later.

In February 1983, Gingrich began meeting regularly with other young conservatives in an organization they called the Conservative Opportunity Society—a name designed to contrast with "liberal welfare state," the favorite target for their ideological barbs. Gingrich and other young Republicans also gained notoriety for their creative use of the Cable-Satellite Public Affairs Network (C-SPAN), which broadcast live proceedings of the House. This group used the "special orders" period of the House, during which members of Congress may read items into the record, as a platform to denounce Democrats and advance their own views. Although they were actually reading their material before an empty House chamber, Gingrich and his colleagues attempted to create the impression that they were making unchallenged arguments to specific Democrats. House Speaker THOMAS P. ("Tip") O'NEILL, JR. (D-Mass.), responded by ordering the C-SPAN cameras to periodically pan the empty chamber.

By 1984 Gingrich had developed the basic outlines of his conservative philosophy. He published his views in a book, *Window of Opportunity*, cowritten with his wife, Marianne, and David Drake. It remains an excellent guide to Gingrich's thought. In it, he exhibited, in addition to a strong belief in the efficacy of the free market, a strong devotion to technology as an answer to social ills. He wrote of a "window of opportunity" represented by "[b]reakthroughs in computers, biology, and space." Among his futuristic proposals was an ambitious space program, including a lunar research base by the year 2000.

He contrasted this vision of a bright future with a "window of vulnerability" that opened onto an alternative future of Soviet expansionism and U.S. decline. This dystopia was to be prevented by large-scale weapons programs such as Star Wars, also known as the Strategic Defense Initiative, and the dismantling of welfare programs and excessive taxation. The seventh chapter of the book, "Why Balancing the Budget Is Vital," foreshadowed a 1995–96 showdown with President BILL CLINTON over the FEDERAL BUDGET.

At the 1984 Republican National Convention in Dallas, Gingrich gained national attention as he led a move to make the party platform more conservative, successfully inserting planks against tax increases and ABORTION. He won still more influence in 1986, when he became chairman of GOPAC, a Republican political action committee that is a principal source of funding for Republican candidates across the United States. The organization, which Gingrich once called "the Bell Labs of politics," would also be the means for him to spread his conservative gospel. GOPAC has distributed printed and audiovisual works by Gingrich to hundreds of Republican candidates. In the early and mid-1990s, it would come under investigation by the FEDERAL ELECTION COMMISSION for alleged improprieties, including illegal assistance to Gingrich during his 1990 election campaign. Gingrich would step down as the head of GOPAC in 1995.

In 1987, Gingrich took on a major Washington, D.C., figure when he accused House Speaker JIM WRIGHT (D-Tex.)—occupant of the very office Gingrich coveted—of ethics violations. Gingrich claimed that Wright had violated House rules in his dealings with a Texas developer and in the manner by which he had profited from sales of a book. Gingrich's foes immediately attacked him as an irresponsible upstart but he remained unwavering in his attacks. As he later told a newspaper, "I didn't come here to pleasantly rise on an escalator of self-serving compromises." Gingrich won a major coup in 1989 when the House Ethics Committee formally charged Wright with sixty-nine ethics violations and Wright resigned from the House.

That same year Gingrich lobbied for and won (by two votes) the position of House minority whip. This victory represented an important step in his transformation from party pugilist to party leader. However, Gingrich himself soon became the object of a House Ethics Committee probe of alleged violations of House rules on outside gifts and income. The allegations focused on his earnings from two books, including *Window of Opportunity*. Later that year, Gingrich was investigated again by the same committee for improperly transferring congressional staff to work on his reelection campaigns. In both cases, the committee did not find sufficient grounds to reprimand Gingrich.

Gingrich nearly suffered defeat in the elections of 1990 and 1992, winning the former contest by fewer than 1,000 of the 156,000 votes cast. But these narrow victories were followed by a much wider reaching victory for both the man and his party in 1994.

Gingrich had done much to lay the groundwork for this win, particularly through his organization of the CONTRACT WITH AMERICA, a ten-point plan of action that was intended to give Republicans a unified front against their Democratic opponents. The contract called for such measures as tax breaks, a balanced budget amendment to the Constitution, a presidential line-item VETO, term limits for members of Congress, get-tough proposals on crime, reduction of government regulations, WELFARE reform, military budget increases, and more. In September 1994, Gingrich gathered over three hundred Republican candidates for Congress to sign the contract on Capitol grounds.

The big GOP win in 1994 gave the party a gain of fifty-four seats and majority status in the House. In January 1995, Gingrich finally achieved his lifelong dream when he was voted Speaker of the House. His leadership soon led to a dramatic change in House protocol. Wresting control from committee chairs by placing loyal associates—many of them first-year Republican Congress members—on key committees, Gingrich became one of the most powerful speakers since the nineteenth century, at times virtually dictating the content of legislation.

Riding the crest of publicity attached to his new position, Gingrich published two books, *To Renew America* (1995) and *1945* (1995). *To Renew America* was a best-selling work communicating Gingrich's vision for the country. It presents a thesis that cultural elites have torn down the traditional culture of U.S. society. It also contains his already familiar calls to balance the federal budget and decentralize the federal bureaucracy by returning power to states and localities. The book *1945* is a "what if" novel that explores what the consequences would

"WE MUST MAKE GOVERNMENT MORE EFFICIENT, MAKING SURE TAXPAYERS GET THEIR MONEY'S WORTH."

have been if Nazi Germany had been triumphant in World War II.

Gingrich, eager to make his mark as Speaker, initiated a one hundred-day plan to enact the Contract with America into law. He passed nine of the ten items of the contract through the House, but only three—the Congressional Accountability Act (Pub. L. No. 104-1, 109 Stat. 3), the Unfunded Mandate Reform Act (Pub. L. No. 104-4, 109 Stat. 48), and the Paperwork Reduction Act (Pub. L. No. 104-13, 109 Stat. 163)—were signed into law by the president.

Gingrich fought especially hard for one element of the contract: a balanced budget amendment to the Constitution. After its defeat in the Senate, he organized a Republican plan to balance the federal budget in seven years. This plan included tax reductions and deep cuts in federal social programs. Most controversial were provisions requiring large cuts to such programs as Medicare and Medicaid, which provide health care to elderly, disabled, and poor people. Over the course of 1995, President Clinton gradually adopted the goal of a seven-year balanced budget plan—a change of mind that symbolized the pervasive power of the Republican agenda.

When President Clinton vetoed the House budget plan late in 1995, Gingrich and his Republican colleagues refused to compromise their budget priorities. As a result, the federal government was forced to shut down nonessential services for lack of funding. The budget showdown forced national parks, agencies, and other elements of the federal government to close their doors. Gingrich came under fire as people complained of undelivered paychecks and other problems. The impasse ended in January 1996, when Gingrich and Clinton reached a compromise that allowed provisional funding of the federal government and abandoned the seven-year goal of balancing the budget.

In 1995, *Time* magazine named Gingrich its Man of the Year, a fitting recognition of the Speaker's large role in shaping the national political agenda. Such power had not translated into universal public approval for Gingrich, however, particularly given the unpopularity of the federal government shutdown.

CROSS-REFERENCES

Congress of the United States; Dole, Robert Joseph; Election Campaign Financing; Republican Party.

GINNIE MAE See GENERAL NATIONAL MORTGAGE ASSOCIATION.

GINSBURG, DOUGLAS HOWARD Douglas Howard Ginsburg is a U.S. circuit judge for the District of Columbia Circuit. In 1987 his nomination to the SUPREME COURT OF THE UNITED STATES was derailed by questions about his inexperience and about his personal life.

Ginsburg was born May 25, 1946, in Chicago. He grew up in Chicago, where he graduated from the prestigious Latin School in 1963. After high school, he entered Cornell University, in Ithaca, New York, but he left college in the mid-1960s to open the nation's first computerized dating service. After achieving success with the company, which was named Operation Match, Ginsburg sold his interest and returned to Cornell, earning his bachelor's degree in 1970. From there, he went to the University of Chicago Law School, where he received his doctor of jurisprudence degree in 1973.

Ginsburg served as a law clerk to U.S. circuit judge Carl McGowan from 1973 to 1974, and to Justice THURGOOD MARSHALL, of the U.S. Supreme Court, from 1974 to 1975. In 1975, he became an assistant professor of law at Harvard Law School, and in 1981, he was promoted to the rank of professor. He left academia to become a deputy assistant attorney general for regulatory affairs in the U.S. Department of Justice, Antitrust Division, in 1983. A year later, he was appointed administrator for information and regulatory affairs, Executive Office of the President, Office of Management and Budget, where he served for one year before returning to the Antitrust Division of the Justice Department in 1985. In 1986, President RONALD REAGAN named him a judge of the U.S. Court of Appeals for the District of Columbia Circuit.

BIOGRAPHY

DIANA WALKER/GAMMA-LIAISON

Douglas Howard Ginsburg

"IT IS A CARDINAL PRINCIPLE OF OUR SYSTEM OF CRIMINAL LAW THAT THE FACTS ARE SETTLED BY THE TRIER OF FACT, BE IT A JURY OR A JUDGE, AND ARE NOT ORDINARILY TO BE DETERMINED BY A REVIEWING COURT."

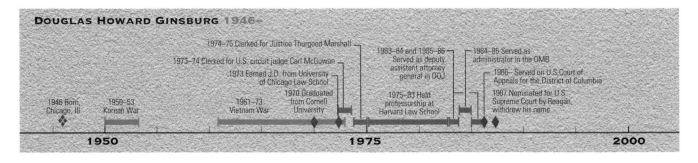

DOUGLAS HOWARD GINSBURG 1946–

1946 Born, Chicago, Ill.

1950–53 Korean War

1961–73 Vietnam War

1970 Graduated from Cornell University

1973 Earned J.D. from University of Chicago Law School

1973–74 Clerked for U.S. circuit judge Carl McGowan

1974–75 Clerked for Justice Thurgood Marshall

1975–83 Held professorship at Harvard Law School

1983–84 and 1985–86 Served as deputy assistant attorney general in DOJ

1984–85 Served as administrator in the OMB

1986– Served on U.S. Court of Appeals for the District of Columbia

1987 Nominated for U.S. Supreme Court by Reagan, withdrew his name

1950   1975   2000

At this point in his career, Ginsburg seemed to be settling into a predictable future on the federal bench. But there was to be a short detour along the way. In 1987, to the surprise of almost everyone, Reagan nominated him to replace retiring Justice LEWIS F. POWELL, JR., on the U.S. Supreme Court.

Ginsburg's nomination followed months of intense, sometimes acrimonious questioning by the Senate Judiciary Committee of Judge ROBERT H. BORK, Reagan's first nominee. During these hearings, the Senate had departed from its traditional "advice-and-consent" role and closely questioned Bork on philosophical and doctrinal matters never before addressed in confirmation proceedings. Bork had a long "paper trail," years of scholarly writings that revealed him to be a strict, conservative constructionist on constitutional matters, just the type of justice Reagan wanted on the Court to carry his vision of judicial restraint into the next century. However, the Senate, wary of upsetting the traditional balance on the Court, saw Bork as an ideologue and ultimately voted not to confirm him.

Stung by the Senate's rejection of Bork, Reagan and his aides were determined to find a nominee who would fulfill their requirement of judicial restraint but who had no "history" that would make their choice vulnerable to attack. They thought they had just the person they needed in Ginsburg and although Ginsburg had less than a year's experience as a judge, Reagan nominated him for the vacancy.

Ginsburg's nomination ran into difficulty almost immediately. Senators raised the obvious issues of his youth and inexperience and voiced concern about how his scanty judicial record made him a tabula rasa on constitutional matters. A CONFLICT-OF-INTEREST question was raised when newspapers reported that at the Justice Department he had handled a major case involving the cable TV industry while he held a $140,000 investment in a Canadian cable TV company. Then, too, it began to look as if he might be opposed by some conservatives because his wife, a physician, had reportedly performed some abortions. The death knell for Ginsburg's nomination sounded when he admitted that he had smoked marijuana "on a few occasions" while he was a student and during his early days on the faculty at Harvard. Faced with the embarrassment of backing a nominee who had admitted illicit drug use, the White House dispatched Secretary of Education William J. Bennett to urge Ginsburg to withdraw his name from consideration. Ginsburg complied, issuing a statement in which he said that the scrutiny of his personal life would continue to draw attention away from more relevant questions. "My views on the law and on what kind of Supreme Court justice I would make have been drowned out in the clamor," he stated. He commended Reagan and his wife, Nancy Reagan, for "leading the fight against illegal drugs," adding, "I fully support their effort and I hope that the young people of this country, including my own daughters, will learn from my mistake and heed their message."

The swift and unfortunate demise of Ginsburg's nomination was a sobering lesson for the Reagan administration. The president reacted by nominating an experienced and uncontroversial moderate, Judge ANTHONY M. KENNEDY, who was quickly and easily confirmed. Many feel that the Senate's handling of the Bork and Ginsburg nominations set a precedent for later investigations of presidential appointees and established a breadth and depth of scrutiny that some say are outside the scope allowed by the Constitution.

After his withdrawal, Ginsburg returned to his position on the District of Columbia Circuit. He is married to Hallee Perkins Morgan Ginsburg and has three children. He is a member of the Illinois State Bar Association, the Massachusetts State Bar Association, the American Economic Association, and the Honor Society of Phi Kappa Phi. He is also an honorary member of the District of Columbia Bar Association.

GINSBURG, RUTH BADER Ruth Bader Ginsburg was appointed associate justice of the U.S. Supreme Court in 1993. Ginsburg was the

BIOGRAPHY

Ruth Bader Ginsburg

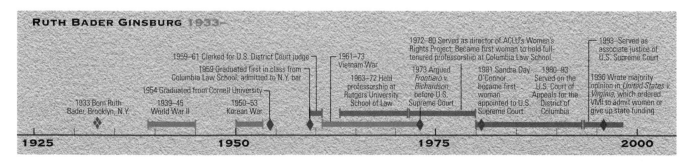

RUTH BADER GINSBURG 1933–

1933 Born Ruth Bader, Brooklyn, N.Y.

1939–45 World War II

1950–53 Korean War

1954 Graduated from Cornell University

1959 Graduated first in class from Columbia Law School; admitted to N.Y. bar

1959–61 Clerked for U.S. District Court judge

1961–73 Vietnam War

1963–72 Held professorship at Rutgers University School of Law

1972–80 Served as director of ACLU's Women's Rights Project; Became first woman to hold full-tenured professorship at Columbia Law School

1973 Argued *Frontiero v. Richardson* before U.S. Supreme Court

1980–93 Served on the U.S. Court of Appeals for the District of Columbia

1981 Sandra Day O'Connor became first woman appointed to U.S. Supreme Court

1993 Served as associate justice of U.S. Supreme Court

1996 Wrote majority opinion in *United States v. Virginia*, which ordered VMI to admit women or give up state funding

1925   1950   1975   2000

first person nominated to the Court by President BILL CLINTON, filling the vacancy created by the retirement of Justice BYRON R. WHITE. As an attorney before her appointment, Ginsburg won distinction for her advocacy of WOMEN'S RIGHTS before the Supreme Court.

Ginsburg was born March 15, 1933, in Brooklyn. She attended New York public schools and then Cornell University. She married Martin Ginsburg after graduating from Cornell in 1954, and gave birth to a daughter, Jane Ginsburg, before entering Harvard Law School in 1956. Ginsburg was an outstanding student and was elected president of her class at the prestigious Harvard Law School. After her second year, she transferred to Columbia Law School, following her husband, who had taken a position with a New York City law firm. Ginsburg was elected to the Columbia Law Review and graduated first in her class. She was admitted to the New York bar in 1959.

Despite her academic brilliance, New York law firms refused to hire her because she was a woman. She finally got a position as a law clerk to a federal district court judge. In 1961 she entered the academic field as a research associate at Columbia Law School. In 1963 she joined the faculty of Rutgers University School of Law, where she served as a professor until 1972.

In 1972 Ginsburg's career shifted to that of an advocate. As the director of the Women's Rights Project of the AMERICAN CIVIL LIBERTIES UNION, she developed and used a strategy of showing that laws that discriminated between men and women were often based on stereotypes that were unfair to both sexes. In the early to mid-1970s, Ginsburg argued six women's rights cases before the U.S. Supreme Court, winning five of them.

Frontiero v. Richardson, 411 U.S. 677, 93 S. Ct. 1764, 36 L. Ed. 2d 583 (1973), illustrates the type of cases Ginsburg argued before the Court. In *Frontiero* a female Air Force officer successfully challenged statutes (10 U.S.C.A. §§ 1072, 1076; 37 U.S.C.A. §§ 401, 403) that allowed a married serviceman to qualify for higher housing benefits even if his wife was not dependent on his income, while requiring a married servicewoman to prove her husband's dependence before receiving the same benefit. The Supreme Court voted 8–1 to overturn the law.

President JIMMY CARTER appointed Ginsburg to the U.S. Court of Appeals for the District of Columbia Circuit in 1980. In this position Ginsburg proved to be a judicial moderate, despite her reputation as a women's rights advocate. She supported women's right to choose

to have an ABORTION, but disagreed with the framework of *Roe v. Wade*, 410 U.S. 113, 93 S. Ct. 705, 35 L. Ed. 2d 147, the 1973 decision that gave women that right. She generally sided with the government in criminal cases, but supported CIVIL RIGHTS issues. She was a model of judicial restraint, preferring legislative solutions to social problems, instead of judge-made solutions.

President Clinton nominated Ginsburg to the Supreme Court in 1993, and she was easily confirmed. Her tenure on the High Court has been consistent with her service on the court of appeals. She has remained a judicial moderate with a strong emphasis on protecting civil rights. In *United States v. Virginia*, __U.S. __, 116 S. Ct. 2264, 135 L. Ed. 2d 735 (1996), Ginsburg wrote the majority opinion, which ordered the all-male Virginia Military Institute (VMI) to admit women or give up state funding. This decision also affected the Citadel, South Carolina's state-run all-male military school, and was a decisive blow to state-sponsored SEX DISCRIMINATION. Ginsburg rejected a proposal by VMI that it establish a separate military program for women. Such a program would be unequal, Ginsburg concluded, because it would rely on stereotypes about women and would not provide an equal education. She stated, "Women seeking and fit for a VMI-quality education cannot be offered anything less under the state's obligation to afford them genuinely equal protection."

GITLOW v. NEW YORK *Gitlow v. New York*, 268 U.S. 652, 45 S. Ct. 625, 69 L. Ed. 1138, is a 1925 decision by the Supreme Court that upheld the constitutionality of criminal anarchy statutes.

The defendant, Benjamin Gitlow, was a member of the Left Wing Section of the Socialist party, a splinter group of that party formed in opposition to its dominant policy of "moderate socialism." This section criticized the mainstream of the party for its acknowledgment of the necessity of the democratic parliamentary state and its insistence on introducing SOCIALISM through the legislative process. The Left Wing Section clearly advocated the necessity of effectuating a Communist revolution by a militant and revolutionary socialism based on the class struggle. It viewed mass industrial revolts as the mechanism by which the parliamentary state would be destroyed and replaced by a system of Communist socialism.

Gitlow was responsible for the publication of these views in writings titled "The Left Wing Manifesto." The "Manifesto" was then published in *The Revolutionary Age*, the official paper of the Left Wing. The opinions expressed in these publications formed the bases for the defendant's convictions under Sections 160 and 161 of the penal law of New York, which were the criminal anarchy statutes.

Section 160 defined criminal anarchy and prescribed that the verbal or written advocacy of the doctrine be treated as a FELONY. Section 161 delineated the conduct that constituted the crime of advocacy of criminal anarchy and stated that its punishment be imprisonment, a fine, or both. The proscribed conduct consisted of the verbal or written advertisement or teaching of the duty, necessity, or propriety of overthrowing organized government by violence, assassination, or other unlawful acts. A person was also prohibited from publishing, editing, knowingly circulating, or publicly displaying any writing embodying this doctrine.

There was a two-count indictment against Gitlow. The first charged that the defendant had advocated, advised, and taught the duty, necessity, and propriety of unlawfully overthrowing organized government through the writings titled "The Left Wing Manifesto." The second count charged that he had printed, published, knowingly circulated, and distributed *The Revolutionary Age*, containing the writings set forth in the first count advocating the doctrine of criminal anarchy.

There was no evidence of any effect ensuing from the publication and circulation of the "Manifesto."

In sustaining the defendant's conviction, the Court assumed that the Due Process Clause of the FOURTEENTH AMENDMENT prevented the states from impairing the freedoms guaranteed by the FIRST AMENDMENT. It thereby departed from its previous position that the Due Process Clause of the Fourteenth Amendment did not apply the guarantees of the Bill of Rights to the states. The Court held, however, that the statutes, as applied in this case, did not deprive the defendant of freedom of expression in violation of the Due Process Clause of the Fourteenth Amendment.

The Court noted that the statutes did not penalize the utterance or publication of abstract doctrine or academic theory having no propensity to incite concrete action. It found that what was proscribed was language advocating, advising, or teaching the overthrow of organized government by unlawful means, and that such language implied an urging to action. The Court held that the "Manifesto" was neither the expression of philosophical abstraction nor the mere prediction of future events; it was the language of direct incitement.

The Court reasoned that the means advocated for engendering the destruction of organized government—mass industrial uprisings, political mass strikes, and revolutionary mass action—necessarily implies the use of force and violence and are inherently unlawful in a democratic system of government. It ruled that freedom of expression does not grant an absolute right to speak or publish, without responsibility, whatever one wishes or an unqualified immunity from punishment for every possible utterance or publication. The state, in the exercise of its POLICE POWER, can indisputably punish those who abuse the FREEDOM OF SPEECH and press by utterances adverse to the public welfare, tending to corrupt public morals, incite to crime, or breach the public peace. In furtherance of its primary and essential right of self-preservation, a state can penalize expression imperiling the foundations of organized government and threatening its overthrow by unlawful means.

The Court also ruled that great deference must be accorded to the determination by the state that utterances advocating the overthrow of organized government by unlawful means are so opposed to the general welfare and involve such danger of substantive evil that they can be penalized in the exercise of its police power. Such police statutes can only be declared unconstitutional if they are arbitrary or unreasonable. In addition, the Court noted that the immediate danger is not diminished because the effect of a particular utterance cannot be precisely foreseen. It indicated that the state need not defer the enactment of protective measures until there is immediate danger of its destruction; it can quash the peril at its onset.

The Court also stated that when the state has ascertained that utterances of a certain type entail such danger of substantive evil that they can be punished, the issue of whether any particular utterance within the ambit of the prohibited class is likely, in and of itself, to bring about the substantive evil, is not subject to consideration. It is sufficient that the statute itself is constitutional and that the use of the language comes within its prohibition.

Additionally, the Court ruled that the general, broad "CLEAR AND PRESENT DANGER" test as used in other cases was inapplicable to cases such as *Gitlow*, where the legislature itself has previously determined the danger of substantive evil arising from specified utterances.

In subsequent cases (for example, *Brandenburg v. Ohio*, 395 U.S. 444, 89 S. Ct. 1827, 23 L. Ed. 2d 430 [1969]; *Hess v. Indiana*, 414 U.S. 105, 94 S. Ct. 326, 30 L. Ed. 2d 303 [1973]), the Court rejected the doctrine it formulated in

Gitlow that incitement to action is implicit in mere advocacy of unlawful acts. The Court subsequently held that freedom of expression does not allow a state to prohibit advocacy of resort to force or unlawful acts except where such advocacy is directed to inciting imminent lawless action and is likely to incite such action.

CROSS-REFERENCES
Anarchism; Communism; Due Process of Law; Incorporation Doctrine.

GLANVILL, RANULF
English COMMON LAW developed partly in response to the pioneering work of Ranulf Glanvill. As chief justiciar, Glanvill was the legal and financial minister of England under HENRY II. He is commonly associated with the first important treatise on practice and procedure in the king's courts: *Tractatus de legibus et consuetudinibus regni Angliae* (Treatise on the laws and customs of the realm of England). Historians agree that Glanvill is probably not the author of the *Tractatus*, which first appeared circa 1188, but he is thought to have been instrumental in its creation. Early U.S. law owes much to English law, which became greatly simplified and available to common people during Glanvill's tenure.

Glanvill was probably born at Stratford St. Andrew, near Saxmundham, Suffolk, England. Although few details are known about his life, it is recorded that he had bumpy political fortunes. He was SHERIFF of Yorkshire from 1163 to 1170, but lost his authority following an official inquiry into the corruption of sheriffs. He regained it by helping raise troops against Scottish invaders in 1173–74, and his reward from King Henry II was a series of increasingly important appointments: justice of the king's court, itinerant justice in the northern circuit, and ambassador to the court in Flanders. In 1180, Glanvill's ascent to power seemed complete when he became legal and financial minister, but a new king, Richard I, threw him in prison. He ransomed his way out, and then died of illness on a Crusade at Acre, in what is now Israel, in 1190.

BIOGRAPHY

"THE LEGAL CONSTITUTION IS BASED ABOVE ALL ON EQUITY; AND JUSTICE, WHICH IS SELDOM ARRIVED AT BY BATTLE . . . , IS MORE EASILY AND QUICKLY ATTAINED THROUGH ITS USE."

For a few centuries before Glanvill became influential, English law was mired in FEUDALISM. Under this political and military system, justice was administered in crude forms: trial by combat, which operated under the assumption that God would favor the righteous party, and trial by ORDEAL, which, in one of its forms, posed the question of innocence as a test of whether a person's wounds could heal within three days. By the twelfth century, feudalistic law was dying. The local courts still adhered to its methods, but the king's courts offered a superior form of justice that was at once less bloody and less superstitious. This was a writ-based, or formulary, system. It allowed litigants to frame a complaint in terms of a particular ACTION, which had its own WRIT and established modes of PLEADING and trial. Although primitive by modern standards, the formulary system represented a considerable advance for its time. But such justice was chiefly available to great lords; commoners had to resort to the local courts.

As chief justiciar, Glanvill sought to extend the benefits of the king's courts to ordinary people. He accomplished this through a system of itinerant royal justices, and the results revolutionized English legal procedure. As the feudal forms fell into disuse, they were replaced with a dominant system of central courts that followed uniform procedure throughout the realm and made English law simpler and better.

The *Tractatus* played a crucial role in this improvement. In fourteen books, it covered each of the eighty distinct writs used in the king's courts. One important writ, for example, was the grand ASSIZE, a procedure for settling land disputes that replaced the feudal practice of battle with a form of JURY system. The treatise offered this commentary on its value: "It takes account so effectively of both human life and civil condition that all men may preserve the rights which they have in any free tenement, while avoiding the doubtful outcome of battle. In this way, too, they may avoid the greatest of all punishments, unexpected and untimely death." As with other writs, the *Trac-*

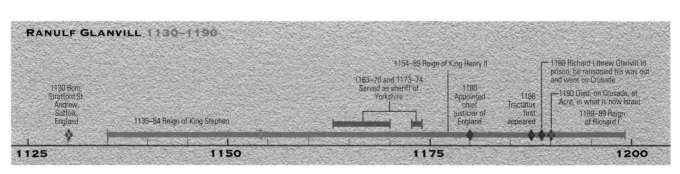

RANULF GLANVILL 1130–1190

1130 Born, Stratford St. Andrew, Suffolk, England

1135–54 Reign of King Stephen

1163–70 and 1173–74 Served as sheriff of Yorkshire

1154–89 Reign of King Henry II

1180 Appointed chief justiciar of England

1188 Tractatus first appeared

1189 Richard I threw Glanvill in prison; he ransomed his way out and went on Crusade

1190 Died, on Crusade, at Acre, in what is now Israel

1189–99 Reign of Richard I

1125   1150   1175   1200

tatus painstakingly spelled out how the grand assize worked. Directed at practitioners of law, the *Tractatus* sought to encourage them to adopt these new "royal benefit[s] granted to the people by the goodness of the king."

The simplicity and clarity of the *Tractatus* helped lead England to a common law. Although records from the period associate Glanvill with the treatise, scholars believe he is unlikely to have written it. The real author may have been his nephew, Hubert Walter, who was the archbishop of Canterbury, or even a later justiciar, Geoffrey Fitzpeter. However, its authorship is of secondary importance to its effect. Besides encouraging the spread of unified procedure, it provided the foundation for later classics, in particular HENRY DE BRACTON's thirteenth-century treatise on English law and custom, *De legibus et consuetudinibus Angliae.*

GLASS, CARTER Carter Glass sponsored important banking laws of the twentieth century, among them the GLASS-STEAGALL ACTS of 1932 and 1933 (48 Stat. 162). He wrote and sponsored the legislation that established the Federal Reserve System in 1913. He was also a key player in making amendments to the system during the decades following its establishment. A Virginia Democrat, he served as secretary of the treasury under WOODROW WILSON and was a member of the House of Representatives and the Senate.

Glass was born January 4, 1858, in Lynchburg, Virginia, the youngest of twelve children. His mother, Augusta Christian Glass, died when he was two years old, and Glass was raised by a sister ten years older than he. His father, Robert H. Glass, was the editor of the *Daily Republic.*

Following the Civil War, Glass's father turned down an offer of reappointment to his old position as postmaster general, because he did not want to be on the payroll of the nation he had just fought. Having lived through a financially strapped childhood during the Reconstruction period, Glass would as an adult consistently oppose strong centralized control

BIOGRAPHY

Carter Glass

by the federal government except in emergencies.

Glass left school at age fourteen to begin a printer's apprenticeship at his father's paper. He completed his apprenticeship in 1876 when the family moved to Petersburg, Virginia. Glass soon moved back to Lynchburg to work as an auditor for the railroad. In 1880 he became the city editor, and then the editor, of the *Lynchburg News.* With savings and the financial backing of friends, he purchased that newspaper in 1888. The same year he married Aurelia McDearmon Caldwell, a teacher. In the early 1890s, Glass bought and consolidated other Lynchburg newspapers.

In 1899 Glass was elected to the Virginia state senate, where he was put on the committee of finance and banking. During his career as a state legislator, he was an active debater on suffrage for African Americans, the subject of the Fourteenth and Fifteenth Amendments to the U.S. Constitution. He supported restricting voting rights for illiterate former slaves on the theory that these votes were used by those in power to maintain their power. He also argued in defense of the Eighteenth Amendment, prohibiting the sale of alcohol. In 1933, however, he voted for its appeal on the grounds that it was futile to maintain a law that could not be enforced.

In 1902 Glass was elected to the U.S. House of Representatives, where he served until 1918. In 1904 he was appointed to the Banking and Currency Committee. He devoted the next several years to studying the topic of banking, and introduced few bills during this period.

The U.S. banking system of the late nineteenth and early twentieth centuries was unstable, leading to a series of banking panics over a thirty-four-year span. By the end of the nineteenth century, banks were largely independent from, and often in competition with, one another. The relatively young U.S. banking system was burdened primarily with a lack of flexibility in lending (or rediscounting) policies and currency availability, as well as

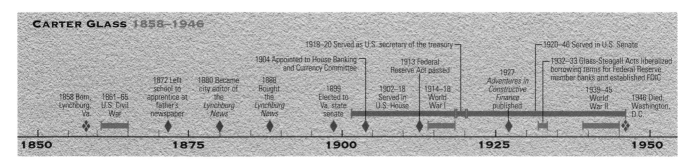

CARTER GLASS 1858–1946

1918–20 Served as U.S. secretary of the treasury
1920–46 Served in U.S. Senate
1904 Appointed to House Banking and Currency Committee
1913 Federal Reserve Act passed
1932–33 Glass-Steagall Acts liberalized borrowing terms for Federal Reserve member banks and established FDIC
1927 *Adventures in Constructive Finance* published
1858 Born, Lynchburg, Va.
1861–65 U.S. Civil War
1872 Left school to apprentice at father's newspaper
1880 Became city editor of the *Lynchburg News*
1888 Bought the *Lynchburg News*
1899 Elected to Va. state senate
1902–18 Served in U.S. House
1914–18 World War I
1939–45 World War II
1946 Died, Washington, D.C.

1850   1875   1900   1925   1950

> "THE MAIN PURPOSE OF THE [GLASS-STEAGALL] BILL . . . WAS TO PREVENT . . . THE USE OF THE FEDERAL RESERVE BANKING FACILITIES FOR STOCK-GAMBLING PURPOSES."

weak supervision and inadequate CHECK collection systems.

In the first decade of the twentieth century, Glass began crafting a bill to address the need for banking reform. In 1912 Democrat Wilson was elected president of the United States. Glass, now chair of the House Banking Committee, enlisted and got Wilson's support for his reform bill.

The Federal Reserve Act, 12 U.S.C.A. § 221 et seq., the most radical banking reform bill in U.S. history, was passed into law December 23, 1913. In presenting his bill to the House, Glass said in his closing remarks, "I have tried to reconcile conflicting views, to compose all friction and technical knowledge of the banker, the wisdom of the philosopher, and the rights of the people."

According to its preamble, Glass's bill was created to "provide for the establishment of Federal reserve banks, to furnish an elastic currency, to afford means of rediscounting COMMERCIAL PAPER, to establish a more effective supervision of banking in the United States, and for other purposes." It provided the establishment of up to twelve Federal Reserve banks (district banks) to develop policy with the seven-member FEDERAL RESERVE BOARD in Washington, D.C. (This board's title was later changed to the Federal Reserve Board of Governors.) Glass's plan also required all nationally chartered banks to be members of the Federal Reserve System and weakened the power of private banks. Although the Federal Reserve System would be criticized for failing to stave off the Great Depression in the 1930s, it would be credited with helping control the effects of a 1987 stock plunge.

During the years leading up to World War I, Glass headed a committee that investigated the act's effectiveness and made amendments as needed. Three test cases in 1923 and 1926 resulted in various changes in the act, which continues to be altered as circumstances dictate.

Glass was appointed Secretary of the Treasury in late 1918 and worked to develop and promote a new "Victory loan" under Wilson's administration (which was renamed "Fifth Liberty Loan" because the V looked like the Roman numeral for 5) as World War I drew to a close. These loans were bonds that the U.S. government encouraged Americans to buy to help generate revenue for war debts and for rebuilding war-torn Europe. In February 1920, Glass resigned as secretary and accepted a vacant seat in the U.S. Senate.

In early 1920, an election year, sentiments against Wilson grew. A movement took hold to select Glass as the Democratic presidential candidate. But Glass, a strong supporter and close friend of Wilson's throughout his lifetime, did not support the effort. WARREN G. HARDING, a critic of the Federal Reserve Board, was elected president in 1920.

In the late 1920s, conditions began to develop that would lead to a stock market crash and the subsequent Great Depression. In fall 1928 Glass wrote an article addressing his concern that the Reserve System was being misused for financial speculation. In early 1929 he gave a speech on the Senate floor warning of financial disaster and urging that action be taken against individuals abusing the system in gambling ventures.

Glass also began work on amendments to reduce the consequences of the disaster he suspected was coming. This work resulted in the Glass-Steagall Acts of 1932 and 1933, sponsored by Glass and Representative Henry B. Steagall. The Glass-Steagall Acts marked the third time in early U.S. history that a major crisis precipitated banking reform. (The first was the Civil War and the development of the National Banking System; the second was the panic of 1907 and the development of the Federal Reserve Act.)

The act of 1932 liberalized terms under which member banks could borrow from the Federal Reserve System. The act of 1933, also called the Banking Act of 1933, established the FEDERAL DEPOSIT INSURANCE CORPORATION. This institution guaranteed bank depositors' savings, separated commercial banking from investment banking and insurance underwriting, regulated interests on time deposits, and increased the power of the Federal Reserve Board.

Glass served in the Senate until 1946. He died May 28, 1946.

See also BANKS AND BANKING.

GLASS-STEAGALL ACT ▥ Legislation passed by Congress in 1933 that prohibits commercial banks from engaging in the investment business. ▥

The Glass-Steagall Act, also known as the Banking Act of 1933 (48 Stat. 162), was enacted as an emergency response to the failure of nearly five thousand banks during the Great Depression. The act was originally part of President FRANKLIN D. ROOSEVELT's New Deal program and became a permanent measure in 1945. It gave tighter regulation of national banks to the Federal Reserve System; prohibited bank sales of SECURITIES; and created the FEDERAL DEPOSIT INSURANCE CORPORATION (FDIC), which insures bank deposits with a pool of money appropriated from banks.

Beginning in the 1900s, commercial banks established security affiliates that floated BOND issues and underwrote corporate STOCK issues. (In underwriting, a bank guarantees to furnish a definite sum of money by a definite date to a business or government entity in return for an issue of bonds or stock.) The expansion of commercial banks into securities underwriting was substantial until the 1929 stock market crash and the subsequent Depression. In 1930 the Bank of the United States failed, reportedly because of activities of its security affiliates that created artificial conditions in the market. In 1933 all the banks throughout the country were closed for a four-day period, and four thousand banks closed permanently.

As a result of the bank closings and already devastated economy, public confidence in the U.S. financial structure was low. To restore the confidence of the U.S. banking public that banks would follow reasonable banking practices, Congress created the Glass-Steagall Act. The act forced a separation of commercial and investment banks by preventing commercial banks from underwriting securities, with the exception of U.S. Treasury and federal agency securities, and municipal and state general obligation securities. More specifically, the act authorizes Federal Reserve banks to use government obligations and COMMERCIAL PAPER as collateral for their note issues, in order to encourage expansion of the currency. Banks can also offer advisory services regarding investments for their customers, as well as buy and sell securities for their customers. However, information gained from providing such services cannot be used by a bank when it acts as a lender. Likewise, investment banks cannot engage in the business of receiving deposits.

A bank is defined as an institution organized under the laws of the United States, any state of the United States, the District of Columbia, any territory of the United States, Puerto Rico, Guam, American Samoa, or the Virgin Islands, that both accepts demand deposits (deposits that the depositor may withdraw by CHECK or similar means for payment to third parties or others) and is engaged in the business of making commercial loans (12 U.S.C.A. § 1841 (c)(1) [1988]). Investment banking consists mostly of securities underwriting and related activities; making a market in securities; and setting up corporate mergers, acquisitions, and restructuring. Investment banking also includes services provided by brokers or dealers in transactions in the secondary market. A secondary market is one where securities are bought and sold subsequent to their original issuance.

Despite attempts to reform Glass-Steagall, the legislature has not passed any major changes—although it has passed bills that relax restrictions. Banks may now set up brokerage subsidiaries, and UNDERWRITE a limited number of issues such as asset-backed securities, corporate bonds, and commercial paper.

The Glass-Steagall Act restored public confidence in banking practices during the Great Depression. However, many historians believe that the commercial bank securities practices of the time had little actual effect on the already devastated economy and were not a major contributor to the Depression. Some legislators and bank reformers argue that the act was never necessary, or that it has become outdated and should be repealed.

CROSS-REFERENCES

Banks and Banking; Federal Reserve Board; Glass, Carter.

GLOSS 📖 An ANNOTATION, explanation, or commentary on a particular passage in a book or document, which is ordinarily placed on the same page or in the margin to elucidate or amplify the passage. 📖

GOING CONCERN VALUE 📖 The value inherent in an active, established company as opposed to a firm that is not yet established.

The value of the ASSETS of a business considered as an operating whole. 📖

As a component of business value, going concern value recognizes the many advantages that an existing business has over a new business, such as avoidance of start-up costs and improved operating efficiency. In this sense, the going concern value of a firm represents the difference between the value of an established firm and the value of a start-up firm.

Going concern value also indicates the value of a firm as an operating, active whole, rather than merely as distinct items of property. U.S. BANKRUPTCY law, for example, has recognized the need to preserve going concern value when reorganizing businesses in order to maximize recoveries by creditors and shareholders (11 U.S.C.A. § 1101 et seq.). Bankruptcy laws seek to preserve going concern value whenever possible by promoting the REORGANIZATION, as opposed to the LIQUIDATION, of businesses.

Going concern value also implies a firm's ability to generate income without interruption, even when ownership has changed (*Butler v. Butler*, 541 Pa. 364, 663 A.2d 148 [Pa. 1995]).

Going concern value is distinguished from the concept of GOOD WILL, which refers to the excess value of a business that arises from the favorable disposition of its customers. Good will may include the value of such business elements as TRADE NAMES, trade brands, and established location.

GOING PUBLIC Altering the organization of a CORPORATION from ownership and control by a small group of people, as in a close corporation, to ownership by the general public, as in a publicly held corporation.

When a corporation goes public, it opens up the sale of shares of its stock to the public at large.

GOLDBERG, ARTHUR JOSEPH Arthur Joseph Goldberg served as a justice of the U.S. Supreme Court from 1962 to 1965. A distinguished labor law attorney, Goldberg also served as secretary of labor in the administration of President JOHN F. KENNEDY from 1961 until his judicial appointment and as ambassador to the UNITED NATIONS from 1965 to 1968 during the administration of President LYNDON B. JOHNSON. Johnson persuaded a reluctant Goldberg to resign from the Supreme Court to accept the U.N. assignment.

Goldberg was born August 8, 1908, in Chicago, to Russian immigrants. He graduated from Northwestern University Law School in 1929 and entered the field of labor law in Chicago. Goldberg gained national attention in 1939 as counsel to the Chicago Newspaper Guild during a strike. He served in the Office of Strategic Services during World War II and then returned to his labor practice in 1944.

In 1948 he became general counsel for the United Steelworkers of America, a position he held until 1961. The steelworkers union was an important union during a time when U.S. heavy industry was thriving. STRIKES or the threat of strikes in the steel industry had national repercussions. Goldberg proved adept in his role as general counsel, skillfully negotiating strike settlements, consolidating gains through COLLECTIVE BARGAINING, and helping with public relations.

From 1948 to 1955, Goldberg also was general counsel for the Congress of Industrial Organizations (CIO), which contained most nontrade unions, such as those controlling

manufacturing and mining jobs. The CIO had been created when the trade union members of the American Federation of Labor (AFL) showed no interest in organizing these industries. There was a great deal of friction between the CIO and the AFL, yet the leadership of both organizations realized that a unified labor movement was a necessity. Goldberg was a principal architect of the 1955 merger of the CIO and AFL into the AFL-CIO. He then served as a special counsel to the AFL-CIO's industrial union department from 1955 to 1961.

In 1961 President Kennedy appointed Goldberg secretary of labor. During the less than two years that Goldberg held this office, he saw congressional approval of an increase in the minimum wage, and the reorganization of the Office of Manpower Administration (now the Employment and Training Administration). When Justice FELIX FRANKFURTER retired from the Supreme Court in 1962, Kennedy appointed Goldberg to the "Jewish seat." The so-called Jewish seat began with the 1939 appointment of Felix Frankfurter, who was Jewish, to succeed Justice BENJAMIN CARDOZO, also Jewish. It was assumed that for political reasons, Democratic presidents would appoint a Jewish person to that vacancy. This tradition ended with the appointment of ABE FORTAS.

The appointment of the liberal Goldberg, replacing the conservative Frankfurter, turned a four-justice liberal minority on the Court into a five-justice liberal majority, which was led by Chief Justice EARL WARREN. Goldberg became known as an innovative judicial thinker who moved the Court toward liberal activism. He usually joined the majority of Warren Court justices in extending the Court's rulings into areas previously considered the realm of the states and of Congress. He was also an able negotiator within the Court, helping to smooth the way in reaching difficult and controversial decisions.

Goldberg was a firm supporter of CIVIL RIGHTS and civil liberties. His best-known opinion came in the areas of CRIMINAL LAW and CRIMINAL PROCEDURE, when he wrote the major-

BIOGRAPHY

Arthur Joseph Goldberg

"LAW NOT SERVED BY POWER IS AN ILLUSION; BUT POWER NOT RULED BY LAW IS A MENACE WHICH OUR NUCLEAR AGE CANNOT AFFORD."

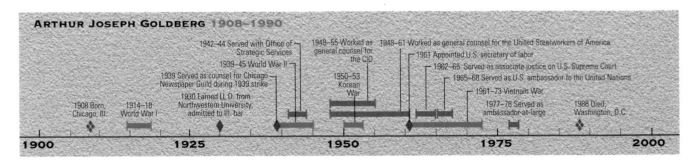

ARTHUR JOSEPH GOLDBERG 1908–1990

1908 Born, Chicago, Ill.
1914–18 World War I
1930 Earned LL.D. from Northwestern University; admitted to Ill. bar
1939 Served as counsel for Chicago Newspaper Guild during 1939 strike
1939–45 World War II
1942–44 Served with Office of Strategic Services
1948–55 Worked as general counsel for the CIO
1950–53 Korean War
1948–61 Worked as general counsel for the United Steelworkers of America
1961 Appointed U.S. secretary of labor
1962–65 Served as associate justice on U.S. Supreme Court
1965–68 Served as U.S. ambassador to the United Nations
1961–73 Vietnam War
1977–78 Served as ambassador-at-large
1988 Died, Washington, D.C.

1900   1925   1950   1975   2000

ity opinion in *Escobedo v. Illinois*, 378 U.S. 478, 84 S. Ct. 1758, 12 L. Ed. 2d 977 (1964). In this case the Court struck down a murder conviction because the defendant had been denied the right to confer with his lawyer after his arrest. This decision was a major step toward the landmark decision in *Miranda v. Arizona*, 384 U.S. 436, 86 S. Ct. 1602, 16 L. Ed. 2d 694 (1966), which gave suspects the right to be advised of their constitutional rights to remain silent, to have a lawyer appointed, and to have a lawyer present during interrogation.

Goldberg believed in the constitutional right of DUE PROCESS. In a dissenting opinion in *United States v. Barnett*, 376 U.S. 681, 84 S. Ct. 984, 12 L. Ed. 2d 23 (1964), he argued that federal judges should not be allowed to use their CONTEMPT power to send persons to jail. When punishment for contempt of court could be meted out, the person held in contempt should be entitled to a jury trial. Although he did not prevail in *Barnett*, his dissent drew attention to the abuses of this practice and helped reduce it.

In 1965 Goldberg appeared to have a promising judicial career. Yet he became one of the few justices to give up his lifetime appointment to the Supreme Court for a reason other than retirement. In the summer of 1965, President Johnson asked Goldberg to resign from the Court and accept the U.S. ambassadorship to the United Nations, promising a larger role in foreign policy than was traditionally given to the U.N. delegate. Goldberg did so reluctantly and regretfully. When Johnson appointed his friend and political confidant Abe Fortas to replace Goldberg, many believed this had been the primary motive in offering Goldberg the U.N. post.

Goldberg's major achievement as U.N. ambassador was his aid in drafting Security Council Resolution No. 242 (22 SCOR 8–9, U.N. Doc. S/INF/Rev. 2), passed in November 1967, concerning peace measures in the Middle East. Goldberg tried continually and unsuccessfully to make the United Nations play a role in a peace process that would end the Vietnam War. His efforts were met with disfavor by Johnson and by Johnson's advisers. Frustrated and disappointed by the failure of these efforts and the escalation of the war, Goldberg resigned his U.N. position in 1968.

After his resignation Goldberg joined a New York City law firm and also served in 1968 and 1969 as president of the American Jewish Committee, a national human rights organization. He ran for governor of New York in 1970 as the Liberal-Democrat candidate, but incumbent Nelson A. Rockefeller soundly defeated him.

He then returned to Washington, D.C., where he resumed a private law practice.

In 1977 and 1978, Goldberg was a U.S. ambassador-at-large in the administration of President JIMMY CARTER. Following this assignment, he became deeply involved in the international HUMAN RIGHTS movement, a cause he pursued until his death.

Goldberg wrote several books, including *AFL-CIO Labor United* (1956), *Defense of Freedom* (1966), and *Equal Justice: The Warren Era of the Supreme Court* (1972).

Goldberg died January 19, 1990, in Washington, D.C.

GOLDEN PARACHUTE An agreement that provides key executives with generous severance pay and other benefits in the event that their employment is terminated as a result of a change of ownership at their employer CORPORATION; known more formally as a change-of-control agreement.

Golden parachutes are provided by a firm's BOARD OF DIRECTORS and, depending on the laws of the state in which the company is incorporated, may require shareholder approval. These agreements compensate executives in the event that they lose their job or quit because they have suffered a reduction in power or status following a change of ownership of their employer corporation. Some golden parachutes are triggered even if the control of the corporation does not change completely; such parachutes open after a certain percentage of the corporation's stock is acquired.

Golden parachutes have been justified on three grounds. First, they may enable corporations that are prime TAKEOVER targets to hire and retain high-quality executives who would otherwise be reluctant to work for them. Second, since the parachutes add to the cost of acquiring a corporation, they may discourage takeover bids. Finally, if a takeover bid does occur, executives with a golden parachute are more likely to respond in a manner that will benefit the shareholders. Without a golden parachute, executives might resist a takeover that would be in the interests of the shareholders, in order to save their own job.

As golden parachutes have grown increasingly lucrative, they have come under criticism from shareholders who argue that they are a waste of corporate assets. These shareholders point out that managers already have a FIDUCIARY duty to act in the best interests of their shareholders and should not require golden parachutes as an incentive. Especially suspect are large parachutes that are awarded once a takeover bid has been announced. Critics charge that these last-minute parachutes are little more than going-away presents for the executives and may encourage them to work for the takeover at the expense of the shareholders.

As the practice of offering golden parachutes became more and more common in the 1980s, efforts to place restrictions on the agreements increased. Many of these efforts stemmed from the realization that the practice, which had once showed a positive stock return for shareholders, was now producing negative stock returns.

On February 6, 1996, the FEDERAL DEPOSIT INSURANCE CORPORATION (FDIC) issued a final rule that restricted troubled banks, thrifts, and holding companies from making golden parachute payments. Exceptions to the rule are allowed for individuals who have qualified for pension and retirement plans. Other exceptions permit the FDIC to enforce the spirit of the law by allowing legitimate payments but stopping payments that might be considered abusive or improper. The rule also prevents FDIC-insured institutions from paying the legal expenses of employees who are the subject of related enforcement proceedings. The rule went into effect on April 1, 1996.

GOLDMAN, EMMA

Emma Goldman was a crusader for ANARCHISM, feminism, and the labor movement. She was also an essayist and is best known as the first editor of *Mother Earth*, a magazine providing a forum for feminist and anarchist writers.

Goldman was born June 27, 1869, in Kaunas, Russia, when Russia was in transition from czarism to COMMUNISM. The seeds of the Bolshevik revolt were already being sown in the towns and villages throughout the country where discontent with czarist rule was strongest. Goldman, who described herself as a born rebel, came into the world as the third daughter of Abraham Goldman and Taube Goldman. Her parents' marriage, like many Jewish Orthodox unions of the time, had been arranged. Goldman suffered the fate of being a female in a culture that valued males. When she was young, her father made no effort to disguise his disappointment at having still another daughter instead of the much-prized son he hoped for. He

BIOGRAPHY

Emma Goldman

has been described as hot tempered and impatient, particularly with Goldman's rebelliousness, which she showed at an early age. He was a traditional Jewish father and he planned to arrange a marriage for his daughter when she was fifteen. Goldman, however, had different ideas: she longed for an education and hoped someday to marry someone she loved. Goldman described her mother as cold and distant, but also strong and assertive, and she may have served as a role model for Goldman's own forthright manner.

After spending her childhood in Kaunas, Königsberg, and St. Petersburg, Goldman emigrated to the United States in 1886 with a sister. They joined another sister who had settled in Rochester, New York, where Goldman found work in a coat factory, sewing ten-and-a-half hours daily at a salary of $2.50 a week. She lived in a crowded apartment with her two sisters and her brother-in-law. Their working and living conditions, as well as those of others even more destitute, sparked her interest in anarchism and the labor movement, which was in its infancy. She joined radical groups agitating for an eight-hour workday and other improvements in factory conditions.

Goldman was intensely interested in the Haymarket Square incident in Chicago in 1886. A labor rally called by a small group of anarchists was interrupted by a bomb explosion and gunfire. When it was over, seven police officers and four spectators were dead and one hundred were injured. Eight anarchists were tried and convicted of inciting a riot. Four of the convicted were hanged, one committed suicide in prison, and the other three served prison sentences. Spurred by her outrage at this alleged injustice, Goldman began attending anarchist meetings and reading the militant anarchist newspaper *Die Freiheit* (Freedom). She felt herself irresistibly drawn to the movement, and in the summer of 1889, at the age of twenty, she moved to New York to be near the center of anarchist activity.

After arriving in New York, Goldman befriended Johann J. Most, a well-known anarchist and publisher of *Die Freiheit*. She also met

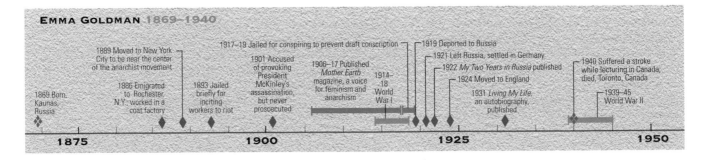

EMMA GOLDMAN 1869–1940

1869 Born, Kaunas, Russia

1886 Emigrated to Rochester, N.Y.; worked in a coat factory

1889 Moved to New York City to be near the center of the anarchist movement

1893 Jailed briefly for inciting workers to riot

1901 Accused of provoking President McKinley's assassination, but never prosecuted

1906–17 Published *Mother Earth* magazine, a voice for feminism and anarchism

1914–18 World War I

1917–19 Jailed for conspiring to prevent draft conscription

1919 Deported to Russia

1921 Left Russia, settled in Germany

1922 *My Two Years in Russia* published

1924 Moved to England

1931 *Living My Life*, an autobiography, published

1939–45 World War II

1940 Suffered a stroke while lecturing in Canada; died, Toronto, Canada

1875   1900   1925   1950

Alexander Berkman, who became her lover and with whom she remained close throughout her life. By this time, she was known as Red Emma, and she was followed by detectives wherever she went. She wrote, traveled, and lectured to promote anarchism and the labor movement. In 1893, she was briefly jailed for inciting workers to riot. After her release from jail, she traveled to Vienna to train as a nurse and midwife. She then returned to New York and resumed her lecturing. In 1901 she was accused of provoking the ASSASSINATION of President WILLIAM McKIN-LEY, because the assassin had attended one of her lectures. No charges were ever brought against her, but newspapers throughout the United States portrayed her as an evil traitor because of her controversial ideas.

In 1906 Goldman published the first issue of a magazine that was to serve as a platform for feminist and anarchist ideas. She called her venture *Mother Earth*, and within six months, it became a leading voice for feminism and anarchism. With Berkman, Goldman published the magazine until 1917, while she continued to travel, write, and lecture. During this time, she carried on an eight-year relationship with Ben Reitman, Chicago's King of the Hobos, a well-known anarchist and labor activist who became her manager. Goldman had long since given up her idealistic notions about marriage. She had been married twice to the same man, both times with disastrous results, and had carried on a number of love affairs. Goldman preferred the impermanence and freedom of short-term affairs and wrote in more than one essay that marriage was women's greatest enemy because it robbed them of their independence.

The United States' entry into World War I in 1917 precipitated a wave of hostility toward leftists, pacifists, anarchists, and foreigners. Legislation like the Selective Service Act, the Espionage Act, and the Sedition Act was passed during 1917 and 1918 to suppress opposition to the war or the draft and to restrict civil liberties. Heedless of the repressive mood of the country, Goldman and Berkman, along with Leonard D. Abbott and Eleanor Fitzgerald, organized the No-Conscription League to oppose "all wars by capitalist governments." In the June 1917 issue of *Mother Earth*, they declared, "We will resist conscription by every means in our power, and we will sustain those who ... refuse to be conscripted." As a result of their antiwar activities, Goldman and Berkman were arrested and charged with conspiring to prevent draft registration. They were tried and convicted and each received the maximum sentence of two years in prison and $10,000 in fines. In December 1919, in the wake of a Red scare that led to the arrest

and deportation of hundreds of leftists, anarchists, and labor organizers, Goldman and Berkman were deported to Russia.

Goldman was optimistic about resuming life in Russia now that the czar had been toppled by the Bolsheviks, but her hopes quickly dissipated as the realities of the new government became apparent. In her opinion, "the old cruel regime ... had simply been replaced by a new, equally cruel one." She and Berkman left Russia in 1921 and eventually went to Germany. During their years in Germany, Goldman lectured and wrote a book, *My Two Years in Russia*, detailing her disillusionment with Bolshevik rule.

In 1924, Goldman moved to England, but she longed to return to the United States. Accepting an offer of marriage to James Colton, a staunch Scottish anarchist she had known for many years, provided her with an opportunity for British citizenship and the possibility of obtaining a British passport. She hoped to make her way to Canada and somehow gain entry into the United States. During the 1920s and 1930s, she traveled through Europe, writing and lecturing, and in 1931, she published her autobiography, *Living My Life*.

Goldman's wish to return to the United States was granted for a brief ninety-day lecture tour in 1934, after which she returned to Europe. In 1940, while on a trip to Canada to enlist support for the anti-Franco forces in Spain, Goldman suffered a stroke. She died several months later, on May 14, 1940, in Toronto. Her body was allowed to be returned to the United States for burial in Chicago near the graves of other anarchists she admired.

See also HAYMARKET RIOT.

GOLDWATER, BARRY MORRIS

Barry Morris Goldwater is a former U.S. senator and presidential nominee. During almost forty years in public life, he became the outspoken and controversial leader of the conservative wing of the REPUBLICAN PARTY.

Goldwater was born January 1, 1909, in Phoenix. His paternal ancestors were Orthodox Jewish innkeepers who emigrated from Poland in the mid-1800s to join the California gold rush.

Goldwater's father, Baron Goldwater, managed the family's general store in Phoenix. This store was the humble beginning of what would become an enormously profitable chain, Goldwater's Department Stores. Goldwater's mother, Josephine Williams, was a nurse who raised Goldwater and his siblings in her Episcopalian faith. A woman who loved outdoor activities, she took her children hiking and camping throughout Arizona and taught them the colorful history of the region. From her Goldwater acquired an

"ALL WARS ARE WARS AMONG THIEVES WHO ARE TOO COWARDLY TO FIGHT AND WHO THEREFORE INDUCE THE YOUNG MANHOOD OF THE WHOLE WORLD TO DO THE FIGHTING FOR THEM."

BIOGRAPHY

Barry Morris Goldwater

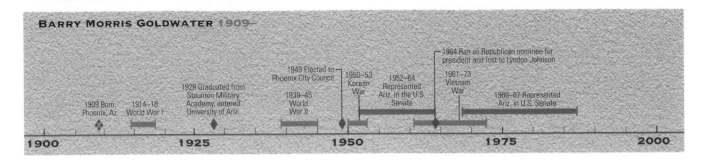

BARRY MORRIS GOLDWATER 1909–

1909 Born, Phoenix, Az.

1914–18 World War I

1928 Graduated from Staunton Military Academy, entered University of Ariz.

1939–45 World War II

1949 Elected to Phoenix City Council

1950–53 Korean War

1952–64. Represented Ariz. in the U.S. Senate

1961–73 Vietnam War

1964 Ran as Republican nominee for president and lost to Lyndon Johnson

1968–87 Represented Ariz. in U.S. Senate

1900   1925   1950   1975   2000

abiding love of the Southwest and a deep appreciation of its people and its beauty.

Goldwater was a mediocre student who preferred sports and socializing to studying. At Phoenix Union High School, he was elected president of his first-year class, but the principal advised his father that Goldwater should probably attend school elsewhere the following year. Against his strenuous objections, his parents sent him to Staunton Military Academy, in Virginia. There, he excelled at athletics and did better academically than anyone expected, being named best all-around cadet in 1928.

Goldwater loved the military and dreamed of attending West Point. But when he graduated from Staunton, his father was in ill health, and Goldwater instead enrolled at the University of Arizona, at Tucson, to be near his home. His father died before he had finished his first year in college. Goldwater left school a year later to enter the family business.

With his father gone, Goldwater turned to his uncle Morris for advice and direction. He quickly worked his way up from junior clerk, to general manager in 1936, and to president in 1937. Under his leadership, Goldwater's became Phoenix's premier department store and leading specialty shop. Goldwater pioneered the five-day workweek and instituted many progressive fringe benefits for his employees, including health and life insurance, profit sharing, and use by employees of a vacation ranch. Also, Goldwater's was the first Phoenix store to hire African Americans as salesclerks.

Goldwater entered politics in 1949 when he was elected to the Phoenix City Council as a reform candidate. He was surprised to find that he loved politics. In 1950, he managed Howard Pyle's successful campaign for governor of Arizona. In 1952, he was elected to the U.S. Senate on the strength of voter dissatisfaction with Democratic president HARRY S. TRUMAN and the war in Korea. Elected as a Republican, Goldwater described himself as "not a me-too Republican" but one "opposed to the superstate and to gigantic, bureaucratic, centralized authority." He quickly developed a reputation for "outspo-

"A GOVERNMENT THAT IS BIG ENOUGH TO GIVE YOU ALL YOU WANT IS BIG ENOUGH TO TAKE IT ALL AWAY."

ken unreliability" because even his Republican colleagues could not predict what he might say. A maverick who speaks his mind regardless of consequences, Goldwater is the personification of the Western ideal of rugged individualism. He opposes any intrusion by the federal government in what he considers the state's domain. While in the Senate, he consistently opposed federal spending for social programs, argued that contributions to SOCIAL SECURITY should be voluntary, and contended that medical programs for poor and elderly people would lead to socialized medicine. "I do not undertake to promote welfare, for I propose to extend freedom," he said. Throughout his career, Goldwater sought to reduce the role of government in citizens' lives by eliminating unnecessary laws and social programs.

One of Goldwater's most controversial actions in the Senate was his staunch defense of Senator JOSEPH R. MCCARTHY, a notorious Communist hunter whose committee, through innuendo and guilt by association, ruined the lives and careers of many U.S. citizens by labeling them Communists or Communist sympathizers. Goldwater was criticized for trying to forestall a Senate vote on censuring McCarthy and then voting against the censure.

In 1958 Goldwater was easily reelected to the Senate despite a concerted campaign to defeat him by organized labor, a group he distrusted and criticized. By that time he had established himself as the outspoken leader of conservative Republicans. His statements were frequently off-the-cuff, sometimes contradictory, and always quotable. He has been credited with saying that Walter P. Reuther, a labor movement leader, was a bigger threat than the Communists; that Supreme Court chief justice EARL WARREN, noted for his liberal opinions, was a socialist; and that Cuban premier Fidel Castro was just another Communist who needed a shave. He was notoriously disdainful of what he called the Eastern establishment, who, according to him, were elitist and out of touch with the rest of the United States. He supported a strong military and opposed efforts to lower defense spending and increase social spending. His detractors scoffed at him, but his followers were fiercely devoted, perhaps because his nonintellectual, candid style reflected their own values.

While in the Senate, Goldwater befriended JOHN F. KENNEDY, and, though they disagreed vehemently, they remained close friends until Kennedy's death. Goldwater had hoped to run against Kennedy in 1964; the two had discussed the possibility of traveling the country together on an old-fashioned debating tour. When Kennedy was assassinated, Goldwater lost his desire to run. He felt he could not beat LYNDON B. JOHNSON. Nonetheless, he was persuaded to run.

At the 1964 Republican convention in San Francisco, Goldwater was unanimously nominated after an intense floor fight. In his acceptance speech, he uttered the words that would haunt him during the coming campaign and paint him, perhaps unfairly, as a one-dimensional warmonger. "I would remind you," he said, "that extremism in the defense of liberty is no vice. And let me remind you also that moderation in the pursuit of justice is no virtue." Johnson and the Democrats blasted Goldwater as a trigger-happy extremist who was willing to drop bombs whenever and wherever necessary to defend the United States' interest.

Capitalizing on the country's growing unease with the war in Vietnam, the Johnson campaign developed a television commercial that many feel ushered in a new era of negative campaign advertising. The commercial showed a young girl standing in a field plucking petals from a daisy. A background voice recited an ominous countdown. Finally, the child evaporated in a mushroom cloud, and viewers were urged to vote for Johnson because, "The stakes are too high for you to stay home." Goldwater acknowledged later that the Johnson campaign effectively exploited the public's fear of his militancy. "In fact," he said with sardonic wit, "if I hadn't known Goldwater, I'd have voted against the s.o.b. myself."

Goldwater was defeated by Johnson in a landslide, carrying only Arizona and five southern states. He was unapologetic about his "extremism" speech, saying, "[P]rotecting freedom is what this country has been about. We'll go to any extent to protect it. I know people were thinking 'nuclear' when I said [extremism,] but . . . I think it had to be said, and I never lost any sleep over it." The final irony, of course, is that Johnson escalated the war in Vietnam, and it dragged on until 1973. According to Goldwa-ter, Johnson's Vietnam policy cost the country far more money and lives than if Goldwater, the supposed warmonger, had been elected.

After his loss to Johnson, Goldwater returned to Arizona and private life. Although his defeat was stunning, and he was treated like a pariah by other Republicans, he was undaunted. "Politics has never been the making or breaking point of my life," he said. "I worked hard to make Arizona a better state and my country a better country. If I failed, I've taken the criticism." He returned to politics in 1968 when he easily won the Senate seat vacated by retiring Democrat Carl Hayden. As an older and somewhat more moderate statesman, he relished his positions as chair of the Armed Services Committee, the Intelligence Committee, the Communications Subcommittee, and the Indian Affairs Committee. He continued to work against big government and for a free market economy. Summing up his opposition to federal control, he said, "All the great civilizations fell when people lost their initiative because government moved in to do things for them."

Goldwater served in the Senate for almost twenty additional years and left with his reputation and his convictions intact. "I was luckier than hell—politics is mostly luck—and I made a lot of friends," he said. "It would be hard for me to name an enemy in Congress. People disagreed with me violently, but we remained very good friends." In addition to a loyal conservative following, Goldwater's friends have included liberal Democrats Morris Udall, Daniel Inouye, EDWARD M. KENNEDY, Walter F. Mondale, and HUBERT H. HUMPHREY. One conservative Goldwater removed from his list of friends was RICHARD M. NIXON. Unable to accept Nixon's failings or forgive his deceptions during the WATERGATE crisis, Goldwater called Nixon "one of the saddest moments of my life. For twenty years or so, he and I worked hand in glove all over this land—not to help Nixon, not to help Goldwater, but to help the Republican Party and our country. But I was slow to see the real Nixon."

Goldwater retired from the Senate in 1987 and returned to his home in Paradise Valley, Arizona, overlooking Phoenix. He remained active, although slowed somewhat by arthritis. In the 1990s, he took up an unlikely new cause: gay rights. "The big thing is to make this country . . . quit discriminating against people just because they're gay," he asserted. "You don't have to agree with it, but they have a constitutional right to be gay. And that's what brings me into it." Always a strict constructionist when it comes to the Constitution, Goldwater feels that his defense of gay rights is consistent with his lifelong devotion to individual freedom. Then governor of Oregon Barbara Roberts said that because people do not expect someone like Goldwater to speak up for gay rights, they look at the issue in a new light when he does. "He causes people to focus on the real issue," she said. "Should the country that celebrates life, liberty and the pursuit of happiness allow discrimination for a group of Americans based on sexual preference?" Goldwater's position on gay rights puts the former conservative standard-bearer squarely in conflict with religious conservatives who oppose any effort to outlaw discrimination against homosexuals. See also GAY AND LESBIAN RIGHTS.

Goldwater is a member of many organizations, including the Royal Photographic Society, the American Association of Indian Affairs, and the Veterans of Foreign Wars. He is honorary cochairman of Americans against Discrimination, a lobbying effort aimed at securing gay rights. He and his second wife, Susan Goldwater, live in Paradise Valley.

GOOD BEHAVIOR 📖 Orderly and lawful action; conduct that is deemed proper for a peaceful and law-abiding individual. 📖

The definition of good behavior depends upon how the phrase is used. For example, what constitutes good behavior for an elected public officer may be quite different from that expected of a prisoner who wants to have his or her sentence reduced or to earn privileges.

The Constitution of the United States provides that federal judges shall hold their offices during good behavior, which means that they cannot be discharged but can be IMPEACHED for misconduct.

GOOD CAUSE 📖 Legally adequate or substantial grounds or reason to take a certain action. 📖

The term *good cause* is a relative one and is dependent upon the circumstances of each individual case. For example, a party in a legal ACTION who wants to do something after a particular STATUTE OF LIMITATIONS has expired must show good cause, or justification for needing additional time. A serious illness or accident might, for example, constitute good cause.

An employee is said to be discharged for good cause if the reasons for the termination are work related. However, if the employer simply did not like the employee's personality, this would not ordinarily constitute good cause, unless the employee held a position, such as a salesperson, for which a likable personality was required.

GOOD FAITH 📖 Honesty; a sincere intention to deal fairly with others. 📖

Good faith is an abstract and comprehensive term that encompasses a sincere belief or motive without any MALICE or the desire to DEFRAUD others. It derives from the translation of the Latin term *bona fide*, and courts use the two terms interchangeably.

The term *good faith* is used in many areas of the law but has special significance in commercial law. A good faith purchaser for VALUE is protected by the UNIFORM COMMERCIAL CODE, which every state has adopted. Under sections 1-201(9) and 2-403 of the code, a merchant may keep possession of goods that were bought from a seller who did not have TITLE to the goods, if the merchant can show he or she was a good faith purchaser for value. To meet this test, the person must be a merchant, must have demonstrated honesty in the conduct of the transaction concerned, and must have observed reasonable commercial standards of fair dealing in the trade. A buyer would likely meet these requirements if the purchase proceeded in the ordinary course of business. If, on the other hand, the purchase took place under unusual or suspicious circumstances, a court might conclude that the buyer lacked good faith.

Where a nonmerchant purchases property that the seller lacks LEGAL TITLE to convey, the issue of good faith is known both as the INNOCENT PURCHASER doctrine and as the bona fide purchaser doctrine. If the purchaser acquires the property by an honest CONTRACT or agreement and without knowledge of any defect in the title of the seller, or means of knowledge sufficient to charge the buyer with such knowledge, the purchaser is deemed innocent.

In both commercial and noncommercial law, persons who in good faith pay a fraudulent seller valuable CONSIDERATION for PROPERTY are protected from another person who claims legal title to the property. If a court establishes the purchaser's good faith defense, the person who claims title has recourse only against the fraudulent seller. Strong PUBLIC POLICY is behind the good faith defense. Good faith doctrines enhance the flow of goods in commerce, as under them, buyers are not required, in the ordinary course of business, to go to extraordinary efforts to determine whether sellers actually have good title. A purchaser can move quickly to close a deal with the knowledge that a fraudulent seller and a legitimate titleholder will have to sort the issue out in court. Of course, the purchaser will be required to demonstrate to the court evidence of good faith.

Good faith is also central to the COMMERCIAL PAPER (CHECKS, DRAFTS, PROMISSORY NOTES, CERTIFICATES OF DEPOSIT) concept of a HOLDER IN DUE COURSE. A holder is a person who takes an instrument, such as a check, subject to the reasonable belief that it will be paid and that there are no legal reasons why payment will not occur. If the holder has taken the check for value and in good faith believes the check to be good, she or he is a holder in due course, with sole right to recover payment. If, on the other hand, the holder accepts a check that has been dishonored (stamped with terms such as "insufficient funds," "account closed," and "payment stopped"), she or he has knowledge that something is wrong with the check and therefore cannot allege the check was accepted in the good faith belief that it was valid.

In LABOR LAW, the National Labor Relations Act of 1935 (29 U.S.C.A. § 151 et seq.) mandates good faith bargaining by every union and employer in order to reach agreement. In corporate law, the BUSINESS JUDGMENT RULE is based on good faith. This principle makes officers, directors, managers, and other AGENTS of a CORPORATION immune from liability to the corporation for losses incurred in corporate transactions that are within their authority and power to make, when sufficient evidence demonstrates that those transactions were made in good faith. As in commercial law, the use of good faith in this case enhances corporate business practices, as agents of a corporation are free to act quickly, decisively, and sometimes wrongly to advance the interests of the corporation. Good faith insulates corporate officers from disgruntled shareholders.

GOODS 📖 Items; CHATTELS; things; any PERSONAL PROPERTY. 📖

Goods is a term of flexible context and meaning and extends to all tangible items.

GOOD SAMARITAN DOCTRINE 📖 A principle of TORT law that provides that a person who sees another individual in imminent and serious danger or peril cannot be charged with NEGLIGENCE if that first person attempts to aid or rescue the injured party, provided the attempt is not made recklessly. 📖

The Good Samaritan doctrine is used by rescuers to avoid civil liability for injuries arising from their negligence. Its purpose is to encourage emergency assistance by removing the threat of LIABILITY for damage done by the assistance. However, the assistance must be reasonable; a rescuer cannot benefit from the Good Samaritan doctrine if the assistance is reckless or grossly negligent.

Three key elements support a successful invocation of the Good Samaritan doctrine: (1) the care rendered was performed as the result of the emergency, (2) the initial emergency or injury was not caused by the person invoking the defense, and (3) the emergency care was not given in a grossly negligent or reckless manner.

Assume that a person has slipped on ice and broken a vertebra. The victim is unconscious, the accident has occurred in a desolate area, and the weather is dangerously cold. A passerby finds the injured person and moves the person to warmth and safety, but in the process aggravates the spinal injury. In a civil suit by the victim seeking damages for the additional injury, the passerby may successfully defeat the claims under the Good Samaritan doctrine.

The Good Samaritan doctrine is also used as a defense by persons who act to prevent or contain property damage. Assume that a passerby notices a fire has started just outside a cabin in the wilderness. If the passerby breaks into the cabin to look for a fire extinguisher, the passerby will not be liable for damage resulting from the forced entry. However, if the passerby runs down the cabin with a bulldozer to extinguish the fire, this will probably be considered grossly negligent or reckless, and the Good Samaritan doctrine will not provide protection from a civil suit for damages to the cabin.

The line separating negligence from GROSS NEGLIGENCE or RECKLESSNESS is often thin. *Hardingham v. United Counseling Service of Bennington County*, 672 A. 2d 480 (Vt. 1995), illustrates the negligent acts that the Good Samaritan doctrine protects. In this case, the plaintiff, David Hardingham, sued United Counseling Service (UCS) when he became blind after drinking windshield wiper fluid. Hardingham, a recovering alcoholic, was employed by UCS as an emergency services counselor. When Hardingham began drinking again, employees of UCS went to his apartment and discovered him in an inebriated condition. During their visit, they saw Hardingham drink windshield wiper fluid. They called the police, who took Hardingham

The Good Samaritan doctrine holds that a passerby who attempts to revive an unconscious person by performing CPR cannot be held liable for unintentional damage to the victim.

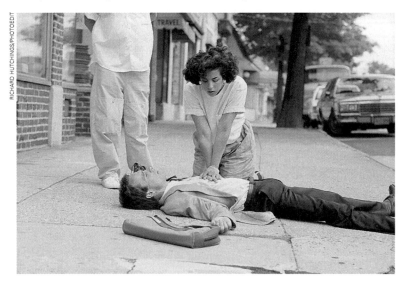

RICHARD HUTCHINGS/PHOTOEDIT

to a hospital. At the hospital, none of the UCS workers informed medical authorities that Hardingham had drunk the dangerous fluid. Doctors did not learn until the next day that Hardingham had overdosed on methanol, a component of windshield wiper fluid, and Hardingham eventually lost his sight.

Hardingham never got a chance to present his case to a JURY. The Chittenden Superior Court granted SUMMARY JUDGMENT to UCS, holding that there was insufficient evidence to support an allegation of gross negligence by the organization. The Supreme Court of Vermont affirmed this decision. According to the court, the actions of the defendants "probably saved plaintiff's life." Although the defendants may have been negligent in failing to disclose that Hardingham had swallowed enough methanol to threaten his life, "no reasonable person could conclude that defendants showed indifference to plaintiff or failed to exercise even a slight degree of care."

Justice John Dooley dissented, arguing that the case presented a QUESTION OF FACT for a jury to decide. The defendants "failed to tell the emergency room physician the most significant fact that wasn't obvious from plaintiff's condition—that plaintiff had consumed windshield wiper fluid." Dooley lamented that "the greatest difficulty plaintiff faces in this case is to persuade us to accept that 'good samaritans' should ever be liable."

Section 324 of the Second Restatement of Torts describes the Good Samaritan doctrine in an inverse fashion. According to section 324, a person is subject to liability for physical harm resulting from the failure to exercise reasonable care if the failure increases the risk of harm, if the rescuer has a duty to render care, or if others are relying on the rescuer.

Many states are content to follow the Good Samaritan doctrine through their COMMON LAW or through similar previous cases. Some states have general statutes mandating the doctrine. Utah, for example, has a Good Samaritan act, which provides in part that

> [a] person who renders emergency care at or near the scene of, or during an emergency, gratuitously and in good faith, is not liable for any civil damages or penalties as a result of any act or omission by the person rendering the emergency care, unless the person is grossly negligent or caused the emergency. (Utah Code Ann. § 78-11-22).

Some states have enacted statutes that protect specific emergency care or assistance. Indiana, for example, protects the emergency care of veterinarians (Ind. Code § 15-5-1.1-31). Alabama provides IMMUNITY to those who assist or advise in the mitigation of the effects of the discharge of hazardous materials (Ala. Code § 6-5-332.1). Some states also provide protection to those participating in the cleanup of oil spills. In 1990, Congress passed the Oil Pollution Act (Pub. L. No. 101-380, 33 U.S.C.A. §§ 2701–2761 [1994]), which gave immunity from liability to persons who participate in oil cleanup efforts. Like any Good Samaritan law, the statute does not protect a person who is grossly negligent or reckless.

GOOD WILL The favorable reputation and clientele of an established and well-run business.

The value of good will is ordinarily determined as the amount a purchaser will pay for a business beyond the monetary value of its TANGIBLE property and money owed to it.

Good will is regarded as a PROPERTY interest in and of itself, although it exists only in connection with other property, such as the name or location of the operation. Good will exists even in a situation where the business is not operating at a profit. Certain courts refuse to recognize good will that arises out of the personal qualities of the owner. For example, a physician cannot sell good will when selling the office building and other physical assets of his or her practice, since the physician's reputation is based solely upon personal professional abilities.

A transfer of good will from one individual to another can take place as a bequest in a WILL or through a SALE. Ordinarily, when an individual sells the property to which good will is connected, it is automatically transferred to the buyer. However, the buyer and seller can alter this arrangement or specify details in their sale agreement. A former owner of a business has no right to interfere with the subsequent owner's enjoyment of good will following a sale transferring good will, even in the event that the sales CONTRACT does not specifically so indicate. In the event that the purchaser wants to prevent the seller from establishing a competing business in the same vicinity, the purchaser must bargain for such a provision in the contract. An agreement not to compete, sometimes called RESTRICTIVE COVENANT, differs from good will. However, an individual who sells the good will of his or her business is not permitted to solicit former clients or customers or lead them to believe that he or she is still running the same business.

GOVERNMENT INSTRUMENTALITY DOCTRINE 📖 A rule that provides that any organization run by a branch of the government is immune from TAXATION. 📖

GOVERNMENT NATIONAL MORTGAGE ASSOCIATION The Government National Mortgage Association (GNMA), also known as Ginnie Mae, is a CORPORATION wholly owned by the federal government. Created by the Housing and Urban Development Act of 1968, 825 Stat. 491, GNMA is designed to support the federal government's housing programs by establishing a secondary market for the sale and purchase of residential MORTGAGES.

During the late 1960s, the federal government expressed concern that available credit for low-income housing was insufficient to meet the growing demand. In response GNMA began issuing certificates to obtain additional funds for government-backed low-income mortgages. GNMA certificates entitle their holders to receive a portion of the income derived from a residential mortgage pool approved by the government.

A residential mortgage pool consists of a group of mortgages that are issued by private lenders, including commercial banks and savings and loan institutions. The mortgages in this group have similar terms and interest rates. If the pool is approved by GNMA, it is placed into a trust, from which it is sold to investors by securities dealers. Some pools include more than one thousand residential mortgages.

The revenue generated by the sale of these pools helps make additional credit available for low-income residential mortgages insured by government agencies such as the Federal Housing Administration (FHA), the VETERANS ADMINISTRATION (VA), and the Farmers Home Administration. The Department of HOUSING AND URBAN DEVELOPMENT, which is responsible for administering GNMA, oversees the entire program.

GNMA mortgage pools are considered stable investments by securities dealers and investors alike. The timely payment of principal and interest on each mortgage is guaranteed by GNMA and the full faith and credit of the federal government. GNMA enjoys unlimited authority to borrow funds from the U.S. Treasury in order to make good on this guarantee.

By developing a stable and viable secondary market for government-backed residential mortgages, GNMA has originated more than $1 trillion in securities trading. The revenue generated through this secondary market has enabled more than 19 million low-income families to purchase homes, and provided the U.S. Treasury with annual receipts sometimes exceeding $400 million.

In 1994 President BILL CLINTON outlined the National Homeowners Strategy, which spurred GNMA to undertake an intense and sweeping review of its practices and programs. In addition, GNMA has been working to satisfy internal mandates that require it to enhance its customer service, improve its relations with other businesses, and better market its securities. GNMA has incorporated the latest technology and automation to achieve these goals, and hired consultants to market its residential mortgage pools.

GOVERNMENT PRINTING OFFICE
Since the mid–nineteenth century, one government establishment has existed to fill the printing, binding, and distribution needs of the federal government. Established on June 23, 1860, by Congressional Joint Resolution No. 25, the Government Printing Office (GPO) has provided publication supplies and services to the U.S. CONGRESS, the executive departments, and all other agencies of the federal government. The definition of the duties set forth in the 1860 resolution has stayed essentially the same over the years, with only one amendment in all that time, 44 U.S.C.A. § 101 et seq.

The GPO is overseen by the Congressional Joint Committee on Printing. The head of the GPO works under the title *public printer* and is appointed by the president of the United States with the consent of the Senate. The public printer is also legally required to be a "practical printer versed in the art of bookbinding" (44 U.S.C.A. § 301).

The GPO uses a variety of printing and binding processes, including electronic photo composition; letterpress printing; Linotype and hand composition; photopolymer platemaking; offset photography; stripping, platemaking, and presswork; and manual and machine bookbinding. The GPO also provides supplies like blank paper and ink to federal agencies, prepares catalogs, and sells and distributes some publications to civilians.

The GPO offers catalogs that detail publications available to the public. All catalogs are available from the superintendent of documents at the GPO. The *GPO Sales Publications Reference File*, which is issued biweekly on magnetic tape, lists the author, the title, and subject information for each new publication. A more comprehensive listing, the *Monthly Catalog of U.S. Government Publications*, serves as an index to all the publications handled by the GPO.

Government Printing Office

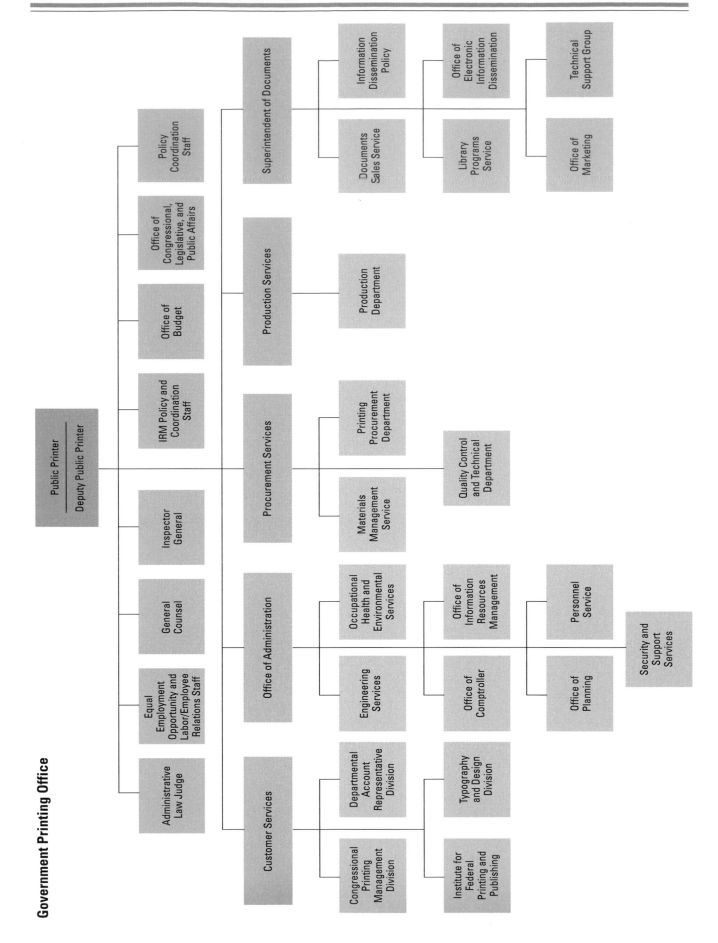

The GPO also offers two free catalogs for people who are interested in new or popular publications: *U.S. Government Books* and *New Books*. The first lists the titles of best-selling government publications, and the second is a bimonthly listing of government publications for sale.

The approximately twenty thousand publications listed in these catalogs can be purchased by mail from the GPO's superintendent of documents. In addition, the books and catalogs published by the GPO can be purchased at the approximately two dozen GPO bookstores open to the public. Most of the bookstores are located in government hub cities such as Washington, D.C., Atlanta, Chicago, Dallas, Houston, and Los Angeles. Publications are also available for public perusal at select depository libraries around the United States.

Owing to the large volume of documents produced by the various federal agencies, the GPO does not handle 100 percent of the printing and binding services for the government. In some instances, the GPO takes bids from commercial suppliers and awards contracts to those with the lowest bids. From there, the GPO serves as a connection between ordering agencies and contractors. The booklet *How to Do Business with the Government Printing Office* provides a background and instructions for contracting with the GPO and submitting bids. The booklet can be requested from any GPO regional printing procurement office. Any printing or binding contract inquiries can be directed to one of these thirteen offices, located in Atlanta; Boston; Chicago; Columbus, Ohio; Dallas; Denver; Hampton, Virginia; Los Angeles; New York; Philadelphia; St. Louis; San Francisco; and Seattle.

GRAB LAW State statutory provisions and COMMON-LAW principles that govern the aggressive use of legal and equitable remedies, such as ATTACHMENT and GARNISHMENT, by CREDITORS to collect payment from DEBTORS.

State laws governing debtor and creditor transactions emphasize the importance of prompt action by creditors to ensure payment of the debtor's outstanding debts. For example, the first creditor to attach the debtor's property is most likely to be paid. The quicker the creditor acts to seize or "grab" the debtor's assets, the greater the chance the creditor's claims will be satisfied. As a result, grab law has come to designate aggressive, but legal, methods used by creditors to enforce their rights to payment against delinquent debtors.

GRACE PERIOD In INSURANCE law, a period beyond the due date of a premium (usually thirty or thirty-one days) during which the insurance is continued in force and during which the payment may be made to keep the policy in good standing. The grace period for payment of the premium does not provide free insurance or operate to continue the policy in force after it expires by agreement of the parties. *Grace period* may also refer to a period of time provided for in a loan agreement during which DEFAULT will not occur even though a payment is overdue.

GRADUATED TAX Tax structured so that the rate increases as the amount of income of taxpayer increases.

GRAFT A colloquial term referring to the unlawful acquisition of public money through questionable and improper transactions with public officials.

Graft is the personal gain or advantage earned by an individual at the expense of others as a result of the exploitation of the singular status of, or an influential relationship with, another who has a position of public trust or confidence. The advantage or gain is accrued without any exchange of legitimate compensatory services.

Behavior that leads to graft includes BRIBERY and dishonest dealings in the performance of public or official acts. Graft usually implies the existence of THEFT, corruption, FRAUD, and the lack of integrity that is expected in any transaction involving a public official.

GRANDFATHER CLAUSE A portion of a statute that provides that the law is not applicable in certain circumstances due to pre-existing facts.

Grandfather clauses, which were originally intended to prevent black people from voting, were named for provisions adopted by the constitutions of some states. Such amendments sought to interfere with an individual's right to vote by setting forth difficult requirements. For example, common requirements were ownership of a large amount of land or the ability to read and write portions of the state and federal constitutions. The name *grandfather clause* arose from the exceptions that were made for veterans of the Civil War. If the veterans were qualified to vote prior to 1866, their descendants were also qualified. Thus, in effect, if a person's grandfather could vote, he could vote without further restrictions.

These statutes accomplished precisely what was intended, since nearly all slaves and their descendants were disqualified from voting because they could not satisfy the statutory requirements.

In the 1915 case of *Guinn v. United States*, 238 U.S. 347, 35 S. Ct. 926, 59 L. Ed. 1340, the Supreme Court of the United States examined a grandfather clause that was added to the Oklahoma constitution shortly following its admission to the Union. The 1910 constitutional amendment required that prospective voters pass a literacy test in order to qualify to vote. However, anyone who was entitled to vote on January 1, 1866, or any time earlier under any form of government, or who at that time lived in a foreign country, was exempt from satisfying the literacy test requirement. The lineal descendants of such exempted persons also were exempt from such a requirement. In reality, the amendment recreated and perpetuated the very conditions that the FIFTEENTH AMENDMENT was intended to destroy, even though race was never mentioned as a voter qualification.

The Court held that the clause was in violation of the Fifteenth Amendment, which states that "the right of citizens of the United States to vote shall not be denied or abridged by the United States or by any State on account of race, color, or previous condition of servitude." Oklahoma argued that states had the power to set forth voter qualifications. Therefore, the statute in controversy did not violate the Fifteenth Amendment since race was not mentioned as a voter qualification. The Supreme Court was in agreement that states have the right to determine who is qualified to vote; however, they are permitted to do so only within constitutional limits. The limit that proscribes consideration of the race of voters extends to sophisticated as well as simpleminded discrimination, and equality under the law cannot be based upon whether a person's grandfather was a free man.

Oklahoma undertook to change its law following this decision. The revised statute said that everyone who was able to vote as a result of the grandfather clause automatically continued to be eligible and those who had been denied VOTING RIGHTS were given twelve days in 1916 to register to vote. If they were out of the county where they resided or if they were prevented from registering by sickness or unavoidable circumstances, they were given an additional fifty days in 1916 to register. After that time black persons who tried to register to vote were turned away, since the time to register outside the grandfather clause had ended in 1916.

In the 1939 case of *Lane v. Wilson*, 307 U.S. 268, 59 S. Ct. 872, 83 L. Ed. 1281, the Supreme Court rejected Oklahoma's new scheme, calling it another example of an attempt by a state to thwart equality in the right to vote regardless of race or color. The Court ruled that the proposed remedy, in the form of such a limited registration period, was inadequate. A group of citizens who lacked the habits and traditions of political independence deserved a greater opportunity to register to vote.

The term *grandfather clause* in its current application refers to a legislative provision that permits an exemption based upon a preexisting condition. For example, through the application of grandfather clauses, certain prerogatives are extended to those regularly engaged in a particular profession, occupation, or business that is regulated by statute or ordinance. Such a clause might allow an individual, who has been in continuous practice in a particular profession for a specific period, to circumvent certain licensing requirements.

GRAND JURY 📖 A panel of citizens that is convened by a court to decide whether it is appropriate for the government to indict (proceed with a prosecution against) someone suspected of a crime. 📖

An American institution since the colonial days, the grand jury has long played an important role in CRIMINAL LAW. The FIFTH AMENDMENT to the U.S. Constitution says that a person suspected of a federal crime cannot be tried until a grand jury has determined that there is enough reason to charge the person. Review by a grand jury is meant to protect suspects from inappropriate prosecution by the government, since grand jurors are drawn from the general population. It has been criticized at times as failing to serve its purpose.

The grand jury system originated in twelfth-century England, when King HENRY II enacted the Assize of Clarendon in order to take control of the courts from the Catholic Church and local nobility. The proclamation said that a person could not be tried as a criminal unless a certain number of local citizens appeared in court to accuse her or him of specific crimes. This group of citizens, known as the grand ASSIZE, was very powerful: it had the authority to identify suspects, present evidence personally held by individual jurors, and determine whether to make an accusation. Trial was by ORDEAL, so accusation meant that conviction was very likely. (Trial by ordeal involved subjecting the defendant to some physical test to determine guilt or innocence. For example, in ordeal by water, a suspect was thrown into deep water: if she or he floated, the verdict was guilty; if the suspect sank, the verdict was innocent.) See also CLARENDON, CONSTITUTIONS OF.

The grand assize was not designed to protect suspects, and it changed very little over the next five hundred years. Then, in 1681, its reputation began to change. An English grand jury denied King Charles II's wish for a public hearing in the cases of two Protestants accused of TREASON for opposing his attempts to reestablish the Catholic Church. The grand jury held a private session and refused to indict the two suspects. This gave the grand jury new respect as a means of protection against government bullying (although ultimately in those particular cases, the king found a different grand jury willing to indict the suspects).

After this small act of rebellion, the grand jury became known as a potential protector of people facing baseless or politically motivated prosecution. The early colonists brought this concept to America, and by 1683, all colonies had some type of grand jury system in place. Over the next century, grand juries became more sympathetic to those who resisted British rule. In 1765, for example, a Boston grand jury refused to indict leaders of protests against the STAMP ACT, a demonstration of resistance to colonialism.

The grand jury was considered important enough to incorporate it into the U.S. Constitution created after the Revolutionary War, and has remained largely unchanged. Grand juries are used in the federal and most state courts. Federal grand juries use a standard set of rules. States are free to formulate their own pretrial requirements, and vary greatly in the number of grand jurors they seat, the limits placed on the deliberations of those jurors, and whether a grand jury is used at all. FEDERAL COURTS use a grand jury that consists of twenty-three citizens but can operate with a QUORUM of sixteen.

Twelve jurors' votes are required for an INDICTMENT. States use a grand jury consisting of as few as five but no more than twenty-three members. Grand juries are chosen from lists of qualified state residents of legal age, who have not been convicted of a crime, and who are not biased against the subject of the investigation.

The usual role of a grand jury is to review the adequacy of EVIDENCE presented by the PROSECUTOR and then decide whether to indict the suspect. In some cases, a grand jury decides which charges are appropriate. Generally, grand jurors do not lead investigations, but can question WITNESSES to satisfy themselves that evidence is adequate and usable. The prosecutor prepares a BILL OF INDICTMENT (a list explaining the case and possible charges) and presents evidence to the grand jury. The jurors can call witnesses, including the target of the investigation, without revealing the nature of the case. They call witnesses by using a document called a SUBPOENA. A person who refuses to answer the grand jury's questions can be punished for CONTEMPT of court. However, no witness need answer incriminating questions unless that witness has been granted IMMUNITY. In federal courts, the jurors may accept HEARSAY and other evidence that is normally not admissible at trial.

If the grand jury agrees that there is sufficient reason to charge the suspect with a crime, it returns an indictment carrying the words *true bill*. If there is insufficient evidence to satisfy the grand jury, it returns an indictment carrying the words *no bill*.

Hearsay Evidence: Admissible before a Grand Jury?

The rules of evidence prohibit the introduction of most hearsay evidence in a criminal trial. (Hearsay is evidence given by a person concerning what someone else said outside of court.) However, when Frank Costello, alias Francisco Castaglia, a notorious organized crime figure of the 1940s and 1950s, argued that his conviction for federal income tax evasion should be overturned because the grand jury that indicted him heard only hearsay evidence, the Supreme Court rejected his claim (*Costello v. United States,* 350 U.S. 359, 76 S. Ct. 406, 100 L. Ed. 397 [1956]).

Prior to his trial, Costello asked to inspect the grand jury record. He claimed there could have been no legal or competent evidence before the grand jury that indicted him. The judge refused the request. At trial, Costello's attorneys established that three investigating officers were the only witnesses to testify before the grand jury. These officers summarized the vast amount of evidence compiled by their investigation and introduced computations showing, if correct, that Costello had received far greater income than he had reported. Their summaries clearly constituted hearsay, since the three officers had no firsthand knowledge of the transactions upon which their computations were based. Therefore, Costello alleged a violation of the Fifth Amendment, and asked that hearsay evidence be barred from grand jury proceedings.

Justice Hugo L. Black, in his majority opinion, rejected these claims, noting that "neither the Fifth Amendment nor any other constitutional provision prescribes the kind of evidence upon which grand juries must act."

Seldom do grand juries issue documents. However, when given a judge's permission to do so, they may use a report to denounce the conduct of a government figure or organization against whom an indictment is not justified or allowed. This occurred in 1973, when U.S. district court judge John J. Sirica allowed the grand jury investigating the WATERGATE scandals to criticize President RICHARD NIXON's conduct in covering up the involvement of his administration in the June 17, 1972, burglary of the Democratic National Committee headquarters in the Watergate Apartment and Hotel complex. The judge recommended that the report be forwarded to the House Judiciary Committee to assist in proceedings to IMPEACH the president. Many states allow the issuance of grand jury reports, but limit their use: the target must be a public official or institution who can be denounced only where statutory authority exists, and the resulting document can be released publicly only with a judge's approval.

In February 1996, for the first time in history, a first lady of the United States was required to appear before a grand jury. HILLARY RODHAM CLINTON testified for four hours before a federal grand jury on the disappearance and reappearance of billing records related to her representation of a failed investment institution that was under scrutiny when she was an attorney in Arkansas. Her testimony was part of the Whitewater investigation, which examined past financial dealings of Hillary Rodham Clinton, President BILL CLINTON, and others.

Critics have complained that the grand jury offers witnesses and suspected criminals insufficient protection. The cause of the controversy is the set of rules that govern the operation of federal grand juries. A prosecutor (a public attorney whose job is to prove a defendant's guilt) manages the work of the grand jury, which is to investigate and determine the adequacy of evidence against a suspect. Grand juries have broad powers in order to accomplish their goals, and they meet in secret. Critics say this combination leaves room for abuse by prosecutors.

Among a federal grand jury's powers is the authority to call witnesses, including suspects, without identifying the exact nature of the investigation. Witnesses cannot have an attorney present when they testify. Prosecutors are required to present, on behalf of the suspect, information that they feel is exculpatory (so strong that it could create a REASONABLE DOUBT that the suspect committed the crime). In arguing that the suspect should be charged, prosecutors may make arguments and use information that would not be ADMISSIBLE during a trial. A formal record of federal grand jury proceedings is not usually provided to the suspect even after indictment. Among the actions a grand jury cannot take are gathering evidence solely for a civil, or noncriminal, lawsuit, and obtaining evidence against someone who has already been indicted.

Critics of the current system claim that justice is ill served by these rules. They say that ambitious prosecutors can misuse the powers of a nonprofessional grand jury to harass, trap, or wear down witnesses. For example, activists who opposed the Vietnam War during the 1960s and 1970s accused the Justice Department of abusing the grand jury system as it searched for information about political dissidents. The activists believed that the department used the power and secrecy of the grand jury to intimidate witnesses and fish for evidence. Many other groups, such as the news media, the business community, and organized labor, have also criticized the institution.

Supporters of the current system say that the secrecy of the grand jury's work prevents suspects from escaping, prevents attempts to influence the jurors, prevents the coaching or intimidation of witnesses, encourages candid TESTIMONY, and protects the PRIVACY of innocent suspects who are later cleared. Regarding witnesses' lack of legal representation, supporters of the status quo point out that delay, disruption, and rehearsed testimony would lessen the efficiency of the grand jury's work and would result in a minitrial. Similar arguments have been made against limiting evidence that would not be admissible at trial. In addition, federal courts have held that because the rights of a suspect are adequately protected during trial, where the strength or weakness of evidence determines the VERDICT, no examination of grand jury indictment proceedings is necessary.

Grand juries also face criticism in the area of jury selection, especially with high-profile cases. Criticism focuses on bias and a lack of balance in the selection process. The requirement that grand juries be unbiased has evolved since the indictment of Vice President AARON BURR as a traitor in 1807, when he insisted that the evidence against him be heard by an "impartial" jury as guaranteed in the SIXTH AMENDMENT to the Constitution. He successfully challenged many jurors on the all-Republican grand jury that had been selected. Burr was willing to

SHOULD THE GRAND JURY BE ABOLISHED?

Though the grand jury has existed in the United States since the colonial period, and the Fifth Amendment to the U.S. Constitution requires its use in federal criminal proceedings, it has come under increasing attack. Critics charge that it no longer serves the functions the Framers intended, and therefore should be abolished. Defenders admit there may be some problems with it today, but contend that these can be remedied.

Critics aim their attacks at both federal and state grand juries. They note that a grand jury has two functions. One is to review evidence of criminal wrongdoing and to issue an indictment if the evidence is sufficient. The other is to be an investigative arm of the government, helping the prosecutor gather evidence. Critics contend that in both areas contemporary grand juries have failed.

In reviewing evidence of criminal wrongdoing, a grand jury is supposed to act as a shield against ill-conceived or malicious prosecutions. Yet critics charge that grand juries typically rubber-stamp the prosecution's moves, indicting anyone the prosecutor cares to bring before it.

Historically the grand jury was not dominated by a professional prosecutor. Without a strong attorney leading the way, the grand jury was forced to be independent and diligent in reviewing evidence brought before it.

Critics note that many states abolished all or part of the grand jury's jurisdiction at the end of the nineteenth century, in large part because the process had come increasingly under the control of prosecutors. States acknowledged that a professional criminal prosecutor did not need a grand jury's assistance in the charging process. The prosecutor was capable of making an independent, disinterested review of the need to bring charges. Though forty-eight states have grand juries as part of their criminal justice system, many of these judicial bodies are now reserved for serious felonies, usually first-degree murder.

Those who favor abolition of the grand jury argue that the domination of the prosecutor has led to a passivity that destroys the legitimacy of the grand jury concept. Most grand jurors have little background in law and must rely on the prosecutor to educate them about the applicable law and help them apply the law. In addition, at the federal level, there are very complex criminal laws, like the Racketeer Influenced and Corrupt Organizations statute. Even lawyers find many of these laws difficult to fathom, yet grand jurors are expected to understand them and apply them to intricate fact situations. Not surprisingly, charge the critics, the grand jury tends to follow the prosecution's advice.

Critics point out that though the Fifth Amendment requires a grand jury indictment for all federal crimes, the accused may waive this requirement and accept charges filed by a prosecutor alone on all but capital crimes. Waivers are frequent, and most prosecutions of even serious offenses are initiated by federal prosecutors. Therefore, critics argue that it makes no sense to take additional time and money for a grand jury to convene and participate in a hollow ritual.

For its critics the grand jury has declined from a proactive community voice to a passive instrument of the prosecution. Though the U.S. Supreme Court may talk about the historic importance of the grand jury in Anglo-American justice, few academics defend the institution based on its current performance. Faced with this poor performance, the critics argue that abolition is the best course. It would make the prosecutor directly accountable for the charging decision and remove the illusion that grand jurors are in control.

Defenders of the grand jury acknowledge that there are problems with the modern system, but insist the grand jury is worth saving. Despite its shortcomings the grand jury still allows citizens to help make important community decisions. Though critics may deplore prosecutorial domination of grand juries, they overgeneralize when they call the grand juries rubber stamps for the state. Congress recognized the competency and importance of citizen input when, in the Organized Crime Control Act of 1970 (18 U.S.C.A. §§ 3332–3333), it authorized the creation of "special" grand juries to investigate organized crime, return indictments if warranted, and issue reports on the results of their investigations.

Supporters also believe that the critics overemphasize the importance of the grand jury in acting as a shield against government oppression. The key function of the grand jury is to enhance the legitimacy of the criminal charges that are returned. Prosecutors use the grand jury to gain community support for charges that might otherwise be perceived as based on racial bias, political motivation, or prosecutorial vindictiveness. A grand jury review may also help a prosecutor avoid bringing charges where the formal requisites of a crime are present but the community's moral sense would regard charges as unjust.

Some supporters of the grand jury admit that it could be improved by severing the close tie between prosecutor and jurors. They point out that Hawaii provides grand juries with their own attorney. Such a "grand jury counsel" provides independent legal advice and acts as a buffer between jurors and prosecutors. This, in turn, makes grand juries more independent and gives their indictments more credibility. Some scholars have argued that though using such a system nationwide would cost more, the added expense would be a small price to pay to reinvigorate the grand jury and restore it to its proper role as a voice of the community.

IN FOCUS

accept jurors who were familiar with some details of his famous case but claimed not to have drawn any conclusions about it. (Although he was indicted, Burr was eventually acquitted at trial.)

Today, an unbiased grand jury means one that comprises people who have no prior familiarity with the facts of the case. Critics of this requirement say that it greatly limits the quality of people who are chosen to sit, since many intelligent, engaged, and otherwise ideal candidates for a grand jury also follow the news. On June 24, 1994, a California state judge dismissed a grand jury that was considering whether to indict former athlete and media personality O. J. Simpson for the murder of his ex-wife and her friend. The judge was responding to concerns, of both the prosecutor and the defendant, that grand jurors had been exposed to PRETRIAL PUBLICITY that might prejudice them—such as transcripts of 911 calls made by Simpson's ex-wife after he broke down the back door to her house.

After numerous struggles to balance juries—including grand juries—racially and by gender, federal case law provides that "a defendant may challenge the array of grand jurors . . . on the ground that the grand jury was not selected, drawn or summoned in accordance with law, and may challenge an individual juror on the ground that the juror is not legally qualified" (*Estes v. United States*, 335 F.2d 609, *cert. denied*, 379 U.S. 964, 85 S. Ct. 656, 13 L. Ed. 2d 559).

There have been suggestions that the federal grand jury be abolished, but this action seems unlikely because it would change the Bill of Rights for the first time. In addition, the investigative and indicting roles of the courts have to be performed by some entity, and an alternative entity may be less desirable than the grand jury. Some states have abolished grand juries or provided alternatives. For example, in some states, prosecutors are allowed to file an INFORMATION, which is a formal list of charges, usually submitted with notice of some kind of PROBABLE CAUSE hearing.

Other suggestions for change at the federal level may experience more success. Among those promoted by the AMERICAN BAR ASSOCIATION and others are the following:

- Better instructions from judges to jurors about the grand jury's powers and its independence from prosecutors
- Reports by prosecutors on the performance of the grand jury system
- Increased access to grand jury transcripts for suspects who are eventually indicted
- Expanded safeguards against abuse of witnesses, including education about their rights and the presence of their attorneys
- Notification of targets of investigations that they are targets
- Optional rather than mandatory appearances by targets of investigations
- An end to the requirement that prosecutors present defense evidence, and replacement with a requirement that grand jurors be informed that the defense was not represented in the hearing.

GRAND LARCENY ▥ A category of LARCENY—the offense of illegally taking the property of another—in which the value of the property taken is greater than that set for PETIT LARCENY. ▥

At COMMON LAW, the punishment for grand larceny was death. Today, grand larceny is a statutory crime punished by a fine, imprisonment, or both.

GRANGER MOVEMENT The Granger Movement was begun in the late 1860s by farmers who called for government regulation of railroads and other industries whose prices and practices, they claimed, were monopolistic and unfair. Their efforts contributed to a growing public sentiment against monopolies, which culminated in the passage of the Sherman Act (or SHERMAN ANTI-TRUST ACT) of 1890, 15 U.S.C.A. §§ 1–7.

In 1867, the American farmer was in desperate straits. Needing better educational opportunities and protection from exorbitant prices charged by middlemen, the farmers decided to form an independent group to achieve their goals.

Oliver Hudson Kelley, a former employee of the Department of Agriculture, organized a group called the Patrons of Husbandry. Membership was open to both men and women, and each local group was known as a Grange. Each Grange chose officers, and the goal of each meeting was to present news of educational value to the farmer.

Kelley traveled across the country establishing Granges; he found his greatest support in Minnesota. The Granges soon evolved into the national Granger Movement. By 1873, all but four states had Granges.

The main problems confronting the Granger Movement concerned corporate ownership of grain elevators (used for the storage of crops) and railroads. These corporations charged high prices for the distribution and marketing of agricultural goods, and the farmer had no recourse but to pay. By 1873, the movement was becoming political, and the farmers formed an alliance, promising to support only political candidates who shared the interests of farmers; if that failed, they vowed to form their own parties.

Granger-supported candidates won political victories, and, as a result, much legislation protective of their interests was passed. Their biggest gain occurred in 1876, when the U.S. Supreme Court decreed in *Munn v. Illinois*, 94 U.S. (4 Otto.) 113, 24 L. Ed. 77, that states had the right to intervene in the regulation of public businesses. The law affected the prices of elevator charges, grain storage, and other services vital to the livelihood of the farmers.

In addition to political involvement, the Grangers established stores and cooperative elevators and employed the services of agents who secured special prices for the Grangers. These endeavors were not as successful as their previous undertakings, and the attempt to manufacture farm machinery depleted the finances of the movement. As a result, the Granger Movement began to wane in 1876.

See also AGRICULTURAL LAW.

GRANT To confer, give, or bestow. A gift of legal rights or privileges, or a recognition of asserted rights, as in treaty.

In the law of PROPERTY, the term *grant* can be used in a DEED to convey land, regardless of the number and types of rights conferred or the promises made by the transferor to the transferee. It is a comprehensive term that encompasses more specific words of transfer, such as ASSIGN, BARGAIN, and DEVISE.

A *public land grant* is a conveyance of ownership or other rights and privileges in publicly owned property to members of the general public who come under the qualifications of the statute that makes the land available. Such a grant is ordinarily noted in a public record, such as a CHARTER or PATENT. In order to properly trace the ownership of property, it is sometimes necessary to determine each successive owner following the first grant.

A *private grant* is a grant of PUBLIC LAND by a public official to a private individual as a type of reward or prize.

BIOGRAPHY

Ulysses Simpson Grant

"THE WAR IS OVER—THE REBELS ARE OUR COUNTRYMEN AGAIN."

GRANT, ULYSSES SIMPSON Ulysses Simpson Grant, originally known as Hiram Ulysses Grant, was a U.S. general, the commander of the Union army during the last part of the Civil War, and the president of the United States from 1869 to 1877. During his presidency Grant's reputation was tarnished by political corruption and scandal in his administration. Though he was never personally involved with any scandal, his failure to choose trustworthy advisers hurt his presidency.

Grant was born April 27, 1822, in Point Pleasant, Ohio. Raised in nearby Georgetown, he was educated at local and boarding schools. In 1839 he accepted an appointment to the Army's military academy at West Point, though he did not intend to become a soldier. The appointment allowed him to obtain the education he could not afford otherwise. He graduated in 1843 and began his military career with a tour of duty during the Mexican War of 1846–48, in which he distinguished himself in battle. After the war he was assigned to Fort Humboldt, California. During his time in California, Grant became lonely, and it has been alleged he had a drinking problem. He resigned his commission in 1854 and made several unsuccessful attempts at alternative careers, including farming and real estate. In 1860 he moved to Galena, Illinois, where he worked in his father's leather goods store.

With the outbreak of the Civil War in 1861, Grant returned to the military as a colonel in the Illinois Volunteers. He soon was promoted to brigadier general. Grant's first major victory came in February 1862, when his troops captured Forts Henry and Donelson, Tennessee, forcing General Simon B. Buckner, of the Confederacy, to accept unconditional surrender. As a result Grant was promoted to major general.

Grant fought in the Battles of Shiloh and Corinth before forcing the surrender of Vicksburg, Mississippi, on July 4, 1862. In 1863 his forces triumphed over those of General Braxton Bragg, of the Confederacy, at Chattanooga, Tennessee.

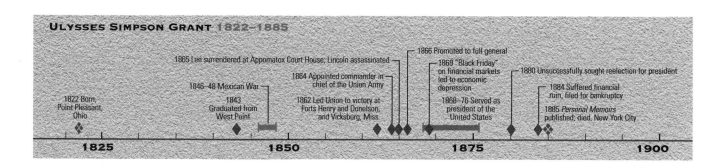

ULYSSES SIMPSON GRANT 1822–1885

1822 Born, Point Pleasant, Ohio

1843 Graduated from West Point

1846–48 Mexican War

1862 Led Union to victory at Forts Henry and Donelson, and Vicksburg, Miss.

1864 Appointed commander in chief of the Union Army

1865 Lee surrendered at Appomatox Court House; Lincoln assassinated

1866 Promoted to full general

1868–76 Served as president of the United States

1869 "Black Friday" on financial markets led to economic depression

1880 Unsuccessfully sought reelection for president

1884 Suffered financial ruin, filed for bankruptcy

1885 *Personal Memoirs* published; died, New York City

1825   1850   1875   1900

Grant's leadership was welcomed by President ABRAHAM LINCOLN, who had endured a succession of commanders of the Union army who refused to wage an aggressive war. In March 1864 Lincoln promoted Grant to lieutenant general and gave him command over the entire Union army. In that year Grant scored another major military triumph. He commanded the Army of the Potomac against the forces of General Robert E. Lee, of the Confederacy, in the Wilderness Campaign, a series of violent battles that took place in Virginia. Battles at Spotsylvania, Cold Harbor, Petersburg, and Richmond produced heavy Union casualties, but Lee's smaller army was devastated. On April 9, 1865, at Appomattox Courthouse, Lee surrendered his forces, signaling an end to the Civil War.

After the war Grant enforced the Reconstruction laws of Congress in the Southern military divisions. President ANDREW JOHNSON appointed him secretary of war in 1867, but Grant soon had a falling out with the president. Grant aligned himself with the Republican party and became its presidential candidate in 1868. He defeated Democrat Horatio Seymour, former governor of New York, by a small popular vote margin. At age forty-six, he was the youngest man yet elected president. He was reelected in 1872, easily defeating Horace Greeley.

Though Grant's intentions were good, it soon became clear that his political and administrative skills did not match his military acumen. Despite his interest in CIVIL SERVICE reform, he followed his predecessors in using political patronage to fill positions in his administration. Many of his appointees were willing to use their office for personal profit.

Grant's reputation was first tarnished in 1869 when financiers Jay Gould and James Fisk attempted to corner the gold market and drive up the price. Their plan depended on keeping the federal government's gold supply off the market. They used political influence within the Grant administration to further their scheme. When Grant found out about it, he ordered $4 million of government gold sold on the market. On September 24, 1869, known as Black Friday, the price of gold plummeted, which caused a financial panic.

During Grant's second term, more scandal erupted. Vice President Schuyler Colfax was accused of taking bribes in the CRÉDIT MOBILIER SCANDAL, which involved a diversion of profits from the Union Pacific Railroad. And Grant's private secretary, Orville E. Babcock, was one of 238 persons indicted in the Whiskey Ring CONSPIRACY, which sought to defraud the federal government of liquor taxes. Babcock was acquitted after Grant testified on his behalf. Finally, Grant accepted the resignation of Secretary of War William W. Belknap shortly before Belknap was IMPEACHED on charges of accepting a bribe.

In domestic policy Grant attempted to resolve the tensions between North and South. He supported AMNESTY for Confederate leaders, and he tried to enforce federal CIVIL RIGHTS legislation that was intended to protect the newly freed slaves. In foreign policy he settled long-standing difficulties with Great Britain, in the 1871 Treaty of Washington.

After leaving office in 1877, Grant spent his time traveling and writing. He made a world tour in 1878 and 1879. In 1880 he unsuccessfully sought the Republican party's nomination for president. In 1881 he bought a home in New York City and became involved in the investment firm of Grant and Ward, in which his son, Ulysses S. Grant, Jr., was a partner. He invested his personal fortune with the firm and encouraged others to invest as well. In 1884 the firm collapsed. Partner Ferdinand Ward had swindled all the funds from the investors. Grant was forced to file for BANKRUPTCY.

Needing money, Grant contracted with his friend Mark Twain to write his memoirs. Despite the debilitations of throat cancer, Grant was able to complete his *Personal Memoirs* shortly before his death on July 23, 1885, in Mount McGregor, New York. His memoir was well received and is now recognized as a classic military autobiography. Grant and his wife, Julia Dent Grant, are buried in Grant's Tomb, in New York City, which was proclaimed a national memorial in 1959.

GRANTEE An individual to whom a transfer or CONVEYANCE of property is made.

In a case involving the sale of land, the buyer is commonly known as the grantee.

GRANTING CLAUSE The portion of an instrument of CONVEYANCE, such as a DEED, containing the words that transfer a present interest from the grantor to the grantee.

GRANTOR An individual who conveys or transfers ownership of property.

In REAL PROPERTY law, an individual who sells land is known as the grantor.

GRANTOR-GRANTEE INDEX A master reference book, ordinarily kept in the office of official records of a particular COUNTY, which lists all recorded DEEDS as evidence of ownership of REAL PROPERTY.

This index contains the volume and page number where an instrument can be found in the record books. The grantor-grantee index is frequently used to conduct a TITLE SEARCH on property. By consulting the index, an individual can trace the conveyance history of the property and determine whether or not it is encumbered.

GRATUITOUS Bestowed or granted without consideration or exchange for something of value.

The term *gratuitous* is applied to DEEDS, BAILMENTS, and other contractual agreements.

A *gratuity* is something given by someone who has no obligation to give and can be used in reference to a bribe or tip.

GRATUITOUS LICENSEE An individual who is permitted, although not invited, to enter another individual's property and who provides no CONSIDERATION in exchange for such permission.

For example, a person who obtains the permission of the owner of a parcel of land to park his or her car on such land for a few hours is a gratuitous licensee. Since the driver of the vehicle was not invited by the owner, he or she is not an INVITEE, and since the driver has obtained the owner's permission, he or she is not committing a TRESPASS. If the driver does not pay for the permission to park, the LICENSE to do so is thereby considered gratuitous.

GRAVAMEN The basis or essence of a grievance; the issue upon which a particular controversy turns.

The gravamen of a criminal charge or COMPLAINT is the material part of the charge.

In English ecclesiastical law, the term *gravamen* referred to a grievance of which the clergy complained before the bishops in convocation.

GRAY, HORACE Horace Gray gained prominence as a Massachusetts jurist and a U.S. Supreme Court justice. In his fifty-three-year career as a lawyer and judge, Gray earned a reputation as an expert on legal history and PRECEDENT.

Gray was born in the prosperous Beacon Hill neighborhood of Boston on March 24, 1828. His grandfather, William Gray, was a prominent merchant and shipowner, and his father, Horace Gray, was a successful manufacturer. His uncle, Francis Calley Gray, gained fame for discovering the original Liberties of the Massachusetts Colony in New England, the first constitution of the colony, which was drawn up by NATHANIEL WARD and adopted in 1641.

Gray attended Harvard College, in Cambridge, Massachusetts. In 1848 he entered Harvard Law School; he received his law degree one year later. After two years of working in various law offices, Gray opened his own firm in Boston, where he practiced law until 1864. In addition to practicing law, Gray worked as reporter and editor of the *Massachusetts Reports*, a collection of court opinions and commentary on Massachusetts CASE LAW.

The position of reporter of the *Massachusetts Reports* traditionally led to a seat on the state supreme court, and that tradition played out for Gray. In 1864 he was named to the Supreme Judicial Court of Massachusetts by Governor John A. Andrew. At age thirty-six, Gray was the youngest appointee in the history of that court.

As a justice, Gray was formal and stern. He required conservative dress in his court, and he lectured lawyers on their conduct. He demanded that attorneys arrive prepared, and he asked frequent questions from the bench. Gray's opinions were thorough and well documented. In 1873 Gray assumed the position of chief justice of the Supreme Judicial Court of Massachusetts.

In 1881 President JAMES GARFIELD was looking for a nominee for the U.S. Supreme Court, to replace the ailing justice NATHAN CLIFFORD. Garfield was considering Gray and asked for copies of his opinions. Considering such self-promotion unseemly, Gray refused to send anything to Garfield. After Garfield's death in September 1881, Senator George F. Hoar recommended Gray to the new president, CHESTER A. ARTHUR, and Arthur nominated Gray as Clifford's replacement.

Gray authored many opinions on important issues of the day, including cases involving industry, immigration, and state-federal rela-

BIOGRAPHY

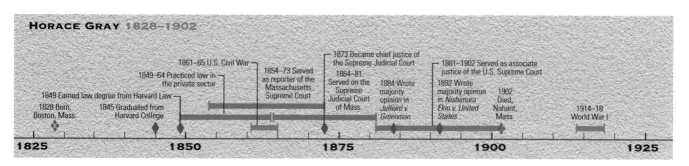

HORACE GRAY 1828–1902

1828 Born, Boston, Mass.
1845 Graduated from Harvard College
1849 Earned law degree from Harvard Law
1849–64 Practiced law in the private sector
1854–73 Served as reporter of the Massachusetts Supreme Court
1861–65 U.S. Civil War
1864–81 Served on the Supreme Judicial Court of Mass.
1873 Became chief justice of the Supreme Judicial Court
1881–1902 Served as associate justice of the U.S. Supreme Court
1884 Wrote majority opinion in *Juilliard v. Greenman*
1892 Wrote majority opinion in *Nishimura Ekiu v. United States*
1902 Died, Nahant, Mass.
1914–18 World War I

1825   1850   1875   1900   1925

tions. One lasting opinion written by Gray involved the power of the federal government to issue paper money. In *Juilliard v. Greenman*, 110 U.S. 421, 4 S. Ct. 122, 28 L. Ed. 204 (1884), the High Court established that the United States, through Congress, had the power to issue paper money against its own credit during times of peace as well as times of war.

The *Juilliard* opinion revealed Gray's strong nationalist sentiment, which became a hallmark of Gray's service on the Court. Gray tended to promote the rights of the United States in its own endeavors and in its relations with other countries. He led the Court in upholding a federal law limiting the immigration of Chinese into the United States (*Nishimura Ekiu v. United States*, 142 U.S. 651, 12 S. Ct. 336, 35 L. Ed. 1146 [1892]). In *Fong Yue Ting v. United States*, 149 U.S. 698, 13 S. Ct. 1016, 37 L. Ed. 905 (1893), Gray dismissed the notion that resident ALIENS could claim the protection of the U.S. Constitution. Gray also wrote the opinion in *Hilton v. Guyot*, 159 U.S. 113, 16 S. Ct. 139, 40 L. Ed. 95 (1895), in which the Court held that the United States did not have to recognize JUDGMENTS obtained in France, because France did not recognize judgments obtained in the United States.

Gray never attained the legendary status enjoyed by some Supreme Court justices, perhaps because of his unwillingness to stray beyond the bounds of precedent and author far reaching opinions that change the course of the law.

Gray died September 15, 1902, in Nahant, Massachusetts.

GRAY, JOHN CHIPMAN

John Chipman Gray was born July 14, 1839, in Brighton, Massachusetts. He attended Harvard University and earned a bachelor of arts degree in 1859 and a bachelor of laws degree in 1861. He also received honorary doctor of laws degrees from Yale University in 1894 and Harvard in 1895.

After his admission to the bar in 1862, Gray served a tour of military duty in the Civil War before establishing his legal practice in Boston

"IT BEHOOVES THE COURT TO BE CAREFUL THAT IT DOES NOT UNDERTAKE TO PASS UPON POLITICAL QUESTIONS."

BIOGRAPHY

NATIONAL ARCHIVES

William H. Gray III

BIOGRAPHY

NEW YORK PUBLIC LIBRARY

John Chipman Gray

in 1865. Four years later, he became a member of the faculty of the Harvard Law School, serving as a lecturer of law from 1869 to 1871, as a law professor from 1875 to 1883, and as a Royall professor of law from 1883 to 1913. His specialty was real property law, and he favored the CASE METHOD of presentation of legal principles.

As an author, Gray wrote several publications but his most noteworthy is *The Nature and Sources of the Law* (1909). Gray died June 28, 1915, in Boston.

GRAY, WILLIAM H. III

From 1979 to 1991 William H. Gray III served as U.S. representative from Pennsylvania's Second Congressional District. Gray, a liberal Democrat, chaired the powerful House Budget Committee during his last six years in Congress. In those years, he fought against the administrations of Republican presidents RONALD REAGAN and GEORGE BUSH to preserve Democratic spending priorities. An African American, Gray also became a leader on U.S. policy toward Africa. He helped create and pass laws that imposed harsh SANCTIONS on South Africa for its policies of apartheid, or racial segregation.

Gray was born August 20, 1941, in Baton Rouge, Louisiana. His father, William H. Gray, Jr., was a clergyman and an educator who served as president of Florida Normal and Industrial College, in St. Augustine, and of Florida A&M College, in Tallahassee. His mother, Hazel Yates Gray, worked as a high school teacher. In 1949, the family moved to Philadelphia, where Gray's father became pastor of Bright Hope Baptist Church. Gray's grandfather had served in the same post since 1925, and Gray would follow his grandfather and father to the Bright Hope pulpit in 1972.

Gray attended Franklin and Marshall College, in Lancaster, Pennsylvania, where he served an internship in the office of Representative Robert N. C. Nix, Jr. (D-Pa.). Although Gray felt stimulated by his brief experience in politics, he followed his father and grandfather into the ministry after his graduation in 1963. In 1964, he became assistant pastor of the

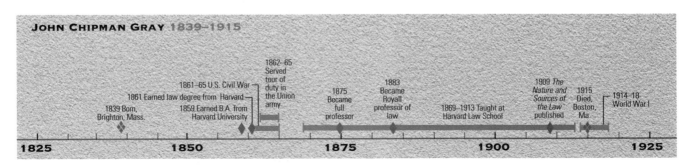

JOHN CHIPMAN GRAY 1839–1915

1839 Born, Brighton, Mass.

1859 Earned B.A. from Harvard University

1861 Earned law degree from Harvard

1861–65 U.S. Civil War

1862–65 Served tour of duty in the Union army

1875 Became full professor

1883 Became Royall professor of law

1869–1913 Taught at Harvard Law School

1909 *The Nature and Sources of the Law* published

1915 Died, Boston, Ma.

1914–18 World War I

1825   1850   1875   1900   1925

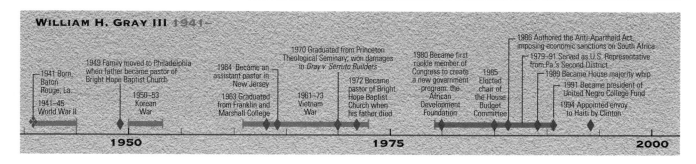

WILLIAM H. GRAY III 1941–

1941 Born, Baton Rouge, La.

1941–45 World War II

1949 Family moved to Philadelphia when father became pastor of Bright Hope Baptist Church

1950–53 Korean War

1964 Became an assistant pastor in New Jersey

1963 Graduated from Franklin and Marshall College

1970 Graduated from Princeton Theological Seminary; won damages in *Gray v. Serruto Builders*

1961–73 Vietnam War

1972 Became pastor of Bright Hope Baptist Church when his father died

1980 Became first rookie member of Congress to create a new government program: the African Development Foundation

1985 Elected chair of the House Budget Committee

1986 Authored the Anti-Apartheid Act, imposing economic sanctions on South Africa

1979–91 Served as U.S. Representative from Pa.'s Second District

1989 Became House majority whip

1991 Became president of United Negro College Fund

1994 Appointed envoy to Haiti by Clinton

1950   1975   2000

Union Baptist Church, in Montclair, New Jersey. He went on to earn a master of divinity degree from Drew Theological School, in Madison, New Jersey, in 1966, and a master of theology degree from Princeton Theological Seminary in 1970.

While working as a minister, Gray became active in community projects, winning particularly high praise for his efforts to improve housing for low-income African Americans. In 1970, he brought suit against a landlord in Montclair who had refused to rent to him because of his race. The New Jersey Superior Court awarded Gray financial damages in a decision that set a national precedent (*Gray v. Serruto Builders, Inc.*, 110 N.J. Super. 297, 265 A.2d 404 [1970]). Gray also served as a lecturer at several New Jersey colleges and as an assistant professor at Saint Peter's College, in Jersey City, New Jersey.

After his father's death in 1972, Gray became pastor of Bright Hope Baptist Church and continued his involvement in community politics. Convinced that he could accomplish more in a position of greater power, Gray decided to challenge his former employer, Nix, in 1976 for the Democratic nomination to represent Pennsylvania's Second Congressional District. He lost the primary by only 339 votes. In 1978, he challenged Nix in the primary again and won, and then earned a decisive victory over his Republican opponent in the general election.

In the House, Gray became a member of the Foreign Affairs, District of Columbia, and Budget Committees and was an active member of the Congressional Black Caucus. On the Budget Committee, he brokered crucial budget compromises between the House and Senate and developed a keen understanding of the intricacies of the federal government's money matters. An unapologetic liberal, he fought doggedly against the conservative policies of President Reagan.

On January 4, 1985, Gray was elected chairman of the powerful Budget Committee. During budget negotiations that year, he salvaged many programs that the Reagan administration

"THE DIFFERENCE BETWEEN MYSELF AND OLD-LINE FOLKS IS THAT I UNDERSTAND THAT THE POLITICAL PROCESS IS PUTTING TOGETHER COALITIONS."

and the Republican-controlled Congress sought to cancel, including Urban Development Action grants and the Appalachian Development Program. He also froze the defense budget at the previous year's level in order to reduce the budget deficit. Gray opposed the Gramm-Rudman-Hollings Act (also known as the Balanced Budget and Emergency Deficit Control Act) (1 § 251 et seq. [2 U.S.C.A. § 901 et seq.]), however, calling it a "flawed doomsday machine" that would destroy worthwhile programs. The law mandated automatic budget cuts unless specific deficit-reduction targets were met. Gray argued that the act led to budget padding and discouraged efficient management.

In 1987, Gray whittled the budget deficit down to $137 billion, $7 billion under the Gramm-Rudman-Hollings ceiling. He accomplished this through military spending reductions and tax increases. In negotiations for the budget of fiscal year 1989—the year in which the FEDERAL BUDGET first exceeded $1 trillion—Gray successfully lobbied for more tax increases to meet the Gramm-Rudman-Hollings targets.

Gray worked throughout his congressional career to increase aid to black Africa. In 1980, he became the first rookie member of Congress to create a new government program, when he sponsored the bill that established the African Development Foundation (22 U.S.C.A. 290h-1). The foundation sent aid directly to African villages. In 1984, he sponsored legislation that sent emergency food aid to Ethiopia. Gray also exerted a great deal of influence over African affairs, authoring and promoting passage of the Anti-Apartheid Act (22 U.S.C.A. § 5001 et seq.), which imposed economic sanctions on South Africa for its policies of racial segregation. The act passed in 1986 over President Reagan's veto. In addition, Gray worked to foster better relations between African and Jewish Americans.

As he rose in the House, Gray became increasingly influential in the DEMOCRATIC PARTY. In 1988, he chaired the panel that drafted the party platform at the Democratic National

Convention. The following year, he was named to the powerful position of House majority whip.

Gray encountered difficulties when unconfirmed rumors of financial wrongdoing surfaced in 1988. He left Congress in 1991, surprising many who had predicted that he would continue to rise in the House. The same year, he became president of the United Negro College Fund.

Following his congressional career, Gray has continued to be active in public affairs. In 1994, President Bill Clinton appointed him envoy to Haiti. Gray advocated using economic sanctions against that country's military dictatorship in order to restore President Jean-Bertrand Aristide to power.

Gray was awarded the Martin Luther King, Jr., Award for Public Service in 1985. He has received honorary degrees from more than fifty colleges. Despite his heavy work schedule over the years, he has continued to preach sermons at Bright Hope Baptist Church, in Philadelphia, at least two Sundays a month.

Gray married Andrea Dash in 1971. The couple has three sons.

GRAY PANTHERS Founded in 1970, the Gray Panthers is a national organization dedicated to social justice for old and young people alike. The Gray Panthers is best known for work on behalf of older persons. It has lobbied and litigated against AGE DISCRIMINATION in the areas of retirement, housing, and health care. The group's broad liberal agenda reflects the politics of its founder, Margaret E. ("Maggie") Kuhn (1905–95), who built the fledgling organization into a powerful force in local and national politics. Kuhn's success as an organizer, leader, spokeswoman, and author left the Gray Panthers, at the time of her death in 1995,

with seventy thousand members in eighty-five chapters nationwide. Although the organization is strongest at the grassroots level, its relatively small seven-member national staff has effected significant changes in federal law.

The protest era of the Vietnam War gave rise to the Gray Panthers. In 1970 the sixty-five-year-old Kuhn was forced by the federal mandatory retirement law to end her twenty-two-year career in the United Presbyterian Church. However, she did not want to retire. In response Kuhn helped form a loose-knit organization called Consultation of Older and Younger Adults for Social Change. Its primary goals were changing the mandatory retirement age and uniting people of all ages to seek an end to the Vietnam War. As the group gained recognition, the press coined the term "gray panthers," comparing it to the radical black activist group, the BLACK PANTHERS. Kuhn adopted the name in 1972.

The Gray Panthers developed a broad political agenda. Among its goals were affordable housing, the creation of a national health system, nursing home reform, and CONSUMER PROTECTION.

Lobbying efforts soon established the group's reputation on Capitol Hill. In 1978 it helped secure passage of an amendment to the Age Discrimination in Employment Act of 1967, which raised the mandated retirement age from sixty-five to seventy. In 1981, the Gray Panthers added a representative to the United Nations' Economic and Social Council.

Throughout the 1980s and early 1990s, the Gray Panthers backed efforts ranging from the passage of gay civil rights legislation to the legalization of the medical use of marijuana by those who are ill. They also lobbied strongly during the first term of President BILL CLINTON for the creation of a national health care system.

The organization was also active in the courts. It joined numerous cases by filing FRIEND-OF-THE-COURT briefs and brought its own suits. Perhaps its most significant victory came in 1980, in *Gray Panthers v. Schweiker,* 652 F.2d 146 (D.C. Cir. 1980), a CLASS ACTION suit brought to change Medicare regulations. At issue was how the government informed older patients when Medicare reimbursements were denied: under federal law, benefits of less than $100 could be denied for reimbursement with only a form letter, which was thick with jargon (42 U.S.C.A. § 1395 et seq.). In 1979, the Gray Panthers contended that this notification scheme was an unconstitutional violation of their DUE PROCESS rights. The defendant, the Department of Health, Education, and Welfare,

The Gray Panthers support a variety of issues, including affordable housing, creation of a national health system, and lower military spending.

maintained that it had a congressional mandate to set restraints on the program; any further form of notification would be too expensive, it argued. After losing the initial court case, the Gray Panthers successfully argued on appeal for improved written communication and an oral hearing at which they could explain their side of the dispute.

The Gray Panthers continues to hold monthly meetings in state chapters and to publish its bimonthly newsletter, *Network*.

GREENBERG, JACK

Jack Greenberg is a CIVIL RIGHTS attorney and professor of law who was on the front lines of the struggle to eliminate racial DISCRIMINATION in U.S. society. He served for thirty-five years as an assistant counsel and as director-counsel of the NATIONAL ASSOCIATION FOR THE ADVANCEMENT OF COLORED PEOPLE's (NAACP's) Legal Defense and Educational Fund (LDF).

Greenberg was born December 22, 1924, in New York City. His parents, Bertha Rosenberg and Max Greenberg, were immigrants from Eastern Europe who stressed the importance of education for their children. Although they were not involved in civil rights or politics, they inculcated in their children a deep concern for disadvantaged people. This early awareness of the plight of society's less fortunate ignited Greenberg's desire to take up the civil rights cause.

Greenberg grew up in Brooklyn and the Bronx, and was educated at public elementary and high schools before receiving his bachelor of arts from Columbia University in 1945. He then entered the Navy and served in the Pacific as a deck officer, participating in the invasion of Iwo Jima. After the war ended, he enrolled at Columbia Law School, and earned his bachelor of laws in 1948. While in law school, Greenberg enrolled in a seminar called "Legal Survey," which set the direction of his future career. The course offered students the opportunity to work for civil liberties and civil rights organizations, doing legal research and writing memorandums, complaints, and briefs. While taking the course, Greenberg became ac-

BIOGRAPHY

Jack Greenberg

"I THINK THAT THE LAW HAS BEEN AN IMMENSE FORCE FOR SOCIAL CHANGE WITH REGARD TO RACE."

quainted with THURGOOD MARSHALL, who at the time was the fund's director. When an LDF staff attorney resigned her position, Greenberg was recommended as a replacement. His career in civil rights, as well as his lasting friendship with Marshall, was launched.

Greenberg began his work at the LDF with only a vague idea of the cases he would handle. He was quickly plunged into the ugly reality of racial discrimination. His first cases required him to travel regularly to the South to defend blacks against various racially motivated charges. On those trips, he experienced racial discrimination firsthand. The African American lawyers with whom he traveled were not allowed to stay at hotels for whites or eat at restaurants for whites. Greenberg, who is white, saw for himself the deplorable accommodations black people were forced to accept because of legal segregation.

Greenberg soon realized that the LDF had a definite plan underlying its apparently random selection of disparate cases. The fund's ambitious goal was nothing less than the complete repudiation of *Plessy v. Ferguson*, 163 U.S. 537, 16 S. Ct. 1138, 41 L. Ed. 256, the infamous 1896 Supreme Court case that established the "SEPARATE-BUT-EQUAL" doctrine, which legitimized segregation at all levels of society.

During the 1930s and 1940s, NAACP and LDF lawyers concentrated on desegregating higher education. Greenberg was involved in important cases that allowed the integration of professional schools in Maryland, Missouri, Oklahoma, Texas, Louisiana, North and South Carolina, and many other states. The LDF then set its sights on state-supported undergraduate schools. The first big case that Greenberg handled on his own was the integration of the University of Delaware. The LDF's assault on segregated education culminated with the landmark 1954 Supreme Court decision in *Brown v. Board of Education*, 349 U.S. 294, 75 S. Ct. 753, 99 L. Ed. 1083, in which Greenberg was a major participant.

Greenberg and the LDF argued on behalf of African Americans in countless cases, with

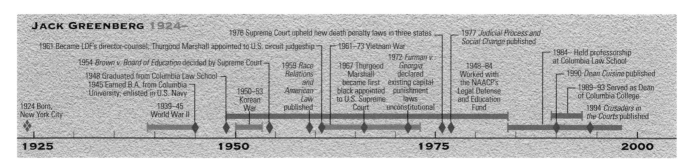

JACK GREENBERG 1924–

1924 Born, New York City

1939–45 World War II

1945 Earned B.A. from Columbia University; enlisted in U.S. Navy

1948 Graduated from Columbia Law School

1950–53 Korean War

1954 *Brown v. Board of Education* decided by Supreme Court

1959 *Race Relations and American Law* published

1961 Became LDF's director-counsel; Thurgood Marshall appointed to U.S. circuit judgeship

1961–73 Vietnam War

1967 Thurgood Marshall became first black appointed to U.S. Supreme Court

1972 *Furman v. Georgia* declared existing capital punishment laws unconstitutional

1976 Supreme Court upheld new death penalty laws in three states

1977 *Judicial Process and Social Change* published

1948–84 Worked with the NAACP's Legal Defense and Education Fund

1984– Held professorship at Columbia Law School

1989–93 Served as Dean of Columbia College

1990 *Dean Cuisine* published

1994 *Crusaders in the Courts* published

1925   1950   1975   2000

Greenberg appearing before the U.S. Supreme Court more than forty times. The fund launched a full-scale effort during the 1960s and 1970s to abolish the death penalty because of its disproportionate effect on blacks. The LDF was ultimately successful, but the victory was short-lived. By the 1980s, most states that had used CAPITAL PUNISHMENT before the Supreme Court outlawed it had reinstated it under new terms considered constitutionally acceptable. During the 1960s and 1970s, Greenberg also won important cases abolishing discrimination in housing, health care, employment, and public accommodations.

In 1961, when Marshall was appointed to the federal judiciary, Greenberg was named director-counsel of the LDF, a position he held until he resigned in 1984 to become a professor at Columbia Law School. During his last ten years at the LDF, he concentrated the group's energies on preventing the reversal of laws and court rulings that had finally outlawed discrimination in all forms. In 1989, Greenberg was named dean of Columbia College, a post he held until 1993, when he returned to the faculty of the law school.

Greenberg's being one of a small number of white lawyers involved in the LDF's struggles against racial discrimination was not a point of contention until 1982, when he was asked to co-teach a course in race and legal issues at Harvard Law School. The Black Law Students Association picketed the opening of the course, protesting the use of a white lawyer to present it. Greenberg led the course as planned, although some students boycotted. He encountered similar hostility when he was slated to teach a similar course at Stanford the following year, and so he declined the Stanford position. The protests were apparently a reflection of the feelings of younger black students and lawyers that whites had no credibility to speak about the African American struggle for equality. Greenberg was unfazed by the objections.

Greenberg is a man of many and varied interests. He is the author of three books: *Race Relations and American Law* (1959), *Judicial Process and Social Change*, (1977), and *Crusaders in the Courts: How a Dedicated Band of Lawyers Fought for the Civil Rights Revolution*. He has also coauthored a cookbook, *Dean Cuisine, or the Liberated Man's Guide to Fine Cooking* (1990), and studies Mandarin Chinese. He was married from 1950 to 1969 to Sema Ann Tanzer, and they have four children. He lives in Manhattan with Deborah M. Cole, whom he married in 1970. They have two children.

CROSS-REFERENCES
Brown v. Board of Education of Topeka, Kansas; Plessy v. Ferguson; School Desegregation.

GREEN CARD ◫ The popular name for the Alien Registration Receipt Card issued to all immigrants entering the United States on a non-temporary VISA who have registered with and been fingerprinted by the Immigration and Naturalization Service. The name *green card* comes from the distinctive coloration of the card. ◫

See also ALIENS.

GREENMAIL ◫ A corporation's attempt to stop a takeover bid by paying a price above MARKET VALUE for STOCK held by the aggressor. ◫

Greenmail is a practice in corporate mergers and acquisitions. Like BLACKMAIL, the concept after which it is named, greenmail is money paid to an aggressor to stop an act of aggression. In the case of greenmail, the aggressor is an investor attempting to take over a CORPORATION by buying up a majority of its stock, and the money is paid to stop the takeover. The corporation under attack pays an inflated price to buy stock from the aggressor, known popularly as a corporate raider. After the greenmail payment, the takeover attempt is halted. The raider is richer; the corporation is poorer but retains control. During a great wave of corporate mergers in the 1980s, the practice of paying greenmail became controversial. Critics viewed it as harmful to U.S. business interests. Portraying the transaction as little more than a bribe, they argued that some corporate raiders began takeover bids simply to earn profits through greenmail. Corporate shareholders also protested the practice. By the mid-1990s, state legislatures had taken the lead in opposing greenmail through legislation.

The increase in corporate mergers in the 1980s made the hostile corporate takeover a familiar event. Before the decade's multi-billion-dollar takeovers, corporate mergers usually involved a mutual agreement. In contrast, hostile takeovers ignore the target corporation's management. One form of hostile takeover involves stock. Whoever owns the most stock controls the corporation. Instead of entering negotiations with management, corporate raiders go to the corporation's stockholders with offers to buy their stock. Not only the means but also the goals of these acquisitions differ from those of earlier acquisitions. Prior to the 1980s, mergers generally occurred when larger interests bought up smaller competitors in similar industries, with an eye toward dominating a

Investor Saul Steinberg earned a profit of $60 million when Disney bought his stock to prevent a takeover. Disney stockholders later sued Steinberg and his profit was placed in a trust.

particular market. In hostile takeovers, corporate raiders often intend to break up and sell a corporation after the takeover is complete. Their interest commonly lies in earning enormous short-term profits from selling a company's ASSETS, motivating corporations to try to protect themselves against takeovers.

Greenmail is one of an array of strategies, ranging from changing corporate bylaws to acquiring debt that makes the corporation a less attractive target, used to deter raiders. It is an expensive alternative, as was illustrated when investor Saul P. Steinberg attempted to take over the Disney Corporation in 1984. Steinberg was known for his concerted efforts in the takeover field, having previously targeted Chemical Bank and Quaker State. In March 1984, his purchase of 6.3 percent of Disney's stock triggered concern at the corporation that a takeover was in progress. Disney management quickly announced an approximately $390 million acquisition of its own that would make the company less attractive. After this maneuver failed, Disney's DIRECTORS ultimately bought Steinberg's stock to stop the takeover. Steinberg earned a profit of about $60 million.

The Disney case illustrates a major criticism of greenmail: other stockholders blame corporate directors for showing undue favoritism to corporate raiders, who are paid exorbitant sums for stock whereas the stockholders are not. This criticism formed the basis of a lawsuit that produced one of the few court decisions condemning greenmail outright. In 1984, Disney stockholders sued the corporation's directors as well as Steinberg and his fellow investors, seeking to recover the amount paid as greenmail. They won an INJUNCTION from the Superior Court of Los Angeles County, which placed Steinberg's profits from the sale in a TRUST. The verdict was upheld on appeal (*Heckmann v. Ahmanson*, 168 Cal. App. 3d 119, 214 Cal. Rptr. 177 [Cal. Ct. App. 1985]). In ordering the profits put in a trust, the court sought "to prevent unjust enrichment" that would otherwise "reward [Steinberg] for his wrongdoing." In 1989, Steinberg settled with the plaintiffs for approximately $21.1 million.

Although greenmail's heyday was in the 1980s, it continued to be controversial in the 1990s. Criticism of greenmail grew out of a larger condemnation of the way in which corporate raiders had rewritten the rules of mergers and acquisitions in an avaricious, short-sighted manner. Some critics viewed this trend harshly. In his 1995 work on the subject, Professor David C. Bayne portrayed greenmail as a pact involving EMBEZZLEMENT by corporate directors and blackmail by corporate raiders. Bayne said greenmail is "nothing other than a recondite species of the broader genus Corporate Bribery, and as such is intrinsically illegitimate." States increasingly viewed greenmail in the same light. Most states had enacted anti-takeover laws, and several had anti-greenmail provisions. The Ohio and Pennsylvania laws were among the toughest, requiring raiders to return greenmail profits to the target corporation (Ohio Rev. Code Ann. § 1707.043 [Anderson Supp. 1990]; 15 Pa. Cons. Stat. Ann. §§ 2571–2576 [Purdon Supp. 1991]). Some people doubt the constitutionality of these laws, and the issue of greenmail remains far from settled.

GREEN PARTY The Green party blossomed as an outgrowth of the environmental and conservation movement of the 1970s and 1980s. In 1970 Charles Reich published *The Greening of America*, a popular extended essay that effectively inserted environmentalism into politics. Reich, along with anarchist Murray Bookchin, helped inspire a worldwide environmental movement. Throughout the 1970s and 1980s, environmental activists, calling themselves Greens, began to work within the political system to advance environmental causes around the globe.

The Green party first achieved electoral success in Germany in the early 1980s. German

Green party candidates were elected to public office on platforms that stressed four basic values: ecology, social justice, grassroots democracy, and nonviolence. In the mid-1990s, the Green party was established in over fifty countries, and Green party politicians held seats in approximately nine European parliaments.

In the United States, Greens originally were reluctant to move into electoral politics. Throughout the 1970s and most of the 1980s, they teamed with military and nuclear power protesters to promote their agendas from outside the formal political system. In 1984 the Greens began to discuss the organization of a political party, and in 1988 the U.S. Green party fielded its first candidates for elective office in Wisconsin and Connecticut.

The U.S. Green party offers a proactive approach to government based on ten key values: ecology; grassroots democracy; social justice; nonviolence; common leadership (as opposed to powerful, charismatic leadership); small-scale, community based economic structures; feminism; respect for diversity; personal and global responsibility; and a focus on the future.

In 1996 the party fielded candidates in twenty-four states and in the District of Columbia. It increased its national profile the same year by nominating RALPH NADER as its candidate for president. Nader accepted the nomination, but stipulated that he would not become a member of the Green party and that he would not feel obliged to follow faithfully its political platform. Nader ran a no-frills campaign, eschewing advertising and usually traveling alone to speak at various locales. He accepted no taxpayer money and spent approximately $5,000 on the campaign. With political activist Winona LaDuke as his running mate, Nader appeared on the ballot in twenty-one states and in the District of Columbia. The ticket also received write-in votes in all but five states. Nader and LaDuke lost to the Democratic incumbents, President BILL CLINTON and Vice President Al Gore.

The young Green party has realized almost immediate electoral success on the local level, especially in California.

In 1996 Arcata, California, became the first town in the United States to be controlled by the Green party. There, Green party politicians held three of the five seats on the city council. In all, Green party candidates in California won six city council seats in 1996.

See also ENVIRONMENTAL LAW; INDEPENDENT PARTIES.

BIOGRAPHY

LIBRARY OF CONGRESS

Thomas Watt Gregory

"CRITICISM OF THE COURTS FOR THEIR ADMINISTRATION OF THE WAR LAWS CAN HARDLY BE CALLED AN ATTACK ON THE FORM OF GOVERNMENT OF THE UNITED STATES."

GREGORY, THOMAS WATT Thomas Watt Gregory served as attorney general of the United States under President WOODROW WILSON from 1914 to 1919. Because his term of office coincided with the entry of the United States into World War I, Gregory's Department of Justice experienced tremendous growth. He presided over the creation of a war emergency division within the Department of Justice, and he watched the FEDERAL BUREAU OF INVESTIGATION (FBI) grow to five times its prewar size as he worked to enforce U.S. laws pertaining to ESPIONAGE, SEDITION, SABOTAGE, trading with the enemy, and selective service compliance—in addition to pursuing the general interests of the U.S. government.

It is fitting that Gregory's service to the United States came in a time of war. Born November 6, 1861, in Crawfordsville, Mississippi, he was, in many ways, a child of war. His father, Francis Robert Gregory, a physician and Confederate army captain, was killed during the early days of the Civil War. His mother, Mary Cornelia Watt Gregory, a delicate woman mourning the loss of her first child, was unable to cope with news of her husband's death. As she drifted in and out of melancholy, the upbringing of her remaining child, Gregory, fell to her father, Major Thomas Watt, a Mississippi planter.

By all accounts, Gregory's grandfather was a stern taskmaster with a strong commitment to education. Gregory graduated from Southwestern Presbyterian University, in Clarksville, Tennessee, in 1883. Driven to please his grandfa-

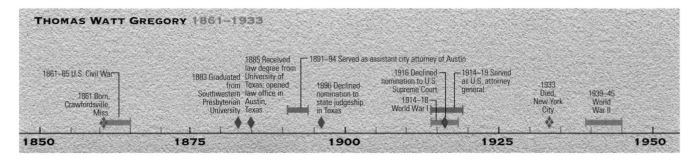

THOMAS WATT GREGORY 1861–1933

1861–65 U.S. Civil War

1861 Born, Crawfordsville, Miss.

1883 Graduated from Southwestern Presbyterian University

1885 Received law degree from University of Texas; opened law office in Austin, Texas

1891–94 Served as assistant city attorney of Austin

1896 Declined nomination to state judgeship in Texas

1914–18 World War I

1916 Declined nomination to U.S. Supreme Court

1914–19 Served as U.S. attorney general

1933 Died, New York City

1939–45 World War II

1850   1875   1900   1925   1950

ther, he had completed his course work in just two years. From 1883 to 1884, he studied law at the University of Virginia. In 1885, he received a bachelor of laws degree from the University of Texas. Later that year, he opened a law office in Austin, Texas.

In the early 1890s, Gregory began forming some important partnerships. On February 22, 1893, he married Julia Nalle, the daughter of Captain Joseph Nalle, an Austin native. They had two sons, Thomas Watt Gregory, Jr., and Joseph Nalle Gregory, and two daughters, Jane Gregory and Cornelia Gregory. He also formed a law partnership with Robert L. Batts. Together, they successfully represented the state of Texas against Waters-Pierce Oil Company, a subsidiary of Standard Oil of New York, charged with violating Texas ANTITRUST LAWS. The company was found guilty and enjoined from doing further business in Texas. The case was appealed, and was ultimately affirmed by the U.S. Supreme Court (*Waters-Pierce Oil Co. v. Texas*, 212 U.S. 86, 29 S. Ct. 220, 53 L. Ed. 417 [1909]). The company paid a heavy fine and ceased to operate in Texas.

While partnered with Batts, Gregory also served as assistant city attorney of Austin, from 1891 to 1894. As his reputation grew, he was offered a number of political appointments, including the assistant attorney generalship of Texas in 1892 and a state judgeship in 1894. Wanting to serve on a national level, he declined them all.

To further his personal and professional goals, Gregory served as a Texas delegate to the Democratic national conventions of 1904 and 1912. In 1910, he began working in Democratic party circles to secure a presidential nomination for Wilson. He actively promoted a Wilson candidacy throughout his state—and because of Gregory's considerable influence, Texas went on to elect a delegation that would hold fast for Wilson at the Baltimore convention. In 1913, Gregory was rewarded for his efforts. President Wilson's attorney general, JAMES C. MCREYNOLDS, made Gregory a special assistant and asked him to spearhead an action against the New York, New Haven, and Hartford Railroad for monopolizing transportation in New England. Using his experience from the *Waters-Pierce* case in Texas, Gregory negotiated a settlement. As a result of his work, the railroad gave up control of several rail lines, trolley lines, and coastal shipping interests.

Gregory was named attorney general of the United States by President Wilson in 1914. McReynolds, his predecessor (and former University of Virginia classmate), created the vacancy by accepting Wilson's appointment to the U.S. Supreme Court.

When World War I broke out in Europe, the first act of the Department of Justice was to create a war emergency division responsible for circumventing the work of agents of foreign governments, and preventing or suppressing violations of U.S. neutrality. When the United States entered the war, the roles and responsibilities of the Department of Justice and the FBI were expanded to deal with the enforcement of espionage, sedition, sabotage, and trading-with-the-enemy laws. The passage of selective service legislation further increased the department's reach. Reports from Gregory's tenure reveal that his officers arrested sixty-three hundred spies and conspirators; detained twenty-three hundred ALIENS in Army detention camps; filed 220,747 actions against men who failed to comply with draft laws; and uncovered the activities of a group securing government and supply contracts through illegal means.

Under Gregory, the Department of Justice also organized and oversaw the operations of a volunteer secret service called the American Protective League. In addition to his wartime responsibilities, Gregory continued to watch domestic issues. He initiated several antitrust suits, including actions against the International Harvester Company and anthracite coal operators. Gregory also secured reforms in the administration of federal prisons while in office.

Like his predecessor, Gregory was eventually offered a Supreme Court appointment by President Wilson; unlike his predecessor, he declined. In refusing the vacancy created by the resignation of Justice CHARLES E. HUGHES in 1916, Gregory cited his failing hearing and his inability to tolerate the confining life dictated by the position. Gregory liked to speak his mind and thought he would be unable to temper the expression of his opinions.

On March 4, 1919, Gregory resigned from the cabinet at the request of President Wilson. During the war, Gregory had treated pacifists and other opponents of the war ruthlessly; his tough, no-compromise demeanor had been suited to the times. But, as the war drew to a close, Wilson and others wanted to replace him with an attorney general more suited to postwar needs abroad and peacetime needs at home.

In a gesture of respect and esteem, President Wilson invited Gregory to attend the postwar Paris Peace Conference as an adviser. In the spirit of reconciliation, Gregory urged Wilson to enlist the support of Republican business leaders in the peace efforts and to include them on the advisory team.

Upon his return from the peace conference, Gregory remained in Washington, D.C., and returned to the practice of law. But ill health and age forced a retirement after just a few years. He spent his last years in Houston, Texas, where he continued to advise local attorneys on antitrust matters and to lecture at the University of Texas.

Gregory died of pneumonia on February 26, 1933, in New York City, while on a trip to meet with president-elect FRANKLIN D. ROOSEVELT.

GRIER, ROBERT COOPER Robert Cooper Grier served as an associate justice of the U.S. Supreme Court from 1846 to 1870. Grier is best remembered for his unusual actions during the deliberation of *Dred Scott v. Sandford*, 60 U.S. (19 How.) 393, 15 L. Ed. 691 (1857).

Grier was born March 5, 1794, in Cumberland County, Pennsylvania. He graduated from Dickinson College in 1812 and was admitted to the bar in Bloomsburg, Pennsylvania, in 1817. A year later, he relocated to Danville, Pennsylvania, and established a successful law practice. In 1833, he was appointed judge of the Allegheny County, Pennsylvania, district court, where he remained until 1846.

With the death in 1844 of Supreme Court justice HENRY BALDWIN, who was a Pennsylvania native, President JAMES POLK sought to appoint a Democrat from that state. After failing to find a candidate who could pass Senate confirmation, Polk turned in 1846 to the noncontroversial and relatively unknown Grier.

During his term on the Supreme Court, Grier held a centrist position. A strong believer in STATES' RIGHTS, he generally was opposed to federal legislation that intruded on state police powers. This philosophy led him to side with the Southern states in upholding their right to keep slaves and to recapture runaway slaves who had escaped to Northern states.

Grier has been criticized for his actions during the deliberation of *Dred Scott*, generally recognized as the most important pre–Civil War case concerning the legitimacy of SLAVERY

Robert Cooper Grier

"THE EVIDENCE OF [FRAUD] IS ALMOST ALWAYS CIRCUMSTANTIAL. NEVERTHELESS . . . IT PRODUCES CONVICTION IN THE MIND OFTEN OF MORE FORCE THAN DIRECT TESTIMONY."

and the rights of African Americans. The circumstances of the ruling as well as the ruling itself increased the division between the Northern and Southern states.

Dred Scott was a slave owned by an army surgeon, John Emerson, who resided in Missouri. In 1836, Emerson took Scott to Fort Snelling, in what is now Minnesota but was then a territory in which slavery had been expressly forbidden by the MISSOURI COMPROMISE legislation of 1820. In 1846, Scott sued for his freedom in Missouri state court, arguing that his residence in a free territory released him from slavery. The Missouri Supreme Court rejected his argument, and Scott appealed to the U.S. Supreme Court.

Grier and the other members of the Court heard arguments on *Dred Scott* in 1855 and 1856. A key issue was whether African Americans could be CITIZENS of the United States, even if they were not slaves. Grier did not want to address the citizenship issue, but other justices who were Southerners wanted the Court's vote to transcend sectional lines. Justice JOHN CATRON took the unusual and unethical step of asking President JAMES BUCHANAN to lobby Grier on this issue. Buchanan wrote to Grier, who in turn breached the separation between the executive and judicial branches by replying to the president. Grier agreed to side with the majority, which held that there was no power under the Constitution to grant African Americans citizenship. Grier set out in detail how the Court would rule on the case. Buchanan, in his inaugural address on March 4, 1857, mentioned the case. When the decision was released two days later, opponents of the decision attributed the president's remarks to inside information provided by Chief Justice ROGER B. TANEY. In fact, Grier was the informer.

Although Grier was sympathetic to Southern concerns, he remained a Unionist. During the Civil War, Grier voted to support the power of the president to enforce a BLOCKADE of the Confederate shoreline. The *Prize* cases, 67 U.S. 635, 17 L. Ed. 459; 70 U.S. 451, 18 L. Ed. 197; 70 U.S. 514, 18 L. Ed. 200; 70 U.S. 559, 18 L.

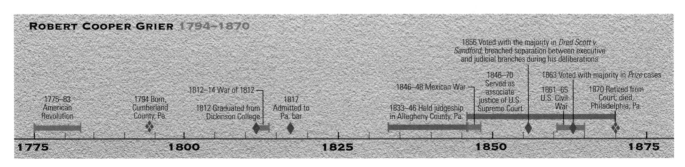

ROBERT COOPER GRIER 1794–1870

1856 Voted with the majority in *Dred Scott v. Sandford*; breached separation between executive and judicial branches during his deliberations

1846–70 Served as associate justice of U.S. Supreme Court

1863 Voted with majority in *Prize* cases

1846–48 Mexican War

1861–65 U.S. Civil War

1870 Retired from Court, died, Philadelphia, Pa

1775–83 American Revolution

1794 Born, Cumberland County, Pa

1812–14 War of 1812

1812 Graduated from Dickinson College

1817 Admitted to Pa. bar

1833–46 Held judgeship in Allegheny County, Pa.

1775   1800   1825   1850   1875

Ed. 220 (1863), involved the disposition of vessels captured by the Union navy during the blockade of Southern ports ordered by President ABRAHAM LINCOLN in the absence of a congressional declaration of war. Under existing laws of war, the Union could claim the vessels as property only if the conflict was a declared war. The Supreme Court rejected prior law and ruled that the president has the authority to resist force without the need for special legislative action. Grier noted that the "[p]resident was bound to meet [the Civil War] in the shape it presented itself, without waiting for the Congress to baptize it with a name; and no name given to it by him or them could change the fact."

Grier's health began to fail in 1867. He retired in 1870, after members of the Court requested that he resign because he could no longer carry out his duties. He died on September 25, 1870, in Philadelphia.

See also DRED SCOTT V. SANDFORD.

GRIEVANCE PROCEDURE 📖 A term used in LABOR LAW to describe an orderly, established way of dealing with problems between employers and employees. 📖

Through the grievance procedure system, workers' complaints are usually communicated through their union to management for consideration by the employer.

GRIGGS, JOHN WILLIAM John William Griggs was a prominent New Jersey lawyer and politician who served as attorney general of the United States under President WILLIAM MCKINLEY.

Griggs was born July 10, 1849, near Newton, Sussex County, New Jersey. His father, Daniel Griggs, descended from the colonial founders of Griggstown, New Jersey. His mother, Emeline Johnson Griggs, also had early roots in New Jersey; she descended from militiaman and Revolutionary War soldier Henry Johnson.

As a young man, Griggs attended the Collegiate Institute, in Newton. He later entered Lafayette College, and graduated in 1868. After college, he studied law in Newton with Repre-

sentative Robert Hamilton, of New Jersey, and Socrates Tuttle. Griggs completed his legal studies in 1871 and entered into practice with Tuttle.

In 1874, Griggs was established well enough to marry Carolyn Webster Brandt, the daughter of a successful Newton businessman. They had three children.

Griggs's early association with Congressman Hamilton sparked a lifelong interest in politics. While working for Hamilton, Griggs established himself as an able campaigner and gifted speech maker. By 1874, Griggs had decided to stop campaigning for others and to throw his own hat into the ring. In 1875, he was elected to the New Jersey Assembly, the lower house of the New Jersey Legislature, where he became chairman of the Committee on the Revision of the Laws. Griggs's special area of expertise was the laws governing elections. He returned to the assembly for a final term in 1877.

At the end of his final term, Griggs opened a law office in Paterson, New Jersey, and resolved to take a break from politics. His resolve was short-lived. In 1879, he was appointed to the Board of Chosen Freeholders of Passaic County, and he served as legal counsel to the city of Paterson from 1879 to 1882.

In 1882, Griggs was elected to the first of two terms in the New Jersey state senate. He served as president of the senate in 1886, and in that capacity presided over several high-profile IMPEACHMENT trials resulting from allegations of corruption in state government.

As a state senator, Griggs worked to pass legislation forcing railroads and other large corporations to bear a larger share of the state's tax burden. He was known as a centrist who moderated many of the radical measures proposed by New Jersey's liberal Democratic governor Leon Abbett.

Griggs was a delegate to the Republican National Convention of 1888, and he worked actively to further the political agenda of presidential candidate BENJAMIN HARRISON. After the election, he was among those considered for a Supreme Court nomination by President Har-

BIOGRAPHY

John William Griggs

IBRARY OF CONGRESS

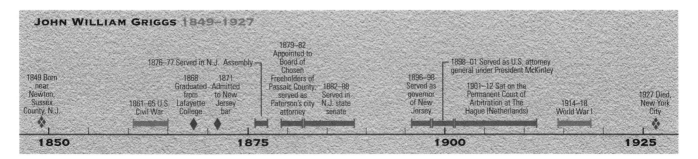

JOHN WILLIAM GRIGGS 1849–1927

1849 Born near Newton, Sussex County, N.J.	
1861–65 U.S. Civil War	
1868 Graduated from Lafayette College	
1871 Admitted to New Jersey bar	
1876–77 Served in N.J. Assembly	
1879–82 Appointed to Board of Chosen Freeholders of Passaic County, served as Paterson's city attorney	
1882–88 Served in N.J. state senate	
1896–98 Served as governor of New Jersey	
1898–01 Served as U.S. attorney general under President McKinley	
1901–12 Sat on the Permanent Court of Arbitration at The Hague (Netherlands)	
1914–18 World War I	
1927 Died, New York City	

1850   1875   1900   1925

rison. When the nomination did not materialize, Democratic governor George Theodore Werts offered him a seat on New Jersey's highest court. Historians have speculated that Griggs discouraged the Supreme Court nomination, and declined appointment to the New Jersey high court, because of his wife's ill health. She died in 1891.

In 1893, Griggs married Laura Elizabeth Price, with whom he eventually had two children. With the support of his new wife and of campaign manager Garret A. Hobart, Griggs made a run for the governor's office in 1894. In 1895, he became the first Republican to be elected governor of New Jersey since the Civil War.

The victory brought Griggs to national prominence. In 1898, he resigned his office to accept President McKinley's appointment as attorney general of the United States.

As attorney general, Griggs rendered early opinions on the controversial practice of presidential IMPOUNDMENT, which is an action or failure to act by the president that effectively prevents the use of congressionally appropriated funds and thereby thwarts the effectiveness of legislation that should have been funded. Griggs advised the president to look beyond a bill's specific language and consider the intent of Congress in determining whether an expenditure of funds was mandatory or discretionary. Upon examination of intent, Griggs often counseled against impoundment (see 22 Op. Att'y Gen. 295, 297 [1899]).

Griggs's work with a body of litigation known as the *Insular* cases established some of the guiding principles of INTERNATIONAL LAW by defining geographic limits to the protections afforded by the U.S. Constitution. (The *Insular* cases concerned disputes involving the island possessions of the U.S. government.)

Because of his expertise in the field of international law, Griggs was among the first members appointed to the Permanent Court of Arbitration at The Hague. He served, when called on, from 1901 to 1912. While on the court, he also maintained a law practice in New York City and was involved in many lucrative business ventures. Griggs served as president of the Marconi Wireless Telegraph Company prior to its dissolution, and he was general counsel and director of the Radio Corporation of America at the time of his death in New York City on November 28, 1927.

GRISWOLD v. CONNECTICUT *Griswold v. Connecticut*, 381 U.S. 479, 85 S. Ct. 1678, 14 L. Ed. 2d 510 (1965), was a landmark Supreme Court decision that recognized that a married couple has a right of PRIVACY that cannot be infringed upon by a state law making it a crime to use contraceptives.

Two Connecticut statutes provided that any person who used, or gave information or assistance concerning the use of, contraceptives was subject to a fine, imprisonment, or both. Estelle T. Griswold, an executive with the state Planned Parenthood League, and a physician who worked at a league center were arrested for violating these laws, even though they gave such information to married couples.

They were convicted and fined $100 each. The state appellate courts upheld their convictions and they appealed to the Supreme Court on the ground that the statutes violated the FOURTEENTH AMENDMENT. The Supreme Court recognized that the appellants had STANDING to raise the issue of the constitutional rights of married couples since they had a professional relationship with such people.

Addressing the propriety of its review of such legislation, the Court reasoned that although it is loath to determine the need for state laws affecting social and economic conditions, these statutes directly affected sexual relations between a married couple and the role of a physician in the medical aspects of such a relationship. Such a relationship is protected from intrusion by the government under the theory of a right to privacy. This right, while not specifically guaranteed by the Constitution, exists because it may be reasonably construed from certain amendments contained in the Bill of Rights.

The FIRST AMENDMENT guarantees of FREEDOM OF SPEECH and press implicitly create the right of freedom of association since one must be allowed to freely associate with others in order to fully enjoy these specific guarantees. The THIRD AMENDMENT prohibition against the quartering of soldiers in a private home without the owner's consent is an implicit acknowledgment of the owner's right to privacy. Both the FOURTH AMENDMENT protection against unreasonable SEARCHES AND SEIZURES and the Fifth Amendment SELF-INCRIMINATION Clause safeguard a person's privacy in his or her home and life against government demands. The NINTH AMENDMENT states that the enumerated constitutional rights should not be interpreted as denying any other rights retained by the people.

The Court created the right of privacy from the PENUMBRAS of these specific rights, which it deemed created zones of privacy. The statutory regulation of a marital relationship by the state was an invasion of the constitutional right of a married couple to privacy in such a relationship, a relationship that historically American law has held sacred. The means by which the state chose to regulate contraceptives—by outlawing their use, rather than their sale and manufacture—was clearly unrelated to its goal and would detrimentally affect the marital relationship. The question of enforcement of such statutes also was roundly criticized since it would mandate government inquiry into "marital bedrooms."

Because of the invalidity of such laws, the Supreme Court reversed the judgments of the state trial and appellate courts and the convictions of the appellants.

See also HUSBAND AND WIFE.

GROESBECK, WILLIAM SLOCOMB

Thrust into the national spotlight by the IM-PEACHMENT trial of President ANDREW JOHNSON in 1868, defense attorney William Slocomb Groesbeck won wide renown for his stirring defense of the president. Prior to the trial, Groesbeck was known chiefly for his law practice in Ohio and for a single term in Congress. His friendship with Johnson led to his last-minute substitution on the president's defense team. Delivered while he was ill, Groesbeck's CLOSING ARGUMENT is remembered for its brilliance and passion.

Groesbeck was born July 24, 1815, in Schenectady, New York, and studied law at Miami University, in Ohio. After graduating in 1834, he began practicing at the age of nineteen in Cincinnati. As a liberal Republican, he served in Congress from 1857 to 1859, then lost his bid for reelection. He remained active in party politics as a leader of the Union Democrats, served as a delegate at the fruitless peace convention in 1861 that sought to prevent the Civil War, and won election as a senator in the Ohio state legislature in 1862.

Groesbeck befriended Johnson during the war, and became a natural choice for defending Johnson during his 1868 impeachment trial. Johnson trusted and respected the younger man. He had even briefly considered ousting treasury secretary Hugh McCulloch and giving Groesbeck McCulloch's job. When the distinguished lawyer JEREMIAH SULLIVAN BLACK re-

BIOGRAPHY

*William Slocomb
Groesbeck*

"EVEN IF [PRESIDENT ANDREW JOHNSON] HAD COMMITTED A CRIME AGAINST THE LAWS. HIS SERVICES TO THE COUNTRY ENTITLE HIM TO SOME CONSIDERATION."

signed from Johnson's impeachment defense team amid scandal, Johnson turned to Groesbeck.

Like the rest of Johnson's defense team, Groesbeck served without a fee. The task facing the attorneys was immense. After assuming the presidency in 1865 following ABRAHAM LINCOLN's assassination, Johnson had embarked on a moderate, slow-paced policy of reform. The bitter politics of the Reconstruction era, however, had sapped both his popularity and his power. Radical Republicans in Congress overruled his policies, and in 1867, with the stage set for a dramatic confrontation, they established the TENURE OF OFFICE ACT (14 Stat. 430) over his VETO. This law severely limited executive power. It required the president to ask the Senate for permission before removing any federal official whose appointment the Senate had approved, and it also provided that presidential CABINET members would serve one month past the expiration of the president's term.

In August 1867, Johnson rejected the authority of the act when he requested the removal of Secretary of War EDWIN M. STANTON, on the ground that Stanton had secretly conspired with Johnson's political enemies. Stanton refused to step down, so Johnson removed him from office and replaced him with ULYSSES S. GRANT. The Radical Republicans swiftly sought revenge. Three days later, the House of Representatives voted to impeach Johnson, making him the first president in U.S. history to stand trial on impeachment charges. The U.S. Senate then adopted eleven articles of impeachment, the most serious of which was violation of the Tenure of Office Act.

Groesbeck played a key role in trial preparation. Like his colleagues, he advised Johnson not to appear at trial—a recommendation the president followed. Groesbeck remained silent in the Senate until all the evidence had been presented, and on April 25 he delivered the second closing argument. (Because there was no precedent for an impeachment trial of a president, the Senate allowed several defense attorneys to present closing arguments.)

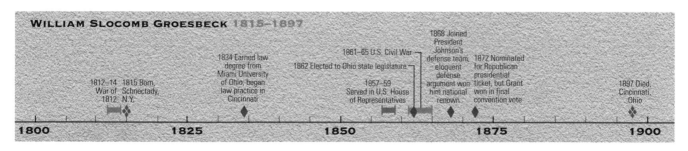

WILLIAM SLOCOMB GROESBECK 1815–1897

1812–14 War of 1812

1815 Born, Schenectady, N.Y.

1834 Earned law degree from Miami University of Ohio, began law practice in Cincinnati

1857–59 Served in U.S. House of Representatives

1861–65 U.S. Civil War

1862 Elected to Ohio state legislature

1868 Joined President Johnson's defense team; eloquent defense argument won him national renown

1872 Nominated for Republican presidential ticket, but Grant won in final convention vote

1897 Died, Cincinnati, Ohio

1800   1825   1850   1875   1900

Groesbeck's speech was a masterpiece of simplicity and eloquence. He noted that there had only been five impeachment trials since the organization of the government, and urged the Senate to leave political judgments to the citizenry. Despite suffering from an illness, he deftly countered each of the eleven charges.

When Groesbeck came to the Tenure of Office Act, he turned the tables on the Senate. He argued that the Senate had always had the power to deal with Stanton's dismissal and replacement without resorting to impeachment. What Johnson had done, argued Groesbeck, was simply to remove a member of the cabinet who had been unfriendly to him, both personally and politically. Johnson had made an AD INTERIM (temporary) appointment to last for a single day, an appointment the Senate could have terminated whenever it saw fit. The Senate, argued Groesbeck, had had the power to control the situation all along. Surely, in light of this, Johnson's act was no crime.

Groesbeck continued with a peroration comparing Johnson to Lincoln and even invoking Christ's crucifixion. Then he praised Johnson's contribution to the nation in time of war: "How his voice rang out in this hall for the good cause, and in denunciation of rebellion. But he . . . was wanted for greater peril, and went into the very furnace of the war . . . Who of you have done more? Not one."

The speech stunned the Senate. Supporters surrounded Groesbeck. His argument was praised in the national press, with the *New York Herald* calling it "the most eloquent . . . heard in the Senate since the palmy days of oratory" (as quoted in Bowers 1929, 189) and the *Nation* regarding it as the defense's most effective moment. Johnson, too, was deeply pleased, and Groesbeck assured him that he would be acquitted. When the Senate voted on May 16 and May 26, Johnson escaped impeachment by a margin of one vote.

Following the trial, Groesbeck's political fortunes briefly soared. In 1872, he was nominated for the presidency by liberal Republicans but failed to garner enough support. He died July 7, 1897, in Cincinnati.

GROSS Great; culpable; general; absolute. A thing *in gross* exists in its own right, and not as an appendage to another thing. Before or without diminution or deduction. Whole; entire; total; as in the gross sum, amount, weight—as opposed to net. Not adjusted or reduced by deductions or subtractions.

Out of all measure; beyond allowance; flagrant; shameful; as a gross dereliction of duty, a gross injustice, gross carelessness or negligence. Such conduct as is not to be excused.

GROSS ESTATE All the real and personal property owned by a DECEDENT at the time of his or her death.

The calculation of the value of the gross estate is the first step in the computation that determines whether any estate tax is owed to federal or state governments. Federal and state laws define gross estate for purposes of taxation. Under federal law, the gross estate includes proceeds of life INSURANCE policies that are payable to the decedent's estate, as well as policies to which the decedent retained "incidents of ownership" until his or her death, such as the right to change beneficiaries or to borrow against the CASH SURRENDER VALUE of the policy.

See also ESTATE AND GIFT TAXES.

GROSS INCOME The financial gains received by an individual or a business during a fiscal year.

For INCOME TAX purposes, gross income includes any type of monetary benefit paid to an individual or business, whether it be earned as a result of personal services or business activities or produced by investments and CAPITAL ASSETS. The valuation of gross income is the first step in computing whether any federal or state income tax is owed by the recipient.

GROSS NEGLIGENCE An indifference to, and a blatant violation of, a legal DUTY with respect to the rights of others.

Gross negligence is a conscious and voluntary disregard of the need to use reasonable care, which is likely to cause foreseeable grave injury or harm to persons, property, or both. It is conduct that is extreme when compared with ordinary NEGLIGENCE, which is a mere failure to exercise reasonable care. Ordinary negligence and gross negligence differ in degree of inattention, while both differ from WILLFUL and WANTON conduct, which is conduct that is reasonably considered to cause injury. This distinction is important, since contributory negligence—a lack of care by the plaintiff that combines with the defendant's conduct to cause the plaintiff's injury and completely bar his or her ACTION—is not a DEFENSE to willful and wanton conduct but is a defense to gross negligence. In addition, a finding of willful and wanton misconduct usually supports a recovery of PUNITIVE DAMAGES, whereas gross negligence does not.

GROTIUS, HUGO Hugo Grotius, also known as Huigh de Groot, achieved prominence as a Dutch jurist and statesman and is regarded as the originator of INTERNATIONAL LAW.

Grotius was born April 10, 1583, in Delft,

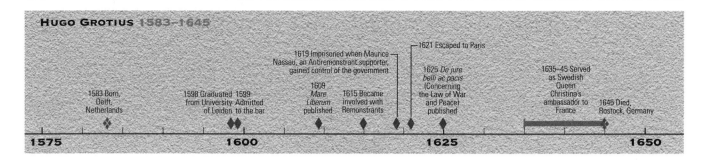

1619 Imprisoned when Maurice Nassau, an Antiremonstrant supporter, gained control of the government

1621 Escaped to Paris

1583 Born, Delft, Netherlands

1598 Graduated 1599 from University Admitted of Leiden to the bar

1609 *Mare Liberum* published

1615 Became involved with Remonstrants

1625 *De jure belli ac pacis* (Concerning the Law of War and Peace) published

1635–45 Served as Swedish Queen Christina's ambassador to France

1645 Died, Rostock, Germany

1575   1600   1625   1650

Netherlands. A brilliant student, Grotius attended the University of Leiden, received a law degree at the age of fifteen, and was admitted to the bar and began his legal practice at Delft in 1599. It was at this time that he became interested in international law, and, in 1609, wrote a preliminary piece titled *Mare Liberum*, which advocated freedom of the seas to all countries.

In 1615, Grotius became involved in a religious controversy between two opposing groups, the Remonstrants, Dutch Protestants who abandoned Calvinism to follow the precepts of their leader, Jacobus Arminius, and the Anti-Remonstrants, who adhered to the beliefs of Calvinism. The dispute extended to politics, and when Maurice of Nassau gained control of the government, the Remonstrants lost popular support. Grotius, a supporter of the Remonstrants, was imprisoned in 1619. Two years later he escaped, seeking safety in Paris.

In Paris, Grotius began his legal writing, and, in 1625, produced *De jure belli ac pacis*, translated as "Concerning the Law of War and Peace." This work is regarded as the first official text of the principles of international law, wherein Grotius maintained that NATURAL LAW is the basis for legislation for countries as well as individuals. He opposed war in all but extreme cases and advocated respect for life and the ownership of property. The main sources for his theories were the Bible and history.

Grotius spent the remainder of his years in diplomatic and theological endeavors. From 1635 to 1645, he represented Queen Christina of Sweden as her ambassador to France. He pursued his religious interests and wrote several theological works. Grotius died August 28, 1645, in Rostock, Germany.

GROUND RENT 📖 Perpetual CONSIDERATION paid for the use and occupation of REAL PROPERTY to the individual who has transferred such property, and subsequently to his or her descendants or someone to whom the interest is conveyed. 📖

Ground rent agreements have sometimes required the payment of rent for a term of

BIOGRAPHY

Hugo Grotius

"WHAT THE CONSENT OF ALL MEN MAKES KNOWN AS THEIR WILL IS LAW."

ninety-nine years, with renewal at the option of the party who pays it. In this type of agreement, the LESSOR retains TITLE to the property. Large structures, such as hotels and office buildings, are ordinarily built on land under ground rent LEASES.

The concept of a ground rent arrangement is English in origin. Its original purpose was an attempt by feudal TENANTS to put themselves in the role of lords over lower tenants. This was proscribed by a law passed in 1290 that made every tenant a subject only to the overlord.

In the United States, the only states where the ground rent system has been used to any great extent are Maryland and Pennsylvania. These agreements were initially popular as a method of encouraging renters to improve the property, since they could own the buildings while paying rent on the land. The courts enforced the ground rent agreements, and they gained popularity with investors who purchased and sold shares in ground rent agreements.

Although the ground rent system was not used in New York, the state courts did recognize comparable *manorial* or *perpetual* leases. A DEED setting up a ground rent arrangement might indicate that it is to last for ninety-nine years, but since most agreements are automatically renewable, ground rents can last forever.

An obligation to pay the rent can terminate if (1) the individual entitled to receive rent forfeits such a right in a deed or other instrument; (2) the land is taken by EMINENT DOMAIN and the individual entitled to receive rent is compensated for the loss; (3) the agreement setting up the rent is breached and is thereafter unenforceable; or (4) the landowner also becomes the individual entitled to receive the rent or buys back the right to receive rents.

Under the COMMON LAW, rents that were not demanded for a number of years could not be collected, since the law assumed that they had been paid.

The term *ground rent* is currently applied to a lease for land upon which the tenant constructs a building. While the LANDLORD continues to own the land, the tenant owns all of the structures and pays rent for the ground only.

GROUNDS 📖 The basis or foundation; reasons sufficient in law to justify relief. 📖

Grounds are more than simply reasons for wanting a court to order relief. They are the reasons specified by the law that will serve as a basis for demanding relief. For example, a woman may sue her neighbor for TRESPASS on the ground that his fence was erected beyond his boundary line. Her real reason for suing may be that she does not like the loud music that he plays on his stereo, and she wants to cause him trouble. If his fence actually encroaches on her property, however, she has grounds for a CAUSE OF ACTION based on the trespass.

GROUP LEGAL SERVICES 📖 Legal services provided under a plan to members, who may be employees of the same company, members of the same organization, or individual consumers. 📖

Group legal services resembles group health insurance. It is an all-purpose, general coverage: for an annual fee, members are entitled to low-cost or free consultation with an attorney. Several forms of group legal services exist, ranging from employee-provided benefits to commercially marketed plans. These vary in scope, price, and availability. The first plans appeared in the early 1970s, for unions, which negotiated for them as employee benefits and have remained their primary users. Over the following two decades, the concept expanded as lawyers saw an opportunity for a nontraditional way to market their services. By the mid-1980s, the rise of commercial plans aimed at other groups sparked considerable interest in the legal profession, the media, and the public. Approximately 10 percent of U.S. citizens belonged to some form of plan in the 1990s, and observers expected that percentage to increase as more vendors entered the market to cater to consumers.

For several decades, the legal profession resisted the plans and sought to restrict them. State bars opposed them because the organization of the plans requires the imposition of an intermediary between the attorney and the client, which they saw as violative of the traditional attorney-client relationship. As the first groups to realize the advantages of using the plans, unions encountered stiff opposition in several states. Beginning in the early 1960s, however, the CIVIL RIGHTS MOVEMENT and a series of U.S. Supreme Court decisions removed these barriers.

The Court's decision in *NAACP v. Button,* 371 U.S. 415, 83 S. Ct. 328, 9 L. Ed. 2d 405 (1963), struck down a Virginia law that had prevented the NATIONAL ASSOCIATION FOR THE ADVANCEMENT OF COLORED PEOPLE from providing staff lawyer services to members. *Brotherhood of Railroad Trainmen v. Virginia ex rel. Virginia State Bar,* 377 U.S. 1, 84 S. Ct. 1113, 12 L. Ed. 2d 89 (1964), struck down an INJUNCTION that prohibited legal services activities of the union on FIRST and FOURTEENTH AMENDMENT grounds. In *United Mine Workers District 12 v. Illinois State Bar Ass'n,* 389 U.S. 217, 88 S. Ct. 353, 19 L. Ed. 2d 426 (1967), the Court permitted the union to collectively sponsor legal services for members' WORKERS' COMPENSATION claims, holding that restrictions imposed by the Illinois State Bar Association were unconstitutional under the First Amendment. In response, the legal profession slowly loosened restrictions in its Model Code of Professional Responsibility and Model Rules of Professional Conduct. By the mid-1970s, most of the special restrictions were gone.

These trends cleared the way for a broad expansion of group legal services. The chief benefit of such plans is discounted legal fees. Legal advice is often expensive. As in group health insurance, volume produces savings: the buying power of a large membership can lower the costs to individuals. This feature figured prominently in an expansion of the plans into commercial markets in the 1980s. Moreover, although individuals with low incomes are sometimes entitled to legal aid, and affluent individuals can usually afford a lawyer, members of the middle class are often hit hard by legal bills. Thus, marketers of group legal services have tried to appeal to middle-class consumers through such outlets as banks and credit card companies.

Federal and state regulations govern plans for group legal services. Employer-provided plans fall under the EMPLOYEE RETIREMENT INCOME SECURITY ACT (ERISA) (29 U.S.C.A. § 1001 et seq.). Enacted in 1974, ERISA protects employees' pension rights and imposes strict FIDUCIARY requirements on their group legal services. Other types of plans are subject to state laws, which generally impose light regulation and follow the legal profession's Model Rules of Professional Conduct in such areas as ethics and ATTORNEY-CLIENT PRIVILEGE.

GRUNDY, FELIX Felix Grundy served as U.S. attorney general from 1838 to 1839. A prominent criminal attorney, Grundy also served as a judge, state legislator, and U.S.

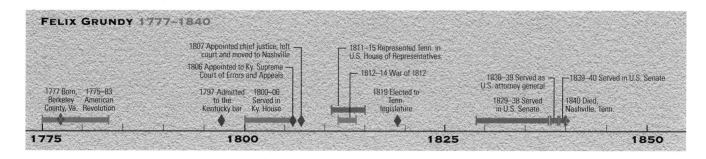

FELIX GRUNDY 1777–1840

1807 Appointed chief justice, left court and moved to Nashville

1806 Appointed to Ky. Supreme Court of Errors and Appeals

1811–15 Represented Tenn. in U.S. House of Representatives

1812–14 War of 1812

1838–39 Served as U.S. attorney general

1839–40 Served in U.S. Senate

1777 Born, Berkeley County, Va.

1775–83 American Revolution

1797 Admitted to the Kentucky bar

1800–06 Served in Ky. House

1819 Elected to Tenn. legislature

1829–38 Served in U.S. Senate

1840 Died, Nashville, Tenn.

1775   1800   1825   1850

senator. His brief service as attorney general took place during the administration of President MARTIN VAN BUREN.

Grundy was born September 11, 1777, in Berkeley County, Virginia (now West Virginia). His family moved to Kentucky in 1780. Although he had little early formal education, he studied law and was admitted to the Kentucky bar in 1797. An able advocate, he soon developed a reputation as an outstanding criminal lawyer.

In 1799 he was elected a delegate to the Kentucky state constitutional convention, where he played a prominent role. In 1800 he was elected to the Kentucky House of Representatives. He served in the house until 1806, when he was appointed associate justice of the state supreme court of errors and appeals. He was made chief justice in 1807, but left the court that same year and moved to Nashville.

Grundy established a law practice in Nashville before politics again became paramount. He was elected to the U.S. House of Representatives in 1811 and was reelected in 1813 During these years in Congress, Grundy was a strong advocate of territorial expansion, seeking to add Florida and Canada to the United States. He was also a supporter of the War of 1812, against Great Britain.

After resigning from Congress in 1815, Grundy returned to Nashville and his law practice. JAMES POLK, future president of the United States, apprenticed under Grundy during this period. In 1819 Grundy was elected to the Tennessee legislature, and in 1820 he acted as a commissioner to settle the boundary line between Kentucky and Tennessee.

BIOGRAPHY

"THE PROSECUTOR'S STATEMENT WAS BUT ANOTHER ILLUSTRATION OF COLD-BLOODED YANKEE CHARACTER."

During the 1820s Grundy concentrated on his law practice, while working to strengthen the Democratic party and to promote the candidacy of Tennessean ANDREW JACKSON for president. Though Jackson lost his first bid in 1824, he easily won in 1828 and 1832. In 1829 Grundy was appointed to a vacancy in the U.S. Senate, and in 1833 he was reelected.

Grundy remained in the Senate until 1838, when President Van Buren appointed him to serve as attorney general. Van Buren, who had been Jackson's vice president, had little success as president. An economic depression, called the Panic of 1837, crippled the U.S. economy for most of his four-year term. Grundy, sensing the fading political fortunes of Van Buren, resigned his position in December 1839 and returned to his seat in the Senate.

Grundy died in Nashville December 19, 1840.

GUARANTEE One to whom a GUARANTY is made. This word is also used, as a noun, to denote the contract of guaranty or the obligation of a guarantor, and, as a verb, to denote the action of assuming the responsibilities of a guarantor.

GUARANTY As a verb, to agree to be responsible for the payment of another's DEBT or the performance of another's DUTY, LIABILITY, or OBLIGATION if that person does not perform as he or she is legally obligated to do; to assume the responsibility of a guarantor; to warrant.

As a noun, an undertaking or promise that is COLLATERAL to the primary or principal obligation and that binds the guarantor to performance in the event of nonperformance by the principal obligor.

A sample guaranty

For value received, _____ hereby guarantee the payment of the within note at maturity, or at any time thereafter, with interest at the rate of _____ per cent per annum until paid, waiving demand, notice of nonpayment and protest. *[Signature]*

A guaranty is a CONTRACT that some particular thing shall be done exactly as it is agreed to be done, whether it is to be done by one person or another, and whether there be a prior or principal contractor or not.

GUARANTY CLAUSE A provision contained in a written document, such as a CONTRACT, DEED, or MORTGAGE, whereby one individual undertakes to pay the OBLIGATION of another individual.

The stipulation contained in Article IV, Section 4, of the U.S. Constitution, in which the federal government promises a republican form of government to every state and the defense and protection of the federal government if domestic violence occurs.

GUARDIAN A person lawfully invested with the power, and charged with the obligation, of taking care of and managing the property and rights of a person who, because of age, understanding, or self-control, is considered incapable of administering his or her own affairs.

GUARDIAN AD LITEM A guardian appointed by the court to represent the interests of INFANTS, the unborn, or incompetent persons in legal actions.

Guardians are adults who are legally responsible for protecting the well-being and interests of their WARD, who is usually a MINOR. A guardian ad litem is a unique type of guardian in a relationship that has been created by a court order only for the duration of a legal action. Courts appoint these special representatives for infants, minors, and mentally incompetent persons, all of whom generally need help protecting their rights in court. Such court-appointed guardians figure in divorces, child neglect and abuse cases, paternity suits, contested inheritances, and so forth, and are usually attorneys.

The concept of guardian ad litem grew out of developments in U.S. law in the late nineteenth century. Until then, the COMMON LAW had severely restricted who could bring lawsuits in FEDERAL COURTS; it was easiest to sue in states through EQUITY courts. Changes in the 1870s relaxed these standards by bringing federal codes in line with state codes, and in 1938, the Federal Rules of Civil Procedure removed the old barriers by establishing one system for CIVIL ACTIONS. Rule 17(c) addresses the rights of children and incompetent persons in three ways. First, it permits legal guardians to sue or defend on the behalf of minors or incompetent individuals. Second, it allows persons who do not have such a representative to name a "next friend," or guardian ad litem, to sue for them. And third, it states that federal courts "shall appoint a guardian ad litem for an infant or incompetent person not otherwise represented in an action or shall make such other order as it deems proper for [his or her] protection." In practice, the courts have interpreted this last provision broadly: the term *infants* is taken to mean unborn children and all minors. In addition, courts can exercise discretion; they are not required to appoint a guardian ad litem.

In the 1970s and 1980s, the importance of the guardian ad litem grew in response to increased concern about children's welfare. Two social developments brought about this growth: a rise in DIVORCE cases, and greater recognition of the gravity of CHILD ABUSE and neglect. Because states had generally modeled their civil court processes on the Federal Rules of Civil Procedure, the role of guardian ad litem was well established. But now, states began moving toward stronger legislation of their own. By the 1990s, many states had enacted laws specifying the guardians' qualifications, duties, and authority. Equally important, these laws spelled out requirements for the appointment of guardians ad litem in abuse cases. As a leader in the area, Florida enacted legislation in 1990 providing funding for the training of guardians ad litem (State of Florida Guardian Ad Litem Program Guidelines for Family Law Case Appointment, Fla. Stat. § 61.104). In 1993, after hearing an appeal in a particularly horrifying abuse case, the Supreme Court of West Virginia set forth guidelines for guardians ad litem in its decision (*In Re Jeffrey R. L.*, 190 W. Va. 24, 435 S.E.2d 162 [1993]).

Guardians ad litem have extensive power and responsibility. Their duties are greatest in cases involving children, where they investigate, attend to the child's emotional and legal needs, monitor the child's family, and seek to shield the child from the often bruising experience of a lawsuit. Their function as OFFICERS OF THE COURT is also extensive: in addition to compiling relevant facts, interviewing witnesses, giving testimony, and making recommendations to the court on issues of custody and visitation, they ensure that all parties comply with court orders. Given the rigors of the task, which is often voluntary or low paid, it is not surprising that courts have traditionally had difficulty finding adequate numbers of qualified individuals to serve as guardians ad litem.

In the mid-1990s, the role of guardian ad litem provoked new concerns. Whereas many attorneys perceived a need for guardians ad litem to be appointed in all CHILD CUSTODY proceedings, others expressed caution about the risk of lawsuits. Particularly for attorneys serving as guardians ad litem in divorce cases, this risk was high: parents upset with the result of a custody ruling might sue the guardian, just as a number of parties had in the 1980s brought action against government agencies involved in child welfare cases. Lawyers worried that the guardian ad litem system had become potentially dangerous for those whose rights it had been designed to protect, some of society's weakest members.

See also CIVIL PROCEDURE.

GUARDIAN AND WARD 📖 The legal relationship that exists between a person (the GUARDIAN) appointed by a court to take care of and manage the PROPERTY of a person (the WARD) who does not possess the legal CAPACITY to do so, by reason of age, comprehension, or self-control. 📖

The term *guardian* refers to a person appointed by a court to manage the affairs of another person who is unable to conduct those affairs on her or his own behalf. The term is most often applied to a person who is responsible for the care and management of an INFANT, which in legal terms is a person below the AGE OF MAJORITY. Thus, children who have not reached adulthood (usually age eighteen or twenty-one) must, with some exceptions, have a legal guardian.

Courts also appoint guardians to supervise the property and personal well-being of adults who cannot manage their affairs. Persons incapacitated because of mental or physical illness, drug or alcohol abuse, or other disability may require the appointment of a guardian to ensure the conservation of their PERSONAL PROPERTY and to oversee their day-to-day personal care. The term *conservator* is often used for a person designated to manage the property of an adult who is unable to do so.

The law of guardianship is based on the COMMON LAW and has been the province of state government. This law has been modified by state statutes. For example, section V of the UNIFORM PROBATE CODE, a model set of procedures governing the administration of TRUSTS and ESTATES, contains rules that guide courts in managing guardianships. The Uniform Probate Code, adopted by virtually every state, has done much to streamline PROBATE law. Nevertheless, a new set of procedures, titled the Uniform Guardianship and Protective Proceedings Act, has been proposed to codify guardianship issues among the states.

There are two basic types of guardians: of the person and of the property. A guardian of the person has custody of the ward and responsibility for the ward's daily care. A guardian of the property has the right and the duty to hold and manage all property belonging to the ward. A ward usually has a general guardian, who supervises both the person and the property, but in some circumstances it is necessary and convenient to divide responsibilities.

Persons for Whom a Guardian Is Appointed A guardian cannot be appointed for a person unless that person is in need of supervision by a representative of the court. The natural guardian of a child is the child's parent. A parent can lose this status by neglect or abandonment. In addition, when both parents die, leaving a minor child, the court will often appoint a guardian.

Guardians can also be appointed in medical emergencies. If a parent refuses to permit necessary treatment for a child, such as a blood transfusion or vaccination, the court can name a temporary guardian to consent to such treatment. An adult has the right to refuse medical treatment, even if her or his life is in immediate danger. However, if there is evidence that the adult is not thinking clearly or is not making the decision voluntarily, a guardian can be appointed to make the decision.

Selection of a Guardian Courts of GENERAL JURISDICTION in most states have the authority to appoint guardians. Typically, probate courts and juvenile courts hear cases involving guardianship. Probate courts, which oversee the administration of the estates of DECEDENTS, are the most common forum for the appointment of guardians. Juvenile courts decide on the appointment of guardians when a child has been removed from the home because of abuse or neglect, or has been declared a ward of the court. Generally, a court can appoint a guardian for a minor wherever the child lives. If a child lives in one state and has title to REAL

The natural guardian of a child is the child's parent.

ROBERT BURKE/LIAISON INTERNATIONAL

ESTATE in another state, a guardian can be appointed where the property is, in order to manage it.

A parent can appoint a guardian, usually by naming the guardian in a WILL. Some state laws allow a child to choose his or her own guardian if the child is over a certain age, usually fourteen. A court must approve the choice if the proposed guardian is suitable, even if the court believes someone else would be a better choice. Before approving the child's choice, however, the court must satisfy itself that the child understands the effect of the nomination and that the choice is not detrimental to the child's interests or contrary to law.

Guardianship statutes specify which persons have the right to ask a court to appoint a guardian for a certain child. Most of these laws list people who would be expected to have an interest in the child's welfare, usually relatives. Some statutes are more general, permitting applications to be filed by "any person." A court must examine a petition to determine whether the person applying for appointment as guardian really has the child's interest at heart.

Factors in Choosing a Guardian The choice of a guardian for a child is guided by the needs of the ward. The ward's age, affections for certain people, education, and morals are all important considerations. Courts prefer to allow a child to remain with a competent person who has been caring for the child rather than disrupt a stable home. Courts also examine the financial condition, health, judgment, morals, and character of the person who seeks guardianship of the ward. Although age alone is not a determining factor, it may be material to the individual's ability to fulfill the duties of guardian for the entire period of guardianship. Affluence is not a prerequisite for a guardian, although a guardian must be reasonably secure financially. As a rule, courts attempt to entrust the care of a child to someone with the same religious background as the child's.

A divorced parent is not disqualified from appointment as guardian of a child's property simply because the DIVORCE decree has awarded the other parent custody. The court almost always favors a parent over other relatives or someone not related to the child unless there is reason to believe the parent is not a fit guardian. A close family member is not disqualified from caring for a child whose property she or he is eligible to inherit, unless it appears that she or he is unkind to the child or concerned only with the wealth to be gained from the child's property.

Sometimes the responsibilities of guardianship are divided between two people. In one case, a mother continued to have custody of her children after her husband's death, but the court refused her request to be appointed guardian of the children's estates because she dissipated the family allowance. A parent can also be disqualified under different statutes for "notoriously bad conduct," by "willfully and knowingly abandoning the child," or for "failing to maintain the child" when he or she has the financial ability to contribute to the child's support.

Manner and Length of Appointment Once a guardian is selected, she or he can be required to take an OATH of office before performing the duties of guardian. Statutes generally require a guardian to post a BOND, that is, pay the court a sum of money out of which a ward can be reimbursed if the guardian fails to perform the duties faithfully. These laws also permit the court to waive this requirement if the ward's property is of relatively little value or if the guardian managing the property is a financial corporation, such as a bank or a trust company.

The formal appointment of a guardian is completed when the court issues the guardian a certificate called letters of guardianship. The naming of a guardian in a parent's will is only a nomination. The court must issue the letters of guardianship before a guardian has the legal authority to act.

Generally, a guardian's authority continues as long as the ward is below the legal age of majority. If the ward marries before reaching the age of majority, guardianship of the person ends. Under the law of some states, guardianship of the property continues until he or she reaches the age of majority. For an adult ward, guardianship ends when a court determines the ward no longer needs supervision.

A guardian can be divested of authority whenever a court is convinced that he or she has neglected the duties of guardian or mismanaged property. In some cases, courts have ordered partial removal. For example, a father who has squandered money that should have remained in his children's bank accounts can continue to have personal guardianship of them, while someone else acts as guardian of their property.

Duties and Responsibilities of a Guardian Generally, a guardian acts as guardian of both the person and the property of the ward, but in some circumstances these duties are split. When acting as guardian of the person, a guardian is entitled to custody and control of the ward. Some statutes make a specific exception when a child has a living parent who is suitable to provide daily care. The guardian then manages the child's property, and the parent retains custody. The rights and responsibilities associated with the child's daily care belong to the parent, but the guardian makes major decisions affecting long-term planning for the minor.

A guardian of the person of a child can prevent certain people from seeing the ward, but a court will not allow unreasonable restrictions. A guardian also has the right to move to a different state with the child, but can be required to appear in court prior to relocation and give assurances regarding the child's care. A guardian has the duty to provide for the child's support, education, and religious training. Courts permit a guardian to use income and interest earned by the child's assets to pay for the child's needs, but they are reluctant to permit the guardian to spend the principal. A parent is primarily responsible for the support of a child, so when a parent is living, his or her money must be used before the child's resources are spent. The child has a right to receive all his or her property upon reaching the age of majority, unless restrictions are imposed by a will or a trust instrument.

A general guardian or a guardian of the property is considered a FIDUCIARY—a person who occupies a position of trust and is legally obligated to protect the interests of the ward in the same manner as her or his own interests. A guardian cannot invest the ward's money in speculative ventures, agree not to sue someone who owes the ward money, or neglect legal proceedings, tax bills, or the maintenance of land, crops, or buildings that are part of the ward's estate. In addition, a guardian cannot maintain a business that the ward inherited or permit someone else to hold on to property belonging to the ward, without supervising such transactions. A guardian must earn income from the ward's property by making secure investments.

A guardian must take INVENTORY and collect all the ASSETS of the ward. Where permitted by law, TITLE is taken in the ward's name. Otherwise, the guardian owns the property "as guardian" for the ward, which indicates that the guardian has the legal right to hold or sell the property but must not use it for his or her personal benefit. The guardian must determine the value of the property and file a list of assets and their estimated value with the court. The

guardian must collect the assets promptly, and is liable to the ward's estate for any loss incurred owing to a failure to act promptly.

In general, a guardian does not have the authority to make CONTRACTS for the ward without specific permission from the court. If the child is party to a lawsuit, a guardian cannot assent to a settlement without first submitting the terms to the court for approval. A guardian must deposit any money held for the ward into an interest-bearing bank account separate from the guardian's own money. A guardian is also prohibited from making gifts from the ward's estate.

Generally, a guardian cannot tie up the ward's money by purchasing real estate, but can lend the money to someone else buying real estate if the property is sufficient security for the loan. A guardian cannot borrow money for personal use from the ward's estate. A guardian can LEASE property owned by the ward, but ordinarily the lease cannot extend beyond the time the ward reaches the age of majority. A guardian cannot MORTGAGE real property or permit a LIEN on personal property of the ward. A guardian can sell items of the ward's personal property, but must receive the permission of the court to sell the ward's real estate.

At the end of the guardianship period, a guardian must account for all transactions involving the ward's estate. The guardian is usually required to file interim reports periodically with the court, but a final report must be filed and all property turned over to the ward when the ward has reached the age of majority. If the guardian has not managed the property in an ethical manner, the ward, upon reaching adulthood, may sue for WASTE, CONVERSION, or EMBEZZLEMENT. If the management of the ward's

Adoptive parents are the guardians of those children they have formally adopted.

DAVID YOUNG-WOLFF/PHOTOEDIT

assets was not illegal but resulted in losses, the guardian must reimburse the ward. If the guardian has managed the assets correctly, the guardian is entitled to be paid out of the ward's estate for his or her services.

Finally, whenever a guardian participates in a lawsuit for the ward, she or he sues or is sued only "as guardian," and not personally. For example, if the ward sues a physician for malpractice and recovers damages, the money does not belong to the guardian even though she or he initiated the lawsuit for the ward. In the same way, if someone obtains a JUDGMENT for DAMAGES against the ward, the money must come from the ward's property, not from the guardian. If both the guardian and the ward are parties in one lawsuit, the guardian participates in the action as both a guardian and an individual.

GUEST STATUTES Widely adopted in the 1920s and 1930s, guest statutes were state laws that strictly limited LIABILITY in car accidents. These laws curtailed the legal rights of "guests"—nonpaying passengers such as friends or neighbors—who brought lawsuits against drivers after being hurt. Generally speaking, they prevented guests from suing car drivers or owners except in cases of a very high degree of NEGLIGENCE. Mere ordinary carelessness was an insufficient ground for a suit: if a guest was injured when a driver momentarily failed to pay attention and crashed the car, most states would reject a lawsuit. The net effect of guest statutes was to protect drivers and INSURANCE companies while leaving injured passengers, for the most part, out of luck. Constitutional challenges to the laws frequently appeared in state and federal courts throughout the middle of the twentieth century, but courts waited until the 1970s and

Guest statutes, which limited the liability of a driver in the case of an accident, have been repealed or overturned. Today in nearly all states passengers can sue a driver for negligence and recover damages.

1980s to begin narrowing and ultimately striking down the statutes in wholesale numbers.

The first guest statutes appeared in 1927, in Connecticut and Iowa (1927 Conn. Pub. Acts 4404, ch. 308, § 1 [repealed 1937]; Iowa Code Ann. § 321.494 [Supp. 1983]). Coinciding with a burst in manufacturing that increased the number of AUTOMOBILES produced, the laws arose to meet the growing number of suits resulting from car accidents. By 1939, the last year in which a guest statute was enacted, thirty-three states had such laws or court precedents of comparable effect. The rationale behind the statutes was that a driver's liability should be limited: mere carelessness was seen as so commonplace that drivers in all accidents would be held liable for hurting their passengers were that the standard. For an injured passenger to surmount the barriers of a guest statute, greater evidence would have to be shown. A lawsuit would have to prove that the driver's actions were much more than careless—that they were grossly or willfully negligent. Other states went further, setting the standard as WILLFUL or WANTON misconduct. In essence, little short of an utter disregard for safety or a desire to run someone off the road would hold up in court in a civil suit.

Thus, in one typical 1943 case, the Iowa guest statute prevented a passenger from recovering for injury. On May 30, 1942, a four-door Plymouth carrying five teenagers along a narrow, twisty gravel road went out of control, hit a bridge, and turned over. Driving was seventeen-year-old Fabian Gehl. Seconds before the accident, Gehl had leaned over to pick up a cigarette from the floor of the car. John Neyens, an eighteen-year-old passenger who was injured in the accident, sued Gehl. Under the guest statute, Neyens had to convince a jury that Gehl's behavior was reckless. At trial, the jury ruled in favor of the defendant, finding that reaching down for a cigarette, smashing the car into a bridge, and rolling it over was something short of reckless. On appeal, Neyens lost again (*Neyens v. Gehl et al.*, 235 Iowa 115, 15 N.W.2d 888 [1944]).

Over the years, guest statutes caused considerable controversy. When they were defended at all, it was to argue that they were needed to prevent drivers and passengers from colluding to bring fraudulent claims against insurers. Critics took a different tack: they argued that guest statutes unfairly protected drivers and insurance companies, while leaving injured passengers and the survivors of dead passengers with no compensation for their losses. The

DAVID YOUNG-WOLFF/PHOTOEDIT

distinction between paying and nonpaying passengers seemed arbitrary: why should friends given a ride in a car be unable to recover damages when, for example, commuters riding in a bus were able to do so? In many states, even cattle being transported to market enjoyed greater legal protection than a guest in a car. But such arguments fell on deaf ears for many years. As early as 1929, the U.S. Supreme Court rejected a constitutional challenge to a guest statute on DUE PROCESS grounds (*Silver v. Silver*, 280 U.S. 117, 50 S. Ct. 57, 74 L. Ed. 221), and as late as 1977, it refused to hear another challenge because it did not pose a substantial FEDERAL QUESTION (*Hill v. Garner*, 434 U.S. 989, 98 S. Ct. 623, 54 L. Ed. 2d 486 [mem.]).

Nonetheless, the death knell for guest statutes began in the 1970s. As the concept of liability evolved, state legislatures began providing other means for passengers to seek compensation, and a few repealed their guest laws. Reacting to these changes, courts began to carve out exceptions in existing guest statutes, and ultimately to overturn the laws on constitutional grounds. Thus, the Supreme Court of Utah said, when striking down Utah's guest statute in 1984, "The original scope of the guest statute has been substantially narrowed, and its application to any particular guest is both problematic and irrational" (*Malan v. Lewis*, 693 P.2d 661). By 1996, only Alabama still had a guest statute (Ala. Code § 32-1-2).

GUILTY 📖 Blameworthy; culpable; having committed a TORT or CRIME; devoid of innocence. 📖

An individual is guilty if he or she is responsible for a delinquency or a criminal or civil offense. When an ACCUSED is willing to accept legal responsibility for a criminal act, he or she pleads guilty. Similarly, a JURY returns a VERDICT of guilty upon finding that a defendant has committed a crime. In the event that a jury is not convinced that a defendant has committed a crime, jurors can return a verdict of *not guilty*, which does not mean that the individual is innocent or that the jurors are so convinced, but rather that they do not believe sufficient evidence has been presented to prove that the defendant is guilty.

In civil lawsuits, the term *guilty* does not imply criminal responsibility but refers to misconduct.

GUN CONTROL 📖 Government regulation of the manufacture, sale, and possession of firearms. 📖

The SECOND AMENDMENT to the U.S. Constitution is at the heart of the issue of gun control. The Second Amendment declares that, "A well

Murder—Weapons Used or Cause of Death: 1993

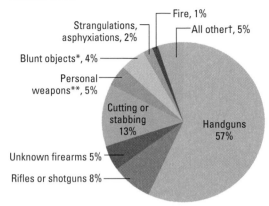

* Refers to club, hammer, etc.
**Refers to hands, fists, feet, etc.
† Includes poison, drowning, explosives, narcotics, and unknown causes.

Source: Federal Bureau of Investigation, *FBI Supplemental Homicide Report*, annual; *Crime in the United States*, annual.

regulated Militia, being necessary to the security of a free State, the right of the people to keep and bear Arms, shall not be infringed."

To many, the language of the amendment appears to grant to the people the absolute right to bear arms. However, the U.S. Supreme Court has held that the amendment merely protects the right of states to form a state MILITIA (*United States v. Miller*, 307 U.S. 174, 59 S. Ct. 816, 83 L. Ed. 1206 [1939]).

Even before the *Miller* opinion defined the Second Amendment in 1939, Congress, state legislatures, and local governing bodies were passing laws that infringed on the right to bear arms. Kentucky passed the first state legislation prohibiting the carrying of concealed weapons, in 1813. By 1993 firearms were regulated by approximately twenty-three thousand federal, state, and local laws.

State and local firearms laws vary widely. Thirteen states prohibit only the carrying of concealed handguns. At the other end of the spectrum, three Chicago suburbs—Morton Grove, Oak Park, and Evanston—ban handgun ownership outright. Generally, firearms regulations are more restrictive in large metropolitan areas.

State and local firearms laws and ordinances include outright bans of certain firearms, prohibitions on the alteration of certain firearms, and restrictions on the advertising of guns. State gun control laws also address the THEFT of handguns, INHERITANCE of firearms, use of firearms as COLLATERAL for loans, possession of firearms by ALIENS, discharge of firearms in a public area, and alteration of numbers or other

TAKE THAT! AND THAT! THE GUN CONTROL DEBATE CONTINUES

Gun control motivates one of U.S. law's fiercest duels.

Arguments favoring control range from calls for regulation to support for total disarmament. At the most moderate point of the spectrum is the idea that government should regulate who owns guns and for what purpose, a position held by the lobby Handgun Control Incorporated (HGI), which helped write the Brady law. This kind of monitoring is far too little for one antigun group, the Coalition to Stop Gun Violence, which demands a complete ban on manufacturing and selling guns to the general public. The opposition leaves room for only very slight compromise. The National Rifle Association (NRA)—the most powerful opponent of gun control—generally fights any restrictive measure. The NRA has opposed efforts to ban so-called cop-killer bullets, which can pierce police safety vests. It has supported background checks at the time of purchase, yet only if these are done instantly so as not to inconvenience the vast majority of gun buyers. Even more adamant is the group Gun Owners of America, which opposes any legal constraints.

With so many laws on the books, the question of gun control's constitutionality would seem already settled. Yet this is where the gun control debate begins. The Second Amendment reads, "A well regulated Militia, being necessary to the security of a free State, the right of the people to keep and bear Arms, shall not be infringed." Does this mean citizens have a constitutional right to own guns? The gun lobby says yes.

A minority of legal scholars believe that the framers of the Bill of Rights meant to include citizens along with "a

well regulated Militia" in the right to bear arms. One supporter of this view is Professor Sanford Levinson, of the University of Texas, who argues that the Second Amendment is intended to tie the hands of government in restricting private ownership of guns. He charges that liberal academics who support gun control read only the Constitution's Second Amendment so narrowly.

IN FOCUS

The majority view is more restrictive in its reading. It pictures the Second Amendment as tailored to a specific right, namely, that of states to equip and maintain a state national guard. Harvard law professor Laurence Tribe argues that "[t]he Second Amendment's preamble makes it clear that it is not designed to create an individual right to bear arms outside of the context of a state-run militia."

This argument has a leading advantage over the minority position: it is what the U.S. Supreme Court has consistently held for over fifty years. In the 1939 case of *United States v. Miller*, 307 U.S. 174; 59 S. Ct. 816, 83 L. Ed. 1206 (1939)—the only modern Supreme Court case to address the issue—a majority of the Court refused to find an individual constitutional right to bear arms.

Since the meaning of the Second Amendment seems well settled, the dispute has turned to pragmatics. How well does gun control work, if it works at all? Measuring lives saved by gun control is practically impossible; it is only possible to count how many lives are lost to gun violence. Advocates generally claim that the fact that lives are lost to guns and the possibility that even one life may be saved through gun

control are justification enough for legislation. They can quantify gains of another sort under the Brady law. In early 1995, the Justice Department estimated that background checks had kept forty thousand felons from buying handguns, a figure derived from information provided by the state and local authorities who ran the checks.

Opponents say gun control is a gross failure. They argue that it never has kept criminals from buying guns illegally. Instead, they say, prohibition efforts have only been nuisances for law-abiding gun owners: city ordinances like Chicago's that ban handgun sales send buyers to the suburbs, and the Brady law's five-day waiting period amounts to another unfair penalty. Moreover, opponents rebut arguments about gun violence by insisting that guns are actually used to protect their owners from harm. The NRA's chief lobbyist has argued that the self-defense effectiveness of guns is proved by "the number of crimes thwarted, lives protected, injuries prevented, medical costs saved and property preserved."

Settling the gun control debate is no more likely than solving the problem of crime itself. In fact, only the latter could ever bring about the former. After all, it is violent crime, more than accidental gun deaths involving children, that animates the gun control movement. On this point, the two sides agree briefly and then diverge once again. Both want tougher action on crime. The key difference is that gun control opponents want such measures to include almost every traditional means available—more police officers, more prisons, and longer prison sentences—except the control of guns. Advocates believe there can be no effective anticrime measures without gun control.

identifying markings on firearms. States generally base their power to control firearms on the police power provisions of their constitutions, which grant to the states the right to enact laws for public safety.

Congress finds its power to regulate firearms in the Commerce Clause, in Article I, Section 8, Clause 3, of the U.S. Constitution. Under the Commerce Clause, Congress may regulate commercial activity between the states and commerce with foreign countries. In reviewing federal legislation enacted pursuant to the COMMERCE CLAUSE, the U.S. Supreme Court has given Congress tremendous leeway. Under the Commerce Clause, Congress may enact criminal statutes regarding firearms if the activity at issue relates to interstate transactions, affects interstate commerce, or is such that control is necessary and proper to carry out the intent of the Commerce Clause.

In 1927, Congress passed the Mailing of Firearms Act, 18 U.S.C.A. § 1715, which banned the shipping of concealable handguns through the mail. Congress followed this with the National Firearms Act of 1934 (ch. 757, 48 Stat. 1236–1240 [26 U.S.C.A. § 1132 et seq.]), which placed heavy taxes on the manufacture and distribution of firearms. One year later, Congress prohibited unlicensed manufacturers and dealers from shipping firearms across state borders, with the Federal Firearms Act of 1938 (ch. 850, § 2(f), 52 Stat. 1250, 1251).

In 1968, after the ASSASSINATIONS of President JOHN F. KENNEDY, civil rights activists MALCOLM X and MARTIN LUTHER KING, JR., and Senator ROBERT F. KENNEDY, Congress responded to the public outcry by passing the Gun Control Act of 1968 (Pub. L. No. 90-615, § 102, 82 Stat. 1214 [codified at 18 U.S.C.A. §§ 921–928]). This act repealed the Federal Firearms Act and replaced it with increased federal control over firearms. Title I of the act requires the federal licensing of anyone manufacturing or selling guns or ammunition. Title I also prohibits the interstate mail-order sale of guns and ammunition, the sale of guns to MINORS or persons with criminal records, and the importation of certain firearms. Title II of the act imposes the same restrictions on other destructive devices, such as bombs, grenades, and other explosive materials.

Between 1979 and 1987, a total of 693,000 people in the United States were assaulted by criminals armed with handguns. Statistics such as this as well as high profile shootings, such as that of President RONALD REAGAN and his aide, James Brady, in 1982, led to pressure for further gun control measures.

In November 1993 Congress passed the Brady Handgun Violence Prevention Act (18 U.S.C.A. §§ 921–922 [1994]). The Brady Act imposes a five-day waiting period before a handgun may be taken home by a purchaser. During the waiting period, the seller is required to check the background of the buyer. Under the act, the waiting period will be phased out, to be replaced by a national computerized system for background checks.

In August 1994, Congress passed legislation banning so-called assault weapons under title XI of the Public Safety and Recreational Firearms Use Protection Act (Pub. L. No. 103-322, 108 Stat. 1796 [codified as amended in scattered sections of 42 U.S.C.A.]). This act bans the manufacture, sale, and use of nineteen types of semiautomatic weapons and facsimiles, as well as certain high-capacity ammunition magazines.

In 1995 the U.S. Supreme Court set a limit on gun control with its decision in *United States v. Lopez*, 514 U.S. 549, 115 S. Ct. 1624, 131 L. Ed. 2d 626. In *Lopez*, the Court ruled that Congress had exceeded its authority under the Commerce Clause in passing a law that criminalized the possession of a firearm within one thousand feet of a school (Gun-Free School Zones Act of 1990 [18 U.S.C.A. § 922(1)(1)(A)]). The Court held that because such gun possession was not an economic activity that significantly affected interstate commerce, it was beyond Congress's power to regulate.

See also WEAPONS.

HABEAS CORPUS

HABEAS CORPUS 📖 [*Latin, You have the body.*] A WRIT (court order) that commands an individual or a government official who has restrained another to produce the prisoner at a designated time and place so that the court can determine the legality of CUSTODY and decide whether to order the prisoner's release. 📖

A writ of habeas corpus directs a person, usually a prison warden, to produce the prisoner and justify the prisoner's detention. If the prisoner argues successfully that the incarceration is in violation of a constitutional right, the court may order the inmate's release. Habeas corpus relief may also be used to obtain custody of a child or to gain the release of a detained person who is insane, is a drug addict, or has an infectious disease. Usually, though, it is a response to imprisonment by the criminal justice system.

A writ of habeas corpus is authorized by statute in federal courts and in all state courts. An inmate in state or federal prison asks for the writ by filing a PETITION with the court that sentenced him or her. In most states, and in FEDERAL COURTS, the inmate is given the opportunity to present a short oral argument in a HEARING before the court. The petitioner may also receive an evidentiary hearing to establish evidence for the petition.

The habeas corpus concept was first expressed in the MAGNA CHARTA, a constitutional document forced on King John by English landowners at Runnymede on June 15, 1215. Among the liberties declared in the Magna Charta was this: "No free man shall be seized, or imprisoned, or disseised, or outlawed, or exiled, or injured in any way, nor will we enter on him or send against him except by the lawful judgment of his peers, or by the law of the land." This principle evolved to mean that no person should be deprived of freedom without DUE PROCESS OF LAW.

The writ of habeas corpus was first used by the COMMON-LAW courts in thirteenth- and fourteenth-century England. These courts, composed of legal professionals, were in competition with feudal courts, which were controlled by local landowners, or "lords." The feudal courts lacked procedural consistency, and on this basis, the common-law courts began to issue writs demanding the release of persons imprisoned by them. From the late fifteenth to the seventeenth centuries, the common-law courts used the writ to order the release of persons held by royal courts, such as the CHANCERY, Admiralty courts, and the STAR CHAMBER.

The only reference to the writ of habeas corpus in the U.S. Constitution is contained in Article I, Section 9, Clause 2. This clause provides, "The Privilege of the Writ of Habeas Corpus shall not be suspended, unless when in Cases of Rebellion or Invasion the public Safety may require it." The writ was suspended by President ABRAHAM LINCOLN during the Civil War in 1861 when he authorized his generals to arrest anyone thought dangerous. It was also suspended by Congress in 1863 to allow the Union army to hold people temporarily until trial in the civilian courts. The Union army reportedly ignored the statute suspending the writ and conducted trials under martial law.

In 1789, Congress passed the JUDICIARY ACT OF 1789 (ch. 20, § 14, 1 Stat. 73 [codified in title 28 of the U.S.C.A.]), which granted to federal courts the power to hear the habeas corpus petitions of federal prisoners. In 1867, Con-

Ruben ("Hurricane") Carter

Federal courts grant writs of habeas corpus only when grave constitutional violations have occurred. The granting of Ruben ("Hurricane") Carter's habeas petition in 1985 freed him from almost twenty years of imprisonment for a crime he maintains he did not commit.

Carter was the number 1–ranked contender for the U.S. middleweight boxing title when he and John Artis were arrested in 1966 for murdering three people in Paterson, New Jersey. Carter and Artis were African American; the victims were white. Carter and Artis claimed they were innocent and the victims of racism and a police frame-up, but they were convicted of murder and sentenced to life imprisonment.

Carter fought his conviction in state court, but the verdict was upheld. In 1974 he published *The Sixteenth Round: From Number 1 Contender to Number 45472*. The book became a national best-seller and drew attention to his case. In 1975 Bob Dylan wrote and recorded the song "Hurricane," which recounted Carter's arrest and trial and characterized Carter as an innocent man. This publicity, along with an investigation by the New Jersey public defenders' office, led to a motion for a new trial. The motion was granted, but Carter and Artis were convicted again in 1976. Carter remained imprisoned, and Artis was paroled.

After all state appeals were exhausted, it appeared the case was closed. However, in 1985 Carter and Artis filed a petition for a writ of habeas corpus in New Jersey federal court. In November 1985 Judge H. Lee Sarokin ruled that the second murder trial convictions were unconstitutional because the prosecution had improperly argued racial hatred as a motive and had withheld critical evidence from Carter and Artis that would have helped show their innocence (*Carter v. Rafferty*, 621 F. Supp. 533 [D.N.J. 1985]). Therefore, he granted habeas corpus and overturned the convictions. Carter was released and moved to Canada.

gress passed the Habeas Corpus Act of February 5 (ch. 28, 14 Stat. 385 [28 U.S.C.A. § 2241 et seq.]). This act gave federal courts the power to issue habeas corpus writs for "any person . . . restrained in violation of the Constitution, or of any treaty or law of the United States." The U.S. Supreme Court has interpreted this statute to mean that federal courts may hear the habeas corpus petitions of state prisoners as well as federal prisoners.

The writ of habeas corpus is an extraordinary remedy because it gives a court the power to release a prisoner after the prisoner has been processed through the criminal justice system, with all its procedural safeguards and appeals. For this reason, the burden is initially on the petitioning prisoner to prove that he or she is being held in violation of a constitutional right. If the petitioner can meet this burden with sufficient evidence, the burden shifts to the warden to justify the imprisonment.

A prisoner may file a petition for a writ of habeas corpus with the sentencing court only after exhausting all APPEALS and MOTIONS. Federal courts may receive a petition from a state prisoner, but not until the petitioner has attempted all available appeals and motions and habeas corpus petitions in the state courts. Federal prisoners must exhaust all available appeals and motions in the federal sentencing court and federal appeals courts before filing a habeas corpus petition with the sentencing court. If the first petition is denied, the inmate may petition the appeals courts.

A petition for a writ of habeas corpus is a CIVIL ACTION against the jailer. It is not an appeal and not a continuation of the criminal case against the inmate. It is not used to determine guilt or innocence. Rather, the purpose of the suit is solely to determine whether the confinement is in violation of a constitutional right. This is significant because it limits the scope of complaints a petitioner may use as a basis for the writ.

Violation of the Due Process Clauses of the Fifth and FOURTEENTH AMENDMENTS is the most common basis for a writ of habeas corpus. Prosecutorial misconduct, juror MALFEASANCE, and ineffective assistance of counsel are common due process grounds for the writ. FIFTH AMENDMENT grounds include failure of the police to give *Miranda* warnings before in-custody questioning, in violation of the right against SELF-INCRIMINATION, and multiple trials, in violation of the DOUBLE JEOPARDY prohibition. The EIGHTH AMENDMENT right against CRUEL AND UNUSUAL PUNISHMENT is another common ground for habeas corpus relief, especially in cases involving the death penalty or a lengthy prison term.

A sample form for use in applications for habeas corpus

Name _____

Prison number _____

Place of confinement _____

United States District Court _____ District of _____

Case No. _____

(To be supplied by Clerk of U.S. District Court)

_____, PETITIONER

(Full name)

v.

_____, RESPONDENT

(Name of Warden, Superintendent, Jailor, or authorized person having custody of petitioner)

and

THE ATTORNEY GENERAL OF THE STATE OF _____,
ADDITIONAL RESPONDENT.

(If petitioner is attacking a judgment which imposed a sentence to be served in the *future*, petitioner must fill in the name of the state where the judgment was entered. If petitioner has a sentence to be served in the *future* under a federal judgment which he wishes to attack, he should file a motion under 28 U.S.C. § 2255, in the federal court which entered the judgment.)

PETITION FOR WRIT OF HABEAS CORPUS BY A
PERSON IN STATE CUSTODY

Instructions—Read Carefully

(1) This petition must be legibly handwritten or typewritten, signed by the petitioner and sworn to before a notary public or institutional officer authorized to administer an oath. Any false statement of a material fact may serve as the basis for prosecution and conviction for perjury. All questions must be answered concisely in the proper space on the form.

(2) Additional pages are not permitted except with respect to the *facts* which you rely upon to support your grounds for relief. No citation of authorities need be furnished. If briefs or arguments are submitted, they should be submitted in the form of a separate memorandum.

(3) Upon receipt of a fee of $5 your petition will be filed if it is in proper order.

(4) If you do not have the necessary filing fee, you may request permission to proceed *in forma pauperis*, in which event you must execute the affidavit on the last page, setting forth information establishing your inability to prepay the fees and costs or give security therefor. If you wish to proceed *in forma pauperis*, you must have an authorized officer at the penal institution complete the certificate as to the amount of money and securities on deposit to your credit in any account in the institution. If your prison account exceeds $_____, you must pay the filing fees as required by the rule of the district court.

(5) Only judgments entered by one court may be challenged in a single petition. If you seek to challenge judgments entered by different courts either in the same state or in different states, you must file separate petitions as to each court.

(6) Your attention is directed to the fact that you must include all grounds for relief and all facts supporting such grounds for relief in the petition you file seeking from any judgment of conviction.

A sample form for use in applications for habeas corpus (continued)

(7) When the petition is fully completed, *the original and two copies* must be mailed to the Clerk of the United States District Court whose address is _____

(8) Petitions which do not conform to these instructions will be returned with a notation as to the deficiency.

PETITION

1. Name and location of court which entered the judgment of conviction under attack

    _____

2. Date of judgment of conviction _____

3. Length of sentence _____

4. Nature of offense involved (all counts) _____

    _____

    _____

    _____

5. What was your plea? (Check one)
    (a) not guilty   ☐
    (b) Guilty   ☐
    (c) Nolo contendere   ☐
    If you entered a guilty plea to one count or indictment, and a not guilty plea to another count or indictment, give details:

    _____

    _____

    _____

6. Kind of trial: (Check one)
    (a) Jury   ☐
    (b) Judge only   ☐

7. Did you testify at the trial?
    Yes ☐   No ☐

8. Did you appeal from the judgment of conviction?
    Yes ☐   No ☐

    [Portions omitted for purpose of illustration.]

12. State *concisely* every ground on which you claim that you are being held unlawfully. Summarize *briefly* the *facts* supporting each ground. If necessary, you may attach pages stating additional grounds and *facts* supporting same.

    Caution: In order to proceed in the federal court, you must ordinarily first exhaust your state court remedies as to each ground on which you request action by the federal court. If you fail to set forth all grounds in this petition, you may be barred from presenting additional grounds at a later date.

    For your information, the following is a list of the most frequently raised grounds for relief in habeas corpus proceedings. Each statement preceded by a letter constitutes a separate ground for possible relief. You may raise any grounds which you may have other than those listed if you have exhausted your state court remedies with respect to them. However, *you should raise in this petition all available grounds* (relating to this conviction) on which you base your allegations that you are being held in custody unlawfully.

    Do not check any of these listed grounds. If you select one or more of these grounds for relief, you must allege facts. The petition will be returned to you if you merely check (a) through (j) or any one of these grounds.

A sample form for use in applications for habeas corpus (continued)

(a) Conviction obtained by plea of guilty which was unlawfully induced or not made voluntarily with understanding of the nature of the charge and the consequences of the plea.

(b) Conviction obtained by use of coerced confession.

(c) Conviction obtained by use of evidence gained pursuant to an unconstitutional search and seizure.

(d) Conviction obtained by use of evidence obtained pursuant to an unlawful arrest.

(e) Conviction obtained by a violation of the privilege against self-incrimination.

(f) Conviction obtained by unconstitutional failure of the prosecution to disclose to the defendant evidence favorable to the defendant.

(g) Conviction obtained by a violation of the protection against double jeopardy.

(h) Conviction obtained by action of a grand or petit jury which was unconstitutionally selected and impaneled.

(i) Denial of effective assistance of counsel.

(j) Denial of right of appeal.

[Portions omitted for purpose of illustration.]

17. Do you have any future sentence to serve after you complete the sentence imposed by the judgment under attack?

Yes ☐   No ☐

(a) If so, give name and location of court which imposed sentence to be served in the future: _____

(b) And give date and length of sentence to be served in the future: _____

(c) Have you filed, or do you contemplate filing, any petition attacking the judgment which imposed the sentence to be served in the future?

Yes ☐   No ☐

Wherefore, petitioner prays that the Court grant petitioner relief to which he may be entitled in this proceeding.

Executed at _____

on _____, 19___.

_____   _____
   Signature of Attorney (if any)   Signature of Petitioner

There are several notable restrictions on the writ's application. FOURTH AMENDMENT violations of the right against unreasonable SEARCH AND SEIZURE cannot be raised in a habeas corpus petition. Inmates are not entitled to a court-appointed attorney for habeas corpus petitions. Newly developed constitutional principles will not be applied retroactively in habeas corpus cases except where doubt is cast on the guilt of the prisoner. Delay in filing a habeas petition may result in its dismissal, if the government is prejudiced (made less able to respond) by the delay. In addition, the petitioner must be in custody to request a writ of habeas corpus. This rule prevents an inmate from challenging a conviction through habeas corpus after serving out a prison term for the conviction.

The law of habeas corpus is ever changing. In the 1990s, the U.S. Supreme Court took steps to further limit the writ's application. In *Keeney v. Tamayo-Reyes*, 504 U.S. 1, 112 S. Ct. 1715, 118 L. Ed. 2d 318 (1992), the Court held that a habeas corpus petitioner is not entitled to an evidentiary hearing in federal court unless she or he can show two things: a reason for failing to develop evidence at trial, and actual PREJUDICE to the inmate's defense as a result of the failure. In *Herrera v. Collins*, 506 U.S. 390, 113 S. Ct. 853, 122 L. Ed. 2d 203 (1993), the Court held that a claim of actual innocence is not a basis for federal habeas corpus relief. This means that newly discovered evidence alone does not entitle a petitioner to federal habeas corpus relief.

The availability and import of habeas corpus in state courts is also subject to change through judicial decisions and new laws. For example, in 1995, the Texas Legislature passed a law that made the habeas corpus process concurrent with appeals (Tex. Crim. Proc. Code Ann. art. 11.071). This law effectively limited the number of times a Texas state prisoner could challenge the disposition of a criminal case. Significantly, the law applied to all criminal defendants, including defendants facing the death penalty. Under the legislation, a death row inmate has only one round of review in Texas state courts before seeking relief in federal court.

In 1996 Congress passed a law restricting access to habeas corpus relief (Pub. L. No. 104-132). Under the new law, if a state provides a convict with competent postconviction counsel, there is a six month statute of limitations on filing a habeas petition. If counsel is not provided, the convict has a one year limitations period for investigating and filing the petition. The new law limits the time a federal court can spend on the case, limits its ability to hold evidentiary hearings or challenge factual determinations of the state court, and curtails the possibility of successive habeas petitions. In addition, the law eliminated federal funding for death penalty resource centers, which assist death row inmates with appeals.

Many states have also begun restricting time limits and other aspects of the postconviction review process.

HABEAS CORPUS ACT

An English statute enacted in 1679 during the reign of King Charles II and subsequently amended and supplemented by enactments of Parliament that permitted, in certain cases, a person to challenge the legality of his or her imprisonment before a court that ordered the person to appear before it at a designated time so that it could render its decision.

The Habeas Corpus Act served as the precursor of HABEAS CORPUS provisions found in federal and state constitutions and statutes that safeguard the valuable guarantee of personal liberty.

HABENDUM CLAUSE

The portion of a DEED to REAL PROPERTY that begins with the phrase *To have and to hold* and that provides a description of the ownership rights of the transferee of such property.

Whereas a GRANTING CLAUSE contains the words of transfer of an interest, a habendum clause defines the ESTATE granted and declares the extent of the interest conveyed. For example, such a clause might say: "To have and to hold the premises herein granted unto the party of the second part, and to the female heirs of the party of the second part forever." This particular habendum clause qualifies the estate granted by limiting its inheritability to the female heirs of the GRANTEE.

HABITABILITY

Fitness for occupancy. The requirement that rented premises, such as a house or apartment, be reasonably fit to occupy.

A WARRANTY of habitability is an implied promise by a LANDLORD of residential premises that such premises are fit for human habitation. It exists in a majority of states, either by statute or case law, and implies that the premises are free from any condition that is unsafe or unsanitary. A breach of this warranty would, for example, occur if none of the toilets were in working order or if the roof of a house was in total disrepair.

A warranty of habitability begins at the commencement of the TENANCY and continues for its duration.

HABITUAL

Regular or customary; usual.

A *habitual* DRUNKARD, for example, is an individual who regularly becomes intoxicated as opposed to a person who drinks infrequently. A *habitual criminal* is a legal category that has been created by a number of state statutes by which serious penalties can be imposed on individuals who have been repeatedly convicted of a designated crime.

HAGUE TRIBUNAL

An ARBITRATION court established for the purpose of facilitating immediate recourse for the settlement of international disputes.

The Hague Tribunal was established by the Hague Peace Conference in 1899 to provide a permanent court accessible at all times for the resolution of international differences. The court was granted JURISDICTION over all arbitration cases, provided the parties thereto did not decide to institute a special tribunal. In addition, an international bureau was established to act as a registry for the tribunal and to serve as the channel of communications with respect to the meetings of the court.

The Hague Tribunal is considered permanent due to the fact that there is a permanent list of members from among whom the arbitrators are chosen. In 1907 at the Second Hague Conference it was provided that of the two arbitrators selected by each of the parties, only one could be a national of the state appointing him or her.

See also INTERNATIONAL LAW.

HAMER, FANNIE LOU TOWNSEND

Fannie Lou Hamer worked for voter registration for African Americans in the U.S. South and helped establish the Mississippi Freedom Democratic party (MFDP), which successfully challenged the all-white DEMOCRATIC PARTY in Mississippi.

BIOGRAPHY

THE GRANGER COLLECTION, NEW YORK

Fannie Lou Townsend Hamer

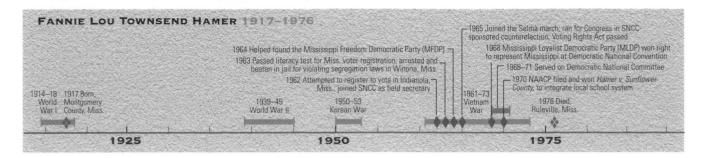

FANNIE LOU TOWNSEND HAMER 1917–1976

1965 Joined the Selma march; ran for Congress in SNCC-sponsored counterelection; Voting Rights Act passed

1964 Helped found the Mississippi Freedom Democratic Party (MFDP)

1968 Mississippi Loyalist Democratic Party (MLDP) won right to represent Mississippi at Democratic National Convention

1963 Passed literacy test for Miss. voter registration; arrested and beaten in jail for violating segregation laws in Winona, Miss.

1968–71 Served on Democratic National Committee

1962 Attempted to register to vote in Indianola, Miss.; joined SNCC as field secretary

1970 NAACP filed and won *Hamer v. Sunflower County* to integrate local school system

1914–18
World
War I

1917 Born,
Montgomery
County, Miss.

1939–45
World War II

1950–53
Korean War

1961–73
Vietnam
War

1976 Died,
Ruleville, Miss.

1925   1950   1975

Hamer was born October 6, 1917, in Montgomery County, Mississippi. She was the twentieth and youngest child of Jim Townsend and Lou Ella Townsend, who were sharecroppers in rural Mississippi. Hamer grew up in a tar paper shack and slept on a cotton sack stuffed with dry grass. She first went into the cotton fields to work when she was six years old, picking thirty pounds of cotton a week. By the time she was thirteen years old, Hamer was picking two hundred to three hundred pounds of cotton each week. Because of her family's poverty, she was forced to end her formal education after the sixth grade.

In 1944, when she was twenty-seven, Hamer married Perry ("Pap") Hamer, a sharecropper on a nearby plantation owned by the Marlowe family, near Ruleville, Mississippi. Hamer spent the next eighteen years working in the fields chopping cotton. Her husband also ran a small saloon, and they made liquor to sell.

In August 1962, Hamer attended a meeting sponsored by the SOUTHERN CHRISTIAN LEADERSHIP CONFERENCE (SCLC) and the STUDENT NONVIOLENT COORDINATING COMMITTEE (SNCC, pronounced Snick). The SCLC was founded in 1957 by a group of black ministers led by MARTIN LUTHER KING, JR., and coordinated the CIVIL RIGHTS activities of ministers. SNCC was organized in 1960 by students and other young people, and SNCC workers had recently come to Ruleville to organize voter registration drives. At that time, only five percent of African Americans in Mississippi who were old enough to vote had been allowed to register. Ten days later, a group of white men rode through the town and fired sixteen shots into the homes of those involved in the black voting drive. That night Hamer fled to her niece's house forty miles away. A few weeks later, SNCC workers brought her to the SNCC annual conference in Nashville. She later returned to the Marlowe plantation, where she found that her husband had been fired from his job and her family had lost its car, furniture, and house.

Hamer then became a field secretary for SNCC in Ruleville, earning $10 a week, and

"IF THIS IS A GREAT
SOCIETY, I'D HATE TO
SEE A BAD ONE."

began organizing a poverty program. She worked with the local people, educating them about their right to vote, and she became an effective fund-raiser for SNCC, traveling to northern towns to speak about life as an African American in Mississippi, and participating in civil rights demonstrations across the country. Hamer and her associates were often harassed, intimidated, and even beaten.

Hamer helped found the Council of Federated Organizations, which brought large numbers of white northerners into Mississippi in the summer of 1964, known as Freedom Summer. These volunteers helped with voter registration and other civil rights activities, and their work focused national attention on the segregation still rampant in the South.

In April 1964, Hamer helped found the Mississippi Freedom Democratic party. The MFDP was organized as an alternative to the all-white Mississippi Democratic party, which barred African Americans from its activities. The MFDP planned to challenge the regular Democratic party's right to represent Mississippi at the Democratic National Convention in Atlantic City, New Jersey, in August 1964 and hoped to win the right to be seated as the state's legal delegation. Before leaving for Atlantic City, the MFDP held its own convention and elected sixty-four African Americans and four whites as delegates to the national convention. Hamer was elected vice chairwoman.

Democratic president LYNDON B. JOHNSON, who was running for reelection in 1964, became worried that the MFDP would disrupt party unity and cause him to lose the election to Republican senator BARRY M. GOLDWATER. Johnson went to work to stop the MFDP by having his supporters threaten and harass MFDP supporters on the Credentials Committee, which was scheduled to hear the MFDP's case at the convention. In nationally televised proceedings before the committee, Hamer testified about the difficult life of African Americans in Mississippi and how they were prevented from participating in the political process. She also described a brutal beating she received while in jail for violating segregation laws. The beating left Hamer nearly blind in one eye.

Following Hamer's testimony, viewers from across the United States telegrammed their delegates, urging them to support the MFDP. Realizing he would now have to deal with the new party, Johnson worked out a settlement that called for the seating of two at-large delegates from the MFDP and a pledge that segregated delegations would not be seated at the 1968 convention. Hamer spoke out strongly against the compromise, and the delegation voted to reject it.

Following the 1964 convention, Hamer continued her work in the civil rights movement. In March 1965, she joined King and hundreds of others in a fifty-four-mile march from Selma, Alabama, to Montgomery, Alabama. She also traveled with a SNCC delegation to Africa.

Back in Ruleville, Hamer and two other women ran for Congress against white congressmen in a special counterelection organized by SNCC. In the Democratic primary, their names were not on the ballot because the Mississippi election commission said they did not have enough signatures of registered voters on their petitions, and the white candidates won. In the SNCC election, however, the women's names were listed on the ballot, and they won. The women pressed their claim to be seated in Congress in Washington, D.C. They argued that Mississippi county registrars had refused to certify the signatures of black voters on their petitions. In September 1965, after nine months of investigation into their claim that the state had illegally obstructed their attempts to place their names on the ballot, the U.S. House of Representatives rejected their challenge by a margin of eighty-five votes.

In August 1968, Hamer again traveled to the Democratic National Convention in Chicago as a member of the alternative Mississippi delegation, renamed the Mississippi Loyalist Democratic party (MLDP). Again, the party went before the Credentials Committee seeking recognition, and again, a compromise was offered,

this time to seat twenty-one members of each delegation. The MLDP refused to compromise, and this time, the regular delegation was unseated. When Hamer finally took her seat at the convention, she received a standing ovation.

Hamer went on to serve on the Democratic National Committee from 1968 until 1971. She also continued her civil rights work in Mississippi. In May 1970, Hamer and officials of the NATIONAL ASSOCIATION FOR THE ADVANCEMENT OF COLORED PEOPLE in Indianola filed a class action lawsuit in federal district court, claiming that the Sunflower County, Mississippi, school districts maintained a dual school system for black and white students and that black teachers and principals were not adequately protected against losing their jobs. The suit asked the court to order that one integrated school system be established and maintained. In *Hamer v. Sunflower County* (N.D. Miss., June 15, 1970), the district court, relying heavily on data in a report from a biracial committee headed by Hamer, ordered the county to merge its schools into one public school system. The U.S. Court of Appeals for the Fifth Circuit affirmed the district court in *United States v. Sunflower County School District*, 430 F.2d 839 (5th Cir. 1970).

Hamer continued to work for the poor in Ruleville, organizing poverty programs, raising money for low-income housing, and starting a day care center. Her favorite project was the Freedom Farm Cooperative. She started the farm with 40 acres, which eventually increased to 650 acres on which five thousand people grew their own food.

In 1976, Hamer was honored in Ruleville on Fannie Lou Hamer Day. She died the following year from heart disease, cancer, and diabetes. Engraved on the headstone of her grave in Ruleville are the words I Am Sick and Tired of Being Sick and Tired.

See also CIVIL RIGHTS MOVEMENT; VOTING RIGHTS.

HAMILTON, ALEXANDER

CULVER PICTURES

Alexander Hamilton

Alexander Hamilton, as a lawyer, politician, and statesman, left an enduring impression on U.S. gov-

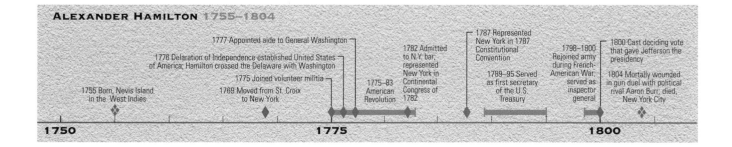

ALEXANDER HAMILTON 1755–1804

1755 Born, Nevis Island in the West Indies

1769 Moved from St. Croix to New York

1775 Joined volunteer militia

1776 Delaration of Independence established United States of America; Hamilton crossed the Delaware with Washington

1777 Appointed aide to General Washington

1775–83 American Revolution

1782 Admitted to N.Y. bar; represented New York in Continental Congress of 1782

1787 Represented New York in 1787 Constitutional Convention

1789–95 Served as first secretary of the U.S. Treasury

1798–1800 Rejoined army during French-American War; served as inspector general

1800 Cast deciding vote that gave Jefferson the presidency

1804 Mortally wounded in gun duel with political rival Aaron Burr; died, New York City

1750   1775   1800

ernment. His birth was humble, his death tragic. His professional life was spent forming basic political and economic institutions for a stronger nation. As a New York delegate at the Constitutional Convention, Hamilton advocated certain powers for the central government. His principles led to his rise as chief spokesperson for the Federalist party. The party had a short life span, but Hamilton's beliefs carried on through his famous *Federalist Papers.* In these documents he advocated broad constitutional powers for the federal government, including national defense and finance. According to Hamilton, a lesser degree of individual human liberties and CIVIL RIGHTS would follow federal powers. His deemphasis of freedom put him at odds with other Founders, especially THOMAS JEFFERSON's Democrats. However, he backed his beliefs with a strong record of public service from the Revolution onward. Through his contributions in the U.S. Army, in the Department of the Treasury, and as a lawyer, many still recognize him as a commanding architect of the United States government.

Hamilton was born January 11, 1755, on Nevis Island, in the West Indies. His parents never married. His father, the son of a minor Scottish noble, drifted to the West Indies early in his life and worked odd jobs throughout the Caribbean. His mother died in the Indies when he was eleven. Hamilton spent his early years in poverty, traveling to different islands with his father. At the age of fourteen, while visiting the island of St. Croix, he met a New York trader who recognized his natural intelligence and feisty spirit. The trader made it possible for Hamilton to go to New York in pursuit of an education.

Hamilton attended a preparatory school in New Jersey and developed contacts with men who had created a movement seeking colonial independence. When he later entered King's College (now Columbia University), he became active in the local patriot movement. The American Revolution had been brewing in the background, and Hamilton took a keen interest in the battles that flared between the colonists and the British around Boston in 1775. Instead of graduating from college, he opted to join a volunteer militia company.

He reported for orders to General GEORGE WASHINGTON's chief of artillery, Colonel Henry Knox. In his duties, Hamilton assisted in the famous crossing of the ice-jammed Delaware River on Christmas Night, 1776. Knox called Hamilton to Washington's attention. In March 1777, Hamilton was appointed aide to the commander in chief. With Washington, Hamilton learned his first lessons on the need for central administration in dealing with crises.

He also took advantage of his contacts with General Philip Schuyler, a wealthy and influential man within the military. In March 1780, Schuyler's young daughter, Elizabeth Schuyler, agreed to marry Hamilton. The relationship provided Hamilton with both additional contacts inside U.S. politics and generous financial gifts from his father-in-law.

Hamilton came to resent the limits of his position as aide to Washington and aspired to greater challenges. A minor reprimand afforded him the opportunity to resign from his services in April 1781. Hamilton had already received an education beyond anything that King's or any other college could have offered. However, he went to New York with his wife and took up the study of law in early 1782. In July of that year, he was admitted to the bar.

As a lawyer and as an intellectual who commanded growing respect, Hamilton represented New York in the Continental Congress of 1782, in Philadelphia. Here, he spoke with an ally, a young Virginian, JAMES MADISON. The two expounded on the merits of strong central administration. Most of the other delegates represented the common fears of citizens in the United States—apprehensions about the abusive tendencies of strong central powers and, more important, the possibility of oppression in the future. Hamilton and Madison failed to sway a majority of the delegates to vote for their ideas. In the end, the Congress adopted the ARTICLES OF CONFEDERATION, a body of principles intended to knit the new states into a union that was only loosely defined.

Hamilton left Philadelphia frustrated. He returned to New York, built a thriving law practice, and gained fame as a legal theorist. In 1787, he spent a term in the New York Legislature and joined the movement designed to create a new Constitution. During this time, Madison and JOHN JAY (a future chief justice of the Supreme Court) helped Hamilton draft a series of essays called *The Federalist Papers.* The essays still stand as fundamental statements of U.S. political philosophy.

The Articles of Confederation had already begun to show inadequacies, as the federal government had no real power to collect the money necessary for its own defense. The authors of *The Federalist Papers* argued that a strong federal government would constitute not a tyranny but an improvement over the current system of relatively weak rule. Their arguments helped allay the commonly held fears about central power.

"REAL LIBERTY IS NEITHER FOUND IN DESPOTISM OR THE EXTREMES OF DEMOCRACY, BUT IN MODERATE GOVERNMENTS."

At the 1787 Constitutional Convention in Philadelphia, Hamilton again served as a delegate from New York. This time, his ideas were received with more favor. In the drafting of the new Constitution, and the creation of a more effective government, many of Hamilton's Federalist beliefs came into play. In the area of defense, for example, Article I, Section 8, of the Constitution read, "The Congress shall have Power . . . To raise and support Armies . . . To provide and maintain a Navy . . . To provide for organizing, arming, and disciplining, the Militia." The role of the government in raising finances to do these things would put Hamilton's ideas to the test.

Hamilton took on the test personally. In 1789, when President Washington began to assemble the new federal government, he asked Hamilton to become the nation's first secretary of the treasury. For the following six years, Hamilton developed a fiscal and economic system based on a national coinage, a national banking system, a revenue program to provide for the repayment of the national debt, and measures to encourage industrial and commercial development. He sought a vigorous, diversified economy that would also provide the nation with the means to defend itself. He stirred a considerable amount of controversy with certain proposals, such as the need for TARIFFS on imports, several kinds of excise taxes, the development of natural resources, a friendship with England, and opposition to France during the French Revolution. However, without such a concrete agenda, many historians have argued, the United States could not have survived its years of initial development.

Because of Hamilton's decisive stance on some issues, a split occurred between, and even within, political parties. Hamilton and JOHN ADAMS spoke the ideas of the Federalists. Madison joined Jefferson in the Democratic-Republican party. Even though Hamilton had previously worked alongside Secretary of State Jefferson, the two were now, as Washington noted, "daily pitted in the cabinet like two cocks." Hamilton stressed the need for a strong central government, while Jefferson emphasized individuals' rights. Their rivalry, among the most famous political clashes in U.S. history, led to a significant and ongoing level of frustration for both sides. Because of the deadlock, Hamilton retired from his secretarial position in 1795.

He went back to practicing law. Through his service in government and his connections with the Schuyler family, Hamilton became a prominent and prosperous lawyer. His practice extended to wealthy clients in New York and in other states, both individuals and partnerships. It resembled the practices of modern corporate lawyers, since he also represented banks and companies.

The bulk of his civil practice took place in maritime litigation, which boomed with European interests in the U.S. market. His most important ADMIRALTY case involved the sale and export to Europe of large quantities of cotton and indigo. Defendants Gouveneur and Kemble had incurred damages to the head merchant in their trade, Le Guen. Hamilton took on the case as attorney for Le Guen. He was assisted by AARON BURR, with whom he had formerly worked in New York.

In *Le Guen v. Gouveneur,* Hamilton helped the merchant successfully sue his agents for $120,000—at the time, one of the largest awards in a personal damage suit. JAMES KENT, chancellor of the New York bar, remembered Hamilton's performance in the trial as displaying "his reasoning powers . . . his piercing criticism, his masterly analysis, and . . . his appeals to the judgment and conscience of the tribunal." A grateful Le Guen wanted to pay Hamilton a fee commensurate with the size of the judgment. Hamilton refused anything more than $1,500. Burr took a much larger fee at his own discretion. This was the beginning of strained developments between Hamilton and Burr that would result in a future, climactic confrontation.

As a private citizen, Hamilton had amassed considerable power. In letters to politicians and newspapers, he continued to make a number of government-related proposals. At least four of them figured into future developments in the U.S. political structure. First, he suggested dividing each state into judicial districts as subdivisions of the federal government's judicial branch. Second, he proposed consolidating the federal government's revenues, ships, troops, officers, and supplies as assets under its control. Third, he pushed for the enlargement of the legal powers of the government by making certain already existing laws permanent, particularly the law authorizing the government to summon MILITIAS to counteract subversive activities and insurrections. Finally, he proposed the addition of laws that would give the courts power to punish sedition. Through letters to leaders and citizens, as through his *Federalist Papers,* Hamilton's ideas were received, although not always easily, into the political mainstream.

In 1798 the United States prepared for war with France. Hamilton decided to rejoin the

Army as a major general. He was assigned the additional duties of inspector general until 1800. In 1800, Jefferson campaigned for president with Hamilton's former partner in the Le Guen settlement, Burr, as his running mate. The two received identical numbers of electoral votes for the 1800 presidential election. At that time all candidates ran for the presidency. The winner became president and the individual in second place became vice president. Hamilton, an elector for New York, refused to go along with the Federalists' plans to deny Jefferson the presidency. Hamilton voted for Jefferson instead of Burr, partly because he could stand Burr even less than his ideological rival. Jefferson won the election.

In 1804, Burr ran for governor of New York and became embittered by more of Hamilton's insults during the campaign. When Burr lost again, he challenged Hamilton to a duel. On July 11, 1804, the two men met at Weehawken Heights, New Jersey. Hamilton received a mortal wound from Burr's pistol shot, and died in New York City the next day.

As the United States evolved in political, legal, and economic dimensions, Hamilton's contributions remained part of its basic structure. His legacy went on to affect the way the rest of the world interpreted the proper role of government. Numerous political experiments took place in the following centuries, but still, Hamilton's notions of a strong central government made other systems appear weak in comparison. In a letter to the *Washington Post* on January 28, 1991, biographer Robert A. Hendrickson asserted that Hamilton's doctrine lives up to its model status as "a beacon of freedom and financial success in the modern world. It has peacefully discredited agrarianism, communism, and totalitarianism."

CROSS-REFERENCES

Constitution of the United States; *Federalist Papers.*

HAND, BILLINGS LEARNED Learned Hand served as a U.S. district court judge from 1909 to 1924, and on the U.S. Circuit Court of

Appeals from 1924 to 1951. Although he was a great and respected legal figure, he was never appointed to the U.S. Supreme Court.

Hand cannot be classified as a liberal or conservative because he did not allow his personal biases to affect his judicial positions. He was careful to base his decisions on public policy and laws as he understood them, and he did not believe it was the court's job to create public policy. To Hand's way of thinking, human values are relative. Although one value—such as protecting young people from OBSCENITY—may prevail in a certain case, it might not prevail in another. And he felt that the role of court decisions should be to provide realistic guidelines on which to base future decisions.

Hand was born January 27, 1872, in Albany, New York. His was a distinguished family, with both his grandfather and his father being lawyers and Democrats. He was an only child, and his father died when he was fourteen. Hand attended private schools, and graduated with honors and a degree in philosophy from Harvard in 1893. He graduated from Harvard Law School with honors in 1896. A year later he began practicing law in the state of New York.

In 1902 Hand married Frances A. Fincke and moved to New York City. Although successful, he found law practice to be boring. In 1909 newly elected president WILLIAM HOWARD TAFT appointed Hand to a federal judgeship. At age thirty-seven, Hand was one of the youngest appointees ever. He served the court for fifteen years.

A few years after his appointment, Hand supported THEODORE ROOSEVELT's Bull Moose party presidential candidacy against Taft, and became the Progressive party's candidate for chief judge of the New York Court of Appeals. He undertook this first and last political venture of his career because of a concern that big business would control the nation. Whatever Hand's reasons, Taft never forgot Hand's "disloyalty," and many believe that this act cost Hand his first chance to serve on the Supreme Court in 1922. Taft, who was then the chief

BIOGRAPHY

Learned Hand

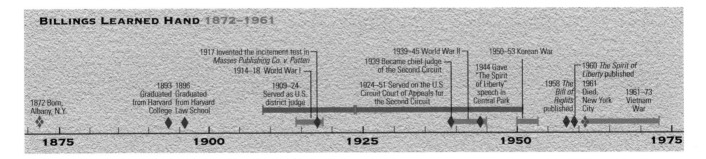

BILLINGS LEARNED HAND 1872–1961

1872 Born, Albany, N.Y.

1893 Graduated from Harvard College

1896 Graduated from Harvard Law School

1909–24 Served as U.S. district judge

1914–18 World War I

1917 Invented the incitement test in *Masses Publishing Co. v. Patten*

1924–51 Served on the U.S. Circuit Court of Appeals for the Second Circuit

1939 Became chief judge of the Second Circuit

1939–45 World War II

1944 Gave "The Spirit of Liberty" speech in Central Park

1950–53 Korean War

1958 *The Bill of Rights* published

1960 *The Spirit of Liberty* published

1961 Died, New York City

1961–73 Vietnam War

1875 1900 1925 1950 1975

justice of the U.S. Supreme Court, urged President WARREN G. HARDING not to nominate Hand.

Throughout his career, Hand chose to follow his conscience while knowing he would forfeit promotions as a result. For example, in 1917 Hand decided *Masses Publishing Co. v. Patten*, 244 F. 535 (S.D.N.Y. 1917), *rev'd* 246 F. 24 (2d Cir. 1917). *Masses* was the first test of a new law, the Espionage Act of 1917 (Act of June 15, 1917, ch. 30, 40 Stat. 217). This act outlawed making "false statements with intent to interfere with the operation or success of the military or naval forces . . . when the United States is at war." It also allowed the U.S. mail to ban materials containing such statements. Editors of an antiwar magazine, *The Masses*, took the New York City postmaster, Thomas G. Patten, to court for refusing to distribute the magazine. Patten argued that the Espionage Act allowed him to ban the publication.

The *Masses* case came before the Second District at the beginning of World War I, when the government viewed criticism of the war as a threat to national security. It came also when Hand was being considered for appointment to the Second Circuit Court of Appeals.

At that time, the legality of written or spoken words was usually judged by the probable result of the words—that is, if the words had the tendency to produce unlawful conduct, then they could be banned. Hand took a different approach: his solution focused on the words themselves, rather than on a guess at the public's reaction to them. He invented what became known as the incitement test: if the words told someone to break the law, if they instructed the person that it was a duty or interest to do so, then they could be banned. *The Masses* magazine praised CONSCIENTIOUS OBJECTORS and antiwar demonstrators, but it never actually told readers they should behave similarly. For this reason, Hand ruled that the postmaster could not ban the magazine.

Masses was just one of the many opinions Hand wrote that decided issues for which no precedent existed at the Supreme Court level. It is an early example of Hand's strong opinions about free speech—that it should be protected and defined as a critical ingredient to democracy. He struggled for the rest of his career to convince his colleagues of the importance and complexity of issues relating to the FIRST AMENDMENT to the U.S. Constitution.

Hand correctly predicted the consequences of his decision in *Masses* before he announced it. The decision was immediately appealed and reversed by the Second Circuit Court of Appeals, and he did not receive the appointment to that court. But over time the climate of the country and the courts would change, and in the late 1960s, the Supreme Court would adopt Hand's incitement test as the standard for evaluating whether speech threatened security.

In 1924 Hand was appointed to the U.S. Circuit Court of Appeals for the Second Circuit. On the court, Hand served with many famous judges, including conservative judge Thomas Walter Swan, Hand's first cousin Augustus Noble Hand, Harrie Brigham Chase, Charles Edward Clark, and JEROME N. FRANK.

With his cousin and Swan, Hand made many widely respected decisions. Some observers credit the craftsmanship of these decisions to the use of preconference memos, which were unique to the Second Circuit at that time. Under this method, each judge reviewed each case and drafted a tentative opinion without consulting the others. Only after each judge had reached an independent conclusion did all the conferring judges exchange memos and meet to discuss the case. This led to more diverse and thorough thinking than with the usual method of approaching cases, in which one judge took the lead early on and drafted a single opinion.

As a circuit court judge, Hand was limited to applying PRECEDENTS of the Supreme Court and federal statutes in appeals before his court. He felt responsible to the precedents, and once he was sure he understood the basic reason for a law, he stood his ground despite any negative effects the decision might cause.

Hand was again considered for the Supreme Court in 1931, this time by President HERBERT HOOVER. But Hoover felt obliged to offer the position to CHARLES E. HUGHES first, with the intention of appointing Hand when Hughes refused. To Hoover's surprise, Hughes accepted.

Hand became chief judge of the circuit court in 1939 when his predecessor, Martin T. Manton, was indicted and eventually imprisoned for accepting bribes. This was the highest position that Hand was to hold in the courts.

Hand's final close call with the Supreme Court came in 1942, when FRANKLIN D. ROOSEVELT was seeking a replacement for Justice James F. Byrnes, whom he had appointed to a cabinet position. Hand was in the running, and his colleagues organized a strong campaign to persuade the president to choose him. However, in January 1943—the month that Hand turned seventy-one—Roosevelt appointed

"IF WE ARE TO KEEP OUR DEMOCRACY, THERE MUST BE ONE COMMANDMENT: THOU SHALT NOT RATION JUSTICE."

Wiley B. Rutledge, of Iowa. The reason? Rutledge was only forty-eight years old, and Roosevelt had insisted in 1937 that justices should not serve past age seventy. Ironically, Rutledge died in 1949, whereas Hand was still active and productive for another twelve years.

Hand influenced the Supreme Court profoundly, though he did not serve on it. He was quoted in Supreme Court opinions and widely cited in legal journals. Even during his lifetime, he was widely regarded as one of the greatest judges in the English-speaking world.

In 1944 Hand delivered a public speech that brought his thinking to the attention of people in nonlegal circles. His address, "The Spirit of Liberty," was delivered in New York's Central Park to over 1 million people. The *New Yorker*, the *New York Times, Life,* and *Reader's Digest* all reprinted portions of his address. Hand also publicly denounced McCarthyism during an address in Albany in 1952.

Hand served on the council of the American Law Institute, a group of law teachers, judges, and lawyers that restates laws and constructs model codes on many legal subjects. He helped shape the way the group thought, and also helped improve procedural rules of CRIMINAL LAW.

When Hand retired from the second Circuit in 1951, he had served as a federal judge longer than anyone else in U.S. history.

During his career he had written almost three thousand legal opinions. They are famous for their careful construction and sharp understanding of all forces at work. He showed an ability to clarify legal concepts, even those in specialized areas such as admiralty (shipping) law, patent law, and immigration law.

After he retired Hand still sat on the federal bench, wrote opinions, and handled a nearly full workload. Toward the end of his life, he complained to a friend that he was only writing twenty to twenty-five opinions a month, instead of his customary fifty to sixty. He was the author of *The Bill of Rights* (1958) and *The Spirit of Liberty* (1960), which is a collection of his papers and speeches.

Hand died of a heart attack in New York City on August 18, 1961, after more than fifty years of service on the federal bench.

HARBOR 📖 As a noun, a haven, or a space of deep water so sheltered by the adjacent land and surroundings as to afford a safe anchorage for ships.

As a verb, to afford lodging to, to shelter, or to give a refuge to. To clandestinely shelter, succor, and protect improperly admitted aliens. It may be aptly used to describe the furnishing of shelter, lodging, or food clandestinely or with concealment, and under certain circumstances may be equally applicable to those acts divested of any accompanying secrecy. Harboring a criminal is a crime under both federal and state statutes and a person who harbors a criminal is an ACCESSORY after the fact. 📖

HARDING, GEORGE George Harding is known as the greatest U.S. PATENT attorney of the late nineteenth century.

Harding was born in Philadelphia on October 26, 1827. He was the son of Jesper Harding, publisher of the *Pennsylvania Inquirer.* Harding attended public schools and graduated from the University of Pennsylvania in 1846. After graduating, he worked as an intern for John Cadwalader, who later became a U.S. district judge, before starting his own law practice.

Harding was admitted to the bar in 1849, and elected secretary of the Law Academy of Philadelphia the same year. Two years later he assisted EDWIN M. STANTON in *Pennsylvania v. Wheeling & Belmont Bridge Co.,* 54 U.S. (13 How.) 518, 14 L. Ed. 249 (1851), before the Supreme Court. With this case he began to gain fame as a patent attorney.

Harding successfully represented Samuel F. Morse in lengthy litigation over Morse's telegraph patent (*O'Reilly v. Morse,* 56 U.S. [15 How.] 62, 14 L. Ed. 601 [1853]). In this case Morse was found to be the "true and original inventor of the Electro-Magnetic Telegraph, worked by the motive power of electromagnetism, and of the several improvements thereon."

In the Cyrus H. McCormick reaper litigation, *McCormick v. Talcott,* 61 U.S. (20 How.)

BIOGRAPHY

George Harding

THE HISTORICAL SOCIETY OF PENNSYLVANIA

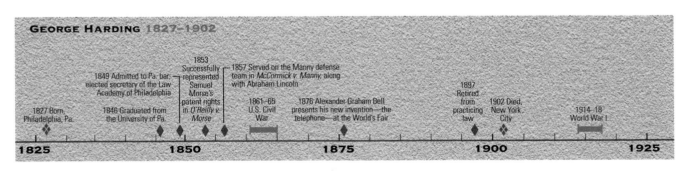

GEORGE HARDING 1827–1902

1827 Born, Philadelphia, Pa.

1846 Graduated from the University of Pa.

1849 Admitted to Pa. bar; elected secretary of the Law Academy of Philadelphia

1853 Successfully represented Samuel Morse's patent rights in *O'Reilly v. Morse*

1857 Served on the Manny defense team in *McCormick v. Manny,* along with Abraham Lincoln

1861–65 U.S. Civil War

1876 Alexander Graham Bell presents his new invention—the telephone—at the World's Fair

1897 Retired from practicing law

1902 Died, New York City

1914–18 World War I

1825   1850   1875   1900   1925

402, 15 L. Ed. 930 (1857), the attorney on retainer for defendant John Manny was ABRAHAM LINCOLN. Harding and his associates, lead attorneys for the defense, considered Lincoln too inexperienced to handle the litigation but kept him on because they needed to have a local attorney of record. They promptly removed him to the status of little more than an observer. Historians report that Lincoln was devastated by the treatment he received from the famous lawyers from Philadelphia.

Relying on his expertise in mechanics and chemistry, Harding became known for his courtroom demonstrations. To explain some of the patent issues being litigated, he would perform chemical experiments or demonstrate working models of the machines in question. Some of the models he brought into the courtroom were a miniature telephone system, a miniature grain field and reaper, and a furnace. In *Burr v. Duryee*, 68 U.S. (1 Wall.) 531, 17 L. Ed. 650 (1863), Justice ROBERT C. GRIER noted that the "large museum of exhibits in the shape of machines and models" brought in by Harding were critical to giving the Court "a proper understanding of the merits of the controversy."

Harding was as much a showman as an orator and was able to use humor to create interest in patent litigation. He was listed as counsel in over one hundred cases heard before the federal circuit courts of appeal and the Supreme Court.

Harding retired from practice in 1897 at age seventy. He died five years later, in New York City.

HARDING, WARREN GAMALIEL

Warren Gamaliel Harding served as the twenty-ninth president of the United States, from 1921 to 1923. Harding, who also served one term in the U.S. Senate, presided over an administration that achieved little and that was tainted by political corruption.

Harding was born November 2, 1865, in Corsica (now Blooming Grove), Ohio, the eldest of eight children. He attended Ohio Central College. Harding then tried teaching, reading the law, selling insurance, and working as a journalist. He became the editor and publisher of the *Marion Star*, in Ohio, in 1884.

In 1891, Harding married Florence Kling DeWolfe, the daughter of a prominent Marion banker. DeWolfe was a divorcée, five years Harding's senior, with great ambitions for Harding. She helped build the *Marion Star* into a prosperous newspaper and encouraged Harding to enter Republican party politics.

Harding was elected to the Ohio Senate in 1898, and was elected lieutenant governor of the state in 1903. He ran unsuccessfully for governor in 1910. His national political standing rose over the next decade. At the Republican National Convention in 1912, he was selected to nominate President WILLIAM HOWARD TAFT for a second term. (In 1921, he would nominate Taft to serve as chief justice of the U.S. Supreme Court.) In 1914, he was elected to the U.S. Senate. Regarded as a fine public speaker, he gave the keynote address at the 1916 Republican National Convention.

As a U.S. senator, Harding was well liked by his colleagues but demonstrated little interest in the legislative process. He introduced no major bills during his six-year term, and was frequently absent. His politics followed the Republican mainstream: favoring high TARIFFS on imports and opposing the LEAGUE OF NATIONS and the federal regulation of commerce.

At the 1920 Republican National Convention, in Chicago, most of the delegates favored Governor Frank O. Lowden, of Illinois; Major General Leonard Wood, formerly army chief of staff; or Senator Hiram W. Johnson, of California, for president. After four ballots, the convention was deadlocked. Early in the morning, in what Harding campaign manager Harry M. Daugherty called a smoke-filled room, the party leaders agreed on Harding as a compromise candidate. The convention agreed to the selection and nominated Governor CALVIN COOLIDGE, of Massachusetts, as Harding's vice presidential running mate.

Harding defeated the Democratic party nominee, Governor James M. Cox, of Ohio, in the November 1920 election. Harding cam-

BIOGRAPHY

LIBRARY OF CONGRESS

Warren Gamaliel Harding

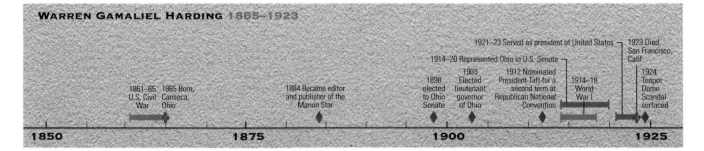

WARREN GAMALIEL HARDING 1865–1923

1861–65 U.S. Civil War

1865 Born, Canseca, Ohio

1884 Became editor and publisher of the Marion Star

1898 elected to Ohio Senate

1903 Elected lieutenant governor of Ohio

1912 Nominated President Taft for a second term at Republican National Convention

1914–20 Represented Ohio in U.S. Senate

1914–18 World War I

1921–23 Served as president of United States

1923 Died, San Francisco, Calif.

1924 Teapot Dome Scandal surfaced

1850   1875   1900   1925

paigned from the front porch of his home in Marion, avoiding any specifics on his domestic political agenda. Instead, he promised the United States a return to "normalcy."

Harding's presidency was marked by the delegation of responsibilities to his cabinet chiefs. Rejecting the strong executive leadership style of Presidents THEODORE ROOSEVELT and WOODROW WILSON, Harding relied on a distinguished group of men, including Secretary of Commerce HERBERT HOOVER, Secretary of State CHARLES EVANS HUGHES, and Secretary of Agriculture Henry C. Wallace. These and other cabinet heads helped lead the government away from wartime emergency conditions. In 1921, Secretary Hughes convened the Washington Conference on Naval Disarmament. The members of the conference—England, France, Italy, Japan, and the United States—agreed to limit their naval warships in fixed ratios.

In June 1923, Harding began a cross-country speaking tour, in hopes of reviving Republican party fortunes, which had taken a beating in the 1922 congressional election. On the trip, he received a secret telegram that disclosed an impending scandal for his administration concerning a Senate investigation of oil leases. In Seattle, Harding fell ill, presumably of food poisoning. His train stopped in San Francisco, where doctors reported Harding had pneumonia. On August 2, Harding died. No autopsy was made, leaving the exact cause of death unknown. Vice President Coolidge succeeded Harding as president.

The scandals that stained the Harding administration largely became public after Harding's death. One involved Attorney General Daugherty, who in 1926 was tried twice on charges he had committed improprieties in administering the Office of the Alien Property Custodian. Both trials ended in a HUNG JURY (the jury was unable to reach a decision).

The most troubling scandal, called TEAPOT DOME, involved Secretary of the Interior Albert B. Fall. Fall, a wealthy New Mexico attorney, had left the U.S. Senate in 1921 to join Hard-

"AMERICANS OUGHT EVER BE ASKING THEMSELVES ABOUT THEIR CONCEPT OF THE IDEAL REPUBLIC."

BIOGRAPHY

John Marshall Harlan

PHOTOGRAPHER: HANDY STUDIOS. COLLECTION OF THE SUPREME COURT OF THE UNITED STATES

ing's cabinet. In 1924, he was indicted for criminal CONSPIRACY and BRIBERY. It was alleged that he accepted a $100,000 bribe from oil producers Harry F. Sinclair and Edward Doheny in exchange for leasing government-owned oil reserves at Teapot Dome, Wyoming, and Elk Hills, California, to the pair's oil companies at unusually favorable terms. Fall was acquitted of the conspiracy charge in 1926, but was convicted of bribery in 1929. He served two years in prison and paid a fine.

President Harding's short term of office and the scandals that befell his political appointees have left his administration remembered more for its corruption than for its achievements.

HARLAN, JOHN MARSHALL John Marshall Harlan served as justice of the U.S. Supreme Court from 1877 to 1911. Harlan, a native of Kentucky, is best remembered for his dissenting opinions in cases that upheld restrictions on the CIVIL RIGHTS of African Americans, most notably in *Plessy v. Ferguson*, 163 U.S. 537, 16 S. Ct. 1138, 41 L. Ed. 256 (1896). Harlan's DISSENTS served to enlarge his judicial reputation as attitudes and laws changed concerning state-mandated segregation.

Harlan was born in Boyle County, Kentucky, on June 1, 1833. The son of a prominent lawyer and politician, Harlan graduated from Centre College and then studied law at Transylvania University, both located in Kentucky. He was admitted to the Kentucky bar in 1853. As a young man, Harlan sought his own political career. He was elected a county judge in 1858, but relocated to Louisville in 1861 to establish a successful law practice.

With the beginning of the Civil War in 1861, Harlan joined the Union army as a lieutenant colonel and commanded a company of infantry volunteers. Upon the death of his father, he resigned his commission and returned to his law practice in Louisville. There, he became an active member of the Republican party. He made two unsuccessful efforts at getting himself elected governor of Kentucky, but proved more successful at helping others,

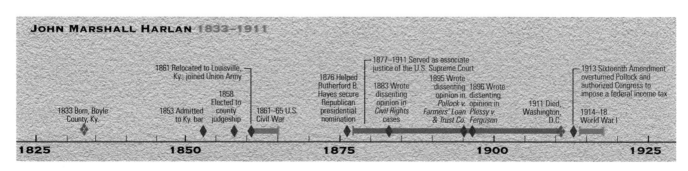

JOHN MARSHALL HARLAN 1833–1911

1833 Born, Boyle County, Ky.

1853 Admitted to Ky. bar

1858 Elected to county judgeship

1861 Relocated to Louisville, Ky; joined Union Army

1861–65 U.S. Civil War

1876 Helped Rutherford B. Hayes secure Republican presidential nomination

1877–1911 Served as associate justice of the U.S. Supreme Court

1883 Wrote dissenting opinion in *Civil Rights* cases

1895 Wrote dissenting opinion in *Pollock v. Farmers' Loan & Trust Co.*

1896 Wrote dissenting opinion in *Plessy v. Ferguson*

1911 Died, Washington, D.C.

1913 Sixteenth Amendment overturned Pollock and authorized Congress to impose a federal income tax

1914–18 World War I

1825   1850   1875   1900   1925

securing the presidential nomination of RUTH-ERFORD B. HAYES at the 1876 Republican National Convention.

Hayes took office in 1877, after a difficult election. One of his first acts was to appoint Harlan to the U.S. Supreme Court. Harlan, at age forty-four, joined a Court that, for the length of his tenure, was economically conservative and philosophically opposed to the enlargement of federal power. In addition, the Court deferred to the policies of southern states on racial segregation.

During his long tenure on the bench, Harlan gained prominence as a frequent dissenter. With a temperament that was better suited to leading than following, Harlan did not have the ability to negotiate compromise. Instead, he relied on his dissenting opinions to voice his often prophetic judgments.

In *Pollock v. Farmers' Loan & Trust Co.*, 157 U.S. 429, 15 S. Ct. 673, 39 L. Ed. 759 (1895), the Court held that the federal INCOME TAX was unconstitutional. Harlan dissented, arguing that the Court was ignoring PRECEDENT and acting as a legislator rather than a court. He noted that "the practical effect of the decision today is to give to certain kinds of property a position of favoritism and advantage." Harlan was vindicated in 1913 when the SIXTEENTH AMENDMENT overturned *Pollock* and authorized Congress to impose a federal income tax.

In 1883, the Supreme Court struck down Congress's attempt to outlaw racial discrimination in places of public accommodation, including hotels, taverns, restaurants, theaters, streetcars, and railroad passenger cars. The majority decided in the *Civil Rights* cases, 109 U.S. 3, 3 S. Ct. 18, 27 L. Ed. 835 (1883), that the CIVIL RIGHTS ACT of 1875 violated the FOURTEENTH AMENDMENT. It determined that the amendment prohibited only official, state-sponsored discrimination and could not reach discrimination practiced by privately owned places of public accommodation.

Justice Harlan, in his dissent, argued that segregation in public accommodations was a "badge of slavery" for the recently freed African Americans, and that the act could be constitutionally justified by looking to the THIRTEENTH AMENDMENT. This amendment gave Congress the authority to outlaw all "badges and incidents" of SLAVERY. Harlan pointed out that before the Civil War, the Supreme Court protected the rights of slaveholders. Less than twenty years after the abolition of slavery, the Court refused to extend its power and authority to protect the former slaves. Not until the

passage of title II of the Civil Rights Act of 1964 (42 U.S.C.A. § 2000a et seq.) would the federal government ultimately achieve the desegregation of public accommodations.

Harlan's most famous dissent came in *Plessy*. At issue in this case was an 1890 Louisiana law that required passenger trains operating within the state to provide "equal but separate" accommodations for "white and colored races." The Supreme Court upheld the law on a 7–1 vote, thus putting a stamp of approval on all laws that mandated racial segregation. In his majority opinion, Justice HENRY B. BROWN concluded that the Fourteenth Amendment "could not have intended to abolish distinctions based upon color, or to enforce social, as distinguished from political, equality."

Justice Harlan, the lone dissenter, responded that the "arbitrary separation of citizens on the basis of race" was equivalent to the imposition of a "badge of servitude" on African Americans. He cut through the legal arguments to proclaim that the real intent of the law was not to give equal accommodations but to compel African Americans "to keep to themselves." He concluded that this was unacceptable because "our Constitution is color-blind, and neither knows nor tolerates classes among citizens."

Sixty years later, Harlan's vision was embraced by the Supreme Court in *Brown v. Board of Education*, 347 U.S. 483, 74 S. Ct. 686, 98 L. Ed. 873 (1954), when it overturned *Plessy* and rejected the "SEPARATE-BUT-EQUAL" doctrine. With *Brown*, the modern CIVIL RIGHTS MOVEMENT gained its first major victory, setting the stage for the dismantling of the JIM CROW LAWS, which had required racial discrimination in the South.

Justice Harlan also taught constitutional law at Columbian University (now George Washington University) and served on the Bering Sea Arbitration Tribunal of 1893, which resolved a dispute between the United States and Great Britain over the hunting of seals inhabiting the Bering Sea area of Alaska.

Harlan died October 14, 1911. His grandson, John Marshall Harlan II, also served on the Supreme Court.

CROSS-REFERENCES

Brown v. Board of Education of Topeka, Kansas; Civil Rights Cases; Plessy v. Ferguson; Pollock v. Farmers' Loan & Trust Co.

HARLAN, JOHN MARSHALL II John Marshall Harlan II served as an associate justice of the U.S. Supreme Court from 1955 to 1971. Harlan was the grandson of Supreme Court

"OUR CONSTITUTION IS COLOR-BLIND, AND NEITHER KNOWS NOR TOLERATES CLASSES AMONG CITIZENS. IN RESPECT OF CIVIL RIGHTS, ALL CITIZENS ARE EQUAL BEFORE THE LAW."

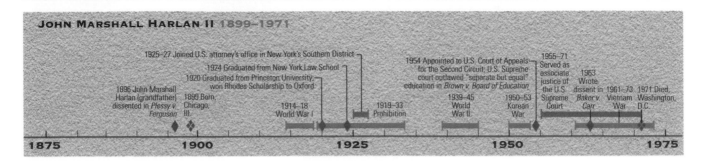

JOHN MARSHALL HARLAN II 1899–1971

1925–27 Joined U.S. attorney's office in New York's Southern District
1924 Graduated from New York Law School
1920 Graduated from Princeton University; won Rhodes Scholarship to Oxford
1954 Appointed to U.S. Court of Appeals for the Second Circuit; U.S. Supreme court outlawed "separate but equal" education in *Brown v. Board of Education*
1955–71 Served as associate justice of the U.S. Supreme Court
1896 John Marshall Harlan (grandfather) dissented in *Plessy v. Ferguson*
1899 Born, Chicago, Ill.
1963 Wrote dissent in *Baker v. Carr*
1971 Died, Washington, D.C.
1914–18 World War I
1919–33 Prohibition
1939–45 World War II
1950–53 Korean War
1961–73 Vietnam War

1875   1900   1925   1950   1975

justice JOHN MARSHALL HARLAN. He was a conservative voice during the Warren Court era, arguing for judicial restraint in the face of court decisions that changed the landscape of U.S. civil and criminal law.

Harlan was born May 20, 1899, in Chicago. His father, John Maynard Harlan, was a successful lawyer and reform Republican politician who served as a Chicago alderman. Harlan was educated at boarding schools in Canada and Princeton University. After graduating from Princeton in 1920, he attended Oxford University on a Rhodes Scholarship and studied jurisprudence.

On his return to the United States, Harlan was hired by Root, Clark, Buckner, and Howard, a prominent New York City law firm. Emory Buckner, a partner in the firm and its chief litigator, encouraged Harlan to attend law school. Harlan graduated from New York Law School in 1924 and was admitted to the bar in 1925.

At Root, Clark, Harlan worked assiduously to master the fine points of litigation. His attention to detail and careful preparation won him Buckner's admiration. In 1925, when Buckner became U.S. attorney for New York's Southern District, Harlan joined his legal staff. One of Harlan's primary duties was enforcing the National Prohibition Act, 41 Stat. 305, which outlawed the possession, sale, transportation of, and importation of intoxicating liquors.

Harlan returned to Root, Clark in 1927. During the 1930s, he emerged as the law firm's top trial attorney. He became the attorney of choice for many major U.S. corporations.

During World War II, Harlan headed the Army Air Corps' operations analysis section, which developed ways of improving the accuracy of military bombings of Germany. Following the war, he returned to his law practice.

Harlan's connections with Republican party politicians, including President DWIGHT D. EISENHOWER'S attorney general, Herbert Brownell, Jr., led to a judicial career. In 1954, Eisenhower accepted Brownell's recommenda-

BIOGRAPHY

John Marshall Harlan II

"OUR CONSTITUTION IS NOT A PANACEA FOR EVERY BLOT UPON THE PUBLIC WELFARE NOR SHOULD THIS COURT, ORDAINED AS A JUDICIAL BODY, BE THOUGHT OF AS A GENERAL HAVEN FOR REFORM MOVEMENTS."

tion and appointed Harlan to the U.S. Court of Appeals for the Second Circuit.

Harlan's tenure on the circuit court of appeals was unremarkable and brief. When Justice ROBERT H. JACKSON died in October 1954, Eisenhower appointed Harlan to the U.S. Supreme Court. Harlan was confirmed by the U.S. Senate in 1955.

Harlan took his seat at a time when the Supreme Court, under Chief Justice EARL WARREN, had aroused the anger of advocates of racial segregation. The previous year, in *Brown v. Board of Education*, 347 U.S. 483, 74 S. Ct. 686, 98 L. Ed. 873 (1954), a unanimous Court had rejected the concept of SEPARATE BUT EQUAL, signaling the end of the JIM CROW LAWS, which had required racial discrimination throughout the South. The decision vindicated Harlan's grandfather, who had written the lone dissent to the Supreme Court's decision in *Plessy v. Ferguson*, 163 U.S. 537, 16 S. Ct. 1138, 41 L. Ed. 256 (1896), upholding an 1890 Louisiana law requiring passenger trains to provide "equal but separate" accommodations for "white and colored races."

In his first years on the Court, Harlan and Justice FELIX FRANKFURTER often voted together, counseling judicial restraint. They believed in the concepts of FEDERALISM (the division of power between the state and federal governments) and SEPARATION OF POWERS (the division of power between the legislative, executive, and judicial branches of the federal government). After Frankfurter left the Court in 1962, Harlan became the lone advocate of these concepts. As the Warren Court reshaped U.S. law, Harlan often dissented, arguing that the Court was granting too much power to the federal government and to the judicial branch.

As a conservative jurist, Harlan respected PRECEDENT (the prior rulings of the Court). He sought to limit the reach of decisions by linking constitutional interpretation with the facts of a case. In this way, lower courts would be restrained from applying an interpretation to other contexts. This refusal to overgeneralize an interpretation led him to dissent in the ONE-PERSON, ONE-VOTE case of *Baker v. Carr,* 369 U.S. 186, 82 S. Ct. 691, 7 L. Ed. 2d 663 (1962). The majority in *Baker* held that the federal district court had JURISDICTION to consider a claim that a state statute apportioning state legislative districts violated the plaintiffs' right to EQUAL PROTECTION guaranteed by the FOUR-TEENTH AMENDMENT. Noting that the majority has disregarded considerable precedent, the dissent asserted that the claim was a nonjusticiable "POLITICAL QUESTION."

Harlan died December 29, 1971, in Washington, D.C.

CROSS-REFERENCES

Apportionment; *Baker v. Carr;* Judicial Review.

HARMLESS ERROR

The legal doctrine of harmless error is found in the Federal Rules of Criminal Procedure, extensive CASE LAW, and state statutes. It comes into use when a litigant appeals the decision of a judge or jury, arguing that an ERROR of law was made at trial that resulted in an incorrect decision or VERDICT. The APPELLATE COURT then must decide whether the error was serious enough to strike down the decision made at trial. Review for harmless error involves a complicated test that applies to state and federal laws as well as rules of procedure. If an error is held to be serious, the appellate court is likely to set aside the decision of the trial court and may order a new trial. If it deems the error harmless, the appellate court affirms the lower court's decision. The doctrine of harmless error thus prevents an unnecessary new trial when the error alleged would not have affected the outcome at trial.

Harmless error jurisprudence grew out of a late-nineteenth-century development in English law. Before 1873, English courts automatically reversed decisions in cases where an error was committed at trial. In 1873, Parliament put an end to this practice in civil cases by permitting reversals only in cases of substantial error. As the author Raymond A. Kimble has noted, U.S. law slowly adopted the idea in order to limit the number of retrials in U.S. courts.

In 1919, Congress first applied the harmless error doctrine to federal appellate courts, ordering them "to give judgment after an examination of the record without regard to errors or defects which do not affect the substantial rights of the parties" (28 U.S.C.A. § 2811 [1988]). By the midtwentieth century, harmless error jurisprudence was growing. The U.S. Supreme Court first moved toward establishing harmless error analysis in the 1946 case of

Kotteakos v. United States, 328 U.S. 750, 66 S. Ct. 1239, 90 L. Ed. 1557, but left doubt about its applicability to constitutional errors. It began to remove this doubt in 1967 in the landmark case of *Chapman v. California,* 386 U.S. 18, 87 S. Ct. 824, 17 L. Ed. 2d 705. The Court in *Chapman* ruled that defendants were not necessarily entitled to a new trial simply because constitutional violations had occurred at trial. It directed appellate courts to dismiss arguments about certain constitutional errors when these "are so unimportant and insignificant that they may, consistent with the Federal Constitution, be deemed harmless, not requiring automatic reversal of a conviction." However, the Supreme Court put an important condition on this analysis: the appellate court had to be certain BEYOND A REASONABLE DOUBT that the error did not affect the outcome of the case.

Even decades after *Chapman,* determining whether a constitutional error is harmless remains a complicated task. This is because harmless error has no single, uniform definition. Courts must resort to one of two distinct tests—and sometimes a third that combines both of them. The first test asks whether the error influenced the verdict. If the error did not have even a minimal effect on the verdict, it is harmless. The second test considers the EVIDENCE of guilt found in the trial record. If the evidence is overwhelming and untainted, the defendant's guilt is considered to be the most important factor, and the error is harmless. The third test is a BALANCING test in which the court weighs the error's effect on the verdict against the untainted evidence. The court may emphasize either element in this test, and the outcome of the test will reflect which is considered stronger.

The harmless error doctrine has continued to evolve since the late 1960s. For many years, there was still uncertainty about which constitutional errors at trial could be subject to harmless error analysis, but the Supreme Court has clarified this by allowing most constitutional errors to be reviewed under the doctrine. Some of its decisions have proved controversial. In the 1991 case of *Arizona v. Fulminante,* 499 U.S. 279, 111 S. Ct. 1246, 113 L. Ed. 2d 302, for example, it included coerced CONFESSIONS under the scope of harmless error review. This decision curtailed the ability of criminal defendants to overturn their conviction by arguing that the police used physical or emotional force to win a confession. As a result, appellate courts are free to determine if the jury had enough evidence besides the challenged confession to convict a defendant. As part of a general trend, this expansion of the scope of harmless error analysis has raised complaints about the proper role of appellate review.

See also CRIMINAL PROCEDURE.

HARMON, JUDSON Judson Harmon was an attorney, judge, and two-time Ohio governor with presidential aspirations. He served as attorney general of the United States under President GROVER CLEVELAND from 1895 to 1897.

Harmon was born February 3, 1846, in Newton, Hamilton County, Ohio, the oldest of eight children of Benjamin Franklin Harmon and Julia Bronson Harmon. Because his father was a teacher, the young Harmon was schooled at home. Later, when his father entered the ministry, Harmon attended public schools. An apt student, he was enrolled at Denison University by the age of sixteen, and he graduated in 1866.

The Civil War was an ever present intrusion on Harmon's college years. Funds for education were scarce, and young men were needed on the battlefield, not in the classroom. Harmon often earned money between terms by serving with local MILITIA units responsible for defending his home district against Southern raids. He was profoundly affected by the ASSASSINATION of President ABRAHAM LINCOLN in 1865. When Lincoln's body lay in state in Springfield, Ohio, Harmon went through the line of mourners three times. Years later, he said that he had been in awe—and that he had never seen such a crowd of sad and disheartened people.

After graduating from college, Harmon moved to Columbus, Ohio, and followed his father into the teaching profession. He lasted a year. Upon deciding to pursue a legal career, he moved to Cincinnati and read law in the office of George Hoadly. He received his law degree at Cincinnati Law School in 1869, and he was admitted to the Ohio bar the following year. In June 1870, Harmon married Olivia Scobey, of Hamilton, Ohio, and settled into the life of a successful young attorney.

Judson Harmon

"THE FUNDAMENTAL PRINCIPLE OF INTERNATIONAL LAW IS THE ABSOLUTE SOVEREIGNTY OF EVERY NATION, AS AGAINST ALL OTHERS, WITHIN ITS OWN TERRITORY."

After seven years of practice, Harmon was elected judge of the common pleas court in Cincinnati; two years later, he was elected to the local superior court. He left the bench in 1887 when his teacher and mentor, Hoadly, was elected governor of Ohio. To help his old friend with the transition to public office, Harmon assumed Hoadly's caseload at the firm of Hoadly, Johnson, and Colston. At Hoadly's urging, Harmon also took a greater interest in national politics. Though Harmon had originally supported the Republican party on war issues, he found himself unable to support its program of Reconstruction after the Civil War. By 1887, Harmon was closely associated with Hoadly's supporters, the conservative faction of the Democratic party in Ohio.

Harmon's ties to the governor and the state Democratic party reaped rewards. In June 1895, President Cleveland appointed Harmon to succeed RICHARD OLNEY as attorney general of the United States. In this office, Harmon established a national reputation as a lawyer. As attorney general, he directed several major ANTITRUST prosecutions, including one against the Trans-Missouri Freight Association (*United States v. Trans-Missouri Freight Ass'n*, 166 U.S. 290, 17 S. Ct. 540, 41 L. Ed. 1007 [1897]) and one against the Addyston Pipe and Steel Company (*United States v. Addyston Pipe & Steel Co.*, 78 Fed. 712 [E.D. Tenn. 1897]).

In *United States v. Texas*, 162 U.S. 1, 16 S. Ct. 725, 40 L. Ed. 867 (1896), a WATER RIGHTS case, he espoused a theory of absolute territorial SOVEREIGNTY that has come to be known as the Harmon doctrine. Harmon said, "[T]he rules, principles and precedents of international law imposed no liability or obligation on the United States" to let parts of the waters that were diverted upstream by the United States flow to Mexico. According to Harmon, nations had exclusive jurisdiction and control over the uses of all waters within their boundaries. (Since Harmon's time, the Harmon doctrine has been largely superseded by the concepts of state responsibility and global citizenship.)

Following his term as attorney general, Har-

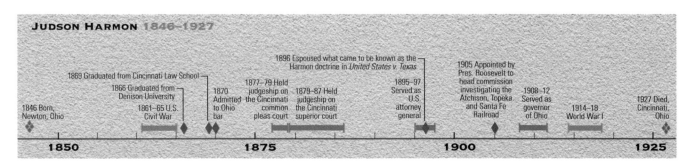

JUDSON HARMON 1846–1927

1846 Born, Newton, Ohio

1861–65 U.S. Civil War

1866 Graduated from Denison University

1869 Graduated from Cincinnati Law School

1870 Admitted to Ohio bar

1877–79 Held judgeship on the Cincinnati common pleas court

1879–87 Held judgeship on the Cincinnati superior court

1896 Espoused what came to be known as the Harmon doctrine in *United States v. Texas*

1895–97 Served as U.S. attorney general

1905 Appointed by Pres. Roosevelt to head commission investigating the Atchison, Topeka, and Santa Fe Railroad

1908–12 Served as governor of Ohio

1914–18 World War I

1927 Died, Cincinnati, Ohio

1850   1875   1900   1925

mon resumed practice in Cincinnati, but he was never far from the national spotlight. In 1905, he was appointed by President THEODORE ROOSEVELT to head a commission investigating the business practices of the Atchison, Topeka, and Santa Fe Railroad. Harmon helped to trace a million dollars in KICKBACKS—or REBATES, as they were then called—to a railroad traffic manager named Paul Morton. The commission's findings embarrassed the president because Morton had left the railroad to become Roosevelt's secretary of the Navy. Harmon urged prosecution of the responsible railroad officials, but Roosevelt interceded, and charges were never brought. Harmon was disappointed in the president's actions. He believed that individuals were accountable for their activities, even when those activities were carried out on behalf of a corporate entity. Harmon's observation that "guilt is always personal" became a theme in his subsequent political campaigns.

By 1908, Harmon had reasserted himself in the politics of his home state. His reputation as a conservative Democrat made him the logical person to help the Democrats challenge the long-standing Republican control of Ohio state politics.

At the Ohio state Democratic convention of May 1908, Harmon became the nominee of his party. He went on to win the gubernatorial election over a Republican incumbent—even though a Republican presidential candidate, WILLIAM HOWARD TAFT, carried the state. In his first term as governor, Harmon waged war on corporate GRAFT and corruption and created a state office of business administration.

Harmon won a second term easily—even though former president Roosevelt, still bearing a grudge from the Morton incident, came to Ohio to assist the opposition. In his second term, Harmon remained conservative but began to feel the pressures of the Progressive wave sweeping the nation. This Progressive movement was made up of those who supported more government involvement and oversight in programs aimed at helping ordinary citizens. Bowing to that pressure, his administration supported a number of popular measures, including a federal INCOME TAX amendment; a law consolidating boards overseeing the state's penal, benevolent, and reformatory institutions; and a corrupt practices act to safeguard against voting violations. Harmon's signature was also attached to a model WORKERS' COMPENSATION act, a measure for the direct popular election of U.S. senators, and a statute creating a PUBLIC UTILITY commission.

In 1912, Harmon decided to seek his party's nomination for president of the United States at the Democratic National Convention in Baltimore. After he declared his opposition to the statewide application of INITIATIVE and REFERENDUM in Ohio, many Progressive leaders in his home state doubted his viability as a national candidate. (Initiative is the power of the people to propose bills and laws and to enact or reject them at the polls independent of legislative assembly; referendum is the process of referring constitutional or legislative proposals to the electorate for decision.) WILLIAM JENNINGS BRYAN, leader of the national Progressive movement, denounced Harmon as a reactionary. Harmon nevertheless went to the national convention assured of support from both Ohio and New York delegates, but he failed to win the nomination.

By throwing his hat into the national ring, Harmon had given up the opportunity to run for a third term as governor of Ohio. The election of James M. Cox as governor later in 1912 marked the end of Harmon's political career.

Harmon returned to Cincinnati, resumed practice, and began teaching at Cincinnati Law School. He was often asked to reconsider his withdrawal from public life, but he firmly declined all opportunities to do so.

Harmon died in Cincinnati on February 22, 1927.

HARRISON, BENJAMIN On March 4, 1889, Benjamin Harrison was sworn in as the twenty-third president of the United States. Forty-eight years to the day earlier, his grandfather, WILLIAM H. HARRISON, had become the

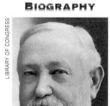

BIOGRAPHY

LIBRARY OF CONGRESS

Benjamin Harrison

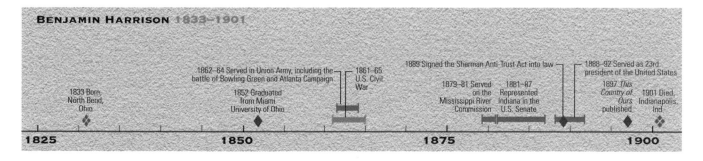

BENJAMIN HARRISON 1833–1901

1833 Born, North Bend, Ohio

1852 Graduated from Miami University of Ohio

1862–64 Served in Union Army, including the battle of Bowling Green and Atlanta Campaign

1861–65 U.S. Civil War

1879–81 Served on the Mississippi River Commission

1881–87 Represented Indiana in the U.S. Senate

1889 Signed the Sherman Anti-Trust Act into law

1888–92 Served as 23rd president of the United States

1897 *This Country of Ours* published

1901 Died, Indianapolis, Ind.

1825   1850   1875   1900

ninth U.S. president. His grandfather's presidency ended after only one month when he died from complications due to a pneumonia he developed after delivering his inaugural address in the rain. Harrison's presidency lasted a full four-year term, ushering in sweeping legislative changes, signaling a return of the Republican party to the White House, and laying the groundwork for the foreign policy of the late 1800s.

Harrison was born August 20, 1833, in Ohio. After graduating from Miami University, in Oxford, Ohio, he moved to Indianapolis to practice law. There he became involved in Republican politics, serving as city attorney, secretary of the Republican state committee, and supreme court reporter for Indiana. During the Civil War, he joined the Union Army. Within a month he was promoted to colonel and commanding officer of the Seventieth Indiana Regiment. He fought under General William T. Sherman and was promoted to brevet brigadier general in February 1865. After the war he returned to Indianapolis to pursue his legal career.

Harrison lost the race for governor of Indiana in 1876, but made a successful bid for a Senate seat in 1881. He held his Senate position for only one term, failing to win reelection in 1887. This loss did not deter ardent Republican supporters who wanted to see Harrison in the White House.

In 1888 Harrison ran against the incumbent Democratic president, GROVER CLEVELAND. Harrison was the surprise nominee of the Republican party, a second choice after James G. Blaine, who declined to run again after having lost to Cleveland in 1884. Following a very close race, Harrison won 233 electoral votes; although Cleveland took the popular vote, he won only 168 electoral votes.

In the 1888 election, the Republican party gained control of Congress. During the first two years of Harrison's presidency, Congress enacted into law almost everything contained in the 1888 Republican platform. This was one of the most active Congresses in history. The central themes of Harrison's campaign had been nationalism and TARIFF protection. The Democrats favored tariff reduction, whereas the Republicans steadfastly favored a system of protection. The tariff existing at the time Harrison took office produced more income than was needed to run the government and was the cause of much bipartisan debate. In 1889 Harrison signed the McKinley Tariff Act, which raised CUSTOMS DUTIES to an average of 49.5 percent, higher than any previous tariff. The act

contained over four hundred amendments, including provisions for reciprocal trade agreements. It found favor with few Republicans, causing a rift within the party.

One issue in Harrison's term that enjoyed bipartisan support was ANTITRUST legislation. During the late 1800s, business combinations known as trusts were created and began taking over large shares of the market. Both Republicans and Democrats perceived trusts as destructive of competition, and each party's platform was antimonopoly in 1888. In 1889 Senator JOHN SHERMAN introduced antitrust legislation to restrain interstate trusts. On July 2, 1889, Harrison signed the SHERMAN ANTI-TRUST ACT into law. This was the first major piece of legislation enacted during his term, and it remains in effect more than one hundred years after its adoption. Historians view the Sherman Anti-Trust Act as the most important piece of legislation of the Fifty-first Congress.

During Harrison's term legislation providing for federal supervision of all congressional elections was defeated several times. The legislation had been drafted to ensure the VOTING RIGHTS of blacks as mandated by the FIFTEENTH AMENDMENT. Harrison was a strong supporter of the bill and also of legislation to ensure education for southern blacks, which was also defeated. These were the last significant attempts to provide these CIVIL RIGHTS until the 1930s.

With regard to foreign policy, Harrison had an aggressive attitude and little patience for drawn-out diplomatic negotiations. He helped convince several European countries to lift their restrictions on the importation of U.S. pork products, thus increasing U.S. exports of pork from approximately 47 million pounds in 1891 to 82 million pounds in 1892. Harrison also played a part in solving disputes between the United States, England, and Canada regarding seal hunting in the Bering Sea. And his tenacity proved successful in avoiding a war with Chile in 1892. Harrison's attitude toward foreign relations was emulated by THEODORE ROOSEVELT and other politicians.

When Harrison sought reelection in 1892, Cleveland once again opposed him. This time Cleveland emerged the victor.

Harrison has been described as an aloof loner, lacking in personal magnetism, but a man of great intellect. After he failed to secure a second term as president, he was revered as an elder statesman, giving lectures and acting as chief counsel for Venezuela in a boundary dispute with British Guiana.

After a bout with pneumonia, Harrison died March 13, 1901, in Indianapolis, Indiana.

"THE BOTTOM PRINCIPLE . . . OF OUR STRUCTURE OF GOVERNMENT IS THE PRINCIPLE OF CONTROL BY THE MAJORITY. EVERYTHING ELSE ABOUT OUR GOVERNMENT IS APPENDAGE, IT IS ORNAMENTATION."

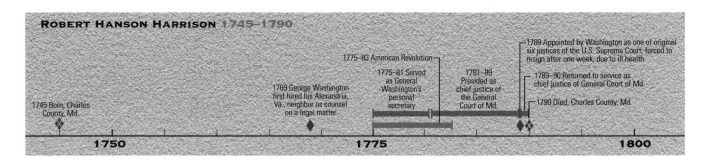

ROBERT HANSON HARRISON 1745–1790

1789 Appointed by Washington as one of original six justices of the U.S. Supreme Court; forced to resign after one week, due to ill health

1775–83 American Revolution

1775–81 Served as General Washington's personal secretary

1781–89 Presided as chief justice of the General Court of Md.

1789–90 Returned to service as chief justice of General Court of Md.

1769 George Washington first hired his Alexandria, Va., neighbor as counsel on a legal matter

1745 Born, Charles County, Md.

1790 Died, Charles County, Md.

1750   1775   1800

HARRISON, ROBERT HANSON Robert Hanson Harrison was a lawyer and judge who was one of GEORGE WASHINGTON's original six appointments to the U.S. Supreme Court.

Harrison was born in 1745, in Charles County, Maryland. Though little has been written about his upbringing and education, it is known that he established a successful law practice in Alexandria, Virginia, where Washington became a client and close friend. Harrison later served as Washington's personal secretary throughout much of the Revolutionary War. He resigned from this post in March 1781 to become chief justice of the General Court of Maryland.

On September 24, 1789, President Washington signed the JUDICIARY ACT OF 1789 into law. This act established the Supreme Court, consisting of a chief justice and five associate justices. The act also established lower federal circuit and district courts and gave the Supreme Court the power to review, as well as affirm or reverse, the rulings of those courts. On the day the law was enacted, Washington nominated his longtime friend Harrison to the Court.

The Senate confirmed Harrison's nomination two days later with little debate. Harrison initially declined the appointment because of poor health, but Washington persuaded him to accept the seat. A week after Harrison departed for New York City to begin work on the Court, he was stricken with a sudden illness and was forced to again decline the appointment. Washington eventually appointed JAMES IREDELL to the seat intended for Harrison.

Despite illness, Harrison remained chief jus-

BIOGRAPHY

Robert Hanson Harrison

BIOGRAPHY

William Henry Harrison

tice of the General Court of Maryland until his death on April 20, 1790. During his tenure on the Maryland court, Harrison dealt mainly with real estate law and other legal matters; he had little opportunity to write about more sweeping issues of constitutional law. As a result, his legal record indicates little about the effect he would have had if he had been able to serve his appointed term on the U.S. Supreme Court.

HARRISON, WILLIAM HENRY William Henry Harrison was the ninth president of the United States. He served the shortest term of any U.S. president, dying just a month after assuming office.

Harrison was born February 9, 1773, in Charles City County, Virginia, the youngest of seven children in a distinguished plantation family. His father, Benjamin Harrison V, served in the House of Burgesses before the American Revolution, was later a member of the CONTINENTAL CONGRESS, and was a signer of the DECLARATION OF INDEPENDENCE. Harrison was tutored at home in his early years. In 1787, at age fourteen, he entered Hampden Sidney College for premedical studies, intending to become a doctor. In 1791, he enrolled at the University of Pennsylvania Medical School to study under Dr. Benjamin Rush, a noted physician. Later that year, following his father's death and without funds to continue school, Harrison decided to enlist in the Army and was commissioned an ensign in the First Infantry, serving in the Northwest Territory.

Harrison rose quickly through the ranks of the military, becoming a lieutenant in 1792 and acting as aide-de-camp to Major General An-

---

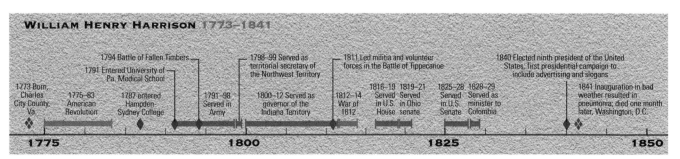

WILLIAM HENRY HARRISON 1773–1841

1794 Battle of Fallen Timbers

1791 Entered University of Pa. Medical School

1798–99 Served as territorial secretary of the Northwest Territory

1811 Led militia and volunteer forces in the Battle of Tippecanoe

1840 Elected ninth president of the United States; first presidential campaign to include advertising and slogans

1773 Born, Charles City County, Va.

1775–83 American Revolution

1787 entered Hampden-Sydney College

1791–98 Served in Army

1800–12 Served as governor of the Indiana Territory

1812–14 War of 1812

1816–19 Served in U.S. House

1819–21 Served in Ohio senate

1825–28 Served in U.S. Senate

1828–29 Served as minister to Colombia

1841 Inauguration in bad weather resulted in pneumonia; died one month later, Washington, D.C.

1775   1800   1825   1850

thony ("Mad Anthony") Wayne, who was responsible for pacifying the Ottawa, Chippewa, Shawnee, and Pottawatomie tribes. At the Battle of Fallen Timbers, in August 1794, Harrison was responsible for holding the line against the tribes and received an official commendation from General Wayne for his efforts. He was later promoted to captain, but in 1798 resigned from the Army.

Following his distinguished military service, Harrison was appointed territorial secretary of the Northwest Territory by President JOHN ADAMS. The position paid well ($1,200 a year), but Harrison did not find it particularly challenging. In 1799, he was appointed the territory's first delegate to Congress, a nonvoting position that authorized him only to introduce legislation and participate in debate. Harrison made the most of his office, introducing and lobbying for passage of the Harrison Land Act of 1800, which opened the Northwest Territory to settlers and offered land for sale in small, affordable tracts and on reasonable credit terms.

In 1800, Harrison was appointed governor of the Indiana Territory. In his twelve years in the post, Harrison successfully negotiated a number of Indian treaties that opened to white settlers millions of acres in southern Indiana and Illinois. Despite the treaties, the threat of uprisings continued, and in November 1811, Harrison led a force of a thousand men, largely militiamen and volunteers from Kentucky and Indiana, against the Indian confederacy. Harrison's troops, taken by surprise, were attacked by the confederacy forces in an early morning raid. In more than two hours of intense fighting, Harrison's men beat back their opponents, suffering more than two hundred casualties. The conflict, known as the Battle of Tippecanoe, put an end to Native American resistance to white settlement in the region—and earned Harrison the nickname Old Tippecanoe.

Soon after the War of 1812 broke out, Harrison was again on the front lines of a major military operation. He was commissioned a major general of the Kentucky militia, then made a brigadier general in command of the Northwest frontier. In 1813, he was promoted to major general. Harrison's biggest battle of the war was at the Thames River, in Ontario, where he defeated a force of seventeen hundred British troops and secured the Northwest for the United States. Harrison was proclaimed a national hero and left the military to resume a career in politics.

In 1816, Harrison won a seat in the U.S. House of Representatives, where he served as chairman of the Militia Committee, advocating

"SEE THAT THE GOVERNMENT DOES NOT ACQUIRE TOO MUCH POWER. KEEP A CHECK UPON YOUR RULERS. DO THIS, AND LIBERTY IS SAFE."

universal military training and sponsoring a relief bill for veterans and war widows. He also opposed laws that would restrict SLAVERY. In 1819, Harrison left the House to serve as an Ohio state senator. After a year in office, he ran for the U.S. Senate but was defeated. He also lost a close election for the U.S. House in 1822. In 1825, he was elected to the U.S. Senate. As a senator, Harrison once again focused on military issues, using his influence as chairman of the Committee on Military Affairs to lobby for increases in Army pay and an expansion of the Navy.

After three years in the Senate, Harrison turned to foreign service, accepting an appointment as minister to Colombia. Harrison's tenure in South America was brief, because of political instability within Colombia and concerns within the U.S. government that he was sympathetic to revolutionaries plotting to overthrow the Colombian president. He was recalled to Washington, D.C., in February 1830.

After returning to the United States, Harrison retired to his farm in Ohio and suffered a series of financial setbacks and family tragedies, including the death of his oldest son. But he remained interested in politics. In 1836, he ran unsuccessfully for president, losing to MARTIN VAN BUREN. In 1840, he again ran against Van Buren, with JOHN TYLER as his running mate. The race has been viewed by historians as the first modern presidential campaign, one with advertising and slogans, including the famous Tippecanoe and Tyler, Too, a reference to Harrison's strong military record on the frontier. Harrison and Tyler won the election with 53 percent of the popular vote.

Harrison was inaugurated amid great enthusiasm and gave one of the longest inaugural speeches in history (nearly an hour and a half) outdoors in early March without a hat, gloves, or an overcoat. He soon came down with a cold, which grew progressively worse and eventually developed into pneumonia. He died less than a month later, on April 4, 1841, in Washington, D.C., at age sixty-eight.

HASTIE, WILLIAM HENRY William Henry Hastie was one of the twentieth century's leading African American lawyers and jurists. He served on the U.S. Court of Appeals for the Third Circuit from 1949 to 1971, becoming the first African American to sit on a federal APPELLATE COURT. Hastie also distinguished himself as an educator, a CIVIL RIGHTS attorney, and a public servant. He successfully argued major civil rights cases before the U.S. Supreme Court and was a leader in the effort to desegregate the U.S. military during World War II. With

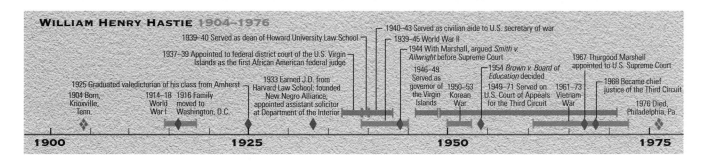

WILLIAM HENRY HASTIE 1904-1976

1904 Born, Knoxville, Tenn.

1914–18 World War I

1916 Family moved to Washington, D.C.

1925 Graduated valedictorian of his class from Amherst

1933 Earned J.D. from Harvard Law School; founded New Negro Alliance; appointed assistant solicitor at Department of the Interior

1937–39 Appointed to federal district court of the U.S. Virgin Islands as the first African American federal judge

1939–40 Served as dean of Howard University Law School

1939–45 World War II

1940–43 Served as civilian aide to U.S. secretary of war

1944 With Marshall, argued *Smith v. Allwright* before Supreme Court

1946–49 Served as governor of the Virgin Islands

1950–53 Korean War

1949–71 Served on U.S. Court of Appeals for the Third Circuit

1954 *Brown v. Board of Education* decided

1961–73 Vietnam War

1967 Thurgood Marshall appointed to U.S. Supreme Court

1968 Became chief justice of the Third Circuit

1976 Died, Philadelphia, Pa.

1900   1925   1950   1975

CHARLES HAMILTON HOUSTON, his second cousin, Hastie dramatically improved the standing and reputation of Howard University Law School during the 1930s and 1940s.

Hastie was born in Knoxville, Tennessee, on November 17, 1904. In 1916 his family moved to Washington, D.C., so that he could attend Dunbar High School. Thus began an education at the same schools Houston had attended before him. Hastie graduated from Dunbar as class valedictorian in 1921 and went on to distinguish himself at Amherst College, where he graduated in 1925, again as valedictorian.

After college Hastie spent two years teaching mathematics and science at a New Jersey school, then enrolled at Harvard Law School. There he served on the editorial board of the *Harvard Law Review*, becoming only the second African American to do so. He received a bachelor of laws degree from Harvard in 1930 and a doctor of jurisprudence degree in 1933.

Hastie then joined Houston's Washington, D.C., law firm. He also worked as an instructor at Howard University Law School, where Houston served as vice dean. Together, Hastie and Houston mentored scores of young black lawyers, including THURGOOD MARSHALL, who would become a leading civil rights lawyer and a U.S. Supreme Court justice.

Throughout the 1930s and 1940s, Hastie worked as an activist for African American civil rights. In 1933 he founded the New Negro Alliance, a group that organized pickets and BOYCOTTS of white businesses to force increased hiring of African Americans. He worked with Houston, Marshall, and other members of the NATIONAL ASSOCIATION FOR THE ADVANCEMENT OF COLORED PEOPLE (NAACP) to devise legal strategies to fight racism in employment, housing, and education. With regard to segregation in schools, Hastie and his NAACP colleagues focused first on graduate education. Hastie unsuccessfully argued one of the first SCHOOL DESEGREGATION cases, *Hocutt v. Wilson* (N.C. Super. Ct. 1933), *unreported*, which involved the attempt of a student, Thomas R. Hocutt, to enter the University of North Carolina.

BIOGRAPHY

William Henry Hastie

"ALWAYS BE PREPARED. YOUR OPPONENT WILL HAVE THE ADVANTAGE OF COLORLESSNESS."

In 1933 Secretary of the Interior Harold L. Ickes recruited Hastie to work for the Department of the Interior as assistant solicitor. While in that position, Hastie fought against segregated dining facilities in the department and helped draft the Organic Act of 1936 (48 U.S.C.A. § 1405 et seq.), which restructured the government of the Virgin Islands and gave that territory greater autonomy. In 1937, as a result of this work, he was appointed to the federal district court of the Virgin Islands, becoming the first African American to be named a federal judge.

Hastie left this position in 1939 when he was named dean of Howard University Law School. A year later he returned to government service as civilian aide to the secretary of war. Charged with rooting out racial DISCRIMINATION in the military, Hastie identified and attacked discrimination against African Americans such as unequal promotion, segregation in unequal training facilities, and violent assaults by police officers and civilians. Unsatisfied with the government response to his proposals to eliminate discrimination, Hastie resigned from his position in protest in 1943. However, his reports on racism in the military attracted national notice, and in 1944 the Army high command ordered that African American officers be trained alongside white officers.

Following his work in the military, Hastie continued to practice law and plead civil rights cases for the NAACP. Hastie and Marshall won several key cases before the U.S. Supreme Court. In *Smith v. Allwright*, 321 U.S. 649, 64 S. Ct. 757, 88 L. Ed. 2d 987 (1944), Hastie and Marshall persuaded the Court that the practice of holding all-white party primaries, which effectively denied African Americans the right to vote, was unconstitutional. The case set a vital precedent for later Supreme Court civil rights decisions.

Hastie and Marshall won another major victory in *Morgan v. Virginia*, 328 U.S. 373, 66 S. Ct. 1050, 90 L. Ed. 1317 (1946), in which the Court struck down a Virginia law (Virginia Code of 1942, §§ 4097z–4097dd) requiring racial segregation on buses. Hastie and Marshall argued that the law imposed an improper burden on interstate commerce. Despite this ruling de facto (actual) segregation continued on buses in the South.

From 1946 to 1949, Hastie served as governor of the Virgin Islands. In 1949 President HARRY S. TRUMAN appointed Hastie to the U.S. Court of Appeals for the Third Circuit. He was sworn in as an interim appointee that year and was confirmed by the Senate in 1950. In 1968 Hastie was named chief justice of the court of appeals. After retiring from the court in 1971, Hastie devoted himself to PUBLIC INTEREST law, including programs to provide legal aid for consumers, environmentalists, and minorities. He died April 14, 1976 in Philadelphia, Pennsylvania.

Hastie was awarded over twenty honorary degrees, including ones from Amherst and Harvard. He received the NAACP's Spingarn Medal in 1943 and was elected a fellow of the American Academy of Arts and Sciences in 1952.

HATCH ACT Enacted in 1939, the Hatch Act (5 U.S.C.A. 7324) curbs the political activities of employees in federal, state, and local governments. The law's goal is to enforce political neutrality among civil servants: the act prohibits them from holding public office, influencing ELECTIONS, participating in or managing political campaigns, and exerting undue influence on government hiring. Penalties for violations range from warnings to dismissal. The law's restrictions have always been controversial. Critics have long argued that the act violates the FIRST AMENDMENT freedoms of government employees. The U.S. Supreme Court has disagreed, twice upholding the law's constitutionality. Congress has amended the Hatch Act several times since 1939. In 1993, a number of amendments to the act sought to limit the effects of political PATRONAGE in federal hiring.

The Hatch Act grew out of nineteenth-century concerns about the political activities of federal employees. As early as 1801, President THOMAS JEFFERSON issued an executive order that said federal workers should neither "influence the votes of others, nor take part in the business of electioneering." He saw such activities as "inconsistent with the spirit of the Constitution." Jefferson was primarily concerned with what government employees did while in office; subsequently, concerns developed in another area. Throughout the nineteenth century, appointments to the federal bureaucracy were viewed as the natural spoils of political success. The prevalent awarding of jobs for political

loyalty created a so-called spoils system and, ultimately, a reaction against it.

The long process of neutralizing politics in federal employment continued into the twentieth century. Attempts began with the Pendleton Act of 1883 (22 Stat. 403), a comprehensive anti-patronage law named after its sponsor, Senator GEORGE H. PENDLETON, who argued that "the spoils system needs to be killed or it will kill the republic" (14 Cong. Rec. 206 [1882]). The law sought to eliminate patronage by insulating federal employees from coercion. It provided that they could not be fired for refusing to work on behalf of a candidate or for choosing not to make campaign contributions. In 1907, President THEODORE ROOSEVELT instituted even broader controls through Executive Order 642. Its two major prohibitions addressed employees in the executive CIVIL SERVICE and the larger class of federal civil servants. The former were forbidden to use their authority to interfere in elections, and the latter were barred from taking part in political management or campaigning. This order marked the first time that federal employees had limits placed on their First Amendment right to engage in political speech.

The passage of the Hatch Act in 1939 combined the prohibitions of earlier EXECUTIVE ORDERS and the Pendleton Act. The act includes restrictions on political activity for the whole federal bureaucracy. The act stated, "[N]o of-

Federal employees, such as those who work for the U.S. Fish and Wildlife Service, may not engage in political activities that would imply that they are not politically neutral.

ficer or employee in the Executive Branch of the Federal government, or in any agency or department thereof, shall take any active part in political management or in political campaigns" (ch. 410, § 9(a)). The measure received bipartisan support in a response to concern about the New Deal—President FRANKLIN D. ROOSEVELT's economic program for relieving the effects of the Great Depression—which significantly increased the ranks of federal employees. Congress wanted to rein in Roosevelt's power, especially following allegations that he had used Works Progress Administration employees to influence the 1938 congressional elections. Opponents of patronage in general and enemies of Roosevelt in particular thought the New Deal represented an opportunity for the president to meddle with elections while perpetuating his hold on the White House.

Congress increased the scope of the Hatch Act in 1940 by extending its restrictions to employees of state and local governments that receive federal funds (Act of July 19, 1940, ch. 640, 54 Stat. 767), although it cut back certain applications of this measure in 1974. At various times it has also increased or decreased the penalties for Hatch Act violations—notably, by including suspension without pay as a lesser penalty. In 1993, Congress made yet more changes aimed at curtailing patronage in jobs: amendments to 5 U.S.C.A. § 3303 restricted elected officials from making unsolicited recommendations for job applicants seeking federal employment. States, meanwhile, have broadly incorporated the principles of the Hatch Act in their own statutes, which have also undergone revision over time.

Debate over the Hatch Act has been vigorous since its inception. Critics have portrayed it as an unfair restriction on the First Amendment rights of government employees, especially violative of their fundamental right to engage in political speech. This argument formed the basis of an early suit that the U.S. Supreme Court heard in 1947, *United Public Workers of America v. Mitchell*, 330 U.S. 75, 67 S. Ct. 556, 91 L. Ed. 754. In sustaining the legality of the Hatch Act, the Court balanced individual speech rights against the "elemental need for order," and found the latter more important. The Court rejected another challenge to the law in 1973 in *United States Civil Service Commission v. National Ass'n of Letter Carriers*, 413 U.S. 548, 93 S. Ct. 2880, 37 L. Ed. 2d 796. Opponents continued to attack these rulings throughout the 1990s. "Unfortunately for those individuals who have chosen a career in the federal public service," argued author Michael Bridges in a 1993 law review article, "the Court has found that Congress may place an asterisk beside their First Amendment rights."

MILESTONES IN THE LAW

NEW YORK TIMES V. SULLIVAN

ISSUE

Freedoms of Speech and Press

MATERIALS

Opinion of the Supreme Court of Alabama, August 30, 1962
Briefs to the Supreme Court
Opinion of the Supreme Court, March 9, 1964

HOW TO USE MILESTONES IN THE LAW

In this section, the reader is invited to study the court opinions and briefs* that shaped a major facet of First Amendment law. As you read the following pages, you may wish to consider these issues:

- What were the inaccuracies upon which Sullivan's claims of libel were based?
- What about the advertisement made Sullivan believe it was directed at him?
- How did the descriptions of the issues before the Court, and of their significance, differ as presented by the different parties?
- What facts and legal principles did the Alabama Supreme Court rely on for its decision, and how was the U.S. Supreme Court's approach different?
- What sorts of misstatements about a government official do you think would be permissible, and impermissible, under this case?

---

*The Court heard the cases between Sullivan and the Times, and Sullivan and the four clergymen, together. Both sets of briefs are included.

THIS CASE IN HISTORY

New York Times v. Sullivan, handed down in the midst of the civil rights movement, changed the inquiry for libel actions, strengthening the freedoms of speech and press when directed at government behavior. L. B. Sullivan, a city commissioner in Montgomery, Alabama, sued the *Times* and four black clergymen over an advertisement placed by the Committee to Defend Martin Luther King and the Struggle for Freedom in the South. The full page ad, which described abuses that students and civil rights activists had suffered at the hands of police and state authorities in various southern cities, contained several inaccuracies. Though the inaccuracies were minor, the Supreme Court of Alabama upheld a judgment of $500,000 against the defendants. In a unanimous 9–0 decision, the U.S. Supreme Court reversed, holding that public officials cannot recover damages for false statements regarding their official conduct unless they can prove actual malice—that is, that the defendant or defendants knew the statements were false or made them with reckless disregard as to whether they were true or false. The decision freed the press and others to comment on government conduct by reducing fears of enormous damage awards based on minor inaccuracies.

NEW YORK TIMES COMPANY v. SULLIVAN   Ala.   25
Cite as 144 So.2d 25

The NEW YORK TIMES COMPANY et al.

v.

L. B. SULLIVAN.

3 Div. 961.

Supreme Court of Alabama.

Aug. 30, 1962.

Suit for libel against nonresident, corporate, newspaper publisher and others. The Circuit Court, Montgomery County, Walter B. Jones, J., entered a judgment for the plaintiff and the defendants appealed. The Supreme Court, Harwood, J., held that the publication of libelous matter in another state and the distribution of such matter within Alabama gave rise to a cause of action for libel in Alabama, and the evidence justified an award of $500,000 damages.

Affirmed

1. Corporations ⬅642(4½)

Activities of foreign corporation, which published newspaper and sent representatives into Alabama to solicit advertisements and gather news stories, were amply sufficient to meet minimal standards required for service of process in libel suit on corporation's resident "stringer" correspondent who was paid only for such articles as were accepted by corporation. Laws 1953, p. 347.

2. Constitutional Law ⬅309(2)

Corporations ⬅641

Statute providing for substituted service on nonresident corporations fully meets requirements of due process. Laws 1953, p. 347.

3. Corporations ⬅668(14)

Affidavit filed by plaintiff, suing foreign newspaper corporation for libel, stated sufficient facts to invoke statute providing for substituted service on nonresident corporation. Laws 1953, p. 347.

4. Process ⬅74

Legislature's purpose in calling for affidavit to invoke substituted service statute was not to require detailed quo modo of business done but to furnish Secretary of State with sufficient information so that he could perform duties imposed on him. Laws 1953, p. 347.

5. Corporations ⬅642(1)

Ultimate determination of whether nonresident corporation has done business in state or performed work or services in state, and whether cause of action accrues from such acts, thereby coming within substituted service statute, is judicial and not ministerial. Laws 1953, p. 347.

6. Libel and Slander ⬅25

When nonresident prints libel beyond boundaries of state and distributes published libel in Alabama, cause of action for libel arises in Alabama as well as in state of printing or publishing of libel.

7. Libel and Slander ⬅25

Where foreign newspaper corporation published libelous advertisement in New York and sent its papers into Alabama with carrier as its agent, freight prepaid, and with title passing on delivery to consignee, cause of action for libel arose from acts of newspaper in Alabama. Code 1940, Tit. 57, § 25; Laws 1953, p. 347.

8. Process ⬅69

Scope of substituted service is as broad as permissible limits of due process. Laws 1953, p. 347.

9. Corporations ⬅669

Nonresident corporation, by including in motion to quash service of process, prayer that court dismiss action as to corporation for lack of jurisdiction of subject matter of action, went beyond question of jurisdiction over corporate person and made a general appearance which waived any defects in service of process and sub mitted its corporate person to jurisdiction of court.

10. Pleading ⚷106(1)

Pleadings based on lack of jurisdiction of person are in their nature pleas in abatement which find no special favor in law, are purely dilatory and amount to no more than declaration that defendant is in court in proper action, after actual notice, but because of defect in service he is not legally before court.

11. Libel and Slander ⚷6(1)

Where words published tend to injure person libeled by them in his reputation, profession, trade or business, or charge him with indictable offense, or tend to bring individual into public contempt words are libelous per se.

12. Libel and Slander ⚷19

Publication is not to be measured by its effect when subjected to critical analysis of trained legal mind, but must be construed and determined by its natural and probable effect upon mind of average lay reader.

13. Libel and Slander ⚷21, 123(5)

Impersonal reproach of indeterminate class is not actionable but if words may by any reasonable application import charge against several defendants, under some general description or general name, it is for jury to decide whether charge has personal application averred by plaintiff.

14. Evidence ⚷25(2), 29

Court would judicially know that City of Montgomery operates under commission form of government and that by provision of statute executive and administrative powers are distributed into departments of public health and public safety; streets, parks and public property and improvements; accounts, finances, and public affairs; and that assignments of commissioners may be changed at any time by

majority of board. Laws 1931, p. 30; Code 1940, Tit. 37, § 51.

15. Evidence ⚷5(2)

It is common knowledge that average person knows that municipal agents such as police and firemen are under control and direction of city governing body, and more particularly under direction and control of a single commissioner. Code 1940, Tit. 37, § 51.

16. Libel and Slander ⚷10(3), 21

Advertisement which falsely recounted activities of city police on college campus and elsewhere was libelous per se, and libelous matter was of and connected with plaintiff police commissioner.

17. Libel and Slander ⚷86(2), 89(1)

Where advertisement was libelous per se it was not necessary to allege special damages and complaint could be very simple and brief and there was no need to set forth innuendo.

18. Libel and Slander ⚷85

Complaint referring to false advertisement concerning police activities was sufficient to state a cause of action for libel in favor of plaintiff police commissioner.

19. Jury ⚷131(6)

Broad right of parties to interrogate jurors as to interest or bias is limited by propriety and pertinence and is exercised within sound discretion of trial court. Code 1940, Tit. 30, § 52.

20. Jury ⚷131(6)

Refusal to allow newspaper sued for libel to ask certain questions of jury venire as to bias against newspaper was not an abuse of discretion where prospective jurors had already indicated that there was no reason which would cause them to hesitate to return a verdict for newspaper. Code 1940, Tit. 30, § 52.

NEW YORK TIMES COMPANY v. SULLIVAN Ala. 27

Cite as 144 So.2d 25

21. Jury ⟨⟩131(4)

Refusal to allow defendant newspaper, being sued for libel, to ask of jury venire if any of them had been plaintiffs in litigation in court was not an abuse of discretion, considering completeness of qualification of prospective jurors and remoteness of question. Code 1940, Tit. 30, § 52.

22. Constitutional Law ⟨⟩82

First Amendment of United States Constitution does not protect libelous publications. U.S.C.A.Const. Amend. 1.

23. Constitutional Law ⟨⟩251

Fourteenth Amendment of United States Constitution is directed against state and not private action. U.S.C.A.Const. Amend. 14.

24. Libel and Slander ⟨⟩33, 88

Where words are actionable per se complaint need not specify damages and proof of pecuniary injury is not required since such injury is implied.

25. Libel and Slander ⟨⟩105(4)

Testimony of witnesses that they associated libelous statements in advertisement with plaintiff who was suing defendant newspaper was admissible. Code 1940, Tit. 7, § 910.

26. Witnesses ⟨⟩245

Admission of testimony by witnesses, who had already testified that they had associated plaintiff with libelous advertisement, that if they had believed matter contained in advertisement they would have thought less of plaintiff was not error on ground that answers were hypothetical and implied that witness thought ad was published of and concerning plaintiff.

27. Appeal and Error ⟨⟩1170(7)

Proof of common knowledge is harmless though it is unnecessary to offer such proof. Supreme Court Rules, rule 45.

144 So.2d—2

28. Evidence ⟨⟩5(2)

It is matter of common knowledge that publication of matter that is libelous per se would, if believed, lessen person in eyes of any recipient of libel.

29. Appeal and Error ⟨⟩1170(6)

Court's reference to witness for defendant newspaper in libel action as a very high official of newspaper was not, in view of witness' background and state of record, reversible error. Supreme Court Rules, rule 45.

30. Appeal and Error ⟨⟩207

Where no objections were interposed to argument of counsel nothing was presented for review by claim of prejudicial statements of counsel in argument.

31. Appeal and Error ⟨⟩236(1), 237(1)

Defendant newspaper could not predicate error in libel trial because of hostile newspaper articles where at no time did defendant suggest continuance or change of venue.

32. Appeal and Error ⟨⟩201(1)

Defendant newspaper could not predicate error in libel trial due to presence of photographers in courtroom where at no time was an objection interposed to their presence.

33. New Trial ⟨⟩157

Where newly discovered evidence was not basis of motion for new trial court was confined, upon hearing motion, to matters contained in record of trial.

34. Trial ⟨⟩295(1)

Court's oral charge must be considered as whole and if instruction as a whole states law correctly there is no reversible error even though part of instruction, when considered alone, might be erroneous.

35. Trial ⟨⟩295(5)

Charge of court, when considered as whole, was a fair, accurate, and clear expression of governing principles and that portion of charge which referred to libelous advertisement aimed at plaintiff did not remove from jury question of whether advertisement was of and concerning plaintiff.

36. Appeal and Error ⊕273(6)

Statement that counsel excepted to described portions of court's charge was descriptive of subject matter only and was too indefinite to invite review.

37. Trial ⊕234(3)

Charges instructing jury that if the jury "find" or "find from the evidence" were refused without error in that predicate for jury's determination in civil suit is "reasonably satisfied from the evidence."

38. Trial ⊕261

Court cannot be reversed for refusal of charges which are not expressed in exact and appropriate terms of law.

39. Appeal and Error ⊕1064(4), 1067

Judgment will not be reversed or affirmed because of refusal, or giving, of "belief" charges.

40. Appeal and Error ⊕233(2), 261

Refusal to sustain individual defendant's objection in libel action to way one of plaintiff's counsel pronounced word "Negro" presented nothing for review where no further objections were interposed after colloquy between court and counsel and no exceptions were reserved.

41. Appeal and Error ⊕170(1)

Claims that error infected record in libel action because courtroom was segregated during trial and because judge was not legally elected due to alleged deprivation of Negro voting rights could not be presented for review where such matters were not presented in trial below.

42. Appeal and Error ⊕170(1)

Claim that parties were deprived of fair trial in that judge was, by virtue of

statute, member of jury commission must be considered waived where it was not raised in trial below.   Loc.Laws 1939, p. 66.

43. Appeal and Error ⊕304

Where there are no judgments on motion for new trial and such motions had become discontinued, assignments attempting to raise questions as to weight of evidence and excessiveness of damages were ineffective and presented nothing for review on appeal.

44. Appeal and Error ⊕294(1), 295

Questions as to weight of evidence and excessiveness of damages can be presented only by motion for new trial.

45. Libel and Slander ⊕121(1)

Evidence authorized award of $500,-000 damages against defendant newspaper for publication of libelous advertisement and against individual defendants who subscribed their names to such advertisement.

46. Appeal and Error ⊕930(1)

There is presumption of correctness of verdict where trial judge has refused to grant new trial.

———◆———

T. Eric Embry, Beddow, Embry & Beddow and Fred Blanton, Birmingham, and Lord, Day & Lord and Herbert Wechsler, New York City, for appellant New York Times.

Chas. S. Conley and Vernon Z. Crawford, Montgomery, for individual appellants.

R. E. Steiner, III, Sam Rice Baker, M. R. Nachman, Jr., Steiner, Crum & Baker and Calvin M. Whitesell, Montgomery, for appellee.

HARWOOD, Justice.

This is an appeal from a judgment in the amount of $500,000.00 awarded as damages in a libel suit.   The plaintiff below

NEW YORK TIMES COMPANY v. SULLIVAN   Ala.   29
Cite as 144 So.2d 25

was L. B. Sullivan, a member of the Board of Commissioners of the City of Montgomery, where he served as Police Commissioner. The defendants below were The New York Times, a corporation, and four individuals, Ralph D. Abernathy, Fred L. Shuttlesworth, S. S. Seay, Sr., and J. E. Lowery.

Service of the complaint upon The New York Times was by personal service upon Dan McKee as an agent of the defendant, and also by publication pursuant to the provisions of Sec. 199(1) of Tit. 7, Code of Alabama 1940.

The Times moved to quash service upon it upon the grounds that McKee was not its agent, and The Times, a foreign corporation, was not doing business in Alabama, and that service under Sec. 199(1) was improper, and to sustain either of the services upon it would be unconstitutional.

After hearing upon the motion to quash, the lower court denied such motion.

In this connection the plaintiff presented evidence tending to show The Times gathers news from national press services, from its staff correspondents, and from string correspondents, sometimes called "stringers."

The Times maintained a staff correspondent in Atlanta, Claude Sitton, who covered eleven southern states, including Alabama.

During the period from 1956 through April 1960, regular staff correspondents of The Times spent 153 days in Alabama to gather news articles for submission to The Times. Forty-nine staff news articles so gathered were introduced in evidence.

Sitton himself was assigned to cover in Alabama, at various times, the so-called "demonstrations," the hearings of the Civil Rights Commission in Montgomery, and proceedings in the United States District Court in Montgomery. During his work in Alabama, he also conducted investigations and interviews in such places as Clayton and Union Springs. On some of his visits to Alabama, Sitton would stay as long as a week or ten days.

In May of 1960, he came to Alabama for the purpose of covering the Martin Luther King trial. After his arrival in Montgomery, he "understood" an attempt would be made to serve him. He contacted Mr. Roderick McLeod, Jr., an attorney representing The Times, and was advised to leave Alabama. Shortly after this he called McKee, the "stringer" in Montgomery, and talked generally about the King trial with him.

In addition, The Times made an active effort to keep a resident "stringer" in Montgomery at all times, and as a matter of policy wanted to have three "stringers" in Alabama at all times.

The work of "stringers" was outlined by Sitton as follows: "When The Times feels there is a news story of note going on in an area where a particular stringer lives, * * * The Times calls on a stringer for a story."

"Stringers" fill out blank cards required by The Times, which refer to them as "our correspondents." Detailed instructions are also given to "stringers" by The Times.

"Stringers" also on occasions initiate stories to The Times by telephone recordation. If these stories were not accepted, The Times pays the telephone tolls.

A "stringer" is usually employed by another newspaper, or news agency and is called upon for stories occasionally, or offers stories upon his own. A "stringer" is paid at about the rate of a penny a word. No deductions are made from these payments for such things as income tax, social security, insurance contributions, etc., and "stringers" are not carried on the payroll of The Times. Up to July 26 for the year 1960, The Times had paid Chadwick, the "stringer" in Birmingham, $135.00 for stories accepted, and paid McKee $90.00.

It further appears that upon receipt of a letter from the plaintiff Sullivan demanding a retraction and apology for the statements appearing in the advertisement, which is the basis of this suit, the general counsel of The Times in New York requested the Assistant Managing Editor of The Times to have an investigation made of the correctness of the facts set forth in the advertisement in question. The Times thereupon communicated with McKee and asked for a report. After his investigation, McKee sent a lengthy wire to The Times setting forth facts which demonstrated with clarity the utter falsity of the allegations contained in the advertisement. McKee was also paid $25.00 by The Times for help given Harrison Salisbury, a staff correspondent of The Times when he was in Alabama on an assignment in the spring of 1960.

The Times also has a news service and sells to other papers stories sent it by its staff correspondents, "stringers," and local reporters. In this connection the lower court observed:

> "Obviously, The Times considered the news gathering activities of these staff correspondents and 'stringers' a valuable and unique complement to the news gathering facilities of the Associated Press and other wire services of which The Times is a member. The stories of the 'stringers' appear under the 'slug' 'Special to The New York Times,' and there were 59 such 'specials' in the period from January 1, 1956, through April of 1960."

Advertising

About three quarters of the revenue of The Times comes from advertisements. In 1956, The New York Times Sales, Inc., was set up. This is a wholly owned subsidiary of The Times and its sole function is to solicit advertising for The Times only.

All of the officials of "Sales" are also officials of The Times.

Two solicitors for "Sales," as well as two employees of The Times have at various times come into Alabama seeking advertising for The Times. Between July 1959 and June 3, 1960, one representative spent over a week in this State, another spent a week and a third spent three days. Advertising business was solicited in Birmingham, Montgomery, Mobile, and Selma. Between January 1, 1960 and May 1960, inclusive, approximately seventeen to eighteen thousand dollars worth of advertising was thus sold in Alabama, while in the period of 1956 through April 1960, revenues of $26,801.64 were realized by The Times from Alabama advertisers.

Circulation

The Times sends about 390 daily, and 2,500 Sunday editions into Alabama.

Shipments are made by mail, rail, and air, with transportation charges being prepaid by The Times. Dealers are charged for the papers.

Credit is given for unsold papers and any loss in transit is paid by The Times.

Claims for losses are handled by baggagemen in Alabama, and The Times furnishes claim cards to dealers who bring them to the baggagemen, The Times paying for losses or incomplete copies upon substantiation by the local Alabama baggagemen.

Account cards of various Alabama Times dealers show that credit was thus given for unsold merchandise.

We are here confronted with the question of in personam jurisdiction acquired by service upon an alleged representative of a foreign corporation.

The severe limitations of the doctrine of Bank of Augusta v. Earle (1839) 13 Pet. 519, 13 U.S. 519, 10 L.Ed.2d 274, that a corporation "must dwell in the place of its creation, and cannot migrate to another sovereignty," proving unsatisfactory, the courts, by resort to fictions of "presence," "consent," and "doing business," attempted

NEW YORK TIMES COMPANY v. SULLIVAN   Ala. 31
Cite as 144 So.2d 25

to find answers compatible with social and economic needs. Until comparatively recent years these bases of jurisdictions have tended only to confuse rather than clarify, leading the late Judge Learned Hand to remark that it was impossible to determine any established rule, but that "we must step from tuft to tuft across the morass." Hutchinson v. Chase and Gilbert, (2 Cir.) 45 F.2d 139.

In Pennoyer v. Neff, 95 U.S. 714, 24 L. Ed. 565, the court held that the Fourteenth Amendment to the Federal Constitution required a relationship between the State and the person upon whom the State seeks to exercise personal jurisdiction, and there must be a reasonable notification to the person upon whom the State seeks to exercise its jurisdiction. The required relationship between the State and the person was held to be presence within the State, and as a corollary, no state could "extend its process beyond that territory so as to subject either persons or property to its decisions."

In Hess v. Pawloski, 274 U.S. 352, 47 S. Ct. 632, 71 L.Ed. 1091 (1927), the United States Supreme Court sustained the validity of a non-resident motorist statute which provided that the mere act of driving an automobile in a state should be deemed an appointment of a named state official as agent to receive service in a suit arising out of the operation of the motor vehicle on the highway of such state. The dangerous nature of a motor vehicle was deemed to justify the statute as a reasonable exercise of police power to preserve the safety of the citizens of the state, and the consent for service exacted by the State for use of its highways was reasonable.

In 1935 the same reasoning was applied in upholding a state statute permitting service on an agent of a non-resident individual engaged in the sale of corporate securities in the state in claims arising out of such business. Henry L. Doherty and Co. v. Goodman, 294 U.S. 623, 55 S.Ct. 553, 79 L.Ed. 1097.

Corporations being mere legal entities and incapable of having physical presence as such in a foreign state, and its agents being limited by the scope of their employment, neither the "presence" theory nor the "consent" theory could satisfactorily be applied as a basis for personal jurisdiction.

As to personal jurisdiction over non-resident corporations, the rule therefore evolved that such jurisdiction could be based upon the act of such corporations "doing business" in a state, though echoes of the "presence" and "consent" doctrines may be found in some decisions purportedly applying the "doing business" doctrine in suits against foreign corporations. See Green v. Chicago Burlington and Quincy Ry., 205 U.S. 530, 27 S.Ct. 595, 51 L.Ed. 916, when "presence" of a corporation was found to exist from business done in a state, and Old Wayne Mutual Life Ass'n. of Indianapolis v. McDonough, 204 U.S. 8, 27 S.Ct. 236, 51 L.Ed. 345, where implied consent to jurisdiction was said to arise from business done in the state of the forum.

The term "doing business" carries no inherent criteria. It is a concept dependent upon each court's reaction to facts. These reactions were varied, and the conflicting decisions evoked the observation of Judge Learned Hand, then fully justified, but no longer apt since the "morass" has been considerably firmed up by subsequent decisions of the United States Supreme Court.

In International Shoe Co. v. State of Washington et al., 326 U.S. 310, 66 S.Ct. 154, 90 L.Ed. 95, the old bases of personal jurisdiction were re-cast, the court saying:

"To say that the corporation is so far 'present' there as to satisfy due process requirements * * * is to beg the question to be decided. For the terms 'present' or 'presence' are used merely to symbolize those activities of the corporations's agent within the state which courts will deem to be sufficient to satisfy the demands of due process. * * * Those demands may be met by such contacts of the corporation with the state of the forum as make it reasonable, in the context of our federal system of government, to require the corporation to defend the particular suit which is brought there. An 'estimate of the inconveniences' which would result to the corporation from a trial away from its 'home' or principal place of business is relevant in this connection."

That the new test enunciated is dependent upon the degree of contacts and activities exercised in the forum state is made clear, the court saying:

"* * * due process requires only that in order to subject a defendant to a judgment *in personam*, if he be not present within the territory of the forum, we have certain minimum contacts with it such that the maintenance of the suit does not offend 'traditional notions of fair play and substantial justice.' "

In accord with the above doctrine is our case of Boyd v. Warren Paint and Color Co., 254 Ala. 687, 49 So.2d 559.

In 1957 the United States Supreme Court handed down its opinion in McGee v. International Life Insurance Co., 355 U.S. 220, 78 S.Ct. 199, 2 L.Ed.2d 223. This case involved the validity of a California judgment rendered in a proceeding where service was had upon the defendant company by registered mail addressed to the respondent at its principal place of business in Texas. A California statute subjecting foreign corporations to suit in California on insurance contracts with California residents even though such corporations could not be served with process within its borders.

The facts show that petitioner's son, a resident of California, bought a life insurance policy from an Arizona corporation, naming petitioner as beneficiary. Later, respondent, a Texas corporation, agreed to assume the insurance obligations of the Arizona company, and mailed a re-insurance certificate to the son in California, offering to insure him in accordance with his policy. He accepted the offer and paid premiums by mail from California to the company's office in Texas. Neither corporation ever had any office in California, nor any agent therein, nor had solicited or done any other business in that state. Petitioner sent proofs of her son's death to respondent, but it refused to pay the claim.

The Texas court refused to enforce the California judgment holding it void under the Fourteenth Amendment because of lack of valid service. McGee v. International Life Insurance Company, Tex.Civ.App., 288 S.W.2d 579.

In reversing the Texas Court, the United States Supreme Court wrote:

"Since Pennoyer v. Neff, 95 U.S. 714, 24 L.Ed. 565, this Court has held that the Due Process Clause of the Fourteenth Amendment places some limit on the power of state courts to enter binding judgments against persons not served with process within their boundaries. But just where this line of limitation falls has been the subject of prolific controversy, particularly with respect to foreign corporations. In a continuing process of evolution this Court accepted and then abandoned 'consent,' 'doing business,' and 'presence' as the standard for measuring the extent of state judicial power over such corporations. See Henderson, The Position of Foreign Corporations in American Constitutional Law, c. V. More recently in International Shoe Co. v. State of Washington, 326 U.S. 310, 66 S.Ct. 154, 90 L.Ed. 95, the Court decided that 'due process requires only that in order to subject a defendant to a judgment *in personam*, if he be not present within the territory of the forum, he have certain minimum contacts with it such that the maintenance of the suit does not offend " 'traditional notions of fair play and substantial justice.' " ' 326 U.S. at 316, 66 S.Ct. at 158.

"Looking back over this long history of litigation a trend is clearly discernible toward expanding the permissible scope of state jurisdiction over foreign corporations and other nonresidents. In part this is attributable to the fundamental transformation of our national economy over the years. Today many commercial transactions touch two or more States and may involve parties separated by the full continent. With this increasing nationalization of commerce has come a great increase in the amount of business conducted by mail across state lines. At the same time modern transporation and communication have made it much less burdensome for a party sued to defend himself in a State where he engages in economic activity."

[1] Under the above and more recent doctrines, we are clear to the conclusion that the activities of The New York Times, as heretofore set out, are amply sufficient to more than meet the minimal standards required for service upon its representative McKee.

The adjective "string" in McKee's designation is redundant, and in no wise lessens his status as a correspondent and agent of The New York Times in Alabama. Justice demands that Alabama be permitted to protect its citizens from tortious libels, the effects of such libels certainly occurring to a substantial degree in this State.

Substituted Service

By Act No. 282, approved 5 August 1953 (Acts of Alabama, Reg.Sess.1953, page 347) amending a prior Act of 1949, it was provided that any non-resident person, firm, partnership or corporation, not qualified to do business in this State, who shall do any business or perform any character of work or service in this State shall by so doing, be deemed to have appointed the Secretary of State to be his lawful attorney or agent of such non-resident, upon whom process may be served in any action accruing from the acts in this State, or incident thereto, by any non-resident, or his or its agent, servant or employee.

The act further provides that service of process may be made by service of three copies of the process on the Secretary of State, and such service shall be sufficient service upon the non-resident, provided that notice of such service and a copy of the process are forthwith sent by registered mail by the Secretary of State to the defendant, at his last known address, which shall be stated in the affidavit of the plaintiff, said matter so mailed shall be marked "Deliver to Addressee Only" and "Return Receipt Requested," and provided further that such return receipt shall be received by the Secretary of State purporting to have been signed by the said non-resident.

It is further provided in the Act that any party desiring to obtain service under the Act shall make and file in the cause an affidavit stating facts showing that this Act is applicable.

[2] A mere reading of the above Act demonstrates the sufficiency of the provisions for notice to the non-resident defendant, and that service under the provisions of the Act fully meet the requirements of due process.

Counsel for appellant argues however that the service attempted under Act 282, supra, is defective in two aspects. First, that the affidavit accompanying the complaint is conclusionary and does not show facts bringing the Act into operation, and second, that the Act complained of did not accrue from acts done in Alabama.

The affidavit filed by the plaintiff avers that the defendant " * * * has actually done and is doing business or performing work or services in the State of Alabama; that this cause of action has arisen out of the doing of such business or as an incident thereof by said defendant in the State of Alabama."

[3–5] The affidavit does state facts essential to the invocation of Act 282, supra. We do not think the legislative purpose in requiring the affidavit was to require a detailed quo modo of the business done, but rather was to furnish the Secretary of State with information sufficient upon which to perform the duties imposed upon that official. The ultimate determination of whether the non-resident has done business or performed work or services in this State, and whether the cause of action accrues from such acts, is judicial, and not ministerial, as demonstrated by appellant's motion to quash.

As to appellant's second contention that the cause did not accrue from any acts of The Times in Alabama, it is our conclusion that this contention is without merit.

Equally applicable to newspaper publishing are the observations made in Consolidated Cosmetics v. D–A Pub. Co., Inc., et al., 7 Cir., 186 F.2d 906 at 908, relative to the functions of a magazine publishing company:

"The functions of a magazine publishing company, obviously, include gathering material to be printed, obtaining advertisers and subscribers, printing, selling and delivering the magazines for sale. Each of these, we think, constitutes an essential factor of the magazine publication business. Consequently if a non-resident corporation sees fit to perform any one of those essential functions in a given jurisdiction, it necessarily follows that it is conducting its activities in such a manner as to be subject to jurisdiction."

[6, 7] It is clear under our decisions that when a non-resident prints a libel beyond the boundaries of the State, and distributes and publishes the libel in Alabama, a cause of action arises in Alabama, as well as in the State of the printing or publishing of the libel. Johnson Publishing Co. v. Davis, 271 Ala. 474, 124 So.2d 441; Weir v. Brotherhood of Railroad Trainmen, 221 Ala. 494, 129 So. 267; Bridwell v. Brotherhood of Railroad Trainmen, 227 Ala. 443, 150 So. 338; Collins v. Brotherhood of Railroad Trainmen, 226 Ala. 659, 148 So. 133.

[8] The scope of substituted service is as broad as the permissible limits of due process. Boyd v. Warren Paint & Color Co., 254 Ala. 687, 49 So.2d 559; Ex parte Emerson, 270 Ala. 697, 121 So.2d 914.

The evidence shows that The Times sent its papers into Alabama, with its carrier as its agent, freight prepaid, with title passing on delivery to the consignee. See Tit. 57, Sec. 25, Code of Alabama 1940; 2 Williston on Sales, Sec. 279(b), p. 90. Thence the issue went to newsstands for sale to the public in Alabama, in accordance with a long standing business practice.

The Times or its wholly owned advertising subsidiary, on several occasions, had agents in Alabama for substantial periods of time soliciting, and procuring in substantial amounts advertising to appear in The Times.

Furthermore, upon the receipt of the letter from the plaintiff demanding a retraction of the matter appearing in the advertisement, The Times had its string correspondent in Montgomery, Mr. McKee, investigate the truthfulness of the assertions in the advertisement. The fact that McKee was not devoting his full time to the service of The Times is "without constitutional significance." Scripto Inc. v. Carson, Sheriff, et al., 362 U.S. 207, 80 S.Ct. 619, 4 L.Ed.2d 660.

In WSAZ, Inc. v. Lyons, 254 F.2d 242 (6 Cir.), the defendant television corporation was located in West Virginia. Its broadcasts covered several counties in Kentucky, and the defendant contracted for advertising in the Kentucky counties, all contracts for such advertising being sent to the corporation in West Virginia for acceptance.

The alleged libel sued upon occurred during a news broadcast.

Service was obtained by serving the Kentucky Secretary of State under the provisions of a Kentucky statute providing for such service upon a foreign corporation doing business in Kentucky where the action arose out of or was "connected" with the business done by such corporation in Kentucky.

In sustaining the judgment awarded the plaintiff, the court wrote in connection with the validity of the service to support the judgment:

> "All that is necessary here is that the cause of action asserted shall be 'connected' with the business done. Defendant asserts that the alleged libel has no connection with its business done in Kentucky. But in view of its admission that its usual business was the business of telecasting and that this included news programs, and in view of the undisputed fact that the alleged libel was part of news programs regularly broadcast by defendant, this contention has no merit.

> "The question of due process would seem to be settled by the case of McGee v. International Life Insurance Co. (citation), as well as by International Shoe Co. v. State of Washington, supra. While defendant was not present in the territory of the forum, it certainly had substantial contacts with it. It sought and executed contracts for the sale of advertising service to be performed and actually performed by its own act within the territory of the forum. We conclude that the maintenance of the suit does not offend 'traditional notions of fair play and substantial justice.'"

In the present case the evidence shows that the publishing of advertisements was a substantial part of the business of The Times, and its newspapers were regularly sent into Alabama. Advertising was solicited in Alabama. Its correspondent McKee was called upon by The Times to investigate the truthfulness or falsity of the matters contained in the advertisement after the letter from the plaintiff. The acts therefore disclose not only certain general conditions with reference to newspaper publishing, but also specific acts directly connected with, and directly incident to the business of The Times done in Alabama.

The service acquired under the provisions of Act No. 282, supra, was valid.

General Appearance by The Times

[9] The trial court also found that The Times, by including as a ground of the prayer in its motion to quash, the following, " * * * that this court dismiss this action as to The New York Times Company, A Corporation, for lack of jurisdiction of the subject matter of said action * * *" did thereby go beyond the question of jurisdiction over the corporate person of The Times, and made a general appearance, thereby waiving any defects in service of process, and thus submitted its corporate person to the jurisdiction of the court.

The conclusions of the trial court in this aspect are in accord with the doctrines of a majority of our sister states, and the doctrines of our own decisions.

[10] Pleadings based upon lack of jurisdiction of the person are in their nature pleas in abatement, and find no special favor in the law. They are purely dilatory and amount to no more than a declaration by a defendant that he is in court in a proper action, after actual notice, but because of a defect in service, he is not legally before the court. See Olcese v. Justice's Court, 156 Cal. 82, 103 P. 317.

In Roberts v. Superior Court, 30 Cal.App. 714, 159 P. 465, the court observed:

> "The motion to dismiss the complaint on the ground that the court was with-

out jurisdiction of the subject-matter of the action amounted, substantially or in legal effect, to a demurrer to the complaint on that ground. At all events, a motion to dismiss on the ground of want of jurisdiction of the subject-matter of the action necessarily calls for relief which may be demanded only by a party to the record. It has been uniformly so held, as logically it could not otherwise be held, and, furthermore, that where a party appears and asks for such relief, although expressly characterizing his appearance as special and for the special purpose of objecting to the jurisdiction of the court over his person, he as effectually submits himself to the jurisdiction of the court as though he had legally been served with process."

The reason dictating such conclusion is stated by the Supreme Court of North Carolina, in Dailey Motor Co. v. Reaves, 184 N.C. 260, 114 S.E. 175, to be:

"Any course that, in substance, is the equivalent of an effort by the defendants to try the matter and obtain a judgment on the merits, in any material aspect of the case, while standing just outside the threshold of the court, cannot be permitted to avail them. A party will not be allowed to occupy so ambiguous a position. He cannot deny the authority of the court to take cognizance of his action for want of jurisdiction of the person or proceeding, and at the same time seek a judgment in his favor on the ground that there is no jurisdiction of the cause of action.

*   *   *   *   *   *

"We might cite cases and authorities indefinitely to the same purpose and effect, but those to which we have briefly referred will suffice to show how firmly and unquestionably it is established, that it is not only dangerous, but fatal, to couple with a demurrer, or other form of objection based upon the ground that the court does not have jurisdiction of the person, an objection in the form of a demurrer, answer, or otherwise, which substantially pleads to the merits, and, as we have seen, such an objection is presented when the defendant unites with his demurrer for lack of jurisdiction of the person, a cause of demurrer for want of jurisdiction of the cause or subject of the action, and that is exactly what was done in this case."

We will not excerpt further from the decisions from other jurisdictions in accord with the doctrine of the above cases, but point out that innumerable authorities from a large number of states may be found set forth in an annotation to be found in 25 A.L.R.2d, pages 838 through 842.

In Thompson v. Wilson, 224 Ala. 299, 140 So. 439, this court stated:

"If there was a general appearance made in this case, the lower court had jurisdiction of the person of the appellant. (Authorities cited.)

"The filing of a demurrer, unless based solely on the ground of lack of jurisdiction of the person, constitutes a general appearance."

Again, in Blankenship v. Blankenship, 263 Ala. 297, 82 So.2d 335, the court reiterated the above doctrine.

Thus the doctrine of our cases is in accord with that of a majority of our sister states that despite an allegation in a special appearance that it is for the sole purpose of questioning the jurisdiction of the court, if matters going beyond the question of jurisdiction of the person are set forth, then the appearance is deemed general, and defects in the service are to be deemed waived.

We deem the lower court's conclusions correct, that The Times, by questioning the jurisdiction of the lower court over the subject matter of this suit, made a general appearance, and thereby submitted itself to the jurisdiction of the lower court.

NEW YORK TIMES COMPANY v. SULLIVAN Ala. 37

Cite as 144 So.2d 25

Appellant's assignment No. 9 is to the effect that the lower court erred in overruling defendant's demurrers as last amended to plaintiff's complaint.

The defendant's demurrers contain a large number of grounds, and the argument of the appellant is directed toward the propositions that:

"1. As a matter of law, the advertisement was not published of and concerning the plaintiff, as appears in the face of the complaint.

"2. The publication was not libelous per se.

"3. The complaint was defective in failing to allege special damages

"4. The complaint was defective in failing to allege facts or innuendo showing how plaintiff claimed the article had defamed him.

"5. The complaint was bad because it stated two causes of action."

Both counts of the complaint aver among other things that " * * * defendants falsely and maliciously published in the City of New York, State of New York, and in the City of Montgomery, Alabama, and throughout the State of Alabama, of and concerning the plaintiff, in a paper entitled The New York Times, in the issue of March 29, 1960, on page 25, in an advertisement entitled 'Heed Their Rising Voices' (a copy of said advertisement being attached hereto and made a part hereof as Exhibit 'A'), false and defamatory matter or charges reflecting upon the conduct of the plaintiff as a member of the Board of Commissioners of the City of Montgomery, Alabama, and imputing improper conduct to him, and subjecting him to public contempt, ridicule and shame, and prejudicing the plaintiff in his office, profession, trade or business, with an intent to defame the plaintiff, and particularly the following false and defamatory matter contained therein:

" 'In Montgomery, Alabama, after students sang "My Country 'Tis of Thee" on the State Capitol steps, their leaders were expelled from school, and truckloads of police armed with shotguns and tear-gas ringed the Alabama State College Campus. When the entire student body protested to state authorities by refusing to re-register, their dining hall was padlocked in an attempt to starve them into submission.

* * * * * *

" 'Again and again the Southern violators have answered Dr. King's peaceful protests with intimidation and violence. They have bombed his home almost killing his wife and child. They have assaulted his person. They have arrested him seven times—for "speeding," "loitering," and similar "offenses." And now they have charged him with "perjury"—a *felony* under which they could imprison him for *ten years.*' "

[11] Where the words published tend to injure a person libeled by them in his reputation, profession, trade or business, or charge him with an indictable offense, or tends to bring the individual into public contempt are libelous per se. White v. Birmingham Post Co., 233 Ala. 547, 172 So. 649; Iron Age Pub. Co. v. Crudup, 85 Ala. 519, 5 So. 332.

[12] Further, "the publication is not to be measured by its effects when subjected to the critical analysis of a trained legal mind, but must be construed and determined by its natural and probable effect upon the mind of the average lay reader." White v. Birmingham Post Co., supra.

We hold that the matter complained of is, under the above doctrine, libelous per se, if it was published of and concerning the plaintiff.

In "Dangerous Words—A Guide to the Law of Libel," by Philip Wittenberg, we find the following observations, at pages 227 and 228:

"There are groupings which may be finite enough so that a description of the body is a description of the members. Here the problem is merely one of evaluation. Is the description of the member implicit in the description of the body, or is there a possibility that a description of the body may consist of a variety of persons, those included within the charge, and those excluded from it?

* * * * * *

"The groupings in society today are innumerable and varied. Chances of recovery for libel of the members of such groups diminish with increasing size, and increase as the class or group decreases. Whenever a class decreases so that the individuals become obvious, they may recover for a libel descriptive of the group. In cases where the group is such that it is definite in number; where its composition is easily recognizable and the forms of its organization are apparent, then recognition of individuals libeled by group defamation becomes clear."

[13] The same principle is aptly stated in Gross v. Cantor, 270 N.Y. 93, 200 N.E. 592, as follows:

"An action for defamation lies only in case the defendant has published the matter 'of and concerning the plaintiff.' * * * Consequently an impersonal reproach of an indeterminate class is not actionable. * * * 'But if the words may by any reasonable application, import a charge against several individuals, under some general description or general name, the plaintiff has the right to go on to trial, and it is for the jury to decide, whether the charge has the personal application averred by the plaintiff.'

"We cannot go beyond the face of this complaint. It does not there appear that the publication was so scattered a generality or described so large a class as such that no one could have been personally injured by it. Perhaps the plaintiff will be able to satisfy a jury of the reality of his position that the article was directed at him as an individual and did not miss the mark."

And in Wofford v. Meeks, 129 Ala. 349, 30 So. 625, we find this court saying:

"Mr. Freeman, in his note to case of Jones v. State, (Tex.Cr.App.) 43 S.W. 78, 70 Am.St.Rep. 756, after reviewing the cases, says: 'We apprehend the true rule is that, although the libelous publication is directed against a particular class of persons or a group, yet any one of that class or group may maintain an action, upon showing that the words apply especially to him.' And, further, he cites the cases approvingly which hold that each of the persons composing the class may maintain the action. We think this the correct doctrine, and it is certainly supported by the great weight of authority. 13 Am. & Eng.Enc.Law, 392, and note 1; Hardy v. Williamson, 86 Ga. 551, 12 S.E. 874, 22 Am.St.Rep. 479."

[14] We judicially know that the City of Montgomery operates under a commission form of government. (See Act 20, Gen.Acts of Alabama 1931, page 30.) We further judicially know that under the provisions of Sec. 51, Tit. 37, Code of Alabama 1940, that under this form of municipal government the executive and administrative powers are distributed into departments of (1) public health and public safety, (2) streets, parks and public property and improvements, and, (3) accounts, finances, and public affairs; and that the assignments of the commissioners may be changed at any time by a majority of the board.

The appellant contends that the word "police" encompasses too broad a group to permit the conclusion that the statement in the advertisement was of and concerning the plaintiff since he was not mentioned by name.

NEW YORK TIMES COMPANY v. SULLIVAN   Ala.   39
Cite as 144 So.2d 25

[15] We think it common knowledge that the average person knows that municipal agents, such as police and firemen, and others, are under the control and direction of the city governing body, and more particularly under the direction and control of a single commissioner. In measuring the performance or deficiencies of such groups, praise or criticism is usually attached to the official in complete control of the body. Such common knowledge and belief has its origin in established legal patterns as illustrated by Sec. 51, supra.

In De Hoyos v. Thornton, 259 App.Div. 1, 18 N.Y.S.2d 121, a resident of Monticello, New York, a town of 4000 population, had published in a local newspaper an article in which she stated that a proposed acquisition of certain property by the municipality was "another scheme to bleed the taxpayers and force more families to lose their homes. * * * It seems to me it might be better to relieve the tension on the taxpayers right now and get ready for the golden age * * * and not be dictated to by gangsters and Chambers of Commerce."

The mayor and the three trustees of Monticello brought libel actions. The court originally considering the complaint dismissed the actions on the grounds that the plaintiffs were not mentioned in the article, and their connection with the municipality was not stated in the complaint. In reversing this decision the Appellate Division of the Supreme Court wrote: "There is no room for doubt as to who were the objects of her attack. Their identity is as clear to local readers from the article itself as if they were mentioned by name."

[16] The court did not err in overruling the demurrer in the aspect that the libelous matter was not of and concerning the plaintiffs.

[17] The advertisement being libelous per se, it was not necessary to allege special damages in the complaint. Iron Age Pub. Co. v. Crudup, 85 Ala. 519, 5 So. 332.

[18] Where, as in this case, the matter published is libelous per se, then the complaint may be very simple and brief (Penry v. Dozier, 161 Ala. 292, 49 So. 909), and there is no need to set forth innuendo. White v. Birmingham Post Co., 233 Ala. 547, 172 So. 649. Further, a complaint in all respects similar to the present was considered sufficient in our recent case of Johnson Publishing Co. v. Davis, 271 Ala. 474, 124 So.2d 441.

The Johnson case, supra, is also to the effect that where a newspaper publishes a libel in New York, and by distribution of the paper further publishes the libel in Alabama, a cause of action arises in Alabama, as well as in New York, and that the doctrine of Age-Herald Pub. Co. v. Huddleston, 207 Ala. 40, 92 So. 193, 37 A.L.R. 898, concerned venue, and venue statutes do not apply to a foreign corporation not qualified to do business in Alabama.

In view of the principles above set forth, we hold that the lower court did not err in overruling the demurrer to the complaint in the aspects contended for and argued in appellant's brief.

Assignments of error Nos. 14, 15, 16 and 17, relate to the court's refusal to permit certain questions to be put to the venire in qualifying the jurors.

The appellant contends that The Times was unlawfully deprived of its right to question the jury venire to ascertain the existence of bias or prejudice. The trial court refused to allow four questions which were in effect, (1) Do you have any conviction, opinion or pre-disposition which would compel you to render a verdict against The Times? (2) Have any of you been plaintiffs in litigation in this court? (3) If there is no evidence of malice, would you refuse to punish The Times? (4) Is there any reason which would cause you to hesitate to return a verdict in favor of The Times?

The prospective jurors had already indicated that they were unacquainted with any of the facts in the case, that they had not discussed the case with anyone nor had it been discussed in their presence nor were they familiar in any manner with the contentions of the parties. Appellant was permitted to propound at some length other questions designed to determine whether there was any opinion or pre-disposition which would influence the juror's judgment. The jurors indicated that there was no reason whatsoever which would cause them to hesitate to return a verdict for The Times.

[19, 20] Sec. 52, Tit. 30, Code of Alabama 1940, gives the parties a broad right to interrogate jurors as to interest or bias. This right is limited by propriety and pertinence. It is exercised within the sound discretion of the trial court. We cannot say that this discretion has been abused where similar questions have already been answered by the prospective jurors. Dyer v. State, 241 Ala. 679, 4 So.2d 311.

[21] Only the second question could have conceivably revealed anything which was not already brought out by appellant's interrogation of the prospective jurors. Considering the completeness of the qualification and the remoteness of the second question, the exclusion of that inquiry by the trial court will not be regarded as an abuse of discretion. Noah v. State, 38 Ala. App. 531, 89 So.2d 231.

Appellant contends that without the right to adequately question the prospective jurors, a defendant cannot adequately ensure that his case is being tried before a jury which meets the federal constitutional standards laid down in such decisions as Irvin v. Dowd, 366 U.S. 717, 81 S.Ct. 1639, 6 L.Ed. 751. It is sufficient to say that the jurors who tried this case were asked repeatedly, and in various forms, by counsel for The Times about their impartiality in every reasonable manner.

Appellant's assignment of error 306 pertains to the refusal of requested charge T. 22, which was affirmative in nature.

It is appellant's contention that refusal of said charge contravenes Amendment One of the United States Constitution and results in an improper restraint of freedom of the press, and further, that refusal of said charge is violative of the Fourteenth Amendment of the federal constitution.

In argument in support of this assignment, counsel for appellant asserts that the advertisement was only an appeal for support of King and "thousands of Southern Negro students" said to be "engaged in widespread non-violent demonstrations in positive affirmation of the right to live in human dignity as guaranteed by the U. S. Constitution and the Bill of Rights."

The fallacy of such argument is that it overlooks the libelous portions of the advertisement which are the very crux of this suit.

[22] The First Amendment of the U. S. Constitution does not protect libelous publications. Near v. Minnesota, 283 U.S. 697, 51 S.Ct. 625, 75 L.Ed. 1357; Konigsberg v. State Bar of California, 366 U.S. 36, 81 S.Ct. 997, 6 L.Ed.2d 105; Times Film Corporation v. City of Chicago, 365 U.S. 43, 81 S.Ct. 391, 5 L.Ed.2d 403; Chaplinsky v. New Hampshire, 315 U.S. 568, 62 S.Ct. 766, 86 L.Ed. 1031; Beauharnais v. Illinois, 343 U.S. 250, 72 S.Ct. 725, 96 L.Ed. 919.

[23] The Fourteenth Amendment is directed against State action and not private action. Collins v. Hardyman, 341 U.S. 651, 71 S.Ct. 937, 95 L.Ed. 1253.

Assignment of error No. 306 is without merit.

Appellant's assignment of error No. 94 also pertains to the court's refusal of its requested charge T. 22.

Appellant's argument under this assignment asserts it was entitled to have charge T. 22 given because of the plaintiff's failure to plead or prove special damages.

NEW YORK TIMES COMPANY v. SULLIVAN   Ala.   **41**

[24] In libel action, where the words are actionable per se, the complaint need not specify damages (Johnson v. Robertson, 8 Port. 486), nor is proof of pecuniary injury required, such injury being implied. Johnson Publishing Co. v. Davis, supra.

[25] Assignments 18, 19, 21, 23, 25, 27, 30, and 32, relate to the action of the court in overruling defendant's objections to questions propounded to six witnesses presented by the plaintiff as to whether they associated the statements in the advertisement with the plaintiff. All of the witnesses answered such questions in such manner as to indicate that they did so associate the advertisement.

Without such evidence the plaintiff's cause would of necessity fall, for that the libel was of or concerning the plaintiff is the essence of plaintiff's claim.

Section 910 of Title 7, Code of Alabama 1940, pertaining to libel, among other things, provides that " * * * and if the allegation be denied, the plaintiff must prove, on the trial, the facts showing that the defamatory matter was published or spoken of him." This statute would seem to require the proof here admitted. And in Wofford v. Meeks, 129 Ala. 349, 30 So. 625, 55 L.R.A. 214, the court stated that where the libel is against a group, any one of that group may maintain an action "upon showing that the words apply specially to him," and in Chandler v. Birmingham News Co., 209 Ala. 208, 95 So. 886, this court said, "Any evidence which tended to show it was not intended 'of and concerning him' was material and relevant to the issue."

In Hope v. Hearst Consolidated Publications, (2 Cir.1961), 294 F.2d 681, the court said as to the admissibility of testimony that a witness believed the defamatory matter referred to the plaintiff:

"In this regard it appears that the New York exclusionary rule represents a distinct, if not a lone, minority voice.

The vast majority of reported cases, from both American state and British courts, espouse the admission of such evidence; the text writers similarly advocate its admissibility.

*   *   *   *   *   *

"The plaintiff, as a necessary element in obtaining relief, would have to prove that the coercive lies were understood, by customers, to be aimed in his direction. In a case where the plaintiff was not specifically named, the exact issue now before us would be presented."

In accord with the doctrine that the instant evidence was admissible may be cited, among other authorities Marr v. Putnam Oil Co., 196 Or. 1, 246 P.2d 509; Red River Valley Pub. Co., Inc. v. Bridges, (Tex. Civ.App.) 254 S.W.2d 854; Colbert v. Journal Pub. Co., 19 N.M. 156, 142 P. 146; Prosser v. Callis et al., 117 Ind. 105, 19 N.E. 735; Martin County Bank v. Day, 73 Minn. 195, 75 N.W. 1115; Ball v. Evening American Pub. Co., 237 Ill. 592, 86 N.E. 1097; Children v. Shinn, 168 Iowa 531, 150 N.W. 864.

[26] Appellant's assignments of error 22, 26, 28, 31, 33, and 34, relate to the action of the court in overruling objections to certain questions propounded to plaintiff's witnesses Blackwell, Kaminsky, Price, Parker, and White, which questions were to the effect that if the witnesses believed the matter contained in the advertisement, would they have thought less of the plaintiff.

Counsel for appellant argues that the questions " * * * inescapably carried the implication that the witness thought the ad was published of and concerning the plaintiff." Each and every one of the above named witnesses had testified previous to the instant questions, that they had associated the City Commissioners, or the plaintiff, with the advertisement upon reading it. The questions were therefore based upon the witnesses' testimony that they associated the advertisement with the plaintiff, and not merely an implication that might be read into the question.

Counsel further argues that the question is hypothetical in that none of the witnesses testified they believed the advertisement, or that they thought less of the plaintiff.

While we think such evidence of small probative value, yet it would have relevancy not only as to its effect upon the recipient, but also as to the effect such publication may reasonably have had upon other recipients. See "Defamation," 69 Harv.L.R., 877, at 884.

[27] This aside, we cannot see that the answers elicited were probably injurious to the substantial rights of the appellant. Sup. Court Rule 45. Proof of common knowledge is without injury, though it be unnecessary to offer such proof.

[28] Clearly we think it common knowledge that publication of matter libelous per se would, if believed, lessen the person concerned in the eyes of any recipient of the libel. See Tidmore v. Mills, 33 Ala. App. 243, 32 So.2d 769, and cases cited therein.

[29] Assignment of error No. 63 asserts error arising out of the following instance during the cross-examination of Gershon Aronson, a witness for The Times, which matter, as shown by the record, had been preceded by numerous objections, and considerable colloquy between counsel and court:

"Q Would you state now sir, what that word means to you; whether it has only a time meaning or whether it also to your eye and mind has a cause and effect meaning?

"MR. EMBRY: Now, we object to that, Your Honor. That's a question for the jury to determine—

"THE COURT: Well, of course, it probably will be a question for the jury,

but this gentleman here is a very high official of The Times and I should think he can testify—

"MR. DALY: I object to that, Your Honor. He isn't a high official of The Times at all—

"MR. EMBRY: He is just a man that has a routine job there, Your Honor. He is not—

"THE COURT: Let me give you an exception to the Court's ruling.

"MR. EMBRY: We except."

We do not think it can be fairly said that the record discloses a ruling by the trial court on counsel's objection to the use of the term "very high official." The ruling made by the court is palpably to the question to which the objection was interposed. Counsel interrupted the court to object to the term "very high official," and second counsel added, "He is just a man that has a routine job there, Your Honor." Apparently this explanation satisfied counsel, as the court's use of the term was not pursued to the extent of obtaining a ruling upon this aspect, and the court's ruling was upon the first, and main objection.

Mr. Aronson testified that he had been with The Times for twenty-five years, and was Assistant Manager of the Advertising Acceptability Department of The Times, and was familiar with the company's policies regarding advertising in all its aspects, that is, sales, acceptability, etc., and that advertisements of organizations and committees that express a point of view comes within the witness's particular duties.

In view of the above background of Mr. Aronson, and the state of the record immediately above referred to, we are unwilling to cast error upon the lower court in the instance brought forth under assignment No. 63.

Assignment of error No. 81 is to the effect that the lower court erred in denying appellant's motion for a new trial. Such an

NEW YORK TIMES COMPANY v. SULLIVAN   Ala.   **43**
Cite as 144 So.2d 25

assignment is an indirect assignment of all of the grounds of the motion for a new trial which appellant sees fit to bring forward and specify as error in his brief.

The appellant under this assignment has sought to argue several grounds of its motion for a new trial.

Counsel, in this connection, seeks to cast error on the lower court because of an alleged prejudicial statement made by counsel for the appellee in his argument to the jury.

[30] The record fails to show any objections were interposed to any argument by counsel for any of the litigants during the trial. There is therefore nothing presented to us for review in this regard. Woodward Iron Co. v. Earley, 247 Ala. 556, 25 So.2d 267, and cases therein cited.

Counsel also argues two additional grounds contained in the motion for a new trial, (1) that the appellant was deprived of due process in the trial below because of hostile articles in Montgomery newspapers, and (2) because of the presence of photographers in the courtroom and the publication of the names and pictures of the jury prior to the rendition of the verdict.

[31] As to the first point, the appellant sought to introduce in the hearing on the motion for a new trial newspaper articles dated prior to, and during, the trial. The court refused to admit these articles.

At no time during the course of the trial below did the appellant suggest a continuance, or a change of venue, or that it did not have knowledge of said articles.

[32] Likewise, at no time was any objection interposed to the presence of photographers in the courtroom.

[33] Newly discovered evidence was not the basis of the motion for a new trial. This being so, the court was confined upon the hearing on the motion to matters con-

tained in the record of the trial. Thomason v. Silvey, 123 Ala. 694, 26 So. 644; Alabama Gas Co. v. Jones, 244 Ala. 413, 13 So.2d 873.

Assignment of error 78 pertains to an alleged error occurring in the court's oral charge.

In this connection the record shows the following:

"MR. EMBRY: We except, your Honor. We except to the oral portions of Your Honor's Charge wherein Your Honor charged on libel per se. We object to that portion of Your Honor's Charge wherein Your Honor charged as follows: 'So, as I said, if you are reasonably satisfied from the evidence before you, considered in connection with the rules of law the Court has stated to you, you would come to consider the question of damages and, where as here, the Court has ruled the matter complained of proved to your reasonable satisfaction and aimed at the plaintiff in this case, is libelous per se then punitive damages may be awarded by the jury even though the amount of actual damages is neither found nor shown.'

"THE COURT: Overruled and you have an exception."

Preceding the above exception the court had instructed the jury as follows:

"Now, as stated, the defendants say that the ad complained of does not name the plaintiff, Sullivan, by name and that the ad is not published of and concerning him. * * * The plaintiff, Sullivan, as a member of the group referred to must show by the evidence to your reasonable satisfaction that the words objected to were spoken of and concerning him. The reason for this being that while any one of a class or group may maintain an action because of alleged libelous words, he must show to the reasonable satisfaction of the jury that the words he complained of apply especially to him or are published of and concerning him.

*   *   *   *   *   *

"So, at the very outset of your deliberations you come to this question: Were the words complained of in counts 1 and 2 of this complaint spoken of and concerning the plaintiff, Sullivan? That's the burden he has. He must show that to your reasonable satisfaction and if the evidence in this case does not reasonably satisfy you that the words published were spoken of or concerning Sullivan or that they related to him, why then of course he would not be entitled to any damages and you would not go any further."

In addition the court gave some eleven written charges at defendant's request, instructing the jury in substance that the burden was upon the plaintiff to establish to the reasonable satisfaction of the jury that the advertisement in question was of and concerning the plaintiff, and that without such proof the plaintiff could not recover.

It is to be noted that in the portion of the complained of instructions excerpted above, the court first cautioned the jury they were to consider the evidence in connection with the rules of law stated to them. The court had previously made it crystal clear that the jury were to determine to their reasonable satisfaction from the evidence that the words were spoken of and concerning the plaintiff.

Counsel for appellant contend that because of the words "and aimed at the plaintiff in this case," the instruction would be taken by the jury as a charge that the advertisement was of and concerning the plaintiff, and hence the instruction was invasive of the province of the jury.

Removed from the full context of the court's instructions the charge complained of, because of its inept mode of expression, might be criticized as confused and misleading.

[34] However, it is basic that a court's oral charge must be considered as a whole and the part excepted to should be considered in the light of the entire instruction. If as a whole the instructions state the law correctly, there is no reversible error even though a part of the instructions, if considered alone, might be erroneous.

Innumerable authorities enunciating the above doctrines may be found in 18 Ala.Dig. Trial ☞295(1) through 295(11).

Specifically, in reference to portions of oral instructions that might be criticized because tending to be invasive of the province of the jury, we find the following stated in 89 C.J.S. Trial § 438, the text being amply supported by citations:

"A charge which, taken as a whole, correctly submits the issues to the jury will not be held objectionable because certain instructions, taken in their severalty, may be subject to criticism on the ground they invade the province of the jury, * * *."

To this same effect, see Abercrombie v. Martin and Hoyt Co., 227 Ala. 510, 150 So. 497; Choctaw Coal and Mining Co. v. Dodd, 201 Ala. 622, 79 So. 54.

[35] We have carefully read the court's entire oral instruction to the jury. It is a fair, accurate, and clear expression of the governing legal principles. In light of the entire charge we consider that the portion of the charge complained of to be inconsequential, and unlikely to have affected the jury's conclusions. We do not consider it probable that this appellant was injured in any substantial right by this alleged misleading instruction in view of the court's repeated and clear exposition of the principles involved, and the numerous written charges given at defendant's request further correctly instructing the jury in the premises.

NEW YORK TIMES COMPANY v. SULLIVAN   Ala.   **45**

Cite as 144 So.2d 25

The individual appellants, Ralph D. Abernathy, Fred L. Shuttlesworth, S. S. Seay, Sr., and J. E. Lowery have also filed briefs and arguments in their respective appeals. Many of the assignments of error in these individual appeals are governed by our discussion of the principles relating to the appeal of The Times. We therefore will now confine our review in the individual appeals to those assignments that may present questions not already covered.

[36] In their assignment of error No. 41, the individual appellants assert that the lower court erred in it oral instructions as to ratification of the use of their names in the publication of the advertisement. The instructions of the court in this regard run for a half a page or better. The record shows that an exception was attempted in the following language:

"Lawyer Gray: Your Honor, we except to the Court's charge dealing with ratification as well as the Court's charge in connection with the advertisement being libelous per se in behalf of each of the individual defendants."

The above attempted exception was descriptive of the subject matter only, and is too indefinite to invite our review. Birmingham Ry. Light and Power Co. v. Friedman, 187 Ala. 562, 65 So. 939; Conway v. Robinson, 216 Ala. 495, 113 So. 531; Birmingham Ry. Light and Power Co. v. Jackson, 198 Ala. 378, 73 So. 627.

The refusal of a large number of charges applicable only to the individual appellants are also made the bases of numerous assignments of error. We have read all such refused charges, and each and every one is faulty.

[37, 38] Several of the charges instruct the jury that if the jury "find" etc., while others use the term "find from the evidence." These charges were refused without error in that the predicate for the jury's determination in a civil suit is "reasonably satisfied from the evidence." A court can-

not be reversed for its refusal of charges which are not expressed in the exact and appropriate terms of the law. W. P. Brown and Sons Lumber Co. v. Rattray, 238 Ala. 406, 192 So. 851, 129 A.L.R. 526.

[39] Others of the refused charges, not affirmative in nature, are posited on "belief," or "belief from the evidence." A judgment will not be reversed or affirmed because of the refusal, or giving, of "belief" charges. Sovereign Camp, W. O. W. v. Sirten, 234 Ala. 421, 175 So. 539; Pan American Petroleum Co. v. Byars, 228 Ala. 372, 153 So. 616; Casino Restaurant v. McWhorter, 35 Ala.App. 332, 46 So.2d 582.

[40] Specification of error number 6 asserts error in the court's action in refusing to sustain the individual defendants' objection to the way one of the plaintiff's counsel pronounced the word "negro." When this objection was interposed, the court instructed plaintiff's counsel to "read it just like it is," and counsel replied, "I have been pronouncing it that way all my life." The court then instructed counsel to proceed. No further objections were interposed, nor exceptions reserved.

We consider this assignment mere quibbling, and certainly nothing is presented for our review in the state of the record.

[41] Counsel have also argued assignments to the effect that error infects this record because, (1) the courtroom was segregated during the trial below, and (2) the trial judge was not duly and legally elected because of alleged deprivation of voting rights to negroes.

Neither of the above matters were presented in the trial below, and cannot now be presented for review.

[42] Counsel further argues that the appellants were deprived of a fair trial in that the trial judge was, by virtue of Local Act No. 118, 1939 Local Acts of Alabama, p. 66, a member of the jury commission of

Montgomery County. This act is constitutional. Reeves v. State, 260 Ala. 66, 68 So.2d 14.

Without intimating that any merit attaches to this contention, it is sufficient to point out that this point was not raised in the trial below, and must be considered as having been waived. De Moville v. Merchants & Farmers Bank of Greene County, 237 Ala. 347, 186 So. 704.

Assignments 42, 121, 122, assert error in the court's refusal to hear the individual appellants' motions for new trials, and reference in brief is made to pages 2058–2105 of the record in this connection.

These pages of the record merely show that the individual appellants filed and presented to the court their respective motions for a new trial on 2 December 1960, and the same were continued until 16 December 1960. On 16 December 1960, the respective motions were continued to 14 January 1961. No further orders in reference to the motions of the individual appellants appear in the record, and no judgment on any of the motions of the individual appellants appears in the record.

The motions of the individual appellants therefore became discontinued after 14 January 1961.

[43, 44] There being no judgments on the motion for a new trial of the individual appellants, and they having become discontinued, those assignments by the individual appellants attempting to raise questions as to the weight of the evidence, and the excessiveness of the damages are ineffective and present nothing for review. Such matters can be presented only by a motion for a new trial. See 2 Ala.Dig. Appeal and Error ⊂294(1) and 295, for innumerable authorities.

Other matters are argued in the briefs of the individual appellants. We conclude they are without merit and do not invite discussion, though we observe that some of the matters attempted to be brought forward are insufficiently presented to warrant review.

Evidence on the Merits

The plaintiff first introduced the depositional testimony of Harding Bancroft, secretary of The Times.

Mr. Bancroft thus testified that one John Murray brought the original of the advertisement to The Times where it was delivered to Gershon Aronson, an employee of The Times. A Thermo-fax copy of the advertisement was turned over to Vincent Redding, manager of the advertising department, and Redding approved it for insertion in The Times. The actual insertion was done pursuant to an advertising insertion order issued by the Union Advertising Service of New York City.

Redding determined that the advertisement was endorsed by a large number of people whose reputation for truth he considered good.

Numerous news stories from its correspondents, published in The Times, relating to certain events which formed the basis of the advertisement and which had been published from time to time in The Times were identified. These news stories were later introduced in evidence as exhibits.

Also introduced through this witness was a letter from A. Philip Randolph certifying that the four individual defendants had all given permission to use their names in furthering the work of the "Committee to Defend Martin Luther King and the Struggle for Freedom in the South."

Mr. Bancroft further testified that The Times received a letter from the plaintiff dated 7 April 1960, demanding a retraction of the advertisement. They replied by letter dated 15 April 1960, in which they asked Mr. Sullivan what statements in the advertisement reflected on him.

After the receipt of the letter from the plaintiff, The Times had McKee. its "string"

NEW YORK TIMES COMPANY v. SULLIVAN   Ala.   **47**
Cite as 144 So.2d 25

correspondent in Montgomery, and Sitton, its staff correspondent in Atlanta, investigate the truthfulness of the allegations in the advertisement. Their lengthy telegraphic reports, introduced in evidence showed that the Alabama College officials had informed them that the statement that the dining room at the College had been padlocked to starve the students into submission was absolutely false; that all but 28 of the 1900 students had re-registered and meal service was furnished all students on the campus and was available even to those who had not registered, upon payment for the meals; that the Montgomery police entered the campus upon request of the College officials, and then only after a mob of rowdy students had threatened the negro college custodian, and after a college policeman had fired his pistol in the air several times in an effort to control the mob. The city police had merely tried to see that the orders of the Alabama College officials were not violated.

Sitton's report contained the following pertinent statements:

"* * * Paragraph 3 of the advertisement, which begins, 'In Montgomery, Alabama, after students sang' and so forth, appears to be virtually without any foundation. The students sang the National Anthem. Never at any time did police 'ring' the campus although on three occasions they were deployed near the campus in large numbers. Probably a majority of the student body was at one time or another involved in the protest but not the 'entire student body.' I have been unable to find any one who has heard that the campus dining room was padlocked. * * * In reference to the 6th paragraph, beginning: 'Again and again the Southern violators' and so forth, Dr. King's home was bombed during the bus boycott some four years ago. His wife and child were there but were not (repeat not) injured in any way. King says that the only as-

sault against his person took place when he was arrested some four years ago for loitering outside a courtroom. The arresting officer twisted King's arm behind the minister's back in taking him to be booked. * * *.' "

These reports further show that King had been arrested only twice by the Montgomery police. Once for speeding on which charge he was convicted and paid a $10.00 fine, and once for "loitering" on which charge he was convicted and fined $14.00, this fine being paid by the then police commissioner whom the plaintiff succeeded in office.

Mr. Bancroft further testified that upon receipt of a letter from John Patterson, Governor of Alabama, The Times retracted the advertisement as to Patterson, although in The Times' judgment no statement in the advertisement referred to John Patterson either personally or as Governor of Alabama. However, The Times felt that since Patterson held the high office of Governor of Alabama and believed that he had been libeled, they should apologize.

Grover C. Hall, Jr., Arnold D. Blackwell, William H. MacDonald, Harry W. Kaminsky, H. M. Price, Sr., William M. Parker, Jr., and Horace W. White, all residents of the city of Montgomery, as well as the plaintiff, testified over the defendant's objections that upon reading the advertisement they associated it with the plaintiff, who was Police Commissioner.

E. Y. Lacy, Lieutenant of detectives for the city of Montgomery, testified that he had investigated the bombings of King's home in 1955. This was before the plaintiff assumed office as Commissioner of Police. One bomb failed to explode, and was dismantled by Lacy. In attempting to apprehend the bombers, "The Police Department did extensive research work with overtime and extra personnel and we did everything that we knew including inviting and working with other departments throughout the country."

O. M. Strickland, a police officer of the city of Montgomery, testified that he had arrested King on the loitering charge after King had attempted to force his way into an already overcrowded courtroom, Strickland having been instructed not to admit any additional persons to the courtroom unless they had been subpoenaed as a witness. At no time did he nor anyone else assault King in any manner, and King was permitted to make his own bond and was released.

In his own behalf the plaintiff, Sullivan, testified that he first read the advertisement in the Mayor's office in Montgomery. He testified that he took office as a Commissioner of the City of Montgomery in October 1959, and had occupied that position since. Mr. Sullivan testified that upon reading the advertisement he associated it with himself, and in response to a question on cross-examination, stated that he felt that he had been greatly injured by it.

Mr. Sullivan gave further testimony as to the falsity of the assertions contained in the advertisement.

For the defense, Gershon Aronson, testified that the advertisement was brought to him by John Murray and he only scanned it hurriedly before the advertisement was sent to the Advertising Acceptability Department of The New York Times. As to whether the word "they" as used in the paragraph of the advertisement charging that "Southern violators" had bombed King's home, assaulted his person, arrested him seven times, etc., referred to the same people as "they" in the paragraph wherein it was alleged that the Alabama College students were padlocked out of their dining room in an attempt to starve them into submission and that the campus was ringed with police, armed with shotguns, tear gas, etc., Aronson first stated, "Well, it may have referred to the same people. It is rather difficult to tell" and a short while later Aronson stated, "Well, I think now it probably refers to the same people."

The Times was paid in the vicinity of $4,800 for publishing the advertisement.

D. Vincent Redding, assistant to the manager of the Advertising Acceptability Department of The Times, testified that he examined the advertisement and approved it, seeing nothing in it to cause him to believe it was false, and further he placed reliance upon the endorsers "whose reputations I had no reason to question." On cross-examination Mr. Redding testified he had not checked with any of the endorsers as to their familiarity with the events in Montgomery to determine the accuracy of their statements, nor could he say whether he had read any news accounts concerning such events which had been published in The Times. The following is an excerpt from Mr. Redding's cross-examination:

"Q Now, Mr. Redding, wouldn't it be a fair statement to say that you really didn't check this ad at all for accuracy?

"A That's a fair statement, yes."

Mr. Harding Bancroft, Secretary of The Times, whose testimony taken by deposition had been introduced by the plaintiff, testified in the trial below as a witness for the defendants. His testimony is substantially in accord with that given in his deposition and we see no purpose in an additional delineation of it.

As a witness for the defense, John Murray testified that he was a writer living in New York City. He was a volunteer worker for the "Committee to Defend Martin Luther King," etc., and as such was called upon, together with two other writers, to draft the advertisement in question.

These three were given material by Bayard Rustin, the Executive Director of the Committee, as a basis for composing the advertisement. Murray stated that Rustin is a professional organizer, he guessed along the line of raising funds. Murray knew that Rustin had been affiliated with the War Resisters League, among others.

After the first proof of the advertisement was ready, Rustin called him to his office and stated he was dissatisfied with it as it did not have the kind of appeal it should have if it was to get the response in funds the Committee needed.

Rustin then stated they could add the names of the individual defendants since by virtue of their membership in the Southern Christian Leadership Conference, which supported the work of the Committee, he felt they need not consult them.

The individual defendants' names were then placed on the advertisement under the legend "We in the South who are struggling daily for dignity and freedom warmly endorse this appeal."

Murray further testified that he and Rustin rewrote the advertisement "to get money" and "to project the ad in the most appealing form from the material we were getting."

As to the accuracy of the advertisement, Murray testified:

"Well, that did not enter the—it did not enter into consideration at all except we took it for granted that it was accurate—we took it for granted that it was accurate—they were accurate—and if they hadn't been—I mean we would have stopped to question it—I mean we would have stopped to question it. We had every reason to believe it."

The individual defendants all testified to the effect that they had not authorized The New York Times, Philip Randolph, the "Committee to Defend Martin Luther King," etc., nor any other person to place their names on the advertisement, and in fact did not see the contents of the advertisement until receipt of the letter from the plaintiff.

They all testified that after receiving the letter demanding a retraction of the advertisement they had not replied thereto, nor had they contacted any person or group concerning the advertisement or its retraction.

Amount of Damages

[45] Under assignment of error No. 81, The Times argues those grounds of its motion for a new trial asserting that the damages awarded the plaintiff are excessive, and the result of bias, passion, and prejudice.

In Johnson Publishing Co. v. Davis, supra, Justice Stakely in a rather definitive discussion of a court's approach to the question of the amount of damages awarded in libel actions made the following observations:

"* * * The punishment by way of damages is intended not alone to punish the wrongdoer, but as a deterrent to others similarly minded. Liberty National Life Insurance Co. v. Weldon, supra; Advertiser Co. v. Jones, supra [267 Ala. 171, 100 So.2d 696, 61 A.L.R.2d 1346]; Webb v. Gray, 181 Ala. 408, 62 So. 194.

"Where words are libelous per se and as heretofore stated we think the published words in the present case were libelous per se, the right to damages results as a consequence, because there is a tendency of such libel to injure the person libeled in his reputation, profession, trade or business, and proof of such pecuniary injury is not required, such injury being implied. Advertiser Co. v. Jones, supra [169 Ala. 196, 53 So. 759]; Webb v. Gray, supra; Brown v. Publishers: George Knapp & Co., 213 Mo. 655, 112 S.W. 474; Maytag Co. v. Meadows Mfg. Co., 7 Cir., 45 F.2d 299.

"Because damages are presumed from the circulation of a publication which is libelous per se, it is not necessary that there be any correlation between the actual and punitive damages. Advertiser Co. v. Jones, supra; Webb

v. Gray, supra; Whitcomb v. Hearst Corp., 329 Mass. 193, 107 N.E.2d 295.

"The extent of the circulation of the libel is a proper matter for consideration by the jury in assessing plaintiff's damages. Foerster v. Ridder, Sup., 57 N.Y.S.2d 668; Whitcomb v. Hearst Corp., supra.

* * * * * *

"In Webb v. Gray, supra [181 Ala. 408, 62 So. 196], this court made it clear that a different rule for damages is applicable in libel than in malicious prosecution cases and other ordinary tort cases. In this case the court stated in effect that in libel cases actual damages are presumed if the statement is libelous per se and accordingly no actual damages need be proved.

* * * * * *

"In Advertiser Co. v. Jones, supra, this Court considered in a libel case the claim that the damages were excessive and stated: 'While the damages are large in this case we cannot say that they were excessive. There was evidence from which the jury might infer malice, and upon which they might award punitive damages. This being true, neither the law nor the evidence furnishes us any standard by which we can ascertain certainly that they were excessive. The trial court heard all of this evidence, saw the witnesses, observed their expression and demeanor, and hence was in a better position to judge of the extent of punishment which the evidence warranted than we are, who must form our conclusions upon the mere narrative of the transcript. This court, in treating of excessive verdicts in cases in which punitive damages could be awarded, through Justice Haralson spoke and quoted as follows: " 'There is no legal measure of damages in cases of this character.' "

* * * * *

"The Supreme Court of Missouri considered the question in Brown v. Publishers: George Knapp & Co., 213 Mo. 655, 112 S.W. 474, 485, and said: 'The action for libel is one to recover damages for injury to man's reputation and good name. It is not necessary, in order to recover general damages for words which are actionable per se, that the plaintiff should have suffered any actual or constructive pecuniary loss. In such action, the plaintiff is entitled to recover as general damages for the injury to his feelings which the libel of the defendant has caused and the mental anguish or suffering which he had endured as a consequence thereof. *So many considerations enter into the awarding of damages by a jury in a libel case that the courts approach the question of the excessiveness of a verdict in such case with great reluctance.* The question of damages for a tort especially in a case of libel or slander is peculiarly within the province of the jury, and unless the damages are so unconscionable as to impress the court with its injustice, and thereby to induce the court to believe the jury were actuated by prejudice, partiality, or corruption, it rarely interferes with the verdict.' " (Emphasis supplied.)

In the present case the evidence shows that the advertisement in question was first written by a professional organizer of drives, and rewritten, or "revved up" to make it more "appealing." The Times in its own files had articles already published which would have demonstrated the falsity of the allegations in the advertisement. Upon demand by the Governor of Alabama, The Times published a retraction of the advertisement insofar as the Governor of Alabama was concerned. Upon receipt of the letter from the plaintiff demanding a retraction of the allegations in the advertisement, The Times had investigations made by a staff correspondent, and by its "string" correspondent. Both made a report demonstrating the falsity of the allegations. Even in the face of these reports, The Times adamantly refused to right the wrong it knew it had done the plaintiff. In the trial below none of the defendants questioned the falsity of the allegations in the advertisement.

On the other hand, during his testimony it was the contention of the Secretary of The Times that the advertisement was "substantially correct." In the face of this cavalier ignoring of the falsity of the advertisement, the jury could not have but been impressed with the bad faith of The Times, and its maliciousness inferable therefrom.

While in the Johnson Publishing Co. case, supra, the damages were reduced by way of requiring a remittitur, such reduction was on the basis that there was some element of truth in part of the alleged libelous statement. No such reason to mitigate the damages is present in this case.

It is common knowledge that as of today the dollar is worth only 50 cents or less of its former value.

The Times retracted the advertisement as to Governor Patterson, but ignored this plaintiff's demand for retraction. The matter contained in the advertisement was equally false as to both parties.

The Times could not justify its nonretraction as to this plaintiff by fallaciously asserting that the advertisement was substantially true, and further, that the advertisement as presented to The Times bore the names of endorsers whose reputation for truth it considered good.

The irresponsibility of these endorsers in attaching their names to this false and malicious advertisement cannot shield The Times from its irresponsibility in printing the advertisement and scattering it to the four winds.

[46] All in all we do not feel justified in mitigating the damages awarded by the jury, and approved by the trial judge below, by its judgment on the motion for a new trial, with the favorable presumption which attends the correctness of the verdict of the jury where the trial judge refuses to grant a new trial. Housing Authority of City of Decatur v. Decatur Land Co., 258 Ala. 607, 64 So.2d 594.

In our considerations we have examined the case of New York Times Company v. Conner, (5CCA) 291 F.2d 492 (1961), wherein the Circuit Court of Appeals for the Fifth Circuit, relying exclusively upon Age Herald Publishing Co. v. Huddleston, 207 Ala. 40, 92 So. 193, 37 A.L.R. 898, held that no cause of action for libel arose in Alabama where the alleged libel appeared in a newspaper primarily published in New York.

This case overlooks, or ignores, the decision of this court in Johnson Publishing Co. v. Davis, 271 Ala. 474, 124 So.2d 441, wherein this court rejected the argument that the whole process of writing, editing, printing, transportation and distribution of a magazine should be regarded as one libel, and the locus of such libel was the place of primary publication. This court further, with crystal clarity, held that Age Herald Publishing Co. v. Huddleston, supra, concerned a venue statute, and that venue statutes do not apply to foreign corporations not qualified to do business in Alabama.

The statement of Alabama law in the Conner case, supra, is erroneous in light of our enunciation of what is the law of Alabama as set forth in the Johnson Publishing Company case, supra. This erroneous premise, as we interpret the Conner case, renders the opinion faulty, and of no persuasive authority in our present consideration.

"The laws of the several states, except where the Constitution or treaties of the United States or Acts of Congress otherwise require or provide, shall be regarded as rules of decision

52   Ala.   144 SOUTHERN REPORTER, 2d SERIES

in civil actions in the courts of the United States, in cases where they apply." Sec. 1652, Title 28, U.S.C.A., 62 Stat. 944.

It is our conclusion that the judgment below is due to be affirmed, and it is so ordered.

Affirmed.

LIVINGSTON, C. J., and SIMPSON and MERRILL, JJ., concur.

IN THE
SUPREME COURT OF THE UNITED STATES
OCTOBER TERM, 1963

No. 39

THE NEW YORK TIMES COMPANY, PETITIONER,

v.

L. B. SULLIVAN, RESPONDENT

ON WRIT OF CERTIORARI TO THE SUPREME COURT OF ALABAMA

BRIEF FOR THE PETITIONER

LOUIS M. LOEB
T. ERIC EMBRY
MARVIN E. FRANKEL
RONALD S. DIANA
DORIS WECHSLER
LORD, DAY & LORD
BEDDOW, EMBRY & BEDDOW

Of Counsel

HERBERT BROWNELL
THOMAS F. DALY
25 Broadway
New York 4, New York

HERBERT WECHSLER
435 West 116th St.
New York 27, New York

Attorneys for Petitioner
The New York Times Company

INDEX

IN THE
SUPREME COURT OF THE
UNITED STATES
OCTOBER TERM, 1963
NO. 39

THE NEW YORK TIMES COMPANY, PETITIONER,

V.

L. B. SULLIVAN, RESPONDENT.

ON WRIT OF CERTIORARI TO THE
SUPREME COURT OF ALABAMA

BRIEF FOR THE PETITIONER

OPINIONS BELOW

The opinion of the Supreme Court of Alabama (R. 1139) is reported in 273 Ala. 656, 144 So. 2d 25. The opinion of the Circuit Court, Montgomery County, on the petitioner's motion to quash service of process (R. 49) is unreported. There was no other opinion by the Circuit Court.

JURISDICTION

The judgment of the Supreme Court of Alabama (R. 1180) was entered August 30, 1962. The petition for a writ of certiorari was filed November 21, 1962 and was granted January 7, 1963. 371 U.S. 946. The jurisdiction of this Court is invoked under 28 U.S.C. 1257 (3).

QUESTIONS PRESENTED

1. Whether, consistently with the guarantee of freedom of the press in the First Amendment as embodied in the Fourteenth, a State may hold libelous *per se* and actionable by an elected City Commissioner published statements critical of the conduct of a department of the City Government under his general supervision, which are inaccurate in some particulars.

2. Whether there was sufficient evidence to justify, consistently with the constitutional guarantee of freedom of the press, the determination that published statements naming no individual but critical of the conduct of the "police" were defamatory as to the respondent, the elected City Commissioner with jurisdiction over the Police Department, and punishable as libelous *per se*.

3. Whether an award of $500,000 as "presumed" and punitive damages for libel constituted, in the circumstances of this case, an abridgment of the freedom of the press.

4. Whether the assumption of jurisdiction in a libel action against a foreign corporation publishing a newspaper in another State, based upon sporadic news gathering activities by correspondents, occasional solicitation of advertising and minuscule distribution of the newspaper within the forum state, transcended the territorial limitations of due process, imposed a forbidden burden on interstate commerce or abridged the freedom of the press.

Constitutional and statutory provisions involved

The constitutional and statutory provisions involved are set forth in Appendix A, *infra*, pp. 91–95.

STATEMENT

On April 19, 1960, the respondent, one of three elected Commissioners of the City of Montgomery, Alabama, instituted this action in the Circuit Court of Montgomery County against *The New York Times*, a New York corporation, and four co-defendants resident in Alabama, Ralph D. Abernathy, Fred L. Shuttlesworth, S. S. Seay, Sr., and J. E. Lowery. The complaint (R. 1) demanded $500,000 as damages for libel allegedly contained in two paragraphs of an advertisement (R. 6) published in *The New York Times* on March 29, 1960. Service of process was attempted by delivery to an alleged agent of *The Times* in Alabama and by substituted service (R. 11) pursuant to the "long-arm" statute of the State. A motion to quash, asserting constitutional objections to the jurisdiction of the Circuit Court (R. 39, 43–44, 47, 129) was denied on August 5, 1960 (R. 49). A demurrer to the complaint (R. 58, 67) was overruled on November 1, 1960 (R. 108) and the cause proceeded to a trial by jury, resulting on November 3 in a verdict against all defendants for the full $500,000 claimed (R. 862). A motion for new trial (R. 896, 969) was denied on March 17, 1961 (R. 970). The Supreme Court of Alabama affirmed the judgment on August 30, 1962 (R. 1180).* The Circuit Court and the Supreme

---

*Libel actions based on the publication of the same statements in the same advertisement were also instituted by Governor Patterson of Alabama, Mayor James of Montgomery, City Commissioner Parks and former Commissioner Sellers. The James case is pending on motion for new trial after a verdict of $500,000. The Patterson, Parks and Sellers cases, in which the damages demanded total $2,000,000, were removed by petitioner to the District Court. That court sustained the removal (195 F. Supp. 919 [1961]) but the Court of Appeals, one judge dissenting, reversed and ordered a remand (308 F. 2d 474 [1962]). A petition to review that decision on certiorari is now pending in this Court. *New York Times Company* v. *Parks and Patterson*, No. 687, October Term, 1962, No. 52, this Term.

Court both rejected the petitioner's contention that the liability imposed abridged the freedom of the press.

1. The nature of the publication

The advertisement, a copy of which was attached to the complaint (R. 1, 6), consisted of a full page statement (reproduced in Appendix B, *infra* p. 97) entitled "Heed Their Rising Voices", a phrase taken from a *New York Times* editorial of March 19, 1960, which was quoted at the top of the page as follows: "The growing movement of peaceful mass demonstrations by Negroes is something new in the South, something understandable . . . Let Congress heed their rising voices, for they will be heard."

The statement consisted of an appeal for contributions to the "Committee to Defend Martin Luther King and the Struggle for Freedom in the South" to support "three needs—the defense of Martin Luther King—the support of the embattled students—and the struggle for the right-to-vote." It was set forth over the names of sixty-four individuals, including many who are well known for achievement in religion, humanitarian work, public affairs, trade unions and the arts. Under a line reading "We in the South who are struggling daily for dignity and freedom warmly endorse this appeal" appeared the names of twenty other persons, eighteen of whom are identified as clergymen in various southern cities. A New York address and telephone number were given for the Committee, the officers of which were also listed, including three individuals whose names did not otherwise appear.

The first paragraph of the statement alluded generally to the "non-violent demonstrations" of Southern Negro students "in positive affirmation of the right to live in human dignity as guaranteed by the U.S. Constitution and the Bill of Rights." It went on to charge that in "their efforts to uphold these guarantees, they are being met by an unprecedented wave of terror by those who would deny and negate that document which the whole world looks upon as setting the pattern for modern freedom. . . . "

The second paragraph told of a student effort in Orangeburg, South Carolina, to obtain service at lunch counters in the business district and asserted that the students were forcibly ejected, tear-gassed, arrested en masse and otherwise mistreated.

The third paragraph spoke of Montgomery, Alabama and complained of the treatment of students who sang on the steps of the State Capitol, charging that their leaders were expelled from school, that truckloads of armed police ringed the Alabama State College Campus and that the College dining-hall was padlocked in an effort to starve the protesting students into submission.

The fourth paragraph referred to "Tallahassee, Atlanta, Nashville, Savannah, Greensboro, Memphis, Richmond, Charlotte and a host of other cities in the South," praising the action of "young American teenagers, in face of the entire weight of official state apparatus and police power," as "protagonists of democracy."

The fifth paragraph speculated that "The Southern violators of the Constitution fear this new, non-violent brand of freedom fighter . . . even as they fear the upswelling right-to-vote movement," that "they are determined to destroy the one man who more than any other, symbolizes the new spirit now sweeping the South—the Rev. Dr. Martin Luther King, Jr., world-famous leader of the Montgomery Bus Protest." It went on to portray the leadership role of Dr. King and the Southern Christian Leadership Conference, which he founded, and to extol the inspiration of "his doctrine of non-violence".

The sixth paragraph asserted that the "Southern violators" have repeatedly "answered Dr. King's protests with intimidation and violence" and referred to the bombing of his home, assault upon his person, seven arrests and a then pending charge of perjury. It stated that "their real purpose is to remove him physically as the leader to whom the students and millions of others—look for guidance and support, and thereby to intimidate *all* leaders who may rise in the South", concluding that the defense of Dr. King "is an integral part of the total struggle for freedom in the South."

The remaining four paragraphs called upon "men and women of good will" to do more than "applaud the creative daring of the students and the quiet heroism of Dr. King" by adding their "moral support" and "the material help so urgently needed by those who are taking the risks, facing jail and even death in a glorious reaffirmation of our Constitution and its Bill of Rights".

2. The allegedly defamatory statements

Of the ten paragraphs of text in the advertisement, the third and a portion of the sixth were the basis of respondent's claim of libel.

(a) The third paragraph was as follows:

"In Montgomery, Alabama, after students sang 'My Country, 'Tis of Thee' on the State Capitol steps, their leaders were expelled from school, and truckloads of police armed with shot-guns and tear-gas ringed the Alabama State College Campus. When the entire student body protested to state authorities by refusing to re-register, their dining hall was padlocked in an attempt to starve them into submission."

Though the only part of this statement that respondent thought implied a reference to him was the assertion about "truckloads of police" (R. 712), he undertook and was permitted to deal with the paragraph in general by adducing evidence depicting the entire episode involved. His evidence consisted mainly of a story by Claude Sitton, the southern correspondent of *The Times*, published on March 2, 1960 (R. 655, 656–7, Pl. Ex. 169, R. 1568), a report requested by *The Times* from Don McKee, its "stringer" in Montgomery, after institution of this suit was threatened (R. 590–593, Pl. Ex. 348, R. 1931–1935), and a later telephoned report from Sitton to counsel for *The Times*, made on May 5, after suit was brought (R. 593–595, Pl. Ex. 348, R. 1935–1937).

This evidence showed that a succession of student demonstrations had occurred in Montgomery, beginning with an unsuccessful effort by some thirty Alabama State College students to obtain service at a lunch counter in the Montgomery County Court House. A thousand students had marched on March 1, 1960, from the College campus to the State Capitol, upon the steps of which they said the Lord's Prayer and sang the National Anthem before marching back to the campus. Nine student leaders of the lunch counter demonstration were expelled on March 2 by the State Board of Education, upon motion of Governor Patterson, and thirty-one others were placed on probation (R. 696–699, Pl. Ex. 364, R. 1972–1974), but the singing at the Capitol was not the basis of the disciplinary action or mentioned at the meeting of the Board (R. 701). Alabama State College students stayed away from classes on March 7 in a strike in sympathy with those expelled but virtually all of them returned to class after a day and most of them re-registered or had already done so. On March 8, there was another student demonstration at a church near the campus, followed by a march upon the campus, with students dancing around in conga lines and some becoming rowdy. The superintendent of grounds summoned the police and the students left the campus, but the police arrived as the demonstrators marched across the street and arrested thirty-two of them for disorderly conduct or failure to obey officers, charges on which they later pleaded guilty and were fined in varying amounts (R. 677–680, 681, 682).

A majority of the student body was probably involved at one time or another in the protest but not the "entire student body". The police did not at any time "ring" the campus, although they were deployed near the campus on three occasions in large numbers. The campus dining hall was never "padlocked" and the only students who may have been barred from eating were those relatively few who had neither signed a pre-registration application nor requested temporary meal tickets (R. 594, 591).

The paragraph was thus inaccurate in that it exaggerated the number of students involved in the protest and the extent of police activity and intervention. If, as the respondent argued (R. 743), it implied that the students were expelled for singing on the steps of the Capitol, this was erroneous; the expulsion was for the demand for service at a lunch counter in the Courthouse. There was, moreover, no foundation for the charge that the dining hall was padlocked in an effort to starve the students into submission, an allegation that especially aroused resentment in Montgomery (R. 605, 607, 949, 2001, 2002, 2007).

(b) The portion of the sixth paragraph of the statement relied on by respondent read as follows:

> "Again and again the Southern violators have answered Dr. King's peaceful protests with intimidation and violence. They have bombed his home, almost killing his wife and child. They have assaulted his person. They have arrested him seven times—for 'speeding', 'loitering' and similar 'offenses'. And now they have charged him with 'perjury'—a *felony* under which they could imprison him for *ten* years."

As to this paragraph, which did not identify the time or place of the events recited, but which respondent read to allude to himself because it also "describes police action" (R. 724), his evidence showed that Dr. King's home had in fact been bombed twice when his wife and child were at home, though one of the bombs failed to explode—both of the occasions antedating the respondent's tenure as Commissioner (R. 594, 685, 688); that Dr. King had been arrested only four times, not seven, three of the arrests preceding the respondent's service as Commissioner (R. 592, 594–595, 703); that Dr. King had in fact been indicted for perjury on two counts, each carrying a possible sentence of five years imprisonment (R. 595), a charge on which he subsequently was acquitted (R. 680). It also showed that while Dr. King claimed to have been assaulted when he was arrested some four years earlier for loitering outside a courtroom (R. 594), one of the officers participating in arresting him and carrying him to a detention cell at headquarters denied that there was a physical assault (R. 692–693)—this incident also antedating the respondent's tenure as Commissioner (R. 694).

On the theory that the statement could be read to charge that the bombing of Dr. King's home was the work of the police (R. 707), respondent was permitted to call evidence that the police were not involved; that they in fact dismantled the bomb that did not explode; and that they did everything they could to apprehend the perpetrators of the bombings (R. 685–687)—also before respondent's tenure as Commissioner (R. 688). In the same vein, respondent testified himself that the police had not bombed the King home or assaulted Dr. King or condoned the bombing or assaulting; and that he had had nothing to do with procuring King's indictment (R. 707–709).

3. The impact of the statements on respondent's reputation

As one of the three Commissioners of the City of Montgomery since October 5, 1959, specifically Commissioner of Public Affairs, respondent's duties were the supervision of the Police Department, Fire Department, Department of Cemetery and Department of Scales (R. 703). He was normally not responsible, however, for day-to-day police operations, including those during the Alabama State College episode referred to in the advertisement, these being under the immediate supervision of Montgomery's Chief of Police—though there was one occasion when the Chief was absent and respondent supervised directly (R. 720). It was stipulated that there were 175 full time policemen in the Montgomery Police Department, divided into three shifts and four divisions, and 24 "special traffic directors" for control of traffic at the schools (R. 787).

As stated in respondent's testimony, the basis for his role as aggrieved plaintiff was the "feeling" that the advertisement, which did not mention him or the Commission or Commissioners or any individual, "reflects not only on me but on the other Commissioners and the community" (R. 724). He felt particularly that statements referring to "police activities" or "police action" were associated with himself, impugning his "ability and integrity" and reflecting on him "as an individual" (R. 712, 713, 724). He also felt that the other statements in the passages complained of, such as that alluding to the bombing of King's home, referred to the Commissioners, to the Police Department and to him because they were contained in the same paragraphs as statements mentioning police activities (R. 717–718), though he conceded that as "far as the expulsion of students is concerned, that responsibility rests with the State Department of Education" (R. 716).

In addition to this testimony as to the respondent's feelings, six witnesses were permitted to express their opinions of the connotations of the statements and their effect on respondent's reputation.

Grover C. Hall, editor of the Montgomery Advertiser, who had previously written an editorial attacking the advertisement (R. 607, 613, 949), testified that he thought he would associate the third paragraph "with the City Government—the Commissioners" (R. 605) and "would naturally think a little more about the police commissioner" (R. 608). It was "the phrase about starvation" that led to the association; the "other didn't hit" him "with any particular force" (R. 607, 608). He thought "starvation is an instrument of reprisal and would certainly be indefensible . . . in any case" (R. 605).

Arnold D. Blackwell, a member of the Water Works Board appointed by the Commissioners (R. 621) and a businessman engaged in real estate and insurance (R. 613), testified that the third paragraph was associated in his mind with "the Police Commissioner" and the "people on the police force"; that if it were true that the dining hall was padlocked in an effort to starve the students into submission, he would "think that the people on our police force or the heads of our police force were acting without their jurisdiction and would not be competent for the position" (R. 617, 624). He also associated the statement about "truck-loads of police" with the police force and the Police Commissioner (R. 627). With respect to the "Southern violators" passage, he associated the statement about the arrests with "the police force" but not the "sentences above that" (R. 624) or the statement about the charge of perjury (R. 625).

Harry W. Kaminsky, sales manager of a clothing store (R. 634) and a close friend of the respondent (R. 644), also associated the third paragraph with "the Commissioners" (R. 635), though not the statement about the expulsion of the students (R. 639). Asked on direct examination about the sentences in the sixth paragraph, he said that he "would say that it refers to the same people in the paragraph that we look at before", i.e., to "The Commissioners", including the respondent (R. 636). On cross-examination, however, he could not say that he associated those statements with the respondent, except that he thought that the reference to arrests "implicates the Police Department . . . or the authorities that would do that—arrest folks for speeding and loitering and such as that" (R. 639-640). In general, he would "look at" the respondent when he saw "the Police Department" (R. 641).

H. M. Price, Sr., owner of a small food equipment business (R. 644), associated "the statements contained" in both paragraphs with "the head of the Police Department", the respondent (R. 646). Asked what it was that made him think of the respondent, he read the first sentence of the third paragraph and added: "Now, I would just automatically consider that the Police Commissioner in Montgomery would have to put his approval on those kind of things as an individual" (R. 647). If he believed the statements contained in the two paragraphs to be true, he would "decide that we probably had a young Gestapo in Montgomery" (R. 645–646).

William M. Parker, Jr., a friend of the respondent and of Mayor James (R. 651), in the service station business, associated "those statements in those paragraphs" with the City Commissioners (R. 650) and since the respondent "was the Police Commissioner", he "thought of him first" (R. 651). If he believed the statements to be true, he testified that he would think the respondent "would be trying to run this town with a strong arm—strong armed tactics, rather, going against the oath he took to run his office in a peaceful manner and an upright manner for all citizens of Montgomery" (R. 650).

Finally, Horace W. White, proprietor of the P. C. White Truck Line (R. 662), a former employer of respondent (R. 664), testified that both of the paragraphs meant to him "Mr. L. B. Sullivan" (R. 663). The statement in the advertisement that indicated to him that it referred to the respondent was that about "truck-loads of police", which made him think of the police and of respondent "as being the head of the Police Department" (R. 666). If he believed the statements, he doubted whether he "would want to be associated with anybody who would be a party to such things" (R. 664) and he would not re-employ respondent for P. C. White Truck Line if he thought that "he allowed the Police Department to do the things the paper say he did" (R. 667, 664, 669).

None of the six witnesses testified that he believed any of the statements that he took to refer to respondent and all but Hall specifically testified that they did not believe them (R. 623, 636, 647, 651, 667). None was led to think less kindly of respondent because of the advertisement (R. 625, 638, 647, 651, 666). Nor could respondent point to any injury that he had suffered or to any sign that he was held in less esteem (R. 721–724).

Four of the witnesses, moreover, Blackwell, Kaminsky, Price and Parker, saw the publication first when it was shown to them in the office of respondent's counsel to equip them as witnesses (R. 618, 637, 643, 647, 649). Their testimony should, therefore, have been disregarded under the trial court's instruction that the jury should "disregard . . . entirely" the testimony of any witness "based upon his reading of the advertisement complained of here, only after having been shown a copy of same by the plaintiff or his attorneys" (R. 833). White did not recall when he first saw the advertisement; he believed, though he was not sure, that "somebody cut it out of the paper and mailed it" to him or left it on his desk (R. 662, 665, 668). Only Hall, whose testimony was confined to the phrase about starving students into submission (R. 605, 607), received the publication in ordinary course at *The Montgomery Advertiser* (R. 606, 726–727).

4. The circumstances of the publication

The advertisement was published by *The Times* upon an order from the Union Advertising Service, a reputable New York advertising agency, acting for the Committee to Defend Martin Luther King (R. 584–585, 737, Pl. Ex. 350, R. 1957). The order was dated March 28, 1960, but the proposed typescript of the ad had actually been delivered on March 23 by John Murray, a writer acting for the Committee, who had participated in its composition (R. 731, 805). Murray gave the copy to Gershon Aaronson, a member of the National Advertising Staff of *The Times* specializing in "editorial type" advertisements (R. 731, 738), who promptly passed it on to technical departments and sent a thermo-fax copy to the Advertising Acceptability Department, in charge of the screening of advertisements (R. 733, 734, 756). D. Vincent Redding, the manager of that department, read the copy on March 25 and approved it for publication (R. 758). He gave his approval because he knew nothing to cause him to believe that anything in the proposed text was false and because it bore the endorsement of "a number of people who are well known and whose reputation" he "had no reason to question" (R. 758, 759–760, 762–763). He did not make or think it necessary to make any further check as to the accuracy of the statements (R. 765, 771).

When Redding passed on the acceptability of the advertisement, the copy was accompanied by a letter from A. Philip Randolph, Chairman of the Committee, to Aaronson, dated March 23 (R. 587, 757, Def. Ex. 7, R. 1992) and reading:

> "This will certify that the names included on the enclosed list are all signed members of the

Committee to Defend Martin Luther King and the Struggle for Freedom in the South.

"Please be assured that they have all given us permission to use their names in furthering the work of our Committee."

The routine of *The Times* is to accept such a letter from a responsible person to establish that names have not been used without permission and Redding followed that practice in this case (R. 759). Each of the individual defendants testified, however, that he had not authorized the Committee to use his name (R. 787–804) and Murray testified that the original copy of the advertisement, to which the Randolph letter related, did not contain the statement "We in the South . . . warmly endorse this appeal" or any of the names printed thereunder, including those of these defendants. That statement and those names were added, he explained, to a revision of the proof on the suggestion of Bayard Rustin, the Director of the Committee. Rustin told Murray that it was unnecessary to obtain the consent of the individuals involved since they were all members of the Southern Christian Leadership Conference, as indicated by its letterhead, and "since the SCLC supports the work of the Committee . . . he [Rustin] . . . felt that there would be no problem at all, and that you didn't even have to consult them" (R. 806–809). Redding did not recall this difference in the list of names (R. 767), though Aaronson remembered that there "were a few changes made . . . prior to publication" (R. 739).

The New York Times has set forth in a booklet its "Advertising Acceptability Standards" (R. 598, Pl. Ex. 348, Exh. F, R. 1952) declaring, *inter alia*, that *The Times* does not accept advertisements that are fraudulent or deceptive, that are "ambiguous in wording and . . . may mislead" or "[a]ttacks of a personal character". In replying to the plaintiff's interrogatories, Harding Bancroft, Secretary of *The Times*, deposed that "as the advertisement made no attacks of a personal character upon any individual and otherwise met the advertising acceptability standards promulgated" by *The Times*, D. Vincent Redding had approved it (R. 585).

Though Redding and not Aaronson was thus responsible for the acceptance of the ad, Aaronson was cross-examined at great length about such matters as the clarity or ambiguity of its language (R. 741–753), the court allowing the interrogation on the stated ground that "this gentleman here is a very high official of *The Times*", which he, of course, was not (R. 744). In the course of this colloquy, Aaronson contradicted himself on the question whether the word "they" in the "Southern violators" passage refers to "the same people" throughout or to different people, saying first "It is rather difficult to tell" (R. 745) and later: "I think now that it probably refers to the same people" (R. 746). Redding was not interrogated on this point, which respondent, in his Brief in Opposition, deemed established by what Aaronson "conceded" (Brief in Opposition, p. 7).

The Times was paid "a little over" $4800 for the publication of the advertisement (R. 752). The total circulation of the issue of March 29, 1960, was approximately 650,000, of which approximately 394 copies were mailed to Alabama subscribers or shipped to newsdealers in the State, approximately 35 copies going to Montgomery County (R. 601–602, Pl. Ex. 348, R. 1942–1943).

5. The response to the demand for a retraction

On April 8, 1960, respondent wrote to the petitioner and to the four individual defendants, the letters being erroneously dated March 8 (R. 588, 671, 776, Pl. Ex. 348, 355–358, R. 1949, 1962–1968). The letters, which were in identical terms, set out the passages in the advertisement complained of by respondent, asserted that the "foregoing matter, and the publication as a whole charge me with grave misconduct and of [*sic*] improper actions and omissions as an official of the City of Montgomery" and called on the addressee to "publish in as prominent and as public a manner as the foregoing false and defamatory material contained in the foregoing publication, a full and fair retraction of the entire false and defamatory matter so far as the same relates to me and to my conduct and acts as a public official of the City of Montgomery, Alabama."

Upon receiving this demand and the report from Don McKee, the *Times* stringer in Montgomery referred to above (p. 7), petitioner's counsel wrote to the respondent on April 15, as follows (R. 589, Pl. Ex. 363, R. 1971):

Dear Mr. Commissioner:

Your letter of April 8 sent by registered mail to The New York Times Company has been referred for attention to us as general counsel.

You will appreciate, we feel sure, that the statements to which you object were not made by The New York Times but were contained in an advertisement proffered to The Times by responsible persons.

We have been investigating the matter and are somewhat puzzled as to how you think the statements in any way reflect on you. So far, our investigation would seem to indicate that the statements are substantially correct with the sole exception that we find no justification for the statement that the dining hall in the State College was "padlocked in an attempt to starve them into submission."

We shall continue to look into the subject matter because our client, The New York Times, is always desirous of correcting any statements which appear in its paper and which turn out to be erroneous.

In the meanwhile you might, if you desire, let us know in what respect you claim that the statements in the advertisement reflect on you.

Very truly yours,
LORD, DAY & LORD

The respondent filed suit on April 19, without answering this letter.

Subsequently, on May 9, 1960, Governor John Patterson of Alabama, sent a similar demand for a retraction to *The Times*, asserting that the publication charged him "with grave misconduct and of [*sic*] improper actions and omissions as Governor of Alabama and Ex-Officio Chairman of the State Board of Education of Alabama" and demanding publication of a retraction of the material so far as it related to him and to his conduct as Governor and Ex-Officio Chairman.

On May 16, the President and Publisher of *The Times* wrote Governor Patterson as follows (R. 773, Def. Ex. 9, R. 1998):

Dear Governor Patterson:

In response to your letter of May 9th, we are enclosing herewith a page of today's New York Times which contains the retraction and apology requested.

As stated in the retraction, to the extent that anyone could fairly conclude from the advertisement that any charge was made against you, The New York Times apologizes.

Faithfully yours,
ORVIL DRYFOOS

The publication in *The Times* (Pl. Ex. 351, R. 1958), referred to in the letter, appeared under the headline "Times Retracts Statement in Ad" and the subhead "Acts on Protest of Alabama Governor Over Assertions in Segregation Matter". After preliminary paragraphs reporting the Governor's protest and quoting his letter in full, including the specific language of which he complained, the account set forth a "statement by The New York Times" as follows:

The advertisement containing the statements to which Governor Patterson objects was received by The Times in the regular course of business from and paid for by a recognized advertising agency in behalf of a group which included among its subscribers well-known citizens.

The publication of an advertisement does not constitute a factual news report by The Times nor does it reflect the judgment or the opinion of the editors of The Times. Since publication of the advertisement, The Times made an investigation and consistent with its policy of retracting and correcting any errors or misstatements which may appear in its columns, herewith retracts the two paragraphs complained of by the Governor.

The New York Times never intended to suggest by the publication of the advertisement that the Honorable John Patterson, either in his capacity as Governor or as ex-officio chairman of the Board of Education of the State of Alabama, or otherwise, was guilty of "grave misconduct or improper actions and omission". To the extent that anyone can fairly conclude from the statements in the advertisement that any such charge was made, The New York Times hereby apologizes to the Honorable John Patterson therefor.

The publication closed with a recapitulation of the names of the signers and endorsers of the advertisement and of the officers of the Committee to Defend Martin Luther King.

In response to a demand in respondent's pre-trial interrogatories to "explain why said retraction was made but no retraction was made on the demand of the plaintiff", Mr. Bancroft, Secretary of *The Times*, said that *The Times* published the retraction in response to the Governor's demand "although in its judgment no statement in said advertisement referred to John Patterson either personally or as Governor of the State of Alabama, nor referred to this plaintiff [Sullivan] or any of the plaintiffs in the companion suits. The defendant, however, felt that on account of the fact that John Patterson held the high office of Governor of the State of Alabama and that he apparently believed that he had been libeled by said advertisement in his capacity as Governor of the State of Alabama, the defendant should apologize" (R. 595–596, Pl. Ex. 348, R. 1942). In further explanation at the trial, Bancroft testified: "We did that because we didn't want anything that was published by The Times to be a reflection on the State of Alabama and the Governor was, as far as we could see, the embodiment of the State of Alabama and the proper representative of the State and, furthermore, we had by that time learned more of the actual facts which the ad purported to recite and, finally, the ad did refer to the action of the State authorities and the Board of Education presumably of which the Governor is ex-officio chairman . . . " (R. 776–777). On the other hand, he did not think that "any of the language in there referred to Mr. Sullivan" (R. 777).

This evidence, together with Mr. Bancroft's further testimony that apart from the statement in the advertisement that the dining hall was padlocked, he thought that "the tenor of the content, the material of those two paragraphs in the ad . . . are . . . substantially correct" (R. 781, 785), was deemed by the Supreme Court of Alabama to lend support to the verdict of the jury and the size of its award (R. 1178).

6. The rulings on the merits

The Circuit Court held that the facts alleged and proved sufficed to establish liability of the defendants, if the jury was satisfied that the statements complained of by respondent were published of and concerning him. Overruling a demurrer to the complaint (R. 108) and declining to direct a verdict for petitioner (R. 728–729, 818), the court charged the jury (R. 819–826) that the statements relied on by the plaintiff were "libelous per se"; that "the law implies legal injury from the bare fact of the publication itself"; that "falsity and malice are presumed"; that "[g]eneral damages need not be alleged or proved but are presumed" (R. 824); and that "punitive damages may be awarded by the jury even though the amount of actual damages is neither found nor shown" (R. 825). While the court instructed, as requested, that "mere negligence or carelessness is not evidence of actual malice or malice in fact, and does not justify an award of exemplary or punitive damages" (R. 836), it refused to instruct that the jury must be "convinced" of malice, in the sense of "actual intent" to harm or "gross negligence and recklessness" to make such an award (R. 844). It also declined to require that a verdict for respondent differentiate between compensatory and punitive damages (R. 846).

Petitioner challenged these rulings as an abridgment of the freedom of the press, in violation of the First and the Fourteenth Amendments, and also contended that the verdict was confiscatory in amount and an infringement of the constitutional protection (R. 73–74, 898, 929–930, 935, 936–937, 945–946, 948). A motion for new trial, assigning these grounds among others (R. 896–949), was denied by the Circuit Court (R. 969).

The Supreme Court of Alabama sustained these rulings on appeal (R. 1139, 1180). It held that where "the words published tend to injure a person libeled by them in his reputation, profession, trade or business, or charge him with an indictable offense, or tends to bring the individual into public contempt," they are "libelous per se"; that "the matter complained of is, under the above doctrine, libelous per se, if it was published of and concerning the plaintiff" (R. 1155); and that it was actionable without "proof of pecuniary injury . . ., such injury being implied" (R. 1160–1161). It found no error in the trial court's ruling that the complaint alleged and the evidence established libelous statements which the jury could find were "of and pertaining to" respondent (R. 1158, 1160), reasoning as follows (R. 1157):

> "We think it common knowledge that the average person knows that municipal agents, such as police and firemen, and others, are under the control and direction of the city governing body, and more particularly under the direction and control of a single commissioner. In measuring the performance or deficiencies of such groups, praise or criticism is usually attached to the official in complete control of the body."

The Court also approved the trial court's charge as "a fair, accurate and clear expression of the governing legal principles" (R. 1167) and sustained its determination that the damages awarded by the verdict were not excessive (R. 1179). On the latter point, the Court endorsed a statement in an earlier opinion that there "is no legal measure of damages in cases of this character" (R. 1177) and held to be decisive that "The Times in its own files had articles already published which would have demonstrated the falsity of the allegations in the advertisement"; that "The Times retracted the advertisement as to Governor Patterson, but ignored this plaintiff's demand for retraction" though the "matter contained in the advertisement was equally false as to both parties"; that in "the trial below none of the defendants questioned the falsity of the allegations in the advertisement" and, simultaneously, that "during his testimony it was the contention of the Secretary of The Times that the advertisement was 'substantially correct'" (R. 1178).

Petitioner's submissions under the First and the Fourteenth Amendments (assignments of error 81, 289–291, 294, 296, 298, 306–308, 310; R. 1055, 1091–1094, 1096–1097, 1098) were summarily rejected with the statements that the "First Amendment of the U.S. Constitution does not protect libelous publications" and the "Fourteenth Amendment is directed against State action and not private action" (R. 1160).

7. The jurisdiction of the Alabama courts

Respondent sought to effect service in this action (R. 11) by delivery of process to Don McKee, the *New York Times* stringer in Montgomery, claimed to be an agent under § 188, Alabama Code of 1940, title 7 (Appendix A, *infra*, pp. 91–92), and by delivery to the Secretary of State under § 199(1), the "long-arm" statute of the State (Appendix A, *infra*, pp. 92–95). Petitioner, appearing specially and only for this purpose, moved to quash the service on the ground, among others, that the subjection of *The Times* to Alabama jurisdiction in this action would transcend the territorial limitations of due process in violation of the Fourteenth Amendment, impose a burden on interstate commerce forbidden by the Commerce Clause and abridge the freedom of the press (R. 39, 43–44, 47; see also, *e.g.*, R. 129).

The evidence adduced upon the litigation of the motion (R. 130–566) established the following facts:

Petitioner is a New York corporation which has not qualified to do business in Alabama or designated anyone to accept service of process there (R. 134–135). It has no office, property or employees resident in Alabama (R. 146, 403–404, 438–439). Its staff correspondents do, however, visit the State as the occasion may arise for purposes of newsgathering. From the beginning of 1956 through April, 1960, nine correspondents made such visits, spending, the courts below found, 153 days in Alabama, or an average of some thirty-six man-days per year. In the first five months of 1960, there were three such visits by Claude Sitton, the staff correspondent stationed in Atlanta (R. 311–314, 320, Pl. Ex. 91–93, R. 1356–1358) and one by Harrison Salisbury (R. 145, 239, Pl. Ex. 117, R. 1382). *The Times* also had an arrangement with newspapermen, employed by Alabama journals, to function as "stringers", paying them for stories they sent in that were requested or accepted at the rate of a cent a word and also using them occasionally to furnish information to the desk (*e.g.*, R. 175, 176) or to a correspondent (R. 136–137, 140, 153, 154). The effort was to have three such stringers in the State, including one in Montgomery (R. 149, 309) but only two received payments from *The Times* in 1960, Chadwick of *South Magazine*, who was paid $155 to July 26, and McKee of *The Montgomery Advertiser*, who was paid $90, covering both dispatches and assistance given Salisbury (R. 140, 143, 155, 159, 308–309, 441). McKee was also asked to investigate the facts relating to respondent's claim of libel, which he did (R. 202, 207). The total payments made by petitioner to stringers throughout the country during the first five months of 1960 was about $245,000 (R. 442). Stringers are not treated as employees for purposes of taxes or employee benefits (R. 439–440, 141–143).

The advertisement complained of in this action was prepared, submitted and accepted in New York, where the newspaper is published (R. 390–393, 438). The total daily circulation of *The Times* in March, 1960, was 650,000, of which the total sent to Alabama was 394—351 to mail subscribers and 43 to dealers. The Sunday circulation was 1,300,000, of which the Alabama shipments totaled 2,440 (Def. Ex. No. 4, R. 1981, R. 401–402). These papers were either mailed to subscribers who had paid for a subscription in advance (R. 427) or they were shipped prepaid by rail or air to Alabama newsdealers, whose orders were unsolicited (R. 404–408, 444) and with whom there was no contract (R. 409). *The Times* would credit dealers for papers which were unsold or arrived late, damaged or incomplete, the usual custom being for the dealer to get the irregularities certified by the railroad baggage man upon a card provided by *The Times* (R. 408–409, 410–412, Pl. Ex. 276–309, R. 1751–1827, R. 414, 420–426), though this formality had not been observed in Alabama (R. 432–436). Gross revenue from this Alabama circulation was approximately $20,000 in the first five months of 1960 of a total gross from circulation of about $8,500,000 (R. 445). *The Times* made absolutely no attempt to solicit or promote its sale or distribution in Alabama (R. 407–408, 428, 450, 485).

The Times accepted advertising from Alabama sources, principally advertising agencies which sent their copy to New York, where any contract for its publication was made (R. 344–349, 543); the agency would then be billed for cost, less the amount of its 15% commission (R. 353–354). The New York Times Sales, Inc., a wholly-owned subsidiary corporation, solicited advertisements in Alabama, though it had no office or resident employees in the State (R. 359–361, 539, 482). Two employees of Sales, Inc. and two employees of *The Times* spent a total of 26 days in Alabama for this purpose in 1959; and one of the Sales, Inc. men spent one day there before the end of May in 1960 (R. 336–338, Def. Ex. 1, R. 1978, 546, 548–551). Alabama advertising linage, both volunteered and solicited, amounted to 5471 in 1959 of a total of 60,000,000 published; it amounted to 13,254 through May of 1960 of a total of 20,000,000 lines (R. 342–344, 341, Def. Ex. 2, R. 1979). An Alabama supplement published in 1958 (R. 379, Pl. Ex. 273, R. 1689–1742) produced payments by Alabama advertisers of $26,801.64 (R. 380). For the first five months of 1960 gross revenue from advertising placed by Alabama agencies or advertisers was $17,000 to $18,000 of a total advertising revenue of $37,500,000 (R. 443). The gross from Alabama advertising and circulation during this period was $37,300 of a national total of $46,000,000 (R. 446).

On these facts, the courts below held that petitioner was subject to the jurisdiction of the Circuit Court in this action, sustaining both the service on McKee as a claimed agent and the substituted service on the Secretary of State and rejecting the constitutional objections urged (R. 49, 51–57, 1139, 1140–1151). Both courts deemed the newsgathering activities of correspondents and stringers, the solicitation and publication of advertising from Alabama sources and the distribution of the paper in the State to constitute sufficient Alabama "contacts" to support the exercise of jurisdiction (R. 56–57, 1142–1147). They also held that though petitioner had appeared specially upon the motion for the sole purpose of presenting these objections, as permitted by the Alabama practice, the fact that the prayer for relief asked for dismissal for "lack of jurisdiction of the subject matter" of the action, as well as want of jurisdiction of the person of defendant, constituted a general appearance and submission to the jurisdiction of the Court (R. 49–51, 1151–1153).

SUMMARY OF ARGUMENT

I

Under the doctrine of "libel per se" applied below, a public official is entitled to recover "presumed" and punitive damages for a publication found to be critical of the official conduct of a governmental agency under his general supervision if a jury thinks the publication "tends" to "injure" him "in his reputation" or to "bring" him "into public contempt" as an official. The publisher has no defense unless he can persuade the jury that the publication is entirely true in all its factual, material particulars. The doctrine not only dispenses with proof of injury by the complaining official, but presumes malice and falsity as well. Such a rule of liability works an abridgment of the freedom of the press.

The court below entirely misconceived the constitutional issues, in thinking them disposed of by the propositions that "the Constitution does not protect libelous publications" and that the "Fourteenth Amendment is directed against State action and not private action" (R. 1160). The requirements of the First Amendment are not satisfied by the "mere labels" of State law. *N.A.A.C.P.* v. *Button*, 371 U.S. 415, 429 (1963); see also *Beauharnais* v. *Illinois*, 343 U.S. 250, 263–264 (1952). The rule of law and the judgment challenged by petitioner are, of course, state action within the meaning of the Fourteenth Amendment.

If libel does not enjoy a talismanic insulation from the limitations of the First and Fourteenth Amendments, the principle of liability applied below infringes "these basic constitutional rights in their most pristine and classic form." *Edwards* v. *South Carolina*, 372 U.S. 229, 235 (1963). Whatever other ends are also served by freedom of the press, its safeguard "was fashioned to assure unfettered interchange of ideas for the bringing about of political and social changes desired by the people." *Roth* v. *United States*, 354 U.S. 476, 484 (1957). It is clear that the political expression thus protected by the fundamental law is not delimited by any test of truth, to be administered by juries, courts, or by executive officials. *N.A.A.C.P.* v. *Button, supra,* at 445; *Cantwell* v. *Connecticut*, 310 U.S. 296, 310 (1940). It also is implicit in this Court's decisions that speech or publication which is critical of governmental or official action may not be repressed upon the ground that it diminishes the reputation of those officers whose conduct it deplores or of the government of which they are a part.

The closest analogy in the decided cases is provided by those dealing with contempt, where it is settled that concern for the dignity and reputation of the bench does not support the punishment of criticism of the judge or his decision, whether the utterance is true or false. *Bridges* v. *California*, 314 U.S. 252, 270 (1941); *Pennekamp* v. *Florida*, 328 U.S. 331, 342 (1946); *Wood* v. *Georgia*, 370 U.S. 375 (1962). Comparable criticism of an elected, political official cannot consistently be punished as a libel on the ground that it diminishes his reputation. If political criticism could be punished on the ground that it endangers the esteem with which its object is regarded, none safely could be uttered that was anything but praise.

That neither falsity nor tendency to harm official reputation, nor both in combination, justifies repression of the criticism of official conduct was the central lesson of the great assault on the short-lived Sedition Act of 1798, which the verdict of history has long deemed inconsistent with the First Amendment. The rule of liability applied below is even more repressive in its function and effect than that prescribed by the Sedition Act: it lacks the safeguards of criminal sanctions; it does not require proof that the defendant's purpose was to bring the official into contempt or disrepute; it permits, as this case illustrates, a multiplication of suits based on a single statement; it allows legally limitless awards of punitive damages. Moreover, reviving by judicial decision the worst aspect of the Sedition Act, the doctrine of this case forbids criticism of the government as such on the theory that top officers, though they are not named in statements attacking the official conduct of their agencies, are presumed to be hurt because such critiques are "attached to" them (R. 1157).

Assuming, without conceding, that the protection of official reputations is a valid interest of the State and that the Constitution allows room for the "accommodation" of that interest and the freedom of political expression, the rule applied below is still invalid. It reflects no compromise of the competing interests; that favored by the First Amendment has been totally rejected, the opposing interest totally preferred. If there is scope for the protection of official reputation against criticism of official conduct, measures of liability far less destructive of the freedom of expression are available and adequate to serve that end. It might be required, for example, that the official prove special damage, actual malice, or both. The Alabama rule embraces neither mitigation. Neither would allow a judgment for respondent on the evidence that he presents.

The foregoing arguments are fortified by the privilege the law of libel grants to an official if he denigrates a private individual. It would invert the scale of values vital to a free society if citizens discharging the "political duty" of "public discussion" (Brandeis, J., concurring in *Whitney* v. *California*, 274 U.S. 357, 375 [1927]) did not enjoy a fair equivalent of the immunity granted to officials as a necessary incident of the performance of official duties.

Finally, respondent's argument that the publication is a "commercial advertisment", beyond the safeguard of the First Amendment, is entirely frivolous. The statement was a recital of grievances and protest against claimed abuse dealing squarely with the major issue of our time.

II

Whether or not the rule of liability is valid on its face, its application in this case abridges freedom of the press. For nothing in the evidence supports a finding of the type of injury or threat to the respondent's reputation that conceivably might justify repression of the publication or give ground for the enormous judgment rendered on the verdict.

Complaining broadly against suppression of Negro rights throughout the South, the publication did not name respondent or the Commission of which he is a member and plainly was not meant as an attack on him or any other individual. Its protests and its targets were impersonal: "the police", "the state authorities", "the Southern violators". The finding that these collective generalities embodied an allusion to respondent's personal identity rests solely on

the reference to "the police" and on his jurisdiction over that department. But the police consisted of too large a group for such a personal allusion to be found. The term "police" does not, in fact, mean all policemen. No more so does it mean the Mayor or Commissioner in charge. This fatal weakness in the claim that the respondent was referred to by the publication was not cured by his own testimony or that of his six witnesses; they did no more than express the opinion that "police" meant the respondent, because he is Commissioner in charge. These "mere general asseverations" (*Norris* v. *Alabama*, 294 U.S. 587, 595 [1935]) were not evidence of what the publication said or what it reasonably could be held to mean.

Even if the statements that refer to "the police" could validly be taken to refer to the respondent, there was nothing in those statements that suffices to support the judgment. Where the publication said that "truckloads" of armed police "ringed the Alabama State College Campus", the fact was that only "large numbers" of police "were deployed near the campus" upon three occasions, without ringing it on any. And where the statement said "They have arrested him seven times", the fact was that Dr. King had been arrested only four times. That these exaggerations or inaccuracies cannot rationally be regarded as tending to injure the respondent's reputation is entirely clear. The advertisement was also wrong in saying that when "the entire student body protested to state authorities by refusing to re-register, their dining hall was padlocked in an attempt to starve them into submission." Only a few students refused to re-register and the dining hall was never padlocked. But none of these erroneous assertions had a thing to do with the police and even less with the respondent. It was equally absurd for respondent to claim injury because the publication correctly reported that some unidentified "they" had twice bombed the home of Dr. King, and to insist on proving his innocence of that crime as the trial court permitted him to do.

That the respondent sustained no injury in fact from the publication, the record makes entirely clear.

Even if there were in this record a basis for considering the publication an offense to the respondent's reputation, there was no rational relationship between the gravity of the offense and the size of the penalty imposed. A "police measure may be unconstitutional merely because the remedy, although effective as means of protection, is unduly harsh or oppressive." Brandeis, J., concurring in *Whitney* v. *California*, 274 U.S. 357, 377 (1927). The proposition must apply with special force when the "harsh" remedy has been explicitly designed as a deterrent of expression. Upon this ground alone, this monstrous judgment is repugnant to the Constitution.

III

The assumption of jurisdiction in this action by the Circuit Court, based on service of process on McKee and substituted service on the Secretary of State, transcended the territorial limits of due process, imposed a forbidden burden on interstate commerce and abridged the freedom of the press.

There was no basis for the holding by the courts below that petitioner forfeited these constitutional objections by making an involuntary general appearance in the cause. The finding of a general appearance was based solely on the fact that when petitioner appeared specially and moved to quash the attempted service for want of jurisdiction of its person, as permitted by the Alabama practice, the prayer for relief concluded with a further request for dismissal for "lack of jurisdiction of the subject matter of said action." That prayer did not manifest an intention to "consent" or to make "a voluntary submission to the jurisdiction of the court", which the Alabama cases have required to convert a special into a general appearance. *Ex parte Cullinan*, 224 Ala. 263, 266 (1931). The papers made entirely clear that the sole ruling sought by the petitioner was that it was not amenable to Alabama jurisdiction, as a New York corporation having no sufficient contact with the State to permit the assertion of jurisdiction *in personam* in an action based upon a publication in New York.

Moreover, even if petitioner could validly be taken to have made an involuntary general appearance, that appearance would not bar the claim that in assuming jurisdiction of this action the state court imposed a forbidden burden on interstate commerce or that it abridged the freedom of the press. *Davis* v. *Farmers Co-operative Co.*, 262 U.S. 312 (1923); *Michigan Central R. R. Co.* v. *Mix*, 278 U.S. 492, 496 (1929); *Denver & R. G. W. R. Co.* v. *Terte*, 284 U.S. 284, 287 (1932).

The decisions of this Court do not support the holding that the sporadic newsgathering activities of correspondents and stringers of *The Times* in Alabama, the occasional solicitation and publication of advertising from Alabama sources and the minuscule shipment of the newspaper to subscribers and newsdealers in the State constitute sufficient Alabama contacts to satisfy the requirements of due process.

The petitioner's peripheral relationship to Alabama does not involve "continuous corporate operations" which are "so substantial and of such a nature as to justify suit against it on causes of action arising from dealings entirely distinct from those activities." *International Shoe Co.* v. *Washington*, 326 U.S. 310, 318 (1945); *Perkins* v. *Benguet Mining Co.*, 342 U.S. 437 (1952). Hence, if the jurisdiction is sustained, it must be on the ground that the cause of action alleged is so "connected with" petitioner's "activities within the state" as to "make it reasonable, in the context of our federal system of government, to require the corporation to defend the particular suit which is brought there." *International Shoe Co.* v. *Washington*, *supra*, at 319, 317. There is no such connection. Here, as in *Hanson* v. *Denckla*, 357 U.S. 235, 252 (1958), the "suit cannot be said to be one to enforce an obligation that arose from a privilege the defendant exercised in" the State. The liability alleged is not based on any activity of correspondents or stringers of *The Times* in covering the news in Alabama; and such activity does not rest on a privilege the State confers, given the rights safeguarded by the Constitution. Nor is this claim connected with the occasional solicitation of advertisements in Alabama. Finally, the negligible circulation of *The Times* in Alabama does not involve an act of the petitioner within the State. Copies were mailed in New York to Alabama subscribers or shipped in New York to newsdealers who were purchasers, not agents of *The Times*.

Even if the shipment of the paper may be deemed an act of the petitioner in Alabama, it does not sustain the jurisdiction here affirmed. The standard of *International Shoe* is not "simply mechanical or quantitative"; its application "must depend rather upon the quality and nature of the activity in relation to the fair and orderly administration of the laws which it was the purpose of the due process clause to insure" (326 U.S. at 319). Measured by this standard, a principle which would require, in effect, that almost every newspaper defend a libel suit in almost any jurisdiction of the country, however trivial its circulation there may be, would not further the "fair and orderly administration of the laws". To the extent that this submission prefers the interest of the publisher to that of the plaintiff, the preference is one supported by the First Amendment. It also is supported by the fact that the plaintiff's grievance rests but fancifully on the insubstantial distribution of the publication in the forum, as distinguished from its major circulation out of state.

The decision in *McGee v. International Life Ins. Co.*, 355 U.S. 220 (1957) does not govern the disposition here. The contract executed in *McGee* constituted a continuing legal relationship between the insurer and the insured within the State, a relationship which the States, with the concurrence of Congress, have long deemed to require special regulation. *Hanson v. Denckla, supra,* at 252; *Travelers Health Assn. v. Virginia,* 339 U.S. 643 (1950). *Scripto v. Carson,* 362 U.S. 207 (1960), relied on by respondent, is totally irrelevant to the problem of judicial jurisdiction.

The need for reciprocal restraints upon the power of the States to exert jurisdiction over men and institutions not within their borders is emphasized in our society by the full faith and credit clause of the Constitution. An Alabama judgment in this case would have no practical importance were it not enforceable as such in States where the petitioner's resources are located. Thus jurisdictional delineations must be based on grounds that command general assent throughout the Union. No standard worthy of such general assent sustains the jurisdiction here.

If negligible state circulation of a paper published in another state suffices to establish jurisdiction of a suit for libel threatening the type of judgment rendered here, such distribution interstate cannot continue. So, too, if the interstate movement of correspondents provides a factor tending to sustain such jurisdiction, as the court below declared, a strong barrier to such movement has been erected. In the silence of Congress, such movement and distribution are protected by the commerce clause against burdensome state action, unsupported by an overriding local interest. Such a burden has been imposed here.

Newsgathering and circulation are both aspects of the freedom of the press, safeguarded by the Constitution. Neither can continue unimpaired if they subject the publisher to foreign jurisdiction on the grounds and of the scope asserted here. Accordingly, the jurisdictional determination is also repugnant to the First Amendment.

ARGUMENT

The decision of the Supreme Court of Alabama, sustaining the judgment of the Circuit Court, denies rights that are basic to the constitutional conception of a free society and contravenes a postulate of our federalism.

We submit, first (Points I and II), that the decision gives a scope and application to the law of libel so restrictive of the right to protest and to criticize official conduct that it abridges the protected freedom of the press.

We argue, secondly (Point III), that in requiring petitioner to answer in this action in the courts of Alabama, the decision violates the territorial restrictions that the Constitution places on State process, casts a forbidden burden on interstate commerce and also abridges freedom of the press.

I. The decision rests upon a rule of liability for criticism of official conduct that abridges freedom of the press.

Under the law of libel as declared below, a public official is entitled to recover "presumed" and punitive damages for a publication found to be critical of the official conduct of a governmental agency under his general supervision if a jury thinks the publication "tends" to "injure" him "in his reputation" or to "bring" him "into public contempt" as an official. The place of the official in the governmental hierarchy is, moreover, evidence sufficient to establish that his reputation has been jeopardized by statements that reflect upon the agency of which he is in charge. The publisher has no defense unless, as respondent noted in his Brief in Opposition (p. 18, n. 10), he can persuade the jury that the publication is entirely true in all its factual, material particulars. *Ferdon v. Dickens,* 161 Ala. 181, 185, 200–201 (1909); *Kirkpatrick v. Journal Publishing Company,* 210 Ala. 10, 11 (1923); *Alabama Ride Company v. Vance,* 235 Ala. 263, 265 (1938); *Johnson Publishing Co. v. Davis,* 271 Ala. 474, 495 (1960). Unless he can discharge this burden as to stated facts, he has no privilege of comment. *Parsons v. Age-Herald Pub. Co.,* 181 Ala. 439, 450 (1913). Good motives or belief in truth, however reasonable, are relevant only in mitigation of punitive damages if the jury chooses to accord them weight. *Johnson Publishing Co. v. Davis, supra,* at 495. A claim of truth which is regarded as unfounded affords evidence of malice, fortifying the presumption that applies in any case (R. 1178).

We submit that such a rule of liability works an abridgment of the freedom of the press, as that freedom has been defined by the decisions of this Court.

First: The State Court's misconception of the constitutional issues The reasons assigned by the Court below give no support to its rejection of petitioner's constitutional objections.

The accepted proposition that "[t]he Fourteenth Amendment is directed against State action and not private action" (R. 1160) obviously has no application to the case. The petitioner has challenged a State rule of law applied by a State court to render judgment carrying the full coercive power of the State, claiming full faith and credit through the Union solely on that ground. The rule and judgment are, of course, State action in the classic sense of the subject of the Amendment's limitations. See *N.A.A.C.P.* v. *Alabama*, 357 U.S. 449, 463 (1958); *Barrows* v. *Jackson*, 346 U.S. 249, 254 (1953); *Shelley* v. *Kraemer*, 334 U.S. 1, 14 (1948).

There is no greater merit in the other reason stated in the Court's opinion, that "the Constitution does not protect libelous publications." Statements to that effect have, to be sure, been made in passing in opinions of this Court. See *Konigsberg* v. *State Bar of California*, 366 U.S. 36, 49 (1961); *Times Film Corporation* v. *City of Chicago*, 365 U.S. 43, 48 (1961); *Roth* v. *United States*, 354 U.S. 476, 486 (1957); *Beauharnais* v. *Illinois*, 343 U.S. 250, 266 (1952); *Pennekamp* v. *Florida*, 328 U.S. 331, 348–349 (1946); *Chaplinsky* v. *New Hampshire*, 315 U.S. 568, 572 (1942); *Near* v. *Minnesota*, 283 U.S. 697, 715 (1931). But here, no less than elsewhere, a "great principle of constitutional law is not susceptible of comprehensive statement in an adjective." *Carter* v. *Carter Coal Co.*, 298 U.S. 238, 327 (1936) (dissenting opinion of Cardozo, J.).

The statements cited meant no more than that the freedom of speech and of the press is not a universal absolute and leaves the States some room for the control of defamation. None of the cases sustained the repression as a libel of expression critical of governmental action or was concerned with the extent to which the law of libel may be used for the protection of official reputation. The dictum in *Pennekamp* that "when the statements amount to defamation, a judge has such remedy in damages for libel as do other public servants" left at large what may amount to defamation and what remedy a public servant has. *Beauharnais* alone dealt with the standards used in judging any kind of libel, sustaining with four dissenting votes a state conviction for a publication held to be both defamatory of a racial group and "liable to cause violence and disorder". Mr. Justice Frankfurter's opinion took pains to reserve this Court's "authority to nullify action which encroaches on freedom of utterance under the guise of punishing libel"—adding that "public men are, as it were, public property," that "discussion cannot be denied and the right, as well as the duty, of criticism must not be stifled." 343 U.S. at 263–264. Those reservations, rather than the judgment, are apposite here.

Throughout the years this Court has measured by the standards of the First Amendment every formula for the repression of expression challenged at its bar. In that process judgment has been guided by the meaning and the purpose of the Constitution, interpreted as a "continuing instrument of government" (*United States* v. *Classic*, 313 U.S. 299, 316 [1941]), not by the vagaries or "mere labels" of state law. *N.A.A.C.P.* v. *Button*, 371 U.S. 415, 429 (1963). See also Mr. Chief Justice Warren in *Trop* v. *Dulles*, 356 U.S. 86, 94 (1958). Hence libel, like sedition, insurrection, contempt, advocacy of unlawful acts, breach of the peace, disorderly conduct, obscenity or barratry, to name but prime examples, must be defined and judged in terms that satisfy the First Amendment. The law of libel has no more immunity than other law from the supremacy of its command.

Second: Seditious libel and the Constitution
If libel does not enjoy a talismanic insulation from the limitations of the First and Fourteenth Amendments, the principle of liability applied below, resting as it does on a "common law concept of the most general and undefined nature" (*Cantwell* v. *Connecticut*, 310 U.S. 296, 308 [1940]), infringes "these basic constitutional rights in their most pristine and classic form." *Edwards* v. *South Carolina*, 372 U.S. 229, 235 (1963).

Whatever other ends are also served by freedom of the press, its safeguard, as this Court has said, "was fashioned to assure unfettered interchange of ideas for the bringing about of political and social changes desired by the people." *Roth* v. *United States*, 354 U.S. 476, 484 (1957). Its object comprehends the protection of that "right of freely examining public characters and measures, and of free communication among the people thereon," which, in the words of the Virginia Resolution, "has ever been justly deemed the only effectual guardian of every other right." 4 *Elliot's Debates* (1876), p. 554. The "opportunity for free political discussion" and "debate" secured by the First Amendment (*Stromberg* v. *California*, 283 U.S. 359, 369 [1931]; *DeJonge* v. *Oregon*, 299 U.S. 353, 365 [1937]; *Terminiello* v. *Chicago*, 337 U.S. 1, 4 [1949]), extends to "vigorous advocacy" no less than "abstract" disquisition. *N.A.A.C.P.* v. *Button*, 371 U.S. 415, 429 (1963). The "prized American privilege to speak one's mind, although not always with perfect good taste," applies at least to such speech "on all public institutions." *Bridges* v. *California*, 314 U.S. 252, 270 (1941). "To many this is, and always will be, folly; but we have staked upon it our all." L. Hand, J., in *United States* v. *Associated Press*, 52 F. Supp. 362, 372 (S.D.N.Y. 1943). That national commitment has been affirmed repeatedly by the decisions of this Court, which have recognized that the Amendment "must be taken as a command of the broadest scope that explicit language, read in the context of a liberty-loving society, will allow" (*Bridges* v. *California, supra*, at 263); and that its freedoms "need breathing space to survive". *N.A.A.C.P.* v. *Button, supra*, at 433.

It is clear that the political expression thus protected by the fundamental law is not delimited by any test of truth, to be administered by juries, courts, or by executive officials, not to speak of a test which puts the burden of establishing the truth upon the writer. Within this sphere of speech or publication, the constitutional protection does not turn upon "the truth, popularity, or social utility of the ideas and beliefs which are offered." *N.A.A.C.P.* v. *Button, supra*, at 445. See also *Speiser* v. *Randall*, 357 U.S. 513, 526 (1958). The Amendment "presupposes that right conclusions are more likely to be gathered out of a multitude of tongues, than through any kind of authoritative selection." *United States* v. *Associated Press, supra*, at 372. As Mr. Justice Roberts said in *Cantwell* v. *Connecticut*, 310 U.S. 296, 310 (1940):

> "In the realm of religious faith, and in that of political belief, sharp differences arise. In both fields the tenets of one man may seem the rankest error to his neighbor. To persuade others to his own point of view, the pleader, as we know, at times, resorts to exaggeration, to vilification of men who have been, or are, prominent in church or state, and even to false statement. But the people of this nation have ordained in the light of history, that, in spite of the probability of excesses and abuses, these liberties are, in the long view, essential to enlightened opinion and right conduct on the part of the citizens of a democracy."

These affirmations are the premises today of any exploration of the scope of First Amendment freedom undertaken by this Court. It is implicit in those premises that speech or publication which is critical of governmental or official action may not be repressed upon the ground that it diminishes the reputation of the officers whose conduct it deplores or of the government of which they are a part.

The closest analogy in the decided cases is provided by those dealing with contempt.* It is settled law that concern for the dignity and reputation of the bench does not support the punishment of criticism of the judge or his

decision (*Bridges* v. *California, supra*, at 270), though the utterance contains "half-truths" and "misinformation" (*Pennekamp* v. *Florida, supra*, 328 U.S. at 342, 343, 345). Any such repression must be justified, if it is justified at all, by danger of obstruction of the course of justice; and such danger must be clear and present. See also *Craig* v. *Harney*, 331 U.S. 367, 373, 376, 389 (1947); *Wood* v. *Georgia*, 370 U.S. 375, 388, 389, 393 (1962). We do not see how comparable criticism of an elected, political official may consistently be punished as a libel on the ground that it diminishes his reputation.** The supposition that judges are "men of fortitude, able to thrive in a hardy climate" (*Craig* v. *Harney, supra*, at 376) must apply to commissioners as well.

These decisions are compelling not alone for their authority but also for their recognition of the basic principle involved. If political criticism could be punished on the ground that it endangers the esteem with which its object is regarded, none safely could be uttered that was anything but praise.

The point was made in classic terms in Madison's Report on the Virginia Resolutions (4 *Elliot's Debates*, p. 575):

> ". . . it is manifestly impossible to punish the intent to bring those who administer the government into disrepute or contempt, without striking at the right of freely discussing public characters and measures; because those who engage in such discussions, must expect and intend to excite these unfavorable sentiments, so far as they may be thought to be deserved. To prohibit the intent to excite those unfavorable sentiments against those who administer the government, is equivalent to a prohibition of the actual excitement of them; and to prohibit the actual excitement of them is equivalent to a prohibition of discussions having that tendency and effect; which, again, is equivalent to a protection of those who administer the government, if they should at any time deserve the contempt or hatred of the people, against being exposed to it, by free animadversions on their characters and conduct. . . . "

If criticism of official conduct may not be repressed upon the ground that it is false or that it tends to harm official reputation, the inadequacy of these separate grounds is not surmounted by their combination. This was the basic lesson of the great assault on the short-lived Sedition Act of 1798, which first crystallized a national awareness of the central meaning of the First Amendment. See, *e.g.*, Levy,

---

*Cf. Kalven, *The Law of Defamation and the First Amendment*, in *Conference on the Arts, Publishing and the Law* (U. of Chi. Law School), p. 4: "It is exactly correct to regard seditious libel, which has been the most serious threat to English free speech, as defamation of government and government officials. It is at most a slight extension of terms to regard contempt of court by publication as a problem of defamation of the judicial process."

**Statements about officials dealing with purely private matters unrelated to their official conduct or competence might raise different questions, not presented here.

Legacy of Suppression (1960), p. 249 *et. seq.*; Smith, *Freedom's Fetters* (1956).

That Act declared it a crime "if any person shall write, print, utter or publish . . . any false, scandalous and malicious writing or writings against the government of the United States, or either house of the Congress . . ., or the President . . ., with intent to defame the said government, or either house of the said Congress, or the said President, or to bring them or either of them, into contempt or disrepute, or to excite against them, or either or any of them, the hatred of the good people of the United States. . . . " It specifically provided that the defendant might "give in evidence in his defence, the truth of the matter contained in the publication charged as a libel", a mitigation of the common law not achieved in England until Lord Campbell's Act in 1843. It also reserved the right of the jury to "determine the law and the fact, under the direction of the court, as in other cases", accepting the reform effected by Fox's Libel Act of 1792. Act of July 14, 1798, Secs. 2, 3; 1 Stat. 596. These qualifications were not deemed sufficient to defend the measure against a constitutional attack that won widespread support throughout the nation.

In the House debate upon the bill, John Nicholas of Virginia warned that a law ostensibly directed against falsehood "must be a very powerful restriction of the press, with respect to the publication of important truths." Men "would be deterred from printing anything which should be in the least offensive to a power which might so greatly harass them. They would not only refrain from publishing anything of the least questionable nature, but they would be afraid of publishing the truth, as, though true, it might not always be in their power to establish the truth to the satisfaction of a court of justice." 8 *Annals of Congress* 2144. Albert Gallatin delineated the same peril, arguing that "the proper weapon to combat error was truth, and that to resort to coercion and punishments in order to suppress writings attacking . . . measures . . ., was to confess that these could not be defended by any other means." *Id.* at 2164. Madison's Report reiterates these points, observing that some "degree of abuse is inseparable from the proper use of every thing; and in no instance is this more true than in that of the press." 4 *Elliot's Debates*, p. 571. Summing up the position in words that have echoed through the years, he asked (*ibid.*):

> "Had Sedition Acts, forbidding every publication that might bring the constituted agents into contempt or disrepute, or that might excite the hatred of the people against the authors of unjust or pernicious measures, been

uniformly enforced against the press, might not the United States have been languishing, at this day, under the infirmities of a sickly Confederation? Might they not, possibly, be miserable colonies, groaning under a foreign yoke?"

Though the Sedition Act was never passed on by this Court, the verdict of history surely sustains the view that it was inconsistent with the First Amendment. Fines levied in its prosecutions were repaid by Act of Congress on this ground. See, *e.g.*, Act of July 4, 1840, c. 45, 6 Stat. 802 (fine imposed on Congressman Matthew Lyon refunded to his heirs).* Its invalidity as "abridging the freedom of the press" was assumed by Calhoun, reporting to the Senate on February 4, 1836, as a matter "which no one now doubts." Report with Senate bill No. 122, 24th Cong., 1st Sess. p. 3. The same assumption has been made upon this Court. Holmes, J., dissenting in *Abrams* v. *United States*, 250 U.S. 616, 630 (1919); Jackson, J., dissenting in *Beauharnais* v. *Illinois*, 343 U.S. 250, 288–289 (1952). See also Cooley, *Constitutional Limitations* (8th ed. 1927), p. 900; Chafee, *Free Speech in the United States* (1941), pp. 27–29. These assumptions reflect a broad consensus that, we have no doubt, is part of present law.

Respondent points to Jefferson's distinction between the right of Congress "to control the freedom of the press", which Jefferson of course denied, and that remaining in the States, which he admitted. Brief in Opposition, p. 19; see *Dennis* v. *United States*, 341 U.S. 494, 522, n. 4 (1961) (concurring opinion). That distinction lost its point with the adoption of the Fourteenth Amendment and the incorporation of the First Amendment freedoms in the "liberty" protected against state action. See, *e.g.*, *Bridges* v. *California*, 314 U.S. 252, 268 (1941); *Edwards* v. *South Carolina*, 372 U.S. 229, 235 (1963). The view that there may be a difference in the stringency of the commands embodied in the two Amendments (Jackson, J., in *Beauharnais* v. *Illinois*, *supra*, 343 U.S. at 288; Harlan, J., concurring in *Alberts* v. *California*, 354 U.S. 476, 501, 503 [1957]) has not prevailed in the

---

*The Committee reporting the bill described its basis as follows (H.R. Rep. No. 86, 26th Cong., 1st Sess., p. 3 (1840)): "All that now remains to be done by the representatives of a people who condemned this act of their agents as unauthorized, and transcending their grant of power, to place beyond question, doubt, or cavil, that mandate of the constitution prohibiting Congress from abridging the liberty of the press, and to discharge an honest, just, moral, and honorable obligation, is to refund from the Treasury the fine thus illegally and wrongfully obtained from one of their citizens. . . ."

See also Acts of June 17, 1844, cc. 136 and 165, 6 Stat. 924 and 931.

decisions of this Court. Even if it had, we think it plain that there could be no reasonable difference in the strength of their protection of expression against "frontal attack or suppression" (Harlan, J., dissenting in *N.A.A.C.P.* v. *Button, supra*, 371 U.S. at 455) of the kind with which we are concerned.

The rule of liability applied below is even more repressive in its function and effect than that prescribed by the Sedition Act. There is no requirement of an indictment and the case need not be proved beyond a reasonable doubt. It need not be shown, as the Sedition Act required, that the defendant's purpose was to bring the official "into contempt or disrepute"; a statement adjudged libelous *per se* is *presumed* to be "false and malicious", as the trial court instructed here (R. 824). There is no limitation to one punishment for one offensive statement, as would be required in a criminal proceeding. Respondent is only one of four commissioners, including one former incumbent, not to speak of the former Governor, who claim damages for the same statement. The damages the jury may award them if it deems the statement to apply to their official conduct are both general and punitive—the former for a "presumed" injury to reputation (R. 1160) and the latter "not alone to punish the wrongdoer, but as a deterrent to others similarly minded" (R. 1176). Such damages, moreover, are fettered by "no legal measure" of amount (R. 1177). It does not depreciate the stigma of a criminal conviction to assert that such a "civil" sanction is a more repressive measure than the type of sentence the Sedition Act permitted for the crime that it purported to define. Here, as in *Bantam Books, Inc.* v. *Sullivan*, 372 U.S. 58, 70 (1963), the "form of regulation . . . creates hazards to protected freedoms markedly greater than those that attend reliance upon the criminal law."

It should be added that the principle of liability, as formulated by the Supreme Court of Alabama, goes even further than to punish statements critical of the official conduct of individual officials; it condemns the critique of government as such. This is accomplished by the declaration that it is sufficient to sustain the verdict that in "measuring the performance or deficiencies" of governmental bodies, "praise or criticism is usually attached to the official in complete control of the body" (R. 1157). On this thesis it becomes irrelevant that the official is not named or referred to in the publication. The most impersonal denunciation of an agency of government may be treated, in the discretion of the jury, as a defamation of the hierarchy of officials having such "complete control". A charge, for example, of "police brutality", instead of calling for investigation and report by supervising officers, gives them a cause of action against the complainant, putting him to proof that will persuade the jury of the truth of his assertion. Such a concept transforms the law of defamation from a method of protecting private reputation to a device for insulating government against attack.

When municipalities have claimed that they were libeled, they have met the answer that "no court of last resort in this country has ever held, or even suggested, that prosecutions for libel on government have any place in the American system of jurisprudence." *City of Chicago* v. *Tribune Co.*, 307 Ill. 595, 601 (1923). See also *City of Albany* v. *Meyer*, 99 Cal. App. 651 (1929). That answer applies as well to converting "libel on government" into libel of the officials of whom it must be composed. The First Amendment, no less than the Fifteenth, "nullifies sophisticated as well as simple-minded modes" of infringing the rights it guarantees. *Lane* v. *Wilson*, 307 U.S. 268, 275 (1939); *Bates* v. *Little Rock*, 361 U.S. 516, 523 (1960); *Louisiana ex rel. Gremillion* v. *N.A.A.C.P.*, 366 U.S. 293, 297 (1961).

If this were not the case, the daily dialogue of politics would become utterly impossible. That dialogue includes, as Mr. Justice Jackson said, the effort "to discredit and embarrass the Government of the day by spreading exaggerations and untruths and by inciting prejudice or unreasoning discontent, not even hesitating to injure the Nation's prestige among the family of nations." *Communications Assn.* v. *Douds*, 339 U.S. 382, 423 (1950) (opinion concurring and dissenting in part). Sound would soon give place to silence if officials in "complete control" of governmental agencies, instead of answering their critics, could resort to friendly juries to amerce them for their words. Mr. Justice Brewer, in calling for the "freest criticism" of this Court, employed a metaphor that is apposite: "The moving waters are full of life and health; only in the still water is stagnation and death." *Government by Injunction*, 15 Nat. Corp. Rep. 848, 849 (1898). The First Amendment guarantees that motion shall obtain.

Third: The absence of accommodation of conflicting interests For the reasons thus far stated we contend that an expression which is critical of governmental conduct is within the "core of constitutional freedom" (*Kingsley Pictures Corp.* v. *Regents*, 360 U.S. 684, 689 [1959]) and may not be prohibited directly to protect the reputation of the government or its officials. A threat to such reputation is intrinsic to the function of such criticism. It is not, therefore, a "substantive evil" that a State has power to prevent by the suppression of the critical expression (cf., e.g., *Schenck* v. *United States*, 249 U.S. 47, 52 [1919]; *Dennis* v. *United States*, 341 U.S. 494, 506–507, 508–510 [1951]); nor does the protection of such reputation provide one of those "conflicting governmental interests" with which the protected freedom must "be reconciled" or to which it may validly be made to yield. *Konigsberg* v. *State Bar*, 366 U.S. 36, 50 n. 11 (1961); *Gibson* v. *Florida Legislative Comm.*, 372 U.S. 539, 546 (1963).

If this submission overstates the scope of constitutional protection, it surely does so only in denying that there may be room for the accommodation of the two "conflicting interests" represented by official reputation and the freedom of political expression. But even under a standard that permits such accommodation, the rule by which this case was judged is inconsistent with the Constitution.

This conclusion follows because Alabama's law of libel *per se*, as applied to the criticism of officials as officials, does not reconcile the conflicting interests; it subordinates the First Amendment freedom wholly to protecting the official. It reflects no compromise of the competing values which we assume, *arguendo*, a State may validly attempt to balance. The interest favored by the First Amendment has been totally rejected, the opposing interest totally preferred. But here, as elsewhere in the area which is of concern to the First Amendment, the breadth of an abridgment "must be viewed in the light of less drastic means for achieving the same basic purpose." *Shelton* v. *Tucker*, 364 U.S. 479, 488 (1960); *Speiser* v. *Randall*, 357 U.S. 513 (1958); cf. *Dean Milk Co.* v. *City of Madison*, 340 U.S. 349, 354 (1951). If there is room for the protection of official reputation against criticism of official conduct, measures of liability far less destructive of the freedom of expression are available and adequate to serve that end.

The Court of Appeals for the District of Columbia adopted such a standard as its version of the common law of libel in *Sweeney* v. *Patterson*, 128 F. 2d 457 (1942), dismissing a complaint based on a statement charging a Congressman with anti-Semitism in opposing an appointment. Judge Edgerton, joined by Judges Miller and Vinson, noted that "the cases are in conflict" but declared that "in our view it is not actionable to publish erroneous and injurious statements of fact and injurious comment or opinion regarding the political conduct and views of public officials, so long as no charge of crime, corruption, gross immorality or gross incompetence is made and no special damage

results. Such a publication is not 'libelous per se.' " The position was placed upon the ground that "discussion will be discouraged, and the public interest in public knowledge of important facts will be poorly defended, if error subjects its author to a libel suit without even a showing of economic loss. Whatever is added to the field of libel is taken from the field of free debate." 128 F. 2d at 458. These are, we argue, grounds which are of constitutional dimension.

The same position was taken by Judge Clark, dissenting in *Sweeney* v. *Schenectady Union Pub. Co.*, 122 F. 2d 288 (2d Cir. 1941), affirmed by an equal division of this Court. 316 U.S. 642 (1942). Deprecating the "dangerous . . . rationale of the decision that a comment leading an appreciable number of readers to hate or hold in contempt the public official commented on is libelous per se," he concluded that "the common-law requirement of proof of special damages gives" the commentator "the protection he needs, while at the same time it does prevent him from causing really serious injury and loss by false and unfair statements." 122 F. 2d at 291, 292.

Other courts have shown solicitude for the freedom to criticize the conduct of officials by requiring that the aggrieved official prove the critic's malice, abrogating the presumptions and strict liability that otherwise obtain.* This approach draws a line between expression uttered with the purpose of harming the official by an accusation known to be unfounded, and expression which is merely wrong in fact, with denigrating implications. It thus makes an essential element of liability an intent similar to that which elsewhere has been deemed necessary to sustain a curb on utterance (see, e.g., *Dennis* v. *United States*, supra, at 516; *Smith* v. *California*,

---

Gough v. *Tribune-Journal Company*, 75 Ida. 502, 510 (1954); *Salinger* v. *Cowles*, 195 Iowa 873, 890–891 (1923); *Coleman* v. *MacLennan*, 78 Kan. 711, 723 (1908) (frequently cited as a leading case); *Bradford* v. *Clark*, 90 Me. 298, 302 (1897); *Lawrence* v. *Fox*, 357 Mich. 134, 142 (1959); *Ponder* v. *Cobb*, 257 N.C. 281, 293 (1962); *Moore* v. *Davis*, 16 S.W. 2d 380, 384 (Tex. Civ. App. 1929). Applying the same rule to candidates for public office, see *Phoenix Newspapers* v. *Choisser*, 82 Ariz. 271, 277 (1957); *Friedell* v. *Blakeley Printing Co.*, 163 Minn. 226, 231 (1925); *Boucher* v. *Clark Pub. Co.*, 14 S.D. 72, 82 (1900). And cf. *Charles Parker Co.* v. *Silver City Crystal Co.*, 142 Conn. 605, 614 (1955) (same privilege against private corporation allegedly libeled in political broadcast). Scholarly opinion, while describing as still a "minority view" in libel law this requirement that a plaintiff officer or candidate prove actual malice, has favored it with substantial unanimity. See, e.g., 1 Harper and James, *The Law of Torts* (1956), pp. 449–450; Noel, *Defamation of Public Officers and Candidates*, 49 Col. L. Rev. 875, 891–895 (1949); cf. *Developments in the Law: Defamation*, 69 Harv. L. Rev. 875, 928 (1956).

361 U.S. 147 [1959]; *cf. Wieman* v. *Updegraff*, 344 U.S. 183 [1952]) and relieves the defendant of an evidential and persuasive burden of a kind that has been held to be excessive (*Speiser* v. *Randall*, 357 U.S. 513 [1958]), assimilating the criteria of libel law in both respects to those demanded by the Constitution in related fields.

Whether either of these mitigated rules of liability for criticism of official conduct, or both in combination, would conform to First Amendment standards, need not be determined in this case. The Alabama rule embraces neither mitigation. Neither would allow a judgment for respondent on the evidence on which he rests his claim.

Fourth: The relevancy of the official's privilege The arguments we have made are fortified by recollection of the privilege the law of libel grants to an official if he denigrates a private individual. In *Barr* v. *Matteo*, 360 U.S. 564, 575 (1959), this Court held the utterance of a federal official absolutely privileged if made "within the outer perimeter" of the official's duties. The States accord the same immunity to statements of their highest officers, though some differentiate their lowlier officials and qualify the privilege they enjoy, taking the position urged by the minority in the *Matteo* case. But all hold that all officials are protected unless actual malice can be proved.*

The ground of the official privilege is said to be that the threat of damage suits would otherwise "inhibit the fearless, vigorous, and effective administration of policies of government", that, in the words of Judge Learned Hand (*Gregoire* v. *Biddle*, 177 F. 2d 579, 581 [2d Cir. 1949]), " 'to submit all officials, the innocent as well as the guilty, to the burden of a trial and to the inevitable danger of its outcome, would dampen the ardor of all but the most resolute, or the most irresponsible, in the unflinching discharge of their duties.' " *Barr* v. *Matteo, supra*, at 571. Mr. Justice Black, concurring, also related the official privilege to the sustenance of "an in-

formed public opinion," dependent on "the freedom people have to applaud or to criticize the way public employees do their jobs, from the least to the most important." 360 U.S. at 577.

It would invert the scale of values vital to a free society if citizens discharging the "political duty" of "public discussion" (Brandeis, J., concurring in *Whitney* v. *California*, 274 U.S. 357, 375 [1927]) did not enjoy a fair equivalent of the immunity granted to officials as a necessary incident of the performance of official duties. The threat of liability for actionable statement is assuredly no less of a deterrent to the private individual (*cf. Farmers Union* v. *WDAY*, 360 U.S. 525, 530 [1959]), who, unlike the official, must rely upon his own resources for defense. And, as Madison observed in words that are remembered, "the censorial power is in the people over the Government, and not in the Government over the people." 4 *Annals of Congress* 934. See also *Report on the Virginia Resolutions* (1799), 4 *Elliot's Debates* (1876), pp. 575–576. "For the same reason that members of the Legislature, judges of the courts, and other persons engaged in certain fields of the public service or in the administration of justice are absolutely immune from actions, civil or criminal, for libel for words published in the discharge of such public duties, the individual citizen must be given a like privilege when he is acting in his sovereign capacity." *City of Chicago* v. *Tribune Co.*, 307 Ill. 595, 610 (1923). The citizen acts in his "sovereign capacity" when he assumes to censure the officialdom.

Fifth: The protection of editorial advertisements Though the point was not taken by the court below, respondent argues that the fact that the statement was a paid advertisement deprives it of protection "as speech and press". Brief in Opposition, p. 19. The argument is wholly without merit.

The decisions invoked by respondent have no bearing on this case. *Breard* v. *Alexandria*, 341 U.S. 622 (1951), dealt with a regulation of the place, manner and circumstances of solicitation of subscriptions, not with the repression of a publication on the basis of its content, the ideas that are expressed. *Valentine* v. *Christensen*, 316 U.S. 52 (1942), involved a handbill soliciting the inspection of a submarine which its owner exhibited to visitors on payment of a stated fee. An ordinance requiring a permit for street distribution of commercial advertising was sustained as applied to him. It is merely cynical to urge that these determinations bar protection of the statement involved here.

The statement published by petitioner was not a "commercial" advertisement, as it is la-

---

E.g., according absolute privilege, *Catron* v. *Jasper*, 303 Ky. 598 (1946) (county sheriff); *Schlinkert* v. *Henderson*, 331 Mich. 284 (1951) (member of liquor commission); *Hughes* v. *Bizzell*, 189 Okla. 472, 474 (1941) (president of state university); *Montgomery* v. *Philadelphia*, 392 Pa. 178 (1958) (deputy commissioner and city architect). Limiting officers below state cabinet rank to a qualified privilege, see, *e.g.*, *Barry* v. *McCollom*, 81 Conn. 293 (1908) (superintendent of schools); *Mills* v. *Denny*, 245 Iowa 584 (1954) (mayor); *Howland* v. *Flood*, 160 Mass. 509 (1894) (town investigating committee); *Peterson* v. *Steenerson*, 113 Minn. 87 (1910) (postmaster). See generally, 1 Harper and James, *The Law of Torts* (1956), pp. 429–30; *Prosser on Torts* (2d ed., 1955), pp. 612–13; *Restatement, Torts*, § 591.

beled by respondent. It was a recital of grievances and protest against claimed abuses dealing squarely with the major issue of our time. The fact that its authors sought to raise funds for defense of Dr. King and his embattled movement, far from forfeiting its constitutional protection, adds a reason why it falls within the freedom guaranteed. *Cf. N.A.A.C.P.* v. *Button, supra,* 371 U.S. at 429–431, 439–440. That petitioner received a payment for the publication is no less immaterial in this connection than is the fact that newspapers and books are sold. *Smith* v. *California,* 361 U.S. 147, 150 (1959); *cf. Bantam Books Inc.* v. *Sullivan,* 372 U.S. 58, 64, n. 6 (1963).

It is, of course, entirely true that the published statement did not represent or purport to represent assertions by petitioner, but rather by the sponsoring Committee and the individuals whose names appeared. But since the publisher is held no less responsible than are the sponsors, it must surely have the same protection they enjoy. *Cf. Barrows* v. *Jackson,* 346 U.S. 249 (1953). The willingness of newspapers to carry editorial advertisements is, moreover, an important method of promoting some equality of practical enjoyment of the benefits the First Amendment was intended to secure. *Cf. Lovell* v. *Griffin,* 303 U.S. 444 (1938); *Schneider* v. *State,* 308 U.S. 147 (1939); *Talley* v. *California,* 362 U.S. 60 (1960). The practice encourages "the widest possible dissemination of information from diverse and antagonistic sources", which the First Amendment deems "essential to the welfare of the public". *Associated Press* v. *United States,* 326 U.S. 1, 20 (1945). It has no lesser claim than any other mode of publication to the freedom that the Constitution guarantees.

II. Even if the rule of liability were valid on its face, the judgment rests on an invalid application.

Assuming, *arguendo,* that the freedom of the press may constitutionally be subordinated to protection of official reputation, as it would be by the rule of liability declared below, the rule is nonetheless invalid as applied, upon the record in this case. Nothing in the evidence supports a finding of the type of injury or threat to the respondent's reputation that, on the assumption stated, justifies repression of the publication. And even if there were a basis for discerning such a threat, there was no ground for the enormous judgment rendered on the verdict.

First: The scope of review   These submissions fall within the settled scope of review by this Court when it is urged that a federal right has been denied "in substance and effect" by a state court. *Norris* v. *Alabama,* 294 U.S. 587, 590

(1935). If the denial rests on findings of fact which are in law determinative of the existence of the federal right, those findings must be adequately sustained by the evidence. *Norris* v. *Alabama, supra; Fiske* v. *Kansas,* 274 U.S. 380 (1927); *Herndon* v. *Lowry,* 301 U.S. 242, 259–261 (1937). If the denial rests on a conclusion or evaluation governing the application of controlling federal criteria, this Court will make its own appraisal of the record to determine if the facts established warrant the conclusion or evaluation made. *Bridges* v. *California,* 314 U.S. 252, 263, 271 (1941); *Pennekamp* v. *Florida,* 328 U.S. 331, 335, 345–346 (1946); *Craig* v. *Harney,* 331 U.S. 367, 373–374 (1947); *Watts* v. *Indiana,* 338 U.S. 49, 50 (1949) (plurality opinion); *Kingsley Pictures Corp.* v. *Regents,* 360 U.S. 684, 708 (1959) (concurring opinion); *Wood* v. *Georgia,* 370 U.S. 375, 386 (1962); *Edwards* v. *South Carolina,* 372 U.S. 229 (1963).

The decision below that the publication libeled the respondent does not, therefore, foreclose the questions whether, on the facts established by the record, it contained a statement "of and concerning" the complainant and, if so, whether such statement injured or jeopardized his reputation to an extent that, as a matter of the First Amendment, justified its punitive repression by the judgment rendered in the Circuit Court. *Bridges* v. *California, supra.* As in the contempt cases, this Court "must weigh the impact of the words against the protection given by the principles of the First Amendment. . . ." *Pennekamp* v. *Florida, supra,* at 349.

Second: The failure to establish injury or threat to respondent's reputation   An appraisal of this record in these terms leaves no room for a determination that the publication sued on by respondent made a statement as to him, or that, if such a statement may be found by implication, it injured or jeopardized his reputation in a way that forfeits constitutional protection.

The publication did not name respondent or the Commission of which he is a member and it plainly was not meant as an attack on him or any other individual. Its protests and its targets were impersonal: "the police", the "state authorities", "the Southern violators". The finding that these collective generalities embodied an allusion to respondent's personal identity rests solely on the reference to "the police" and on his jurisdiction over that department. See pp. 7, 9, 10–14, 23–24, *supra.* But the police consisted of a force of 175 full-time officers, not to speak of a Chief responsible for the direction of their operations. See p. 10, *supra.* Courts have not hitherto permitted the mere designation of a group so large to be regarded as a reference to any member, least of all to one related to it only by an ultimate responsibility for its control or management.* While this result may well involve an element of judgment as to policy, regardful of "the social interest in free press discussion of matters of general concern" (*Service Parking Corp.* v. *Washington Times Co.*, 92 F. 2d at 505), it rests as well upon a common sense perception of the safety that numbers afford against a truly harmful denigration. The term "police" does not in fact mean all policemen. No more so does it mean the Mayor or Commissioner in charge.

This fatal weakness in the allegation that respondent was referred to by the publication was not cured by his own testimony or that of his six witnesses, four of whom first saw the publication in the office of his counsel. See p. 14, *supra*. We have detailed that testimony in the Statement (*supra*, pp. 11–14) and shall not repeat it *in extenso* here. It was at best opinion as to the interpretation of the writing. No witness offered evidence of an extrinsic fact bearing upon the meaning of an enigmatic phrase or the identity of someone mentioned by description. *Cf.*, *e.g.*, *Hope* v. *Hearst Consolidated Publications, Inc.*, 294 F. 2d 681 (2d Cir. 1961). The weight of the testimony does not, therefore, transcend the ground of the opinions, which was no more than the bare *ipse dixit* that "police" meant the respondent, since he is Commissioner in charge.

Respondent's own conception of the meaning of the language went beyond this, to be sure. His view was that if one statement in a paragraph referred to the police, the other statements must be read to make the same allusion. Thus he considered that the declaration "They have bombed his home" meant that the bombing was the work of the police, because the paragraph contained the statement that "[t]hey have arrested him seven times"; and arrests are made by the police. See pp. 9, 11, *supra*.

We think it is enough to say that these "mere general asseverations" (*Norris* v. *Alabama*, 294 U.S. 587, 595 [1935]) were not evidence of what the publication said or what it reasonably could be held to mean. The problem, on this score, is not unlike that posed in *Fiske* v. *Kansas, supra*, where in determining the "situation presented" on the record, this Court read the crucial document itself to see if it possessed the attributes that had produced its condemnation (274 U.S. at 385). So read, this publication was a totally impersonal attack upon conditions, groups and institutions, not a personal assault of any kind.

Even if the statements that refer to "the police" could validly be taken to refer to the respondent, there was nothing in those statements that suffices to support the judgment. Assertions that were shown to have been accurate by the respondent's evidence cannot be relied on to establish injury to his official or his private reputation; if the truth hurts that surely is a hurt the First Amendment calls on him to bear.* Hence, the whole claim of libel rests on two discrepancies between the material statements and the facts. Where the publication said that "truckloads" of armed police "ringed the Alabama State College Campus", the fact was that only "large numbers" of police "were deployed near the campus" upon three occasions, without ringing it on any. See p. 8, *supra*. And where the statement said "They have arrested him seven times", the fact was that Dr. King had been arrested only four times. Three of the arrests had occurred, moreover, before the respondent came to office some six months before the suit was filed. See pp. 9, 10, *supra*. That the exaggerations or inaccuracies in these statements cannot rationally be regarded as tending to injure the respondent's reputation is, we submit, entirely clear.

None of the other statements in the paragraphs relied on by respondent helps to make a colorable case. The advertisement was wrong in saying that when "the entire student body protested to state authorities by refusing to reregister, their dining hall was padlocked in an attempt to starve them into submission." This was, indeed, the gravamen of the resentment that the publication seems to have inspired in

---

*See, *e.g.*, *Service Parking Corp.* v. *Washington Times Co.*, 92 F. 2d 502 (D.C. Cir. 1937); *Noral* v. *Hearst Publications, Inc.*, 40 Cal. App. 2d 348 (1940); *Fowler* v. *Curtis Publishing Co.*, 182 F. 2d 377 (D. C. Cir. 1950); *McBride* v. *Crowell-Collier Pub. Co.*, 196 F. 2d 187 (5th Cir. 1952); *Neiman-Marcus* v. *Lait*, 13 F.R.D. 311, 316 (S.D.N.Y. 1952); *cf. Julian* v. *American Business Consultants, Inc.*, 2 N.Y. 2d 1 (1956); *Weston* v. *Commercial Advertiser Assn.*, 184 N. Y. 479, 485 (1906). See also *Restatement of Torts*, § 564, Comment *c*; *Prosser on Torts* (2d ed. 1955), pp. 583–584.

*This is recognized in part by Alabama law itself, despite the strictness of the rule respecting truth as a defense, since evidence of truth must be received in mitigation under the general issue. Ala. Code of 1940, title 7, § 909; see *Johnson Publishing Co.* v. *Davis*, 271 Ala. 474, 490 (1960). The problem has been met in England by enlarging the defense. See Defamation Act, 1952, 15 & 16 Geo. 6 & 1 Eliz. 2, ch. 66, § 5: "In an action for libel or slander in respect of words containing two or more distinct charges against the plaintiff, a defence of justification shall not fail by reason only that the truth of every charge is not proved if the words not proved to be true do not materially injure the plaintiff's reputation having regard to the truth of the remaining charges." See also *Report of the Committee on the Law of Defamation* (1948) cmd. 7536, p. 21.

Montgomery. See p. 9, *supra*. A majority of students did engage in the protest against the expulsions, but only a few refused to re-register, the dining hall was never "padlocked" and, perforce, there was no "attempt to starve" the students "into submission". See p. 8, *supra*. But none of these admittedly erroneous assertions had a thing to do with the police and even less with the respondent. He testified himself that "as far as the expulsion of students is concerned, that responsibility rests with the State Department of Education" (R. 716). If that was so, as it clearly was, it must have been no less the responsibility of the "State authorities", who are alone referred to in the offending sentence, to have padlocked the dining hall, as it alleged. There certainly is no suggestion, express or implied, that the imaginary padlock was attached by the police.

The statement that "the Southern violators have answered Dr. King's peaceful protests with intimidation and violence" was thought by the respondent to refer to himself only because "it is contained in a paragraph" which also referred to arrests (R. 717–718), a point on which his testimony is, to say the least, quite inexplicit, totally ignoring the fact that the paragraph did not even fix the time of the events recited or purport to place them in Montgomery. But whatever the respondent brought himself to think, or badgered Aaronson to say on cross-examination (see p. 17, *supra*), the statement cannot reasonably bear such a construction. The term "Southern violators of the Constitution" was a generic phrase employed in the advertisement to characterize all those whose alleged conduct gave rise to the grievances recited, whether private persons or officials. There was no suggestion that the individuals or groups were all the same, any more than that they were the same in Orangeburg as in Atlanta or Montgomery.

For the same reason, there was no basis for asserting that the statement that "they" bombed his home, assaulted him and charged him with perjury pointed to respondent as the antecedent of the pronoun, though the trial court pointedly permitted him to prove his innocence upon these points. See p. 10, *supra*. There was, to be sure, disputed evidence respecting a police assault but this related to an incident occurring long before respondent was elected a Commissioner (see pp. 9–10, *supra*). Beyond dispute, there were two bombings of King's home and he was charged with perjury. Indeed, to raise funds to defend him on that charge, which proved to be unfounded, was the main objective of the publication. See p. 6, *supra*.

It is, in sum, impossible in our view to see in this mélange of statements, notwithstanding the inaccuracies noted, any falsehood that related to respondent and portended injury to his official reputation. That he sustained no injury in fact was made entirely clear by his own evidence. The most that his witnesses could say was that they would have thought less kindly of him *if* they had believed the statements they considered critical of his official conduct. They did not in fact believe them and respondent did not fall at all in their esteem. In Alabama, no less than in Virginia, "the militant Negro civil rights movement has engendered the intense resentment and opposition of the politically dominant white community," as this Court said in *N.A.A.C.P.* v. *Button, supra*, 371 U.S. at 435. This publication was, upon its face, made on behalf of sympathizers with that movement. That such a statement could have jeopardized respondent's reputation anywhere he was known as an official must be regarded as a sheer illusion, not a finding that has any tangible support. In the real world, the words were utterly devoid of any "impact" that can weigh "against the principles of the First Amendment." *Pennekamp* v. *Florida, supra*, 328 U.S. at 349.

Respondent adduced as an aspect of his grievance that *The Times* made a retraction on demand of Governor Patterson but failed to do so in response to his demand. See pp. 18–22, *supra*. It is enough to say that if the statement was protected by the Constitution, as we contend it was, no obligation to retract could be imposed. Beyond this, however, there was an entirely reasonable basis for the distinction made. Petitioner selected Governor Patterson as "the proper representative" of Alabama to be formally assured that *The Times* did not intend the publication to reflect upon the State. It also took account of the fact that the Governor was chairman ex-officio of the State Board of Education; and that the "state authorities" had been referred to in the sentence claiming that the dining hall was padlocked. See pp. 21–22, *supra*. A distinction based upon those grounds was not invidious as to respondent. Far from exacerbating any supposed injury to him, as the court below believed (R. 1178), the retraction was a mollifying factor, weakening, if not erasing, the statement as to anyone who thought himself concerned.

Third: The magnitude of the verdict Even if we are wrong in urging that there is no basis on this record for a judgment for respondent, consistently with the protection of the First Amendment, the judgment of $500,000 is so shockingly excessive that it violates the Constitution.

That judgment was rendered, as we have shown, without any proof of injury or special damage. General damages simply were "presumed" and the jury was authorized to levy damages as punishment in its discretion. The trial court refused to charge that the jury should—or even could in its discretion—separately assess compensatory and punitive damages (R. 847, 864, Nos. 59 and 60). Since there was no rational foundation for presuming any damages at all,* it is both legally correct and factually realistic to regard the entire verdict as a punitive award. *Cf. Stromberg* v. *California*, 283 U.S. 359, 367–368 (1931).

Viewing the publication as an offense to the respondent's reputation, as we do for purposes of argument, there was no rational relationship between the gravity of the offense and the size of the penalty imposed. *Cf. Crowell-Collier Pub. Co.* v. *Caldwell*, 170 F. 2d 941, 944, 945 (5th Cir. 1948). The court below declined, indeed, to weigh the elements of truth embodied in the publication in appraising the legitimacy of the verdict, contrary to its action in a recent case involving charges that a private individual was guilty of grave crimes. *Johnson Publishing Co.* v. *Davis*, 271 Ala. 474, 490 (1960). It chose instead to treat petitioner's assertion of belief in the substantial truth of the advertisement, so far as it might possibly have been related to respondent, as evidence of malice and support for the size of the award. See pp. 22, 24, *supra*.

The judgment is repugnant to the Constitution on these grounds. As Mr. Justice Brandeis said, concurring in *Whitney* v. *California*, 274 U.S. 357, 377 (1927), a "police measure may be unconstitutional merely because the remedy, although effective as means of protection, is unduly harsh or oppressive." The proposition must apply with special force when the "harsh" remedy has been explicitly designed as a deterrent of expression. It is, indeed, the underlying basis of the principle that "the power to regulate must be so exercised as not, in attaining a permissible end, unduly to infringe the protected freedom." *Cantwell* v. *Connecticut*, 310 U.S. 296, 304, 308 (1940). That principle has been applied by this Court steadily in recent years as measures burdening the freedoms of

expression have been tested by "close analysis and critical judgment in the light of the particular circumstances" involved. *Speiser* v. *Randall*, 357 U.S. 513, 520 (1958). See also, *e.g.*, *Grosjean* v. *American Press Co.*, 297 U.S. 233 (1936); *N.A.A.C.P.* v. *Alabama*, 357 U.S. 449 (1958); *Smith* v. *California*, 361 U.S. 147, 150–151 (1959); *Bates* v. *Little Rock*, 361 U.S. 516 (1960); *Shelton* v. *Tucker*, 364 U.S. 479 (1960); *cf. Winters* v. *New York*, 333 U.S. 507, 517 (1948).

Even when the crucial freedoms of the First Amendment have not been at stake, this Court has made clear that a penalty or money judgment may deprive of property without due process where it is "so extravagant in amount as to outrun the bounds of reason and result in sheer oppression." *Life & Casualty Co.* v. *McCray*, 291 U.S. 566, 571 (1934). A statutory penalty recoverable by a shipper has not been permitted to "work an arbitrary, unequal and oppressive result for the carrier which shocks the sense of fairness the Fourteenth Amendment was intended to satisfy. . . ." *Chicago & N.W. Ry.* v. *Nye Schneider Fowler Co.*, 260 U.S. 35, 44–45 (1922). See also *Missouri Pacific Ry. Co.* v. *Tucker*, 230 U.S. 340, 350–351 (1913); *St. Louis, I. Mt. & So. Ry. Co.* v. *Williams*, 251 U.S. 63, 66–67 (1919). The idea of government under law is hardly older than the revulsion against "punishment out of all proportion to the offense. . . ." Douglas, J., concurring in *Robinson* v. *California*, 370 U.S. 660, 676 (1962). Such punishment was inflicted here, compounding the affront this judgment offers to the First Amendment.

It is no hyperbole to say that if a judgment of this size can be sustained upon such facts as these, its repressive influence will extend far beyond deterring such inaccuracies of assertion as have been established here. This is not a time—there never is a time—when it would serve the values enshrined in the Constitution to force the press to curtail its attention to the tensest issues that confront the country or to forego the dissemination of its publications in the areas where tension is extreme.

Respondent argued in his Brief in Opposition (pp. 25–26) that the Seventh Amendment bars this Court from considering the size of an award based on the verdict of a jury. The very authorities he cites make clear that any insulation of a verdict from review does not extend to situations where it involves or reflects error of law. See, *e.g.*, *Fairmount Glass Works* v. *Cub Fork Coal Co.*, 287 U.S. 474, 483–485 (1933); *Chicago, B. & Q. Railroad* v. *Chicago*, 166 U.S. 226, 246 (1897). See also *Dimick* v. *Schiedt*, 293 U.S. 474, 486 (1935); *A. & G. Stevedores* v. *Ellerman*

---

*It is relevant in this connection to recall that the entire circulation of *The Times* in Alabama was 394 copies, 35 in Montgomery County (R. 836). Even on the theory of the court below, the reference to "police" could hardly have been read to refer to respondent anywhere but in Montgomery, or at most in Alabama.

Lines, 369 U.S. 355, 364, 366 (1962). Abridgment of the freedom of the press is surely such an error; and in determining if an abridgment has occurred, it makes no difference what branch or agency of the State has imposed the repression. *N.A.A.C.P.* v. *Alabama*, 357 U.S. 449, 463 (1958); *Bantam Books, Inc.* v. *Sullivan*, 372 U.S. 58, 68 (1963). Indeed, the current of authority today regards the Seventh Amendment as inapplicable generally to appellate review of an excessive verdict, viewing the denial of relief below as an error of law. See, *e.g.*, *Southern Pac. Co.* v. *Guthrie*, 186 F. 2d 926, 931 (9th Cir. 1951); *Dagnello* v. *Long Island Rail Road Company*, 289 F. 2d 797, 802 (2d Cir. 1961); *cf. Affolder* v. *New York, Chicago & St. L. R. Co.*, 339 U.S. 96, 101 (1950); 6 *Moore's, Federal Practice* (2d ed. 1953), pp. 3827–3841. That general problem is not presented here because this excess contravenes the First Amendment.

III. The assumption of jurisdiction in this action by the Courts of Alabama contravenes the Constitution.

In sustaining the jurisdiction of the Circuit Court, the courts below held that petitioner made an involuntary general appearance in this action, subjecting its person to the jurisdiction and forfeiting the constitutional objections urged. They also rejected those objections on the merits, holding that petitioner's contacts with Alabama were sufficient to support State jurisdiction in this cause, based either on the service of process on McKee as a purported agent or on the substituted service on the Secretary of State. The decision is untenable on any ground.

First: The finding of a general appearance
The motion to quash stated explicitly that petitioner appeared "solely and specially for the purpose of filing this its motion to quash attempted service of process in this cause and for no other purpose and without waiving service of process upon it and without making a general appearance and expressly limiting its special appearance to the purpose of quashing the attempted service upon it in this case ..." (R. 39, 47). The grounds of the motion related to no other issue than that of petitioner's amenability to Alabama jurisdiction in this action as a New York corporation, neither qualified to do nor doing business in the State (R. 40–45, 47). The prayer for relief (R. 45–46) was not, however, limited to asking that the service or purported service of process be quashed and that the action be dismissed "for lack of jurisdiction of the person" of petitioner. It concluded with a further request for dismissal for "lack of jurisdiction of the subject matter of said action"

(R. 46). That prayer, the courts held, converted the special appearance into a general appearance by operation of the law of Alabama (R. 49–51, 1151–1153).

This ruling lacks that "fair or substantial support" in prior state decisions that alone suffices to preclude this Court's review of federal contentions held to be defeated by a rule of state procedure. *N.A.A.C.P.* v. *Alabama*, 357 U.S. 449, 455–457 (1958). The governing principle of Alabama practice was declared by the court below in *Ex parte Cullinan*, 224 Ala. 263 (1931), holding that a request for "further time to answer or demur or file other motions", made by a party appearing specially, did not constitute a general appearance waiving constitutional objections later made by motion to quash. Noting that a non-resident's objection to the jurisdiction "is not a technical one ... but is an assertion of a fundamental constitutional right", the court said the question involved was one "of consent or a voluntary submission to the jurisdiction of the court", an issue of "intent as evidenced by conduct", as to which "the intent and purpose of the context as a whole must control." 224 Ala. at 265, 266, 267. See also *Ex parte Haisten*, 227 Ala. 183, 187 (1933); *cf. Sessoms Grocery Co.* v. *International Sugar Feed Company*, 188 Ala. 232, 236 (1914); *Terminal Oil Mill Co.* v. *Planters W. & G. Co.*, 197 Ala. 429, 431 (1916). For a waiver to be inferred or implied, when the defendant appears specially to move to set aside service of process, he must have taken some "action in relation to the case, disconnected with the motion, and which recognized the case as in court." *Lampley* v. *Beavers*, 25 Ala. 534, 535 (1854).

Petitioner's prayer for relief neither "recognized the case as in court" nor evidenced "consent or voluntary submission" to the jurisdiction. On the contrary, the papers made entirely clear that the sole ruling sought by the petitioner was that it was not amenable to Alabama's jurisdiction, as a New York corporation having no sufficient contact with the State to permit the assertion of jurisdiction *in personam* in an action based upon a publication in New York.

The doctrine of *Ex parte Cullinan* has not been qualified by any other holding of the court below before the instant case. It is, on the other hand, confirmed by cases in which a defendant appearing specially has joined a motion to quash for inadequate service with a plea in abatement challenging the venue of the action—without the suggestion that the plea amounted to a general appearance, though the question that it raised was characterized by the court below as one of "jurisdiction of the subject matter." *St. Mary's Oil Engine Co. v. Jackson Ice and Fuel Co.*, 224 Ala. 152, 155, 157 (1931). See also *Seaboard Air Line Ry. v. Hubbard*, 142 Ala. 546, 548 (1904); *Dozier Lumber Co. v. Smith-Isburg Lumber Co.*, 145 Ala. 317 (1905); cf. *Johnson Publishing Co. v. Davis*, 271 Ala. 474, 490 (1960); *Ex parte Textile Workers Union of America*, 249 Ala. 136, 142 (1947). Indeed, the precise equivalent of the prayer of the motion in this case was used in *Harrub v. Hy-Trous Corporation*, 249 Ala. 414, 416 (1947), without arousing an objection to adjudication of the issue as to jurisdiction of the person, raised on the special appearance. Beyond this, the late Judge Walter B. Jones, who presided in this case at Circuit, reproduced these very motion papers in the 1962 supplement to his treatise on Alabama practice, as a form of "Motion to Quash Service of Process by Foreign Corporation", without intimation that the prayer addressed to lack of jurisdiction of the subject matter waived the point respecting jurisdiction of the person. 3 Jones, *Alabama Practice and Forms* (1947) § 11207.1a (Supp. 1962).

There is, moreover, a persuasive reason why a foreign corporation challenging its amenability to suit in Alabama by substituted service on the Secretary of State should conceive of its objection as relating in a sense to jurisdiction of the subject matter of the action. The statute (Ala. Code of 1940, title 7, § 199[1]) itself speaks in terms of the sufficiency of service on the Secretary "to give to any of the courts of this state jurisdiction over the cause of action and over such non-resident defendant" (Appendix A, *infra*, p. 94). Hence a contention that the statute is inapplicable or invalid as applied goes, in this sense, to jurisdiction of the cause as well as jurisdiction of the person.* Cf. *St. Mary's Oil Engine Co. v. Jackson Ice & Fuel Co.*, *supra*, at 155; *Boyd v. Warren Paint & Color Co.*, 254 Ala. 687, 691 (1950). The one conclusion is implicit

in the other, not the product of a separate inquiry involving separate grounds.

Against all these indicia of Alabama law, ignored in the decisions of the courts below, the authorities relied on are quite simply totally irrelevant. None involved the alleged waiver of a constitutional objection. Except for *Blankenship v. Blankenship*, 263 Ala. 297, 303 (1955), where the court specifically declined to consider whether the appearance had been general or special, deeming the issue immaterial upon the question posed, none involved a special appearance. In *Thompson v. Wilson*, 224 Ala. 299 (1932), the defendant, a resident of Alabama, had not even purported to appear specially or attempted to question the court's jurisdiction of his person; his sole objection, taken by demurrer, was to the court's competence to deal with the subject matter of the action and to grant relief of the type asked. In *Vaughan v. Vaughan*, 267 Ala. 117, 120, 121 (1957), referred to by the Circuit Court, the movant failed to limit her appearance, leading the court to distinguish *Ex parte Haisten*, *supra*, on this ground. The additional decisions cited by respondent (Brief in Opposition, p. 36) are no less irrelevant. Neither *Kyser v. American Surety Co.*, 213 Ala. 614 (1925) nor *Aetna Insurance Co. v. Earnest*, 215 Ala. 557 (1927) involved a special appearance or dealt with a challenge to service of process on constitutional grounds.

The California and North Carolina cases cited and quoted below (*Olcese v. Justice's Court*, 156 Cal. 82 [1909]; *Roberts v. Superior Court*, 30 Cal. App. 714 [1916]; *Dailey Motor Co. v. Reaves*, 184 N.C. 260 [1922]) and the similar decisions referred to in the annotation cited (25 A.L.R. 2d 838–842), to the extent that they treated a challenge to the jurisdiction of the subject matter as a general appearance, all involved situations where the defendant's objection was deemed to ask for relief inconsistent with the absence of jurisdiction of the person or to raise a separate "question whether, considering the nature of the cause of action asserted and the relief prayed by plaintiff, the court had power to adjudicate concerning the subject matter of the class of cases to which plaintiff's claim belonged." *Davis v. O'Hara*, 266 U.S. 314, 318 (1924); cf. *Constantine v. Constantine*, 261 Ala. 40, 42 (1954). That no such question was presented here the motion papers make entirely clear.

The situation is, indeed, precisely analogous to that presented in the *Davis* case. There the defendant, Director General of Railroads, appeared specially for the purpose of objecting to the jurisdiction of the district court "over the person of the defendant and over the subject

---

*It should be noted also that prior to the enactment of Ala. Code, title 7, § 97 in 1907, Alabama denied her courts jurisdiction over actions against foreign corporations which did not arise within the State. See *McKnett v. St. Louis & San Francisco Ry.*, 292 U.S. 230, 231 (1934). The bar to foreign causes was raised, however, only to suits "in which jurisdiction of the defendant can be legally obtained in the same manner in which jurisdiction could have been obtained if the cause of action had arisen in this state." The claim that McKee was not an "agent" for purposes of service under Ala. Code, title 7, § 188 (Appendix A, *infra*, p. 92), if valid, thus implied a defect of subject matter jurisdiction of this cause of action, which petitioner submitted arose at the place of publication in New York. Compare the statement by the court below upon this point (R. 1179) with *New York Times Company v. Conner*, 291 F. 2d 492, 494 (5th Cir. 1961).

matter of this action," on the ground that in the circumstances the Director was immune to suit in the county where action was brought. The Nebraska courts treated the reference to subject matter as a general appearance, waiving the immunity asserted. *O'Hara* v. *Davis*, 109 Neb. 615 (1923). This Court reversed, holding that there "was nothing in the moving papers to suggest that the Nebraska court had no jurisdiction to try and determine actions, founded on negligence, to recover damages for personal injuries suffered by railway employees while engaged in the performance of their work" (266 U.S. at 318). So here, there was nothing in the papers to suggest that the petitioner questioned the competence of the Circuit Court to "exercise original jurisdiction . . . of all actions for libel. . . ." (Ala. Code, title 13, § 126). The point was only that petitioner, because it is a foreign corporation having only a peripheral relationship to Alabama, was immune to jurisdiction in the action brought.

For the foregoing reasons, we submit that the decision that petitioner made an involuntary general appearance does not constitute an adequate state ground, barring consideration of the question whether Alabama has transcended the due process limitations on the territorial extension of the process of her courts. *Cf. Wright* v. *Georgia*, 373 U.S. 284 (1963); *N.A.A.C.P.* v. *Alabama*, *supra*; *Staub* v. *City of Baxley*, 355 U.S. 313 (1958); *Davis* v. *Wechsler*, 263 U.S. 22 (1923); *Ward* v. *Love County*, 253 U.S. 17 (1920).*

Moreover, even if petitioner could validly be taken to have made an involuntary general appearance by the prayer for dismissal on the ground of lack of jurisdiction of the subject matter, that appearance would not bar the claim that in assuming jurisdiction of this action the state court has cast a burden upon interstate

commerce forbidden by the Commerce Clause. That point is independent of the defendant's amenability to process, as this Court has explicitly decided in ruling that the issue remains open, if presented on "a seasonable motion", notwithstanding the presence of the corporation in the State or its appearance generally in the cause. *Davis* v. *Farmers Cooperative Co.*, 262 U.S. 312 (1923); *Michigan Central R.R. Co.* v. *Mix*, 278 U.S. 492, 496 (1929). See also *Denver & R.G.W.R. Co.* v. *Terte*, 284 U.S. 284, 287 (1932) (attachment); *Canadian Pacific Ry. Co.* v. *Sullivan*, 126 F. 2d 433, 437 (1st Cir.), *cert. denied*, 316 U.S. 696 (1942) (agent designated to accept service); *Zuber* v. *Pennsylvania R. Co.*, 82 F. Supp. 670, 674 (N. D. Ga. 1949); *Pantswowe Zaklady Graviozne* v. *Automobile Ins. Co.*, 36 F. 2d 504 (S.D.N.Y. 1928) (commerce objection relates to jurisdiction of subject matter); 42 Harv. L. Rev. 1062, 1067 (1929); 43 *id.* 1156, 1157 (1930). For the same reason, we submit, an implied general appearance would not bar the litigation of petitioner's contention, seasonably urged upon the motion, that by taking jurisdiction in this action, the courts below denied due process by abridging freedom of the press; that also is an issue independent of the presence of petitioner in Alabama or its amenability to process of the court.

Second: The territorial limits of Due Process   The courts below held that the sporadic newsgathering activities of correspondents and stringers of *The Times* in Alabama, the occasional solicitation and publication of advertising from Alabama sources and the minuscule shipment of the newspaper to subscribers and newsdealers in the State (*supra*, pp. 25–27) constitute sufficient Alabama contacts to permit the exercise of jurisdiction in this action, without transcending the territorial limits of due process.

This assertion of state power finds no sanction in this Court's decisions governing the reach of state authority, despite the relaxation in the limits of due process that we recognize to have occurred in recent years. Neither the "flexible standard" of *International Shoe Co.* v. *Washington*, 326 U.S. 310 (1945), as it was called in *Hanson* v. *Denckla*, 357 U.S. 235, 251 (1958), nor any of its later applications, sustains, in our submission, the extreme determination here.

It is plain, initially, that the petitioner's peripheral relationship to Alabama does not involve "continuous corporate operations" which are "so substantial and of such a nature as to justify suit against it on causes of action arising from dealings entirely distinct from those activities." *International Shoe Co.* v. *Washington*,

---

*It should be noted that the Circuit Court also found a waiver of petitioner's special appearance in its application for mandamus to review an order directing the production of documents demanded by respondent to show the extent of petitioner's activities in Alabama. R. 50–51; see also R. 29–39, Pl. Ex. 311–313, R. 1835–1858. The Supreme Court's opinion is silent on this point, presumably in recognition of the proposition that an action must be "disconnected" with the motion to support an inference of waiver. *Lampley* v. *Beavers*, *supra*; *cf. Ford Motor Co.* v. *Hall Auto Co.*, 226 Ala. 385, 388 (1933). It would obviously thwart essential self-protective measures if an effort to obtain review of an allegedly abusive ancillary order were regarded as a waiver of the prime submission. *Cf. Ex parte Spence*, 271 Ala. 151 (1960); *Ex parte Textile Workers of America*, 249 Ala. 136 (1947); *Ex parte Union Planters National Bank and Trust Co.*, 249 Ala. 461 (1947). See *Fay* v. *Noia*, 372 U.S. 391, 432, n. 41 (1963).

supra, at 318. The case bears no resemblance to *Perkins* v. *Benguet Mining Co.*, 342 U.S. 437 (1952), where the central base of operations of the corporation, including its top management, was in the State where suit was brought. It hardly can be argued that *The New York Times* has such a base in Alabama, where, according to this record, it enjoys 6/100ths of one per cent of its daily circulation and 2/10ths of one per cent of its Sunday circulation and where the sources of 46/1000ths of one per cent of its advertising revenue are found (R. 402, 444–445). The occasional visits of correspondents to the State to report on events of great interest to the nation places *The Times* in Alabama no more than in Ankara or Athens or New Delhi, where, of course, similar visits occur.

Hence, if the jurisdiction here asserted is sustained, it must be on the ground that the alleged cause of action is so "connected with" petitioner's "activities within the state" as to "make it reasonable, in the context of our federal system of government, to require the corporation to defend the particular suit which is brought there." *International Shoe Co.* v. *Washington*, *supra*, at 319, 317. See also *Blount* v. *Peerless Chemicals (P.R.) Inc.*, 316 F. 2d 695, 700 (2d Cir. 1963); *L. D. Reeder Contractors of Ariz.* v. *Higgins Industries, Inc.*, 265 F. 2d 768, 774–775 (9th Cir. 1959); *Partin* v. *Michaels Art Bronze Co.*, 202 F. 2d 541, 545 (3d Cir. 1953) (concurring opinion).

There is, in our view, no such connection. Here, as in *Hanson* v. *Denckla*, *supra*, at 252, the "suit cannot be said to be one to enforce an obligation that arose from a privilege the defendant exercised in" the State. The liability alleged by the respondent certainly is not based on any activity of correspondents or stringers of *The Times* in covering the news in Alabama; and neither entering the State for such reporting, nor the composition nor the filing of reports rests on a privilege the State confers, given the rights safeguarded by the Constitution. Nor is this claim of liability connected with the occasional solicitation of advertisements in Alabama. The advertisement in suit was not solicited and did not reach *The Times* from anyone within the State. There remains, therefore, only the negligible circulation of *The Times* in Alabama on which to mount an argument that this suit relates to the exercise by the petitioner of "the privilege of conducting activities within" the State. *International Shoe Co.* v. *Washington*, *supra*, at 319.

We contend that this circulation did not involve the exercise of such a privilege. Copies of the paper were mailed to subscribers from New York or shipped from there to dealers who were purchasers, not agents of *The Times*. Such mailing and shipment in New York were not activity of the petitioner within the State of Alabama. See, *e.g.*, *Putnam* v. *Triangle Publications, Inc.*, 245 N. C. 432, 443 (1957); *Schmidt* v. *Esquire, Inc.*, 210 F. 2d 908, 915, 916 (7th Cir. 1954), *cert. denied*, 348 U.S. 819 (1954); *Street & Smith Publications, Inc.* v. *Spikes*, 120 F. 2d 895, 897 (5th Cir.), *cert. denied*, 314 U.S. 653 (1941); *Cannon* v. *Time, Inc.*, 115 F. 2d 423, 425 (4th Cir. 1940); *Whitaker* v. *Macfadden Publications, Inc.*, 105 F. 2d 44, 45 (D. C. Cir. 1939); *Buckley* v. *New York Times Co.*, 215 F. Supp. 893 (E. D. La. 1963); *Gayle* v. *Magazine Management Co.*, 153 F. Supp. 861, 864 (M. D. Ala. 1957); *Brewster* v. *Boston Herald-Traveler Corp.*, 141 F. Supp. 760, 761, 763 (D. Me. 1956); *cf. Erlanger Mills* v. *Cohoes Fibre Mills, Inc.*, 239 F. 2d 502 (4th Cir. 1956); *L. D. Reeder Contractors of Ariz.* v. *Higgins Industries, Inc.*, 265 F. 2d 768 (9th Cir. 1959); *Trippe Manufacturing Co.* v. *Spencer Gifts, Inc.*, 270 F. 2d. 821, 823 (7th Cir. 1959). Whether Alabama may, upon these facts, declare the petitioner responsible for an Alabama "publication" by causing or contributing to the dissemination of those papers in the State is not, of course, the issue. That is a problem of the choice of law[*] which is entirely distinct from the question here presented: whether by its shipment in and from New York petitioner "avails itself of the privilege of conducting activities within the forum State, thus invoking the benefits and protections of its laws." *Hanson* v. *Denckla*, *supra*, at 253. A State may be empowered to apply its law to a transaction upon grounds quite insufficient to establish "personal jurisdiction over a non-resident defendant", as *Hanson* (*ibid.*) makes clear. If this were not the case, each of the individual non-resident signers of the advertisement might also be amenable to Alabama's long-arm process, not to speak of every author of a publication sold within the State. See *Calagaz* v. *Calhoon*, 309 F. 2d 248, 254

---

[*] Courts have been no less perplexed than commentators by the conflicts problems incident to multi-state dissemination of an alleged libel; and some have sought to solve them by a "single publication" rule, fixing the time and place of the entire publication when and where the first and primary dissemination occurred. See, *e.g.*, *Hartmann* v. *Time, Inc.*, 166 F. 2d 127 (3d Cir. 1947), *cert. denied*, 334 U.S. 838 (1948); *Insull* v. *New York World-Telegram Corp.*, 273 F. 2d 166, 171 (7th Cir. 1959), *cert. denied*, 362 U.S. 942 (1960); *cf. Mattox* v. *News Syndicate Co.*, 176 F. 2d 897, 900, 904–905 (2d Cir.), *cert. denied*, 338 U.S. 858 (1949). See also, *e.g.*, Prosser, *Interstate Publication*, 51 Mich. L. Rev. 959 (1953); Leflar, *The Single Publication Rule*, 25 Rocky Mt. L. Rev. 263 (1953); Note, 29 U. of Chi. L. Rev. 569 (1962).

(5th Cir. 1962). That would, indeed, entail the "demise of all restrictions on the personal jurisdiction of state courts", an eventuality that this Court has declared the trend of its decisions does not herald. *Hanson* v. *Denckla, supra,* at 251. The avoidance of that outcome calls, at least, for a sharp line between a liability based on an act performed within the State and liability based on an act without, which merely is averred to have an impact felt within.* Surely the papers mailed to subscribers were delivered to them by petitioner when they were posted in New York. *Cf.* 1 *Williston on Contracts* (3d ed. 1957) § 81, p. 268. So, too, the delivery to carriers in New York for shipment to Alabama dealers, pursuant to their orders, can at most be said to have contributed to sales made by the dealers, but those sales were not the acts of the petitioner in Alabama. *Cf. United States* v. *Smith,* 173 Fed. 227, 232 (D. Ind. 1909). That is a matter to be judged in terms of a "practical conception" of the needs of our federalism, not "the 'witty diversities' . . . of the law of sales." Holmes, J., in *Rearick* v. *Pennsylvania,* 203 U.S. 507, 512 (1906).

Assuming, however, that the shipment of *The Times* to Alabama may be deemed an act of the petitioner within that State, we still do not believe the jurisdiction here affirmed can be sustained. In *International Shoe* this Court made clear that the new standard there laid down was not "simply mechanical or quantitative" and that its application "must depend rather upon the quality and nature of the activity in relation to the fair and orderly administration of the

---

Cf. L. Hand, J., in *Kilpatrick* v. *Texas & P. Ry. Co.,* 166 F. 2d 788, 791–792 (2d Cir. 1948): "It is settled that, given the proper procedural support for doing so, a state may give judgment in personam against a non-resident, who has only passed through its territory, if the judgment be upon a liability incurred while he was within its borders. That, we conceive, rests upon another principle. The presence of the obligor within the state subjects him to its law while he is there, and allows it to impose upon him any obligation which its law entails upon his conduct. Had it been possible at the moment when the putative liability arose to set up a piepowder court pro hac vice, the state would have had power to adjudicate the liability then and there; and his departure should not deprive it of the jurisdiction in personam so acquired. On the other hand, in order to subject a non-resident who passes through a state to a judgment in personam for liabilities arising elsewhere, it would be necessary to say that the state had power so to subject him as a condition of allowing him to enter at all, and that for this reason his voluntary entry charged him generally with submission to the courts. As a matter of its own law of conflicts of law, no court of one country would tolerate such an attempt to extend the power of another; and, as between citizens of states of the United States, constitutional doubts would arise which, to say the least, would be very grave. . . ."

laws which it was the purpose of the due process clause to insure" (326 U.S. at 319). See also *Hanson* v. *Denckla, supra,* at 253. The opinion left no doubt that, as Judge Learned Hand had previously pointed out (*Hutchinson* v. *Chase & Gilbert,* 45 F. 2d 139, 141 [2d Cir. 1930]), an " 'estimate of the inconveniences' which would result to the corporation from a trial away from its 'home' or principal place of business is relevant in this connection" (326 U.S. at 317). Measured by this standard, a principle which would require, in effect, that almost every newspaper defend a libel suit in almost any jurisdiction of the country, however trivial its circulation there may be, would not further the "fair and orderly administration of the laws." The special "inconvenience" of the foreign publisher in libel actions brought in a community with which its ties are tenuous need not be elaborated. It was perspicuously noted by the court below in a landmark decision more than forty years ago, confining venue to the county where the newspaper is "primarily published". *Age-Herald Publishing Co.* v. *Huddleston,* 207 Ala. 40, 45 (1921). This record surely makes the "inconvenience" clear.

We do not blink the fact that this submission focuses upon the hardship to the foreign publisher and that the plaintiff faces hardship too in litigating far from home. But if these conflicting interests call for balance in relation to the "orderly administration of the laws", there are substantial reasons why the interest of the publisher ought here to be preferred. In the first place, it is the forum which is seeking to extend its power beyond its own borders, carrying the burden of persuasion that the "territorial limitations on the power of the respective states" (*Hanson* v. *Denckla, supra,* at 251) are respected in the extension made. Secondly, the burden cast upon the publisher can only operate to thwart the object of the First Amendment by demanding the cessation of a circulation that entails at best no economic benefit—depriving the state residents who have an interest in the foreign publication of the opportunity to read. Thirdly, the plaintiff's grievance rests but fancifully on the insubstantial distribution of the publication in the forum, as distinguished from its major circulation out of state. If that grievance is to be assigned a locus, it is hardly where 394 copies were disseminated when the full 650,000 were regarded as relevant to the *ad damnum* (R. 2, 3, 601, 945) and a reason for sustaining the award (R. 1176, 1179). The difficulties presented by libel actions based on multi-state dissemination are notorious enough (see, *e.g., Zuck* v. *Interstate Publishing Corp.,* 317

F. 2d 727, 733 [2d Cir. 1963]), without permitting suit against a foreign publisher in every jurisdiction where a copy of the allegedly offending publication has been sold. Finally, but not the least important, this is not an action merely seeking redress for an injury allegedly inflicted on the plaintiff. Its dominant object is to punish the defendant, as the damages demanded made quite clear. Hence, the considerations that would be decisive against "long-arm" jurisdiction in a criminal proceeding ought to be persuasive here.

The courts below thought the foregoing arguments against the jurisdiction answered by the decision of this Court in *McGee* v. *International Life Ins. Co.*, 355 U.S. 220 (1957), where suit on an insurance contract was sustained in California against a non-resident insurer, based on the solicitation and the consummation of the contract in the State by mail. But that decision certainly does not control the disposition of this case. The contract executed in *McGee* constituted a continuing legal relationship between the insurer and the insured within the State, a relation which the States, with the concurrence of Congress (15 U.S.C. §§ 1011–1015, 59 Stat. 33), have long deemed to require special state regulation. *Hanson* v. *Denckla, supra*, at 252; *Travelers Health Assn.* v. *Virginia*, 339 U.S. 643 (1950). The liability asserted here derives from no such continuing relationship with someone in the State; and newspaper publication, including circulation (*Lovell* v. *Griffin*, 303 U.S. 444 [1938]; *Talley* v. *California*, 362 U.S. 60 [1960]), far from being exceptionally subject to state regulation, is zealously protected by the First Amendment.

Respondent also relies heavily on *Scripto* v. *Carson*, 362 U.S. 207 (1960) (Brief in Opposition, pp. 39, 41) but the reliance plainly is misplaced. That decision dealt with the minimum connection necessary to permit a State to impose on an out-of-state vendor the compensated duty to collect a use tax due from purchasers on property shipped to them in the State. It held the duty validly imposed where sales were solicited within the State, deeming *General Trading Co.* v. *State Tax Comm'n.*, 322 U.S. 335 (1944) controlling though the salesmen were "independent contractors" rather than employees of the vendor. No issue of judicial jurisdiction was involved. This "familiar and sanctioned device" (322 U.S. at 338) of making the distributor the tax collector for the State he exploits as a market plainly casts no burden comparable to the exercise of jurisdiction *in personam*, with the implications such a jurisdiction has. If the problems were analogous, the

relevant decision here would be *Miller Bros. Co.* v. *Maryland*, 347 U.S. 340 (1954), where the imposition of the duty was invalidated because there was "no invasion or exploitation of the consumer market" (*id.* at 347) by the out-of-state vendor. The *New York Times* does not solicit Alabama circulation (*supra*, p. 27); it merely satisfies the very small, local demand.

Viewed in these terms, a different question might be posed if it were shown that the petitioner engaged in activities of substance in the forum state, designed to build its circulation there. *Cf.* Mr. Justice Black, dissenting in part in *Polizzi* v. *Cowles Magazines, Inc.*, 345 U.S. 663, 667, 670 (1953); see also *WSAZ, Inc.* v. *Lyons*, 254 F. 2d 242 (6th Cir. 1958). That would involve a possible analogy to other situations where a foreign enterprise exploits the forum as a market and the cause of action is connected with such effort (*Hanson* v. *Denckla, supra*, at 251–252), though the punitive nature of the action and the special situation of the press must still be weighed. It also would confine the possibilities of litigation to places where the foreign publisher has had the opportunity to build some local standing with the public. No such activities, effort or opportunity existed here.

In a federated nation such as ours, the power of the States to exert jurisdiction over men and institutions not within their borders must be subject to reciprocal restraints on each in the interest of all. *Cf.* L. Hand, J., in *Kilpatrick* v. *Texas & P. Ry. Co.*, p. 81, footnote, *supra*. The need for such restraints is emphasized in our system by the full faith and credit clause of the Constitution. If Alabama stood alone it would be impotent in such a case as this to render any judgment that would be of practical importance to petitioner. What makes this judgment vitally important is the fact that if it is affirmed it is enforceable as such in States where the petitioner's resources are located. Thus jurisdictional delineations must be based on grounds that command general assent throughout the Union; otherwise full faith and credit will become a burden that the system cannot bear. No standard worthy of such general assent sustains the assumption of jurisdiction in this cause.

Third: The burden on commerce In forcing the petitioner to its defense of this case in Alabama, the state court has done more than exceed its territorial jurisdiction. It has also cast a burden on interstate commerce that the commerce clause forbids.

It takes no gift of prophecy to know that if negligible state circulation of a paper published in another state suffices to establish jurisdiction of a suit for libel, threatening the type of judgment rendered here, such distribution interstate cannot continue. So, too, if the interstate movement of correspondents provides a factor tending to sustain such jurisdiction, as the court below declared, a strong barrier to such movement has been erected. Both the free flow of interstate communications and the mobility of individuals are national interests of supreme importance. In the silence of Congress, their protection against burdensome state action, unsupported by an overriding local interest, is the duty of the courts. *Fisher's Blend Station* v. *Tax Commission*, 297 U.S. 650, 654–655 (1936); *Edwards* v. *California*, 314 U.S. 160 (1941). In neither area may a State "gain a momentary respite from the pressure of events by the simple expedient of shutting its gates to the outside world." *Id.* at 173. An attempt to isolate a State from strangers or their publications is no less offensive to the commerce clause than the attempts at economic isolation which have been repeatedly condemned. See, *e.g., Minnesota* v. *Barber*, 136 U.S. 313 (1890); *Baldwin* v. *G. A. F. Seelig, Inc.*, 294 U.S. 511, 527 (1935); *H. P. Hood & Sons* v. *DuMond*, 336 U.S. 525 (1949); *Dean Milk Co.* v. *City of Madison*, 340 U.S. 349 (1951).

This Court has not hitherto considered a case where the mere assumption of jurisdiction in a transitory action threatened an embargo of this kind. It has, however, held that the subjection of a carrier to suit, whether *in personam* or *in rem*, in a jurisdiction where it is engaged in insubstantial corporate activities may impose an excessive burden upon commerce, because of the special inconvenience and expense incident to the defense of litigation there. *Davis* v. *Farmers Co-operative Co.*, 262 U.S. 312 (1923); *Atchison, Topeka & Santa Fe Ry.* v. *Wells*, 265 U.S. 101 (1924); *Michigan Central R.R. Co.* v. *Mix*, 278 U.S. 492 (1929); *Denver & R. G. W. R. Co.* v. *Terte*, 284 U.S. 284, 287 (1932); *cf. International Milling Co.* v. *Columbia Transportation Co.*, 292 U.S. 511 (1934). See also *Sioux Remedy Co.* v. *Cope*, 235 U.S. 197 (1914); *Erlanger Mills* v. *Cohoes Fibre Mills, Inc.*, 239 F. 2d 502 (4th Cir. 1956); *Overstreet* v. *Canadian Pacific Airlines*, 152 F. Supp. 838 (S.D.N.Y. 1957). The burdens deemed excessive in those cases were as nothing compared to the burden imposed here, for which, as we have shown above (pp. 83–84), there is no overriding local interest.

Respondent argued in his Brief in Opposition (p. 42) that the cases holding that jurisdiction may be an excessive burden became moribund with the pronouncement in *International Shoe*. His contention finds no support in that opinion and ignores *Southern Pacific Co.* v. *Arizona*, 325 U.S. 761, 781 (1945), where a few months before the *Shoe* decision Chief Justice Stone alluded to the *Davis* and like cases, otherwise affirming the protective principle for which they stand. The need for that protective principle has, indeed, been increased by the progressive relaxation in due process standards. For the considerations leading to that relaxation have to do with the appropriate relationship between a State and foreign enterprise and individuals. They are entirely inapposite in the situation where an interest of the Nation is impaired.

Fourth: The freedom of the press   We have argued that the jurisdictional determination violates the Constitution, judged by standards that apply to enterprise in general under the constitutional provisions limiting state power in the interest of our federalism as a whole. We need not rest, however, on those standards. Newsgathering and circulation are both aspects of the freedom of the press, safeguarded by the Constitution. Neither can continue unimpaired if they subject the publisher to foreign jurisdiction on the grounds and of the scope asserted here. The decision is, accordingly, repugnant to the First Amendment.

This Court has often held state action inconsistent with the First Amendment, as embodied in the Fourteenth, when it has "the collateral effect of inhibiting the freedom of expression, by making the individual the more reluctant to exercise it" (*Smith* v. *California*, 361 U.S. 147, 151 [1959])—though the action is otherwise consistent with the Constitution. Scienter is not generally deemed a constitutional prerequisite to criminal conviction, but a measure of liability for the possession of obscene publications was invalidated on this ground in *Smith* because of its potential impact on the freedom of booksellers. The allocation of burden of proof in establishing a right to tax-exemption fell in *Speiser* v. *Randall*, 357 U.S. 513 (1958) because it was considered in the circumstances to "result in a deterrence of speech which the Constitution makes free." *Id.* at 526. Compulsory disclosure requires a showing of a more compelling state interest when it tends to inhibit freedom of association than in other situations where disclosure may be forced (see, *e.g., Gibson* v. *Florida Legislative Comm.*, 372 U.S. 539 [1963]; *Talley* v. *California*, 362 U.S. 60 [1960]); and its extent may be more limited. *Shelton* v. *Tucker*, 364 U.S. 479 (1960). Regulation of the legal profession that would raise no question as applied to the solicitation of commercial practice must comply with stricter standards insofar as it inhibits association for the vindication of fundamental rights. *N.A.A.C.P.* v. *Button*, 371 U.S. 415 (1963).

The principle involved in these familiar illustrations plainly applies here. If a court may validly take jurisdiction of a libel action on the basis of sporadic newsgathering by correspondents and trivial circulation of the publication in the State, it can and will do so not only when the plaintiff has a valid cause of action but also when the claim is as unfounded and abusive as the claim presented here. The burden of defense in a community with which the publication has no meaningful connection and the risk of enormous punitive awards by hostile juries cannot be faced with equanimity by any publisher. The inevitable consequence must be the discontinuance of the activities contributing to the assumption of the jurisdiction. The interest of a State in affording its residents the most convenient forum for the institution of such actions cannot justify this adverse impact on the freedom that the First Amendment has explicitly secured. See also pp. 83–84, *supra*. The occasional solicitation of advertising in the State, being wholly unrelated to respondent's cause of action, does not augment the interest of the State in providing the forum challenged here.

CONCLUSION

For the foregoing reasons, the judgment of the Supreme Court of Alabama should be reversed, with direction to dismiss the action.

Respectfully submitted,

Louis M. Loeb
T. Eric Embry
Marvin E. Frankel
Ronald S. Diana
Doris Wechsler
Lord, Day & Lord
Beddow, Embry & Beddow
Of Counsel

Herbert Brownell
Thomas F. Daly
Herbert Wechsler
Attorneys for Petitioner
The New York Times Company

APPENDIX A

CONSTITUTIONAL AND STATUTORY PROVISIONS INVOLVED

Constitution of the United States

Article I, Section 8:
The Congress shall have power * * *

To regulate Commerce with foreign Nations, and among the several States * * *.

* * * * *

Amendment I
Congress shall make no law respecting an establishment of religion, or prohibiting the free exercise thereof; or abridging the freedom of speech, or of the press; or the right of the people peaceably to assemble, and to petition the Government for a redress of grievances.

* * * * *

Amendment XIV
Section 1. All persons born or naturalized in the United States, and subject to the jurisdiction thereof, are citizens of the United States and of the State wherein they reside. No State shall make or enforce any law which shall abridge the privileges or immunities of citizens of the United States; nor shall any State deprive any person of life, liberty, or property, without due process of law; nor deny to any person within its jurisdiction the equal protection of the laws.

Alabama Code of 1940 Title 7

§ 188. **How corporation served** When an action at law is against a corporation the summons may be executed by the delivery of a copy of the summons and complaint to the president, or other head thereof, secretary, cashier, station agent or any other agent thereof. The return of the officer executing the summons that the person to whom delivered is the agent of the corporation shall be prima facie evidence of such fact and authorize judgment by default or otherwise without further proof of such agency and this fact need not be recited in the judgment entry. (1915, p. 607.)

* * * * *

§ 199(1). **Service on non-resident doing business or performing work or service in state** Any non-resident person, firm, partnership, general or limited, or any corporation not qualified under the Constitution and laws of this state as to doing business herein, who shall do any business or perform any character of work or service in this state shall, by the doing of such business or the performing of such work, or services, be deemed to have appointed the secretary of state, or his successor or successors in office, to be the true and lawful attorney or agent of such non-resident, upon whom process may be served [in any action accrued or accruing from the doing of such business, or the performing of such work, or service, or as an incident thereto by any such non-resident, or his, its or their agent, servant or employee.]* Service of such process shall be made by serving three copies of the process on the said secretary of state, and such service shall be sufficient service upon the said non-resident of the state of Alabama, provided that notice of such service and a copy of the process are forthwith sent by registered mail by the secretary of the state to the defendant at his last known address, which shall be stated in the affidavit of the plaintiff or complainant hereinafter mentioned, marked "Deliver to Addressee Only" and "Return Receipt Requested", and provided further that such return receipt shall be received by the secretary of state purporting to have been signed by said non-resident, or the secretary of state shall be advised by the postal authority that delivery of said registered mail was refused by said non-resident; and the date on which the secretary of state receives said return receipt, or advice by the postal authority that delivery of said registered mail was refused, shall be treated and considered as the date of service of process on said non-resident. The secretary of state shall make an affidavit as to the service of said process on him, and as to his mailing a copy of the same and notice of such service to the non-resident, and as to the receipt of said return receipt, or advice of the refusal of said registered mail, and the respective dates thereof, and shall attach said affidavit, return receipt, or advice from the postal authority, to a copy of the process and shall return the same to the clerk or register who issued the same, and all of the same shall be filed in the cause by the clerk or register. The party to a cause filed or pending, or his agent or attorney, desiring to obtain service upon a non-resident under the provisions of this section shall make and file in the cause, an affidavit stating facts showing that this section is applicable, and stating the residence and last known post-office address of the non-resident, and the clerk or register of the court in which the action is filed shall attach a copy of the affidavit to the writ or process, and a copy of the affidavit to each copy of the writ or process, and forward the original writ or process and three copies thereof to the sheriff of Montgomery county for service on the secretary of state and it shall be the duty of the sheriff to serve the same on the secretary of state and to make due return of such service. The court in which the cause is pending may order such continuance of the cause as may be necessary to afford the defendant or defendants reasonable opportunity to make defense. Any person who was a resident of this state at the time of the doing of business, or performing work or service in this state, but who is a non-resident at the time of the pendency of a cause involving the doing of said business or performance of said work or service, and any corporation which was qualified to do business in this state at the time of doing business herein and which is not qualified at the time of the pendency of a cause involving the doing of such business, shall be deemed a non-resident within the meaning of this section, and service of process under such circumstances may be had as herein provided.

The secretary of state of the state of Alabama, or his successor in office, may give such non-resident defendant notice of such service upon the secretary of state of the state of Alabama in lieu of the notice of service hereinabove provided to be given, by registered mail, in the following manner: By causing or having a notice of such service and a copy of the process served upon such non-resident defendant, if found within the state of Alabama, by any officer duly qualified to serve legal process within the state of Alabama, or if such non-resident defendant is found without the state of Alabama, by a sheriff, deputy sheriff, or United States marshal, or deputy United States marshal, or any duly constituted public officer qualified to serve like process in the state of the jurisdiction where such non-resident defendant is found; and the officer's return showing such service and when and where made, which shall be under oath, shall be filed in the office of the clerk or register of the court wherein such action is pending.

Service of summons when obtained upon any such non-resident as above provided for the service of process herein shall be deemed sufficient service of summons and process to give to

---

*Following the decision in *New York Times Company* v. *Conner* 291 F. 2d 492 (5th Cir. 1962) the statute was amended by substituting the following language for the bracketed portion: [in any action accrued, accruing, or resulting from the doing of such business, or the performing of such work or service, or relating to or on an incident thereof, by any such non-resident, or his, its or their agent, servant or employee. And such service shall be valid whether or not the acts done in Alabama shall of and within themselves constitute a complete cause of action.] The amendment applied "only to causes of action arising after the date of the enactment" and therefore has no bearing on this case.

any of the courts of this state jurisdiction over the cause of action and over such non-resident defendant, or defendants, and shall warrant and authorize personal judgment against such non-resident defendant, or defendants, in the event that the plaintiff prevails in the action.

The secretary of state shall refuse to receive and file or serve any process, pleading, or paper under this section unless three copies thereof are supplied to the secretary of state and a fee of three dollars is paid to the secretary of state; and no service shall be perfected hereunder unless there is on file in the office of the secretary of state a certificate or statement under oath by the plaintiff or his attorney that the provisions of this section are applicable to the case. (1949, p. 154, §§ 1, 2, appvd. June 23, 1949; 1951, p. 976, appvd. Aug. 28, 1951; 1953, p. 347, § 1, appvd. Aug. 5, 1953.)

Heed Their Rising Voices

"The growing movement of peaceful mass demonstrations by Negroes is something new in the South, something understandable.... Let Congress heed their rising voices, for they will be heard."

—*New York Times editorial*
Saturday, March 19, 1960

As the whole world knows by now, thousands of Southern Negro students are engaged in widespread non-violent demonstrations in positive affirmation of the right to live in human dignity as guaranteed by the U. S. Constitution and the Bill of Rights. In their efforts to uphold these guarantees, they are being met by an unprecedented wave of terror by those who would deny and negate that document which the whole world looks upon as setting the pattern for modern freedom. . . .

In Orangeburg, South Carolina, when 400 students peacefully sought to buy doughnuts and coffee at lunch counters in the business district, they were forcibly ejected, tear-gassed, soaked to the skin in freezing weather with fire hoses, arrested en masse and herded into an open barbed-wire stockade to stand for hours in the bitter cold.

In Montgomery, Alabama, after students sang "My Country, 'Tis of Thee" on the State Capitol steps, their leaders were expelled from school, and truckloads of police armed with shotguns and tear-gas ringed the Alabama State College Campus. When the entire student body protested to state authorities by refusing to re-register, their dining hall was padlocked in an attempt to starve them into submission.

In Tallahassee, Atlanta, Nashville, Savannah, Greensboro, Memphis, Richmond, Charlotte, and a host of other cities in the South, young American teenagers, in face of the entire weight of official state apparatus and police power, have boldly stepped forth as protagonists of democracy. Their courage and amazing restraint have inspired millions and given a new dignity to the cause of freedom.

Small wonder that the Southern violators of the Constitution fear this new, non-violent brand of freedom fighter . . . even as they fear the upswelling right-to-vote movement. Small wonder that they are determined to destroy the one man who, more than any other, symbolizes the new spirit now sweeping the South—the Rev. Dr. Martin Luther King, Jr., world-famous leader of the Montgomery Bus Protest. For it is his doctrine of non-violence which has inspired and guided the students in their widening wave of sit-ins; and it is this same Dr. King who founded and is president of the Southern Christian Leadership Conference—the organization which is spearheading the surging right-to-vote movement. Under Dr. King's direction the Leadership Conference conducts Student Workshops and Seminars in the philosophy and technique of non-violent resistance.

Again and again the Southern violators have answered Dr. King's peaceful protests with intimidation and violence. They have bombed his home almost killing his wife and child. They have assaulted his person. They have arrested him seven times—for "speeding," "loitering" and similar "offenses." And now they have charged him with "perjury"—a *felony* under which they could imprison him for *ten years*. Obviously, their real purpose is to remove him physically as the leader to whom the students and millions of others—look for guidance and support, and thereby to intimidate *all* leaders who may rise in the South. Their strategy is to behead this affirmative movement, and thus to demoralize Negro Americans and weaken their will to struggle. The defense of Martin Luther King, spiritual leader of the student sit-in movement, clearly, therefore, is an integral part of the total struggle for freedom in the South.

Decent-minded Americans cannot help but applaud the creative daring of the students and the quiet heroism of Dr. King. But this is one of those moments in the stormy history of Freedom when men and women of good will must do more than applaud the rising-to-glory of others. The America whose good name hangs in the balance before a watchful world, the America whose heritage of Liberty these Southern Upholders of the Constitution are defending, is *our* America as well as theirs . . .

We must heed their rising voices—

yes—but we must add our own.

We must extend ourselves above and beyond moral support and render the material help so urgently needed by those who are taking the risks, facing jail, and even death in a glorious re-

affirmation of our Constitution and its Bill of Rights.

We urge you to join hands with our fellow Americans in the South by supporting, with your dollars, this Combined Appeal for all three needs—the

Your Help Is Urgently Needed . . . NOW!!

Stella Adler	Ossie Davis	John Killens	John Raitt
Raymond Pace Alexander	Sammy Davis, Jr.	Eartha Kitt	Elmer Rice
Harry Van Arsdale	Ruby Dee	Rabbi Edward Klein	Jackie Robinson
Harry Belafonte	Dr. Philip Elliott	Hope Lange	Mrs. Eleanor Roosevelt
Julie Belafonte	Dr. Harry Emerson Fosdick	John Lewis	Bayard Rustin
Dr. Algernon Black	Anthony Franciosa	Viveca Lindfors	Robert Ryan
Marc Blitztein	Lorraine Hansbury	Carl Murphy	Maureen Stapleton
William Branch	Rev. Donald Harrington	Don Murray	Frank Silvera
Marlon Brando	Nat Hentoff	John Murray	Hope Stevens
Mrs. Ralph Bunche	James Hicks	A. J. Muste	George Tabori
Diahann Carroll	Mary Hinkson	Frederick O'Neal	Rev. Gardner C. Taylor
Dr. Alan Knight Chalmers	Van Heflin	L. Joseph Overton	Norman Thomas
Richard Coe	Langston Hughes	Clarence Pickett	Kenneth Tynan
Nat King Cole	Morris Iushewitz	Shad Polier	Charles White
Cheryl Crawford	Mahalia Jackson	Sidney Poitier	Shelley Winters
Dorothy Dandridge	Mordecai Johnson	A. Philip Randolph	Max Youngstein

We in the south who are struggling daily for dignity and freedom warmly endorse this appeal

Rev. Ralph D. Abernathy (Montgomery, Ala.)	I. S. Levy (Columbia, S. C.)
Rev. Fred L. Shuttlesworth (Birmingham, Ala.)	Rev. Martin Luther King, Sr. (Atlanta, Ga.)
Rev. Kelley Miller Smith (Nashville, Tenn.)	Rev. Henry C. Bunton (Memphis, Tenn.)
Rev. W. A. Dennis (Chattanooga, Tenn.)	Rev. S. S. Seay, Sr. (Montgomery, Ala.)
Rev. C. K. Steele (Tallahassee, Fla.)	Rev. Samuel W. Williams (Atlanta, Ga.)
Rev. Matthew D. McCollom (Orangeburg, S. C.)	Rev. A. L. Davis (New Orleans, La.)
Rev. William Holmes Borders (Atlanta, Ga.)	Mrs. Katie E. Whickham (New Orleans, La.)
Rev. Douglas Moore (Durham, N. C.)	Rev. W. H. Hall (Hattiesburg, Miss.)
Rev. Wyatt Tee Walker (Petersburg, Va.)	Rev. J. E. Lowery (Mobile, Ala.)
Rev. Walter L. Hamilton (Norfolk, Va.)	Rev. T. J. Jemison (Baton Rouge, La.)

COMMITTEE TO DEFEND MARTIN LUTHER KING AND THE STRUGGLE FOR FREEDOM IN THE SOUTH

312 West 125th Street, New York 27, N. Y. UNiversity 6-1700

Chairmen: A. Philip Randolph, Dr. Gardner C. Taylor; *Chairmen of Cultural Division:* Harry Belafonte, Sidney Poitier; *Treasurer:* Nat King Cole; *Executive Director:* Bayard Rustin; *Chairmen of Church Division:* Father George B. Ford, Rev. Harry Emerson Fosdick, Rev. Thomas Kilgore, Jr., Rabbi Edward E. Klein; *Chairman of Labor Division:* Morris Iushewitz

Please mail this coupon TODAY!

Committee To Defend Martin Luther King
and
The Struggle For Freedom In The South

312 West 125th Street, New York 27, N. Y.
UNiversity 6-1700

I am enclosing my contribution of $_____

for the work of the Committee.

Name _____
(PLEASE PRINT)

Address _____

City _____ Zone _____ State _____

☐ I want to help

☐ Please send further information

Please make checks payable to:

Committee To Defend Martin Luther King

IN THE
SUPREME COURT OF THE UNITED STATES
OCTOBER TERM, 1963

NO. 39

THE NEW YORK TIMES COMPANY, PETITIONER,

v.

L. B. SULLIVAN, RESPONDENT

ON WRIT OF CERTIORARI TO THE SUPREME COURT OF ALABAMA

BRIEF FOR RESPONDENT

STEINER, CRUM & BAKER,
1109-25 First National Bank Building,
Montgomery 1, Alabama,

CALVIN WHITESELL,
Montgomery, Alabama,

Of Counsel.

ROBERT E. STEINER, III,
SAM RICE BAKER,
M. ROLAND NACHMAN, JR.,

Attorneys for Respondent.

INDEX

IN THE
SUPREME COURT OF THE
UNITED STATES
OCTOBER TERM, 1963
NO. 39

THE NEW YORK TIMES COMPANY, PETITIONER,

V.

L. B. SULLIVAN, RESPONDENT.

ON WRIT OF CERTIORARI TO THE
SUPREME COURT OF ALABAMA.

BRIEF FOR RESPONDENT

Respondent adopts petitioner's statement of
"Opinions Below" and "Jurisdiction."

QUESTIONS PRESENTED

1. Does a newspaper corporation have a constitutionally guaranteed absolute privilege to
defame an elected city official in a paid newspaper advertisement so that the corporation is
immune from a private common law libel judgment in a state court in circumstances where,
because of the admitted falsity of the publication, the newspaper is unable to plead or prove
state afforded defenses of truth, fair comment,
privilege or retraction (to show good faith and
eliminate punitive damages), and where the
corporation has retracted the same false material for another admittedly "on a par" with the
city official?

2. When the only claimed invasion of a corporation's constitutional rights is that a city official successfully sued it for damages in a private
civil action for libel in a state court in circumstances described in Question 1, and when the
corporation does not contend that the state trial
proceedings have been unfair, has there been an
abridgement of the corporation's constitutional
rights under the First and Fourteenth Amendments?

3. Are libelous utterances in a paid newspaper
advertisement within the area of constitutionally protected speech and press?

4. When an admittedly false newspaper advertisement published in circumstances described
in Question 1 charges that city police massively
engaged in rampant, vicious, terroristic and
criminal actions in deprivation of rights of others, is a state court holding in a private common
law libel action that such an utterance is libelous

as a matter of state law—leaving to the jury the
questions of publication, identification with the
police commissioner, and damages—an infringement of the newspaper's constitutional rights?

5. When a paid newspaper advertisement published in circumstances described in Question 1
contains admittedly false charges described in
Question 4 about police action in a named city,
may this Court consistently with its decisions
and the Seventh Amendment review on certiorari a state jury finding, in a trial concededly
fair, that the publication is "of and concerning"
the city police commissioner whose name does
not appear in the publication, and an award of
general and punitive damages to him, when this
state jury verdict embodied in a final state
judgment has been approved by the state's
highest appellate court?

6. May this Court consistently with its decisions
and the Seventh Amendment re-examine facts
tried by a state jury in a trial concededly fair, when
those findings have been embodied in a final state
judgment affirmed by the highest state appellate
court, and when review is sought on assertions
that the verdict is wrong and the general and
punitive libel damages merely excessive?

7. When a foreign corporation makes a general
appearance in a private state civil action against
it, according to state law consistent with the
majority view of all states, is there an adequate
independent state ground as to jurisdiction over
this foreign corporation?

8. Even if there had been no general appearance as described in Question 7, when a foreign
newspaper corporation continuously and systematically gathers news by resident and tran-
sient correspondents, solicits advertising in person and by mail, and distributes its newspapers
for sale in the forum state, and when some of
these activities are incident to the cause of
action in suit, has this foreign corporation sufficient contacts with the forum state so that suit
against it is fair in accordance with decisions of
this Court so explicit as to leave no room for
real controversy?

STATUTES INVOLVED

Statutes referred to in this brief are contained
in an appendix hereto.

STATEMENT

In the New York Times of March 29, 1960,
there appeared a full-page advertisement,
"warmly endorsed" by the four petitioners in
No. 40, entitled, "Heed Their Rising Voices."[1]

---

[1] App. B of Petitioner's brief, p. 97.

Charging generally "an unprecedented wave of error," the advertisement said of Montgomery:

> "In Montgomery, Alabama, after students sang 'My Country, 'Tis of Thee' on the State Capitol steps, their leaders were expelled from school, and truckloads of police armed with shotguns and tear-gas ringed the Alabama State College Campus. When the entire student body protested to state authorities by refusing to re-register, their dining hall was padlocked in an attempt to starve them into submission.
>
> *   *   *   *   *   *   *
>
> "Again and again the Southern violators have answered Dr. King's peaceful protests with intimidation and violence. They have bombed his home almost killing his wife and child. They have assaulted his person. They have arrested him seven times—for 'speeding,' 'loitering' and similar 'offenses.' And now they have charged him with 'perjury'—a **felony** under which they could imprison him for **ten years**."

Respondent, police commissioner of Montgomery, asked $500,000 as damages for this libel from the New York Times and the four "warm endorsers."

After a lengthy hearing the trial court held on August 5, 1960, that the New York Times was amenable to suit in Alabama. It had made a general appearance the court found. And, moreover, its business activities in Alabama, some of which had given rise to the cause of action, were sufficient contacts under due process standards to permit service on a Times string correspondent residing in Alabama, and on the Secretary of State under the Alabama Substituted Service Statute[2] (R. 49–57).

After its demurrers had been overruled (R. 108) the Times filed six separate pleas to the complaint (R. 99–105). Although truth regardless of motive is a complete defense to a libel suit in Alabama (see infra), the Times and its co-defendants filed no plea of truth. Although privilege and fair comment are defenses in Alabama in appropriate circumstances (see infra), the Times and its co-defendants did not plead these defenses. At the conclusion of the trial a jury returned a verdict against all defendants for $500,000, and the trial court entered a judgment against all defendants in this amount.[3] Petitioner does not assert here any due process

defects in these trial proceedings, and does not attack the motives and conduct of the jury.

The Times filed a motion for new trial, which was overruled (R. 970); the petitioners in No. 40 filed motions for new trial, but allowed them to lapse (R. 984, 998, 1013, 1028).

The Alabama Supreme Court affirmed the judgment as to all defendants (R. 1180).

The Times complains in this Court: (1) The holdings of the Alabama courts that the publication was libelous per se and the jury verdict that it was "of and concerning" respondent abridged its guaranties under the 1st and 14th Amendments, and (2) it was not amenable to suit in Alabama.

I. Merits

Since the Times has told this Court that the whole libel rests on two discrepancies—mere "exaggerations or inaccuracies"[4] in the course of an "impersonal"[5] discussion "plainly" not meant as an attack on any individual,[6] respondent will state **this** case.[7]

This lawsuit arose because of a wilful, deliberate and reckless attempt to portray in a full-page newspaper advertisement, for which the Times charged and was paid almost $5,000, rampant, vicious, terroristic and criminal police action in Montgomery, Alabama, to a nationwide public of 650,000. The goal was money-raising. Truth, accuracy and long-accepted standards of journalism were not criteria for the writing or publication of this advertisement. The defamatory matter (quoted R. 580–81) describes criminal police action because some college students innocently sang "My Country 'Tis of Thee" from the Alabama State Capitol steps. The innocent singers were expelled from school; police ringed their campus by truck-

---

[2] Title 7, § 199 (1), Code of Alabama. The Times has conceded throughout adequate notice and opportunity to defend.

[3] Of course, this joint judgment is not collectible more than once. The facts giving rise to liability of petitioners in No. 40 will be related in a separate brief.

---

[4] Brief, p. 33.

[5] Brief, p. 32.

[6] Ibid.

[7] Respondent, accordingly, will not dignify beyond this comment the "statement" contained in the briefs of the friends of the Times. They are literally second editions of the advertisement and do not even purport to be confined to accurate summaries of the record.

The American Civil Liberties Union Brief, for example, draws most of its statement from newspaper articles, offered by the Times on its motion for new trial, and excluded below. The correctness and propriety of the ruling are not challenged. The brief simply cites the material as evidence anyway. Such practice presumably fosters the "fair trials" to which the organization is "devoted" (Brief, pp. 1 and 2). The other *amici* briefs are consumed with unrelated cases, entirely outside the record, and with inaccurate and incomplete characterizations of and quotations from a scant fraction of the testimony in this case.

loads armed with shotguns and tear gas;[8] and their dining hall was padlocked to starve the students into submission. All statements charge violation of the students' rights.

The Times is not candid when it tells this Court (Brief p. 7) that "the only part" of the foregoing statement "that Respondent thought implied a reference to him was the assertion about 'truckloads of police.'" Respondent made entirely clear that he considered the padlocking charge—and all other charges except expulsion—as applicable to him as well (R. 716). The Times is also absolutely inaccurate when it tells this Court that respondent's evidence "consisted mainly" (Brief p. 7) of a story by Sitton and a report by McKee. Respondent's evidence also included the Times' answers to interrogatories; respondent's own testimony, and that of his numerous witnesses; the testimony of all of the Times' trial witnesses; the statements and judicial admissions of its attorneys; and the testimony of John Murray who testified for the individual petitioners.

The advertisement in another paragraph charges that the perpetrators of the foregoing alleged barbarisms were the same persons who had intimidated Martin Luther King; bombed his home; assaulted his person; and arrested him. All statements charge criminal conduct. Although the Times' brief tells this Court that the pronoun "they" does not point to respondent, and that such a jury finding is "absurd" (Brief p. 33), the jury was able to make the connection from the Times' own witness, Gershon Aaronson. He conceded that the word "they" as it appeared repeatedly in the quotation in the ad "refers to the same persons" (R. 745).[9] Accordingly, the same police and the same police commissioner committed or condoned these alleged acts. And a jury unanimously agreed with Aaronson.

In a vain attempt to transfer these devastating statements from the constitutionally unprotected area of socially useless libel, where they belong, to the arena of constitutionally protected speech, where they obviously have no place, the Times and its friends employ various soothing phrases to describe the advertisement. It is called "political expression" and "political criticism" (pp. 29 and 30) of "public men" (p. 41); "the daily dialogue of politics" (p. 50); "a critique of government as such"; "criticism of official conduct" and "of the government" (pp. 30 and passim); "the most impersonal denunciation of an agency of government" (p. 50); a "recital of grievances and protests against claimed abuse dealing squarely with the major issue of our time" (pp. 31 and 57); "an expression which is merely wrong in fact with denigrating implications" (p. 54); an "appeal for political and social change" (A.C.L.U. brief, p. 13); a "critique of attitude and method, a value judgment and opinion" (A.C.L.U. brief, p. 29).

But the ordinary, unsophisticated reader of this ad was bound to draw the plain meaning that such shocking conditions were the responsibility of those charged with the administration of the Montgomery Police Department—respondent and the other two city commissioners. Any other conclusion is impossible. The Times itself can suggest no other reference, except to the police generally, and police are under the direct control and supervision of respondent. Indeed, the Times brief (p. 44) characterizes the ad as "criticism of an elected political official ..." and observes that this official should be hardy enough to take it without suing for libel.

A description of such conduct, at war with basic concepts of decency and lawful government, inevitably evokes contempt, indignation, and ridicule for the person charged with the administration of police activities in Montgomery. And obviously this was the precise intent of the authors of the advertisement. One of them, John Murray, so testified.[10]

Significantly, none of the Times' witnesses, and none of the petitioners in No. 40, all of

---

[8] The Times apparently hopes to de-emphasize the ad's false allegations that the police were armed with shotguns and tear gas. It describes the ad as speaking of "truckloads of armed police ..." (Brief, pp. 5 and 62. See also p. 8).

[9] The Times argues here, remarkable to say, that the jury should have disregarded Aaronson's testimony, because another witness, Redding, was *not* interrogated on the point (Brief, p. 17).

[10] "Q. (After reading the first paragraph quoted in the complaint) Was that the way that paragraph was when you first got it with the memorandum or did you give it that added touch for appeal?

"A. Well, it would be a little difficult at this time to recall the exact wording in the memorandum but the sense of what was in the memorandum was certainly the same as what is in here. We may have phrased it a little differently here and there.

"Q. I see. Your purpose was to rev it up a little bit to get money, I take it.

"A. Well, our purpose was to get money and to make the ad as—to project it in the most appealing form from the material we were getting.

"Q. Whether it was accurate or not really didn't make much difference, did it?

"A. Well, that did not enter the—it did not enter into consideration at all except we took it for granted that it was accurate—we took it for granted that it was accurate—they were accurate—and if they hadn't been—I mean we would have stopped to question it. I mean we would have stopped to question it—We had every reason to believe it" (R. 814–815).

whom testified, presented any evidence designed to show that the statements from the ad were true. Certainly, the individual petitioners in No. 40, two of whom lived in Montgomery, had no reason to withhold testimony harmful to respondent.

The reference to respondent as police commissioner is clear from the ad. In addition, the jury heard the testimony of a newspaper editor (R. 602, et seq.); a real estate and insurance man (R. 613, et seq.); the sales manager of a men's clothing store (R. 634, et seq.); a food equipment man (R. 644, et seq.); a service station operator (R. 649, et seq.); and the operator of a truck line for whom respondent had formerly worked (R. 662, et seq.). Each of these witnesses stated that he associated the statements with respondent, and that if he had believed the statements to be true, he would have considered such conduct reprehensible in the extreme.[11]

Unless the Times is asking this Court to assume the functions of a jury and to weigh the credibility of this relevant testimony, nothing could be more irrelevant than the time and place of the witnesses' first inspection of the ad. Even so, the Times has had to adjust the testimony to make its dubious point,[12] and it seems to forget that all of its witnesses were its own employees.

Undoubtedly the demonstrable falsity of the statements prevented pleas of truth or privilege or fair comment. Indeed, the Times published a retraction of the same paragraphs for Governor Patterson on May 16, 1960 (R. 596 and 1958–1961):

> "Since publication of the advertisement, The Times made an investigation and consistent with its policy of retracting and correcting any errors or misstatements which may appear in its columns, herewith retracts the two paragraphs complained of by the Governor."

The Times asked its Montgomery string correspondent, McKee, for an investigation.

On April 14, 1960, five days before suit was filed, McKee advised that the statements in the first quoted paragraph of the ad were false; and that King had been arrested twice by the Montgomery police for loitering and speeding and twice by the Sheriff's office for violation of the State boycott law and on charge of income tax falsification—a charge on which he was subsequently acquitted. Nevertheless, the Times, instead of retracting, wrote respondent that with the exception of the padlocking statement the rest of the quoted material was "substantially correct" (R. 589).

Later the Times directed another investigation by its regional correspondent, Claude Sitton. While the Times now speaks in this Court of "discrepancies" and "inaccuracies" in two instances, Sitton reported on May 4, 1960, that the first quoted paragraph of the advertisement "appears to be virtually without any foundation" (R. 594). There was no suggestion of involvement of respondent or any other city commissioner, or public employee under their charge, in the matters in the second quoted paragraph.

The Times then retracted for Governor Patterson, but not for respondent. The Times attempted to explain its inconsistency:

> "The defendant . . . felt that on account of the fact that John Patterson held the high office of Governor of the State of Alabama and that he apparently believed that he had been libeled by said advertisement in his capacity as Governor of the State of Alabama, the defendant should apologize" (R. 595–596).

When confronted with this answer to interrogatories, Harding Bancroft, then secretary of The New York Times, could give no reason for the different treatment of Governor Patterson and respondent. They were "on a par." But there was a retraction for Patterson and not for respondent (R. 779).[13]

---

[11] One stated, for example: "I don't think there is any question about what I would decide. I think I would decide that we probably had a young Gestapo in Montgomery" (R. 646).

[12] For example, Blackwell testified (R. 619): "He called me into his office and showed me this ad and at that time I indicated that I had seen the ad before but I don't remember just where and under what circumstances . . ." Price testified: " . . . I saw copies of the two paragraphs myself prior to that time" (R. 648). Respondent's counsel himself asked Parker whether he had seen the ad "before in my office" (R. 649) but not whether this was the first occasion; and counsel for the Times did not cross-examine on the point, presumably because its counsel had also talked to Parker before the trial (R. 651).

[13] The Times brief, in its lengthy attempt to explain its inconsistency (pp. 21–22), presents an incomplete and inaccurate summary of Bancroft's testimony. It omits the following (R. 779):
"Q. Is there anything contained in this sentence in the Interrogatories that I just read to you which differentiates in any manner the position of Governor Patterson in his suit with Commissioner Sullivan in the present suit?
"A. As I read the thing, the answer is no.
"Q. They are put on a par, aren't they, Governor Patterson and this Plaintiff?
"A. Yes.
"Q. But there was a retraction for Governor Patterson and there was no retraction for this Plaintiff. That is correct, isn't it?
"A. That is correct."

Undisputed trial testimony showed that respondent and the other commissioners and the Montgomery police had nothing to do with the King bombings; that a city detective had helped dismantle a live bomb which had been thrown on King's front porch (R. 685); and that the department had exerted extraordinary efforts to apprehend the persons responsible (R. 686–687). The occurrence of this event before respondent took office simply compounds the libelous nature of this advertisement which seeks to portray such matters as current actions which "they" took. The ordinary reader, chronologically unsophisticated, would clearly associate the acts with the current city government.

Another police officer testified without contradiction that no one had assaulted King when he had been arrested for loitering outside the courtroom (R. 692–693).

Frank Stewart, State Superintendent of Education, testified without contradiction that students had not been expelled from school for singing on the capitol steps (R. 700).

The uncontroverted testimony of falsity was so overwhelming that counsel for the Times repeatedly brought out from witnesses that the statements quoted from the ad were not true. Moreover, he stated that truth was not in issue in the case because it had not been pleaded (A compendium of counsel's statements is in Appendix B of the brief in opposition, pp. 48–52). Counsel would not and could not have made such statements if the quoted portions of the ad had been true or if they had contained only a few "discrepancies" or "exaggerations."

Undeterred, however, in the teeth of these judicial admissions, Harding Bancroft maintained to the end an equivocal position about the correctness of the ad, with the exception of the padlocking statement.[14] The Times' brief,

on the contrary, candidly recites (pp. 62–65) a chronicle of the ad's falsities in addition to the padlocking statement.

Because of this testimony, when the Times **six months before** had retracted the **same** statements on the basis of the **same** investigation as "errors and misstatements" (R. 595–596, 1958–1961), the court below characterized Bancroft's performance as "cavalier ignoring of the falsity of the advertisement" which surely impressed the jury "with the bad faith of the Times, and its maliciousness inferable therefrom" (R. 1178). The Times is absolutely incorrect when it argues that this statement of the Court was based upon the selected portion of Bancroft's testimony excerpted on pages 21 and 22 of its brief.

Sullivan himself testified that the matters contained in the ad were false (R. 705–709); that the statements reflected "upon my ability and integrity, and certainly it has been established here that they are not true" (R. 713).

The bombing statement "referred to me and to the Police Department and the City Commissioners" (R. 718). Similarly, the other matters contained in the second quoted paragraph of the ad related to him "by virtue of being Police Commissioner and Commissioner of Public Affairs."

When asked on cross-examination whether he felt that the ad had a "direct personal reference" to him, his answer was, and it is the simple answer which any normal reader of the ad would give:

"It is my feeling that it reflects not only on me but on the other Commissioners and the community. . . . When it describes police action, certainly I feel it reflects on me as an individual" (R. 724).

Moreover:

"I have endeavored to try to earn a good reputation and that's why I resent very much the statements contained in this ad which are completely false and untrue" (R. 722).

The circumstances under which this ad was cleared for publication show a striking departure from the Times' usual meticulous screening process. So that it will print only what is "fit to print," the Times has codified an elaborate set of "advertising acceptability standards" (R. 597–601), designed "to exclude misleading,

---

[14] When asked whether the Times took the position that the ad's statements, with this exception, were "substantially correct," Bancroft first said: "I think it is a pretty hard question to answer" (R. 781). Then, the Times . . . "doesn't know anything more than what is set forth in these two responses which our stringer and correspondent there, which are annexed to the Answers to the Interrogatories and we don't have any additional knowledge to that" (R. 782). Next: "I really think I have to answer the question by saying I don't know" (R. 782). Then: "[I]t is awfully difficult to define what The Times thinks," but The Times' lawyers had seemed to indicate on April 15, 1960, that the statements were substantially correct (R. 784). He concluded (R. 785):
"I find it terribly difficult to be able to say that The Times, as such, believes something is true or is not true. Now, all I can tell you is what the sources of The Times' knowledge are, and the sources are The Times' knowledge—the complete sources as far as I know, are the two annexes attached to the Answers to the Interrogatories. Now, if you asked me would I use the words 'substantially correct,' now, I think I probably would,

yes. The tenor of the content, the material of those two paragraphs in the ad which have been frequently read here are not substantially incorrect. They are substantially correct. Now, what sort of words I can use to give you an answer that would satisfy you, I don't know."

inaccurate, and fraudulent advertisements and unfair competitive statements in advertising. The chief purpose of this policy of The Times is to protect the reader and to maintain the high standards of decency and dignity in its advertising columns which The Times has developed over the years."

To be as charitable as possible, it is remarkable that no person connected with The Times investigated charges that as part of "a wave of terror," public officials in Montgomery, because students sang "My Country 'Tis of Thee" from the Capitol steps, expelled the students from school; ringed their campus with truckloads of police armed with shotguns and tear gas; padlocked dining halls to starve them into submission; and thereby maintained continuity with earlier days in which they had bombed King's home, assaulted his person, and arrested him on baseless charges.

Over sixty names appeared on the ad; none of these persons was contacted. A regional correspondent in Atlanta, who the Times admits had written news reports about racial difficulties in Montgomery, was not questioned. The Times had a string correspondent in Montgomery. It directed him to give an immediate report on the demand for retraction. But he was not asked for prior information or investigation.

In its answer to interrogatories, the Times specified sixteen contemporaneous news stories of its own as "relating to certain of the events or occurrences referred to in the advertisement" (R. 586). Aaronson, Redding, and Bancroft—the three Times witnesses—had never bothered to look at any of this news material before publishing the ad.

Aaronson, an employee on the national advertising staff, who first received the ad, testified that he did not read it (R. 741), but simply "scanned it very hurriedly" (R. 742).

Because he knew nothing which would lead him to believe that these monstrous statements were false (R. 758), Vincent Redding, head of the Advertising Acceptability Department, did not check with any of the signers of the ad; or with the regional correspondent in Atlanta; or with the string correspondent in Montgomery; or with the sixteen newspaper stories on file in his office (R. 763–765):

> "Q. Mr. Redding, wouldn't it be a fair statement to say that you really didn't check this ad at all for accuracy?
> "A. That's a fair statement, yes" (R. 765).

One wonders whether the performance of Messrs. Aaronson, Redding and Bancroft inspired the American Civil Liberties Union

comment that the Times had suffered "liability without fault" (Brief, p. 26), and the Washington Post evaluation that " . . . the undisputed record facts disclose that the advertisement was published under circumstances which, by no stretch of the imagination could be characterized as anything other than complete good faith" (Brief, p. 6).

Testimony of John Murray, one of the authors of the ad, and erstwhile Hollywood "scenarist" and Broadway lyricist (R. 815), describing the manner in which the ad was composed, has been quoted previously (Footnote 10, *supra*).

Thus, this "appealing" congeries of monstrous and now undefended falsehoods was sent to The New York Times. Upon payment of almost five thousand dollars, it was published without any investigation as a full-page advertisement in The New York Times of March 29, 1960. Six hundred and fifty thousand copies of it circulated to the nation as part of "All the news that's fit to print." And its purveyors sat back to await the financial return on their investment in "free speech".

II. Jurisdiction

General appearance Petitioner, by moving to dismiss the action because the Alabama court was said to have no jurisdiction of the subject matter, made a general appearance in this case and thereby consented to the jurisdiction of the Alabama courts over its corporate person. This was the holding of both courts below. In addition, the trial court held that by bringing a mandamus action in the Supreme Court of Alabama unrelated to questions of personal jurisdiction, the Times had compounded its general appearance (R. 49–51). The holdings below, as will be demonstrated, accord with Alabama cases as well as those in a majority of the states.

The Times calls this general appearance "involuntary" (Brief, p. 75). But the Times in its brief in the Alabama Supreme Court (p. 54) said:

> "Accordingly, while the motion made it clear that the only grounds for the motion were the defects in the mode of service, the prayer asserted the consequences of these defects—a lack of jurisdiction not only over the person but also over the subject matter."

And the Times still makes the subject matter argument in this Court (Brief, p. 73):

> "Hence a contention that the statute is inapplicable or invalid as applied goes, in this sense, to jurisdiction of the cause as well as jurisdiction of the person."

Validity of service of process on The New York Times The courts below held that service on the string correspondent, McKee, and on the Secretary of State were valid. The trial court held that the Times had been sued on a cause of action "incident to" its business in Alabama (R. 55); and the "manifold contacts which The Times maintains with the State of Alabama" make it amenable to this process and suit in the Alabama courts, commenced by service on McKee and on the Secretary of State, "regardless of its general appearance" (R. 51). The trial court found:

> " . . . an extensive and continuous course of Alabama business activity—news gathering; solicitation of advertising; circulation of newspapers and other products. These systematic business dealings in Alabama give The Times substantial contact with the State of Alabama, considerably in excess of the minimal contacts required by the Supreme Court decisions. . . . The Times does business in Alabama" (R. 56–57).

The Alabama Supreme Court affirmed on this point, after extensive findings regarding the business activities of the Times in Alabama (R. 1140–1147). It adopted, as had the trial court, the test of *Consolidated Cosmetics v. D-A Publishing Company*, 186 F. 2d 906, 908 (7th Cir. 1951):

> "The functions of a magazine publishing company, obviously, include gathering material to be printed, obtaining advertisers and subscribers, printing, selling and delivering the magazines for sale. Each of these, we think, constitutes an essential factor of the magazine publication business. Consequently if a nonresident corporation sees fit to perform any one of those essential functions in a given jurisdiction, it necessarily follows that it is conducting its activities in such a manner as to be subject to jurisdiction."

The court below concluded (R. 1149–1150):

> "The evidence shows that The Times sent its papers into Alabama, with its carrier as its agent, freight prepaid, with title passing on delivery to the consignee. See Tit. 57, Sec. 25, Code of Alabama 1940; 2 Williston on Sales, Sec. 279 (b), p. 90. Thence the issue went to newsstands for sale to the public in Alabama, in accordance with a long standing business practice.
> "The Times or its wholly owned advertising subsidiary, on several occasions, had agents in Alabama for substantial periods of time soliciting, and procuring in substantial amounts advertising to appear in The Times.
> "Furthermore, upon the receipt of the letter from the plaintiff demanding a retraction of the matter appearing in the advertisement, The Times had its string correspondent in Montgomery, Mr. McKee, investigate the truthfulness of the assertions in the advertisement. The fact that Mr. McKee was not devoting his full time to the service of The Times is 'without constitutional significance.' Scripto, Inc. v. Carson, Sheriff, et al., 362 U.S. 207."

Moreover, the court below found (R. 1151):

> "In the present case the evidence shows that the publishing of advertisements was a substantial part of the business of The Times, and its newspapers were regularly sent into Alabama. Advertising was solicited in Alabama. Its correspondent McKee was called upon by The Times to investigate the truthfulness or falsity of the matters contained in the advertisement after the letter from the plaintiff. The acts therefore disclose not only certain general conditions with reference to newspaper publishing, but also specific acts directly connected with, and directly incident to the business of The Times done in Alabama."

The exhaustive findings of fact contained in the opinions of both Alabama courts are fully substantiated in the record, and are not challenged in the Times Brief. In a qualitative sense, the test of *International Shoe Co. v. Washington*, 326 U.S. 310, 319–320, these decisions below were clearly correct. The Times from 1956 through April, 1960, conducted an extensive and continuous course of business activity in Alabama. The annual revenue was over twice as great as the $42,000 which this Court found sufficient to establish adequate Florida contacts in *Scripto v. Carson*, 362 U.S. 207.

SUMMARY OF ARGUMENT

I.

The commercial advertisement in suit sought to, and did, portray criminal and rampant police state activity—an "unprecedented wave of terror"—resulting from students singing "My Country 'Tis of Thee" from the state capitol steps. This falsely alleged "wave of terror" against innocent persons was said to include expulsion from school; ringing of a college campus with truckloads of police armed with shotguns and tear gas; padlocking of the dining hall to starve protesting students into submission; and the arrest of Martin Luther King for loitering and speeding by those who had also bombed his home, assaulted his person and indicted him for perjury. The ad did not name respondent, but massive, terroristic and criminal acts of the police carry the sure meaning to the average, reasonably intelligent reader that the police activity is that of the police commissioner.

A. Alabama libel laws provided petitioner with the absolute defense of truth and with the privilege of fair comment. Petitioner did not plead or attempt to prove truth or fair comment. Its attorneys suggested in open court that the defamatory matter was not true and would not be believed, and that truth was not in issue. The Times itself, in a contemporaneous retraction for another person whom it considered to be "on a par" with respondent, admitted that the material in the ad was erroneous and misleading.

Alabama law provides for untruthful and unprivileged defamers an opportunity to retract and thereby to eliminate all damages except special. Though the Times retracted for another "on a par", it refused to do so for respondent.

The Times makes no claim that it was denied a fair and impartial trial of this libel action, and raises no question of procedural due process.

In these circumstances, no provision of the Constitution of the United States confers an absolute immunity to defame public officials. On the contrary, this Court has repeatedly held that libelous utterances are not protected by the Constitution. *Beauharnais v. Illinois*, 343 U.S. 250; *Near v. Minnesota*, 283 U.S. 697, 715; *Konigsberg v. State Bar of California*, 366 U.S. 36, 49–50; *Roth v. U.S.*, 354 U.S. 476, 483; *Chaplinsky v. New Hampshire*, 315 U.S. 568, 571–572; *Barr v. Matteo*, 360 U.S. 564; *Farmers Union v. WDAY, Inc.*, 360 U.S. 525; and *Pennekamp v. Florida*, 328 U.S. 331, 348–349. Historical commentary on "freedom of the press" accords. See, Thomas Jefferson to Abigail Adams in 1804; Thomas Jefferson's Second Inaugural Address (1805); Chafee, Book Review, 62 Harvard L. Rev. 891, 897, 898 (1949). Moreover, commercial advertisements are not constitutionally protected as speech and press. *Valentine v. Chrestensen*, 316 U.S. 52, 54; and *Breard v. City of Alexandria*, 341 U.S. 622, 643. Because such libelous utterances are not constitutionally protected speech, "it is unnecessary, either for us or for the state courts, to consider the issues behind the phrase 'clear and present danger.' " *Beauharnais v. Illinois*, 343 U.S. 250, 266.

B. It is fantasy for petitioner to argue that the ad which falsely charged respondent, as police commissioner, with responsibility for the criminal and rampant "unprecedented wave of terror" is "the daily dialogue of politics" and mere "political criticism" and "political expression." If the Times prevails, any false statement about any public official comes within this protected category. The absolute immunity would cover false statements that the Secretary of State had given military secrets to the enemy; that the Secretary of the Treasury had embezzled public funds; that the Governor of a state poisoned his wife; that the head of the public health service polluted water with germs; that the mayor and city council are corrupt; that named judges confer favorable opinions on the highest bidder; and that a police commissioner conducted activities so barbaric as to constitute a wave of terror.

C. Since the Times did not invoke Alabama defenses of truth, fair comment or privilege, the question of the constitutional adequacy of these defenses is entirely academic. Nevertheless, Alabama libel law conforms to constitutional standards which this Court has repeatedly set and to the libel laws of most states. "Only in a minority of states is a public critic of Government even qualifiedly privileged where his facts are wrong." *Barr v. Matteo*, 360 U.S. 564, 585 (dissenting opinion of Chief Justice Warren). The constitution has never required that states afford newspapers the privilege of leveling false and defamatory "facts" at persons simply because they hold public office. The great weight of American authority has rejected such a plea by newspapers. *Burt v. Advertiser Company*, 154 Mass. 238, 28 N. E. 1, 4 (opinion by Judge, later Mr. Justice Holmes); *Post Publishing Company v. Hallam*, 59 F. 530, 540 (6th Cir. 1893) (opinion by Judge, later Mr. Chief Justice Taft); *Washington Times Company v. Bonner*, 86 F. 2d 836, 842 (D. C. Cir. 1936); *Pennekamp v. Florida*, 328 U.S. 331, 348–349: "For such injuries, when the statements amount to defamation, a judge has such remedy in damages for libel as do other public servants."

D. Alabama's definition of libel *per se* as a false publication which tends to injure the person defamed in his reputation, which brings him into public contempt as a public official, or which charges him with a crime, is a familiar one and accords with that of most states. This Court approved it in *Beauharnais v. Illinois*, 343 U.S. 250, 257, n. 5, citing *Grant v. Reader's Digest*, 151 F. 2d 733, 735 (2d Cir. 1945), opinion by Judge Learned Hand; *Hogan v. New York Times*, 313 F. 2d 354, 355 (2d Cir. 1963). The presumption of general damages from libel *per se* is the majority rule throughout the country. *Developments in the Law—Defamation*, 69 Harvard L. Rev. 875 at 934 and 937; 3 *Restatement of Torts*, § 621, pp. 313–316.

E. In Alabama, as elsewhere, punitive damages and general damages, where there has been no retraction, are permitted, and the jury is given broad discretion in fixing the amount of the award. *Reynolds v. Pegler,* 123 F. Supp. 36, 38, affirmed 223 F. 2d 429 (2d Cir.), cert. den. 350 U.S. 846; *Faulk v. Aware, Inc.,* 231 N. Y. S. 2d 270; and *Beauharnais v. Illinois,* 343 U.S. 250, 266. In assessing punitive damages, the jury may properly consider the nature and degree of the offense, as well as the higher moral consideration that these damages may deter such illegal practices in the future. The award in this case is but a fraction of two recent libel awards in the *Faulk* case and by a Georgia Federal jury of more than three million dollars, with punitive damages alone of two and one-half million dollars and three million dollars respectively.

This Court has always considered itself barred by the Seventh Amendment of the Constitution from setting aside state and federal damage awards as inadequate or excessive. *Chicago, B. & Q. v. Chicago,* 166 U.S. 226, 242–243; *Fairmount Glass Works v. Cub Fork Coal Co.,* 287 U.S. 474; *Neese v. Southern Ry.,* 350 U.S. 77. Many other cases are cited in this brief.

There is no constitutional infirmity in Alabama procedure which preserves the jury's long-standing common law right to return a general verdict. *Statement of Mr. Justice Black and Mr. Justice Douglas,* 31 F. R. D. 617 at 618–619.

In setting punitive damages, the jury could properly contrast the judicial admissions of the Times' attorneys that the advertisement was false and the Times' retraction of the same matter for another person as misleading and erroneous, with the trial testimony of the secretary of the corporation that the advertisement was substantially correct with the exception of one incident described in the ad.

II.

It is patently frivolous for the Times to argue that no ordinary person of reasonable intelligence could read the advertisement in suit as referring to the Montgomery police commissioner. Certainly the jury is not required as a matter of law to hold that the ad is not of and concerning respondent. Its finding is entitled to all of the safeguards of the Seventh Amendment. *Gallick v. B. & O. R. Co.,* 372 U.S. 108; *Chicago B. & Q. R. Co. v. Chicago,* 166 U.S. 226 at 242–243; and *Fairmount Glass Works v. Cub Fork Coal Co.,* 287 U.S. 474. While the ad's reference is clear enough, the jury heard witnesses who associated respondent with its false allegations. *Hope v. Hearst Consolidated Publications,* 294 F. 2d 681 (2d Cir.), cert. denied 368 U.S. 956; *Chagnon v. Union Leader Corp.,* 103 N. H. 426, 174 A. 2d 825, 831–832, cert. denied 369 U.S. 830.

This Court in *Beauharnais v. Illinois,* 343 U.S. 250, and courts generally, have held that a plaintiff need not be named in a defamatory publication in order to have a cause of action for libel. *Cosgrove Studio, Inc. v. Pane,* 408 Pa. 314, 182 A. 2d 751, 753; *Hope v. Hearst Consolidated Publications,* supra; *Nieman-Marcus v. Lait,* 13 F. R. D. 311 (S. D. N. Y. 1952); *National Cancer Hospital v. Confidential, Inc..* 136 N. Y. S. 2d 921; *Weston v. Commercial Advertisers,* 184 N. Y. 479, 77 N. E. 660; *Bornmann v. Star Co.,* 174 N. Y. 212, 66 N. E. 723; *Chapa v. Abernethy* (Tex. Civ. App.), 175 S. W. 165; *Gross v. Cantor,* 270 N. Y. 93, 200 N. E. 592; *Fullerton v. Thompson,* 119 Minn. 136, 143 N. W. 260; *Children v. Shinn,* 168 Iowa 531, 150 N. W. 864; *Reilly v. Curtiss,* 53 N. J. 677, 84 A. 199; 3 *Restatement of Torts,* § 564 (c), p. 152; and *Developments in the Law—Defamation,* 69 Harvard L. Rev. 894 et seq.

III.

A. The courts below held that under Alabama practice the Times appeared generally in the action because it objected to jurisdiction of the subject matter as well as to jurisdiction of the person. This holding, which accords with the majority rule (25 A. L. R. 2d 835 and 31 A. L. R. 2d 258) is an adequate independent state ground as to jurisdiction over the Times which bars review of that question. *Herb v. Pitcairn,* 324 U.S. 117, 125–126; *Murdock v. Memphis,* 20 Wall. 590, 626; *Fox Film Corporation v. Muller,* 296 U.S. 207, 210; *Minnesota v. National Tea Company,* 309 U.S. 551, 556–557. A state court's interpretation of its own law is binding here. *Fox River Paper Company v. Railroad Commission,* 274 U.S. 651, 655; *Guaranty Trust Company v. Blodgett,* 287 U.S. 509, 513; *United Gas Pipeline Company v. Ideal Cement Company,* 369 U.S. 134.

B. Even if the Times had not made a general appearance in this case, effective service of process on a Times string correspondent residing in Alabama and on the Secretary of State of Alabama under a Substituted Service Statute, Title 7, § 199 (1), Alabama Code of 1940 as amended, is based on decisions of this Court so explicit as to leave no room for real controversy. Suit against the Times in Alabama accorded with traditional concepts of fairness and orderly administration of the laws. *International Shoe Company v. Washington,* 326 U.S. 310, 319; *McGee v. International Insurance Company,* 355 U.S. 220; *Scripto v. Carson,* 362 U.S. 207; *Travelers Health Association v. Virginia,* 339 U.S. 643. The Times maintained three resident string correspondents in Alabama, and, since 1956, carried on an extensive, systematic and continuous course of business activity there, including news gathering, solicitation of advertising and circulation of newspapers and other products. It performed all of the functions of a newspaper outlined in *Consolidated Cosmetics v. D. A. Publishing Company*, 186 F. 2d 906, 908 (7th Cir. 1951). Its business activity produced more than twice the revenue which Scripto derived from Florida (see *Scripto v. Carson*, 362 U.S. 207), and its regular employees combined their efforts with those of independent dealers to produce this result.

It would be manifestly unfair to make respondent bring his libel suit in New York instead of in his home state where the charges were likely to harm him most. See Justice Black's dissenting opinion in *Polizzi v. Cowles Magazines*, 345 U.S. 663, 667.

When other business corporations may be sued in a foreign jurisdiction, so may newspaper corporations on similar facts. This Court has refused newspaper corporations special immunity from laws applicable to businesses in general. *Mabee v. White Plains Publishing Co.*, 327 U.S. 178, 184 (Fair Labor Standards Act); *Associated Press v. N. L. R. B.*, 301 U.S. 103 (National Labor Relations Act); and *Lorain Journal Company v. United States*, 342 U.S. 143 (Antitrust laws).

ARGUMENT
I. The Constitution confers no absolute immunity to defame public officials

The New York Times, perhaps the nation's most influential newspaper, stooped to circulate a paid advertisement to 650,000 readers—an advertisement which libeled respondent with violent, inflammatory, and devastating language. The Times knew that the charges were uninvestigated and reckless in the extreme. It failed to retract for respondent with subsequent knowledge of the falsity of the material in the advertisement. Yet it retracted as misleading and erroneous the same defamatory matter for another "on a par."

Petitioner was unable to plead truth; or fair comment; or privilege. Alabama provides these classic defenses so that the press may be free within the rubric of its libel laws.[15] Since peti-

tioner did not invoke these Alabama defenses, its belated attack on their constitutional adequacy is hollow and entirely academic. Nevertheless, the Alabama law of libel conforms to constitutional standards which this Court has repeatedly set and to the libel laws of most states. "Only in a minority of states is a public critic of Government even qualifiedly privileged where his facts are wrong."[16] Moreover, "[t]he majority of American courts do not give a privilege to a communication of untrue facts, or to a comment based on them, even though due care was exercised in checking their accuracy."[17] *A fortiori* there is no such privilege where there was no check whatever. (See Aaronson, Redding and Bancroft testimony).

The Times' trial attorneys conceded that truth was not in issue; and made plain to the jury that the material was so patently false as to be unbelievable in the community. No defendant attempted to introduce testimony to substantiate the charges. The Times does not claim that it was denied a fair and impartial trial of the libel action. The petition raises no question of procedural due process.

> "This cause was tried in the courts of [the state] in accordance with regular court procedure applicable to such cases. The facts were submitted to a jury as provided by the constitution and laws of that State, and in harmony with the traditions of the people of this nation. Under these circumstances, no proper interpretation of the words 'due process of law' contained in the Fourteenth Amendment can justify the conclusion that appellant has been deprived of its property contrary to that 'due process.'"[18]

Libelous utterances have no constitutional protection The Times does not seek review of a federal question—substantial or otherwise. For libelous utterances have never been protected by the Federal Constitution. Throughout its entire history, this Court has never held that private damage suits for common law libel in state courts involved constitutional questions.[19] Respondent vigorously disputes the Times' assertion that this Court is wrong in its history (Brief, pp. 44–48), and that the constitutional pronouncements in those cases are

---

[15] Substantial truth in all material respects is a complete defense if specially pleaded. *Ferdon v. Dickens*, 161 Ala. 181, 49 So. 888; *Kirkpatrick v. Journal Publishing Company*, 210 Ala. 10, 97 So. 58; *Alabama Ride Company v. Vance*, 235 Ala. 263, 178 So. 438.
Privilege and fair comment, too, are defenses, if specially pleaded. *Ferdon v. Dickens*, supra; *W. T. Grant v. Smith*, 220 Ala. 377, 125 So. 393.
A retraction completely eliminates punitive damages. Title 7, Sections 913–917, Alabama Code (App. A. p. 67).

[16] Chief Justice Warren, dissenting in *Barr v. Matteo*, 360 U.S. 564, 585.
[17] *Developments in the Law—Defamation*, 69 Harvard L. Rev. 877, 927 (1956).
[18] *United Gas Public Service Company v. Texas*, 303 U.S. 123, 153, Black J. concurring.
[19] *Beauharnais v. Illinois*, 343 U.S. 250; *Near v. Minnesota*, 283 U.S. 697, 715; *Konigsberg v. State Bar of California*, 366 U.S. 36, 49–50; *Roth v. U.S.*, 354 U.S. 476, 483; *Chaplinsky v. New Hampshire*, 315 U.S. 568, 571–572.

mere "adjectives" and statements "made in passing" (Brief, p. 40). Respondent is confident that this Court meant what it said in *Roth v. U.S.*, 354 U.S. 476, 483, for example:

"In light of this history it is apparent that the unconditional phrasing of the First Amendment was not intended to protect every utterance. This phrasing did not prevent this Court from concluding that libelous utterances are not within the area of constitutionally protected speech (citation)."

Again in *Konigsberg* this Court pronounced that it "has consistently recognized [that] . . . certain forms of speech [have] been considered outside the scope of constitutional protection." 366 U.S. 36, 50, citing *Beauharnais* and *Roth*.

Moreover, commercial advertisements are not constitutionally protected as speech and press, since there is no real restraint on speech and press where commercial activity is involved. *Valentine v. Chrestensen*, 316 U.S. 52, 54; *Breard v. City of Alexandria*, 341 U.S. 622, 643.[20] The Times has termed the citation of these cases "frivolous" and "cynical" (Brief, pp. 31 and 57). But its analysis of *Valentine v. Chrestensen* is incomplete—the other side of the handbill protested a city department's refusal of wharfage facilities. And the Times itself classified the ad as a commercial one, and submitted it to the Advertising Acceptability Department and to the standards of censorship which that department is supposed to impose. The Times charged the regular commercial advertising rate of almost five thousand dollars, scarcely as "an important method of promoting some equality of practical enjoyment of the benefits the First Amendment was intended to secure" (Brief, p. 58).

This Court last term in *Abernathy v. Patterson*, 368 U.S. 986, declined to review a decision of the Court of Appeals, 295 F. 2d 452, 456–457, which had held this very publication unprotected constitutionally as a libelous utterance. The Court of Appeals stated that the only constitutional claim could be one relating to the conduct of the trial.

In 1804, Thomas Jefferson wrote to Abigail Adams, referring to his condemnation of the Sedition Act of 1798:

"Nor does the opinion of the unconstitutionality and consequent nullity of that law remove all restraint from the overwhelming torrent of slander which is confounding all vice and virtue, all truth and falsehood in the U.S. The power to do that is fully possessed by the several state legislatures. It was reserved to them, and was denied to the general government, by the constitution according to our construction of it. While we deny that Congress have a right to control the freedom of the press, we have ever asserted the right of the states, and their exclusive right, to do so."[21]

Again in his second inaugural address on March 4, 1805, Jefferson said:

"No inference is here intended that the laws provided by the States against false and defamatory publications should not be enforced; he who has time renders a service to public morals and public tranquility in reforming these abuses by the salutary coercions of the law; but the experiment is noted to prove that, since truth and reason have maintained their ground against false opinions in league with false facts, the press, confined to truth, needs no other legal restraint; the public judgment will correct false reasonings and opinions on a full hearing of all parties; and no other definite line can be drawn between the inestimable liberty of the press and its demoralizing licentiousness."[22]

A century and a quarter later, Justices Holmes and Brandeis joined Chief Justice Hughes, who spoke for the Court in *Near v. Minnesota*, 283 U.S. 697, 715:

"But it is recognized that punishment for the abuse of the liberty accorded to the press is essential to the protection of the public, and that the common law rules that subject the libeler to responsibility for the public offense, as well as for the private injury, are not abolished by the protection extended in our constitutions."

Twenty years thereafter, this Court upheld an Illinois criminal group libel statute which had been applied to one who had distributed a pamphlet charging that Negroes as a class were rapists, robbers, carriers of knives and guns, and users of marijuana. *Beauharnais v. Illinois*, 343 U.S. 250, 266:

"Libelous utterances, not being within the area of constitutionally protected speech, it is unnecessary, either for us or for the State courts, to consider the issues behind the phrase 'clear and present danger.'"

---

[20] Lower Federal court decisions accord. *Pollak v. Public Utilities Commission*, 191 F. 2d 450, 457 (D. C. Cir. 1951); *E. F. Drew & Co. v. Federal Trade Commission*, 235 F. 2d 735, 740 (2d Cir. 1956), cert. den. 352 U.S. 969.

[21] Quoted in *Dennis v. U.S.*, 341 U.S. 494, 522, n. 4, and in *Beauharnais v. Illinois*, 343 U.S. 250, 254, n. 4.

[22] I *Messages and Papers of the Presidents*, Joint Committee on Printing, 52nd Congress, pp. 366, 369 (1897).

Since *Beauharnais*, as the table contained in Appendix A of respondent's brief in opposition shows, this Court has declined to review forty-four libel cases coming from the state and federal courts. It has reviewed three. Two of them[23] resulted in a holding that certain lower echelon federal executive personnel had an absolute privilege. The third[24] held that a radio and television station, which gave equal time to all political candidates because of the dictates of § 315 of the Federal Communications Act, was absolutely immune, by virtue of the same act, from state libel suits growing out of any such broadcasts.

The Times and its powerful corporate newspaper friends obviously realize that history and precedent support the holding below that this libelous advertisement is not constitutionally protected. They assert, therefore, at least for themselves and others who conduct the business of mass communication, an absolute privilege to defame all public officials—even in paid advertisements; even when the defamation renders the classic defenses of truth, fair comment and privilege unavailable; even when there is no retraction to show good faith. They urge this Court to write such a fancied immunity into the constitution—at least for themselves, for they are silent on whether this new constitutional protection is to extend to ordinary speakers and writers. The obvious consequence of such a holding would be the confiscation of the rights of those defamed to assert their traditional causes of action for defamation in state courts.

The Times attempts to cloak this defamatory advertisement with constitutional respectability. The ad is called "the daily dialogue of politics" and mere "political criticism" and "political expression." Surely desperation leads the Times so to characterize a charge that respondent, as police commissioner, was responsible for the criminal and rampant "unprecedented wave of terror" which this ad sought to portray falsely.

If the Times prevails, then any statement about any public official becomes "the daily dialogue of politics," "political expression and criticism" and "a critique of attitude and method, a value judgment and opinion." The absolute immunity would cover false statements that the Secretary of State had given military secrets to the enemy; that the Secretary of the Treasury had embezzled public funds; that the Governor of a state poisoned his wife; that the head of the public health service polluted water with germs; that the mayor and city council are corrupt; that named judges confer favorable opinions on the highest bidder; and that a police commissioner conducted activities so barbaric as to constitute a wave of terror. If a state court indulges in "mere labels" without constitutional significance when it holds such utterances libelous, and if such defamatory statements about "public men" are to be protected as legitimate and socially useful speech, then the Times and its friends urge this Court to "convert the constitutional Bill of Rights into a suicide pact."[25]

Clearly, Congress and this Court did not find such a constitutional immunity, hence Section 315 and *Farmers Union v. WDAY*, 360 U.S. 525. The very reason for such Congressionally conferred immunity was the "widely recognized" existence of causes of action for libel by defamed candidates for public office "throughout the states" (360 U.S. 525 at 535). This Court found that Congress had given immunity because broadcasters would have too much difficulty determining whether a particular equal time broadcast was defamatory in terms of relevant state law. 360 U.S. 525 at 530. Surely this Court did not decide *WDAY* on an assumption that the Constitution already provided such immunity absent a "clear and present danger."

Beauharnais, 343 U.S. 250 at 266, disposes of petitioner's "clear and present danger" cases (pp. 13–15) involving criminal prosecutions for breach of peace, criminal syndicalism and contempt of court.[26] Indeed, the background of

---

[23] *Barr v. Matteo*, 360 U.S. 564; and *Howard v. Lyons*, 360 U.S. 593.

[24] *Farmers Union v. WDAY, Inc.*, 360 U.S. 525.

[25] Jackson, J. dissenting in *Terminiello v. Chicago*, 337 U.S. 1, 37.

The Times wrongly argues that Mr. Justice Frankfurter's caveat in *Beauharnais* was designed for such a purpose (Brief, p. 41). He examined the hypothetical dangers of permitting statutes which outlawed libels of political parties. Justice Frankfurter observed that such attempts would "raise quite different problems not now before us" (343 U.S. 250, 264), and it was in this context that he observed that the doctrine of fair comment would come into play "since political parties, like public men, are, as it were, public property." The case at bar, too, presents far different problems.

[26] *Cantwell v. Connecticut*, 310 U.S. 296; *DeJonge v. Oregon*, 299 U.S. 353; *Bridges v. California*, 314 U.S. 252; *Pennekamp v. Florida*, 328 U.S. 331; *Craig v. Harney*, 331 U.S. 367; *Wood v. Georgia*, 370 U.S. 375; *Edwards v. South Carolina*, 372 U.S. 229; *Terminiello v. Chicago*, 337 U.S. 1; *Whitney v. California*, 274 U.S. 357; *Stromberg v. California*, 283 U.S. 359. While *Cantwell* is cited by the Times for the proposition that political expression is not limited by any test of truth, it omits the more relevant observation just following:

"There are limits to the exercise of these liberties. The danger in these times from the coercive activities of those who in the delusion of racial or religious conceit would incite violence and breaches of the peace in order

one of them, *Pennekamp v. Florida*, 328 U.S. 331, 348–349, sharply distinguishes these cases from the one at bar. This Court told Pennekamp that even those hardy judges described by petitioner could bring private suits for defamation in state courts. "For such injuries, when the statements amount to defamation, a judge has such remedy in damages for libel as do other public servants."[27]

Pennekamp—editor of the Miami Herald—ignored this warning. Perhaps he assumed, as does the Times, that the official's remedy was "left at large," and that there was an absolute privilege to level not only fair but false and defamatory criticism at public officials. Pennekamp discovered that he was wrong, and that the remedy had been brought in tow, when his paper libeled a prosecuting attorney who recovered $100,000 in damages. *Miami Herald v. Brautigam* (Fla.), 127 So. 2d 718. Even though Pennekamp and his paper were able to plead fair comment and truth, and claimed the editorial expression as their own,[28] this Court declined to review despite the same First and Fourteenth Amendment arguments which the Times advances in its brief. 369 U.S. 821.

Two of this Court's greatest figures rejected a contention that newspapers should have an absolute privilege to defame public officials and a consequent absolute immunity from private libel suits. Mr. Justice, then Judge Holmes, in *Burt v. Advertiser Company*, 154 Mass. 238, 28 N. E. 1, 4, upholding a trial court charge to the jury that newspaper statements of fact, as distinguished from opinion, if false, were not privileged, said:

> "But what the interest of private citizens in public matters requires is freedom of discussion rather than of statement. Moreover, the statements about such matters which come before the courts are generally public statements, where the harm done by a falsehood is much greater than in the other case.
>
> "If one private citizen wrote to another that a high official had taken a bribe, no one would think good faith a sufficient answer to an

action. He stands no better, certainly, when he publishes his writing to the world through a newspaper, and the newspaper itself stands no better than the writer."

Mr. Chief Justice, then Judge Taft, upholding a similar trial court charge in *Post Publishing Company v. Hallam*, 59 F. 530, 540 (6th Cir., 1893), wrote:

> "[I]f the [absolute] privilege is to extend to cases like that at bar, then a man who offers himself as a candidate must submit uncomplainingly to the loss of his reputation, not with a single person or a small class of persons, but with every member of the public, whenever an untrue charge of disgraceful conduct is made against him, if only his accuser honestly believes the charge upon reasonable ground. We think that not only is such a sacrifice not required of everyone who consents to become a candidate for office, but that to sanction such a doctrine would do the public more harm than good."

Judge Taft rejected the argument, urged here by the Times and its newspaper friends, that the privilege of fair comment "extends to statement of fact as well as comment" when made by one "who has reasonable grounds for believing, and does believe, that [the public officer or candidate] has committed disgraceful acts affecting his fitness for the office he seeks" (59 F. 530 at 540).

Judge Taft's admonitions still obtain, as Chief Justice Warren observed, in the majority of the states which hold that a public critic of government "is not even qualifiedly privileged where his facts are wrong." *Barr v. Matteo*, 360 U.S. 564, 585. Alabama is in accord with the great weight of state and federal authority.[29]

A noted commentator, Professor Zechariah Chafee, an old and close friend of free speech and press, also disagrees with the Times' law and history:

> "Especially significant is the contemporaneous evidence that the phrase 'freedom of the press' was viewed against a background of familiar legal limitations which men of 1791 did not regard as objectionable, such as damage suits for libel. Many state constitutions of this time included guaranties of freedom of speech and press which have been treated as having approximately the same scope as the federal provisions. Some of these, as in Massachusetts, were absolute in terms, while others, as in New York, expressly imposed responsibility for the abuse of the right. The precise nature of the state constitutional language did not matter; the early interpretation was much the

---

to deprive others of their equal right to the exercise of their liberties, is emphasized by events familiar to all. These and other transgressions of those limits the states appropriately may punish" (at p. 310).

[27] Surely the Times does not assert seriously that this Court "left at large" what may amount to defamation and what remedy a public servant has (Brief, p. 41). He has the same remedy under the laws of his state that any other citizen has.

[28] In the Supreme Court of Alabama, the Times literally disavowed the advertisement as its utterance: "The ad was not written by anyone connected with The Times; it was not printed as a report of facts by The Times, nor as an editorial or other expression of the views of The Times" (Reply Brief, p. 12).

[29] See *Washington Times Company v. Bonner*, 86 F. 2d 836, 842 (D. C. Cir. 1936).

same. Not only were private libel suits allowed, but also punishments for criminal libel and for contempt of court. For instance, there were several Massachusetts convictions around 1800 for libels attacking the conduct of the legislature and of public officials. This evidence negatives the author's idea of a firmly established purpose to make all political discussion immune."[30]

The Times can cite no authority holding that the Federal Constitution grants it an absolute privilege to defame a public official.

The advertisement was libelous per se   The Times and its friends complain that the court below has held libelous *per se* a publication which is false, which tends to injure the person defamed in his reputation, which brings him into public contempt as an official, and which charges him with crime. Such a standard, they argue, is a common law concept of the most general and undefined nature. But this Court in *Beauharnais v. Illinois*, 343 U.S. 250, 257, n. 5, approved Judge Learned Hand's definition of libel in *Grant v. Reader's Digest*, 151 F. 2d 733, 735 (2d Cir. 1945), "in accordance with the usual rubric, as consisting of utterances which arose 'hatred, contempt, scorn, obloquy or shame,' and the like." Such a definition, this Court held, was a familiar—not a general and undefined—common law pronouncement.

The Times objects because the court decided the question of whether the publication was libelous *per se*. But the Times' contention opposes *Baker v. Warner*, 231 U.S. 588, 594. And see *Beauharnais*, 343 U.S. 250, 254:

> "Similarly, the action of the trial court in deciding as a matter of law the libelous character of the utterance, leaving to the jury only the question of publication, follows the settled rule in prosecutions for libel in Illinois and other States."

The Times complains because Alabama presumes general damages from a publication libelous *per se*, including the uncertain future damage of loss of job. This is the law generally.[31]

This publication charged a public official in devastating fashion with departing from all civilized standards of law and decency in the administration of his official duties. The correctness of the determination below that it is libelous *per se* is underscored by *Sweeney v. Schenectady Union Publishing Company*, 122 F. 2d 288, affirmed 316 U.S. 642. There a statement that a Congressman opposed a federal judicial appointment because of anti-Semitism was held libelous *per se* as a matter of law.

Very recently this same Court in *Hogan v. New York Times*, 313 F. 2d 354, 355 (2d Cir. 1963), observed that the Times did not even contest on appeal a district court holding that its news article describing a dice game raid of two policemen as a Keystone cop performance was "libelous per se as a matter of law."

Clearly the court below has correctly applied the Alabama common law of libel—law which accords in all relevant particulars with that of many other states.

Damages awarded by the jury may not be disturbed   The Times' objection that punitive damages in libel should not be imposed to deter the libeler and others like him from similar misconduct does not square with *Beauharnais*, 343 U.S. 250, 263. The Alabama test is precisely that of *Reynolds v. Pegler*, 123 F. Supp. 36, 38, affirmed 223 F. 2d 429 (2d Cir.), cert. den. 350 U.S. 846.[32] There the jury brought back one dollar compensatory damages and $175,000 in punitive damages.

In its argument that the size of this verdict impinges its constitutional rights, the Times has ignored a recent New York decision refusing to disturb a verdict of $3,500,000, of which the sum of $2,500,000 was punitive damages, against a publication and another for stating that plaintiff was linked to a Communist con-

---

[30] Chafee, Book Review, 62 Harvard L. Rev. 891, 897–898 (1949) (Footnotes omitted).

[31] Commentators precisely oppose the Times' view. See Note, *Exemplary Damages in the Law of Torts*, 70 Harvard L. Rev. 517, 531 (1957), where it was observed that a requirement of correlation between actual and punitive damages "fails to carry out the punitive function of exemplary damages, since it stresses the harm which actually results rather than the social undesirability of the defendant's behavior."

See, *Developments in the Law—Defamation*, 69 Harvard L. Rev. 875, at 934, et seq. And see ibid. at 937: "Because defamation is a tort likely to cause substantial harm of a type difficult to prove specifically, courts will allow a substantial recovery of general damages on a presumption of harm even though the plaintiff offers no proof of harm." See also 3 *Restatement of Torts*, § 621, pp. 313–316.

[32] "Punitive or exemplary damages are intended to act as a deterrent upon the libelor so that he will not repeat the offense, and to serve as a warning to others. They are intended as punishment for gross misbehavior *for the good of the public* and have been referred to as a 'sort of hybrid between a display of ethical indignation and the imposition of a criminal fine.' *Punitive damages are allowed on the ground of public policy and not because the plaintiff has suffered any monetary damages for which he is entitled to reimbursement; the award goes to him simply because it is assessed in his particular suit.* The damages may be considered expressive of the community attitude towards one who wilfully and wantonly causes hurt or injury to another" (Emphasis supplied; footnotes omitted).

spiracy. *Faulk v. Aware, Inc.*, 231 N. Y. S. 2d 270, 281:

> "In libel suits, of course, punitive damages have always been permitted in the discretion of the jury. The assessment of a penalty involves not only consideration of the nature and degree of the offense but the higher moral consideration that it may serve as a deterrent to anti-social practices where the public welfare is involved. The jury, representing the community, assesses such a penalty as, in its view, is adequate to stop the practices of defendants and others having similar designs."

The New York Times did not condemn the *Faulk* verdict—seven times as great as the one at bar—as heralding the demise of a free press. Instead, the Times applauded the verdict as "having a healthy effect."[33]

Quite recently a Federal jury returned a libel verdict of $3,060,000 in favor of a former college athletic director who was charged with rigging a football game. The specified punitive damages were $3,000,000, even higher than those in the *Faulk* case.[34]

Another commentator has observed that in England "the survival of honorific values and standards of communal decency keep defamation at a minimum and subject it, when it raises its head, to staggering jury verdicts." Riesman, *Democracy and Defamation*, 42 Columbia L. Rev. 727, 730.

It is appropriate here to remind this Court that it has always considered itself barred by the Seventh Amendment from setting aside state and federal jury damage awards as inadequate or excessive. *Chicago, B. & Q. v. Chicago*, 166 U.S. 226, 242–243 ($1 verdict in condemnation proceeding); *Fairmount Glass Works v. Cub Fork Coal Co.*, 287 U.S. 474 (and cases cited); *St. Louis, etc., Ry. Co. v. Craft*, 237 U.S. 648; *Maxwell v. Dow*, 176 U.S. 581, 598; *Southern Ry. v. Bennett*, 233 U.S. 80, 87; *Herencia v. Guzman*, 219 U.S. 44, 45; *Eastman Kodak v. Southern Photo Materials*, 273 U.S. 359; *L. & N. v. Holloway*, 246 U.S. 525; cf. *Neese v. Southern Ry.*, 350 U.S. 77. See also, *Justices v. U.S. ex rel. Murray*, 9 Wall. 274, said by this Court to be one of many cases showing "the uniform course of decision by this Court for over a hundred years in recognizing the legal autonomy of state and federal governments." *Knapp v. Schweitzer*, 357 U.S. 371, 378–379.

In an attempt to avoid this precedent, the Times first cites a series of cases which hold statutory penalties subject to judicial review as excessive—cases obviously having nothing to do with appellate review of jury verdicts.[35]

Next the Times urges that respondent's cases permit appellate review of excessive jury damage awards as errors of law (Brief, p. 69). But the cases themselves are otherwise. They cite, as examples of errors of law, awards which exceed the statutory limits; or are less than the undisputed amount; or are pursuant to erroneous instructions on measure of damages; or are in clear contravention of instructions of the court. *Fairmount Glass Works v. Cub Fork Coal Company*, 287 U.S. 474, 483–484. Another case, *Chicago, B. & Q. RR. v. Chicago*, 166 U.S. 226, 246, holds instead:

> "We are permitted only to inquire whether the trial court prescribed any rule of law for the guidance of the jury that was in absolute disregard of the company's right to just compensation."

Another case, *Dimick v. Schiedt*, 293 U.S. 474, did not hold that the question of excessive or inadequate verdicts was one of law, but on the contrary that it was "a question of fact." 293 U.S. 474 at 486. And *A. & G. Stevedores v. Ellerman Lines*, 369 U.S. 355, 360, cited by the Times, stated that the Seventh Amendment "fashions 'the federal policy favoring jury decisions of disputed fact questions'."

The Times then argues that this Court may review the amount of damages because alleged abridgment of freedom of the press must take precedence over the Seventh Amendment (Brief, p. 69). It cites no authority for this amazing argument—one which scarcely accords with this Court's observation in *Jacob v. City of New York*, 315 U.S. 752 and 753:

> "The right of jury trial in civil cases at common law is a basic and fundamental feature of our system of federal jurisprudence which is protected by the Seventh Amendment. A right so fundamental and sacred to the citizen, whether guaranteed by the Constitution or provided by statute, should be jealously guarded by the courts."

The Times quickly moves on to an argument almost as tenuous, namely, that modern authority "regards the Seventh Amendment as inappli-

---

[33] Editorial of June 30, 1962, p. 18.
[34] *New York Times*, August 21, 1963, p. 1.

---

[35] *Life & Casualty Co. v. McCray*, 291 U.S. 566; *Chicago and N. W. Ry. v. Nye Schneider Fowler Company*, 260 U.S. 35; *Mo. Pac. Ry. Co. v. Tucker*, 230 U.S. 340; *St. Louis, etc. Ry. v. Williams*, 251 U.S. 63. The other case cited for this purpose is a criminal case dealing with the Sixth Amendment. *Robinson v. California*, 370 U.S. 660 (Brief, p. 68).

cable generally to appellate review of an excessive verdict . . ." (Brief, p. 69). The premise clashes with *Neese v. Southern Ry.*, 350 U.S. 77, as well as with such cases as *Fairmount, supra,* 287 U.S. 474, 481:

> "The rule that this Court will not review the action of a federal trial court in granting or denying a motion for a new trial for error of fact has been settled by a long and unbroken line of decisions; and has been frequently applied where the ground of the motion was that the damages awarded by the jury were excessive or were inadequate." (Footnotes omitted.)

Finally, the Times complains that there was constitutional infirmity in the failure of the Alabama court to permit special interrogatories to the jury on damages, and thereby to deprive the jury of its right to return a general verdict.[36] Surely there is no constitutional defect in Alabama's adherence to the common law general verdict so recently eulogized by Justices Black and Douglas when they condemned an extension of the practice of submitting special interrogatories to federal juries:

> "Such devices are used to impair or wholly take away the power of a jury to render a general verdict. One of the ancient, fundamental reasons for having general jury verdicts was to preserve the right of trial by jury as an indispensable part of a free government. Many of the most famous constitutional controversies in England revolved around litigants' insistence, particularly in seditious libel cases, that a jury had the right to render a general verdict without being compelled to return a number of subsidiary findings to support its general verdict. Some English jurors had to go to jail because they insisted upon their right to render general verdicts over the repeated commands of tyrannical judges not to do so."[37]

Accordingly, a review of the damages awarded by the jury in this case is beyond the powers of this Court. Moreover, the verdict, as the court below held, conforms to the general damages suffered by the respondent and to the wrong which the Times committed. The Times does not claim here that the jury was motivated by passion or prejudice or corruption or any improper motive. Two state courts have found that it was not.

The jury was no doubt struck by the amazing lack of concern and contrition exhibited by the Times' representatives at the trial, and it certainly contrasted their conduct. The Times' attorneys did not plead truth; did not attempt to introduce evidence of truth; suggested in cross-examination of respondent's witnesses that the matter was untrue and would not be believed; stated in open court that truth was not in issue; and could not plead fair comment or privilege. The Times retracted the same matter as erroneous and misleading for another person whom it considered to be "on a par" with respondent. But the secretary of the corporation, who had signed its answers to interrogatories, said that with the exception of the padlocking incident he believed the matters in the ad were not substantially incorrect.

Even more recently the conduct of the Times' business has warranted judicial condemnation. *Hogan v. New York Times*, 313 F. 2d 354, 355–356 (2d Cir. 1963):

> "We believe that sufficient evidence existed to sustain the jury verdict on either of the two possible grounds upon which its decision that defendant abused its qualified privilege might have been based: (1) improper purpose in publishing the article, or (2) reckless disregard for the truth or falsity of the story, amounting to bad faith."

The Times had its chance to retract and eliminate punitive damages, but chose not to do so for this respondent though it retracted for another person "on a par." A restriction of respondent to special damages would compound the evils described by Mr. Chafee in the following statement which he quoted with approval:

> " 'To require proof of special damages would mean virtual abolition of legal responsibility for inadvertent newspaper libel. Newspaper slips are usually the result of reprehensible conduct of members of the defendant's organization. To deny plaintiffs recovery for retracted libel unless they prove special damages, is to do away with newspapers' financial interest in accuracy. The tendency towards flamboyance and haste in modern journalism should be checked rather than countenanced. If newspapers could atone legally for their mistakes merely by publishing corrections, the number of mistakes might increase alarmingly. . . .' "[38]

---

[36] *Johnson Pub. Co. v. Davis*, 271 Ala. 474, 496, 124 So. 2d 441; *All States Life Ins. Co. v. Jaudon*, 230 Ala. 593, 162 So. 668; *Little v. Sugg*, 243 Ala. 196, 8 So. 2d 866; *Spry v. Pruitt*, 256 Ala. 341, 54 So. 2d 701.

[37] Statement of Mr. Justice Black and Mr. Justice Douglas on the Rules of Civil Procedure and the Proposed Amendments, 31 F. R. D. 617, at 618–619.

[38] Quoted in Chafee, *Possible New Remedies for Errors in the Press.* 60 Harvard L. Rev., 1, 23.

II. There is no ground for reviewing a jury determination that the advertisement was "of and concerning" the Plaintiff

The Times' assertion that this Court should decide as a matter of constitutional law that the jury which tried this case was wrong in finding that the advertisement was "of and concerning" respondent is astounding. Respondent will not repeat here the thorough discussion of the testimony analyzing the false allegations of the ad and their reference to respondent as police commissioner of Montgomery. Apparently a reading of this testimony has now impressed even the Times. It has omitted from its brief on the merits the cases of *Thompson v. Louisville*, 362 U.S. 199, and *Garner v. Louisiana*, 368 U.S. 157, cited in its petition for certiorari for the proposition that there was no evidence to support the verdict.

Again the Times seeks to overturn imbedded constitutional principles. This case has been tried in a state court according to admittedly proper court procedure, and a jury has decided the facts. This Court simply does not go behind these factual determinations and review a state court judgment, entered on a jury verdict and affirmed by the highest state appellate court. *Chicago, B. & Q. R. Co. v. Chicago*, 166 U.S. 226 at 242–243; *United Gas Public Service Co. v. Texas*, 303 U.S. 123, 152–153 (Black, J., concurring); *Fairmount Glass Works v. Cub Fork Coal Co.*, 287 U.S. 474; *Maxwell v. Dow*, 176 U.S. 581, 598.[39]

When this Court in *Gallick v. B. & O. R. Co.*, 372 U.S. 108, 9 L. Ed. 2d 618, 627, held that its duty was to reconcile state jury findings "by exegesis if necessary," it surely assigned no lesser place to the Seventh Amendment than that described by Justices Black and Douglas:

"The call for the true application of the Seventh Amendment is not to words, but to the spirit of honest desire to see that constitutional right preserved. Either the judge or the jury must decide facts and to the extent that we take this responsibility, we lessen the jury function. Our duty to preserve this one of the Bill of Rights may be peculiarly difficult, for here it is our own power which we must restrain."[40]

Similar principles permeated the judicial philosophy of Judge Learned Hand:

"And so only the most unusual circumstances could justify judicial veto of a legislative act . . . or a jury verdict. Hand's standard for intervention was essentially the same in both cases. It came simply to this: if there was room for doubt, legislation—like a verdict—must stand, however, mistaken it might seem to judges. Ambivalence in the law was the province of jury and legislature—the two authentic voices of the people. Judicial intervention was permissible only when a court was prepared to hold that **no** reasonable mind could have found as the legislature or jury did find."[41]

Regarding falsity, the statements in the ad have been discussed exhaustively in this brief. The Times was unable to plead truth; and conceded falsity before the trial by its retraction to Governor Patterson and at the trial through the statements of its attorneys. It is surely paradoxical for the Times to assert in this Court that the record is so "devoid" of evidence of falsity as to invoke the certiorari jurisdiction of this Court. Nothing could be more idle than to debate with the Times and its friends the question of whether Alabama imposes the burden of proving truth on the wrong party, when the Times by its judicial admissions has conceded falsity.[42]

Moreover, this record reveals this ad's devastating effect on respondent's reputation among those who believed it. Courts have easily and effectively dealt with the Times' argument that the publication was not libelous or injurious because it was not believed in the community (Brief, p. 65).[43] Perhaps the Times would also argue that those in a crowded theater who did

---

[39] The Times seeks to circumvent these cases—and the 7th Amendment—by citing inapposite cases dealing with review here of state court conclusions as to a federal right where facts inadequately support the conclusion. *Norris v. Alabama*, 294 U.S. 587; *Wood v. Georgia*, 370 U.S. 375; *Craig v. Harney*, 331 U.S. 367; *Pennekamp v. Florida*, 328 U.S. 331; *Bridges v. California*, 314 U.S. 252; *Edwards v. South Carolina*, 372 U.S. 229—cases involving state court (not jury) determinations of questions of discrimination in the selection of a grand jury, and of the existence of a clear and present danger; *Watts v. Indiana*, 338 U.S. 49—a state court determination as to a coerced confession; *Herndon v. Lowry*, 301 U.S. 242—a case invalidating a conviction because the criminal statute prescribed "no reasonably ascertainable standard of guilt" (at 264); and *Fiske v. Kansas*, 274 U.S. 380— overturning a conviction under a criminal syndicalism act where the prosecution had introduced no evidence other than a preamble of the constitution of the Industrial Workers of the World which this Court found to be no evidence to support the conviction.

[40] *Galloway v. United States*, 319 U.S. 372, 407 (Black, Douglas and Murphy, JJ., dissenting).
[41] Mendelson, *Learned Hand: Patient Democrat*, 76 Harvard L. Rev. 322, 323–324 (1962).
[42] Completely inapposite, therefore, are the Times' citations of *Speiser v. Randall*, 357 U.S. 513 and *Bantam Books, Inc. v. Sullivan*, 372 U.S. 58, regarding inadequate state procedures where the speech or writing itself may be limited.
[43] See e.g. *Reynolds v. Pegler*, 123 F. Supp. 36, 37–38, affirmed 223 F. 2d 429 (2d Cir.), cert. denied 350 U.S. 846:
" 'A person may be of such high character that the grossest libel would damage him none; but that would be no reason for withdrawing his case from the wholesome, if not necessary, rule in respect of punitive damages . . .'

not see or smell smoke would not believe a person who yelled "fire".

It is patently frivolous for the Times to argue that no ordinary person of reasonable intelligence[44] could possibly read this advertisement as referring to the Montgomery police commissioner. Nor is a jury bound by the Federal Constitution to take the Times' construction of these words after its attorneys have completed a sanitizing operation in an attempt to dull the cutting edges of these words.[45]

Beauharnais v. Illinois, 343 U.S. 250, teaches that a libel plaintiff need not be named in the defamatory publication. There the criminal prosecution was for defamation of the entire Negro race.[46]

It is difficult to believe that the Times is serious when it argues that this record is entirely devoid of evidence to support the jury finding that these defamatory words were of and concerning respondent.

The ad sought to, and did, portray criminal and rampant police state activity resulting from the singing of "My Country, 'Tis of Thee" from the State Capitol steps. It sought to portray, and did, a resultant "wave of terror" against innocent persons—expulsion from school; ringing of the campus of Alabama State College with truckloads of police armed with shotguns and tear gas; and padlocking of the dining hall to starve protesting students into submission. And the ad returned to Montgomery in the second quoted paragraph to charge that pursuant to the same "wave of terror", those who had arrested King for loitering and speeding also had bombed his home, assaulted his person, and indicted him for perjury.[47]

The effect of this publication was as deadly as intended—to instill in the minds of the readers the conclusion that these acts had been perpetrated by Montgomery city officials, specifically the police commissioner. The Times can suggest no one else except the police, whose massive acts in the public mind are surely the work of the commissioner. The connotation is irresistible—certainly not, as the Times argues, completely devoid of rationality.

Moreover, the jury heard witnesses who made the association. *Hope v. Hearst Consolidated Publications*, 294 F. 2d 681 (2d Cir.), cert. denied 368 U.S. 956; *Chagnon v. Union Leader Corp.*, 103 N. H. 426, 174 A. 2d 825, 831–832, cert. denied 369 U.S. 830.

Respondent sued as a member of a group comprising three city commissioners. Libel suits by members of private or public groups of this size are widely permitted. The decision below accords with the law generally.[48]

III. This case provides no occasion for excursions from this record and from accepted constitutional standards.

In a desperate effort to secure review in this Court, the Times and its friends go outside the record and refer this Court to other libel suits pending in Alabama. With the exception of two brought by the other Montgomery commissioners, all are erroneously and uncandidly labeled "companion cases".[49]

To adopt the contrary view ... would mean that a defamer gains a measure of immunity no matter how venomous or malicious his attack simply because of the excellent reputation of the defamed; it would mean that the defamer, motivated by actual malice, becomes the beneficiary of that unassailable reputation and so escapes punishment. It would require punitive damages to be determined in inverse ratio to the reputation of the one defamed."

[44] This is the test everywhere. See *Albert Miller & Co. v. Corte*, 107 F. 2d 432, 435 (5th Cir. 1939), which holds that Alabama cases to this effect accord with libel law generally. See also *Peck v. Tribune Co.*, 214 U.S. 185 (where the wrong person was named); *Grant v. Reader's Digest*, 151 F. 2d 733 (2d Cir. 1945); *Spanel v. Pegler*, 160 F. 2d 619 (7th Cir. 1949); 3 *Restatement of Torts*, § 580, Comments (b) and (c), pp. 205–207.

[45] Authorities in Footnote 44.

[46] See also *Cosgrove Studio, Inc. v. Pane*, 408 Pa. 314, 182 A. 2d 751, 753:

"The fact that the plaintiff is not specifically named in the advertisement is not controlling. A party defamed need not be specifically named, if pointed to by description or circumstances tending to identify him...."

[47] Even Gershon Aaronson of the Times so read "they" as used in this paragraph of the advertisement (R. 745).

[48] *Hope v. Hearst Consolidated Publications*, 294 F. 2d 681 (2d Cir.), cert. denied 368 U.S. 956 (One of Palm Beach's richest men caught his blonde wife in a compromising spot with a former FBI agent); *Nieman-Marcus v. Lait*, 13 F. R. D. 311 (S. D. N. Y. 1952) (immoral acts attributed to department store's 9 models and 25 salesmen); *National Cancer Hospital v. Confidential, Inc.*, 136 N. Y. S. 2d 921 (libelous article about "hospital" gave cause of action to those who conducted hospital); *Weston v. Commercial Advertisers*, 184 N. Y. 479, 77 N. E. 660 (4 coroners); *Bornmann v. Star Co.*, 174 N. Y. 212, 66 N. E. 723 (charges about a hospital stall with 12 doctors in residence); *Chapa v. Abernethy* (Tex. Civ. App.), 175 S. W. 165 (charges about a posse); *Gross v. Cantor*, 270 N. Y. 93, 200 N. E. 592 (12 radio editors); *Fullerton v. Thompson*, 119 Minn. 136, 143 N. W. 260 (State Board of Medical Examiners, of which there were 9); *Children v. Shinn*, 168 Iowa 531, 150 N. W. 864 (Board of Supervisors); *Reilly v. Curtiss*, 53 N. J. 677, 84 A. 199 (an election board).
Commentators have agreed. See 3 *Restatement of Torts*, Sec. 564 (c), p. 152:
"[A] statement that all members of a school board or a city council are corrupt is sufficiently definite to constitute a defamatory publication of each member thereof." And see *Developments in the Law—Defamation*, 69 Harvard L. Rev. 894, et seq.

[49] Times' petition for certiorari, p. 19. Even the Times does not follow the reckless averment of its friends that this suit is part of an "attempt by officials in Alabama to invoke the libel laws against all those who had the

But the effort is as revealing as it is desperate. Clearly, petitioner feels that this case, standing on its own, does not present grounds for review.

These cases are not yet tried. There are different plaintiffs; different defendants; different publications; different communications media; different forums; different attorneys; different issues;[50] no final judgment in any; and a trial on the merits in only one of them. The Times urges this Court to jettison libel laws that have existed since the founding of this Republic, and hold: (a) there is an absolute privilege to defame public officials, at least those living in Alabama; (b) private libel suits for defamation are available to all citizens of the United States in state courts according to state libel laws, but not to persons who happen to hold public office in Alabama; (c) plaintiffs in those cited cases shall be deprived of their rights to have their libel cases heard on their merits.

The Times seems to hint to this Court that because the publication contained statements regarding racial tensions, the law of libel should perforce "confront and be subordinated to" a constitutional privilege to defame.[51] Surely in a field so tense, truthful statements by huge and influential newspapers are imperative. For as this Court said in *Beauharnais*, 343 U.S. 250 at 262:

> "Only those lacking responsible humility will have a confident solution for problems as intractable as the frictions attributable to differences of race, color or religion."

The confrontation which the jury hoped to achieve was the confrontation of the Times with the truth.

The enormity of petitioner's wrong is clear. Hopefully the decision below will impel adherence by this immensely powerful newspaper to high standards of responsible journalism commensurate with its size.

> "A free press is vital to a democratic society because its freedom gives it power. Power in a democracy implies responsibility in its exercise. No institution in a democracy, either governmental or private, can have absolute power. Nor can the limits of power which enforce responsibility be finally determined by the limited power itself. (Citation.) In plain

English, freedom carries with it responsibility even for the press; freedom of the press is not a freedom from responsibility for its exercise. Most State constitutions expressly provide for liability for abuse of the press's freedom. That there was such legal liability was so taken for granted by the framers of the First Amendment that it was not spelled out. Responsibility for its abuse was imbedded in the law. The First Amendment safeguarded the right."[52]

These freedoms are amply protected when a newspaper in a state court can plead and prove truth; can plead and prove fair comment; and can plead and prove privilege. Even when it cannot, it can retract, show its good faith, and eliminate punitive damages. Alabama thus provides the very safeguards which, the Times and its friends argue, are essential to protect petitioner's constitutional rights.

When it can do none of these, and when it has indeed defamed in a commercial advertisement, no constitutional right, privilege or immunity expounded by this Court during its entire history shields a newspaper from damages in a common law libel suit.

The Times and its cohorts would have this Court abandon basic constitutional standards which have heretofore obtained and which Justice Harlan recently described:

> "No member of this Court would disagree that the validity of state action claimed to infringe rights assured by the Fourteenth Amendment is to be judged by the same basic constitutional standards whether or not racial problems are involved."[53]

IV. The Times was properly before the Alabama courts.

1. Because both courts below held that the Times had made a general appearance,[54] an adequate independent state ground as to jurisdiction over the Times in this suit is a bar to review here. *Herb v. Pitcairn*, 324 U.S. 117, 125–126; *Murdock v. Memphis*, 20 Wall. 590, 626; *Fox Film Corporation v. Muller*, 296 U.S. 207, 210; *Minnesota v. National Tea Company*, 309 U.S. 551, 556–557.

---

temerity to criticize Alabama's conduct in the intense racial conflict" (Brief of Washington Post, p. 8).

[50] For example, the Times retracted for Patterson, but not for respondent. Obviously, the Times, while guilty of clear inconsistency, has nevertheless in Patterson's case sought to eliminate punitive damages by retraction, as permitted by Alabama statute.

[51] Times petition, p. 20 and *amici* briefs generally.

---

[52] Frankfurter J., concurring in *Pennekamp v. Florida*, 328 U.S. 331, 355–356 (Footnotes omitted).

[53] *NAACP v. Button*, 371 U.S. 415, 9 L. Ed. 2d 405, 427 (dissenting opinion of Harlan, Clark and Stewart, J. J.).

[54] A state court's interpretation of its own case law is binding here. *Fox River Paper Company v. Railroad Commission*, 274 U.S. 651, 655; *Guaranty Trust Company v. Blodgett*, 287 U.S. 509, 513; *United Gas Pipeline Company v. Ideal Cement Company*, 369 U.S. 134.

Texas, for example, long provided that any appearance at all was a general appearance. *York v. Texas*, 137 U.S. 15, 20.

The Times intended to assert, and did, that the trial court was without jurisdiction of the subject matter of this action. Indeed, the Times still argues in this Court that there was no jurisdiction of the subject matter (Brief, p. 63). This act, alone, is a general appearance in Alabama and in a majority of state courts. In addition, the Times compounded its general appearance by other activities in the Alabama courts unrelated to the claimed lack of personal jurisdiction.

Petitioner argues that the Alabama Supreme Court has incorrectly interpreted its own decisions, and that the decision below is in error. This is obviously the wrong forum for such an argument.[55]

But even if an examination of state law were appropriate, the court below followed its earlier cases. Alabama has held, as have other states, that there is a clear distinction between jurisdiction of the person and subject matter. *Constantine v. Constantine*, 261 Ala. 40, 42, 72 So. 2d 831. A party's appearance in a suit for any purpose other than to contest the court's jurisdiction over the person is a general appearance.[56]

The Alabama cases cited by the Times do not conflict with the decisions below. One case holds that a request for extension of time to file pleadings is not a general appearance;[57] another recognized that defendant might have converted a special appearance into a general appearance, but held that even so a circuit court had authority to set aside a default judgment within thirty days, and denied an extraordinary writ;[58] a third involved a limited attack on "the court jurisdiction over the person of defendant;"[59] one did not even consider the question, since apparently neither the trial judge nor the parties had noticed it;[60] one discussed the

proper way to plead misnomer;[61] and in the last two the defendants conceded jurisdiction of the person.[62]

Moreover, there is nothing novel about the Alabama holding of general appearance. This Court in such cases as *Western Loan & Savings Company v. Butte, etc. Mining Company*, 210 U.S. 368, 370 and *Davis v. Davis*, 305 U.S. 32, 42, as well as leading text writers,[63] and the majority of the jurisdictions of this country have recognized the binding effect of this rule.[64]

Petitioner argues that the general appearance ground is an untenable non-federal one. Its cases simply do not support its contention. No novel state procedure, of which a party could not fairly be deemed to have been apprised, thwarted all means of raising a federal question.[65] Nor is the Alabama rule—in accord with the majority one—an "arid ritual of meaningless form."[66] Clearly beside the point is a case where an admitted special appearance by a party, an officer appointed to run the railroads for the federal government, was not deemed by the state court to be a special appearance for his successor.[67]

Nor do petitioner's cases (pp. 76–77) support the contention that even if there had been jurisdiction by consent because of the general appearance, the commerce clause forbids its exercise. These cases simply hold that a carrier must be given an opportunity to make a seasonable objection to court jurisdiction, and cannot

---

[55] See Footnote 54.

[56] *Kyser v. American Surety Company*, 213 Ala. 614, 616, 105 So. 689; *Blankenship v. Blankenship*, 263 Ala. 297, 303, 82 So. 2d 335; *Thompson v. Wilson*, 224 Ala. 299–300, 140 So. 439; *Aetna Insurance Company v. Earnest*, 215 Ala. 557, 112 So. 145. And see *Vaughan v. Vaughan*, 267 Ala. 117, 121, 100 So. 2d 1:
"[R]espondent . . . by not limiting her appearance and by including non-jurisdictional as well as jurisdictional grounds in her motion to vacate has made a general appearance and has thereby waived any defect or insufficiency of service."

[57] *Ex Parte Cullinan*, 224 Ala. 263, 139 So. 255.

[58] *Ex Parte Haisten*, 227 Ala. 183, 149 So. 213.

[59] *St. Mary's Oil Engine Company v. Jackson Ice & Fuel Company*, 224 Ala. 152, 155, 138 So. 834. See also *Sessoms Grocery Co. v. International Sugar Feed Co.*, 188 Ala. 232; *Terminal Oil Mill Co. v. Planters, etc. Co.*, 197 Ala. 429; and *Dozier Lumber Co. v. Smith-Isberg Lumber Co.*, 145 Ala. 317, also cited by the Times.

[60] *Harrub v. Hy-Trous Corp.*, 249 Ala. 414, 31 So. 2d 567.

[61] *Ex Parte Textile Workers*, 249 Ala. 136, 142, 30 So. 2d 247.

[62] *Seaboard Ry. v. Hubbard*, 142 Ala. 546, and *Johnson Publishing Co. v. Davis*, 271 Ala. 474, 124 So. 2d 441.

[63] *Restatement of Conflict*, § 82, Comment (b); and Kurland, *The Supreme Court, The Due Process Clause and The In Personam Jurisdiction of State Courts*, 25 U. of Chicago L. Rev. 569, 575:
"The mere appearance of a defendant in a lawsuit for a purpose other than to attack the jurisdiction of the court over him is considered a voluntary submission to the court's power."

[64] 25 A. L. R. 2d 835, 838 and 31 A. L. R. 2d 258, 265. New York itself prior to statutory amendment, held in *Jackson v. National Grain Mutual Liability Company*, 299 N. Y. 333, 87 N. E. 2d 283, 285:
"Under its special appearance, the defendant company could do nothing but challenge the jurisdiction of the Justice's court over its person . . . (citation). Hence by its attempt to deny jurisdiction of the subject of the action, the company waived that special appearance and submitted its person to the jurisdiction of the court."
Civil Practice Act, § 273 (a), was necessary to enable a litigant to combine in New York an attack on jurisdiction of the person and of the subject matter without appearing generally in the action. *Ray v. Fairfax County Trust Company*, 186 N. Y. S. 2d 347.

[65] *NAACP v. Alabama*, 357 U.S. 449, and *Wright v. Georgia*, 373 U.S. 284.

[66] *Staub v. City of Baxley*, 355 U.S. 313, 320.

[67] *Davis v. Wechsler*, 263 U.S. 22.

be deprived of doing so by state machinery making a special appearance a general one. Cf. *York v. Texas*, 137 U.S. 15, 20. Alabama does permit a special appearance, and does not prevent a "seasonable motion." But when a foreign corporation makes, instead, a general appearance, the commerce clause does not bar the exercise of court jurisdiction by consent.

Davis v. O'Hara, 266 U.S. 314, 318, discussed by the Times (Brief, pp. 74–75) involved Nebraska, not Alabama law, and held that under Nebraska practice a special appearance was not required to object to jurisdiction over the person.

2. Even if the Times had not made a general appearance in this case, effective service of process is based on decisions of this Court so explicit as to leave no room for real controversy. The Times, having already argued that this Court should cast aside its many decisions permitting libel suits against newspapers, now asks this Court to cast aside its cases permitting tort actions against foreign corporations in states where those corporations do business. In short, the Times seeks absolute immunity on the merits, and jurisdictional immunity from suit outside New York state.

The crucial test is simple. Did the Times have sufficient business contacts with Alabama so that suit against it there accorded with traditional concepts of fairness and orderly administration of the laws? *International Shoe Company v. Washington*, 326 U.S. 310, 319. The court below, and indeed the trial court, after painstaking analysis of the jurisdictional facts of record, held that there were sufficient contacts. The qualitative functions of a newspaper outlined in *Consolidated Cosmetics v. DA Publishing Company*, 186 F. 2d 906, 908 (7th Cir. 1951), were carried on in Alabama.

The Times plainly maintained an extensive and continuous pattern of business activity in Alabama at least since 1956. The resident string correspondents and staff correspondents, who repeatedly came into Alabama, were a unique and valuable complement to the news gathering facilities of the Associated Press and United Press and other wire services upon which smaller newspapers rely. Such widespread news gathering facilities unquestionably increase the scope and detail of the Times' news columns, and enhance, accordingly, its prestige, its circulation, and the prices which it can command in the advertising market. In turn, these far-flung news gathering tentacles subject the Times to potential suit in the states into which they reach. If financial reward comes to the Times from its on-the-spot news coverage in Alabama, it is fair that citizens of Alabama should be able to sue the Times here when it has wronged them.

Scoffing at the quantitative size of its business activities in Alabama, the Times apparently ignored the most recent pronouncement of this Court in *Scripto v. Carson*, 362 U.S. 207, cited by the courts below. *Scripto* derived less than half of the revenue from Florida which the Times has derived from Alabama—and regular employees of the Times have combined their efforts with those of independent dealers to produce this result.

The Times attempts to distinguish *Scripto* by the inaccurate observation that "no issue of judicial jurisdiction was involved" (Brief p. 85). But this Court's opinion in *Scripto* stated that the Florida courts had "held that appellant does have sufficient jurisdictional contacts in Florida [to be made a collector of use tax] . . . We agree with the result reached by Florida's courts" (362 U.S. 207, 208). While the Times would argue that due process standards for jurisdiction to sue are stricter than those for jurisdiction to make a tax collector out of a foreign corporation, objective commentators have not agreed. The due process clause "might well be deemed to impose more stringent limitations on collection requirements than on personal jurisdiction".[68]

One contract negotiated entirely by mail with a predecessor company gave California sufficient contact with a successor insurance company. A default judgment against it was upheld. *McGee v. International Insurance Company*, 355 U.S. 220.[69] Mail transactions alone enabled a Virginia Securities Commission to regulate an out-of-state insurance company. *Travelers Health Association v. Virginia*, 339 U.S. 643. And this Court, as noted in the decision below, commented upon more enlightened concepts resulting in expanded scope of state jurisdiction over foreign corporations. *McGee v. International Insurance Company*, 355 U.S. 220, 222–223. Moreover, state activity through the means of independent contractors, as distinguished from agents or employees, is without

---

[68] *Developments in the Law—Federal Limitations on State Taxation of Interstate Business*, 75 Harvard L. Rev. 953, 998 (1962).

[69] Noteworthy is the fact that the foreign corporation held amenable to California process had never solicited or done any insurance business in California apart from the policy involved. The "continuing legal relationship" on the basis of which the Times attempts to distinguish *McGee* (Brief, p. 84) could not possibly consist of more than transmission of premiums by mail. Such "continuing legal relationship" scarcely compares with the vastly more extensive and continuing relationship which the Times maintained with Alabama according to evidence going back to 1956.

constitutional significance. *Scripto v. Carson*, 362 U.S. 207, 211. The Times does not cite *Scripto* on this point, but it is nevertheless the law.

A recent decision, interpreting Alabama's Substituted Service Statute, *Callagaz v. Calhoon*, 309 F. 2d 248, 256 (5th Cir. 1962) observed:

> "Since [*Travelers Health* and *McGee*] it is established that correspondence alone may establish sufficient contacts with a state to subject a non-resident to a suit in that state on a cause of action arising out of those contacts."

Justice Black's dissenting opinion in *Polizzi v. Cowles Magazines*, 345 U.S. 663, 667, considered a magazine publisher subject to Florida libel suit, under old or new concepts, when its only contact there was two circulation road men who checked retail outlets in a multi-state area which included Florida. Presumably no reporting or advertising solicitation was carried on. Mr. Justice Black's opinion, which has been widely quoted as expressive of the prevailing view, found it manifestly unfair to make the plaintiff "bring his libel suit in a federal district court in the corporation's home state of Iowa . . . [and not] in a federal court in the state where Polizzi lived and where the criminal charges were likely to do him the most harm" (345 U.S. 663 at 668).

Obviously the case at bar does not present an instance of "forum shopping" such as was faced by Judge Hand in *Kilpatrick v. T. & P. Ry. Co.*, 166 F. 2d 788 (2d Cir. 1948). The court's remarks (quoted Brief, p. 81) were directed to a Texas plaintiff, injured in Texas, who had brought his suit in New York. Even so, the district court was reversed for dismissing the plaintiff's action.

McKee, an Alabama resident, conducted all of the usual activities of a stringer for the New York Times. In addition, he performed the delicate task, to which he "naturally" fell heir, of investigating respondent's demand for retraction. The Times was efficaciously brought into court by service on McKee. It is inconceivable, for example, that if while helping Harrison Salisbury obtain material for his Alabama stories, Don McKee had run an automobile into a plaintiff, the Times could have escaped liability by maintaining that McKee was an independent contractor.

Similarly substituted service under the Alabama statute[70] was valid. Alabama business activity of the Times preceded and followed the printing of this libelous material in New York. The ad itself was supposedly cleared on the basis of prior news gathering; it was later sent into Alabama by the Times, with a carrier as its agent, freight prepaid, with title passing on delivery to the consignee. Thence the issue went to newsstands for sale to the Alabama public, in accordance with the longstanding business practice of the Times.[71]

Scripto v. Carson, 362 U.S. 207, lays to rest the significance of any contention that sales to the public in Alabama were through the medium of independent contractors. It is not necessary for this Court to reach the question of whether isolated newsstand sales, disconnected from any other business activity in Alabama, would be a sufficient contact to sustain substituted service. This is not the case. For the Times has also solicited advertising and gathered news in a systematic and continuous fashion, and has thereby established a firm business connection with Alabama.[72]

Due process and the commerce clause do not immunize the Times from Alabama suit.

As *Polizzi* makes clear, newspapers are not to be in a special category. When other corporations may be sued in a foreign jurisdiction, so may they on similar facts. Newspaper corporations are no more entitled to the favored position which the Times and its friends would accord them than they are entitled to many other preferences for which they have unsuccessfully argued. In *Mabee v. White Plains Publishing Co.*, 327 U.S. 178, 184, this Court held: "As the press has business aspects, it has no special immunity from laws applicable to business in general." This case concerned the appli-

---

[70] Title 7, § 199 (1), Code of Alabama.

[71] If the cases cited by the Times (Brief, pp. 79–80) are supposed to conflict with the decision below, they conflict also with the decisions of this Court cited in this section of respondent's brief and by the court below. They conflict, too, with such cases as *Paulos v. Best Securities, Inc.* (Minn.), 109 N. W. 2d 576; *WSAZ v. Lyons*, 254 F. 2d 242 (6th Cir. 1958); *Gray v. American Radiator Corporation*, 22 Ill. 2d 432, 176 N. E. 2d 761; *Sanders Associates, Inc. v. Galion Iron Works*, 304 F. 2d 915 (1st Cir. 1962); *Beck v. Spindler* (Minn.), 99 N. W. 2d 670; and *Smyth v. Twin State Improvement Corporation*, 116 Vt. 569, 80 A. 2d 664. Moreover, the court in *Insull v. New York World-Telegram*, 273 F. 2d 166, 169 (7th Cir. 1959), indicated that its result would have been different if the newspaper "employ[ed] or ha[d] any reporters, advertising solicitors or other persons who are located in Illinois . . ."

[72] A remarkably similar case is *WSAZ v. Lyons*, 254 F. 2d 242 (6th Cir. 1958), cited by the courts below. There the court upheld a Kentucky libel judgment against a foreign television station which had beamed the libelous television matter into Kentucky from outside the state. Service was had under a Kentucky statute covering causes of action "arising out of" or "connected" with the doing of business by foreign corporations in Kentucky. The court cited *McGee* and *International Shoe*. Moreover, it held irrelevant the fact that Kentucky produced only 1.03 per cent of the total annual advertising revenue.

cability of the Fair Labor Standards Act to newspapers. This Court has likewise held newspaper corporations subject to the National Labor Relations Act, *Associated Press v. N. L. R. B.*, 301 U.S. 103 and to the anti-trust laws, *Lorain Journal Company v. United States*, 342 U.S. 143.

Hanson v. Denckla, 357 U.S. 235, relied upon by the Times as contrary to the decisions below, is easily distinguishable. As this Court pointed out, there was no solicitation of business in Florida by the foreign corporation, either in person or by mail. In the case at bar the Times solicited business in both manners. The cause of action in *Hanson v. Denckla* did not arise out of an act done or transaction consummated in the forum. On the contrary, this cause of action arose out of the very distribution of the newspapers by the Times in Alabama. Surely the Times cannot contend that its introduction of these newspapers in Alabama was involuntary.[73] The foreign corporation in *Hanson v. Denckla* had received no benefit from the laws of the forum. The manifold business activities of the Times—news gathering, solicitation of advertising and distribution—have received the protection of Alabama laws.

Finally (Brief, pp. 86–88) the Times suggests that even though it might be amenable to suit in Alabama under due process standards, the commerce clause nevertheless bars the Alabama action. The most recent decision of this Court cited in support of this proposition was handed down in 1932. It seems scarcely necessary to observe that this Court, which has developed enlightened standards giving expanded scope to jurisdiction over foreign corporations in such cases as *International Shoe*, *McGee*, *Travelers Health* and *Scripto* will not grant review to turn the clock back to 1932, and invoke the rigid concepts of earlier days under the aegis of the commerce clause. And the Times must concede that this Court has not "hitherto" held that tort actions against foreign corporations—fairly subject to *in personam* jurisdiction—are unconstitutional as undue burdens on interstate commerce (Brief, p. 87).

Accordingly, even without a general appearance, the Times would have presented no unsettled federal question of jurisdiction for review by this Court on certiorari.

CONCLUSION

For the foregoing reasons it is respectfully submitted that the writ of certiorari should be dismissed as improvidently granted; in the alternative, respondent respectfully submits that this case should be affirmed.

Respectfully submitted,
ROBERT E. STEINER, III,
SAM RICE BAKER,
M. ROLAND NACHMAN, JR.,
Attorneys for Respondent.
STEINER, CRUM & BAKER,
CALVIN WHITESELL,
Of Counsel.

CERTIFICATE

I, M. Roland Nachman, Jr., of Counsel for Respondent, and a member of the bar of this Court, hereby certify that I have mailed copies of the foregoing Brief and of respondent's Brief in No. 40, Abernathy v. Sullivan, air mail, postage prepaid, to Messrs. Lord, Day & Lord, Counsel for petitioner, at their offices at 25 Broadway, New York, New York. I also certify that I have mailed a copy of the foregoing Brief, air mail, postage prepaid, to Edward S. Greenbaum, Esquire, 285 Madison Avenue, New York, New York, as attorney for American Civil Liberties Union and the New York Civil Liberties Union, as *amici curiae*; to Messrs. Kirkland, Ellis, Hodson, Chaffetz & Masters, attorneys for The Tribune Company, as *amicus curiae*, at their offices at 130 East Randolph Drive, Chicago 1, Illinois; and to William P. Rogers, Esquire, attorney for The Washington Post Company, as *amicus curiae*, at his office at 200 Park Avenue, New York 17, New York.

This . . . day of October, 1963.

. . . .

M. Roland Nachman, Jr.,
Of Counsel for Respondent.

APPENDIX A

Title 7, Section 909 of the Code of Alabama:

"TRUTH OF THE WORDS, ETC., EVIDENCE UNDER THE GENERAL ISSUE.—In all actions of slander or libel, the truth of the words spoken or written, or the circumstances under which they were spoken or written, may be given in evidence under the general issue in mitigation of the damages."

Truth specially pleaded is an absolute bar to a civil libel action, *Webb v. Gray*, 181 Ala. 408, 62 So. 194; *Ripps v. Herrington*, 241 Ala. 209, 212, 1 So. 2d 899; *Johnson Publishing Co. v. Davis*, 271 Ala. 474, 124 So. 2d 441.

Title 7, Section 910 of the Code of Alabama:

"LIBEL OR SLANDER; DEFAMATORY MATTER.—In an action for libel or slander, it shall be suffi-

---

[73] But compare Times Brief, p. 81.

cient to state, generally, that the defamatory matter was published or spoken of the plaintiff; and if the allegation be denied, the plaintiff must prove, on the trial, the facts showing that the defamatory matter was published or spoken of him."

Title 7, Section 913 of the Code of Alabama:

"Retraction Mitigates Damages.—The defendant in an action of slander or libel may prove under the general issue in mitigation of damages that the charge was made by mistake or through inadvertence, and that he has retracted the charge and offered amends before suit by publishing an apology in a newspaper when the charge had been thus promulgated, in a prominent position; or verbally, in the presence of witnesses, when the accusation was verbal or written, and had offered to certify the same in writing."

Title 7, Section 914 of the Code of Alabama:

"Aggrieved Person Must Give Notice to Publishers of Alleged Libel Before Vindictive Damages Can Be Recovered.—Vindictive or punitive damages shall not be recovered in any action for libel on account of any publication concerning the official conduct or actions of any public officer, or for the publication of any matter which is proper for public information, unless five days before the bringing of the suit the plaintiff shall have made written demand upon the defendant for a public retraction of the charge or matter published; and the defendant shall have failed or refused to publish within five days in as prominent and public a place or manner as the charge or matter

published occupied, a full and fair retraction of such charge or matter."

Title 7, Section 915 of the Code of Alabama:

"When Actual Damages Only Recoverable.— If it shall appear on the trial of an action for libel that an article complained of was published in good faith, that its falsity was due to mistake and misapprehension, and that a full correction or retraction of any false statement therein was published in the next regular issue of said newspaper, or in case of daily newspapers, within five days after service of said notice aforesaid, in as conspicuous a place and type in said newspaper as was the article complained of, then the plaintiff in such case shall recover only actual damages."

Title 7, Section 916 of the Code of Alabama:

"Recantation and Tender; Effect of.—If the Defendant, after or before suit brought, make the recantation and amends recited in the preceding sections, and also tender to the plaintiff a compensation in money, and bring the same into court, the plaintiff can recover no costs, if the jury believe and find the tender was sufficient."

Title 7, Section 917 of the Code of Alabama:

"Effect of Tender Received.—The receipt of the money tendered, if before suit brought, is a bar to the action; if after suit, releases the defendant from all damages and costs, except the costs which accrued before the tender and receipt of the money."

IN THE
SUPREME COURT OF THE UNITED STATES
OCTOBER TERM, 1963

No. 40

RALPH D. ABERNATHY,

FRED L. SHUTTLESWORTH,

S. S. SEAY, SR., AND

J. F. LOWERY, PETITIONERS,

V.

L. B. SULLIVAN, RESPONDENT

ON WRIT OF CERTIORARI TO THE SUPREME COURT OF ALABAMA

BRIEF FOR THE PETITIONERS

HARRY H. WACHTEL,
SAMUEL R. PIERCE, JR.,
JOSEPH B. RUSSELL,
DAVID N. BRAININ,
STEPHEN J. JELIN,
CLARENCE B. JONES,
DAVID G. LUBELL,
CHARLES B. MARKHAM,
WACHTEL & MICHAELSON,
BATTLE, FOWLER, STOKES & KHEEL,
LUBELL, LUBELL & JONES,

Of Counsel.

I. H. WACHTEL,
CHARLES S. CONLEY,
BENJAMIN SPIEGEL,
RAYMOND S. HARRIS,

Attorneys for Petitioners.
1100 - 17th St., N.W.
Washington, D.C. 20036

INDEX
—»·•·«—

IN THE
SUPREME COURT OF THE
UNITED STATES
OCTOBER TERM, 1963
NO. 40

RALPH D. ABERNATHY,
FRED L. SHUTTLESWORTH,
S. S. SEAY, SR., AND
J. F. LOWERY, PETITIONERS,

V.

L. B. SULLIVAN, RESPONDENT

ON WRIT OF CERTIORARI TO THE
SUPREME COURT OF ALABAMA

BRIEF FOR THE PETITIONERS

Petitioners Abernathy, Shuttlesworth, Seay, and Lowery submit this brief for reversal of the judgment of the Supreme Court of Alabama entered on August 30, 1962, which affirmed a $500,000 libel judgment for punitive damages entered on November 3, 1960 in the Circuit Court of Montgomery County, Alabama against petitioners and The New York Times Company, their co-defendant, in a suit for alleged libel, based on an advertisement (R. 6, 1925; reproduced in Appendix A *infra*, p. 63) printed in The New York Times on March 29, 1960, appealing for contributions to aid the civil rights movement in the South.

OPINIONS BELOW

The Trial Court (Circuit Court of Montgomery County) did not write an opinion. Its judgment is printed at R. 862. The Opinion of the Alabama Supreme Court (R. 1139) affirming said judgment is reported at 273 Ala. 656.

JURISDICTION

The judgment of the Supreme Court of Alabama was entered on August 30, 1962 (R. 1180). The petition for writ of certiorari was filed on November 21, 1962 and was granted on January 7, 1963, 371 U.S. 946 (R. 1194). The jurisdiction of this Court rests upon 28 U. S. C. § 1257(3).[1]

[1] By letter of the Clerk of this Court dated August 9, 1963, the time of petitioners to file this brief has been extended to September 9, 1963.

QUESTIONS PRESENTED[2]

1. May the State of Alabama, under the guise of civil libel prosecutions, suppress criticism of the political conduct of unnamed public officials, consistently with the guaranteed freedoms of speech, press, assembly and association of the First and Fourteenth Amendments?
2. Were petitioners' rights to due process of law, as guaranteed by the Fourteenth Amendment, violated by a $500,000 punitive judgment against them upon a record devoid of evidence of authorization, consent, publication or malice on their part or of pecuniary damage to respondent?
3. Does the rule of law adopted by the State of Alabama below, requiring total strangers to the challenged publication, to procure and study it and, under pain of $500,000 punitive damages, "retract" any claimed libel therein, impose an arbitrary and onerous burden which unconstitutionally infringes petitioners' rights under the First and Fourteenth Amendments?
4. Were the rights of Negro petitioners to equal protection, due process of law and fair and impartial trial under the Fourteenth Amendment violated by the trial of the suit brought against them by a white public official of Montgomery (i) in a segregated Courtroom, rife with racial bias and community hostility, (ii) before an all-white jury (from which Negro citizens were intentionally and systematically excluded), and (iii) before a trial judge, not properly qualified, who has stated from the Bench that the Fourteenth Amendment is inapplicable in Alabama Courts, which are governed by "white man's justice"?[3]

[2] Influenced by the landmark decisions of this Court in the "sit in" cases (n. 6, *infra*), *NAACP* v. *Button*, 371 U.S. 415 and *Johnson* v. *Virginia*, 373 U.S. 61 among others, and the historic events which have taken place since the filing of the petition for writ of certiorari herein on November 21, 1962, petitioners have in this brief consolidated the five questions there presented to this Court so as to focus their argument on the all-pervasive issue of the impingement on and serious threat to their First and Fourteenth Amendment rights.
[3] Judge Jones *On Courtroom Segregation*, 22 The Alabama Lawyer, No. 2, pp. 190–192 (1961), which reprints "Statement made from the Bench of the Circuit Court of Montgomery County, February 1, 1961, . . ." during the trial of the related libel action by Mayor Earl James of Montgomery against The New York Times Company and the four Negro petitioners herein. On March 17, 1961, Judge Jones entered his order denying the new trial application herein (R. 970).

CONSTITUTIONAL AND STATUTORY PROVISIONS INVOLVED

The Constitutional provisions involved are the First, Fourteenth and Fifteenth Amendments to the United States Constitution which are set forth in Appendix B, *infra*, pp. 65–66.

The Statutes involved are Title 7, Sections 913–16 of the Code of Alabama (i.e., the Alabama "Retraction" Statute) and Title 14, Sections 347 and 350 thereof (i.e., the Alabama "Criminal Libel" Statute) which read as follows:

Title 7, Section 913 of the Code of Alabama:

"RETRACTION MITIGATES DAMAGES.—The defendant in an action of slander or libel may prove under the general issue in mitigation of damages that the charge was made by mistake or through inadvertence, and that he has retracted the charge and offered amends before suit by publishing an apology in a newspaper when the charge had been thus promulgated, in a prominent position; or verbally, in the presence of witnesses, when the accusation was verbal or written, and had offered to certify the same in writing."

Title 7, Section 914 of the Code of Alabama:

"AGGRIEVED PERSON MUST GIVE NOTICE TO PUBLISHERS OF ALLEGED LIBEL BEFORE VINDICTIVE DAMAGES CAN BE RECOVERED.—Vindictive or punitive damages shall not be recovered in any action for libel on account of any publication concerning the official conduct or actions of any public officer, or for the publication of any matter which is proper for public information, unless five days before the bringing of the suit the plaintiff shall have made written demand upon the defendant for a public retraction of the charge or matter published; and the defendant shall have failed or refused to publish within five days in as prominent and public a place or manner as the charge or matter published occupied, a full and fair retraction of such charge or matter."

Title 7, Section 915 of the Code of Alabama:

"WHEN ACTUAL DAMAGES ONLY RECOVERABLE.—If it shall appear on the trial of an action for libel that an article complained of was published in good faith, that its falsity was due to mistake and misapprehension, and that a full correction or retraction of any false statement therein was published in the next regular issue of said newspaper, or in case of daily newspapers, within five days after service of said notice aforesaid, in as conspicuous a place and type in said newspaper as was the article complained of, then the plaintiff in such case shall recover only actual damages."

Title 7, Section 916 of the Code of Alabama:

"RECANTATION AND TENDER; EFFECT OF.—If the defendant, after or before suit brought, make the recantation and amends recited in the preceding sections, and also tender to the plaintiff a compensation in money, and bring the same into court, the plaintiff can recover no costs, if the jury believe and find the tender was sufficient."

Title 14, Section 347 of the Code of Alabama:

"LIBEL.—Any person who publishes a libel of another which may tend to provoke a breach of the peace, shall be punished, on conviction, by fine and imprisonment in the county jail, or hard labor for the county; the fine not to exceed in any case five hundred dollars, and the imprisonment or hard labor not to exceed six months."

* * * * * * *

Title 14, Section 350 of the Code of Alabama:

"DEFAMATION.—Any person who writes, prints, or speaks of and concerning any woman, falsely imputing to her a want of chastity; and any person who speaks, writes, or prints of and concerning another any accusation falsely and maliciously importing the commission by such person of a felony, or any other indictable offense involving moral turpitude, shall, on conviction, be punished by fine not exceeding five hundred dollars, and imprisonment in the county jail, or sentenced to hard labor for the county, not exceeding six months; one or both, at the discretion of the jury.

STATEMENT

Numerous recent decisions of this Court[4] have focused sharply on the intense nationwide efforts to secure the constitutional rights of Negroes, and on the numerous unconstitutional acts committed in various Southern states to frustrate these efforts. The four petitioners herein are Negro ministers (resident in Alabama at all relevant times) and religious and spiritual leaders of the movement to secure civil rights in Alabama and throughout the South.

1. The nature of the publication

To enlist public support and raise funds for the legal defense of Dr. Martin Luther King, Jr.

---

[4] *United States* v. *Alabama*, 373 U.S. 545; *United States* v. *Barnett*, 373 U.S. 920; *NAACP* v. *Alabama*, 357 U.S. 449; *Louisiana ex rel. Gremillion* v. *NAACP*, 366 U.S. 293; *Fair* v. *Meredith*, 305 F. 2d 341 (C. A. 5), cert. den., 371 U.S. 828; *Brown* v. *Board of Education*, 347 U.S. 483; *Holmes* v. *City of Atlanta*, 350 U.S. 879; *Cooper* v. *Aaron*, 358 U.S. 1; *Morgan* v. *Virginia*, 328 U.S. 373.

(who shortly before had been indicted in Alabama for perjury)[5], and in aid of the nonviolent demonstrations against racial segregation, a New York group called "The Committee to Defend Martin Luther King and the Struggle for Freedom in the South" ("Committee" hereinafter), with which petitioners had no connection, caused to be printed and published in The New York Times ("*The Times*" hereinafter) on March 29, 1960, an advertisement entitled: "Heed Their Rising Voices" (R. 0; Pl. Ex. 347 at R. 1925, reproduced in full in Appendix "A" p. 63, *infra*). The advertisement commented on the activities of *unnamed* governmental authorities, in cities in a number of Southern states, designed to stifle the then-current protest demonstrations[6] against segregation by students in various Southern institutions (including Alabama State College at Montgomery). In commenting on such activities, the advertisement used the broad, generic term "Southern violators of the Constitution".

The ad referred to the harassments to which Rev. King had been subjected, including arrests, imprisonment, the bombings of his home, and the then-pending perjury indictment, and concluded with an appeal for contributions to be sent to the Committee's office in New York in support of Dr. King's defense, the desegregation movement, and the voter registration drive in the South.

Under the text of the appeal appeared the names of some sixty eminent sponsors (including Mrs. Eleanor Roosevelt, Drs. Harry Emerson Fosdick, Mordecai Johnson, Alan Knight Chalmers and Algernon Black, and Messrs. Raymond Pace Alexander, Elmer Rice and Norman Thomas).

Below the list of sponsors appeared the caption "We in the south who are struggling daily for dignity and freedom warmly endorse this appeal", under which caption were printed the names of eighteen (18) ministers from various Southern states, including the four petitioners.

The appeal concludes with the following plea for funds:

---

[5] Dr. King was later acquitted of this charge (R. 680).
[6] See Pollitt, *Dime Store Demonstrations: Events and Legal Problems of First 60 days*, Duke L. J. 315 (Summer, 1960), describing in detail (at 323–325) repressive acts and statements of Alabama public officials.
This Court has already reversed as unconstitutional a number of such repressive actions of officials of various Southern States including Alabama. *Shuttlesworth* v. *City of Birmingham*, 373 U.S. 262; *Gober* v. *City of Birmingham*, 373 U.S. 374; *Peterson* v. *City of Greenville*, 373 U.S. 244; *Garner* v. *Louisiana*, 368 U.S. 157; *Lombard* v. *Louisiana*, 373 U.S. 267.

"We must extend ourselves above and beyond moral support and render the material help so urgently needed by those who are taking the risks, facing jail, and even death in a glorious re-affirmation of our Constitution and its Bill of Rights.

"We urge you to join hands with our fellow Americans in the South by supporting, with your dollars, this Combined Appeal for all three needs—the defense of Martin Luther King—the support of the embattled students—and the struggle for the right-to-vote."

2. The evidence concerning publication

The undisputed record facts demonstrate that the names of petitioners were added to the advertisement without consultation with them and without their authorization or consent (R. 788–90; 792–4; 797–8; 801–2; 806–10; 824–5; 1175). Indeed, the record is clear that their first knowledge of *The Times* ad came when they received in the mail respondent Sullivan's identical letters which had been posted on or about April 8, 1960, and which were admittedly misdated "March 8, 1960" (Pl. Exs. 355–8, R. 1962–7). Moreover, these letters did not contain a copy of the ad, but merely quoted out of context the two paragraphs on which Sullivan based his complaint, and demanded that each petitioner "publish in as prominent and public a manner" as *The Times* ad, "a full and fair retraction of the entire false and defamatory matter . . ." (R. 1962–8). Petitioners could not possibly comply with this demand; and, before they could consult counsel or even receive appropriate advice in regard thereto, suit was instituted by respondent on April 19, 1960 (R. 789; 793; 798; 801–3).

The undisputed record facts further show a complete lack of connection between petitioners and the publication of the advertisement. The typescript was submitted to *The Times* by one John Murray (R. 732), with a space order from The Union Advertising Service (R. 736). Names of sponsors (the Committee) were typed at the foot (R. 739). Accompanying (or submitted shortly following) the typescript was a letter, signed by A. Philip Randolph, (R. 739, 756–757) purporting to authorize the use of the names of the "signed members of the Committee" as sponsors (R. 1992). It is not disputed that petitioners' names did not appear on the manuscript as submitted (R. 806–7). Petitioners' names were subsequently placed on the advertisement by one Bayard Rustin, on his own motion, without any consultation with petitioners as shown by the undisputed evidence (R. 808–810) and the findings of the Court below (R. 1174–5). No representative of *The Times* ever asked petitioners whether they had consented to this use of their names (R. 754–5, 770, 790, 793, 797–8, 802).

None of the petitioners saw the *full text* of the advertisement prior to the commencement on April 19, 1960 of respondent Sullivan's suit (R. 789, 793, 798, 801); petitioners' first notice of *The Times* ad (and only of the language complained of) came from Sullivan's aforementioned misdated letters mailed on or about April 8, 1960 (R. 789, 793, 798, 802). Petitioners each wholly denied any knowledge of the ad prior to its publication, any consent to the use of their names and any responsibility for its publication (R. 788–90, 792–4, 795, 797–8, 801–2). Respondent in no way disputed these record facts which are confirmed in the opinion of the Court below (R. 1174–5).

3. The alleged libel

The Times ad in suit, without identifying or naming any particular individual or fixing any particular time period, refers to various incidents of claimed repression in numerous cities throughout the South, commencing with "Orangeburg, South Carolina" and continuing on to "Montgomery, Alabama" and "Tallahassee, Atlanta, Nashville, Savannah, Greensboro, Charlotte and a host of other cities in the South. . . ."

On October 5, 1959, respondent Sullivan became one of the City Commissioners of Montgomery, Alabama (R. 694). Nowhere in *The Times* ad in suit was respondent Sullivan or any other southern official referred to by name or office. Many of the repressive actions in Montgomery, referred to in the ad, occurred prior to Sullivan's term of office, as Sullivan himself admitted (R. 703–19).

The entire *gravamen* of Sullivan's complaint (which alleged no special damage but sought $500,000 as punitive damages) concerned the following two paragraphs of the advertisement (*i.e.*, the third and sixth), which were alleged to be defamatory:

"In Montgomery, Alabama, after students sang 'My Country, 'Tis of Thee' on the State Capitol steps, their leaders were expelled from school, and truckloads of police armed with shotguns and tear-gas ringed the Alabama State College Campus. When the entire student body protested to state authorities by refusing to re-register, their dining hall was padlocked in an attempt to starve them into submission."

* * * * * * *

"Again and again the Southern violators have answered Dr. King's peaceful protests with intimidation and violence. They have bombed his home almost killing his wife and child. They have assaulted his person. They have arrested him seven times—for 'speeding', 'loitering' and similar 'offenses'. And now they have charged him with 'perjury'—a *felony* under which they could imprison him for *ten years.*" (R. 2–4).

Although Sullivan's complaint (R. 2–3) and his letters to petitioner demanding retraction (R. 1962–7) suggest that the above quoted paragraphs followed one another in consecutive order in *The Times* ad in suit, the record fact is that the first paragraph quoted is separated from the second by two lengthy paragraphs comprising almost a complete column of the ad—one relating to events in numerous cities in Southern states other than Alabama, and the other lauding Dr. King as the "world famous leader of the Montgomery Bus Protest" and the symbol of "the new spirit now sweeping the South" (Pl. Ex. 347, R. 1923–6, reproduced in full in Appendix "A" hereto).

Moreover, Sullivan's entire claim of libel rests on the following minor discrepancy: whereas the ad said that "truckloads" of armed police "ringed the Alabama State College Campus," the fact was that "on three occasions they [police] were deployed near the Campus in large numbers" (R. 594).

Clearly no distinction of substance can validly be drawn between police "ringing" the campus and being "deployed near the campus in large numbers"—particularly in the context of comment and criticism of official conduct on this most vital public issue.

Further, the ad said that Dr. King was arrested "seven times". The testimony was that he was arrested three or four times in Montgomery, Alabama (three of which arrests admittedly occurred prior to the respondent's term of office) (R. 592, 594–5); but there is nothing in the text or context of the advertisement which either requires or permits the inference that the seven arrests occurred in Montgomery or anywhere else in Alabama. Other alleged inaccuracies in the ad were conceded by respondent Sullivan to refer to matters within the jurisdiction of the State Education Department or other agencies, and to matters occurring long prior to respondent's taking office (R. 684–5, 688, 694, 701, 716, 719, 725).

None of Sullivan's witnesses (four of whom first saw the ad when called to the office of plaintiff's counsel shortly before the trial to be prepared as witnesses) testified that they believed the ad, or that they thought any less of respondent by reason of its publication (R. 623, 625, 636, 638, 644, 647, 651, 667).

4. Biased trial and judgment

Alabama has enacted sweeping racial segregation laws,[7] which reflect the community hostilities and prejudices that were funneled into the Courtroom. Continuous denunciations of the defendants and of the material in the advertisement appeared in Montgomery newspapers prior to the trial, and continued throughout the trial and while the defendants' motions for new trial and appeals were pending (R. 1999–2243; 871 89). The trial itself took place in a carnival-like atmosphere, with press photographers in the Courtroom taking pictures of all the jurors for the two local newspapers (R. 951, 955), and television cameras following the jury to the very door of the juryroom[8] (R. 889–90, 2242). Two Montgomery newspapers, one on its front page, carried the names of the jurors (R. 2079–80, 952).

This suit was tried in November 1960, in Montgomery County, before Judge Walter B. Jones, and an all-white jury. The Trial Judge himself was a member of the jury commission of Montgomery County, the group responsible for the selection of the jury panel (R. 936, 971), from which Negroes have been intentionally and systematically excluded.

Respondent Sullivan's counsel was permitted by the Trial Judge, without restraint, over objections of petitioners' counsel, to indulge in such inflammatory appeals to racial bias as the mispronunciation of the word "Negro" as "Nigra" and "Nigger" in the presence of the jury, (R. 579–80), and in an invidious reference in his summation to purported events in the Congo (R. 929–30, 939–41). The Opinion of the Alabama Supreme Court below, in condoning such conduct, accepts counsel's lame excuse that he pronounced "the word 'negro' " as he

did because that was the way he had pronounced it "all my life"[9] (R. 1168–9).

Throughout the proceedings below, petitioners took all possible steps to preserve their constitutional rights. They demurred to the complaint (R. 15–24) and filed Amended Demurrers (R. 74–99); their demurrers, as amended, were all overruled (R. 108–9). They made numerous proper objections and excepted to the repeated admission of improper testimony of respondent's witnesses (R. 1102–09). They twice moved to exclude plaintiffs' evidence (R. 109–14, 728, 816), which motions were denied (R. 728, 816–17). They made motions for special findings (R. 114–18) and submitted written requests to charge (see R. 827); they made due and timely objections and exceptions to the denial of their motions and requests. Petitioners moved (see, *e.g.*, R. 109–14; 728, 816) for a dismissal at the end of plaintiff's case and for a directed verdict at the conclusion of the entire case, which motions were denied (R. 728, 816–18). Each petitioner duly and timely submitted a motion for new trial (R. 970–1028) on which Judge Jones refused to rule. This evasion of duty by the trial court was, in turn, seized upon by the Alabama Supreme Court as a pretext for denying review (R. 1169–70).

The treatment afforded petitioners' motions for new trial underlines the repeated denial to petitioners of proper opportunity to be heard below. On December 2, 1960 petitioners properly and timely made, filed and submitted motions for new trials. Petitioners duly appeared, in compliance with Title 13, Sec. 119 of the Alabama Code, on December 16, 1960, the day to which said motions (and the motions of their co-defendant, The New York Times) had been continued. On March 3, 1961, the day on which, the general understanding was, the motions of petitioners and The New York Times would be heard together, the Trial Court heard extensive argument on behalf of The New York Times in support of its motion for a new trial and then refused to hear petitioners' counsel, or permit him to argue, or allow him even to make a statement for the record (R. 895–6). Despite the fact that he had petitioners' papers properly before him, Judge Jones erroneously refused repeated demands by petitioners' counsel for rulings on their motions for new trials (R. 984,

---

[7] See Southern School News, August 1960, Vol. 9, No. 2, p. 1, (no desegregation in Alabama schools);
Alabama Code Recompiled 1958, Title 44 § 10 (Segregation of paupers)
id., Title 45 §§ 52, 121–3 (Segregation of prisoners)
id., Title 48 § 186 (Segregation of railroad waiting rooms)
id., Title 48 §§ 196–7 (Segregation of railroad coaches)
id., Title 48 § 301 (31a) (Segregation of motor busses)
id., Title 51 § 244 (Accounts of poll taxes paid by each race must be kept separate)
id., Title 52 § 613(1) (Segregation of delinquents)
id., Title 45 § 4 (Segregation of tubercular patients)
id., Title 45 § 248 (Segregation of patients in mental institutions)
cf. Green v. State, 58 Ala. 190 (no intermarriage).
[8] The Judicial Conference of the United States strongly condemned such practices "as inconsistent with fair judicial proceedings ..." by resolution adopted at its meeting in March 1962 (See New York Law Journal, July 13, 1962, at p. 1).

[9] *Cf. Screws v. United States,* 325 U.S. 91, 135, where Mr. Justice Murphy stated in dissent: "As such, he [Robert Hall, a Negro citizen] was entitled to all the respect and fair treatment that befits the dignity of man, a dignity that is recognized and guaranteed by the Constitution." [Brackets added].

998–9, 1013, 1027–8). On March 17, 1961, Judge Jones denied the Times' motion for a new trial (R. 970); arbitrarily, he never ruled on petitioners' motions (R. 895–6).

All of the foregoing rulings were properly objected to and challenged, and embodied in petitioners' Assignments of Error to the Alabama Supreme Court, duly filed therein and affixed to the certified transcript Record duly submitted and filed with this Court (R. 1100–1132).

In this setting and notwithstanding the complete absence of any evidence of or legal basis for liability of petitioners or any showing of actual damage suffered by respondent, the jury, upon the clearly erroneous instructions of the Trial Judge (R. 819–28), on November 3, 1960 rendered a one sentence verdict in "favor of the plaintiff" in the sum of $500,000 (R. 862), on which the Trial Judge entered judgment[10] (R. 863).

SUMMARY OF ARGUMENT

The State of Alabama and its public officials have developed refined and sophisticated schemes of repression, striking directly at the rights of free speech and press, the roots of our democracy. To silence people from criticizing and protesting their wrongful segregation activities, Alabama officials now seek to utilize civil libel prosecutions which require still less proof than was required under the infamous Sedition Act of 1798, 1 Stat. 596.

The libel prosecutions and enormous judgment herein are clearly induced by Alabama's massive "cradle to grave" statutory system of racial segregation, and clearly constitute another "ingenious" scheme by the State of Alabama and its public officials to suppress criticism of the political conduct of Southern public officials. As such, they clearly constitute prohibited state action and cannot be protected from review by mere labels such as "libel per se."

The preferred First and Fourteenth Amendments' freedoms of speech, press, assembly and association are the very cornerstone of the Bill of Rights. Moreover, the constitutional protection of criticism of the political conduct and actions of public officials extends even to exaggerations and inaccuracies.

Since " . . . public men are as it were, public property" (*Beauharnais* v. *Illinois*, 343 U.S. 250, 263), criticism and defamation of their official conduct is clearly within the protections guaranteed by the First and Fourteenth Amendments. The judgment and proceedings below clearly abridge these basic constitutional protections, especially in view of the vital public interest in the integration struggle, the role of petitioners as spiritual leaders of the nonviolent resistance movement, and the unconscionable penalty imposed below.

In addition to their patent disregard of these preferred constitutional protections, the Alabama Courts rendered and affirmed the judgment below on a record devoid of evidence of publication by petitioners, evidence of their consent to or authorization of publication, or evidence of damage of any kind to respondent due to the publication of the alleged libel. This disregard is all the more flagrant where the libel alleged is based solely on one claimed minor discrepancy in an advertisement (which is substantially correct) that nowhere mentions respondent by name or refers to him by office or title. Further, they attempted to meet petitioners' defenses that they had not published the ad and that it was not libelous, by adopting definitions of libel, libel per se and ratification, so strained, vague and detached from established legal principles as to amount in and of themselves to unconstitutional infringements of petitioners' rights.

Moreover, imposition of such liability because of petitioners' silence abridges petitioners' First Amendment rights of free association and belief.

Coupled with all of these violations of basic rights is the fact that the trial proceedings patently denied petitioners due process and equal protection of laws. Clearly, when four Negro ministers are sued by a white City Commissioner for an ad seeking support for Dr. Martin Luther King, and the case is tried in a segregated court room in Montgomery, Alabama, during a Civil War Centennial, before an all-white jury and a trial judge elected at polls from which Negroes were excluded, and when that very Judge states that "white man's justice" governs in his court and permits respondent's counsel to say "Nigger" and "Nigra" to the jury, then the Fourteenth Amendment does indeed become the "pariah" that the Trial Judge below called it. (See n. 20, pp. 26–27, *infra*; n. 3, p. 3, *supra*).

---

[10] *The Times*' Trial Counsel stated that the Sullivan verdict "could only have been the result of the passion and prejudice revived by that celebration [the Centennial Commemoration] and other events embraced within that Civil War celebration" and the failure of the Court to adjourn the trial even during the day "while ceremonies took place changing the name of the Court Square to "Confederate Square" (R. 2222); and again that plaintiff [Sullivan] "was allowed to present the case to the jury as a sectional conflict rather than as a cause of action for libel" (R. 944).

ARGUMENT

I. This court must nullify schemes which encroach on freedom of utterance under the guise of punishing libel

The century-long struggle of the Negro people for complete emancipation and full citizenship has been met at each step by a distinct pattern of resistance, with only the weapons changing, from lynching, violence and intimidation, through restrictive covenants, Black Codes,[11] and Jim Crow laws, to avoidance, "interposition," "nullification," tokenism and open contempt. Into this pattern, the case at bar fits naturally as a further refinement.

In recent years, when tremendous advances have occurred, "when growing self-respect has inspired the Negro with a new determination to struggle and sacrifice until first-class citizenship becomes a reality" (King, *Stride Toward Freedom* 154 (1958)), when there has come "an awakening moral consciousness on the part of millions of white Americans concerning segregation" (*id.*, p. 154), a national crisis has developed. This crisis was created when the aspirations of the Negroes were met "with tenacious and determined resistance" by "the guardians of the status quo," which "resistance grows out of the desperate attempt of the White South to perpetuate a system of human values that came into being under a feudalistic plantation system which cannot survive" today (*id.*, pp. 155, 156, 158).[12]

Because the essence of this brief is that the civil libel prosecutions involved herein constitute another of the "evasive schemes for racial segregation whether attempted 'ingeniously' or 'ingenuously'" (*Cooper* v. *Aaron*, 358 U.S. 1, 18), we believe it pertinent and material to view this "scheme" historically, in the "mirror"[13] of the Supreme Court's approach and reaction to other, related "schemes" to preserve segregation.

Even if consideration be limited to the fields of education, voting and housing, such "evasive schemes" have been struck down because of this Court's conviction that "constitutional rights would be of little value if they could be thus indirectly denied" (*Smith* v. *Allwright*, 321 U.S. 649, 664).

Thus, the "separate but equal" concept of *Plessy* v. *Ferguson*, 163 U.S. 537 (1896) entrenched segregation in schools until 1954[14] when this Court, in *Brown* v. *Board of Education*, 347 U.S. 483, enunciated the fundamental constitutional principle that racial segregation in the field of public education stamped Negroes with a "badge of inferiority" and violated the equal protection of the laws guaranteed by the Fourteenth Amendment.

For almost a decade, to this very day, there has been "massive resistance" to this decision. (Mendelson, *Discrimination* 40 (1962); also see *id.*, pp. 33–68 *passim*). The State of Alabama has been a leader of the resistance. This Court in 1958 was compelled to observe that the constitutional rights of school children "can neither be nullified openly and directly by state legislators or state executives or judicial officers, nor nullified indirectly by them through evasive schemes for segregation whether attempted '*ingeniously or ingenuously*'" (*Cooper* v. *Aaron*, 358 U.S. 1, 17) [Emphasis added]. In 1960, this Court in a unanimous memorandum made it clear that it would brook no further delay through the series of laws based upon the "concept" of "interposition" (*Bush* v. *Orleans School Board*, 364 U.S. 500). Dilatory requests

---

[11] Immediately following the Civil War, the former slave owners sought to replace the shackles of slavery "with peonage and to make the Negroes an inferior and subordinate economic caste . . . [T]he consequences of slavery were to be maintained and perpetuated." Konvitz, *A Century of Civil Rights* 15 (1961); see also Franklin, *From Slavery to Freedom* 299 (1956); Du Bois, *Black Reconstruction* 381–525 (1935).

[12] "The articulate and organized group, however, was the one favoring the maintenance of the caste system, and it used boycotts, effective appeals to the Southern legislatures, violence and *other means to resist the changes*. In general this group is larger and more effective in the Deep South . . . [Emphasis Added]

"All of the continuing leaders of the Southern resistance are persons with some traditional and legitimate authority. They apparently have a strong racist ideology, and strong personal desires to keep the Negro subordinate . . ." *Postscript Twenty Years Later* to Myrdal, *The American Dilemma* XXXVII (1962).

[13] "The Court is a good mirror, an excellent mirror, of which historians for some reason have little availed themselves, of the struggle of dominant forces outside the Court." Mr. Justice Frankfurter, as quoted in the preface of Vose, *Caucasians Only* (1959).

[14] The 1960 Report of the U.S. Commission on Civil Rights (1863–1963 Freedom to the Free—Century of Emancipation) p. 5, refers to the period of 1875–1900 as "Reaction, Redemption and Jim Crow," when "the former masters would have mastered the techniques of maintaining separation of the races through the agencies of the law." It was the period when "the Supreme Court was becoming attuned to the changing temper of the times" (*Id.*, p. 62). See, *e.g.*, *Slaughterhouse Cases*, 83 U.S. 36 (1873); *United States* v. *Reese*, 92 U.S. 214 (1876); *Cruikshank* v. *United States*, 92 U.S. 542 (1876); *Civil Rights Cases*, 109 U.S. 3 (1883); and *Plessy* v. *Ferguson*, 163 U.S. 537 (1896). But note the sole dissent of the first Mr. Justice Harlan which foreshadowed the reversal in the *Brown* case 58 years later. " . . . [I]n view of the Constitution, in the eye of the law, there is in this country no superior, dominant, ruling class of citizens. There is no caste here. Our Constitution is color-blind, and neither knows nor tolerates classes among citizens. In respect of civil rights, all citizens are equal before the law" (*Id.*, p. 559).

for review have been refused. "Tokenism" as a device is under challenge.[15]

The resistance techniques have taken many forms, some subtle and others overt, including contempt of federal court orders by the Governors of Alabama and Mississippi which required the use of federal troops to enforce basic constitutional rights. Ironically, the resistance took the equitable concept of "all deliberate speed," (*Brown* v. *Board of Education*, 349 U.S. 294, 301), which this Court proffered as a shield, and converted it to a sword. It was employed not for "consideration" of a "prompt and reasonable start towards full compliance" (349 U.S. at 300), but for resistance and nullification. This Court in its last term recognized that the concept of "all deliberate speed" had been abused and subverted. *Watson* v. *City of Memphis*, 373 U.S. 526.[16]

This Court has been vigilant, as it pledged it would be in *Cooper* v. *Aaron, supra,* to invalidate direct and indirect schemes seeking to preserve racial segregation.[17] Such vigilance must now be directed against the "civil libel" scheme so "ingeniously" and "ingenuously" and to date successfully employed as a weapon against the Negro petitioners and The New York Times.

Similarly, in the realm of Negro voting rights and other appurtenances of full citizenship, this Court has exposed the use of "evasive schemes" designed to nullify and sterilize Negro civil rights.

After this Court struck down a Texas law which bluntly denied the Negro the right to vote in a Democratic Party primary (*Nixon* v. *Herndon*, 273 U.S. 536), circumvention and more subtle means were employed. When these too failed to pass this Court's scrutiny (*Nixon* v. *Condon*, 286 U.S. 73), Texas repealed all such laws and fell back successfully to the legal sanctuary of "private action", placing the device beyond the reach of the Fourteenth Amendment (*Grovey* v. *Townsend*, 295 U.S. 45).

But, several years later, in 1944, this Court in *Smith* v. *Allwright*, 321 U.S. 649, overcame the "private action" device by going behind the white primary. Mr. Justice Reed aptly described this Court's searching approach to nullification of constitutional rights by indirection (321 U.S. at 664):

> "The United States is a constitutional democracy. Its organic law grants to all citizens a right to participate in the choice of elected officials without restriction by any state because of race. This grant to the people of the opportunity for choice is not to be nullified by a state through casting its electoral process in a *form* which permits a private organization to practice racial discrimination in the election. *Constitutional rights would be of little value if they could be thus indirectly denied*" (Emphasis added).

Foreshadowing the aftermath of *Brown* v. *Board of Education, supra, Smith* v. *Allwright* "aroused a storm of denunciation in the south, participated in by members of Congress, governors and others who proclaimed that 'white supremacy' must be preserved. They threatened that the decision would be disregarded or circumvented." Fraenkel, *The Supreme Court and Civil Liberties* 31 (1963). Thus, each "evasive scheme" thereafter employed to achieve discrimination in primary machinery was struck down. See *Terry* v. *Adams*, 345 U.S. 461; Fraenkel, *supra*, p. 31; Myrdal, *The American Dilemma* 479–86 (1944).[18]

In addition to the right to vote, full citizenship includes the right of jury service. Southern efforts to restrict and prevent jury service by Negroes reflect a similar pattern of resort to the full arsenal of "evasive schemes" after the passage of direct laws denying Negroes service on

---

[15] "This Court ... condemns the Pupil Placement Act when, with a fanfare of trumpets, it is hailed as the instrument for carrying out a desegregation plan while all the time the entire public knows that in fact it is being used to maintain segregation by allowing a little token desegregation" (*Bush* v. *Orleans Parish School Board*, 308 F. 2d 491, 499 (CA 5)).

[16] Mr. Justice Goldberg stated "*Brown* never contemplated that the concept of 'deliberate speed' would countenance indefinite delay in elimination of racial barriers in schools, let alone other public facilities not involving the same physical problems or comparable conditions. [373 U.S. 526, 530]

" ... Hostility to the constitutional precepts underlying the original decision was expressly and firmly pretermitted as such an operative factor.... [*Id.*, p. 531]

"Most importantly, of course, it must be recognized that even the delay countenanced by *Brown* was a necessary, albeit significant, adaptation of the usual principle that any deprivation of constitutional rights calls for prompt rectification. The rights here asserted are, like all such rights, *present* rights; they are not merely hopes to some *future* enjoyment of some formalistic constitutional promise. The basic guarantees of our Constitution are warrants for the here and now and unless there is an overwhelmingly compelling reason, they are to be promptly fulfilled." (*Id.*, pp. 532–3).

[17] Thus, for example, peonage and involuntary servitude imposed through ingenious subterfuges, whether by contract or otherwise, have been stripped of their "casting" and branded violations of the Thirteenth Amendment. This Court went behind the basic agreement between private individuals—being alert and vigilant to subtle means of reimposing slavery. *Bailey* v. *Alabama*, 219 U.S. 219; *Taylor* v. *Georgia*, 315 U.S. 25; *Pollack* v. *Williams*, 322 U.S. 4.

[18] This text under the heading "Southern Techniques for Disfranchising of Negroes" refers not only to evasive legal schemes but to "violence, terror and intimidation" as the effective means used to disfranchise Negroes in the South (p. 485).

juries was barred by this Court. *Strauder* v. *West Virginia*, 100 U.S. 303. It was in this context that this Court first observed that it would not tolerate discrimination "whether accomplished ingeniously or ingenuously." *Smith* v. *Texas*, 311 U.S. 128, 132; see also *Norris* v. *Alabama*, 294 U.S. 587; *Cassell* v. *Texas*, 339 U.S. 282; *Avery* v. *Georgia*, 345 U.S. 559. Even the finding of a state court that no discrimination existed did not bar this Court from going behind the facade to unmask, after review of the facts, subtle techniques for achieving denial of impartial jury. *Ross* v. *Texas*, 341 U.S. 918; *Shepherd* v. *Florida*, 341 U.S. 50.

Grand jury selections which directly or indirectly discriminated were interdicted. *Smith* v. *Texas, supra; Eubanks* v. *Louisiana*, 356 U.S. 584.

This Court overcame the artifice of gerrymandering which is in essence an "evasive scheme" to disenfranchise Negroes. *Gomillion* v. *Lightfoot*, 364 U.S. 339; and in *Baker* v. *Carr*, 369 U.S. 186, it has begun to grapple with more subtle, deeply entrenched means of effective disenfranchisement. In the same spirit, this Court did not permit voting registrars who committed wrongful acts to be insulated from liability by the designation of "private persons." *United States* v. *Raines*, 362 U.S. 17.

Finally, in the realm of housing, the use of artificial forms and "legalisms" as techniques for perpetuating discrimination was struck down. Racially restrictive zoning ordinances were declared illegal. *Buchanan* v. *Warley*, 245 U.S. 60; *Harmon* v. *Tyler*, 273 U.S. 668. In this field, the label of "private action" on racially restrictive covenants remained an impregnable fortress for discrimination for many decades (cf. *Civil Rights Cases*, 109 U.S. 3; Vose, *Caucasians Only* (1959)). Through racially restrictive covenants, efforts of Negroes to move out of slums and ghettoes to find better homes and schools were effectively and "legally" thwarted.[19]

In *Shelley* v. *Kraemer*, 334 U.S. 1, 19, this Court breached the walls of the fortress protecting these obnoxious covenants and held that the "private action" of contracting parties, when enforced by state courts, resulted in state action, saying: "active intervention of the state courts supported by the full panoply of state power" resulted in state action in the full and complete sense of the phrase.

Again, as with *Smith* v. *Allwright* and *Brown* v. *Board of Education*, both *supra*, a landmark declaration of positive constitutional right and privilege was met by resistance. A search was on to nullify, interpose or circumvent. (Vose, *op. cit., supra*, 227–34). This Court, five years later, in 1953 had to stem a tide of damage suits which had victimized those who "breached" the racial covenants. *Barrows* v. *Jackson*, 346 U.S. 249. Mr. Justice Minton, in a decision which bears close scrutiny as applicable to the case at bar, concluded that the grant of damages by a state court constituted state action under the Fourteenth Amendment; that to allow damages against one who refuses to discriminate "would be to encourage the use of restrictive covenants. To that extent, the State would act to put its sanction behind the covenants . . . [T]he Constitution confers upon no individual the right to demand action by the State which results in the denial of equal protection of laws to other individuals" (346 U.S. at 254–60).

The foregoing discussion of "ingenious" efforts to find "evasive schemes" for segregation was intended to place the case at bar in true perspective. It brings to the fore Mr. Justice Frankfurter's statement, in *Beauharnais* v. *Illinois, supra*, that this Court "retains and exercises authority to nullify action which encroaches on freedom of utterance under the *guise* of punishing libel" (343 U.S. at 263–4) [Emphasis added]. We submit that the civil libel prosecutions involved in the case at bar represent just such a "guise"; that they fall squarely within the pattern of devices and subterfuges which this Court has struck down in the realm of education, peonage, voting rights and housing, and must strike down here.

II. The proceedings below constitute prohibited state action and, together with the concepts of libel enunciated by the Alabama courts, unconstitutionally abridge freedoms of press, speech, assembly and association

A. Prohibited state action is clearly involved

To insulate this case against critical review by this Court, the erroneous assertion was made in the courts below[20] that there is an absence of

---

[19] A leading Negro newspaper, "The Chicago Defender," is quoted in Vose, *Caucasians Only:*
"These covenants have been responsible for more human misery, more crime, more disease and violence than any other factor in our society. They have been used to build the biggest ghettoes in history. They have been used to pit race against race and to intensify racial and religious prejudice in every quarter" (p. 213).

[20] Trial Judge Jones' disregard of the guarantees and requirements of the Fourteenth Amendment is understandable in view of his shockingly biased statement from the Bench during the trial of the related *James* case (n. 3 at p. 3, *supra*):
". . . [T]*he XIV Amendment has no standing whatever in this court, it is a pariah and an outcast,* if it be construed to . . . direct . . . this Court as to the manner in which . . . its internal operations [requiring racial segregation

"state action" and that this is merely a "private action of libel". This contention has no validity.

In *Shelley* v. *Kraemer*, 334 U.S. 1, 14, the Court stated:

> "That the action of *state courts and of judicial officers in their official capacities is to be regarded as action of the State within the meaning of the Fourteenth Amendment, is a proposition which has long been established by decisions of this Court.*" [Emphasis added].
>
> * * * * * * *
>
> "We have no doubt that there has been state action in these cases in the full and complete sense of the phrase." (*Id.*, p. 19).

See *Barrows* v. *Jackson*, 346 U.S. 249, 254 (state court suit between private parties, seeking damages for breach of a racially restrictive covenant, held barred by the Fourteenth Amendment); *American Federation of Labor* v. *Swing*, 312 U.S. 321 (state court's enforcement of a common law policy held state action within the Fourteenth Amendment); accord: *Bridges* v. *California*, 314 U.S. 252; *Wood* v. *Georgia*, 370 U.S. 375.

Moreover, the action by respondent Sullivan and the actions and pronouncements of other public officials (including the Attorney General and Governor of the State of Alabama) *in and of themselves* clearly constitute "State action" within the concepts enunciated by this Court in *Lombard* v. *Louisiana*, 373 U.S. 267.

The record herein notes that the instant case was instituted by Sullivan several days after the public announcement by Attorney General Gallion of Alabama that, on instructions from Governor Patterson, he was examining the legal aspects of damage actions by the State against the New York Times and others based on the advertisement here involved (R. 1999, 2001). The related companion libel suits filed by Mayor James, Commissioner Parks, former Commissioner Sellers and Governor Patterson, as well as the instant case, were instituted soon thereafter. All of these suits were based on substantially identical claims of libel and were instituted against petitioners and The New York Times based on the same advertisement, in the same circuit court of Montgomery County. (See *Parks* v. *New York Times*, 195 F. Supp. 919 (M. D. Ala.), rev'd on other grounds,

308 F. 2d 474 (C. A. 5), cert. pending; *Abernathy* v. *Patterson*, 295 F. 2d 452 (C. A. 5), cert. den., 368 U.S. 986).

Governor Patterson's complaint prays for damages in the sum of $1,000,000, and the Parks and Sellers and James complaints each pray for $500,000 damages.

Four other libel suits were instituted by Birmingham officials, seeking a total of $1,300,000 in damages, based on articles on racial tensions by Harrison Salisbury in *The Times*. Alabama officials have also filed libel actions against the Columbia Broadcasting System, seeking $1,500,000 in damages based on a television news program devoted, in part, to the difficulties experienced by Negro citizens of Montgomery in registering to vote. *Morgan, Connor & Waggoner* v. *CBS, Inc.* (N. D. Ala., So. Div.) Civ. Nos. 10067–10069S; *Willis & Ponton* v. *CBS, Inc.* (M. D. Ala., No. Div.) Civ. Nos. 1790–1791N.

On May 22, 1960, shortly after the institution of the above-described actions against petitioners and *The Times*, the Montgomery Advertiser (a prominent local newspaper) stated editorially:

> "The Advertiser has no doubt that the recent checkmating of The Times in Alabama will impose a restraint upon other publications which have hitherto printed about the South what was supposed to be." (R. 2025).

It is difficult to believe that this flood of libel prosecutions instituted by public officials of the State of Alabama was simply a spontaneous, individual response to a critical newspaper advertisement. One is compelled to conclude that these actions by public officials are part of a concerted, calculated program to carry out a policy of punishing, intimidating and silencing all who criticize and seek to change Alabama's notorious political system of enforced segregation (See n. 7, p. 12, *supra*).

The Sullivan case, considered in conjunction with the activities of the other Alabama city and state officials, is clearly within the state action doctrine enunciated in the *Lombard* case, *supra*. "A State or a city may act as authoritatively through its executive as through its legislative body" (373 U.S. at 273). Clearly, Alabama has interceded, by its judiciary and its city and state officials, to put state sanctions behind its racial segregation practices.

Once the shelter of "private action" is removed from the "libel" judgment below, that judgment and its affirmance are exposed as another "scheme" to abridge the petitioners' basic constitutional rights of free political expression.

---

in seating persons in the courtroom] ... shall be conducted ..."

* * * * * * *

"We will now continue the trial of this case under the laws of the State of Alabama, and not under the XIV Amendment, and in the belief and knowledge that *the white man's justice* ... will give the parties ... equal justice under law." *Judge Jones on Courtroom Segregation*, 22 The Alabama Lawyer, 190 at pp. 191–2 (1961) [Emphasis and brackets added].

B. The First and Fourteenth Amendments protect criticism and discussion of the political conduct and actions of public officials

Since this Court in the public interest accords to public officials immunity from libel (*Barr v. Matteo*, 360 U.S. 564), the same public interest must insure a corresponding protection to those who criticize public officials.[21]

Public officials, backed not only by the full power of their offices but also by the aura of power, must be held to strictest account. To expect such account to be received dispassionately and dealt with in polite phrases by press and public is to deny effective criticism and comment.

---

[21]*Cf.* Chief Justice Warren's comment in his dissent:
" . . . The public interest in limiting libel suits against officers in order that the public might be adequately informed is paralleled by another interest of equal importance: that of preserving the opportunity to criticize the administration of our Government and the action of its officials without being subjected to unfair—and absolutely privileged—retorts. If it is important to permit government officials absolute freedom to say anything they wish in the name of public information, it is at least as important to preserve and foster public discussion concerning our Government and its operation" (at p. 584).
See also *Douglas, The Right of The People* 25 (1961), quoting "as the true spirit of the Bill of Rights":
"In times like those through which we have recently passed, the doctrine of fair comment should be extended as far as the authorities will permit. With unprecedented social and governmental conditions, our own institutions threatened, national legislators who participate in the formation of governmental policies should be held to the strictest official accountability. History has shown that this is promoted through free exercise of the right to criticize official acts. The people furnish the legislators with an extensive and expensive secretariat, give them the right to use the mails at public expense. Their colleagues are generous in granting leave to print. With these opportunities for personal praise and propaganda, opposition newspapers and editorial writers should not be limited to weak, tepid, and supine criticism and discussion" (*Hall v. Binghamton Press Co.*, 263 App. Div. 403, 411, (3d Dept.)).
See also *Hall v. Binghamton, supra*, 263 App. Div. at pp. 412–13 (concurrence of Justice Bliss) for an eloquent dictum on this subject:
"Ours is a representative government, and one who assumes to represent our citizens in a legislative hall must expect that his acts will be commented upon and criticized. . . . Freedom of speech and press are guaranteed to us in our form of government, and it is the right of the free press to criticize severely and of a free citizenry to speak plainly to and of its representatives. . . . If the press or our citizens honestly believe that the acts of a legislative representative lend comfort to our nation's enemies there must be no question about the right to tell him just that in no uncertain terms. Queasy words will not do. How else can a democracy function? If the citizens believe such acts may be setting up a government of Quislings, they must have the right to say so. It is one of the verities of democracy that eternal vigilance is the price of liberty. The courts may not muzzle those who maintain such vigilance. Great issues require strong language."

In *Roth v. United States*, 354 U.S. 476, 484, this Court ruled that the First and Fourteenth Amendments were "fashioned to assure unfettered interchange of ideas for the bringing about of political and social changes desired by the people."

In Justice Hughes' classic statement is found support for the key role of political discussion:

"[I]mperative is the need to preserve inviolate the constitutional rights of free speech, free press and free assembly in order to maintain the opportunity for free political discussion to the end that government may be responsive to the will of the people and that changes, if desired, may be obtained by peaceful means. Therein lies the security of the Republic, the very foundation of constitutional government" (*De Jonge v. Oregon*, 299 U.S. 353, 365).

Such criticism and discussion of the actions of public officials are constitutionally protected not only against prior restraint but also against subsequent punishment. *Wood v. Georgia, supra; Schneider v. State*, 308 U.S. 147; *Bridges v. California*, 314 U.S. 252; *Grosjean v. American Press Co.*, 297 U.S. 233, 243–245; *Near v. Minnesota*, 283 U.S. 697, 707; *Thornhill v. Alabama*, 310 U.S. 88; *Cantwell v. Connecticut*, 310 U.S. 296.

Perhaps more than any other issue in the history of the United States, the demand of Negro Americans to be granted full rights as citizens, from the slave revolts through the Abolition Movement and the Civil War to the present nonviolent movement, has been a most graphic witness to these observations by Justice Jackson:

". . . a function of free speech under our system of government is to invite dispute. It may indeed best serve its high purposes when it induces a condition of unrest, creates dissatisfaction with conditions as they are, or even stirs people to anger. Speech is often provocative and challenging. It may strike at prejudices and preconceptions and have profound unsettling effects as it presses for acceptance of an idea." *Terminello v. Chicago*, 337 U.S. 1, 4.

This Court ruled in *Cantwell, supra*, that the Fourteenth Amendment invalidates state court judgments "based on a common law concept of the most general and undefined nature" (310 U.S. at 308) used by those on one side of "sharp differences" to penalize those on the other side. It concluded that:

". . . the people of this nation have ordained in the light of history, that, in spite of the probability of excesses and abuses, these liberties are, in the long view, essential to enlightened opinion and right conduct on the part of citizens of a democracy" (310 U.S. at 310).

This Court has repeatedly recognized that the preferred First and Fourteenth Amendment freedoms of speech, press, assembly and association are the very cornerstone of the Bill of Rights and our entire democratic heritage (*Wood v. Georgia, supra; Thomas v. Collins,* 323 U.S. 516; *Schneider v. State,* 308 U.S. 147, 161; *De Jonge v. Oregon, supra,* 364); and that the constitutional protection of such criticism of public officials extends even to "half truths", "misinformation", exaggerations and inaccuracies (*Pennekamp v. Florida,* 328 U.S. 331; *Bridges v. California,* 314 U.S. 252; *Cantwell v. Connecticut,* 310 U.S. 296, 310). "Freedom of petition, assembly, speech and press could be greatly abridged by a practice of meticulously scrutinizing every editorial, speech, sermon or other printed matter to extract two or three naughty words on which to hang charges of 'group libel' " (Mr. Justice Black, dissenting, in *Beauharnais v. Illinois,* 343 U.S. 250, 273).

Neither the State of Alabama nor any other state may foreclose the exercise of these basic constitutional rights by the appellation of "libel per se" or any other like label (*NAACP v. Button,* 371 U.S. 415, 429; *Wood v. Georgia,* 370 U.S. 375, 386; *Craig v. Harney,* 331 U.S. 367; *Norris v. Alabama,* 294 U.S. 587).

As this Court ruled in *NAACP v. Button, supra:*

"A State cannot foreclose the exercise of constitutional rights by mere labels" (371 U.S. at 429).

The decision and judgment below clearly conflict with these prior decisions.

Indeed, as emphasized by the context in which they arose, the proceedings below are nothing more than a subterfuge to employ legal sanctions, and the fear of legal sanctions, to silence criticism of the official conduct of public officials, and to thus, revive, in new guise, the heinous, long-proscribed doctrines of "Seditious Libel". This tyrannical device and its civil counterpart, Scandalum Magnatum (described in Odgers, *Libel and Slander* 65 (6th Ed. 1929)), have long been considered barred by the preferred constitutional guarantees of freedom of speech, press, assembly and association embodied in the First and Fourteenth Amendments (see Holmes, J., in *Abrams v. United States,* 250 U.S. 616, 630; *De Jonge v. Oregon,* 299 U.S. 353, 365; *Sillars v. Collier,* 151 Mass. 50; Chafee, *Free Speech in the United States* 27–29 (1941); Schofield, *"Freedom of Press in the United States",* ESSAYS ON CONSTITUTIONAL LAW AND EQUITY 540–541 (1921)). They must not now be permitted resurrection for any purpose, much less that repressive use attempted here.

This Court's recent decision in *Wood v. Georgia, supra,* restates and reaffirms the well-established doctrine that criticism of the official conduct of public officials is protected against state infringement by the First and Fourteenth Amendments. There, the Court found these Amendments protected Sheriff Wood's written accusations to a Grand Jury that the Superior Court Judges of Georgia were guilty of abusing their offices, misusing the state criminal law, attempted intimidation of Negro residents, fomenting racial hatred, "race baiting" and "physical demonstrations such as used by the Ku Klux Klan". In so holding, this Court said, per Mr. Chief Justice Warren:

"Men are entitled to speak as they please on matters vital to them; errors in judgment or unsubstantiated opinions may be exposed, of course, but not through punishment for contempt for the expression. *Under our system of government, counterargument and education are the weapons available to expose these matters, not abridgement of the rights of free speech and assembly.*" (370 U.S. at 389) [Emphasis added].

A fortiori, The Times advertisement, which contained no official's name, no charge of crime or corruption in office, but rather which treated of vital and significant issues of the times, must fall well within that constitutionally protected ambit. Nor can any reasonable representation be made, to remove this case from that protected area, that *The Times* advertisement created any likelihood of immediate danger of conflict or violence. (*Whitney v. California,* 274 U.S. 357).

Further, the enormous sum of $500,000, awarded as punitive damages on a record so thoroughly devoid of crucial evidence, is wholly unconscionable. Such penalty by way of punitive damages (which, the jury was charged, constitutes "punishment" designed to deter defendants and others (R. 825–6)) represents a grave impairment of free expression and an unconstitutional restraint upon "the public need for information and education with respect to the significant issues of the times" (*Thornhill v. Alabama,* 310 U.S. at 102, quoted with approval in *Wood v. Georgia, supra*). The mere threat[22] of such "punishment" is far

---

[22] In *Farmers Ed. & Coop. Union v. WDAY,* 360 U.S. 525, 530, this Court said: "Quite possibly, if a station were held responsible for the broadcast of libelous material, all remarks even faintly objectionable would be excluded out of an excess of caution." See also Riesman, *Democracy and Defamation: Fair Game and Fair Comment,* 42 COLUM. L. REV. 1282 (1943): There is a "need for protecting political and economic criticism against intimidation by

greater than the $400 fine and 20-day sentence for contempt which this Court has reversed as violative of the First and Fourteenth Amendments. (*Wood* v. *Georgia, supra.* See also *Barrows* v. *Jackson,* 346 U.S. 249; *Grosjean* v. *American Press Co.,* 297 U.S. 233).

The Alabama Supreme Court sustained the $500,000 verdict and judgment solely as proper "punitive damages" (R. 1175–9).[23] The technical and formal distinction that this huge penalty was imposed through civil rather than criminal libel prosecution is, in this situation, disingenuous at best, and lends no support to the judgment below.

For both this Court and the Circuit Court of Appeals have recognized that both civil and criminal libel prosecutions may encroach on the preferred rights guaranteed by the First and Fourteenth Amendments. See, *e.g., Beauharnais* v. *Illinois,* 343 U.S. 250, 263–4 (criminal); *Sweeney* v. *Patterson,* 128 F. 2d 457 (C. A., D. C.), cert. den., 317 U.S. 678 (civil).

In *Beauharnais* this Court stated:

> " 'While this Court sits' it retains and exercises authority to nullify action which encroaches on freedom of utterance under the guise of punishing libel. Of course discussion cannot be denied and the right, as well as the duty, of criticism must not be stifled." (343 U.S. at 263, 264)

and significantly added in a footnote:

> "If a statute sought to outlaw libels of political parties, quite different problems not now before us would be raised. For one thing, the whole doctrine of fair comment as indispensable to the democratic political process would come into play [citing cases]. Political parties, like public men, are, as it were, public property." (*Id.,* p. 263, n. 18).

Criticism and discussion of the actions of public officials are a *sine qua non* of the democratic process.[24] It may fairly be said that the

genius of our Bill of Rights lies precisely in its guarantee of the right to speak freely on public issues and to criticize public officials' conduct on the assumption that only an informed people is fit to govern itself. First Amendment freedoms are "the most cherished policies of our civilization"[25] "vital to the maintenance of democratic institutions".[26]

This Court has recognized that the right to speak out for the civil rights of Negro citizens, and against those in public or private life who would deny them, is under bitter attack in Southern States, and has acted to protect that right in a long line of cases. *Gibson* v. *Florida Legislative Investigation Committee,* 372 U.S. 539; *NAACP* v. *Button,* 371 U.S. 415; *Shelton* v. *Tucker,* 364 U.S. 479; *Bates* v. *City of Little Rock,* 361 U.S. 516; *NAACP* v. *Alabama,* 357 U.S. 449.

In *Button,* this Court stated:

> "We cannot close our eyes to the fact that the militant Negro civil rights movement has engendered the intense resentment and opposition of the politically dominant white community . . ." (371 U.S. at 435).

In *Bates,* this Court noted that:

> "Freedoms such as these are protected not only against heavy-handed frontal attack, but also from being stifled by more subtle governmental interference." (361 U.S. at 523).

The award of punitive damages to a criticized official may well be more subversive of the freedom to criticize the government than is compelled disclosure of affiliation, which this Court has ruled inconsistent with the First Amendment in the cases cited above. See also *Gibson, supra; West Va. Board of Education* v. *Barnette,* 319 U.S. 624.

Indeed, "punishment by way of damages . . . not alone to punish the wrongdoer, but as a deterrent to others similarly minded,"[27] where such damages are subject to "no legal measure,"[28] exceeds even the criminal punishment of Seditious Libel. For here the "fine" is limited only by the complainant's *ad damnum* clause, and may be imposed without indictment or proof beyond a reasonable doubt. The Alabama courts require neither an intent to bring the

---

the libel laws" (at p. 1309) " . . . smaller journals, struggling along on subsidies or barely managing on their own, are, of course, highly vulnerable to a libel suit . . ." (at p. 1310).

[23] Sullivan proved no special damages. Moreover, his testimony and that of his witnesses left little doubt that there was no injury to his reputation or standing in the community; more than likely, the contrary was true (R. 625, 638, 647, 651, 666, 721–4).

[24] "In dealing with governmental affairs, or the fitness of a political candidate for office, the law, however, has come to recognize a very broad privilege to comment freely and even criticize harshly. On matters of public concern, the expression of ideas may not be suppressed just because someone decides that the ideas are false. In that way we encourage the widest and broadest debate

on public issues." Douglas, *A Living Bill of Rights* 26 (1961).

[25] *Bridges* v. *California,* 314 U.S. 252, 260.

[26] *Schneider* v. *State,* 308 U.S. 147, 161.

[27] Ala. Sup. Ct. (R. 1176)

[28] *Ibid.* (R. 1177)

official "into contempt or disrepute," as in the Sedition Act (Act of July 14, 1798, 1 Stat. 596), nor any proof of actual injury to reputation. The Trial Court below ruled the ad libelous *per se*, and instructed the jury (R. 823) that it was to be presumed to be "malicious." Further, the Court below ruled it was legally sufficient to constitute libel *per se* that the criticism, "if believed",[29] would "tend to injure . . . [the official] in his reputation."[30]

Were the libel theory of the Alabama courts below allowed to stand, the danger to freedom of written expression would be tremendous. Its infection would spread quickly and disastrously, bringing suit next for slander for spoken words. A veritable blackout of criticism, a deadening conformity, would follow inexorably. It requires little imagination to picture the destructiveness of such weapons in the hands of those who, only yesterday, used dogs and fire hoses in Birmingham, Alabama against Negro petitioners leading non-violent protests against segregation practices.

C. Vagueness and indefiniteness of standards require reversal of the judgment below Such vague rules of liability, as were employed in the Trial Court's judgment and upheld in the Alabama Supreme Court's affirmance, restrict the exercise of First Amendment rights more seriously than would have the penalties stricken down in *Wood*, *supra*, or *Cantwell*, *supra*, or the compulsory disclosure prohibited in *Gibson*, *supra*. For the uncertainty created thereby is even greater than that involved in the following cases in which this Court has found vagueness constitutionally offensive.

In *NAACP* v. *Button*, 371 U.S. 415, a Virginia statute was condemned on the ground that the conduct it prohibited was "so broad and uncertain" as to "lend itself to selective enforcement against unpopular causes." As the Court said in *Button, supra*:

> "Broad prophylactic rules in the area of free expression are suspect [citing cases]. Precision of regulation must be the touchstone in an area so closely touching our most precious freedoms." (371 U.S. at 435).

Similarly, in *Bantam Books, Inc.* v. *Sullivan*, 372 U.S. 58, 71, the Court struck down a statute ostensibly designed to shield youthful readers from obscenity on the ground that the statutory mandate was "vague and uninformative", leaving the distributor of books "to specu-

late" as to whether his publication fell within the statute.

Perhaps the most telling of all statements on this point is contained in the dissent of Messrs. Justice Reed and Douglas in *Beauharnais*:

> " . . . Racial, religious, and political biases and prejudices lead to charge and countercharge, acrimony and bitterness. If words are to be punished criminally, the Constitution at least requires that only words or expressions or statements that can be reasonably well defined, or that have through long usage an accepted meaning, shall furnish a basis for conviction.
>
> "These words—'virtue,' 'derision,' and 'obloquy'—have neither general nor special meanings well enough known to apprise those within their reach as to limitations on speech [citing case]. Philosophers and poets, thinkers of high and low degree from every age and race have sought to expound the meaning of virtue, but each teaches his own conception of the moral excellence that satisfies standards of good conduct. Are the tests of the Puritan or the Cavalier to be applied, those of the city or the farm, the Christian or non-Christian, the old or the young? Does the Bill of Rights permit Illinois to forbid any reflection on the virtue of racial or religious classes which a jury or a judge may think exposes them to derision or obloquy, words themselves of quite uncertain meaning as used in the statute? I think not. A general and equal enforcement of this law would restrain the mildest expressions of opinion in all those areas where 'virtue' may be thought to have a role. Since this judgment may rest upon these vague and undefined words, which permit within their scope the punishment of incidents secured by the guarantee of free speech, the conviction should be reversed." *Beauharnais* v. *Illinois*, 343 U.S. 250, 283–284.

Accordingly, on grounds of vagueness and uncertainty alone, the judgment below must be reversed.

D. Respondent's erroneous contentions as to the defense of truth Respondent, in opposing certiorari, contended that the availability of the defense of truth suffices to protect the First Amendment freedoms against encroachment by a common law libel action. This argument has been rejected by the courts and by history. *Sweeney* v. *Patterson*, 128 F. 2d 457, 458 (C. A., D. C.), cert. den., 317 U.S. 678, held:

> "Cases which impose liability for *erroneous reports of the political conduct of officials* reflect the obsolete doctrine that the governed must not criticize their governors . . . Information and discussion will be discouraged, and the public interest in public knowledge of important facts will be poorly defended if error subjects its author to a libel suit without even a showing of economic loss. *Whatever is added to the field of libel is taken from the field of free debate*." [Emphasis added].

---

[29] *Ibid.* (R. 1162–3)
[30] *Ibid.* (R. 1155)

To the same argument, raised in defense of the Sedition Act of 1798, James Madison replied:

" . . . [A] very few reflections will prove that [the Sedition Act's] baneful tendency is little diminished by the privilege of giving in evidence the truth of the matter contained in political writings.

* * * * *

"But in the next place, it must be obvious to the plainest minds, that opinions, and inferences, and conjectural observations, are not only in many cases inseparable from the facts, but may often be more the objects of the prosecution than the facts themselves; or may even be altogether abstracted from particular facts; and that opinions and inferences, and conjectural observations, cannot be subjects of that kind of proof which appertains to facts, before a court of law." (*Kentucky-Virginia Resolutions and Mr. Madison's Report of 1799*, Virginia Commission on Constitutional Government 71 (1960)).

Respondent's case confirms Madison's observations, resting as it does on one minor inaccuracy in *The Times* ad and the strained inferences therefrom of respondent and his witnesses.

Nor, as this Court has expressly stated in *NAACP* v. *Button*, *supra*, is the truth of ideas and beliefs a precondition for their constitutional protection:

" . . . For the Constitution protects expression and association without regard to the race, creed or political or religious affiliation of the members of the group which invokes its shield, or to the truth, popularity or social utility of the ideas and beliefs which are offered." (371 U.S. at 444–5).

And the use by the Alabama Supreme Court (R. 1178) of the testimony of the Secretary of The Times, that the advertisement was "substantially correct" (R. 785), to sustain both an inference of malice and the $500,000 verdict, is best rebutted by Judge Clark in his cogent dissent in *Sweeney* v. *Schenectady Union Pub. Co.*, 122 F. 2d 288, 292 (C. A. 2), aff'd per curiam by an equally divided Court, 316 U.S. 642.

"I do not think it an adequate answer to such a threat against public comment, which seems to me necessary if democratic processes are to function, to say that it applies only to false statements. For this is comment and inference, . . . and hence not a matter of explicit proof or disproof. The public official will always regard himself as not bigoted, and will so testify, sincerely enough. And then the burden of proving the truth of the defense will rest upon the commentator, who must sustain the burden of proving his inference true. If he fails in

even a minority of the suits against him—as the sporting element in trials to juries susceptible to varying shades of local opinion would make probable—he is taught his lesson, and a serious brake upon free discussion established."

In sum, this Court must not permit a discredited technique of oppression, no matter how "subtle" or sophisticated or refined its new guise (*Bates* v. *Little Rock*, *supra*, at 523) to be restored as an effective device for men in office to

" . . . injure and oppress the people under their administration, provoke them to cry out and complain; and then make that very complaint the foundation for new oppression and prosecutions."[31]

III. The judgment and proceedings below violate petitioners' First and Fourteenth Amendment rights in that the record is devoid of evidence of authorization or publication of the ad in suit, and they require of total strangers to the publication expression of disbelief and disavowal

A. Lack of evidence as denial of Due Process of Law   The record below is devoid of probative evidence of authorization or publication by any of the petitioners of the alleged libel or of any malice on their part (see pp. 8–12, *supra*).

In examining this record, District Judge Johnson, in *Parks* v. *New York Times Co.*, 195 F. Supp. 919 (M. D. Ala.), rev'd on other grounds by a two to one decision, 308 F. 2d 474 (C. A. 5), petition for cert. pending, (No. 687, 1962 Term, renumbered No. 52, 1963 Term), found and ruled as follows (pp. 922–3):

"This Court reaches the conclusion that from the evidence presented upon the motion to remand in each of these cases there is no legal basis whatsoever for the claim asserted against the resident defendants Abernathy, Shuttlesworth, Seay, Sr., and Lowery [petitioners herein]. *From the facts available to this Court, no liability on the part of the four resident defendants existed under any recognized theory of law; this is true even with the application of the Alabama 'scintilla rule'.*"

* * * * *

"They were neither officers nor members of the Committee, and had not authorized the committee, or Murray, or The New York Times, or anyone else to use their names in such a manner. *Neither resident defendant knew his name had been used until some time after the publication of the article in question. The theory that the article was authorized and that the individual resident defendants had authorized the use*

---

[31] Andrew Hamilton, Argument to the Jury, *Zenger's Trial*, 17 How. St. Tr. 675, 721–2.

of their names through the Southern Christian Leadership Conference is without any evidentiary basis whatsoever. As a matter of fact, all the evidence is to the contrary and uncontradicted." [Emphasis and brackets supplied].[32]

The courts below relied on the unfounded premise that the petitioners were linked with the advertisement in question by the letter from A. Philip Randolph (R. 1948–9; 1992), which the Alabama Supreme Court seized upon and characterized as a certification that the petitioners had consented to the use of their names in the advertisement (R. 1170). On the contrary, however, it is undisputed that the letter referred to "signed members of the Committee" and that the petitioners' names were not attached thereto (R. 805–10, 818).

Therefore, as their names were used without their knowledge or consent (R. 754–5, 806–10), the assertion of the court below (R. 1170) that the Randolph letter certified petitioners' permission to use their names is clearly groundless and constitutes distorted fact finding.

In *Stein* v. *New York*, 346 U.S. 156, 181, this Court set forth the established rule:

"Of course, this Court cannot allow itself to be completely bound by state court determination of any issue essential to decision of a claim of federal right, else federal law could be frustrated by distorted fact finding."

Accord: *Wood* v. *Georgia*, 370 U.S. 375; *Craig* v. *Harney*, 331 U.S. 367; *Pennekamp* v. *Florida*, 328 U.S. 331.

As indicated, the judgment against petitioners clearly lacks any rational connection with, and is in fact directly contrary to, the undisputed record facts. Accordingly, the result below conflicts with this Court's decisions in *Thompson* v. *Louisville*, 362 U.S. 199; *Postal Tele-*

graph Cable Co. v. *City of Newport, Ky.*, 247 U.S. 464; *Tot* v. *United States*, 319 U.S. 463.[33]

Since there is no rational evidentiary support in the record for the finding that petitioners authorized the use of their names as sponsors of the advertisements, the judgment below clearly violates the "due process" requirements of the Fourteenth Amendment and must be set aside for lack of evidence. *Garner* v. *Louisiana*, 368 U.S. 157; *Thompson* v. *Louisville*, 362 U.S. 199.

B. Prejudicial rulings below concerning "ratification"; silence as consent Absent any evidence that petitioners published or authorized publication of the advertisement at issue, and in the face of uncontroverted evidence that petitioners' names were used without authorization or consent, the trial court improperly charged the jury (R. 824–5):

"... although you may believe ... that they did not sign this advertisement and did not authorize it, yet it is the contention of the plaintiff ... that the four individuals ... after knowing of the publication of the advertisement and after knowing of its content, ratified the use of their names ... and we here define ratification as the approval by a person of a prior act which did not bind him but which was professedly done on his account or in his behalf whereby the act, the use of his name, the publication, is given effect as if authorized by him in the very beginning. Ratification is really the same as a previous authorization and is a confirmation or approval of what has been done by another on his account."

Petitioners duly excepted, and the Trial Judge duly granted an exception, to this crucial and prejudicial portion of the oral charge (R. 829); but the Supreme Court of Alabama nevertheless refused to rule thereon, on the purported ground that the "attempted exception was descriptive of the subject matter only, and is too indefinite to invite our review" (R. 1168).

The quoted oral charge rests solely on the silence of petitioners for approximately eight days, between their receipt, on or about April 11, 1960 (R. 799), of respondent's demand for retraction, and April 19, 1960, the date of commencement of respondent's suit; for the record is wholly devoid of any other act or

---

[32] The majority decision of the 5th Circuit Court of Appeals in *Parks* v. *New York Times, supra,* is clearly shown by the Opinion to rest on matters not contained in the Record in this case (see 308 F. 2d 478, at 479, 482), and the issue there considered was the question of "colorable liability" of petitioners to defeat removal to the federal courts of other libel suits.

In fact, the two majority judges in the *Parks* case had before them the complete Record in the *Sullivan* case at bar and took no issue with District Judge Johnson's findings and decision that, on that Record, there was not a scintilla of evidence or any "recognized theory of law" to support any claim against petitioners (195 F. Supp. 919, 922). This is further confirmed by the dissenting Opinion of Judge Ainsworth in the *Parks* case, which states in relevant part:

"The majority opinion apparently agrees with the principal findings of fact of the court below [*i.e.*, of District Judge Johnson as quoted above] ...", 308 F. 2d 474, 483 [brackets added].

[33] In *Williams* v. *Tooke*, 108 F. 2d 758, 759 (C. A. 5), cert. den., 311 U.S. 655, the established rule was cogently restated as follows:

"[I]f a case between private parties is arbitrarily and capriciously decided, in violation of settled principles of law and contrary to undisputed facts, though the court so deciding had jurisdiction over the suit, the judgment may be in violation of the 14th Amendment. *Postal Telegraph Cable Co.* v. *Newport, Ky.*, 247 U.S. 464, 38 S. Ct. 566, 62 L. ed. 1215."

omission of petitioners subsequent to the publication of the advertisement. Thus, the charge invited the jury to impose liability on petitioners solely on the basis of their silence subsequent to publication of the advertisement. But such silence does not have sufficient rational connection with the publication of the advertisement to satisfy the Due Process Clause of the Fourteenth Amendment, nor can the erroneous refusal of the Alabama Supreme Court to rule on petitioners' exceptions and Assignments of Error preclude review by this Court.

Moreover, the trial judge, contrary to established principles, in effect directed the jury to find the New York Times' ad in suit "libelous per se" (R. 823); and the Supreme Court of Alabama, while finding this charge "confused" and "invasive" of the province of the jury (R. 1166–7), still refused to find prejudice to petitioners (R. 1167).

Such erroneous and prejudicial rulings by the courts below unconstitutionally infringed petitioners' basic rights in their gross misapplication of controlling decisions of this Court, and in the oppressive and unreasonable judgment they buttressed. No state court can, particularly on such evidence, exact a price of $500,000 for *eight* days' silence and remain consistent with the First and Fourteenth Amendments.

Nor do petitioners' failures to reply constitute a ratification. Governing authority is clear that a prerequisite of "ratification" (even in contract cases) is knowledge by the "ratifying" party of all the relevant facts involved. Petitioners did not have such knowledge here (R. 787–804). Neither respondent nor the Courts below cited any applicable authority to negate this accepted definition of ratification. (*Cf. A. B. Leach & Co.* v. *Peirson*, 275 U.S. 120; and see *Angichiodo* v. *Cerami*, 127 F. 2d 849, 852 (C. A. 5)).

C. Compulsory disclosure of belief   Moreover, any such attempt to require petitioners to retract or deny publication fatally conflicts with the freedoms of thought and association guaranteed by the Constitution and the decisions of this Court. *Gibson* v. *Florida Legislative Investigation Committee; NAACP* v. *Button; Talley* v. *California; Bates* v. *City of Little Rock; NAACP* v. *Alabama; West Va. Board of Education* v. *Barnette; De Jonge* v. *Oregon,* all *supra.*

The applicability of the doctrine of these cases to a failure to retract or deny cannot be seriously disputed. It is patent that compelled expression of disbelief, such as would result from imposition of liability for failure to retract a publication neither made nor authorized, is at least as dangerous as compulsion to disclose belief (*Talley* v. *California, supra; NAACP* v. *Alabama, supra*) or express belief (*West Va. Board of Education* v. *Barnette, supra*). This Court has ruled such compulsions unconstitutional.

These cases guarantee petitioners freedom to believe in the aims of the advertisement as well as freedom to associate themselves with others to accomplish such aims. As this Court said in *Gibson* (*supra,* 544):

> "This Court has repeatedly held that rights of association are within the ambit of the constitutional protections afforded by the First and Fourteenth Amendments (citing cases). The respondent Committee does not contend otherwise, nor could it, for, as was said in *NAACP* v. *Alabama, supra,* 'it is beyond debate that freedom to engage in association for the advancement of beliefs and ideas is an inseparable aspect of the "liberty" assured by the Due Process Clause of the Fourteenth Amendment, which embraces freedom of speech.' 357 U.S. at 460. *And it is equally clear that the guarantee encompasses protection of privacy of association . . ."* [Emphasis added].

Respondent, abetted by the coercive power of the State of Alabama, cannot constitutionally compel petitioners to decide within an *eight* day period whether or not to associate themselves publicly with, or dissociate themselves from, an advertisement seeking to achieve goals which petitioners may constitutionally support, especially under penalty of imputing malice to them and of punitive damages. Certainly no such compulsion can be constitutionally imposed on petitioners to make such disavowal of an ad, the full text of which they had not seen. Any such application of the Alabama retraction statutes cited by respondent (Title 7, Sections 913–16 of the Code of Alabama, at pp. 4–5, *supra*), or any such "rule of evidence" as respondent seeks to apply, would deprive petitioners of their right to obtain a copy of the advertisement, study the content thereof, investigate the accuracy of the statements claimed to be false, analyze the effect of the advertisement, consult with legal counsel, and—in the light of such study, investigation, analysis and consultation— decide either to deny publication, support the advertisement, remain silent or adopt some other course of conduct consistent with their consciences and beliefs.

The Alabama statutes as herein applied compelled petitioners to choose between public dissociation from beliefs and ideas and the legal imputation that they are associated with such beliefs and ideas. The First and Fourteenth Amendments, as interpreted in the controlling decisions cited above, prohibit such compulsory disclosure of association or dissociation.

Moreover, the Alabama "retraction statute" requires in part that defendant shall "publish . . . in as prominent and public a place or manner as the charge or matter published occupied, a full and fair retraction of such charge or matter." (Title 7, Section 914 of the Code of Alabama, set forth in full at p. 4, *supra*).

Assuming *arguendo* that petitioners might have been willing to "retract," it was clearly impossible for them to meet the conditions imposed by the Alabama statute. To make such retraction would require petitioners to place and pay for an advertisement in *The Times*. The record (together with the subsequent attachments and levies on petitioners made by respondent Sullivan) indicates that the limited salaries of petitioners would probably have made the cost of such an advertisement prohibitive to them. Accordingly, the Alabama retraction statute, as applied in the case at bar, clearly appears to discriminate against the indigent and in favor of the wealthy. It is, thus, apparent that the Alabama retraction statutes, as so applied against petitioners, deny equal protection of law in violation of the Fourteenth Amendment. *Cf. Gideon* v. *Wainwright*, 372 U.S. 335.

This Court has repeatedly held that freedom of thought and belief is absolute (*Cf. Cantwell* v. *Connecticut*, *supra*, 303; *West Va. Board of Education* v. *Barnette*, *supra*). Whatever may be the power of the State to restrict or compel actions, the right to remain silent as to a choice of such conflicting beliefs is absolutely protected. The statement at issue here is a constitutionally protected expression of opinion on important public issues. However, even if this case involved a statement not within the safeguards of the First and Fourteenth Amendments, failure during an *eight* day period to deny publication could not sustain liability for publication of a claimed libel, without unconstitutionally restricting freedom of belief and association. *Gibson*, *supra*; *NAACP* v. *Alabama*, *supra*.

IV. Petitioners' rights to Due Process and Equal Protection of Law and to a fair and impartial trial as guaranteed by the Fourteenth Amendment were flagrantly violated and abridged by the proceedings below

Petitioners submit that their trial below was a "race trial", in which they were from first to last placed in a patently inferior position because of the color of their skins.

Throughout the trial below, the jury had before it an eloquent assertion of the inequality

of the Negro in the segregation of the one room, of all rooms, where men should find equality, before the law. This Court's landmark decision in *Brown* v. *Board of Education*, *supra*, gave Constitutional recognition to the principle that segregation is inherently unequal; that it denies Negroes the equal protection of the law, stamps them with a "badge of inferiority" and deprives them of the full benefits of first-class citizenship.

In *Johnson* v. *Virginia*, *supra*, this Court specifically held:

> "Such a conviction [for contempt for refusing to sit in a Negro section of the court room] cannot stand, for it is no longer open to question that a State may not constitutionally require segregation of public facilities [Citing cases]. State-compelled segregation in a court of justice is a manifest violation of the State's duty to deny no one the equal protection of its laws." 373 U.S. at 62 [Brackets added].

Where Sullivan, a white public official, sued Negro petitioners represented by Negro counsel before an all-white jury, in Montgomery, Alabama, on an advertisement seeking to aid the cause of integration, the impact of courtroom segregation could only denote the inferiority of Negroes and taint and infect all proceedings, thereby denying petitioners the fair and impartial trial to which they are constitutionally entitled. And such courtroom segregation has been judicially noted to be a long-standing practice in the state courts of Alabama,[34] as well as throughout the South.[35]

In such a context and in light of Alabama's massive system of segregation,[36] the segregated courtroom, even if it be the immediate result of the acts of private persons in "voluntarily" segregating themselves, must be viewed as the direct result of state action and policy in contravention of the Equal Protection Clause. *Lombard* v. *Louisiana*, 373 U.S. 267. Here, as in *Lombard*, state policy and action has dictated, and is legally responsible for, the "private act" of segregation.

State courts and judges have an affirmative duty to secure the equal protection of laws (*Gibson* v. *Mississippi*, 162 U.S. 565, 586), which duty cannot be sidestepped, as below, by ignoring, or merely failing to discharge, the obligation. *Burton* v. *Wilmington Parking Authority*, 365 U.S. 715. Such duty can only be a more

---

[34] See *U.S. ex rel Seals* v. *Wiman*, 304 F. 2d 53 (C. A. 5), cert. den., 372 U.S. 915.
[35] See *Johnson* v. *Virginia*, *supra*.
[36] See n. 7, p. 12, *supra*.

stringent obligation when the violation of equal protection occurs within the judge's own courtroom.

Compounding this unconstitutional segregation were the racial animosities of the community which the Trial Judge permitted, indeed encouraged, to enter and pervade the courtroom. See pp. 12–15, *supra*. The conclusion is inescapable that the trial denied petitioners equal protection and due process of law. *Irvin v. Dowd*, 366 U.S. 717, *Marshall v. United States*, 360 U.S. 310; *Shepherd v. Florida*, 341 U.S. 50, 54–5; *Craig v. Harney*, 331 U.S. 367.[37]

The conduct of the trial itself emphasized the race and racial inferiority of petitioners. In his summation to the jury, respondent's counsel, without so much as a rebuke from the Bench, made the following highly prejudicial and inflammatory remark:

> "In other words, all of these things that happened did not happen in Russia where the police run everything, they did not happen in the Congo where they still eat them, they happened in Montgomery, Alabama, a law-abiding community." (R. 929–30, 941).

Respondent's counsel was also permitted by the Trial Judge, without restraint and over the objections of petitioners' counsel, to mispronounce the word "Negro" as "Nigra" and "Nigger" in the presence of the jury (R. 579–80). The acceptance by the Court below of the lame excuse that this was "the way respondent's counsel had always pronounced it all his life" (R. 580) is directly in conflict with the decisions of this Court. Customs or habits of an entire community (and, *a fortiori*, of an individual) cannot support the denial of constitutional rights. *Cooper* v. *Aaron*, 358 U.S. 1; *Eubanks* v. *Louisiana*, 356 U.S. 584, 588.

More than fifty years ago in *Battle* v. *United States*, 209 U.S. 36, 39, Justice Holmes noted that racist epithets should never be permitted in a court of law, and that the trial judge should prevent such prejudicial and offensive conduct:

> "Finally, an exception was taken to an interruption of the judge, asking the defendant's counsel to make an argument that did not tend to degrade the administration of justice. The reference was to an appeal to race prejudice and to such language as this: 'You will believe a white man not on his oath before you will a negro who is sworn. You can swallow those

niggers if you want to, but John Randolph Cooper will never swallow them.' The interruption was fully justified."

The very use of the term "Nigger" in referring to a defendant or a witness has been recognized by numerous state appellate courts to constitute prejudicial, reversible error. See, *e.g.*, *Taylor* v. *State*, 50 Tex. Crim. Rep. 560, *Harris* v. *State*, 96 Miss. 379; *Collins* v. *State*, 100 Miss. 435; *Roland* v. *State*, 137 Tenn. 663; *Hamilton* v. *State*, 12 Okla. Crim. Rep. 62.

Perhaps the most subtle and personally offensive example of racial derogation is the seeming difference in the Judge's forms of address to the various trial attorneys. Petitioners' trial counsel, all of whom are Negroes, were never addressed or referred to as "Mister" but always impersonally; indeed, in the transcript they are peculiarly referred to as "Lawyer" (*e.g.*, "Lawyer Gray", "Lawyer Crawford"); whereas all white attorneys in the case were consistently and properly addressed as "Mister" (see, *e.g.*, R. 787–90). Such suggested purposeful differentiation by the Judge himself not only would appear to classify Negro petitioners and their counsel as somehow different; it strongly intimates to all present, including the jurors, that in Alabama courts the Negro practitioner at the bar may be a "lawyer" but is not quite a man to be dignified as "mister".

Furthermore, the systematic and intentional exclusion of Negroes from the jury panel itself again stamped the Negro petitioners inferior and unequal, and inevitably denied them a fair trial. From *Norris* v. *Alabama*, 294 U.S. 587, decided by this Court in 1935, through the recent *U.S. ex rel. Seals* v. *Wiman*, 304 F. 2d 53, cert. den., 372 U.S. 915, the federal judiciary has struck down, as violative of the Equal Protection Clause, the systematic exclusion of Negroes from the jury panels of Alabama.

Such exclusion is "an evil condemned by the Equal Protection Clause" (*Akins* v. *Texas*, 325 U.S. 398, 408), which violates the basic constitutional guarantee of a "fair trial in a fair tribunal" (*In re Murchison*, 349 U.S. 133, 136). For such exclusion deprived petitioners of a tribunal of impartial and indifferent jurors from the locality without discrimination (*Strauder* v. *West Virginia*, 100 U.S. 303; see *Irvin* v. *Dowd*, 366 U.S. 717), and firmly rooted in the minds of all those within the courtroom (most significantly, the twelve white jurors) that Negroes are unqualified to sit and render justice over their fellow citizens (*Strauder* v. *West Virginia*, *supra*; see *Cassell* v. *Texas*, 339 U.S. 282).

The denial of a fair trial is still further evidenced by the illegal election of the trial

---

[37] Nor does it matter whether the cause of such denial was state action or private action (see *Moore* v. *Dempsey*, 261 U.S. 86, 91) such as inflammatory local newspaper reports. See *Irvin* v. *Dowd*, *supra*.

judge, even under the Alabama Constitution, which requires the lawful election of a judge as a prerequisite to his exercise of judicial power.[38] Yet, as the federal judiciary has recognized, the State of Alabama unconstitutionally deprives Negroes of their franchise. *Alabama* v. *United States*, 304 F. 2d 583, aff'd 371 U.S. 37.[39] And the United States Civil Rights Commission has documented in detail the county by county exclusion of qualified Negroes from the Alabama electorate.[40]

Such long-standing exclusion of Negroes from voting in elections for State judges insured that the Trial Judge, in whom was vested "justice" in the form of the "atmosphere of the court room",[41] would reflect, as in fact he did, the prejudice of the dominant, white community that elected him.

In this atmosphere of hostility, bigotry, intolerance, hatred and "intense resentment of the . . . white community . . .,"[42] can anyone expect or believe that an all-white jury could render a true and just verdict? It is inconceivable that these twelve men, with the attention of the whole community of their friends and neighbors focused on them, would be able to give their attention to the complex shadings of "truth", malice, fair comment and to the nuances of libel *per se*, injury to reputation and punitive damages despite the absence of proof of pecuniary damages. These twelve men were not, in fact or probably in their own minds, a jury of "peers" of petitioners, but rather an instrumentality for meting out punishment to critics of the political activities of their elected City Commissioner.

The provision of Section 2 of the Fourteenth Amendment, providing for reduction in representation in the event of denial of the right to vote in a federal election or in the election of "the Executive and Judicial officers of a State" is, in part, an implicit recognition that those so elected cannot sit as representatives of those discriminated against, and, therefore, cannot claim full representation. (*Cf. Baker* v. *Carr*, 369 U.S. 186).

In the case at bar, the Trial Judge was not only passively elected by a dominant, prejudiced, white electorate; he actively participated in the perpetuation of white supremacy within the State courts of Alabama. At the very time Trial Judge Jones was considering petitioners' motions for a new trial, he stated in a companion libel case to this one that the Fourteenth Amendment was "a pariah," and inapplicable in proceedings in Alabama State courts which are governed by "white man's justice."[43]

Given the cumulative pressure of all of these forms and techniques of emphasizing petitioners' racial inequality, it is clear that petitioners could not possibly receive a fair trial. The answer prescribes the remedy; for "the apprehended existence of prejudice was one inducement which led to the adoption of the Fourteenth Amendment", *U.S. ex rel. Goldsby* v. *Harpole*, 263 F. 2d 71, 81 (C. A. 5), cert. den., 361 U.S. 838; see also *Shelley* v. *Kraemer, supra*. **Jurisdiction to redress flagrant violations of fundamental constitutional rights "is not to be defeated under the name of local practice"**[44] Petitioners properly presented numerous objections to all these violations of fundamental rights, to the segregated courtroom, the racial bias and community hostility which pervaded the trial, the improper newspaper and television coverage of the trial,[45] the intentional and systematic exclusion of Negroes from the jury and from voting, the illegal election and improper qualification of the presiding Trial Judge and the *ad hominem* appeals of respondent's attorneys. Such abridgments of due process and equal protection were not and could not be waived, and, under established authority, are properly before this Court for review.

These violations are inherent and implicit in the trial transcript, and too obvious for this Court not to notice. And, they are shockingly manifest outside the transcript as well. For, three decades after the decision in *Norris* v. *Alabama, supra*, one need only read *U.S. ex rel. Seals* v. *Wiman, supra*, to learn that Alabama still excludes Negroes from juries; *Alabama* v. *United*

---

[38] Ala. Const. of 1901, Sec. 152.

[39] Thereinbelow the U.S. District Court stated (192 F. Supp. 677, 679 (M. D. Ala.)):
"The evidence in this case is overwhelming to the effect that the State of Alabama, acting through its agents, including former members of the Board of Registrars of Macon County, has deliberately engaged in acts and practices designed to discriminate against qualified Negroes in their efforts to register to vote."

[40] 1961 Report of U.S. Civil Rights Commission (see p. 26 for paragraph summary of voting registration discrimination in Montgomery County). The detailed factual findings of this eminent government agency are entitled to consideration by this court. See *H. J. Heinz Co.* v. *NLRB*, 311 U.S. 514. The attempt to conceal the voting record of Montgomery County from federal government inspection is a fact also known to the federal courts. See *Alabama* v. *Rogers*, 187 F. Supp. 848 (M. D. Ala.), aff'd 285 F. 2d 430 (C. A. 5), cert. den. 366 U.S. 913.

[41] Judge Learned Hand in *Brown* v. *Walter*, 62 F. 2d 798, 799–800 (C. A. 2); See also *Herron* v. *Southern P. Co.*, 283 U.S. 91, 95.

[42] *NAACP* v. *Button, supra* at 435.

[43] See n. 3, p. 3, *supra* and n. 20, pp. 26–7, *supra*.

[44] *Davis* v. *Wechsler*, 263 U.S. 22, 24.

[45] See pp. 12–15, *supra* and n. 10 at p. 15, *supra*.

States, 304 F. 2d 583 (C. A. 5), aff'd 371 U.S. 37, to learn that Negroes are still excluded from voting in Alabama. In fact, state enforced racial segregation is the rule for all areas of public and civil activity,[46] a rule that will not, assuredly, be changed voluntarily by the officials of that state, if recent history is any accurate basis for prediction.[47]

This Court has held repeatedly that violations of fundamental constitutional rights, which plainly appear on the record, are properly reviewable whether or not state "local forms" of practice have been complied with. *Fay* v. *Noia*, 372 U.S. 391; *Williams* v. *Georgia*, 349 U.S. 375; *Terminello* v. *Chicago*, 337 U.S. 1; *Patterson* v. *Alabama*, 294 U.S. 600; *Blackburn* v. *Alabama*, 361 U.S. 199; *U.S. ex rel. Goldsby* v. *Harpole*, 263 F. 2d 71 (C. A. 5), cert. den., 361 U.S. 838.

Moreover, where, as hereinabove shown, petitioners have raised objections as best they can, and have put the issues plainly before this Court, established authority requires review of these objections, even if they were not raised strictly in accordance with local forms of practice and procedural technicalities. *Rogers* v. *Alabama*, 192 U.S. 226. In *Rogers*, a Negro's objection to the selection of the Grand Jury, because Negroes had been excluded from the list of eligible persons, was stricken by the Alabama Court as not in statutorily prescribed form.

---

[46] See n. 7, p. 12, *supra*.

[47] Desegregation of the State University of Alabama was only achieved with the direct assistance of federal law enforcement authorities, and in the face of vigorous dissent by Alabama public officials. *Alabama* v. *United States*, 373 U.S. 545.

Public facilities in Alabama have been desegregated only after court litigation, and over strenuous opposition of state and local authorities. See: *Browder* v. *Gayle*, 142 F. Supp. 707 (M. D. Ala.), aff'd 352 U.S. 903, reh. den., 352 U.S. 950; *Baldwin* v. *Morgan*, 251 F. 2d 780 (C. A. 5); *Baldwin* v. *Morgan*, 287 F. 2d 750 (C. A. 5); *Gilmore* v. *City of Montgomery*, 176 F. Supp. 776 (M. D. Ala.), modified and aff'd, 277 F. 2d 364 (C. A. 5); *Boman* v. *Birmingham Transit Co.*, 280 F. 2d 531 (C. A. 5); *Lewis* v. *The Greyhound Corp.*, 199 F. Supp. 210 (M. D. Ala.); *Sawyer* v. *City of Mobile, Alabama*, 208 F. Supp. 548 (S. D. Ala.); *Shuttlesworth* v. *Gaylord*, 202 F. Supp. 59 (N. D. Ala.), aff'd *sub. nom. Hanes* v. *Shuttlesworth*, 310 F. 2d 303 (C. A. 5); *Cobb* v. *Montgomery Library Board*, 207 F. Supp. 880 (M. D. ala.).

Alabama has failed to desegregate its public school system in compliance with the mandate of this Court in *Brown* v. *Board of Education*, *supra*, and has purposefully passed a series of statutes designed to evade compliance therewith. (See Alabama Code, Title 52 § 61 (13) authorizing the closing of integration-threatened schools by boards of education; *Id.*, Title 52 § 197(1)–(30) providing for secession of individual schools from local and state systems and for their organization into independent districts; *Id.*, Title 52 § 61(20) permitting allocation of education funds to private schools, etc.) See also *Statistical Summary, November 1961*, Southern Education Reporting Service, 5–6.

This Court reviewed the objection and reversed the judgment below, even though it "assume[d] that this section was applicable to the motion," saying (p. 230):

> "It is a necessary and well-settled rule that the exercise of jurisdiction by this court to protect constitutional rights cannot be declined when it is plain that the fair result of a decision is to deny the rights."

Accord: *Brown* v. *Mississippi*, 297 U.S. 278, 285; *Davis* v. *Wechsler, supra; American Ry. Express Co.* v. *Levee*, 263 U.S. 19, 21; *Ward* v. *Love County*, 253 U.S. 17, 22.

As this Court held in *Davis* v. *Wechsler, supra*, at p. 24:

> " ... the assertion of Federal rights, when plainly and reasonably made, is not to be defeated under the name of local practice."

CONCLUSION

Petitioners respectfully submit that the headlong clash between the proceedings and judgment below and the United States Constitution as interpreted by this Court requires reversal of the judgment and dismissal of respondent's suit herein, in order to preserve and protect those rights which are the Constitution's greatest gift.

Respectfully submitted,
I. H. WACHTEL,
CHARLES S. CONLEY,
BENJAMIN SPIEGEL,
RAYMOND S. HARRIS,
Attorneys for Petitioners.
1100 - 17th St., N.W.
Washington, D.C. 20036
HARRY H. WACHTEL,
SAMUEL R. PIERCE, JR.,
JOSEPH B. RUSSELL,
DAVID N. BRAININ,
STEPHEN J. JELIN,
CLARENCE B. JONES,
DAVID G. LUBELL,
CHARLES B. MARKHAM,
WACHTEL & MICHAELSON,
BATTLE, FOWLER, STOKES & KHEEL,
LUBELL, LUBELL & JONES,
Of Counsel.

APPENDIX B
Constitutional and statutory provisions involved

The constitutional provisions herein involved are the First, Fourteenth and Fifteenth Amendments to the Constitution of the United States, which read as follows:

* * * * *

Amendment I

Congress shall make no law respecting an establishment of religion, or prohibiting the free exercise thereof; or abridging the freedom of speech, or of the press; or the right of the people peaceably to assemble, and to petition the Government for a redress of grievances.

* * * * *

Amendment XIV

Section 1. All persons born or naturalized in the United States, and subject to the jurisdiction thereof, are citizens of the United States and of the State wherein they reside. No State shall make or enforce any law which shall abridge the privileges or immunities of citizens of the United States; nor shall any State deprive any person of life, liberty, or property, without due process of law; nor deny to any person within its jurisdiction the equal protection of the laws.

Section 2. Representatives shall be apportioned among the several States according to their respective numbers, counting the whole number of persons in each State, excluding Indians not taxed. But when the right to vote at any election for the choice of electors for President and Vice President of the United States, Representatives in Congress, the Executive and Judicial officers of a State, or the members of the Legislature thereof, is denied to any of the male inhabitants of such State, being twenty-one years of age, and citizens of the United States, or in any way abridged, except for participation in rebellion, or other crime, the basis of representation therein shall be reduced in the proportion which the number of such male citizens shall bear to the whole number of male citizens twenty-one years of age in such State.

Section 3. No person shall be a Senator or Representative in Congress, or elector of President and Vice President, or hold any office, civil or military, under the United States, or under any State, who, having previously taken an oath, as a member of Congress, or as an officer of the United States, or as a member of any State legislature, or as an executive or judicial officer of any State, to support the Constitution of the United States, shall have engaged in insurrection or rebellion against the same, or given aid or comfort to the enemies thereof. But Congress may by a vote of two-thirds of each House, remove such disability.

Section 4. The validity of the public debt of the United States, authorized by law, including debts incurred for payment of pensions and bounties for services in suppressing insurrection or rebellion, shall not be questioned. But neither the United States nor any State shall assume or pay any debt or obligation incurred in aid of insurrection or rebellion against the United States, or any claims for the loss or emancipation of any slave; but all such debts, obligations and claims shall be held illegal and void.

Section 5. The Congress shall have power to enforce, by appropriate legislation, the provisions of this article.

Amendment XV

Section 1. The right of citizens of the United States to vote shall not be denied or abridged by the United States or by any State on account of race, color, or previous condition of servitude.

Section 2. The Congress shall have power to enforce this article by appropriate legislation.

IN THE
SUPREME COURT OF THE UNITED STATES
OCTOBER TERM, 1963

NO. 40

RALPH D. ABERNATHY ET AL., PETITIONERS,

V.

L. B. SULLIVAN, RESPONDENT

ON WRIT OF CERTIORARI TO THE SUPREME COURT OF ALABAMA

BRIEF FOR RESPONDENT

STEINER, CRUM & BAKER,
1109–25 First National Bank Building,
Montgomery 1, Alabama,

CALVIN WHITESELL,
Montgomery, Alabama,
Of Counsel.

ROBERT E. STEINER, III.,
SAM RICE BAKER,
M. ROLAND NACHMAN, JR.,

Attorneys for Respondent

INDEX

IN THE
SUPREME COURT OF THE
UNITED STATES
OCTOBER TERM, 1963
NO. 40

RALPH D. ABERNATHY ET AL., PETITIONERS,

V.

L. B. SULLIVAN, RESPONDENT

ON WRIT OF CERTIORARI TO THE
SUPREME COURT OF ALABAMA

BRIEF FOR RESPONDENT[1]

OPINIONS BELOW

The opinion of the Supreme Court of Alabama (R. 1139) is reported in 273 Ala. 656, 144 So. 2d 25.

JURISDICTION

Petitioners have sought to invoke this Court's jurisdiction under 28 U.S.C., § 1257 (3).

QUESTIONS PRESENTED

1. Will this Court review a state jury verdict in a private common law libel action, embodied in a final state judgment and affirmed by a state's highest appellate court, when alleged federal questions asserted in this Court were not timely raised below in accordance with state procedure, and when there is nothing in the record to support the allegations of the petition and brief?

2. Is there a constitutionally guaranteed absolute privilege to defame an elected city official, under guise of criticism, in a paid newspaper advertisement so that participants in the publication of this defamation are immune from private common law libel judgment in a state court in circumstances where, because of the admitted falsity of the publication, the participants are unable to plead truth, privilege or retraction (to show good faith and eliminate punitive damages)?

3. Are libelous utterances in a paid newspaper advertisement within the area of constitutionally protected speech and press?

4. When persons whose names appear on a defamatory newspaper advertisement as "warm

endorsers" of the advertisement do not deny participation in its publication in response to a demand for retraction which charges publication, and ratify by silence, and when there is other evidence of authority for use of their names on the advertisement, will this Court re-examine a state jury verdict of liability in a private common law libel action, embodied in a final judgment affirmed by the highest state appellate court on a record which a Federal Court of Appeals has found to contain state questions of "substance" which could "go either way", on a bare assertion that the same record is totally devoid of evidence of petitioners' participation in the publication of this defamatory advertisement?

5. When an admittedly false newspaper advertisement charges that city police massively engaged in rampant, vicious, terroristic and criminal actions in deprivation of the rights of others, is a state court holding in a private common law libel action that such an utterance is libelous as a matter of state law—leaving to the jury the questions of publication, identification with the police commissioner, and damages—an infringement of constitutional rights of a participant in the publication of the libel?

6. When a paid newspaper advertisement published in circumstances described in Questions 2 and 4 contains admittedly false charges described in Question 5 about police action in a named city, may this Court consistently with its decisions and the 7th Amendment review on certiorari a state jury finding that the publication is "of and concerning" the city police commissioner whose name does not appear in the publication, and an award of general and punitive damages to him, when this state jury verdict embodied in a final state judgment has been approved by the state's highest appellate court?

7. May this Court consistently with its decisions and the 7th Amendment re-examine facts tried by a state jury when those findings have been embodied in a final state judgment affirmed by the highest state appellate court, and when review is sought on assertions that the verdict is wrong and the general and punitive libel damages merely excessive?

STATUTES INVOLVED

Statutes referred to in this brief are contained in an appendix.

STATEMENT

Petitioners, whose names appeared in a paid advertisement in the New York Times of March 29, 1960 (described in No. 39) as "warm en-

---

[1] To conserve the time of this Court the brief filed by this respondent in No. 39, New York Times Company v. Sullivan, will be referred to throughout this brief when the same issues have been covered there.

dorsers" of the material contained in the advertisement, were joined as co-defendants in a common law libel action against The New York Times. The nature of the ad as a defamation, and not a political expression; its extensive falsity, not one "minor discrepancy" (Brief pp. 11, 17 and 42);[2] its reference to respondent; the questions of libel *per se* and truth as a limitation on libelous utterances; the circumstances of the ad's composition, publication and distribution; and other relevant facts of record are fully discussed in respondent's brief in No. 39. As observed there, these petitioners, two residents of Montgomery, and all residents of Alabama, introduced no testimony whatever to attempt to substantiate in any manner the truth of the defamatory material in the advertisement. Nor did they plead specially truth, or privilege.

The jury returned a joint verdict against The New York Times and petitioners in accordance with Alabama procedure,[3] for Five Hundred Thousand Dollars, and the trial court entered a judgment thereon.

In the case which was tried below, as distinguished from the case which petitioners attempt to bring in this Court, the only alleged defect of due process which petitioners asserted at the trial was a contention that there was an entire absence of evidence connecting them with the publication of the advertisement.

Petitioners filed motions for new trial but allowed them to lapse (R. 984, 999, 1013, 1028). Petitioners' assertion that there was a "general understanding" (Brief, pp. 14–15) which should have prevented this lapse and which was violated by the trial court and presumably by respondent's attorneys is absolutely contrary to fact. The record is barren of even a hint of such an understanding. The record shows that petitioners' then attorneys (none of whom have appeared in this Court) made no attempt to continue the motion within each thirty day period as required by Alabama statutory and case law. The Times' attorneys obviously were unaware of such an "understanding" since they continued The Times' motion from January 14, 1961 to February 10, 1961 (R. 968) and from February 10, 1961 to March 3, 1961 (R. 968), when the motion was heard. More-

over, none of the assignments of error in the Supreme Court of Alabama relating to their motion for new trial (R. 1100–1132) even mentioned that there was any "understanding". Clearly there was not. And clearly the motion lapsed.[4]

The court below affirmed the judgment as to all defendants.

At the trial petitioners denied any connection with the publication of the advertisement. But contrary to what petitioners would have this Court believe, their denial was far from "undisputed", as this record and the following summary of it make clear. Certainly the jury was not required as a matter of law to believe petitioners' protestations of innocence.

Respondent showed at the trial that the names of the petitioners were on the advertisement. They did not reply to respondent's demand for retraction, and their silence in the face of the demand's inculpatory charges that each published the libel under circumstances normally calling for a reply, was evidence from which a jury could find that they had admitted the statements contained in the demand, namely, that they had published the material in the ad. Their failure to deny publication—not their failure to retract—is the basis of the admission.

Moreover, petitioners' silence, and their failure in any manner to disavow the advertisement, constituted a ratification.

In addition, a letter from A. Philip Randolph (R. 587) went to the jury without objection from petitioners as part of The Times' answer to an interrogatory asking for authorization from the signers of the advertisement.[5]

Though petitioners recite that "undisputed" evidence (Brief, pp. 8 and 46) established that their names were not on the Randolph letter, and called the contrary finding below "distorted", the sworn answers to the interrogatories were in evidence, and Times witness Redding, according to the Times' brief in this Court, "did not recall this difference in the list of names . . ." (Times Brief in No. 39, p. 16).

A witness for the Times, Aaronson, testified without objection from petitioners, that the

---

[2] Petitioners are entirely inaccurate in their observation that other "alleged inaccuracies in the ad were conceded by respondent Sullivan to refer to matters within the jurisdiction of the State Education Department or other agencies, or to matters occurring long prior to respondent's taking office" (Brief, p. 12).

[3] Such a joint verdict against joint tort-feasors is required by Alabama procedure, *Bell v. Riley Bus Lines,* 257 Ala. 120, 57 So. 2d 612. It is, of course, collectible only once.

[4] Title 13, § 119, Code of Alabama, 1940 (App. A. p. 29); *Mount Vernon Woodbury Mills v. Judges,* 200 Ala. 168, 75 So. 916; *Ex parte Margart,* 207 Ala. 604, 93 So. 505; *Southern Ry. Co. v. Blackwell,* 211 Ala. 216, 100 So. 215.
[5] This letter stated:
"This will certify that the names included on the enclosed list are all signed members of the Committee to Defend Martin Luther King and The Struggle for Freedom in the South. Please be assured that they have all given me permission to use their names in furthering the work of our Committee."

Randolph letter was a "written communication confirming the fact that the persons whose names were given here had authorized it" (R. 739), and that such a letter was "our usual authorization" (R. 740). Murray, the author of the ad, a witness for petitioners, testified that the executive director of the committee which inserted the ad, one Bayard Rustin, had stated that the southern ministers, including petitioners, did not have to be contacted or consulted since they were all members of the Southern Christian Leadership Conference, and supported the work of the committee (R. 809).

While not in this record, the report of *Abernathy v. Patterson*, 295 F. 2d 452 (5th Cir.), cert. den. 368 U.S. 986, shows that the complaint of these petitioners in that case verified by oath of Petitioner Abernathy strongly underlines the correctness of the jury verdict.[6]

The foregoing states the facts relating to this case.

The following matters, stated by petitioners to be in this case, are not.

A. Matters outside the record which petitioners did not raise in the trial court, but

---

[6] The painstaking analysis of the Court of Appeals revealed:

1. "(The complaint) alleges that on or about March 29, 1960, 'supporters of the plaintiffs and the movement for equality which they lead' inserted in The New York Times a paid advertisement . . ." (295 F. 2d at 453).

2. The advertisement "purports to be signed by twenty ministers including the four plaintiffs" (295 F. 2d at 454).

3. "The complaint then alleges: 'The defendants . . . conspired and planned . . . to deter and prohibit the plaintiffs and their supporters as set forth above, from utilizing their constitutional rights and in particular their right to access to a free press, by instituting fraudulent actions in libel against the plaintiffs . . .' " (295 F. 2d at 454).

4. "Irreparable damage is alleged, as follows: ' . . . (b) . . . the plaintiffs herein . . . will be deterred from using the media of a free press and all other rights guaranteed under the 1st Amendment . . .' " (295 F. 2d at 454).

5. "The relief prayed for is as follows: ' . . . (c) . . . Restraining each of the defendants . . . from engaging in the aforesaid conspiracy designed to deter and prohibit the plaintiffs from exercising rights guaranteed by the 1st and 14th Amendments with respect to freedom of speech, press . . .' " (295 F. 2d at 455).

6. "As has been noted (on page 454), the plaintiffs' claim of irreparable injury and loss is based (1) upon the claim that 'the plaintiffs and the Negro citizens of the State of Alabama will be deterred from using the media of a free press . . .' " (295 F. 2d at 456).

7. "Libelous utterances or publications are not within the area of constitutionally protected speech and press. The plaintiffs' claim that they will be deterred from using the media of a free press must therefore be predicated upon their claims of denial of a fair and impartial trial of the libel actions and the absence of a plain, adequate and complete remedy at law" (295 F. 2d at 456–457).

attempted to raise for the first time in the Supreme Court of Alabama

1. An alleged racially segregated court room. There is nothing in the record to support this. It was not raised in the trial court. Had it been, respondent would have strongly controverted the allegation as entirely untrue.[7]

2. An alleged "atmosphere of racial bias, passion and hostile community pressures" (Petition, p. 2). This was not raised in the trial court. There was no motion for change of venue, continuance, or for mistrial, though three lawyers represented the petitioners and five represented The New York Times at the trial (R. 567–568). Their silence in this regard speaks eloquently for the fair and impartial manner in which the trial judge conducted the trial. There is nothing in the record to support this allegation.

3. Alleged improper newspaper and television coverage at the trial. This was not raised in the trial court, nor were there motions for mistrial, change of venue, or continuance. There is nothing in the record to support the allegations. Had there been timely trial motions attacking the propriety of newspaper and television coverage of the trial, respondent would have strongly controverted them.

4. Alleged intentional and systematic exclusion of Negroes from the jury. This was not raised in the trial court and there is nothing in the record to support the allegation. Had the allegation been made, respondent would have strongly controverted it.[8]

5. Alleged unqualified trial judge—illegally elected and illegally a member of the county jury commission. This matter was not raised in the trial court. There was no motion seeking disqualification of the trial judge. There is nothing in the record to support the allegation. Had the charge been made in timely fashion, it would have been strongly controverted.

---

[7] Petitioners tell this Court that court room segregation "has been judicially noted to be a longstanding practice in the state courts of Alabama . . ." (Brief, p. 53). They cite *U.S. ex rel. Seals v. Wiman*, 304 F. 2d 53 (5th Cir. 1962). But that case specifically held that the question of a segregated courthouse, there sought to be raised, "[was] not presented to the State courts on the appeal from the judgment of conviction, on the petition for leave to file coram nobis, or in any other manner. Those questions cannot therefore be considered here" (304 F. 2d at 56).

[8] When this question was appropriately raised in a recent case, the method of selecting Montgomery County juries passed constitutional muster in this Court. *Reeves v. Alabama*, 355 U.S. 368, dismissing the writ of certiorari "as improvidently granted."

6. Alleged improper closing argument of one of the attorneys for respondent. There is nothing in the trial record about this. No objection to any argument of any attorney is in the record. There was no motion for mistrial. Had such objection or motion been made, respondent would have strongly controverted any suggestion of an improper argument. It is noteworthy that the Times makes no such allegation in this Court.

The record references contained in petitioners' brief on some of these points concern testimony offered by The Times in support of its motion for new trial, after petitioners' motion had lapsed. As the court below held, the trial court correctly excluded such evidence under the well-settled Alabama rule that only when newly discovered evidence is the basis for a motion for new trial is the trial court permitted to extend the hearing to matters not contained in the record of the trial.[9] Obviously the Times and these petitioners realize that the trial court ruling was correct. No petitioner challenges the ruling of the courts below here. Unlike the Times, however, these petitioners simply cite this rejected material as evidence anyway, and ask this Court to consider matters outside the record which were not raised in the trial below.

B. Matters outside the record which petitioners did not seek to raise in the trial court or in the Supreme Court of Alabama

1. Petitioners object to the court reporter's transcript designation of their attorneys as "Lawyer." This matter was not raised in either court below. The record was obviously transcribed by the court reporter after the trial was over. It was prepared at the instance of The New York Times; filed by The Times with the clerk of the trial court; and "joined in" by these petitioners (R. 1031). Under Alabama procedure, these petitioners had an opportunity to make any objection to the transcript which they desired, and to bring the matter to the attention of the trial court for ruling.[10] Moreover, the transcript, noting appearances, refers to these, and all other attorneys, as "Esq." (R. 567–568).

Obviously these designations by the court reporter are his own, and were made after the trial had closed. They do not purport to be, nor

are they, quotations of the manner of address used by the attorneys in the case or by the trial judge. A search of the record reveals that only an attorney for the New York Times used this form of address in the proceedings before the trial court without a jury.[11]

2. Petitioners object to an alleged statement by the trial judge regarding "white man's justice", said to have been made by him three months after this trial concluded. The matter was not raised in either court below. There was no motion to disqualify the judge.

But this record **does** reveal that this judge stated to the jury in his oral charge (R. 819–20):

> "Now, one other thing I would like to say although I think it is hardly necessary—one of the defendants in this case is a corporate defendant and some of the others belong to various races and in your deliberation in arriving at your verdict, all of these defendants whether they be corporate or individuals or whether they belong to this race or that doesn't have a thing on earth to do with this case but let the evidence and the law be the two pole stars that will guide you and try to do justice in fairness to all of these parties here. They have no place on earth to go to settle this dispute except to come before a Court of our country and lay the matter before a jury of twelve men in whose selection each party has had the right to participate and out of all the jurors we had here at this term of Court, some fifty jurors, the parties here have selected you because they have confidence in your honesty, your integrity, your judgment and your common sense. Please remember, gentlemen of the jury, that all of the parties that stand here stand before you on equal footing and are all equal at the Bar of Justice."

3. The allegation that there was a "general understanding" about petitioners' motion for new trial has already been covered. The point was not raised in either court below.

4. The allegation that an all-white jury deprived petitioners of their rights. This allegation was not made in either court below. Any such allegation of misconduct on the part of the jury would have been strongly controverted by respondent.

5. The pendency of other libel suits is a matter entirely outside this record; and not presented in either court below. The utter desperation involved in this attempt to bring in other libel suits is fully discussed in respondent's Brief in

---

[9] (R. 1165) citing *Thomason v. Silvey*, 123 Ala. 694, 26 So. 644; and *Alabama Gas Company v. Jones*, 244 Ala. 413, 13 So. 2d 873.
[10] Title 7, § 827 (1a), Alabama Code, Appendix A, p. 27.

[11] "Mr. Embry: . . . I will read Lawyer Gray's examinations" (R. 550).
"Mr. Embry: At this time, your Honor, Lawyer Gray said, 'That's all' " (R. 551).

Opposition in No. 39. The argument will not be repeated here. The baseless and totally unfounded charge that this case is "part of a concerted, calculated program to carry out a policy of punishing, intimidating and silencing all who criticize and seek to change Alabama's notorious political system of enforced segregation" (Brief, p. 29) is simply a figment of the imagination of petitioners and their appellate lawyers. The charge is totally without foundation in the record or in fact. Significantly, none of the numerous attorneys representing the Times and these petitioners at the trial even questioned respondent about such a preposterous matter.

6. Alleged "deliberate, arbitrary, capricious, and discriminatory misapplications of law" (Petition, p. 12). It is impossible to determine what the reference is. It cannot have been raised in either court below.

It is not clear from petitioners' brief whether they claim that these matters outside the record (sub-heads "A" and "B") were raised by "steps" said to have been taken "to preserve their constitutional rights" (Brief, p. 14). Petitioners summarize these "steps" as demurrers to the complaint; objections to the admission of evidence; motions to exclude evidence as insufficient; motions for special jury findings; written requests to charge the jury; and motions for directed verdict in their favor (Brief, p. 14). Obviously, such "steps" could not raise the foregoing points in "A" and "B" under any known rules of practice. It is perfectly plain that the questions were never presented at the trial. And later observations that the questions are "inherent and implicit in the trial transcript" (Brief, p. 59), and "shockingly manifest outside the transcript as well" (Brief, p. 60), reveal clearly that petitioners, too, know these matters were never raised, and are not part of the record before this Court.

C. Matters raised below but concluded to petitioners' apparent satisfaction at the time

This category relates to the pronunciation of the word "Negro". This entirely spurious objection vanished when, whatever the pronunciation had been, the pronouncing attorney was told to "read it just like it is" (R. 579). That was the end of the matter. No further objection was lodged by counsel for these petitioners, even though respondent's counsel spoke the word on at least a dozen additional occasions.[12] More-

over, there is nothing in the record to show precisely how the word was pronounced.

D. Matters foreclosed from the statement of facts by virtue of petitioners' improper procedure below

When petitioners allowed their motions for new trial to lapse, they were foreclosed from raising questions regarding alleged excessiveness of the verdict or alleged insufficiency of the evidence.[13]

SUMMARY OF ARGUMENT[14]

I.

When the only defect of procedural due process asserted at the trial was an alleged entire absence of evidence connecting petitioners with the publication of the ad, they cannot go outside the record and seek to present to this Court new matters—none of which were raised in the trial court, and many of which were not asserted in the Supreme Court of Alabama. Included in this category are those arguments in this Court which allege a segregated trial courtroom; a hostile and prejudiced trial atmosphere; improper newspaper and television coverage of the trial; illegal composition of the jury; improper argument of one of the lawyers for respondent; improper court reporter's designation of petitioners' attorneys in the appellate transcript of the record prepared many months **after** the trial was over; improper statements allegedly made by the trial judge three months **after** the trial had ended; pendency of other libel suits by different plaintiffs, against different defendants, regarding different publications, in different communications media, brought in different forums, with different attorneys, and different issues; illegal election of the trial judge.

Had these allegations been made before or during the trial, they would have been strongly controverted. Since these assertions of alleged federal questions were not made in timely fashion, this Court will not go outside the record to consider them. *Stroble v. California*, 343 U.S. 181, 193–194 (charges of inflammatory newspaper accounts and community prejudice); *Michel v. Louisiana*, 350 U.S. 91 (systematic exclusion of Negroes from grand jury panels

---

[12] R. 580; 581; 592; 593; 631; and 656.

[13] *State v. Ferguson*, 269 Ala. 44, 45, 110 So. 2d 280; *Shelley v. Clark*, 267 Ala. 621, 625, 103 So. 2d 743.
[14] Respondent refers this Court to his summary of argument in New York Times Company v. Sullivan, No. 39, where applicable. Respondent has there set out a summary of the constitutional questions relating to the substantive Alabama law of libel as applied in this case. Those arguments will not be repeated in this brief.

not raised in time); *Edelman v. California*, 344 U.S. 357, 358–359 (vagueness of vagrancy statute not raised at the trial); *Stembridge v. Georgia*, 343 U.S. 541, 547 (federal rights asserted for first time in state appellate court); *Bailey v. Anderson*, 326 U.S. 203, 206–207 (same holding); *Herndon v. Georgia*, 295 U.S. 441, 443 (trial court rulings not preserved in accordance with state practice); *Hanson v. Denckla*, 357 U.S. 235, 243–244.

Since petitioners allowed their motions for new trial to lapse, they may not question the size of the verdict against them or the sufficiency of the evidence. *State v. Ferguson*, 269 Ala. 44, 45, 110 So. 2d 280; *Shelley v. Clark*, 267 Ala. 621, 625, 103 So. 2d 743.

Moreover, it is noteworthy that the Times does not argue that the trial proceedings were defective or that they were other than fair and impartial.

II.

The only federal question of due procedure raised at the trial was whether there was **any** evidence connecting petitioners with the publication of the ad. Positive evidence of authority for the use of their names on the ad, supplemented by evidence of their conduct and admissions, proved the case against petitioners for submission to a jury.

Their names were on the ad; and the Randolph letter, according to the Times' answers to interrogatories, showed authorization.

In addition, petitioners did not reply to Sullivan's demand for retraction which expressly charged them with publication. Their silence in the face of the inculpatory charges contained in this demand, under circumstances normally calling for a reply, was evidence from which a jury could find an admission of the statements contained in the letters demanding retraction. This failure to deny publication—not their failure to retract—is the basis of admission. A litigant will not be heard to say that his extra-judicial statements or conduct, inconsistent with his position taken at the trial, is so little worthy of credence that the trier of fact should not even consider them. *Parks v. New York Times Company*, 308 F. 2d 424 (5th Cir. 1962); *Perry v. Johnston*, 59 Ala. 648, 651; *Peck v. Ryan*, 110 Ala. 336, 17 So. 733; *Craft v. Koonce*, 237 Ala. 552, 187 So. 730; *Sloss-Sheffield Co. v. Sharp*, 156 Ala. 284, 47 So. 279; Annotation 70 A. L. R. 2d 1099; Wigmore on *Evidence*, § 1071; Morgan on Admissions, included in *Selected Writings on Evidence*, p. 829.

Closely allied to the doctrine of silence as admission is the equally well-established principle that one may ratify by silence and acquiescence the act of another, even though the persons involved are strangers. This Alabama rule applies whether or not there is a pre-existing agency relationship. *Parks v. New York Times Company*, 308 F. 2d 424 (5th Cir. 1962); *Birmingham News Co. v. Birmingham Printing Co.*, 209 Ala. 403, 407, 96 So. 336, 340–341; *Goldfield v. Brewbaker Motors* (Ala. App.), 36 Ala. App. 152, 54 So. 2d 797, cert. denied 256 Ala. 383, 54 So. 2d 800; *Woodmen of the World Ins. Co. v. Bolin*, 243 Ala. 426, 10 So. 2d 296; *Belcher Lumber Co. v. York*, 245 Ala. 286, 17 So. 2d 281; 1 *Restatement of Agency 2d*, Sec. 94, page 244; Comments (a) and (b); 3 *Restatement of Agency 2d* (App. pages 168 and 174).

III.

Libelous utterances are not within the area of constitutionally protected speech and press. *Roth v. United States*, 354 U.S. 476, 483; *Beauharnais v. Illinois*, 343 U.S. 250, 256; *Chaplinsky v. New Hampshire*, 315 U.S. 568, 571–572; *Konigsberg v. State Bar of California*, 366 U.S. 36, 49–50; *Near v. Minnesota*, 283 U.S. 697, 715.

ARGUMENT

I. This court will not go outside the record to consider federal questions which were not timely raised in accordance with state procedure

This brief should be stricken for failure to comply with Rule 40 (5) of the Rules of this Court.[15] In addition to the matters outside the record which were not raised in the trial court, and in some instances not even in the Supreme Court of Alabama, petitioners' brief contains lengthy expositions of cases and other materials relating to racial matters involving peonage, education, voting, housing and zoning, public transportation, parks, libraries, petit and grand jury service, municipal boundaries, and reapportionment. In the aggregate, such material and excursions from the record consume almost forty-five per cent of petitioners' brief.

Quite apart from the duty of attorneys to confine issues and discussions to matters appearing in the record, particularly when seeking review in this Court, it is noteworthy that not one of the attorneys appearing here for these petitioners was their counsel in the trial court and none was present there. These appellate

---

[15] "Briefs must be compact, logically arranged with proper headings, concise, and free from burdensome, irrelevant, immaterial, and scandalous matter. Briefs not complying with this paragraph may be disregarded and stricken by the Court."

attorneys are, therefore, peculiarly unqualified to comment on matters not in the record.

This Court will surely note that the brief of The New York Times in No. 39 does not support petitioners' characterization of the trial proceedings. Several of its attorneys were personally present at the trial; participated in it; and know how it was conducted. They make no complaints of trial unfairness.

This is the second time petitioners have brought their baseless charges here. Their petition in *Abernathy v. Patterson*, 368 U.S. 986, climaxed a parade of these same groundless attacks through the entire federal judiciary. The District Court called them "impertinent"; the Court of Appeals upheld that court's dismissal of the complaint, 295 F. 2d 452 and this Court denied certiorari.

It is too elemental for argument that this Court will not go outside the record to consider alleged federal questions which were not timely raised in accordance with state procedure. *Stroble v. California*, 343 U.S. 181, 193–194 (charges of inflammatory newspaper accounts and community prejudice); *Michel v. Louisiana*, 350 U.S. 91 (systematic exclusion of Negroes from grand jury panels not raised in time); *Edelman v. California*, 344 U.S. 357, 358–359 (vagueness of vagrancy statute not raised at the trial); *Stembridge v. Georgia*, 343 U.S. 541, 547 (federal rights asserted for first time in state appellate court); *Bailey v. Anderson*, 326 U.S. 203, 206–207 (same holding); *Herndon v. Georgia*, 295 U.S. 441, 443 (trial court rulings not preserved in accordance with state practice); *Hanson v. Denckla*, 357 U.S. 235, 243–244:

> "We need not determine whether Florida was bound to give full faith and credit to the decree of the Delaware Chancellor since the question was not seasonably presented to the Florida court. Radio Station WOW v. Johnson, 326 U.S. 120, 128."

Thus, aside from the question of whether petitioners have an asserted absolute privilege to defame public officials under the guise of criticism, and thereby to avoid Alabama libel laws—a matter fully discussed in respondent's brief in No. 39, incorporated herein by reference—the only question which petitioners can argue on this record is whether it is "devoid of probative evidence of authorization or publication by any of the petitioners of the alleged libel or of any malice on their part" (Brief, p. 44).

As this Court held in *Garner v. Louisiana*, 368 U.S. 157, 163–164:

> "As in Thompson v. Louisville (citation), our inquiry does not turn on a question of suffi-

ciency of evidence to support a conviction, but on whether these convictions rest upon **any evidence** which would support a finding that the petitioners' acts caused a disturbance of the peace." (Emphasis supplied.)

II. There was ample evidence of petitioners' publication for submission to a jury

Positive evidence of authority for use of their names on the ad, supplemented by evidence of their conduct and admissions, proved the case against petitioners for submission to a jury.

Their names were on the ad; they did not reply to Sullivan's demand for a retraction which expressly charged them with publication, and their silence in the face of the inculpatory charges contained in the demand for retraction, under circumstances normally calling for a reply, was evidence from which a jury could find an admission of the statements contained in the letters demanding retraction. This admission came from their failure to deny publication—not their failure to retract.

Moreover, their silence and their failure in any manner to disavow the ad constituted a ratification.

The Randolph letter, according to The Times' answers to interrogatories, showed authorization. Testimony of Murray and of The Times' witness, Aaronson, has been cited. Clearly such evidence permitted a jury to decide where the truth lay. And, as pointed out, the sworn complaint in *Abernathy v. Patterson*, 295 F. 2d 452 (5th Cir.), cert. denied 368 U.S. 986, strongly corroborated the correctness of this verdict.

The Alabama trial court and Supreme Court held that there was a jury question on the issue of petitioners' liability as participants in the publication. The Court of Appeals in *Parks v. New York Times Company*, 308 F. 2d 474 (5th Cir. 1962), held that the position of this respondent in the state courts had substance, and that on the question of liability of these petitioners the judgment could "go either way" (308 F. 2d at 480–481). This is the classic situation for jury determination.

It is impossible to understand petitioners' assertion here that the Court of Appeals reversed the District Court "on other grounds" (Brief, p. 44). This erroneous assertion is simply in direct conflict with the holding of the Court. Moreover, in view of the Court's extensive and exhaustive discussion of silence in the face of the inculpatory charges in the demand for retraction as evidence from which a jury could "infer ratification or adoption" (308 F. 2d at 479), it is inconceivable that petitioners argue here (Brief, p. 45) that *Parks* "is clearly shown by the Opinion to rest on matters not contained in the Record in this case . . ." The very record on the merits in this case was introduced in the District Court in *Parks*.

The Alabama courts and the Federal Court of Appeals were clearly correct. Petitioners, in their lengthy brief, do not even attempt to challenge the legal authorities cited by respondent in his brief in opposition (pp. 15–18) except to say that they are inapplicable (Brief, pp. 48–49). But they are not, and give solid support to the jury finding of petitioners' liability.

A. Silence as admission

1. Petitioners' silence was an admission. This failure to deny publication—not their failure to retract—is the basis of the admission. Petitioners seem unable to distinguish between a retraction and a denial of publication. It is as simple as the rationale of admissions—that a litigant will not be heard to say that his extra-judicial statements or conduct inconsistent with his position taken at the trial, is so little worthy of credence that the trier of facts should not even consider them.[16]

The Legislature of Alabama, too, has given considerable importance to a demand for retraction in libel cases. Title 7, § 914, Code of Alabama (App. A of Brief in No. 39). The plaintiff in a libel suit such as this may not obtain punitive damages unless he seeks retraction from the defendant; and a defendant may eliminate his liability for punitive damages by retracting.

In much less compelling circumstances, *Gould v. Kramer*, 253 Mass. 433, 149 N. E. 142, 144, held that an admission of the truth of a letter charging defendant with authorship of another letter which had defamed the plaintiff could be considered from the silence of the defendant on receiving the written charge. This suit sought damages for false and malicious statements made by the defendant about the plaintiff in a letter to plaintiff's employer. Defendant contended that he had not signed or authorized the libelous matter contained in the letter.

While the principle of silence as an admission has been held not to obtain when the inculpatory statement was made in an unanswered letter, a well-recognized exception to this letter principle occurs where the unanswered letter contains a demand, or where it is part of a mutual correspondence.[17]

2. The absurd argument in petitioners' brief (pp. 49–52) that this rule of admissions—long a part of the law of evidence throughout this country—somehow violates a fancied federal right deserves no answer. It is undoubtedly based upon the inability of petitioners to distinguish between a denial of publication and a retraction. A denial does not involve a "dissociation" of belief in the underlying subject matter. If one has published a defamatory statement, he can and should be liable for civil damages in a common law libel action. If he had nothing to do with the defamatory publication, he certainly knows it, and is in a position to deny promptly. In short, these petitioners could have done exactly what they did at the trial—deny publication in an answer to the letter charging it.

Moreover, petitioners' argument that the retraction statute imposes too great a financial burden upon them is equally frivolous. If these petitioners had wanted a forum as wide as that of the advertisement, they could have written, most inexpensively, a letter to the New York Times for publication and there explained their alleged innocence.

These petitioners in response to the demand for retraction were not called upon to restate their views of the subject matter if in fact they had not participated in the publication. All the demand required in order to avoid this well established rule of evidence was a denial of publication. This is the rule of liability about which petitioners here complain. It involves no federal question whatever. It is as plain and simple a question of a state rule of evidence as can be imagined.

B. Petitioners ratified and acquiesced in the use of their names on the advertisement

Closely allied to the doctrine of silence as an admission is the equally well established principle that one may ratify by silence and acquiescence the act of another even though the persons involved are strangers. Alabama authorities and those elsewhere are thoroughly explored in *Parks v. New York Times Company*, 308 F. 2d 474, 480 (5th Cir. 1962).[18]

---

[16] See *Perry v. Johnston*, 59 Ala. 648, 651; *Peck v. Ryan*, 110 Ala. 336, 17 So. 733; *Craft v. Koonce*, 237 Ala. 552, 187 So. 730; *Sloss-Sheffield Co. v. Sharp*, 156 Ala. 284, 47 So. 279; Annotation 70 A. L. R. 2d 1099; Wigmore on *Evidence*, § 1071; Morgan on *Admissions*, included in *Selected Writings on Evidence*, p. 829.

[17] See annotations in 8 A. L. R. 1163; 34 A. L. R. 560; 55 A. L. R. 460. Alabama, too, recognizes this exception to the letter rule. See *Denson v. Kirkpatrick Drilling Co.*, 225 Ala. 473, 479–480, 144 So. 86, and *Fidelity & Casualty Co. v. Beeland Co.*, 242 Ala. 591, 7 So. 2d 265. Among the cases cited for this exception to the letter rule in *Beeland* are *Leach & Co. v. Pierson*, 275 U.S. 120, which recognizes an exception to the unanswered letter rule where the letter contains a demand.

[18] These and others are: *Birmingham News Co. v. Birmingham Printing Co.*, 209 Ala. 403, 407, 96 So. 336, 340–341; *Goldfield v. Brewbaker Motors* (Ala. App.), 36

This Alabama rule applies whether or not there is a pre-existing agency relationship, and thereby accords with the law set out in Professor Warren A. Seavey's notes to Restatement of Agency 2d, cited in footnote eighteen.

Obviously, the foregoing matters involve plain questions of state law, and present no occasion for the exercise of certiorari jurisdiction. If there was **any** evidence against petitioners, there is no federal question. Two Alabama Courts and one Federal Court of Appeals have held there was.[19] Apposite is this Court's observation in *Stein v. New York*, 346 U.S. 156, 181:

> "Of course, this Court cannot allow itself to be completely bound by state court determination of any issue essential to decision of a claim of federal right, else federal law could be frustrated by distorted fact finding. But that does not mean that we give no weight to the decision below, or approach the record de novo or with the latitude of choice open to some state appellate courts, such as the New York Court of Appeals."

This case does not entitle petitioners to ask this Court to sit as a jury and substitute its collective judgment for that of the jury which tried this case.

III.

Respondent is reluctant to dignify by comment the statements in petitioners' brief which vilify respondent and his attorneys for bringing this libel suit. Surely, this Court will note the striking fact that nowhere in this lengthy and vituperative document is there the slightest suggestion that these petitioners, or indeed The New York Times, even attempted to introduce any testimony to substantiate the truth of the matters contained in the paid advertisement.

Respondent cares deeply about freedom of press and speech. And he is also concerned that these basic freedoms do not degenerate into a license to lie. As a commentator cited by petitioners has observed: "In the rise of the Nazis to power in Germany, defamation was a major

weapon." Riesman, *Democracy and Defamation*, 42 Columbia L. Rev. 727, 728.

As venerable as John Peter Zenger is the imbedded constitutional principle that libelous utterances are not within the area of constitutionally protected speech and press.[20]

CONCLUSION

For the foregoing reasons it is respectfully submitted that the writ of certiorari should be dismissed as improvidently granted; in the alternative, respondent respectfully submits that this case should be affirmed.

Respectfully submitted,
ROBERT E. STEINER, III,
SAM RICE BAKER,
M. ROLAND NACHMAN, JR.,
Attorneys for Respondent.
STEINER, CRUM & BAKER,
CALVIN WHITESELL,
Of Counsel.

I, M. Roland Nachman, Jr., of Counsel for Respondent, and a member of the bar of this Court, hereby certify that I have mailed copies of the foregoing Brief and of Respondent's Brief in No. 39, The New York Times Company v. Sullivan, air mail, postage prepaid, to I. H. Wachtel, Esquire, Counsel for petitioners, at his office at 1100 17th Street N. W., Washington, D.C. I also certify that I have mailed a copy of the foregoing Brief, air mail, postage prepaid, to Edward S. Greenbaum, Esquire, 285 Madison Avenue, New York, New York, as attorney for American Civil Liberties Union and the New York Civil Liberties Union, as *amici curiae*.

This . . . day of October, 1963.

M. Roland Nachman, Jr.,
Of Counsel for Respondent.

APPENDIX A

Title 7, Section 827 (1), of the Code of Alabama:

> "BILLS OF EXCEPTION ABOLISHED IN CERTAIN COURTS; TRANSCRIPT OF EVIDENCE.—Bills of exception in the trial of cases at law in the circuit court and courts of like jurisdiction and all other courts of record having a full time

---

Ala. App. 152, 54 So. 2d 797. cert. denied 256 Ala. 383, 54 So. 2d 800; *Woodmen of the World Ins. Co. v. Bolin*, 243 Ala. 426, 10 So. 2d 296; *Belcher Lumber Co. v. York*, 245 Ala. 286, 17 So. 2d 281; 1 Restatement of Agency 2d, Sec. 94, page 244, comments (a) and (b); 3 Restatement of Agency 2d (App. pages 168 and 174).

[19] It is, of course, elemental that signers of an advertisement—or those who later ratified the use of their names—would be liable for its publication since every individual participant in the publication of a defamatory statement, except a disseminator, is held strictly liable. *Peck v. Tribune Co.*, 214 U.S. 185; *Developments in the Law—Defamation*, 69 Harvard L. Rev. at 912.

[20] *Roth v. United States*, 354 U.S. 476, 483; *Beauharnais v. Illinois*, 343 U.S. 250, 256; *Chaplinsky v. New Hampshire*, 315 U.S. 568, 571–572; *Konigsberg v. State Bar of California*, 366 U.S. 36, 49–50; *Near v. Minnesota*, 283 U.S. 697, 715.

court reporter and from which appeals lie directly to the court of appeals or the supreme court of Alabama, in the state of Alabama, are hereby abolished. If a party to a cause tried in such court desires to appeal from a judgment rendered, he shall, within five days after he perfects his appeal give notice to the court reporter, in writing, that he desires to appeal and request the evidence to be transcribed. The court reporter shall then promptly transcribe the evidence, including objections, oral motions, rulings of the court, and the oral charge of the court, certify the same and file it with the clerk within sixty days from the date on which the appeal was taken, or within sixty days from the date of the court's ruling on the motion for a new trial, whichever date is later. He shall also identify and copy all documents offered in evidence in the order in which offered. The evidence so transcribed and certified and filed shall be a part of the record, and assignments of error may be made as though the transcript constituted a bill of exceptions. If the reproduction of documents offered in evidence, such as maps or photographs, be difficult or impracticable, the court reporter shall so certify, and the clerk shall thereupon attach the original or a photostatic copy thereof to the transcript on appeal, and such original or photostatic copy thereof shall be a part of the transcript on appeal. If bulky or heavy objects be offered in evidence as exhibits which are not capable of being attached to the transcript, the court reporter shall certify that such exhibits are bulky or heavy objects which are not capable of being attached to the transcript; that he has identified them as part of the transcript on appeal. The court reporter shall include in his certificate a statement that he has notified both parties or their attorneys of record of the filing of the transcript of testimony. (1943, p. 423, § 1, effective Sept. 1, 1943; 1951, p. 1527, § 1, appvd. Sept. 12, 1951; 1956, 1st Ex. Sess., p. 43, § 1, appvd. Feb. 9, 1956.)"

Title 7, Section 827 (1a) of the Code of Alabama:

"Extension of Time for Filing Transcript; Objections to Transcript; Hearing and Rulings Thereon.—The period of time within which the reporter must file the transcript may be extended by the trial court for cause. Within ten (10) days after the filing with the clerk of the certified transcript by the court reporter, either party may file with the clerk objections to the certified transcript, with his certificate that he has notified the opposing party, or attorney of record, that the same will be called to the attention of the trial court at a specified time and place. If no objections are filed within such ten (10) days the transcript shall be conclusively presumed to be correct. The hearing of objections and the ruling of the court thereon shall be concluded within a period of ninety (90) days from the date of the taking of the appeal, provided that this period may be extended by the trial court for cause. The trial court shall endorse its ruling on the transcript, sign the same, all within said ninety (90) days period, except as hereinbefore provided. Any ruling of the trial court upon such requested hearing, as well as any ruling on objections to a succinct statement, provided for in section 827 (c) of this title, shall be reviewable, with error duly assigned by the dissatisfied party upon the appeal of the cause, and the evidence upon such hearing shall be duly certified by the court reporter. (1951, p. 1528, § 2, appvd. Sept. 12, 1951.)"

Title 13, Section 119 of the Code of Alabama:

"Execution on Judgment; New Trial Must Be Asked in Thirty Days.—After the lapse of ten days from the rendition of a judgment or decree, the plaintiff may have execution issued thereon, and after the lapse of thirty days from the date on which a judgment or decree was rendered, the court shall lose all power over it, as completely as if the end of the term had been on that day, unless a motion to set aside the judgment or decree, or grant a new trial has been filed and called to the attention of the court, and an order entered continuing it for hearing to a future day; provided that in any county in which the trial judge did not reside on the date of the trial such motion may be filed in the office of the clerk, or register, of the court of the county having jurisdiction of said cause, within thirty days from the date of the rendition of the judgment or decree, and the court shall lose all power over it sixty days after the date of the rendition of such judgment or decree as completely as if the end of the term had been on that day unless such motion is called to the attention of the court and an order entered continuing it for hearing to a future date. (1915, p. 707; 1939, p. 167.)"

376 U.S. 254

The NEW YORK TIMES COMPANY, Petitioner,

v.

L. B. SULLIVAN.

Ralph D. ABERNATHY et al., Petitioners,

v.

L. B. SULLIVAN.

Nos. 39, 40.

Argued Jan. 6 and 7, 1964.

Decided March 9, 1964.

A New York newspaper published an "editorial" advertisement communicating information, expressing opinion, reciting grievances, protesting claimed abuses, and seeking financial support on behalf of the Negro right-to-vote movement and the Negro student movement. An elected commissioner of the City of Montgomery, Alabama, brought a civil libel action against the publisher of the newspaper and against Negro and Alabama clergymen whose names appeared in the advertisement. The Circuit Court, Montgomery County, Alabama, entered a judgment on a verdict awarding $500,000 to the plaintiff and the defendants appealed. The Supreme Court of Alabama, 273 Ala. 656, 144 So.2d 25, affirmed, and certiorari was granted. The Supreme Court, Mr. Justice Brennan, held that the rule of law applied by the Alabama courts was constitutionally deficient for failure to provide the safeguards for freedom of speech and of the press that are required by the First and Fourteenth Amendments in a libel action brought by a public official against critics of his official conduct, and that under the proper safeguards the evidence presented in the case was constitutionally insufficient to support the judgment for the plaintiff.

Reversed and remanded for further proceedings.

1. Courts ⚷397½

The Supreme Court granted certiorari in case involving the extent to which the constitutional protections for speech and press limit a state's power to award damages in a libel action brought by a public official against critics of his official conduct. U.S.C.A.Const. Amends. 1, 14.

2. Appeal and Error ⚷185(1)

The contention of defendant, a foreign corporation, that assumption of jurisdiction over its corporate person by Alabama courts overreached territorial limits of due process clause was foreclosed from Supreme Court review by ruling of Alabama courts that defendant entered a general appearance in the action and thus waived its jurisdiction objection. U.S.C.A.Const. Amend. 14.

3. Constitutional Law ⚷254

The proposition that Fourteenth Amendment is directed against state action and not private action is inapplicable in case presenting question of extent to which constitutional protections for speech and press limit a state's power to award damages in libel action brought by public official against critics of his official conduct; it matters not that state courts have applied state law in a civil action and that it is common law only, though supplemented by statute; the test is not the form in which state power has been applied but, whatever the form, whether such power has in fact been exercised. U.S.C.A.Const. Amend. 14; Code of Ala., Tit. 7, §§ 908–917.

4. Constitutional Law ⚷274

If allegedly libelous statements criticizing official conduct of public officers would otherwise be constitutionally protected from state court judgment awarding damages, protection is not forfeited because they were published in the form of a paid advertisement, where the advertisement was not a "commercial" advertisement but was an "editorial" advertisement which communicated infor-

376 U.S. 254   **NEW YORK TIMES COMPANY v. SULLIVAN**   **711**

Cite as 84 S.Ct. 710 (1964)

mation, expressed opinion, recited grievances, protested claimed abuses, and sought financial support on behalf of a movement whose existence and objectives were matters of the highest public interest and concern. U.S.C.A.Const. Amends. 1, 14.

5. Constitutional Law ⬤90

Libel can claim no talismanic immunity from constitutional limitations; it must be measured by standards that satisfy the First Amendment. U.S.C.A. Const. Amend. 1.

6. Constitutional Law ⬤90

Freedom of expression upon public questions is secured by the First Amendment. U.S.C.A.Const. Amend. 1.

7. Constitutional Law ⬤90

The constitutional protections for speech and press were fashioned to assure unfettered interchange of ideas for bringing about political and social changes desired by the people. U.S.C.A.Const. Amend. 1.

8. Constitutional Law ⬤90

The maintenance of opportunity for free political discussion to the end that government may be responsive to will of people and that changes may be obtained by lawful means is a fundamental principle of the constitutional system. U.S. C.A.Const. Amend. 1.

9. Constitutional Law ⬤90

There is a national commitment to principle that debate on public issues should be uninhibited, robust, and wideopen, and that it may well include vehement, caustic and sometimes unpleasantly sharp attacks on government and public officials. U.S.C.A.Const. Amend. 1.

10. Constitutional Law ⬤90

The constitutional protections for speech and press do not turn upon the truth, popularity, or social utility of the ideas and beliefs which are offered; there is no exception for any test of truth, whether administered by judges, juries, or administrative officials, and especially not one that puts the burden of proving

truth on the speaker. U.S.C.A.Const. Amend. 1.

11. Constitutional Law ⬤90

Factual error affords no warrant for repressing speech that would otherwise be free; the same is true of injury to official reputation. U.S.C.A. Const. Amend. 1.

12. Constitutional Law ⬤90

Criticism of official conduct of government officials, such as elected city commissioners, does not lose its constitutional protections for speech and press merely because it is effective criticism and hence diminishes their official reputations. U.S.C.A.Const. Amend. 1.

13. Constitutional Law ⬤90

If neither factual error nor defamatory content suffices to remove constitutional shield from criticism of official conduct, the combination of the two elements is no less inadequate. U.S.C.A. Const. Amend. 1.

14. Insurrection and Sedition ⬤2

There is a broad consensus that the Sedition Act, because of the restraint it imposed upon criticism of government and public officials, was inconsistent with First Amendment. Sedition Act of 1798, 1 Stat. 596; U.S.C.A.Const. Amend. 1.

15. Constitutional Law ⬤12

The Fourteenth Amendment made the First Amendment applicable to the states. U.S.C.A.Const. Amends. 1, 14.

16. Libel and Slander ⬤1½

What a state may not constitutionally bring about by means of a criminal statute is likewise beyond the reach of its civil law of libel.

17. Judgment ⬤634

There is no double jeopardy limitation applicable to civil lawsuits.

18. Constitutional Law ⬤274

The Alabama rule of law that words published of and concerning a person are libelous per se if they tend to injure a person in his reputation and that this standard is met if words injure him in his public office or impute misconduct to him in such office and that public officer's reputation is affected by statements that reflect on agency of which he is in charge is inconsistent with First and Fourteenth Amendments, even though the rule allows defense of truth. U.S.C.A.Const. Amends. 1, 14.

19. Constitutional Law ⬥274

The constitutional protections for speech and press require a federal rule that prohibits a public official from recovering damages for a defamatory falsehood relating to his official conduct unless he proves that the statement was made with "actual malice," that is, with knowledge that it was false or with reckless disregard of whether it was false or not. U.S.C.A.Const. Amends. 1, 14.

> See publication Words and Phrases
> for other judicial constructions and
> definitions.

20. Constitutional Law ⬥274
Libel and Slander ⬥48(2)

A conditional privilege immunizing honest mistakes of fact in publication concerning official conduct is required by the First and Fourteenth Amendments. U.S.C.A.Const. Amends. 1, 14.

21. Constitutional Law ⬥274

The Constitution delimits a state's power to award damages for libel in actions brought by public officials against critics of their official conduct. U.S.C.A. Const. Amends. 1, 14.

22. Libel and Slander ⬥5

The Alabama rule that malice is presumed where general damages are concerned in libel action by public official against critics of his official conduct is inconsistent with federal rule prohibiting public official from recovering damages for defamatory falsehood relating to his official conduct unless he proves that statement was made with actual malice.

23. Courts ⬥400

Where trial judge did not instruct jury in libel case to differentiate between general and punitive damages, and it was impossible to know, in view of the general verdict returned, whether the verdict was wholly an award of one or the other, the judgment would be reversed and the case remanded.

24. Courts ⬥399(2)

The Supreme Court's duty is not limited to elaboration of constitutional principles; the court must also in proper cases review the evidence to make certain that those principles have been constitutionally applied.

25. Constitutional Law ⬥47
Courts ⬥399(1)

In cases where the line between speech unconditionally guaranteed and speech which may legitimately be regulated must be drawn, the rule is that the Supreme Court must examine for itself the statements in issue and the circumstances under which they were made to see whether they are of a character which the principles of the First Amendment, as adopted by the due process clause of the Fourteenth Amendment, protect; the Supreme Court must make an independent examination of the whole record so as to assure itself that the judgment does not constitute a forbidden intrusion on the field of free expression; the Seventh Amendment does not preclude such an examination by the court. U.S.C.A. Const. Amends. 1, 7, 14.

26. Courts ⬥399(2)

The Seventh Amendment, providing that "no fact tried by a jury, shall be otherwise reexamined in any court of the United States, than according to the rules of the common law," is applicable to state cases coming to the Supreme Court; but its ban on reexamination of facts does not preclude the Supreme Court from determining whether governing rules of federal law have been properly applied to the facts. U.S.C.A.Const. Amend. 7.

27. Constitutional Law ⬥274
Libel and Slander ⬥112(2)

The evidence, in Alabama libel action by public official against critics of his official conduct, did not support finding of actual malice and hence did not constitutionally sustain judgment for public officer. U.S.C.A.Const. Amends. 1, 14.

28. Constitutional Law ⊂⊃274

The evidence, in Alabama libel action by public official against critics of his official conduct, was constitutionally defective in that it was incapable of supporting the jury's finding that the allegedly libelous statements were made "of and concerning" public officer. U S. C.A.Const. Amends. 1, 14.

29. Constitutional Law ⊂⊃274
Libel and Slander ⊂⊃51(5)

Since the Fourteenth Amendment requires recognition of the conditional privilege for honest misstatement of fact in publication concerning official conduct, a defense of fair comment must also be afforded in libel case for honest expression of opinion based upon privileged, as well as true, statements of fact; both defenses are defeasible if the public official proves actual malice. U.S.C.A. Const. Amend. 14.

———◆———

William P. Rogers and Samuel R. Pierce, Jr., New York City, for petitioner in No. 40.

255

Herbert Wechsler, New York City, for petitioners in No. 39.

M. Roland Nachman, Jr., Montgomery, Ala., for respondent.

256

Mr. Justice BRENNAN delivered the opinion of the Court.

We are required in this case to determine for the first time the extent to which the constitutional protections for speech and press limit a State's power to award damages in a libel action brought by a public official against critics of his official conduct.

Respondent L. B. Sullivan is one of the three elected Commissioners of the City of Montgomery, Alabama. He testified that he was "Commissioner of Public Affairs and the duties are supervision of the Police Department, Fire Department, Department of Cemetery and Department of Scales." He brought this civil libel action against the four individual petitioners, who are Negroes and Alabama clergymen, and against petitioner the New York Times Company, a New York corporation which publishes the New York Times, a daily newspaper. A jury in the Circuit Court of Montgomery County awarded him damages of $500,-000, the full amount claimed, against all the petitioners, and the Supreme Court of Alabama affirmed. 273 Ala. 656, 144 So.2d 25.

Respondent's complaint alleged that he had been libeled by statements in a full-page advertisement that was carried in the New York Times on March 29, 1960.[1] Entitled "Heed Their Rising Voices," the advertisement began by stating that "As the whole world knows by now, thousands of Southern Negro students are engaged in widespread non-violent demonstrations in positive affirmation of the right to live in human dignity as guaranteed by the U. S. Constitution and the Bill of Rights." It went on to charge that "in their efforts to uphold these guarantees, they are being met by an unprecedented wave of terror by those who would deny and negate that document which the whole world looks upon as setting the pattern for modern freedom. * * *" Succeeding

257

paragraphs purported to illustrate the "wave of terror" by describing certain alleged events. The text concluded with an appeal for funds for three purposes: support of the student movement, "the struggle for the right-to-vote," and the legal defense of Dr. Martin Luther King, Jr., leader of the movement, against a perjury indictment then pending in Montgomery.

The text appeared over the names of 64 persons, many widely known for their

---

1. A copy of the advertisement is printed in the Appendix, pages 740 and 741.
84 S.Ct.—45½

activities in public affairs, religion, trade unions, and the performing arts. Below these names, and under a line reading "We in the south who are struggling daily for dignity and freedom warmly endorse this appeal," appeared the names of the four individual petitioners and of 16 other persons, all but two of whom were identified as clergymen in various Southern cities. The advertisement was signed at the bottom of the page by the "Committee to Defend Martin Luther King and the Struggle for Freedom in the South," and the officers of the Committee were listed.

Of the 10 paragraphs of text in the advertisement, the third and a portion of the sixth were the basis of respondent's claim of libel. They read as follows:

Third paragraph:

"In Montgomery, Alabama, after students sang 'My Country, 'Tis of Thee' on the State Capitol steps, their leaders were expelled from school, and truckloads of police armed with shotguns and tear-gas ringed the Alabama State College Campus. When the entire student body protested to state authorities by refusing to re-register, their dining hall was padlocked in an attempt to starve them into submission."

Sixth paragraph:

"Again and again the Southern violators have answered Dr. King's peaceful protests with intimidation and violence. They have bombed his home almost killing his wife and child. They have

258

assaulted his person. They have arrested him seven times—for 'speeding,' 'loitering' and similar 'offenses.' And now they have charged him with 'perjury'—a *felony* under which they could imprison him for *ten years*. * * *"

2. Respondent did not consider the charge of expelling the students to be applicable to him, since "that responsibility rests

Although neither of these statements mentions respondent by name, he contended that the word "police" in the third paragraph referred to him as the Montgomery Commissioner who supervised the Police Department, so that he was being accused of "ringing" the campus with police. He further claimed that the paragraph would be read as imputing to the police, and hence to him, the padlocking of the dining hall in order to starve the students into submission.[2] As to the sixth paragraph, he contended that since arrests are ordinarily made by the police, the statement "They have arrested [Dr. King] seven times" would be read as referring to him; he further contended that the "They" who did the arresting would be equated with the "They" who committed the other described acts and with the "Southern violators." Thus, he argued, the paragraph would be read as accusing the Montgomery police, and hence him, of answering Dr. King's protests with "intimidation and violence," bombing his home, assaulting his person, and charging him with perjury. Respondent and six other Montgomery residents testified that they read some or all of the statements as referring to him in his capacity as Commissioner.

It is uncontroverted that some of the statements contained in the two paragraphs were not accurate descriptions of events which occurred in Montgomery. Although Negro students staged a demonstration on the State Capital steps, they sang the National Anthem and not "My

259

Country, 'Tis of Thee." Although nine students were expelled by the State Board of Education, this was not for leading the demonstration at the Capitol, but for demanding service at a lunch counter in the Montgomery County Courthouse on another day. Not the entire student body, but most of it, had protested the expulsion, not by refusing to register, but by boycotting classes on

with the State Department of Education."

a single day; virtually all the students did register for the ensuing semester. The campus dining hall was not padlocked on any occasion, and the only students who may have been barred from eating there were the few who had neither signed a preregistration application nor requested temporary meal tickets. Although the police were deployed near the campus in large numbers on three occasions, they did not at any time "ring" the campus, and they were not called to the campus in connection with the demonstration on the State Capitol steps, as the third paragraph implied. Dr. King had not been arrested seven times, but only four; and although he claimed to have been assaulted some years earlier in connection with his arrest for loitering outside a courtroom, one of the officers who made the arrest denied that there was such an assault.

On the premise that the charges in the sixth paragraph could be read as referring to him, respondent was allowed to prove that he had not participated in the events described. Although Dr. King's home had in fact been bombed twice when his wife and child were there, both of these occasions antedated respondent's tenure as Commissioner, and the police were not only not implicated in the bombings, but had made every effort to apprehend those who were. Three of Dr. King's four arrests took place before respondent became Commissioner. Although Dr. King had in fact been indicted (he was subsequently acquitted) on two counts of perjury, each of which carried a possible five-year sentence, respondent had nothing to do with procuring the indictment.

260

Respondent made no effort to prove that he suffered actual pecuniary loss as a result of the alleged libel.[3] One of his witnesses, a former employer, testified that if he had believed the statements, he

doubted whether he "would want to be associated with anybody who would be a party to such things that are stated in that ad," and that he would not re-employ respondent if he believed "that he allowed the Police Department to do the things that the paper say he did." But neither this witness nor any of the others testified that he had actually believed the statements in their supposed reference to respondent.

The cost of the advertisement was approximately $4800, and it was published by the Times upon an order from a New York advertising agency acting for the signatory Committee. The agency submitted the advertisement with a letter from A. Philip Randolph, Chairman of the Committee, certifying that the persons whose names appeared on the advertisement had given their permission. Mr. Randolph was known to the Times' Advertising Acceptability Department as a responsible person, and in accepting the letter as sufficient proof of authorization it followed its established practice. There was testimony that the copy of the advertisement which accompanied the letter listed only the 64 names appearing under the text, and that the statement, "We in the south * * * warmly endorse this appeal," and the list of names thereunder, which included those of the individual petitioners, were subsequently added when the first proof of the advertisement was received. Each of the individual petitioners testified that he had not authorized the use of his name, and that he had been unaware of its use until receipt of respondent's demand for a retraction. The manager of the Advertising Acceptability

261

Department testified that he had approved the advertisement for publication because he knew nothing to cause him to believe that anything in it was false, and because it

3. Approximately 394 copies of the edition of the Times containing the advertisement were circulated in Alabama. Of these, about 35 copies were distributed

in Montgomery County. The total circulation of the Times for that day was approximately 650,000 copies.

bore the endorsement of "a number of people who are well known and whose reputation" he "had no reason to question." Neither he nor anyone else at the Times made an effort to confirm the accuracy of the advertisement, either by checking it against recent Times news stories relating to some of the described events or by any other means.

Alabama law denies a public officer recovery of punitive damages in a libel action brought on account of a publication concerning his official conduct unless he first makes a written demand for a public retraction and the defendant fails or refuses to comply. Alabama Code, Tit. 7, § 914. Respondent served such a demand upon each of the petitioners. None of the individual petitioners responded to the demand, primarily because each took the position that he had not authorized the use of his name on the advertisement and therefore had not published the statements that respondent alleged had libeled him. The Times did not publish a retraction in response to the demand, but wrote respondent a letter stating, among other things, that "we * * * are somewhat puzzled as to how you think the statements in any way reflect on you," and "you might, if you desire, let us know in what respect you claim that the statements in the advertisement reflect on you." Respondent filed this suit a few days later without answering the letter. The Times did, however, subsequently publish a retraction of the advertisement upon the demand of Governor John Patterson of Alabama, who asserted that the publication charged him with "grave misconduct and * * * improper actions and omissions as Governor of Alabama and Ex-Officio Chairman of the State Board of Education of Alabama." When asked to explain why there had been a retraction for the Governor but not for respondent, the

262

Secretary of the Times testified: "We did that because we didn't want anything that was published by The Times to be a reflection on the State of Alabama and the Governor was, as far as we could see,

the embodiment of the State of Alabama and the proper representative of the State and, furthermore, we had by that time learned more of the actual facts which the ad purported to recite and, finally, the ad did refer to the action of the State authorities and the Board of Education presumably of which the Governor is the ex-officio chairman * * *." On the other hand, he testified that he did not think that "any of the language in there referred to Mr. Sullivan."

The trial judge submitted the case to the jury under instructions that the statements in the advertisement were "libelous per se" and were not privileged, so that petitioners might be held liable if the jury found that they had published the advertisement and that the statements were made "of and concerning" respondent. The jury was instructed that, because the statements were libelous *per se*, "the law * * * implies legal injury from the bare fact of publication itself," "falsity and malice are presumed," "general damages need not be alleged or proved but are presumed," and "punitive damages may be awarded by the jury even though the amount of actual damages is neither found nor shown." An award of punitive damages —as distinguished from "general" damages, which are compensatory in nature —apparently requires proof of actual malice under Alabama law, and the judge charged that "mere negligence or carelessness is not evidence of actual malice or malice in fact, and does not justify an award of exemplary or punitive damages." He refused to charge, however, that the jury must be "convinced" of malice, in the sense of "actual intent" to harm or "gross negligence and recklessness," to make such an award, and he also refused to require that a verdict for respondent differentiate between compensatory and punitive damages. The judge rejected petitioners' contention

263

that his rulings abridged the freedoms of speech and of the press that are guaranteed by the First and Fourteenth Amendments.

In affirming the judgment, the Supreme Court of Alabama sustained the trial judge's rulings and instructions in all respects. 273 Ala. 656, 144 So.2d 25. It held that "[w]here the words published tend to injure a person libeled by them in his reputation, profession, trade or business, or charge him with an indictable offense, or tends to bring the individual into public contempt," they are "libelous per se"; that "the matter complained of is, under the above doctrine, libelous per se, if it was published of and concerning the plaintiff"; and that it was actionable without "proof of pecuniary injury * * *, such injury being implied." Id., at 673, 676, 144 So.2d, at 37, 41. It approved the trial court's ruling that the jury could find the statements to have been made "of and concerning" respondent, stating: "We think it common knowledge that the average person knows that municipal agents, such as police and firemen, and others, are under the control and direction of the city governing body, and more particularly under the direction and control of a single commissioner. In measuring the performance or deficiencies of such groups, praise or criticism is usually attached to the official in complete control of the body." Id., at 674–675, 144 So.2d at 39. In sustaining the trial court's determination that the verdict was not excessive, the court said that malice could be inferred from the Times' "irresponsibility" in printing the advertisement while "the Times in its own files had articles already published which would have demonstrated the falsity of the allegations in the advertisement"; from

the Times' failure to retract for respondent while retracting for the Governor, whereas the falsity of some of the allegations was then known to the Times and "the matter contained in the advertisement was equally false as to both parties"; and from the testimony of the Times' Secretary that,

264

apart from the statement that the dining hall was padlocked, he thought the two paragraphs were "substantially correct." Id., at 686–687, 144 So.2d, at 50–51. The court reaffirmed a statement in an earlier opinion that "There is no legal measure of damages in cases of this character." Id., at 686, 144 So.2d, at 50. It rejected petitioners' constitutional contentions with the brief statements that "The First Amendment of the U. S. Constitution does not protect libelous publications" and "The Fourteenth Amendment is directed against State action and not private action." Id., at 676, 144 So.2d, at 40.

[1, 2] Because of the importance of the constitutional issues involved, we granted the separate petitions for certiorari of the individual petitioners and of the Times. 371 U.S. 946, 83 S.Ct. 510, 9 L.Ed.2d 496. We reverse the judgment. We hold that the rule of law applied by the Alabama courts is constitutionally deficient for failure to provide the safeguards for freedom of speech and of the press that are required by the First and Fourteenth Amendments in a libel action brought by a public official against critics of his official conduct.[4]

---

4. Since we sustain the contentions of all the petitioners under the First Amendment's guarantees of freedom of speech and of the press as applied to the States by the Fourteenth Amendment, we do not decide the questions presented by the other claims of violation of the Fourteenth Amendment. The individual petitioners contend that the judgment against them offends the Due Process Clause because there was no evidence to show that they had published or authorized the publication of the alleged libel, and that the

Due Process and Equal Protection Clauses were violated by racial segregation and racial bias in the courtroom. The Times contends that the assumption of jurisdiction over its corporate person by the Alabama courts overreaches the territorial limits of the Due Process Clause. The latter claim is foreclosed from our review by the ruling of the Alabama courts that the Times entered a general appearance in the action and thus waived its jurisdictional objection; we cannot say that this ruling lacks "fair or sub-

We

265

further hold that under the proper safeguards the evidence presented in this case is constitutionally insufficient to support the judgment for respondent.

I.

[3] We may dispose at the outset of two grounds asserted to insulate the judgment of the Alabama courts from constitutional scrutiny. The first is the proposition relied on by the State Supreme Court—that "The Fourteenth Amendment is directed against State action and not private action." That proposition has no application to this case. Although this is a civil lawsuit between private parties, the Alabama courts have applied a state rule of law which petitioners claim to impose invalid restrictions on their constitutional freedoms of speech and press. It matters not that that law has been applied in a civil action and that it is common law only, though supplemented by statute. See, e. g., Alabama Code, Tit. 7, §§ 908–917. The test is not the form in which state power has been applied but, whatever the form, whether such power has in fact been exercised. See Ex parte Virginia, 100 U.S. 339, 346–347, 25 L.Ed. 676; American Federation of Labor v. Swing, 312 U.S. 321, 61 S.Ct. 568, 85 L.Ed. 855.

[4] The second contention is that the constitutional guarantees of freedom of speech and of the press are inapplicable here, at least so far as the Times is concerned, because the allegedly libelous statements were published as part of a paid, "commercial" advertisement. The argument relies on Valentine v. Chrestensen, 316 U.S. 52, 62 S.Ct. 920, 86 L.Ed. 1262, where the Court held that a city ordinance forbidding street distribution of commercial and business advertising matter did not abridge the First Amendment freedoms, even as applied to a handbill having a commercial message on one side but a protest against

certain official action on the other. The reliance is wholly misplaced. The Court in Chrestensen reaffirmed the constitutional protection for "the freedom of communicating

266

information and disseminating opinion"; its holding was based upon the factual conclusions that the handbill was "purely commercial advertising" and that the protest against official action had been added only to evade the ordinance.

The publication here was not a "commercial" advertisement in the sense in which the word was used in Chrestensen. It communicated information, expressed opinion, recited grievances, protested claimed abuses, and sought financial support on behalf of a movement whose existence and objectives are matters of the highest public interest and concern. See N. A. A. C. P. v. Button, 371 U.S. 415, 435, 83 S.Ct. 328, 9 L.Ed.2d 405. That the Times was paid for publishing the advertisement is as immaterial in this connection as is the fact that newspapers and books are sold. Smith v. California, 361 U.S. 147, 150, 80 S.Ct. 215, 4 L.Ed.2d 205; cf. Bantam Books, Inc. v. Sullivan, 372 U.S. 58, 64, n. 6, 83 S.Ct. 631, 9 L.Ed. 2d 584. Any other conclusion would discourage newspapers from carrying "editorial advertisements" of this type, and so might shut off an important outlet for the promulgation of information and ideas by persons who do not themselves have access to publishing facilities—who wish to exercise their freedom of speech even though they are not members of the press. Cf. Lovell v. City of Griffin, 303 U.S. 444, 452, 58 S.Ct. 666, 82 L.Ed. 949; Schneider v. State, 308 U.S. 147, 164, 60 S.Ct. 146, 84 L.Ed. 155. The effect would be to shackle the First Amendment in its attempt to secure "the widest possible dissemination of information from diverse and antagonistic sources." Associated Press v. United States, 326 U.S. 1, 20, 65 S.Ct. 1416, 1424, 89 L.Ed. 2013.

---

stantial support" in prior Alabama decisions. See Thompson v. Wilson, 224 Ala. 299, 140 So. 439 (1932); compare N. A.

A. C. P. v. Alabama, 357 U.S. 449, 454–458, 78 S.Ct. 1163, 2 L.Ed.2d 1488.

To avoid placing such a handicap upon the freedoms of expression, we hold that if the allegedly libelous statements would otherwise be constitutionally protected from the present judgment, they do not forfeit that protection because they were published in the form of a paid advertisement.[5]

267

II.

Under Alabama law as applied in this case, a publication is "libelous per se" if the words "tend to injure a person * * in his reputation" or to "bring [him] into public contempt"; the trial court stated that the standard was met if the words are such as to "injure him in his public office, or impute misconduct to him in his office, or want of official integrity, or want of fidelity to a public trust * *." The jury must find that the words were published "of and concerning" the plaintiff, but where the plaintiff is a public official his place in the governmental hierarchy is sufficient evidence to support a finding that his reputation has been affected by statements that reflect upon the agency of which he is in charge. Once "libel per se" has been established, the defendant has no defense as to stated facts unless he can persuade the jury that they were true in all their particulars. Alabama Ride Co. v. Vance, 235 Ala. 263, 178 So. 438 (1938); Johnson Publishing Co. v. Davis, 271 Ala. 474, 494–495, 124 So.2d 441, 457–458 (1960). His privilege of "fair comment" for expressions of opinion depends on the truth of the facts upon which the comment is based. Parsons v. Age-Herald Publishing Co., 181 Ala. 439, 450, 61 So. 345, 350 (1913). Unless he can discharge the burden of proving truth, general damages are presumed, and may be awarded without proof of pecuniary injury. A showing of actual malice is apparently a prerequisite to recovery of punitive damages, and the defendant may in any event forestall a punitive award by a retraction meeting the statutory requirements. Good motives and belief in truth do not negate an inference of malice, but are relevant only in mitigation of punitive damages if the jury chooses to accord them weight. Johnson Publishing Co. v. Davis, supra, 271 Ala., at 495, 124 So.2d, at 458.

268

The question before us is whether this rule of liability, as applied to an action brought by a public official against critics of his official conduct, abridges the freedom of speech and of the press that is guaranteed by the First and Fourteenth Amendments.

[5] Respondent relies heavily, as did the Alabama courts, on statements of this Court to the effect that the Constitution does not protect libelous publications.[6] Those statements do not foreclose our inquiry here. None of the cases sustained the use of libel laws to impose sanctions upon expression critical of the official conduct of public officials. The dictum in Pennekamp v. Florida, 328 U.S. 331, 348–349, 66 S.Ct. 1029, 1038, 90 L.Ed. 1295, that "when the statements amount to defamation, a judge has such remedy in damages for libel as do other public servants," implied no view as to what remedy might constitutionally be afforded to public officials. In Beauharnais v. Illinois, 343 U.S. 250, 72 S.Ct. 725, 96 L.Ed. 919, the Court sustained an Illinois criminal libel statute as applied to a publication held to be both defamatory of a racial group and "liable to cause violence and disorder." But the Court was careful to note that it "retains and

5. See American Law Institute, Restatement of Torts, § 593, Comment b (1938).

6. Konigsberg v. State Bar of California, 366 U.S. 36, 49, and n. 10, 81 S.Ct. 997, 6 L.Ed.2d 105; Times Film Corp. v. City of Chicago, 365 U.S. 43, 48, 81 S.Ct. 391, 5 L.Ed.2d 403; Roth v. United States, 354 U.S. 476, 486–487, 77 S.Ct. 1304, 1 L.Ed.2d 1498; Beauharnais v. Illinois, 343 U.S. 250, 266, 72 S.Ct. 725, 96 L.Ed. 919; Pennekamp v. Florida, 328 U.S. 331, 348–349, 66 S.Ct. 1029, 90 L.Ed. 1295; Chaplinsky v. New Hamphire, 315 U.S. 568, 572, 62 S.Ct. 766, 86 L.Ed. 1031; Near v. Minnesota, 283 U.S. 697, 715, 51 S.Ct. 625, 75 L.Ed. 1357.

exercises authority to nullify action which encroaches on freedom of utterance under the guise of punishing libel"; for "public men, are, as it were, public property," and "discussion cannot be denied and the right, as well as the duty, of criticism must not be stifled." Id., at 263–264, 72 S.Ct. at 734, 96 L.Ed. 919 and n. 18. In the only previous case that did present the question of constitutional limitations upon the power to award damages for libel of a public official, the Court was equally divided and the question was not decided. Schenectady Union Pub. Co. v. Sweeney, 316 U.S. 642, 62 S. Ct. 1031, 86 L.Ed. 1727.

269

In deciding the question now, we are compelled by neither precedent nor policy to give any more weight to the epithet "libel" than we have to other "mere labels" of state law. N. A. A. C. P. v. Button, 371 U.S. 415, 429, 83 S.Ct. 328, 9 L.Ed.2d 405. Like insurrection,[7] contempt,[8] advocacy of unlawful acts,[9] breach of the peace,[10] obscenity,[11] solicitation of legal business,[12] and the various other formulae for the repression of expression that have been challenged in this Court, libel can claim no talismanic immunity from constitutional limitations. It must be measured by standards that satisfy the First Amendment.

[6–8] The general proposition that freedom of expression upon public questions is secured by the First Amendment has long been settled by our decisions. The constitutional safeguard, we have said, "was fashioned to assure unfettered interchange of ideas for the bringing about of political and social changes desired by the people." Roth v. United States, 354 U.S. 476, 484, 77 S.Ct. 1304, 1308, 1 L.Ed.2d 1498. "The maintenance

of the opportunity for free political discussion to the end that government may be responsive to the will of the people and that changes may be obtained by lawful means, an opportunity essential to the security of the Republic, is a fundamental principle of our constitutional system." Stromberg v. California, 283 U.S. 359, 369, 51 S.Ct. 532, 536, 75 L.Ed. 1117. "[I]t is a prized American privilege to speak one's mind, although not always with perfect good taste, on all public institutions," Bridges v. California, 314 U.S. 252, 270, 62 S.Ct. 190, 197, 86 L.Ed. 192, and this opportunity is to be afforded for "vigorous advocacy" no less than "abstract discussion." N. A. A. C. P. v. Button, 371 U.S. 415, 429, 83 S.Ct. 328, 9 L.Ed.2d 405.

270

The First Amendment, said Judge Learned Hand, "presupposes that right conclusions are more likely to be gathered out of a multitude of tongues, than through any kind of authoritative selection. To many this is, and always will be, folly; but we have staked upon it our all." United States v. Associated Press, 52 F.Supp. 362, 372 (D.C.S.D.N.Y.1943). Mr. Justice Brandeis, in his concurring opinion in Whitney v. California, 274 U.S. 357, 375–376, 47 S.Ct. 641, 648, 71 L.Ed. 1095, gave the principle its classic formulation:

"Those who won our independence believed * * * that public discussion is a political duty; and that this should be a fundamental principle of the American government. They recognized the risks to which all human institutions are subject. But they knew that order cannot be secured merely through fear of punishment for its infraction; that it is hazardous to discourage thought,

---

7. Herndon v. Lowry, 301 U.S. 242, 57 S. Ct. 732, 81 L.Ed. 1066.

8. Bridges v. California, 314 U.S. 252, 62 S.Ct. 190, 86 L.Ed. 192; Pennekamp v. Florida, 328 U.S. 331, 66 S.Ct. 1029, 90 L.Ed. 1295.

9. De Jonge v. Oregon, 299 U.S. 353, 57 S.Ct. 255, 81 L.Ed. 278.

10. Edwards v. South Carolina, 372 U.S. 229, 83 S.Ct. 680, 9 L.Ed.2d 697.

11. Roth v. United States, 354 U.S. 476, 77 S.Ct. 1304, 1 L.Ed.2d 1498.

12. N. A. A. C. P. v. Button, 371 U.S. 415, 83 S.Ct. 328, 9 L.Ed.2d 405.

hope and imagination; that fear breeds repression; that repression breeds hate; that hate menaces stable government; that the path of safety lies in the opportunity to discuss freely supposed grievances and proposed remedies; and that the fitting remedy for evil counsels is good ones. Believing in the power of reason as applied through public discussion, they eschewed silence coerced by law—the argument of force in its worst form. Recognizing the occasional tyrannies of governing majorities, they amended the Constitution so that free speech and assembly should be guaranteed."

[9] Thus we consider this case against the background of a profound national commitment to the principle that debate on public issues should be uninhibited, robust, and wide-open, and that it may well include vehement, caustic, and sometimes unpleasantly sharp attacks on government and public officials. See Terminiello v. Chicago, 337 U.S. 1, 4, 69 S.Ct. 894, 93 L.Fd. 1131; De Jonge v. Oregon, 299 U.S. 353,

271

365, 57 S.Ct. 255, 81 L.Ed. 278. The present advertisement, as an expression of grievance and protest on one of the major public issues of our time, would seem clearly to qualify for the constitutional protection. The question is whether it forfeits that protection by the falsity of some of its factual statements and by its alleged defamation of respondent.

[10] Authoritative interpretations of the First Amendment guarantees have consistently refused to recognize an exception for any test of truth—whether administered by judges, juries, or administrative officials—and especially one that puts the burden of proving truth on the speaker. Cf. Speiser v. Randall, 357 U.S. 513, 525–526, 78 S.Ct. 1332, 2 L.Ed. 2d 1460. The constitutional protection does not turn upon "the truth, popularity, or social utility of the ideas and beliefs which are offered." N. A. A. C. P. v. Button, 371 U.S. 415, 445, 83 S.Ct. 328, 344, 9 L.Ed.2d 405. As Madison said,

84 S.Ct.—46

"Some degree of abuse is inseparable from the proper use of every thing; and in no instance is this more true than in that of the press." 4 Elliot's Debates on the Federal Constitution (1876), p. 571. In Cantwell v. Connecticut, 310 U.S. 296, 310, 60 S.Ct. 900, 906, 84 L.Ed. 1213, the Court declared:

"In the realm of religious faith, and in that of political belief, sharp differences arise. In both fields the tenets of one man may seem the rankest error to his neighbor. To persuade others to his own point of view, the pleader, as we know, at times, resorts to exaggeration, to vilification of men who have been, or are, prominent in church or state, and even to false statement. But the people of this nation have ordained in the light of history, that, in spite of the probability of excesses and abuses, these liberties are, in the long view, essential to enlightened opinion and right conduct on the part of the citizens of a democracy."

That erroneous statement is inevitable in free debate, and that it must be protected if the freedoms of expression

272

are to have the "breathing space" that they "need * * * to survive," N. A. A. C. P. v. Button, 371 U.S. 415, 433, 83 S.Ct. 328, 338, 9 L.Ed.2d 405, was also recognized by the Court of Appeals for the District of Columbia Circuit in Sweeney v. Patterson, 76 U.S.App.D.C. 23, 24, 128 F.2d 457, 458 (1942), cert. denied, 317 U.S. 678, 63 S.Ct. 160, 87 L.Ed. 544. Judge Edgerton spoke for a unanimous court which affirmed the dismissal of a Congressman's libel suit based upon a newspaper article charging him with anti-Semitism in opposing a judicial appointment. He said:

"Cases which impose liability for erroneous reports of the political conduct of officials reflect the obsolete doctrine that the governed must not criticize their governors. * * * The interest of the public here outweighs the interest of appellant or any other individual. The protection of the public requires not merely discussion, but information. Political conduct and views which some respectable people approve, and others condemn, are constantly imputed to Congressmen. Errors of fact, particularly in regard to a man's mental states and processes, are inevitable. * * * Whatever is added to the field of libel is taken from the field of free debate." [13]

[11, 12] Injury to official reputation error affords no more warrant for repressing speech that would otherwise be free than does factual error. Where judicial officers are involved, this Court has held that concern for the dignity and reputation of the courts does not justify

273

the punishment as criminal contempt of criticism of the judge or his decision. Bridges v. California, 314 U.S. 252, 62 S. Ct. 190, 86 L.Ed. 192. This is true even though the utterance contains "half-truths" and "misinformation." Pennekamp v. Florida, 328 U.S. 331, 342, 343, n. 5, 345, 66 S.Ct. 1029, 90 L.Ed. 1295. Such repression can be justified, if at all, only by a clear and present danger of the obstruction of justice. See also Craig v. Harney, 331 U.S. 367, 67 S.Ct. 1249, 91 L.Ed. 1546; Wood v. Georgia, 370 U.S. 375, 82 S.Ct. 1364, 8 L.Ed.2d 569. If judges are to be treated as "men of fortitude, able to thrive in a hardy climate," Craig v. Harney, supra, 331 U.S.,

at 376, 67 S.Ct., at 1255, 91 L.Ed. 1546, surely the same must be true of other government officials, such as elected city commissioners.[14] Criticism of their official conduct does not lose its constitutional protection merely because it is effective criticism and hence diminishes their official reputations.

[13, 14] If neither factual error nor defamatory content suffices to remove the constitutional shield from criticism of official conduct, the combination of the two elements is no less inadequate. This is the lesson to be drawn from the great controversy over the Sedition Act of 1798, 1 Stat. 596, which first crystallized a national awareness of the central meaning of the First Amendment. See Levy, Legacy of Suppression (1960), at 258 et seq.; Smith, Freedom's Fetters (1956), at 426, 431 and *passim*. That statute made it a crime, punishable by a $5,000 fine and five years in prison, "if any person shall write, print, utter or publish * * * any false, scandalous and malicious

274

writing or writings against the government of the United States, or either house of the Congress * * *, or the President * * *, with intent to defame * * * or to bring them, or either of them, into contempt or disrepute; or to excite against them, or either or any of them, the hatred of the good people of the United States." The Act allowed the defendant the defense of truth, and provided that the jury were

13. See also Mill, On Liberty (Oxford: Blackwell, 1947), at 47:

"* * * [T]o argue sophistically, to suppress facts or arguments, to misstate the elements of the case, or misrepresent the opposite opinion * * * all this, even to the most aggravated degree, is so continually done in perfect good faith, by persons who are not considered, and in many other respects may not deserve to be considered, ignorant or incompetent, that it is rarely possible, on adequate grounds, conscientiously to stamp the misrepresentation as morally culpable; and still less could law presume to interfere with this kind of controversial misconduct."

14. The climate in which public officials operate, especially during a political campaign, has been described by one commentator in the following terms: "Charges of gross incompetence, disregard of the public interest, communist sympathies, and the like usually have filled the air; and hints of bribery, embezzlement, and other criminal conduct are not infrequent." Noel, Defamation of Public Officers and Candidates, 49 Col.L.Rev. 875 (1949).

For a similar description written 60 years earlier, see Chase, Criticism of Public Officers and Candidates for Office, 23 Am.L.Rev. 346 (1889).

to be judges both of the law and the facts. Despite these qualifications, the Act was vigorously condemned as unconstitutional in an attack joined in by Jefferson and Madison. In the famous Virginia Resolutions of 1798, the General Assembly of Virginia resolved that it

> "doth particularly protest against the palpable and alarming infractions of the Constitution, in the two late cases of the 'Alien and Sedition Acts,' passed at the last session of Congress * * *. [The Sedition Act] exercises * * * a power not delegated by the Constitution, but, on the contrary, expressly and positively forbidden by one of the amendments thereto—a power which, more than any other, ought to produce universal alarm, because it is levelled against the right of freely examining public characters and measures, and of free communication among the people thereon, which has ever been justly deemed the only effectual guardian of every other right." 4 Elliot's Debates, supra, pp. 553–554.

Madison prepared the Report in support of the protest. His premise was that the Constitution created a form of government under which "The people, not the government, possess the absolute sovereignty." The structure of the government dispersed power in reflection of the people's distrust of concentrated power, and of power itself at all levels. This form of government was "altogether different" from the British form, under which the Crown was sovereign and the people were subjects. "Is

275

it not natural and necessary, under such different circumstances," he asked, "that a different degree of freedom in the use of the press should be contemplated?" Id., pp. 569–570. Earlier, in a debate in the House of Representatives, Madison had said: "If we advert to the nature of Republican Government, we shall find that the censorial power is in the people over the Government, and not in the Government over the people." 4 Annals of Congress, p. 934 (1794). Of the exercise of that power by the press, his Report said: "In every state, probably, in the Union, the press has exerted a freedom in canvassing the merits and measures of public men, of every description, which has not been confined to the strict limits of the common law. On this footing the freedom of the press has stood; on this foundation it yet stands * * *." 4 Elliot's Debates, supra, p. 570. The right of free public discussion of the stewardship of public officials was thus, in Madison's view, a fundamental principle of the American form of government.[15]

276

Although the Sedition Act was never tested in this Court,[16] the attack upon its validity has carried the day in the court of history. Fines levied in its prosecution were repaid by Act of Congress on the ground that it was unconstitutional. See, e. g., Act of July 4, 1840, c. 45, 6

---

15. The Report on the Virginia Resolutions further stated:

"[I]t is manifestly impossible to punish the intent to bring those who administer the government into disrepute or contempt, without striking at the right of freely discussing public characters and measures; * * * which, again, is equivalent to a protection of those who administer the government, if they should at any time deserve the contempt or hatred of the people, against being exposed to it, by free animadversions on their characters and conduct. Nor can there be a doubt * * * that a government thus intrenched in penal statutes against the just and natural effects of a culpable administration, will easily evade the responsibility which is essential to a faithful discharge of its duty.

"Let it be recollected, lastly, that the right of electing the members of the government constitutes more particularly the essence of a free and responsible government. The value and efficacy of this right depends on the knowledge of the comparative merits and demerits of the candidates for public trust, and on the equal freedom, consequently, of examining and discussing these merits and demerits of the candidates respectively." 4 Elliot's Debates, supra, p. 575.

16. The Act expired by its terms in 1801.

Stat. 802, accompanied by H.R.Rep.No. 86, 26th Cong., 1st Sess. (1840). Calhoun, reporting to the Senate on February 4, 1836, assumed that its invalidity was a matter "which no one now doubts." Report with Senate bill No. 122, 24th Cong., 1st Sess., p. 3. Jefferson, as President, pardoned those who had been convicted and sentenced under the Act and remitted their fines, stating: "I discharged every person under punishment or prosecution under the sedition law, because I considered, and now consider, that law to be a nullity, as absolute and as palpable as if Congress had ordered us to fall down and worship a golden image." Letter to Mrs. Adams, July 22, 1804, 4 Jefferson's Works (Washington ed.), pp. 555, 556. The invalidity of the Act has also been assumed by Justices of this Court. See Holmes, J., dissenting and joined by Brandeis, J., in Abrams v. United States, 250 U.S. 616, 630, 40 S. Ct. 17, 63 L.Ed. 1173; Jackson, J., dissenting in Beauharnais v. Illinois, 343 U.S. 250, 288–289, 72 S.Ct. 725, 96 L.Ed. 919; Douglas, The Right of the People (1958), p. 47. See also Cooley, Constitutional Limitations (8th ed., Carrington, 1927), pp. 899–900; Chafee, Free Speech in the United States (1942), pp. 27–28. These views reflect a broad consensus that the Act, because of the restraint it imposed upon criticism of government and public officials, was inconsistent with the First Amendment.

[15] There is no force in respondent's argument that the constitutional limitations implicit in the history of the Sedition Act apply only to Congress and not to the States. It is true that the First Amendment was originally addressed only to action by the Federal Government, and

277

that Jefferson, for one, while denying the power of Congress "to controul the freedom of the press," recognized such a power in the States. See the 1804 Letter to Abigail Adams quoted in Dennis v. United States, 341 U.S. 494,

522, n. 4, 71 S.Ct. 857, 95 L.Ed. 1137 (concurring opinion). But this distinction was eliminated with the adoption of the Fourteenth Amendment and the application to the States of the First Amendment's restrictions. See, e. g., Gitlow v. New York, 268 U.S. 652, 666, 45 S.Ct. 625, 69 L.Ed. 1138; Schneider v. State, 308 U.S. 147, 160, 60 S.Ct. 146, 84 L.Ed. 155; Bridges v. California, 314 U.S. 252, 268, 62 S.Ct. 190, 86 L.Ed. 192; Edwards v. South Carolina, 372 U.S. 229, 235, 83 S.Ct. 680, 9 L.Ed.2d 697.

[16, 17] What a State may not constitutionally bring about by means of a criminal statute is likewise beyond the reach of its civil law of libel.[17] The fear of damage awards under a rule such as that invoked by the Alabama courts here may be markedly more inhibiting than the fear of prosecution under a criminal statute. See City of Chicago v. Tribune Co., 307 Ill. 595, 607, 139 N.E. 86, 90 (1923). Alabama, for example, has a criminal libel law which subjects to prosecution "any person who speaks, writes, or prints of and concerning another any accusation falsely and maliciously importing the commission by such person of a felony, or any other indictable offense involving moral turpitude," and which allows as punishment upon conviction a fine not exceeding $500 and a prison sentence of six months. Alabama Code, Tit. 14, § 350. Presumably a person charged with violation of this statute enjoys ordinary criminal-law safeguards such as the requirements of an indictment and of proof beyond a reasonable doubt. These safeguards are not available to the defendant in a civil action. The judgment awarded in this case—without the need for any proof of actual pecuniary loss—was one thousand times greater than the maximum fine provided by the Alabama criminal statute, and one hundred times greater than that provided by the Sedition Act.

278

And since there is no double-jeopardy limitation applicable to civil

17. Cf. Farmers Educational and Cooperative Union of America v. WDAY, 360

U.S. 525, 535, 79 S.Ct. 1302, 3 L.Ed.2d 1407.

lawsuits, this is not the only judgment that may be awarded against petitioners for the same publication.[18] Whether or not a newspaper can survive a succession of such judgments, the pall of fear and timidity imposed upon those who would give voice to public criticism is an atmosphere in which the First Amendment freedoms cannot survive. Plainly the Alabama law of civil libel is "a form of regulation that creates hazards to protected freedoms markedly greater than those that attend reliance upon the criminal law." Bantam Books, Inc. v. Sullivan, 372 U.S. 58, 70, 83 S.Ct. 631, 639, 9 L.Ed.2d 584.

[18] The state rule of law is not saved by its allowance of the defense of truth. A defense for erroneous statements honestly made is no less essential here than was the requirement of proof of guilty knowledge which, in Smith v. California, 361 U.S. 147, 80 S.Ct. 215, 4 L.Ed.2d 205, we held indispensable to a valid conviction of a bookseller for possessing obscene writings for sale. We said:

> "For if the bookseller is criminally liable without knowledge of the contents, * * * he will tend to restrict the books he sells to those he has inspected; and thus the State will have imposed a restriction upon the distribution of constitutionally protected as well as obscene literature. * * * And the bookseller's burden would become the public's burden, for by restricting him the public's access to reading matter would be restricted. * * * [H]is timidity in the face of his absolute criminal liability, thus would tend to restrict the public's access to

forms of the printed word which the State could not constitutionally

279

suppress directly. The bookseller's self-censorship, compelled by the State, would be a censorship affecting the whole public, hardly less virulent for being privately administered. Through it, the distribution of all books, both obscene and not obscene, would be impeded." (361 U.S. 147, 153–154, 80 S.Ct. 215, 218, 4 L.Ed. 2d 205.)

A rule compelling the critic of official conduct to guarantee the truth of all his factual assertions—and to do so on pain of libel judgments virtually unlimited in amount—leads to a comparable "self-censorship." Allowance of the defense of truth, with the burden of proving it on the defendant, does not mean that only false speech will be deterred.[19] Even courts accepting this defense as an adequate safeguard have recognized the difficulties of adducing legal proofs that the alleged libel was true in all its factual particulars. See, e. g., Post Publishing Co. v. Hallam, 59 F. 530, 540 (C.A.6th Cir. 1893) ; see also Noel, Defamation of Public Officers and Candidates, 49 Col.L. Rev. 875, 892 (1949). Under such a rule, would-be critics of official conduct may be deterred from voicing their criticism, even though it is believed to be true and even though it is in fact true, because of doubt whether it can be proved in court or fear of the expense of having to do so. They tend to make only statements which "steer far wider of the unlawful zone." Speiser v. Randall, supra, 357 U.S., at 526, 78 S.Ct. at 1342, 2 L.Ed.2d 1460. The rule thus dampens the vigor and limits the variety of public debate. It is

---

18. The Times states that four other libel suits based on the advertisement have been filed against it by others who have served as Montgomery City Commissioners and by the Governor of Alabama; that another $500,000 verdict has been awarded in the only one of these cases that has yet gone to trial; and that the damages sought in the other three total $2,000,000.

19. Even a false statement may be deemed to make a valuable contribution to public debate, since it brings about "the clearer perception and livelier impression of truth, produced by its collision with error." Mill, On Liberty (Oxford: Blackwell, 1947), at 15; see also Milton, Areopagitica, in Prose Works (Yale, 1959), Vol. II, at 561.

inconsistent with the First and Fourteenth Amendments.

[19, 20] The constitutional guarantees require, we think, a federal rule that prohibits a public official from recovering damages for a defamatory falsehood relating to his official conduct unless he proves that the statement was made with "actual malice"—that is, with knowledge that it was

280

false or with reckless disregard of whether it was false or not. An oft-cited statement of a like rule, which has been adopted by a number of state courts,[20] is found in the Kansas case of Coleman v. MacLennan, 78 Kan. 711, 98 P. 281 (1908). The State Attorney General, a candidate for re-election and a member of the commission charged with the management and control of the state school fund, sued a newspaper publisher for alleged libel in an article purporting to state facts relating to his official conduct in connection with a school-fund transaction. The defendant pleaded privilege and the trial judge, over the plaintiff's objection, instructed the jury that

"where an article is published and circulated among voters for the sole purpose of giving what the defendant

281

believes to be truthful informa-

tion concerning a candidate for public office and for the purpose of enabling such voters to cast their ballot more intelligently, and the whole thing is done in good faith and without malice, the article is privileged, although the principal matters contained in the article may be untrue in fact and derogatory to the character of the plaintiff; and in such a case the burden is on the plaintiff to show actual malice in the publication of the article."

In answer to a special question, the jury found that the plaintiff had not proved actual malice, and a general verdict was returned for the defendant. On appeal the Supreme Court of Kansas, in an opinion by Justice Burch, reasoned as follows (78 Kan., at 724, 98 P., at 286):

"[I]t is of the utmost consequence that the people should discuss the character and qualifications of candidates for their suffrages. The importance to the state and to society of such discussions is so vast, and the advantages derived are so great that they more than counterbalance the inconvenience of private persons whose conduct may be involved, and occasional injury to the reputations of individuals must yield to the public welfare, although at times such injury may be great. The

---

20. E. g., Ponder v. Cobb, 257 N.C. 281, 299, 126 S.E.2d 67, 80 (1962); Lawrence v. Fox, 357 Mich. 134, 146, 97 N.W.2d 719, 725 (1959); Stice v. Beacon Newspaper Corp., 185 Kan. 61, 65–67, 340 P.2d 396, 400–401, 76 A.L.R.2d 687 (1959); Bailey v. Charleston Mail Assn., 126 W.Va. 292, 307, 27 S.E.2d 837, 844, 150 A.L.R. 348 (1943); Salinger v. Cowles, 195 Iowa 873, 889, 191 N.W. 167, 174 (1922); Snively v. Record Publishing Co., 185 Cal. 565, 571–576, 198 P. 1 (1921); McLean v. Merriman, 42 S.D. 394, 175 N.W. 878 (1920). Applying the same rule to candidates for public office, see, e. g., Phoenix Newspapers v. Choisser, 82 Ariz. 271, 276–277, 312 P.2d 150, 154 (1957); Friedell v. Blakely Printing Co., 163 Minn. 226, 230, 203 N.W. 974, 975 (1925). And see Chagnon v. Union-Leader Corp., 103 N.H. 426, 438, 174 A.2d 825, 833 (1961), cert. denied,

369 U.S. 830, 82 S.Ct. 846, 7 L.Ed.2d 795.

The consensus of scholarly opinion apparently favors the rule that is here adopted. E. g., 1 Harper and James, Torts, § 5.26, at 449–450 (1956); Noel, Defamation of Public Officers and Candidates, 49 Col.L.Rev. 875, 891–895, 897, 903 (1949); Hallen, Fair Comment, 8 Tex.L.Rev. 41, 61 (1929); Smith, Charges Against Candidates, 18 Mich.L.Rev. 1, 115 (1919); Chase, Criticism of Public Officers and Candidates for Office, 23 Am.L.Rev. 346, 367–371 (1889); Cooley, Constitutional Limitations (7th ed., Lane, 1903), at 604, 616–628. But see, e. g., American Law Institute, Restatement of Torts, § 598, Comment a (1938) (reversing the position taken in Tentative Draft 13, § 1041(2) (1936)); Veeder, Freedom of Public Discussion, 23 Harv.L.Rev. 413, 419 (1910).

public benefit from publicity is so great and the chance of injury to private character so small that such discussion must be privileged."

The court thus sustained the trial court's instruction as a correct statement of the law, saying:

"In such a case the occasion gives rise to a privilege qualified to this extent. Any one claiming to be defamed by the communication must show actual malice, or go remediless. This privilege extends to a great variety of subjects and includes matters of

282

public concern, public men, and candidates for office." 78 Kan., at 723, 98 P., at 285.

Such a privilege for criticism of official conduct [21] is appropriately analogous to the protection accorded a public official when *he* is sued for libel by a private citizen. In Barr v. Matteo, 360 U.S. 564, 575, 79 S.Ct. 1335, 1341, 3 L.Ed.2d 1434, this Court held the utterance of a federal official to be absolutely privileged if made "within the outer perimeter" of his duties. The States accord the same immunity to statements of their highest officers, although some differentiate their lesser officials and qualify the privilege they enjoy.[22] But all hold that all officials are protected unless actual malice can be proved. The reason for the official privilege is said to be that the threat of damage suits would otherwise "inhibit

the fearless, vigorous, and effective administration of policies of government" and "dampen the ardor of all but the most resolute, or the most irresponsible, in the unflinching discharge of their duties." Barr v. Matteo, supra, 360 U.S., at 571, 79 S.Ct., at 1339, 3 L.Ed.2d 1434. Analogous considerations support the privilege for the citizen-critic of government. It is as much his duty to criticize as it is the official's duty to administer. See Whitney v. California, 274 U.S. 357, 375, 47 S.Ct. 641, 648, 71 L.Ed. 1095 (concurring opinion of Mr. Justice Brandeis), quoted supra, pp. 720, 721. As Madison said, see supra, p. 723, "the censorial power is in the people over the Government, and not in the Government over the people." It would give public servants an unjustified preference over the public they serve, if critics of official conduct

283

did not have a fair equivalent of the immunity granted to the officials themselves.

We conclude that such a privilege is required by the First and Fourteenth Amendments.

III.

[21–23] We hold today that the Constitution delimits a State's power to award damages for libel in actions brought by public officials against critics of their official conduct. Since this is such an action,[23] the rule requiring proof of actual malice is applicable. While

---

21. The privilege immunizing honest misstatements of fact is often referred to as a "conditional" privilege to distinguish it from the "absolute" privilege recognized in judicial, legislative, administrative and executive proceedings. See, e. g., Prosser, Torts (2d ed., 1955), § 95.

22. See 1 Harper and James, Torts, § 5.23, at 429–430 (1956). Prosser, Torts (2d ed., 1955), at 612–613; American Law Institute, Restatement of Torts (1938), § 591.

23. We have no occasion here to determine how far down into the lower ranks of government employees the "public official" designation would extend for purposes of

this rule, or otherwise to specify categories of persons who would or would not be included. Cf. Barr v. Matteo, 360 U.S. 564, 573–575, 79 S.Ct. 1335, 1340–1341, 3 L.Ed.2d 1434. Nor need we here determine the boundaries of the "official conduct" concept. It is enough for the present case that respondent's position as an elected city commissioner clearly made him a public official, and that the allegations in the advertisement concerned what was allegedly his official conduct as Commissioner in charge of the Police Department. As to the statements alleging the assaulting of Dr. King and the bombing of his home, it is immaterial that they might not be considered to involve respondent's official conduct if

Alabama law apparently requires proof of actual malice for an award of punitive damages,[24] where general damages are concerned malice is "presumed." Such a presumption is inconsistent

284

with the federal rule. "The power to create presumptions is not a means of escape from constitutional restrictions," Bailey v. Alabama, 219 U.S. 219, 239, 31 S.Ct. 145, 151, 55 L.Ed. 191; "[t]he showing of malice required for the forfeiture of the privilege is not presumed but is a matter for proof by the plaintiff * *." Lawrence v. Fox, 357 Mich. 134, 146, 97 N.W.2d 719, 725 (1959).[25] Since the trial judge did not instruct the jury to differentiate between general and punitive damages, it may be that the verdict was wholly an award of one or the other. But it is impossible to know, in view of the general verdict returned. Because of this uncertainty, the judgment must be reversed and the case remanded. Stromberg v. California, 283 U.S. 359, 367–368, 51 S.Ct. 532, 535, 75 L.Ed. 1117; Williams v. North Carolina, 317 U.S. 287, 291–292, 63 S.Ct. 207, 209–210, 87 L.Ed. 279; see Yates v. United States, 354 U.S.

298, 311–312, 77 S.Ct. 1064, 1073, 1 L.Ed. 2d 1356; Cramer v. United States, 325 U.S. 1, 36, n. 45, 65 S.Ct. 918, 935, 940, 89 L.Ed. 1441.

[24–26] Since respondent may seek a new trial, we deem that considerations of effective judicial administration require us to review the evidence in the present record to determine

285

whether it could constitutionally support a judgment for respondent. This Court's duty is not limited to the elaboration of constitutional principles; we must also in proper cases review the evidence to make certain that those principles have been constitutionally applied. This is such a case, particularly since the question is one of alleged trespass across "the line between speech unconditionally guaranteed and speech which may legitimately be regulated." Speiser v. Randall, 357 U.S. 513, 525, 78 S.Ct. 1332, 1342, 2 L.Ed.2d 1460. In cases where that line must be drawn, the rule is that we "examine for ourselves the statements in issue and the circumstances under which they were made to see * * * whether they are of a character which the principles of

---

he himself had been accused of perpetrating the assault and the bombing. Respondent does not claim that the statements charged him personally with these acts; his contention is that the advertisement connects him with them only in his official capacity as the Commissioner supervising the police, on the theory that the police might be equated with the "They" who did the bombing and assaulting. Thus, if these allegations can be read as referring to respondent at all, they must be read as describing his performance of his official duties.

24. Johnson Publishing Co. v. Davis, 271 Ala. 474, 487, 124 So.2d 441, 450 (1960). Thus, the trial judge here instructed the jury that "mere negligence or carelessness is not evidence of actual malice or malice in fact, and does not justify an award of exemplary or punitive damages in an action for libel."
The court refused, however, to give the following instruction which had been requested by the Times:
"I charge you * * * that punitive damages, as the name indicates, are de-

signed to punish the defendant, the New York Times Company, a corporation, and the other defendants in this case, * * * and I further charge you that such punitive damages may be awarded only in the event that you, the jury, are convinced by a fair preponderance of the evidence that the defendant * * * was motivated by personal illwill, that is actual intent to do the plaintiff harm, or that the defendant * * * was guilty of gross negligence and recklessness and not of just ordinary negligence or carelessness in publishing the matter complained of so as to indicate a wanton disregard of plaintiff's rights."
The trial court's error in failing to require any finding of actual malice for an award of general damages makes it unnecessary for us to consider the sufficiency under the federal standard of the instructions regarding actual malice that were given as to punitive damages.

25. Accord, Coleman v. MacLennan, supra, 78 Kan., at 741, 98 P., at 292; Gough v. Tribune-Journal Co., 75 Idaho 502, 510, 275 P.2d 663, 668 (1954).

the First Amendment, as adopted by the Due Process Clause of the Fourteenth Amendment, protect." Pennekamp v. Florida, 328 U.S. 331, 335, 66 S.Ct. 1029, 1031, 90 L.Ed. 1295; see also One, Inc., v. Olesen, 355 U.S. 371, 78 S.Ct. 364, 2 L.Ed.2d 352; Sunshine Book Co. v. Summerfield, 355 U.S. 372, 78 S.Ct. 365, 2 L.Ed.2d 352. We must "make an independent examination of the whole record," Edwards v. South Carolina, 372 U.S. 229, 235, 83 S.Ct. 680, 683, 9 L.Ed.2d 697, so as to assure ourselves that the judgment does not constitute a forbidden intrusion on the field of free expression.[26]

[27] Applying these standards, we consider that the proof presented to show actual malice lacks the convincing

286

clarity which the constitutional standard demands, and hence that it would not constitutionally sustain the judgment for respondent under the proper rule of law. The case of the individual petitioners requires little discussion. Even assuming that they could constitutionally be found to have authorized the use of their names on the advertisement, there was no evidence whatever that they were aware of any erroneous statements or were in any way reckless in that regard. The judgment against them is thus without constitutional support.

As to the Times, we similarly conclude that the facts do not support a finding of actual malice. The statement by the Times' Secretary that, apart from the padlocking allegation, he thought the ad-

vertisement was "substantially correct," affords no constitutional warrant for the Alabama Supreme Court's conclusion that it was a "cavalier ignoring of the falsity of the advertisement [from which], the jury could not have but been impressed with the bad faith of The Times, and its maliciousness inferable therefrom." The statement does not indicate malice at the time of the publication; even if the advertisement was not "substantially correct"—although respondent's own proofs tend to show that it was—that opinion was at least a reasonable one, and there was no evidence to impeach the witness' good faith in holding it. The Times' failure to retract upon respondent's demand, although it later retracted upon the demand of Governor Patterson, is likewise not adequate evidence of malice for constitutional purposes. Whether or not a failure to retract may ever constitute such evidence, there are two reasons why it does not here. *First,* the letter written by the Times reflected a reasonable doubt on its part as to whether the advertisement could reasonably be taken to refer to respondent at all. *Second,* it was not a final refusal, since it asked for an explanation on this point —a request that respondent chose to ignore. Nor does the retraction upon the demand of the Governor supply the

287

neces- sary proof. It may be doubted that a failure to retract which is not itself evidence of malice can retroactively become such by virtue of a retraction subsequently made to another party. But in any event that did not happen here, since the

---

26. The Seventh Amendment does not, as respondent contends, preclude such an examination by this Court. That Amendment, providing that "no fact tried by a jury, shall be otherwise reexamined in any Court of the United States, than according to the rules of the common law," is applicable to state cases coming here. Chicago, B. & Q. R. Co. v. Chicago, 166 U.S. 226, 242–243, 17 S.Ct. 581, 587, 41 L.Ed. 979; cf. The Justices v. Murray, 9 Wall. 274, 19 L.Ed. 658. But its ban on re-examination of facts does not preclude us from determining

whether governing rules of federal law have been properly applied to the facts. "[T]his Court will review the finding of facts by a State court * * * where a conclusion of law as to a Federal right and a finding of fact are so intermingled as to make it necessary, in order to pass upon the Federal question, to analyze the facts." Fiske v. Kansas, 274 U.S. 380, 385–386, 47 S.Ct. 655, 656–657, 71 L.Ed. 1108. See also Haynes v. Washington, 373 U.S. 503, 515–516, 83 S.Ct. 1336, 1344, 10 L.Ed.2d 513.

explanation given by the Times' Secretary for the distinction drawn between respondent and the Governor was a reasonable one, the good faith of which was not impeached.

Finally, there is evidence that the Times published the advertisement without checking its accuracy against the news stories in the Times' own files. The mere presence of the stories in the files does not, of course, establish that the Times "knew" the advertisement was false, since the state of mind required for actual malice would have to be brought home to the persons in the Times' organization having responsibility for the publication of the advertisement. With respect to the failure of those persons to make the check, the record shows that they relied upon their knowledge of the good reputation of many of those whose names were listed as sponsors of the advertisement, and upon the letter from A. Philip Randolph, known to them as a responsible individual, certifying that the use of the names was authorized. There was testimony that the persons handling the advertisement saw nothing in it that would render it unacceptable under the Times' policy of rejecting advertisements containing "attacks of a personal character"; [27] their failure to reject it on this ground was not unreasonable. We think

288

the evidence against the Times supports at most a finding of negligence in failing to discover the misstatements, and is constitutionally insufficient to show the recklessness that is required for a finding of actual malice. Cf. Charles Parker Co. v. Silver City Crystal Co., 142 Conn. 605, 618, 116 A.2d 440, 446 (1955); Phoenix Newspapers, Inc. v. Choisser, 82 Ariz.

271, 277–278, 312 P.2d 150, 154–155 (1957).

[28] We also think the evidence was constitutionally defective in another respect: it was incapable of supporting the jury's finding that the allegedly libelous statements were made "of and concerning" respondent. Respondent relies on the words of the advertisement and the testimony of six witnesses to establish a connection between it and himself. Thus, in his brief to this Court, he states:

> "The reference to respondent as police commissioner is clear from the ad. In addition, the jury heard the testimony of a newspaper editor * * *; a real estate and insurance man * * *; the sales manager of a men's clothing store * * *; a food equipment man * * *; a service station operator * * *; and the operator of a truck line for whom respondent had formerly worked * * *. Each of these witnesses stated that he associated the statements with respondent * *."

(Citations to record omitted.)

There was no reference to respondent in the advertisement, either by name or official position. A number of the allegedly libelous statements—the charges that the dining hall was padlocked and that Dr. King's home was bombed, his person assaulted, and a perjury prosecution instituted against him—did not even concern the police; despite the ingenuity of the arguments which would attach this significance to the word "They," it is plain that these statements could not reasonably be read as accusing respondent of personal involvement in the acts

289

in question. The statements upon which re-

---

27. The Times has set forth in a booklet its "Advertising Acceptability Standards." Listed among the classes of advertising that the newspaper does not accept are advertisements that are "fraudulent or deceptive," that are "ambiguous in wording and * * * may mislead," and that contain "attacks of a personal charac-

ter." In replying to respondent's interrogatories before the trial, the Secretary of the Times stated that "as the advertisement made no attacks of a personal character upon any individual and otherwise met the advertising acceptability standards promulgated," it had been approved for publication.

spondent principally relies as referring to him are the two allegations that did concern the police or police functions: that "truckloads of police * * * ringed the Alabama State College Campus" after the demonstration on the State Capitol steps, and that Dr. King had been "arrested * * * seven times." These statements were false only in that the police had been "deployed near" the campus but had not actually "ringed" it and had not gone there in connection with the State Capitol demonstration, and in that Dr. King had been arrested only four times. The ruling that these discrepancies between what was true and what was asserted were sufficient to injure respondent's reputation may itself raise constitutional problems, but we need not consider them here. Although the statements may be taken as referring to the police, they did not on their face make even an oblique reference to

respondent as an individual. Support for the asserted reference must, therefore, be sought in the testimony of respondent's witnesses. But none of them suggested any basis for the belief that respondent himself was attacked in the advertisement beyond the bare fact that he was in overall charge of the Police Department and thus bore official responsibility for police conduct; to the extent that some of the witnesses thought respondent to have been charged with ordering or approving the conduct or otherwise being personally involved in it, they based this notion not on any statements in the advertisement, and not on any evidence that he had in fact been so involved, but solely on the unsupported assumption that, because of his official position, he must have been.[28] This reliance on the bare

290

fact of respondent's

---

28. Respondent's own testimony was that "as Commissioner of Public Affairs it is part of my duty to supervise the Police Department and I certainly feel like it [a statement] is associated with me when it describes police activities." He thought that "by virtue of being Police Commissioner and Commissioner of Public Affairs," he was charged with "any activity on the part of the Police Department." "When it describes police action, certainly I feel it reflects on me as an individual." He added that "It is my feeling that it reflects not only on me but on the other Commissioners and the community."

Grove C. Hall testified that to him the third paragraph of the advertisement called to mind "the City government—the Commissioners," and that "now that you ask it I would naturally think a little more about the police Commissioner because his responsibility is exclusively with the constabulary." It was "the phrase about starvation" that led to the association; "the other didn't hit me with any particular force."

Arnold D. Blackwell testified that the third paragraph was associated in his mind with "the Police Commissioner and the police force. The people on the police force." If he had believed the statement about the padlocking of the dining hall, he would have thought "that the people on our police force or the heads

of our police force were acting without their jurisdiction and would not be competent for the position." "I would assume that the Commissioner had ordered the police force to do that and therefore it would be his responsibility."

Harry W. Kaminsky associated the statement about "truckloads of police" with respondent "because he is the Police Commissioner." He thought that the reference to arrests in the sixth paragraph "implicates the Police Department, I think, or the authorities that would do that—arrest folks for speeding and loitering and such as that." Asked whether he would associate with respondent a newspaper report that the police had "beat somebody up or assaulted them on the streets of Montgomery," he replied: "I still say he is the Police Commissioner and those men are working directly under him and therefore I would think that he would have something to do with it." In general, he said, "I look at Mr. Sullivan when I see the Police Department."

H. M. Price, Sr., testified that he associated the first sentence of the third paragraph with respondent because: "I would just automatically consider that the Police Commissioner in Montgomery would have to put his approval on those kind of things as an individual."

William M. Parker, Jr., testified that he associated the statements in the two paragraphs with "the Commissioners of

official position [29] was made explicit by the Supreme Court of Alabama. That court, in holding that the trial court "did not err in overruling the demurrer [of the Times] in the aspect that the libelous

291

matter was not of and concerning the [plaintiff,]" based its ruling on the proposition that:

> "We think it common knowledge that the average person knows that municipal agents, such as police and firemen, and others, are under the control and direction of the city governing body, and more particularly under the direction and control of a single commissioner. In measuring the performance or deficiencies of such groups, praise or criticism is usually attached to the official in complete control of the body." 273 Ala., at 674–675, 144 So.2d, at 39.

[29] This proposition has disquieting implications for criticism of governmental conduct. For good reason, "no court of last resort in this country has ever held, or even suggested, that prosecutions for libel on government have any place in the American system of jurisprudence." City of Chicago v. Tribune Co.,

the City of Montgomery," and since respondent "was the Police Commissioner," he "thought of him first." He told the examining counsel: "I think if you were the Police Commissioner I would have thought it was speaking of you."

Horace W. White, respondent's former employer, testified that the statement about "truck-loads of police" made him think of respondent "as being the head of the Police Department." Asked whether he read the statement as charging respondent himself with ringing the campus or having shotguns and tear-gas, he replied: "Well, I thought of his department being charged with it, yes, sir. He is the head of the Police Department as I understand it." He further said that the reason he would have been unwilling to re-employ respondent if he had believed the advertisement was "the fact that he allowed the Police Department to do the things that the paper say he did."

307 Ill. 595, 601, 139 N.E.

292

86, 88, 28 A.L. R. 1368 (1923). The present proposition would sidestep this obstacle by transmuting criticism of government, however impersonal it may seem on its face, into personal criticism, and hence potential libel, of the officials of whom the government is composed. There is no legal alchemy by which a State may thus create the cause of action that would otherwise be denied for a publication which, as respondent himself said of the advertisement, "reflects not only on me but on the other Commissioners and the community." Raising as it does the possibility that a good-faith critic of government will be penalized for his criticism, the proposition relied on by the Alabama courts strikes at the very center of the constitutionally protected area of free expression.[30] We hold that such a proposition may not constitutionally be utilized to establish that an otherwise impersonal attack on governmental operations was a libel of an official responsible for those operations. Since it was relied on exclusively here, and there was no other evidence to connect the statements with respondent, the evidence was constitutionally insufficient to support a finding that the statements referred to respondent.

29. Compare Ponder v. Cobb, 257 N.C. 281, 126 S.E.2d 67 (1962).

30. Insofar as the proposition means only that the statements about police conduct libeled respondent by implicitly criticizing his ability to run the Police Department, recovery is also precluded in this case by the doctrine of fair comment. See American Law Institute, Restatement of Torts (1938), § 607. Since the Fourteenth Amendment requires recognition of the conditional privilege for honest misstatements of fact, it follows that a defense of fair comment must be afforded for honest expression of opinion based upon privileged, as well as true, statements of fact. Both defenses are of course defeasible if the public official proves actual malice, as was not done here.

The judgment of the Supreme Court of Alabama is reversed and the case is remanded to that court for further proceedings not inconsistent with this opinion.

Reversed and remanded.

293

Mr. Justice BLACK, with whom Mr. Justice DOUGLAS joins (concurring).

I concur in reversing this half-million-dollar judgment against the New York Times Company and the four individual defendants. In reversing the Court holds that "the Constitution delimits a State's power to award damages for libel in actions brought by public officials against critics of their official conduct." Ante, p. 727. I base my vote to reverse on the belief that the First and Fourteenth Amendments not merely "delimit" a State's power to award damages to "public officials against critics of their official conduct" but completely prohibit a State from exercising such a power. The Court goes on to hold that a State can subject such critics to damages if "actual malice" can be proved against them. "Malice," even as defined by the Court, is an elusive, abstract concept, hard to prove and hard to disprove. The requirement that malice be proved provides at best an evanescent protection for the right critically to discuss public affairs and certainly does not measure up to the sturdy safeguard embodied in the First Amendment. Unlike the Court, therefore, I vote to reverse exclusively on the ground that the Times and the individual defendants had an absolute, unconditional constitutional right to publish in the Times advertisement their criticisms of the Montgomery agencies and officials. I do not base my vote to reverse on any failure to prove that these individual defendants signed the advertisement or that their criticism of the Police Department was aimed at the plaintiff Sullivan, who was then the Montgomery City Commissioner having supervision of the city's police; for present purposes I assume these things were proved. Nor is my reason for reversal

the size of the half-million-dollar judgment, large as it is. If Alabama has constitutional power to use its civil libel law to impose damages on the press for criticizing the way public officials perform or fail

294

to perform their duties, I know of no provision in the Federal Constitution which either expressly or impliedly bars the State from fixing the amount of damages.

The half-million-dollar verdict does give dramatic proof, however, that state libel laws threaten the very existence of an American press virile enough to publish unpopular views on public affairs and bold enough to criticize the conduct of public officials. The factual background of this case emphasizes the imminence and enormity of that threat. One of the acute and highly emotional issues in this country arises out of efforts of many people, even including some public officials, to continue state-commanded segregation of races in the public schools and other public places, despite our several holdings that such a state practice is forbidden by the Fourteenth Amendment. Montgomery is one of the localities in which widespread hostility to desegregation has been manifested. This hostility has sometimes extended itself to persons who favor desegregation, particularly to so-called "outside agitators," a term which can be made to fit papers like the Times, which is published in New York. The scarcity of testimony to show that Commissioner Sullivan suffered any actual damages at all suggests that these feelings of hostility had at least as much to do with rendition of this half-million-dollar verdict as did an appraisal of damages. Viewed realistically, this record lends support to an inference that instead of being damaged Commissioner Sullivan's political, social, and financial prestige has likely been enhanced by the Times' publication. Moreover, a second half-million-dollar libel verdict against the Times based on the same advertisement has already been awarded to another Commissioner. There a jury again gave the full amount claimed. There is no reason to believe that there are not more such huge verdicts lurking just around the corner for the Times or any other newspaper or broadcaster which

295

might dare to criticize public officials. In fact, briefs before us show that in Alabama there are now pending eleven libel suits by local and state officials against the Times seeking $5,600,000, and five such suits against the Columbia Broadcasting System seeking $1,700,000. Moreover, this technique for harassing and punishing a free press—now that it has been shown to be possible—is by no means limited to cases with racial overtones; it can be used in other fields where public feelings may make local as well as out-of-state newspapers easy prey for libel verdict seekers.

In my opinion the Federal Constitution has dealt with this deadly danger to the press in the only way possible without leaving the free press open to destruction—by granting the press an absolute immunity for criticism of the way public officials do their public duty. Compare Barr v. Matteo, 360 U.S. 564, 79 S.Ct. 1335, 3 L.Ed.2d 1434. Stopgap measures like those the Court adopts are in my judgment not enough. This record certainly does not indicate that any different verdict would have been rendered here whatever the Court had charged the jury about "malice," "truth," "good motives," "justifiable ends," or any other legal formulas which in theory would protect the press. Nor does the record indicate that any of these legalistic words would have caused the courts below to set aside or to reduce the half-million-dollar verdict in any amount.

I agree with the Court that the Fourteenth Amendment made the First applicable to the States.[1] This means to me that since the adoption of the Fourteenth Amendment a State has no more power than the Federal Government to use a civil libel law or any other law to impose damages for merely discussing public affairs and criticizing public officials. The power of the United

296

States to do that is, in my judgment, precisely nil. Such was the general view held when the First Amendment was adopted and ever since.[2] Congress never has sought to challenge this viewpoint by passing any civil libel law. It did pass the Sedition Act in 1798,[3] which made it a crime—"seditious libel"—to criticize federal officials or the Federal Government. As the Court's opinion correctly points out, however, ante, pp. 722–723, that Act came to an ignominious end and by common consent has generally been treated as having been a wholly unjustifiable and much to be regretted violation of the First Amendment. Since the First Amendment is now made applicable to the States by the Fourteenth, it no more permits the States to impose damages for libel than it does the Federal Government.

We would, I think, more faithfully interpret the First Amendment by holding that at the very least it leaves the people and the press free to criticize officials and discuss public affairs with impunity. This Nation of ours elects many of its important officials; so do the States, the municipalities, the counties, and even many precincts. These officials are responsible to the people for the way they perform their duties. While our Court has held that some kinds of speech and writings, such as "obscenity,"

---

1. See cases collected in Speiser v. Randall, 357 U.S. 513, 530, 78 S.Ct. 1332, 1344, 2 L.Ed.2d 1460 (concurring opinion).

2. See, e. g., 1 Tucker, Blackstone's Commentaries (1803), 297–299 (editor's appendix). St. George Tucker, a distin-

guished Virginia jurist, took part in the Annapolis Convention of 1786, sat on both state and federal courts, and was widely known for his writings on judicial and constitutional subjects.

3. Act of July 14, 1798, 1 Stat. 596.

Roth v. United States, 354 U.S. 476, 77 S.Ct. 1304, 1 L.Ed.2d 1498, and "fighting words," Chaplinsky v. New Hampshire, 315 U.S. 568, 62 S.Ct. 766, 86 L.Ed. 1061, are not expression within the protection of the First Amendment,[4] freedom to discuss public affairs and public officials

297

is unquestionably, as the Court today holds, the kind of speech the First Amendment was primarily designed to keep within the area of free discussion. To punish the exercise of this right to discuss public affairs or to penalize it through libel judgments is to abridge or shut off discussion of the very kind most needed. This Nation, I suspect, can live in peace without libel suits based on public discussions of public affairs and public officials. But I doubt that a country can live in freedom where its people can be made to suffer physically or financially for criticizing their government, its actions, or its officials. "For a representative democracy ceases to exist the moment that the public functionaries are by any means absolved from their responsibility to their constituents; and this happens whenever the constituent can be restrained in any manner from speaking, writing, or publishing his opinions upon any public measure, or upon the conduct of those who may advise or execute it."[5] An unconditional right to say what one pleases about public affairs is what I consider to be the minimum guarantee of the First Amendment.[6]

---

4. But see Smith v. California, 361 U.S. 147, 155, 80 S.Ct. 215, 219, 4 L.Ed.2d 205 (concurring opinion); Roth v. United States, 354 U.S. 476, 508, 77 S.Ct. 1304, 1321, 1 L.Ed.2d 1498 (dissenting opinion).

5. 1 Tucker, Blackstone's Commentaries (1803), 297 (editor's appendix; cf. Brant, Seditious Libel: Myth and Reality, 39 N.Y.U.L.Rev. 1.

6. Cf. Meiklejohn, Free Speech and Its Relation to Self-Government (1948).

1. I fully agree with the Court that the attack upon the validity of the Sedition Act of 1798, 1 Stat. 596, "has carried the day

I regret that the Court has stopped short of this holding indispensable to preserve our free press from destruction.

Mr. Justice GOLDBERG, with whom Mr. Justice DOUGLAS joins (concurring in the result).

The Court today announces a constitutional standard which prohibits "a public official from recovering damages for a defamatory falsehood relating to his official conduct unless he proves that the statement was made with

298

'actual malice'— that is, with knowledge that it was false or with reckless disregard of whether it was false or not." Ante, at p. 726. The Court thus rules that the Constitution gives citizens and newspapers a "conditional privilege" immunizing nonmalicious misstatements of fact regarding the official conduct of a government officer. The impressive array of history [1] and precedent marshaled by the Court, however, confirms my belief that the Constitution affords greater protection than that provided by the Court's standard to citizen and press in exercising the right of public criticism.

In my view, the First and Fourteenth Amendments to the Constitution afford to the citizen and to the press an absolute, unconditional privilege to criticize official conduct despite the harm which may flow from excesses and abuses. The prized American right "to speak one's

---

in the court of history," ante, at p. 723, and that the Act would today be declared unconstitutional. It should be pointed out, however, that the Sedition Act proscribed writings which were "false, scandalous *and malicious*." (Emphasis added.) For prosecutions under the Sedition Act charging malice, see e. g., Trial of Matthew Lyon (1798), in Wharton, State Trials of the United States (1849), p. 333; Trial of Thomas Cooper (1800), in id., at 659; Trial of Anthony Haswell (1800) in id., at 684; Trial of James Thompson Callender (1800), in id., at 688.

mind," cf. Bridges v. California, 314 U. S. 252, 270, 62 S.Ct. 190, 197, 86 L.Ed. 192, about public officials and affairs needs "breathing space to survive," N. A. A. C. P. v. Button, 371 U.S. 415, 433, 83 S.Ct. 328, 338, 9 L.Ed.2d 405. The right should not depend upon a probing by the jury of the motivation[2] of the citizen or press. The theory

299

of our Constitution is that every citizen may speak his mind and every newspaper express its view on matters of public concern and may not be barred from speaking or publishing because those in control of government think that what is said or written is unwise, unfair, false, or malicious. In a democratic society, one who assumes to act for the citizens in an executive, legislative, or judicial capacity must expect that his official acts will be commented upon and criticized. Such criticism cannot, in my opinion, be muzzled or deterred by the courts at the instance of public officials under the label of libel.

It has been recognized that "prosecutions for libel on government have [no] place in the American system of jurisprudence." City of Chicago v. Tribune Co., 307 Ill. 595, 601, 139 N.E. 86, 88, 28 A.L.R. 1368. I fully agree. Govern-

ment, however, is not an abstraction; it is made up of individuals—of governors responsible to the governed. In a democratic society where men are free by ballots to remove those in power, any statement critical of governmental action is necessarily "of and concerning" the governors and any statement critical of the governors' official conduct is necessarily "of and concerning" the government. If the rule that libel on government has no place in our Constitution is to have real meaning, then libel on the official conduct of the governors likewise can have no place in our Constitution.

We must recognize that we are writing upon a clean slate.[3] As the Court notes, although there have been

300

"statements of this Court to the effect that the Constitution does not protect libelous publications * * * [n]one of the cases sustained the use of libel laws to impose sanctions upon expression critical of the official conduct of public officials." Ante, at p. 719. We should be particularly careful, therefore, adequately to protect the liberties which are embodied in the First and Fourteenth Amendments. It may be urged that deliberately and maliciously false statements have no

---

2. The requirement of proving actual malice or reckless disregard may, in the mind of the jury, add little to the requirement of proving falsity, a requirement which the Court recognizes not to be an adequate safeguard. The thought suggested by Mr. Justice Jackson in United States v. Ballard, 322 U.S. 78, 92–93, 64 S.Ct. 882, 889, 88 L.Ed. 1148, is relevant here: "[A]s a matter of either practice or philosophy I do not see how we can separate an issue as to what is believed from considerations as to what is believable. The most convincing proof that one believes his statements is to show that they have been true in his experience. Likewise, that one knowingly falsified is best proved by showing that what he said happened never did happen." See note 4, infra.

3. It was not until Gitlow v. New York, 268 U.S. 652, 45 S.Ct. 625, 69 L.Ed. 1138, decided in 1925, that it was intimated that the freedom of speech guaranteed by the First Amendment was applicable to the States by reason of the Fourteenth Amendment. Other intimations followed. See Whitney v. California, 274 U.S. 357, 47 S.Ct. 641, 71 L.Ed. 1095; Fiske v. Kansas, 274 U.S. 380, 47 S.Ct. 655, 71 L.Ed. 1108. In 1931 Chief Justice Hughes speaking for the Court in Stromberg v. California, 283 U.S. 359, 368, 51 S.Ct. 532, 535, 75 L.Ed. 1117, declared: "It has been determined that the conception of liberty under the due process clause of the Fourteenth Amendment embraces the right of free speech." Thus we deal with a constitutional principle enunciated less than four decades ago, and consider for the first time the application of that principle to issues arising in libel cases brought by state officials.

conceivable value as free speech. That argument, however, is not responsive to the real issue presented by this case, which is whether that freedom of speech which all agree is constitutionally protected can be effectively safeguarded by a rule allowing the imposition of liability upon a jury's evaluation of the speaker's state of mind. If individual citizens may be held liable in damages for strong words, which a jury finds false and maliciously motivated, there can be little doubt that public debate and advocacy will be constrained. And if newspapers, publishing advertisements dealing with public issues, thereby risk liability, there can also be little doubt that the ability of minority groups to secure publication of their views on public affairs and to seek support for their causes will be greatly diminished. Cf. Farmers Educational & Coop. Union v. WDAY, Inc., 360 U.S. 525, 530, 79 S.Ct. 1302, 1305, 3 L. Ed.2d 1407. The opinion of the Court conclusively demonstrates the chilling effect of the Alabama libel laws on First Amendment freedoms

301

in the area of race relations. The American Colonists were not willing, nor should we be, to take the risk that "[m]en who injure and oppress the people under their administration [and] provoke them to cry out and complain" will also be empowered to "make that very complaint the foundation for new oppressions and prosecutions." The Trial of John Peter Zenger, 17 Howell's St. Tr. 675, 721–722 (1735) (argument of counsel to the jury). To impose liability for critical, albeit erroneous or even malicious, comments on official conduct would effectively resurrect "the obsolete doctrine that the governed must

not criticize their governors." Cf. Sweeney v. Patterson, 76 U.S.App.D.C. 23, 24, 128 F.2d 457, 458.

Our national experience teaches that repressions breed hate and "that hate menaces stable government." Whitney v. California, 274 U.S. 357, 375, 47 S. Ct. 641, 648, 71 L.Ed. 1095 (Brandeis, J., concurring). We should be ever mindful of the wise counsel of Chief Justice Hughes:

> "[I]mperative is the need to preserve inviolate the constitutional rights of free speech, free press and free assembly in order to maintain the opportunity for free political discussion, to the end that government may be responsive to the will of the people and that changes, if desired, may be obtained by peaceful means. Therein lies the security of the Republic, the very foundation of constitutional government." De Jonge v. Oregon, 299 U.S. 353, 365, 57 S. Ct. 255, 260, 81 L.Ed. 278.

This is not to say that the Constitution protects defamatory statements directed against the private conduct of a public official or private citizen. Freedom of press and of speech insures that government will respond to the will of the people and that changes may be obtained by peaceful means. Purely private defamation has little to do with the political ends of a self-governing society. The imposition of liability for private defamation does not

302

abridge the freedom of public speech or any other freedom protected by the First Amendment.[4] This, of course, cannot be said "where

---

4. In most cases, as in the case at bar, there will be little difficulty in distinguishing defamatory speech relating to private conduct from that relating to official conduct. I recognize, of course, that there will be a gray area. The difficulties of applying a public-private standard are, however, certainly, of a different genre from those attending the differentiation

between a malicious and nonmalicious state of mind. If the constitutional standard is to be shaped by a concept of malice, the speaker takes the risk not only that the jury will inaccurately determine his state of mind but also that the injury will fail properly to apply the constitutional standard set by the elusive concept of malice. See note 2, supra.

public officials are concerned or where public matters are involved. * * * [O]ne main function of the First Amendment is to ensure ample opportunity for the people to determine and resolve public issues. Where public matters are involved, the doubts should be resolved in favor of freedom of expression rather than against it." Douglas, The Right of the People (1958), p. 41.

In many jurisdictions, legislators, judges and executive officers are clothed with absolute immunity against liability for defamatory words uttered in the discharge of their public duties. See, e. g., Barr v. Matteo, 360 U.S. 564, 79 S.Ct. 1335, 3 L.Ed.2d 1434; City of Chicago v. Tribune Co., 307 Ill., at 610, 139 N.E., at 91. Judge Learned Hand ably summarized the policies underlying the rule:

"It does indeed go without saying that an official, who is in fact guilty of using his powers to vent his spleen upon others, or for any other personal motive not connected with the public good, should not escape liability for the injuries he may so cause; and, if it were possible in practice to confine such complaints to the guilty, it would be monstrous to deny recovery. The justification for doing so is that it is impossible to know whether the claim is well founded until the

303

case has been tried, and that to submit all officials, the innocent as well as the guilty, to the burden of a trial and to the inevitable danger of its outcome, would dampen the ardor of all but the most resolute, or the most irresponsible, in the unflinching discharge of their duties. Again and again the public interest calls for action which may turn out to be founded on a mistake, in the face of which an official may later find himself hard put to it to satisfy a jury of his good faith. There must indeed be means of punishing public officers who have been truant to their duties; but that

is quite another matter from exposing such as have been honestly mistaken to suit by anyone who has suffered from their errors. As is so often the case, the answer must be found in a balance between the evils inevitable in either alternative. In this instance it has been thought in the end better to leave unredressed the wrongs done by dishonest officers than to subject those who try to do their duty to the constant dread of retaliation. * * *

"The decisions have, indeed, always imposed as a limitation upon the immunity that the official's act must have been within the scope of his powers; and it can be argued that official powers, since they exist only for the public good, never cover occasions where the public good is not their aim, and hence that to exercise a power dishonestly is necessarily to overstep its bounds. A moment's reflection shows, however, that that cannot be the meaning of the limitation without defeating the whole doctrine. What is meant by saying that the officer must be acting within his power cannot be more than that the occasion must be such as would have justified the act, if he had been using his power for any of the purposes on whose account it was vested in him. * * *" Gregoire v. Biddle, 2 Cir., 177 F.2d 579, 581.

304

If the government official should be immune from libel actions so that his ardor to serve the public will not be dampened and "fearless, vigorous, and effective administration of policies of government" not be inhibited, Barr v. Matteo, supra, 360 U.S. at 571, 79 S.Ct. at 1339, 3 L.Ed.2d 1434, then the citizen and the press should likewise be immune from libel actions for their criticism of official conduct. Their ardor as citizens will thus not be dampened and they will

376 U.S. 305   **NEW YORK TIMES COMPANY v. SULLIVAN**   **739**

Cite as 84 S.Ct. 710 (1964)

be free "to applaud or to criticize the way public employees do their jobs, from the least to the most important."[5] If liability can attach to political criticism because it damages the reputation of a public official as a public official, then no critical citizen can safely utter anything but faint praise about the government or its officials. The vigorous criticism by press and citizen of the conduct of the government of the day by the officials of the day will soon yield to silence if officials in control of government agencies, instead of answering criticisms, can resort to friendly juries to forestall criticism of their official conduct.[6]

The conclusion that the Constitution affords the citizen and the press an absolute privilege for criticism of official conduct does not leave the public official without defenses against unsubstantiated opinions or deliberate misstatements. "Under our system of government, counterargument and education are the weapons available to expose these matters, not abridgment * * * of free speech * * *." Wood v. Georgia, 370 U.S. 375,

389, 82 S.Ct. 1364, 1372, 8 L.Ed.2d 569.

305

The public official certainly has equal if not greater access than most private citizens to media of communication. In any event, despite the possibility that some excesses and abuses may go unremedied, we must recognize that "the people of this nation have ordained in the light of history, that, in spite of the probability of excesses and abuses, [certain] liberties are, in the long view, essential to enlightened opinion and right conduct on the part of the citizens of a democracy." Cantwell v. Connecticut, 310 U.S. 296, 310, 60 S.Ct. 900, 906, 84 L.Ed. 1213. As Mr. Justice Brandeis correctly observed, "sunlight is the most powerful of all disinfectants."[7]

For these reasons, I strongly believe that the Constitution accords citizens and press an unconditional freedom to criticize official conduct. It necessarily follows that in a case such as this, where all agree that the allegedly defamatory statements related to official conduct, the judgments for libel cannot constitutionally be sustained.

---

5. Mr. Justice Black concurring in Barr v. Matteo, 360 U.S. 564, 577, 79 S.Ct. 1335, 1342, 3 L.Ed.2d 1434, observed that: "The effective functioning of a free government like ours depends largely on the force of an informed public opinion. This calls for the widest possible understanding of the quality of government service rendered by all elective or appointed public officials or employees.

Such an informed understanding depends, of course, on the freedom people have to applaud or to criticize the way public employees do their jobs, from the least to the most important."

6   See notes 3, 4, supra

7. See Freund, The Supreme Court of the United States (1949), p. 61.

[See pages 740 and 741 for a copy of the advertisement carried in the New York Times on March 29, 1960.]

ABBREVIATIONS

A.	Atlantic Reporter
A. 2d	Atlantic Reporter, Second Series
AAA	American Arbitration Association; Agricultural Adjustment Act of 1933
AAPRP	All African People's Revolutionary Party
ABA	American Bar Association; Architectural Barriers Act, 1968
ABM Treaty	Anti-Ballistic Missile Treaty of 1972; antiballistic missile
ABVP	Anti-Biased Violence Project
A/C	Account
A.C.	Appeal Cases
ACAA	Air Carrier Access Act
ACF	Administration for Children and Families
ACLU	American Civil Liberties Union
ACS	Agricultural Cooperative Service
Act'g Legal Adv.	Acting Legal Advisor
ACUS	Administrative Conference of the United States
ACYF	Administration on Children, Youth, and Families
A.D. 2d	Appellate Division, Second Series, N.Y.
ADA	Americans with Disabilities Act of 1990
ADAMHA	Alcohol, Drug Abuse, and Mental Health Administration
ADC	Aid to Dependent Children
ADD	Administration on Developmental Disabilities
ADEA	Age Discrimination in Employment Act of 1967
ADR	alternative dispute resolution
AEC	Atomic Energy Commission
AECB	Arms Export Control Board
A.E.R.	All England Law Reports
AFDC	Aid to Families with Dependent Children
aff'd per cur.	affirmed by the court
AFIS	automated fingerprint identification system
AFL	American Federation of Labor
AFL-CIO	American Federation of Labor and Congress of Industrial Organizations
AFRes	Air Force Reserve
AFSCME	American Federation of State, County, and Municipal Employees
AGRICOLA	Agricultural Online Access
AIA	Association of Insurance Attorneys
AID	artificial insemination using a third-party donor's sperm; Agency for International Development

AIDS	acquired immune deficiency syndrome
AIH	artificial insemination using the husband's sperm
AIM	American Indian Movement
AIUSA	Amnesty International, U.S.A. Affiliate
AJS	American Judicature Society
ALEC	American Legislative Exchange Council
ALF	Animal Liberation Front
ALI	American Law Institute
ALJ	administrative law judge
All E.R.	All England Law Reports
ALO	Agency Liaison
A.L.R.	American Law Reports
AMA	American Medical Association
Am. Dec.	American Decisions
amdt.	amendment
Amer. St. Papers, For. Rels.	American State Papers, Legislative and Executive Documents of the Congress of the U.S., Class I, Foreign Relations, 1832–1859
AMVETS	American Veterans (of World War II)
ANA	Administration for Native Americans
Ann. Dig.	Annual Digest of Public International Law Cases
ANZUS	Australia–New Zealand–United States Security Treaty Organization
AOA	Administration on Aging
APA	Administrative Procedure Act of 1946
APHIS	Animal and Plant Health Inspection Service
App. Div.	Appellate Division Reports, N.Y. Supreme Court
Arb. Trib., U.S.-British Convention of 1853	Arbitration Tribunal, Claim Convention of 1853, United States and Great Britain
ARS	Advanced Record System
Art.	article
ASCS	Agriculture Stabilization and Conservation Service
ASM	available seatmile
ASPCA	American Society for the Prevention of Cruelty to Animals
Asst. Att. Gen.	Assistant Attorney General
AT&T	American Telephone and Telegraph
ATFD	Alcohol, Tobacco and Firearms Division
ATLA	Association of Trial Lawyers of America
ATTD	Alcohol and Tobacco Tax Division
ATU	Alcohol Tax Unit
AZT	azidothymidine
BALSA	Black-American Law Student Association
BATF	Bureau of Alcohol, Tobacco and Firearms
BCCI	Bank of Credit and Commerce International
BEA	Bureau of Economic Analysis
Bell's Cr. C.	Bell's English Crown Cases
Bevans	United States Treaties, etc. *Treaties and Other International Agreements of the United States of America, 1776–1949* (compiled under the direction of Charles I. Bevans) (1968–76)
BFOQ	bona fide occupational qualification
BI	Bureau of Investigation
BIA	Bureau of Indian Affairs; Board of Immigration Appeals
BJS	Bureau of Justice Statistics
Black.	Black's United States Supreme Court Reports
Blatchf.	Blatchford's United States Circuit Court Reports
BLM	Bureau of Land Management
BLS	Bureau of Labor Statistics
BMD	ballistic missile defense
BOCA	Building Officials and Code Administrators International
BPP	Black Panther Party for Self-Defense

Brit. and For.	British and Foreign State Papers
Burr.	James Burrows, *Report of Cases Argued and Determined in the Court of King's Bench during the Time of Lord Mansfield* (1766–1780)
BVA	Board of Veterans Appeals
c.	Chapter
C³I	Command, Control, Communications, and Intelligence
C.A.	Court of Appeals
CAA	Clean Air Act
CAB	Civil Aeronautics Board
CAFE	corporate average fuel economy
Cal. 2d	California Reports, Second Series
Cal. 3d	California Reports, Third Series
CALR	computer-assisted legal research
Cal. Rptr.	California Reporter
CAP	Common Agricultural Policy
CATV	community antenna television
CBO	Congressional Budget Office
CCC	Commodity Credit Corporation
CCDBG	Child Care and Development Block Grant of 1990
C.C.D. Pa.	Circuit Court Decisions, Pennsylvania
C.C.D. Va.	Circuit Court Decisions, Virginia
CCEA	Cabinet Council on Economic Affairs
CCR	Center for Constitutional Rights
C.C.R.I.	Circuit Court, Rhode Island
CD	certificate of deposit
CDA	Communications Decency Act
CDBG	Community Development Block Grant Program
CDC	Centers for Disease Control and Prevention; Community Development Corporation
CDF	Children's Defense Fund
CDL	Citizens for Decency through Law
CD-ROM	compact disc read-only memory
CDS	Community Dispute Services
CDW	collision damage waiver
CENTO	Central Treaty Organization
CEQ	Council on Environmental Quality
CERCLA	Comprehensive Environmental Response, Compensation, and Liability Act of 1980
cert.	*certiorari*
CETA	Comprehensive Employment and Training Act
C & F	cost and freight
CFC	chlorofluorocarbon
CFE Treaty	Conventional Forces in Europe Treaty of 1990
C.F. & I.	Cost, freight, and insurance
CFNP	Community Food and Nutrition Program
C.F.R.	Code of Federal Regulations
CFTC	Commodity Futures Trading Commission
Ch.	Chancery Division, English Law Reports
CHAMPVA	Civilian Health and Medical Program at the Veterans Administration
CHEP	Cuban/Haitian Entrant Program
CHINS	children in need of supervision
CHIPS	child in need of protective services
Ch.N.Y.	Chancery Reports, New York
Chr. Rob.	Christopher Robinson, *Reports of Cases Argued and Determined in the High Court of Admiralty* (1801–1808)
CIA	Central Intelligence Agency
CID	Commercial Item Descriptions
C.I.F.	Cost, insurance, and freight
CINCNORAD	Commander in Chief, North American Air Defense Command
C.I.O.	Congress of Industrial Organizations

C.J.	chief justice
CJIS	Criminal Justice Information Services
C.J.S.	Corpus Juris Secundum
Claims Arb. under Spec. Conv., Nielsen's Rept.	Frederick Kenelm Nielsen, *American and British Claims Arbitration under the Special Agreement Concluded between the United States and Great Britain, August 18, 1910* (1926)
CLE	Center for Law and Education
CLEO	Council on Legal Education Opportunity
CLP	Communist Labor Party of America
CLS	Christian Legal Society; critical legal studies (movement), Critical Legal Studies (membership organization)
C.M.A.	Court of Military Appeals
CMEA	Council for Mutual Economic Assistance
CMHS	Center for Mental Health Services
C.M.R.	Court of Military Review
CNN	Cable News Network
CNO	Chief of Naval Operations
C.O.D.	cash on delivery
COGP	Commission on Government Procurement
COINTELPRO	Counterintelligence Program
Coke Rep.	Coke's English King's Bench Reports
COLA	cost-of-living adjustment
COMCEN	Federal Communications Center
Comp.	Compilation
Conn.	Connecticut Reports
CONTU	National Commission on New Technological Uses of Copyrighted Works
Conv.	Convention
Corbin	Arthur L. Corbin, *Corbin on Contracts: A Comprehensive Treatise on the Rules of Contract Law* (1950)
CORE	Congress of Racial Equality
Cox's Crim. Cases	Cox's Criminal Cases (England)
CPA	certified public accountant
CPB	Corporation for Public Broadcasting, the
CPI	Consumer Price Index
CPSC	Consumer Product Safety Commission
Cranch	Cranch's United States Supreme Court Reports
CRF	Constitutional Rights Foundation
CRS	Congressional Research Service; Community Relations Service
CRT	critical race theory
CSA	Community Services Administration
CSAP	Center for Substance Abuse Prevention
CSAT	Center for Substance Abuse Treatment
CSC	Civil Service Commission
CSCE	Conference on Security and Cooperation in Europe
CSG	Council of State Governments
CSO	Community Service Organization
CSP	Center for the Study of the Presidency
C-SPAN	Cable-Satellite Public Affairs Network
CSRS	Cooperative State Research Service
CSWPL	Center on Social Welfare Policy and Law
CTA	*cum testamento annexo* (with the will attached)
Ct. Ap. D.C.	Court of Appeals, District of Columbia
Ct. App. No. Ireland	Court of Appeals, Northern Ireland
Ct. Cl.	Court of Claims, United States
Ct. Crim. Apps.	Court of Criminal Appeals (England)
Ct. of Sess., Scot.	Court of Sessions, Scotland
CU	credit union

CUNY	City University of New York
Cush.	Cushing's Massachusetts Reports
CWA	Civil Works Administration; Clean Water Act
Dall.	Dallas' Pennsylvania and United States Reports
DAR	Daughter of the American Revolution
DARPA	Defense Advanced Research Projects Agency
DAVA	Defense Audiovisual Agency
D.C.	United States District Court
D.C. Del.	United States District Court, Delaware
D.C. Mass.	United States District Court, Massachusetts
D.C. Md.	United States District Court, Maryland
D.C.N.D.Cal.	United States District Court, Northern District, California
D.C.N.Y.	United States District Court, New York
D.C.Pa.	United States District Court, Pennsylvania
DCS	Deputy Chiefs of Staff
DCZ	District of the Canal Zone
DDT	dichlorodiphenyltricloroethane
DEA	Drug Enforcement Administration
Decl. Lond.	Declaration of London, February 26, 1909
Dev. & B.	Devereux & Battle's North Carolina Reports
Dig. U.S. Practice in Intl. Law	Digest of U.S. Practice in International Law
Dist. Ct. D.C.	United States District Court, District of Columbia
D.L.R.	Dominion Law Reports (Canada)
DNA	deoxyribonucleic acid
DNase	deoxyribonuclease
DNC	Democratic National Committee
DOC	Department of Commerce
DOD	Department of Defense
Dodson	Dodson's Reports, English Admiralty Courts
DOE	Department of Energy
DOER	Department of Employee Relations
DOJ	Department of Justice
DOS	disk operating system
DOT	Department of Transportation
DPT	diphtheria, pertussis, and tetanus
DRI	Defense Research Institute
DSAA	Defense Security Assistance Agency
DUI	driving under the influence; driving under intoxication
DWI	driving while intoxicated
EAHCA	Education for All Handicapped Children Act of 1975
EBT	examination before trial
ECPA	Electronic Communications Privacy Act of 1986
ECSC	Treaty of the European Coal and Steel Community
EDA	Economic Development Administration
EDF	Environmental Defense Fund
E.D.N.Y.	Eastern District, New York
EDP	electronic data processing
E.D. Pa.	Eastern District, Pennsylvania
EDSC	Eastern District, South Carolina
E.D. Va.	Eastern District, Virginia
EEC	European Economic Community; European Economic Community Treaty
EEOC	Equal Employment Opportunity Commission
EFF	Electronic Frontier Foundation
EFT	electronic funds transfer
Eliz.	Queen Elizabeth (Great Britain)
Em. App.	Temporary Emergency Court of Appeals

ENE	early neutral evaluation
Eng. Rep.	English Reports
EOP	Executive Office of the President
EPA	Environmental Protection Agency; Equal Pay Act of 1963
ERA	Equal Rights Amendment
ERISA	Employee Retirement Income Security Act of 1974
ERS	Economic Research Service
ESF	emergency support function; Economic Support Fund
ESRD	End-Stage Renal Disease Program
ETA	Employment and Training Administration
ETS	environmental tobacco smoke
et seq.	*et sequentes* or *et sequentia;* "and the following"
EU	European Union
Euratom	European Atomic Energy Community
Eur. Ct. H.R.	European Court of Human Rights
Ex.	English Exchequer Reports, Welsby, Hurlstone & Gordon
Exch.	Exchequer Reports (Welsby, Hurlstone & Gordon)
Eximbank	Export-Import Bank of the United States
F.	Federal Reporter
F. 2d	Federal Reporter, Second Series
FAA	Federal Aviation Administration; Federal Arbitration Act
FAAA	Federal Alcohol Administration Act
FACE	Freedom of Access to Clinic Entrances Act of 1994
FACT	Feminist Anti-Censorship Task Force
FAO	Food and Agriculture Organization of the United Nations
FAR	Federal Acquisition Regulations
FAS	Foreign Agricultural Service
FBA	Federal Bar Association
FBI	Federal Bureau of Investigation
FCA	Farm Credit Administration
F. Cas.	Federal Cases
FCC	Federal Communications Commission
FCIA	Foreign Credit Insurance Association
FCIC	Federal Crop Insurance Corporation
FCRA	Fair Credit Reporting Act
FCU	Federal credit unions
FDA	Food and Drug Administration
FDIC	Federal Deposit Insurance Corporation
FDPC	Federal Data Processing Center
FEC	Federal Election Commission
Fed. Cas.	Federal Cases
FEMA	Federal Emergency Management Agency
FFB	Federal Financing Bank
FGIS	Federal Grain Inspection Service
FHA	Federal Housing Authority
FHWA	Federal Highway Administration
FIA	Federal Insurance Administration
FIC	Federal Information Centers; Federation of Insurance Counsel
FICA	Federal Insurance Contributions Act
FIFRA	Federal Insecticide, Fungicide, and Rodenticide Act
FIP	Forestry Incentives Program
FIRREA	Financial Institutions Reform, Recovery, and Enforcement Act
FISA	Foreign Intelligence Surveillance Act of 1978
FMCS	Federal Mediation and Conciliation Service
FmHA	Farmers Home Administration
FMLA	Family and Medical Leave Act of 1993
FNMA	Federal National Mortgage Association, "Fannie Mae"
F.O.B.	free on board

FOIA	Freedom of Information Act
FPC	Federal Power Commission
FPMR	Federal Property Management Regulations
FPRS	Federal Property Resources Service
FR	Federal Register
FRA	Federal Railroad Administration
FRB	Federal Reserve Board
FRC	Federal Radio Commission
F.R.D.	Federal Rules Decisions
FSA	Family Support Act
FSLIC	Federal Savings and Loan Insurance Corporation
FSQS	Food Safety and Quality Service
FSS	Federal Supply Service
F. Supp.	Federal Supplement
FTA	U.S.-Canada Free Trade Agreement, 1988
FTC	Federal Trade Commission
FTS	Federal Telecommunications System
FUTA	Federal Unemployment Tax Act
FWPCA	Federal Water Pollution Control Act of 1948
GAO	General Accounting Office; Governmental Affairs Office
GAOR	General Assembly Official Records, United Nations
GA Res.	General Assembly Resolution (United Nations)
GATT	General Agreement on Tariffs and Trade
Gen. Cls. Comm.	General Claims Commission, United States and Panama; General Claims Commission, United States and Mexico
Geo. II	King George II (Great Britain)
Geo. III	King George III (Great Britain)
GM	General Motors
GNMA	Government National Mortgage Association, "Ginnie Mae"
GNP	gross national product
GOP	Grand Old Party (Republican)
GOPAC	Grand Old Party Action Committee
GPA	Office of Governmental and Public Affairs
GPO	Government Printing Office
GRAS	generally recognized as safe
Gr. Br., Crim. Ct. App.	Great Britain, Court of Criminal Appeals
GRNL	Gay Rights National Lobby
GSA	General Services Administration
Hackworth	Green Haywood Hackworth, *Digest of International Law* (1940–44)
Hay and Marriott	Great Britain. High Court of Admiralty, *Decisions in the High Court of Admiralty during the Time of Sir George Hay and of Sir James Marriott, Late Judges of That Court* (1801)
HBO	Home Box Office
HCFA	Health Care Financing Administration
H.Ct.	High Court
HDS	Office of Human Development Services
Hen. & M.	Hening & Munford's Virginia Reports
HEW	Department of Health, Education, and Welfare
HHS	Department of Health and Human Services
Hill	Hill's New York Reports
HIRE	Help through Industry Retraining and Employment
HIV	human immunodeficiency virus
H.L.	House of Lords Cases (England)
H. Lords	House of Lords (England)
HNIS	Human Nutrition Information Service
Hong Kong L.R.	Hong Kong Law Reports
How.	Howard's United States Supreme Court Reports
How. St. Trials	Howell's English State Trials
HUAC	House Un-American Activities Committee

HUD	Department of Housing and Urban Development
Hudson, Internatl. Legis.	Manley O. Hudson, ed., *International Legislation: A Collection of the Texts of Multipartite International Instruments of General Interest Beginning with the Covenant of the League of Nations* (1931)
Hudson, World Court Reps.	Manley Ottmer Hudson, ed., *World Court Reports* (1934–)
Hun	Hun's New York Supreme Court Reports
Hunt's Rept.	Bert L. Hunt, *Report of the American and Panamanian General Claims Arbitration* (1934)
IAEA	International Atomic Energy Agency
IALL	International Association of Law Libraries
IBA	International Bar Association
IBM	International Business Machines
ICBM	intercontinental ballistic missile
ICC	Interstate Commerce Commission
ICJ	International Court of Justice
IDEA	Individuals with Disabilities Education Act, 1975
IEP	individualized educational program
IFC	International Finance Corporation
IGRA	Indian Gaming Regulatory Act, 1988
IJA	Institute of Judicial Administration
IJC	International Joint Commission
ILC	International Law Commission
ILD	International Labor Defense
Ill. Dec.	Illinois Decisions
ILO	International Labor Organization
IMF	International Monetary Fund
INA	Immigration and Nationality Act
IND	investigational new drug
INF Treaty	Intermediate-Range Nuclear Forces Treaty of 1987
INS	Immigration and Naturalization Service
INTELSAT	International Telecommunications Satellite Organization
Interpol	International Criminal Police Organization
Int'l. Law Reps.	International Law Reports
Intl. Legal Mats.	International Legal Materials
IPDC	International Program for the Development of Communication
IPO	Intellectual Property Owners
IPP	independent power producer
IQ	intelligence quotient
I.R.	Irish Reports
IRA	individual retirement account; Irish Republican Army
IRCA	Immigration Reform and Control Act of 1986
IRS	Internal Revenue Service
ISO	independent service organization
ISSN	International Standard Serial Numbers
ITA	International Trade Administration
ITI	Information Technology Integration
ITO	International Trade Organization
ITS	Information Technology Service
ITU	International Telecommunication Union
IUD	intrauterine device
IWC	International Whaling Commission
IWW	Industrial Workers of the World
JCS	Joint Chiefs of Staff
JDL	Jewish Defense League
JOBS	Jobs Opportunity and Basic Skills
John. Ch.	Johnson's New York Chancery Reports
Johns.	Johnson's Reports (New York)
JP	justice of the peace

K.B.	King's Bench Reports (England)
KGB	Komitet Gosudarstvennoi Bezopasnosti (the State Security Committee for countries in the former Soviet Union)
KKK	Ku Klux Klan
KMT	Kuomintang
LAPD	Los Angeles Police Department
LC	Library of Congress
LD50	lethal dose 50
LDEF	Legal Defense and Education Fund (NOW)
LDF	Legal Defense Fund, Legal Defense and Educational Fund of the NAACP
LEAA	Law Enforcement Assistance Administration
L.Ed.	Lawyers' Edition Supreme Court Reports
LMSA	Labor-Management Services Administration
LNTS	League of Nations Treaty Series
Lofft's Rep.	Lofft's English King's Bench Reports
L.R.	Law Reports (English)
LSAS	Law School Admission Service
LSAT	Law School Aptitude Test
LSC	Legal Services Corporation; Legal Services for Children
LSD	lysergic acid diethylamide
LSDAS	Law School Data Assembly Service
LTBT	Limited Test Ban Treaty
LTC	Long Term Care
MAD	mutual assured destruction
MADD	Mothers against Drunk Driving
MALDEF	Mexican American Legal Defense and Educational Fund
Malloy	William M. Malloy, ed., *Treaties, Conventions, International Acts, Protocols, and Agreements between the United States of America and Other Powers* (1910–38)
Martens	Georg Friedrich von Martens, ed., *Noveau recueil général de traités et autres act es relatifs aux rapports de droit international* (Series I, 20 vols. [1843–75]; Series II, 35 vols. [1876–1908]; Series III [1909–])
Mass.	Massachusetts Reports
MCH	Maternal and Child Health Bureau
Md. App.	Maryland, Appeal Cases
M.D. Ga.	Middle District, Georgia
Mercy	Movement Ensuring the Right to Choose for Yourself
Metc.	Metcalf's Massachusetts Reports
MFDP	Mississippi Freedom Democratic party
MGT	Management
MHSS	Military Health Services System
Miller	David Hunter Miller, ed., *Treaties and Other International Acts of the United States of America* (1931–1948)
Minn.	Minnesota Reports
MINS	minors in need of supervision
MIRV	multiple independently targetable reentry vehicle
Misc.	Miscellaneous Reports, New York
Mixed Claims Comm., Report of Decs.	Mixed Claims Commission, United States and Germany, Report of Decisions
M.J.	Military Justice Reporter
MLAP	Migrant Legal Action Program
MLB	major league baseball
MLDP	Mississippi Loyalist Democratic party
Mo.	Missouri Reports
Mod.	Modern Reports, English King's Bench, etc.
Moore, Dig. Intl. Law	John Bassett Moore, *A Digest of International Law*, 8 vols. (1906)
Moore, Intl. Arbs.	John Bassett Moore, *History and Digest of the International Arbitrations to Which the United States Has Been a Party*, 6 vols. (1898)

Morison	William Maxwell Morison, *The Scots Revised Report: Morison's Dictionary of Decisions* (1908–09)
M.P.	member of Parliament
MPAA	Motion Picture Association of America
mpg	miles per gallon
MPRSA	Marine Protection, Research, and Sanctuaries Act of 1972
M.R.	Master of the Rolls
MS-DOS	Microsoft Disk Operating System
MSHA	Mine Safety and Health Administration
NAACP	National Association for the Advancement of Colored People
NAAQS	National Ambient Air Quality Standards
NABSW	National Association of Black Social Workers
NAFTA	North American Free Trade Agreement, 1993
NARAL	National Abortion Rights Action League
NARF	Native American Rights Fund
NARS	National Archives and Record Service
NASA	National Aeronautics and Space Administration
NASD	National Association of Securities Dealers
NATO	North Atlantic Treaty Organization
NAVINFO	Navy Information Offices
NAWSA	National American Woman's Suffrage Association
NBA	National Bar Association
NBC	National Broadcasting Company
NBLSA	National Black Law Student Association
NBS	National Bureau of Standards
NCA	Noise Control Act; National Command Authorities
NCAA	National Collegiate Athletic Association
NCAC	National Coalition against Censorship
NCCB	National Consumer Cooperative Bank
NCE	Northwest Community Exchange
NCJA	National Criminal Justice Association
NCLB	National Civil Liberties Bureau
NCP	national contingency plan
NCSC	National Center for State Courts
NCUA	National Credit Union Administration
NDA	new drug application
N.D. Ill.	Northern District, Illinois
NDU	National Defense University
N.D. Wash.	Northern District, Washington
N.E.	North Eastern Reporter
N.E. 2d	North Eastern Reporter, Second Series
NEA	National Endowment for the Arts
NEH	National Endowment for the Humanities
NEPA	National Environmental Protection Act; National Endowment Policy Act
NFIP	National Flood Insurance Program
NGTF	National Gay Task Force
NHRA	Nursing Home Reform Act, 1987
NHTSA	National Highway Traffic Safety Administration
Nielsen's Rept.	Frederick Kenelm Nielsen, *American and British Claims Arbitration under the Special Agreement Concluded between the United States and Great Britain, August 18, 1910* (1926)
NIEO	New International Economic Order
NIH	National Institutes of Health, the NIH
NIJ	National Institute of Justice
NIRA	National Industrial Recovery Act; National Industrial Recovery Administration
NIST	National Institute of Standards and Technology, the NIST
NITA	National Telecommunications and Information Administration
N.J.	New Jersey Reports

N.J. Super.	New Jersey Superior Court Reports
NLRA	National Labor Relations Act
NLRB	National Labor Relations Board
No.	Number
NOAA	National Oceanic and Atmospheric Administration
NOW	National Organization for Women
NOW LDEF	National Organization for Women Legal Defense and Education Fund
NOW/PAC	National Organization for Women Political Action Committee
NPDES	National Pollutant Discharge Elimination System
NPL	national priorities list
NPR	National Public Radio
NPT	Non-Proliferation Treaty
NRA	National Rifle Association; National Recovery Act
NRC	Nuclear Regulatory Commission
NSC	National Security Council
NSCLC	National Senior Citizens Law Center
NSF	National Science Foundation
NSFNET	National Science Foundation Network
NTIA	National Telecommunications and Information Administration
NTID	National Technical Institute for the Deaf
NTIS	National Technical Information Service
NTS	Naval Telecommunications System
NTSB	National Transportation Safety Board
N.W.	North Western Reporter
N.W. 2d	North Western Reporter, Second Series
NWSA	National Woman Suffrage Association
N.Y.	New York Court of Appeals Reports
N.Y. 2d	New York Court of Appeals Reports, Second Series
N.Y.S.	New York Supplement Reporter
N.Y.S. 2d	New York Supplement Reporter, Second Series
NYSE	New York Stock Exchange
N.Y. Sup.	New York Supreme Court Reports
NYU	New York University
OAAU	Organization of Afro American Unity
OAP	Office of Administrative Procedure
OAS	Organization of American States
OASDI	Old-age, Survivors, and Disability Insurance Benefits
OASHDS	Office of the Assistant Secretary for Human Development Services
OCED	Office of Comprehensive Employment Development
OCHAMPUS	Office of Civilian Health and Medical Program of the Uniformed Services
OCSE	Office of Child Support Enforcement
OEA	Organización de los Estados Americanos
OFCCP	Office of Federal Contract Compliance Programs
OFPP	Office of Federal Procurement Policy
OICD	Office of International Cooperation and Development
OIG	Office of the Inspector General
OJARS	Office of Justice Assistance, Research, and Statistics
OMB	Office of Management and Budget
OMPC	Office of Management, Planning, and Communications
ONP	Office of National Programs
OPD	Office of Policy Development
OPEC	Organization of Petroleum Exporting Countries
OPIC	Overseas Private Investment Corporation
Ops. Atts. Gen.	Opinions of the Attorneys-General of the United States
Ops. Comms.	Opinions of the Commissioners
OPSP	Office of Product Standards Policy
O.R.	Ontario Reports
OR	Official Records

OSHA	Occupational Safety and Health Administration
OSHRC	Occupational Safety and Health Review Commission
OSM	Office of Surface Mining
OSS	Office of Strategic Services
OST	Office of the Secretary
OT	Office of Transportation
OTA	Office of Technology Assessment
OTC	over-the-counter
OUI	operating under the influence
OWBPA	Older Workers Benefit Protection Act
OWRT	Office of Water Research and Technology
P.	Pacific Reporter
P. 2d	Pacific Reporter, Second Series
PAC	political action committee
Pa. Oyer and Terminer	Pennsylvania Oyer and Terminer Reports
PATCO	Professional Air Traffic Controllers Organization
PBGC	Pension Benefit Guaranty Corporation
PBS	Public Broadcasting Service; Public Buildings Service
P.C.	Privy Council (English Law Reports); personal computer
PCIJ	Permanent Court of International Justice
	Series A—Judgments and Orders (1922–30)
	Series B—Advisory Opinions (1922–30)
	Series A/B—Judgments, Orders, and Advisory Opinions (1931–40)
	Series C—Pleadings, Oral Statements, and Documents relating to Judgments and Advisory Opinions (1923–42)
	Series D—Acts and Documents concerning the Organization of the World Court (1922–47)
	Series E—Annual Reports (1925–45)
PCP	phencyclidine (no need to spell out)
P.D.	Probate Division, English Law Reports (1876–1890)
PDA	Pregnancy Discrimination Act of 1978
PD & R	Policy Development and Research
Perm. Ct. of Arb.	Permanent Court of Arbitration
Pet.	Peters' United States Supreme Court Reports
PETA	People for the Ethical Treatment of Animals
PGM	Program
PHA	Public Housing Agency
Phila. Ct. of Oyer and Terminer	Philadelphia Court of Oyer and Terminer
PHS	Public Health Service
PIC	Private Industry Council
Pick.	Pickering's Massachusetts Reports
PIK	Payment in Kind
PINS	persons in need of supervision
PIRG	Public Interest Research Group
P.L.	Public Laws
PLAN	Pro-Life Action Network
PLI	Practicing Law Institute
PLO	Palestine Liberation Organization
PNET	Peaceful Nuclear Explosions Treaty
POW-MIA	prisoner of war–missing in action
Pratt	Frederic Thomas Pratt, *Law of Contraband of War, with a Selection of Cases from the Papers of the Right Honourable Sir George Lee* (1856)
Proc.	Proceedings
PRP	potentially responsible party
PSRO	Professional Standards Review Organization
PTO	Patents and Trademark Office
PURPA	Public Utilities Regulatory Policies Act

PUSH	People United to Serve Humanity
PWA	Public Works Administration
PWSA	Ports and Waterways Safety Act of 1972
Q.B.	Queen's Bench (England)
Ralston's Rept.	Jackson Harvey Ralston, ed., *Venezuelan Arbitrations of 1903* (1904)
RC	Regional Commissioner
RCRA	Resource Conservation and Recovery Act
RCWP	Rural Clean Water Program
RDA	Rural Development Administration
REA	Rural Electrification Administration
Rec. des Decs. des Trib. Arb. Mixtes	G. Gidel, ed., *Recueil des décisions des tribunaux arbitraux mixtes, institués par les traités de paix* (1922–30)
Redmond	Vol. 3 of Charles I. Bevans, *Treaties and Other International Agreements of the United States of America, 1776–1949* (compiled by C. F. Redmond) (1969)
RESPA	Real Estate Settlement Procedure Act of 1974
RFRA	Religious Freedom Restoration Act
RICO	Racketeer Influenced and Corrupt Organizations
RNC	Republican National Committee
Roscoe	Edward Stanley Roscoe, ed., *Reports of Prize Cases Determined in the High Court of Admiralty before the Lords Commissioners of Appeals in Prize Causes and before the Judicial Committee of the Privy Council from 1745 to 1859* (1905)
ROTC	Reserve Officers' Training Corps
RPP	Representative Payee Program
R.S.	Revised Statutes
RTC	Resolution Trust Company
Ryan White CARE Act	Ryan White Comprehensive AIDS Research Emergency Act of 1990
SAC	Strategic Air Command
SACB	Subversive Activities Control Board
SADD	Students against Drunk Driving
SAF	Student Activities Fund
SAIF	Savings Association Insurance Fund
SALT I	Strategic Arms Limitation Talks of 1969–72
SAMHSA	Substance Abuse and Mental Health Services Administration
Sandf.	Sandford's New York Superior Court Reports
S and L	savings and loan
SARA	Superfund Amendment and Reauthorization Act
Sawy.	Sawyer's United States Circuit Court Reports
SBA	Small Business Administration
SCLC	Southern Christian Leadership Conference
Scott's Repts.	James Brown Scott, ed., *The Hague Court Reports*, 2 vols. (1916–32)
SCS	Soil Conservation Service
SCSEP	Senior Community Service Employment Program
S.Ct.	Supreme Court Reporter
S.D. Cal.	Southern District, California
S.D. Fla.	Southern District, Florida
S.D. Ga.	Southern District, Georgia
SDI	Strategic Defense Initiative
S.D. Me.	Southern District, Maine
S.D.N.Y.	Southern District, New York
SDS	Students for a Democratic Society
S.E.	South Eastern Reporter
S.E. 2d	South Eastern Reporter, Second Series
SEA	Science and Education Administration
SEATO	Southeast Asia Treaty Organization
SEC	Securities and Exchange Commission
Sec.	Section
SEEK	Search for Elevation, Education and Knowledge
SEOO	State Economic Opportunity Office

SEP	simplified employee pension plan
Ser.	Series
Sess.	Session
SGLI	Servicemen's Group Life Insurance
SIP	state implementation plan
SLA	Symbionese Liberation Army
SLBM	submarine-launched ballistic missile
SNCC	Student Nonviolent Coordinating Committee
So.	Southern Reporter
So. 2d	Southern Reporter, Second Series
SPA	Software Publisher's Association
Spec. Sess.	Special Session
SRA	Sentencing Reform Act of 1984
SS	Schutzstaffel (German for Protection Echelon)
SSA	Social Security Administration
SSI	Supplemental Security Income
START I	Strategic Arms Reduction Treaty of 1991
START II	Strategic Arms Reduction Treaty of 1993
Stat.	United States Statutes at Large
STS	Space Transportation Systems
St. Tr.	State Trials, English
STURAA	Surface Transportation and Uniform Relocation Assistance Act of 1987
Sup. Ct. of Justice, Mexico	Supreme Court of Justice, Mexico
Supp.	Supplement
S.W.	South Western Reporter
S.W. 2d	South Western Reporter, Second Series
SWAPO	South-West Africa People's Organization
SWAT	Special Weapons and Tactics
SWP	Socialist Workers party
TDP	Trade and Development Program
Tex. Sup.	Texas Supreme Court Reports
THAAD	Theater High-Altitude Area Defense System
TIA	Trust Indenture Act of 1939
TIAS	Treaties and Other International Acts Series (United States)
TNT	trinitrotoluene
TOP	Targeted Outreach Program
TPUS	Transportation and Public Utilities Service
Tripartite Claims Comm., Decs. and Ops.	Tripartite Claims Commission (United States, Austria, and Hungary), Decisions and Opinions
TRI-TAC	Joint Tactical Communications
TRO	temporary restraining order
TS	Treaty Series, United States
TSCA	Toxic Substance Control Act
TSDs	transporters, storers, and disposers
TTBT	Threshold Test Ban Treaty
TVA	Tennessee Valley Authority
UAW	United Auto Workers; United Automobile, Aerospace, and Agricultural Implements Workers of America
U.C.C.	Uniform Commercial Code; Universal Copyright Convention
U.C.C.C.	Uniform Consumer Credit Code
UCCJA	Uniform Child Custody Jurisdiction Act
UCMJ	Uniform Code of Military Justice
UCPP	Urban Crime Prevention Program
UCS	United Counseling Service
UDC	United Daughters of the Confederacy
UFW	United Farm Workers
UHF	ultrahigh frequency
UIFSA	Uniform Interstate Family Support Act

UIS	Unemployment Insurance Service
UMDA	Uniform Marriage and Divorce Act
UMTA	Urban Mass Transportation Administration
UNCITRAL	United Nations Commission on International Trade Law
UNCTAD	United Nations Conference on Trade and Development
UN Doc.	United Nations Documents
UNDP	United Nations Development Program
UNEF	United Nations Emergency Force
UNESCO	United Nations Educational, Scientific, and Cultural Organization
UNICEF	United Nations Children's Fund
UNIDO	United Nations Industrial and Development Organization
Unif. L. Ann.	Uniform Laws Annotated
UN Repts. Intl. Arb. Awards	United Nations Reports of International Arbitral Awards
UNTS	United Nations Treaty Series
UPI	United Press International
URESA	Uniform Reciprocal Enforcement of Support Act
U.S.	United States Reports
USAF	United States Air Force
U.S. App. D.C.	United States Court of Appeals for the District of Columbia
U.S.C.	United States Code
U.S.C.A.	United States Code Annotated
U.S.C.C.A.N.	United States Code Congressional and Administrative News
USCMA	United States Court of Military Appeals
USDA	U.S. Department of Agriculture
USES	United States Employment Service
USFA	United States Fire Administration
USICA	International Communication Agency, United States
USSC	U.S. Sentencing Commission
U.S.S.R.	Union of Soviet Socialist Republics
UST	United States Treaties
USTS	United States Travel Service
v.	*versus*
VA	Veterans Administration, the VA
VGLI	Veterans Group Life Insurance
Vict.	Queen Victoria (Great Britain)
VIN	vehicle identification number
VISTA	Volunteers in Service to America
VJRA	Veterans Judicial Review Act of 1988
V.L.A.	Volunteer Lawyers for the Arts
VMI	Virginia Military Institute
VMLI	Veterans Mortgage Life Insurance
VOCAL	Victims of Child Abuse Laws
WAC	Women's Army Corps
Wall.	Wallace's United States Supreme Court Reports
Wash. 2d	Washington Reports, Second Series
WAVES	Women Accepted for Volunteer Service
WCTU	Women's Christian Temperance Union
W.D. Wash.	Western District, Washington
W.D. Wis.	Western District, Wisconsin
WEAL	West's Encyclopedia of American Law, Women's Equity Action League
Wend.	Wendell's New York Reports
WFSE	Washington Federation of State Employees
Wheat.	Wheaton's United States Supreme Court Reports
Wheel. Cr. Cases	Wheeler's New York Criminal Cases
Whiteman	Marjorie Millace Whiteman, *Digest of International Law*, 15 vols. (1963–73)
WHO	World Health Organization
WIC	Women, Infants, and Children program
Will. and Mar.	King William and Queen Mary (Great Britain)

WIN	WESTLAW Is Natural; Whip Inflation Now; Work Incentive Program
WIU	Workers' Industrial Union
W.L.R.	Weekly Law Reports, England
WPA	Works Progress Administration
WPPDA	Welfare and Pension Plans Disclosure Act
WWI	World War I
WWII	World War II
Yates Sel. Cas.	Yates' New York Select Cases

BIBLIOGRAPHY

FENWICK, MILLICENT VERNON HAMMOND

Lamson, Peggy. 1979. *In the Vanguard: Six American Women in Public Life*. Boston: Houghton Mifflin.

Stineman, Esther. 1980. *American Political Women*. Littleton, Colo.: Libraries Unlimited.

Women in Congress, 1917–1990. 1991. Washington, D.C.: Government Printing Office.

FERES DOCTRINE

Seidelson, David E. 1994. "From *Feres v. United States* to *Boyle v. United Technologies Corp.*: An Examination of Supreme Court Jurisprudence and a Couple of Suggestions." *Duquesne Law Review* 32.

FERRARO, GERALDINE ANNE

Ferraro, Geraldine. 1985. *Ferraro: My Life*. New York: Bantam Books.

Goldman, Peter, and Tony Fuller. 1985. *The Quest for the Presidency 1984*. Bantam Books.

FETAL RIGHTS

Bates, Kelly F. 1995. "Cesarean Section Epidemic: Defining the Problem, Approaching Solutions." *Boston University Public Interest Law Journal* 4.

Blank, Robert H. 1992. *Mother and Fetus: Changing Notions of Maternal Responsibility*. Westport, Conn.: Greenwood Press.

Condoll, Blair D. 1994. "Extending Constitutional Protection to the Viable Fetus: A Woman's Right to Privacy." *Southern University Law Review* 22 (fall).

Faludi, Susan. 1991. *Backlash: The Undeclared War on American Women*. Crown.

Samuels, Suzanne Uttaro. 1995. *Fetal Rights, Women's Rights: Gender Equality in the Workplace*. Univ. of Wisconsin Press.

FETAL TISSUE RESEARCH

Kluwer. 1994. *The Beginning of Human Life*. Beller, Fritz K., and Robert F. Weir, eds.

Goddard, James E. 1996. "The NIH Revitalization Act of 1993 Washed Away Many Legal Problems with Fetal Tissue Transplantation Research but a Stain Remains." *Southern Methodist University Law Review* 49 (January–February).

FEUDALISM

Hoyt, Robert S., and Stanley Chodorow. *Europe in the Middle Ages*.1976. 3d ed. New York: Harcourt Brace, Jovanovich.

Lazarus, Richard J. 1992. "Debunking Environmental Feudalism: Promoting the Individual through the Collective Pursuit of Environmental Quality." *Iowa Law Review* 77.

FIELD, DAVID DUDLEY

Field, Henry M. 1898. *The Life of David Dudley Field*. New York: Scribner.

Hicks, Frederick C. 1929. *High Finance in the Sixties*. New Haven, Conn.: Yale Univ. Press.

FIELD, STEPHEN JOHNSON

Stephens, Otis H., Jr., and John M. Scheb II. 1993. *American Constitutional Law*. St. Paul: West.

FIFTH AMENDMENT

Helmholz, R. H. 1983. "The Early History of the Grand Jury and the Canon Law." *University of Chicago Law Review* 50.

Hickok, Eugene W., Jr., ed. 1991. *The Bill of Rights: Original Meaning and Current Understanding*. Charlotteville, Va.: University Press of Virginia.

Madison, James. 1787–88. *The Federalist, No. 54*. Ed. Clinton Rossiter, 1961.

Treanor, William M. 1995. "The Original Understanding of the Takings Clause and the Political Process." *Columbia Law Review* 95.

FILLMORE, MILLARD

Grayson, Ben L. 1981. *The Unknown President*. Univ. Press of America.

Rayback, Robert J. 1959. *Millard Fillmore*. Stewart.

Smith, Elbert B. 1988. *The Presidencies of Zachary Taylor and Millard Fillmore*. Lawrence, Kan.: Univ. Press of Kansas.

FINES

Mangan, Lisa Suzanne. 1993. "Aborting the Indecency Standard in Political Programming." *Communication Law Conspectus* 1.

Tecce, James Charles. 1994. "Prisoners Paying for the Costs of Their Own Incarceration: United States Circuit Courts of Appeal Spar over the Validity and Application of United States Sentencing Guideline Section 5E1.2." *Dickinson Law Review* 99 (fall).

FINGERPRINTS

Aitken, C. G. G. 1995. "Evaluating DNA Evidence for Identification." *Southern California Interdisciplinary Law Journal* 4.

Cohen, Peter J. 1996. "How Shall They Be Known? *Daubert v. Merrell Dow Pharmaceuticals* and Eyewitness Identification." *Pace Law Review* 16.

Killerlane, James. J. 1995. "Finger Imaging: A Twenty-first Century Solution to Welfare Fraud at Our Fingertips." *Fordham Urban Law Journal* 22.

Mrowka, Molly J. 1996. "Criminal Procedure: Identification by Use of Thumbprints." *McGeorge School of Law, University of the Pacific* 27.

FIRST AMENDMENT

Bailyn, Bernard. 1992. *The Ideological Origins of the American Revolution.* Cambridge: Harvard Univ. Press.

Corwin, Edwin S. 1978. *The Constitution and What It Means Today.* Princeton, N.J.: Princeton Univ. Press.

Hickok, Eugene W., Jr., ed. 1991. *The Bill of Rights: Original Meaning and Current Understanding.* Charlotteville, Va.: University Press of Virginia.

Levy, Leonard W. 1988. *Original Intent and the Framers Constitution.* New York: Macmillan.

Meyers, Marvin, ed. 1981. *The Mind of the Founder: Sources of Political Thought of James Madison.* University Press of New England.

FISH AND FISHING

Bean, Michael J. 1983. *The Evolution of National Wildlife Law.* New York: Praeger.

Campbell-Mohn, Cynthia, Barry Breen, and J. William Futrell. 1993. *Sustainable Environmental Law.* St. Paul: West.

Cohen, Fay G. 1986. *Treaties on Trial.* Seattle: Univ. of Washington Press.

Greensberg, Eldon V. C., and Michael E. Shapiro. 1982. "Federalism in the Fishery Conservation Zone." *Southern California Law Review* 55.

McManus, Robert J. 1995. "America's Saltwater Fisheries: So Few Fish, So Many Fishermen." *Natural Resources and Environment* 9.

Pevar, Stephen L. 1983. *The Rights of Indians and Tribes.* New York: Bantam Books.

Wilkinson, Charles F. 1991. "To Feel the Summer in the Spring: The Treaty Fishing Rights of the Wisconsin Chippewa." *Wisconsin Law Review.*

FLAG

Cooke, Edward F. 1995. *A Detailed Analysis of the Constitution.* Lanham, Md.: Littlefield Adams.

Dyroff, David. 1991. "Legislative Attempts to Ban Flag Burning." *Washington University Law Quarterly* 69 (fall).

Goldstein, Robert Justin. 1995. *Saving "Old Glory."* Boulder, Colo.: Westview Press.

Padover, Saul. 1995. *The Living U.S. Constitution.* New York: Meridian.

Robinson, Marilyn. 1995. "Book Review: Michael Kent Curtis, Ed., *The Constitution and the Flag, Volume I: The Flag Salute Cases;* and *Volume II: The Flag Burning Cases.*" *American Journal of Legal History* 39 (April).

Walker, Samuel. 1995. "Book Review: Robert Justin Goldstein, *Saving 'Old Glory': The History of the Flag Desecration Controversy.*" *American Journal of Legal History* 39 (July).

FOLTZ, CLARA SHORTRIDGE

Babcock, Barbara Allen. 1991. "Clara Shortridge Foltz: Constitution Maker." *Indiana Law Journal* 66.

———. 1993. "A Place in the Palladium: Women's Rights and Jury Service." *Cincinnati Law Review* 61.

———. 1994. "Clara Shortridge Foltz: 'First Woman.'" *Valparaiso University Law Review* 28.

Elwood-Akers, Virginia. 1984. "Clara Shortridge Foltz, California's First Woman Lawyer." *Pacific Historian* 28.

Foltz, Clara Shortridge. 1897. "Public Defenders." *American Law Review* 31.

Polos, Nicolas C. 1980. "San Diego's 'Portia of the Pacific': California's First Woman Lawyer." *Journal of San Diego History* 2.

Schwartz, Mortimer D., Susan L. Brandt, and Patience Milrod. 1976. "Clara Shortridge Foltz: Pioneer in the Law." *Hastings Law Journal* 27.

FOOD AND DRUG ADMINISTRATION

Burkholz, Herbert. 1994. *The FDA Follies.* New York: Basic Books.

"Center for Drug Evaluation and Research." March 14, 1995. FDA Site. World Wide Web.

Clinton, Bill, and Al Gore. 1995. *Reinventing Drug and Medical Device Regulations.* National Performance Review series (April). Washington, D.C.: U.S. Government Printing Office.

Clinton, Bill, and Al Gore. 1995. *Reinventing the Regulation of Drugs Made from Biotechnology.* National Performance Review series (November). Washington, D.C.: U.S. Government Printing Office.

"FDA Mission Statement: Protect Public Health." March 30, 1995. FDA site. World Wide Web.

"Milestones in U.S. Food and Drug Law History." August 1995. FDA site. World Wide Web.

United States Government Manual, 1995–1996. Washington, D.C.: U.S. Government Printing Office.

U.S. Food and Drug Administration. 1995. *FDA Consumer: From Test Tube to Patient: New Drug Development in the United States.* 2d ed. Washington, D.C.: U.S. Food and Drug Administration.

FOOTNOTE 4

Ackerman, Bruce A. 1985. "Beyond Carolene Products." *Harvard Law Review* 98.

Linzer, Peter. 1995. The "Carolene Products Footnote and the Preferred Position of Individual Rights." *Constitutional Commentary* 12.

FORD, GERALD RUDOLPH

Casserly, John J. 1977. *The Ford White House: The Diary of a Speech Writer.* Boulder: Colorado Associated Univ. Press.

Hartmann, Robert T. 1980. *Palace Politics: An Inside Account of the Ford Years.* New York: McGraw-Hill.

FORENSIC ACCOUNTING
Bologna, G. Jack, and Robert J. Lindquist. 1985. *Fraud Auditing and Forensic Accounting.* 2d ed. New York: Wiley.

FORENSIC SCIENCE
Federal Bureau of Investigation. 1994. *Handbook of Forensic Science.* Washington, D.C.: U.S. Government Printing Office.

Hollien, Harry. 1990. *The Acoustics of Crime: The New Science of Forensic Phonetics.* Plenum.

Marriner, Brian. 1991. *On Death's Bloody Trail: Murder and the Art of Forensic Science.* New York: St. Martin's Press.

Valciukas, José A. 1995. *Forensic Neuropsychology: Conceptual Foundations and Clinical Practice.* Haworth.

Weiner, Irving B., and Allen K. Hess. 1987. *Handbook of Forensic Psychology.* New York: Wiley.

FORFEITURE
Aznavoorian, Vartan. 1995. "Using Racketeering Laws to Control Obscenity: *Alexander v. United States* and the Perversion of RICO." *Boston College Law Review* 36.

Campbell, Christopher Zemp. 1995. "Excessive Means: Applying the Eight Amendment to Civil In Rem Forfeitures under *United States v. Chandler.*" *North Carolina Law Review* 73.

Henry, Sarah. 1994. "The Thin Green Line." *California Law* 46 (September 14).

Lieske, Robert. 1995. "Civil Forfeiture Law: Replacing the Common Law with a Common Sense Application of the Excessive Fines Clause of the Eight Amendment." *William Mitchell Law Review* 21.

Nelson, Scott Alexander. 1994. "The Supreme Court Takes a Weapon from the Drug War Arsenal: New Defenses to Civil Drug Forfeiture." *St. Mary's Law Journal* 26.

Zarkowsky, Aaron. 1995. "The RICO Threat to Artistic Freedoms: An Indirect Consequence of the Anti-Pornography Crusade?" *DePaul-LCA Journal of Art and Entertainment Law* 5.

FORGERY
Bozeman, Pat. 1990. *Forged Documents.* New Castle, Del.: Oak Knoll Books.

Perez, Jacob. 1992. *Forgery and Fraud-Related Offenses in Six States, 1983–1988.* Justice Department. Washington, D.C.: U.S. Government Printing Office.

Rendell, Kenneth W. 1994. *Forging History.* Norman, Okla., and London: Univ. of Oklahoma Press.

Treasury Department. U.S. Secret Service. 1991. *Counterfeiting and Forgery.* Washington, D.C.: U.S. Government Printing Office.

FORTAS, ABE
Stephens, Otis H., Jr., and John M. Scheb II. 1993. *American Constitutional Law.* St. Paul: West.

FOURTEENTH AMENDMENT
Amar, Akhil Reed. 1992. "The Bill of Rights and the Fourteenth Amendment." *Yale Law Journal* 101.

Curtis, Michael Kent. 1993. "The 1859 Crisis over Hinton Helper's Book, *The Impending Crisis: Free Speech, Slavery, and Some Light on the Meaning of the First Section of the Fourteenth Amendment.*" *Chicago-Kent Law Review* 68.

Review of *No State Shall Abridge: The Fourteenth Amendment and the Bill of Rights,* by Michael Kent Curtis. 1988. *Harvard Law Review* 101.

Rierson, Sandra L. "Race and Gender Discrimination: A Historical Case for Equal Treatment under the Fourteenth Amendment." *Duke Journal of Gender Law and Policy* 1.

Stone, Lawrence. 1977. *The Family, Sex, and Marriage in England 1500–1800.* Weidenfeld & Nicolson.

FOURTH AMENDMENT
Cunningham, Clark D. 1988. "A Linguistic Analysis of the Meanings of 'Search' in the Fourth Amendment: A Search for Common Sense." *Iowa Law Review* 73.

LaFave, Wayne and Jerald Israel. 1992. *Criminal Procedure.* 2d ed. St. Paul, Minn.: West/Wadsworth.

Levy, Leonard. 1988. *Original Intent and the Framers' Constitution.* New York: MacMillan.

FRANKFURTER, FELIX
Baker, Leonard. 1984. *Brandeis and Frankfurter: A Dual Biography.* New York: Harper & Row.

Henderson, Lynne M. 1987. "Legality and Empathy." *Michigan Law Review* 85.

Kelso, R. Randall. 1994. "Styles of Constitutional Interpretation and the Four Main Approaches to Constitutional Interpretation in American Legal History." *Valparaiso University Law Review* 29.

FRANKLIN, BENJAMIN
Franklin, Benjamin. 1993. *The Autobiography of Benjamin Franklin.* Edited by Louis P. Masur. New York: St. Martin's Press.

Franklin, Benjamin. 1993. *Benjamin Franklin: Autobiography and Other Writings.* Edited by Ormond Seavoy. New York: Oxford Univ. Press.

Lemay, J. A. Leo. 1993. *Reappraising Benjamin Franklin.* Univ. of Delaware Press.

FREEDOM OF ASSOCIATION
Huget, J. Michael. 1985. "*Roberts v. United States Jaycees:* What Price Freedom of Association?" *Detroit College of Law Review.*

Jameson, Ann H. 1985. "*Roberts v. United States Jaycees:* Discriminatory Membership Policy. . . ." *Catholic University Law Review* 34 (summer).

Moegenburg, Julia A. 1989. "Freedom of Association and the Private Club." *Marquette Law Review* 72, (spring).

FREEDOM OF SPEECH
Haiman, Franklyn S. 1993. *Speech Acts and the First Amendment.* Carbondale, Ill.: Southern Illinois University Press.

Wagman, Robert J. 1991. *The First Amendment Book.* New York: World Almanac.

FREEDOM OF THE PRESS
Wagman, Robert J. 1991. *The First Amendment Book.* New York: World Almanac.

FRIES'S REBELLION

Elsmere, Jane Shaffer. 1979. "The Trials of John Fries." *Pennsylvania Magazine of History and Biography* 103 (October).

Presser, Stephen. 1978. "A Tale of Two Judges. . . ." *Northwestern University Law Review* 73 (March/April).

FRUIT OF THE POISONOUS TREE

McCrackin, Sidney M., 1985. "*New York v. Quarles:* The Public Safety Exception to Miranda." *Tulane Law Review* 59 (March).

FULBRIGHT, JAMES WILLIAM

Halberstam, David. 1972. *The Best and the Brightest.* New York: Random House.

O'Neill, William L. 1971. *Coming Apart: An Informal History of America in the 1960s.* New York: Quadrangle Books.

FULLER, MELVILLE WESTON

Baker, Liva. 1991. *The Justice from Beacon Hill: The Life and Times of Oliver Wendell Holmes.* New York: HarperCollins.

Hall, Kermit L. 1989. *The Magic Mirror.* New York: Oxford Univ. Press.

Review of *The Chief Justiceship of Melville W. Fuller,* by James W. Ely. 1996. *American Journal of Legal History* 40.

Stephens, Otis H., Jr., and John M. Scheb II. 1993. *American Constitutional Law.* St. Paul: West.

FULL FAITH AND CREDIT CLAUSE

Cooke, Edward F. 1995. *A Detailed Analysis of the Constitution.* Lanham, Md.: Littlefield Adams.

Demelis, Linda M. 1994. "Interstate Child Custody and the Parental Kidnapping Prevention Act: The Continuing Search for a National Standard." *Hastings Law Journal* 45.

Olson, Thomas A. 1995. "Rethinking Montana's View of Interstate Custody Disputes." *Montana Lawyer* 20.

FURMAN V. GEORGIA

Stephens, Otis H., Jr., and John M. Scheb II. 1993. *American Constitutional Law.* St. Paul: West.

GAG ORDER

Minnefor, Eileen A. 1995. "Looking for Fair Trials in the Information Age: The Need for More Stringent Gag Orders against Trial Participants." *University of San Francisco Law Review* 30 (fall).

GAG RULE

Miller, William Lee. 1996. *Arguing about Slavery: The Great Battle in the United States Congress.* New York: Knopf.

GAMING

Campion, Kristen M. 1995. "Riverboats: Floating Our Way to a Brighter Fiscal Future?" *Seton Hall Legislative Journal* 19.

Rose, I. Nelson. 1993. "Gambling and the Law—Update 1993." *Hastings Communications and Entertainment Law Journal* 15.

GARLAND, AUGUSTUS HILL

Watkins, Beverly Nettles. 1985. *Augustus Hill Garland, 1832–1899: Arkansas Lawyer to United States Attorney-General.* Auburn Univ.

GARNISHMENT

Lee, Randy. 1994. "Twenty-Five Years after *Goldberg v. Kelly:* Traveling from the Right Spot on the Wrong Road to the Wrong Place." *Capital University Law Review* 23.

IN RE GAULT

Bernard, Thomas J. 1992. *The Cycle of Juvenile Justice.* New York: Oxford Univ. Press.

GAY AND LESBIAN RIGHTS

Eskridge, William N., Jr. 1993. "A History of Same-Sex Marriage." *Virginia Law Review* 79.

Friedman, Lawrence M. 1993. *Crime and Punishment in American History.* New York: Basic Books.

Hall, Kermit L. 1989. *The Magic Mirror.* New York: Oxford Univ. Press.

Stephens, Otis H., Jr., and John M. Scheb II. 1993. *American Constitutional Law.* St. Paul: West.

GENERAL SERVICES ADMINISTRATION

United States Government Manual, 1994–1995. Washington, D.C.: U.S. Government Printing Office.

United States Government Manual, 1995–1996. Washington, D.C.: U.S. Government Printing Office.

GENERAL WELFARE

Rosenthal, Albert J. 1987. "Conditional Federal Spending and the Constitution." *Stanford Law Review* 39.

GENETIC ENGINEERING

Beauchamp, Tom L., and James F. Childress. 1983. *Principles of Biomedical Ethics.* Oxford and New York: Oxford Univ. Press.

Darvall, Leanna. 1993. *Medicine, Law, and Social Change.* Aldershot, England; Brookfield, Wis., U.S.A.; Hong Kong; Singapore; and Sydney: Dartmouth.

Mason, John Kenyon, and R. A. McCall-Smith. 1987. *Butterworths Medico-Legal Encyclopedia.* London: Butterworths.

———. 1994. *Law and Medical Ethics.* London: Butterworths.

Paley, Eric R. 1993. "Rethinking Utility: The Expediency of Granting Patent Protection to Partial CDNA Sequences." *Syracuse Law Review.*

Ratnoff and Smith. 1968. "Human Laboratory Animals: Martyrs for Medicine." *Fordham Law Review* 36.

Smith, George P., II. 1981. *Genetics, Ethics, and the Law.* Gaithersburg, Md.: Associated Faculty Press.

———. 1993. *Bioethics and the Law.* Lanham, Md.; New York; and London: Univ. Press of America.

Williams, R., chmn. Williams Committee. 1976. *Report of the Working Party on the Practice of Genetic Manipulation.* Command No. 6600. London: HMSO.

GENETIC SCREENING

Beauchamp, Tom L., and James F. Childress. 1983. *Principles of Biomedical Ethics.* Oxford and New York: Oxford Univ. Press.

Darvall, Leanna. 1993. *Medicine, Law, and Social Change.* Aldershot, England; Brookfield, Wis., U.S.A.; Hong Kong; Singapore; and Sydney: Dartmouth.

Mason, John Kenyon, and R. A. McCall-Smith. 1987. *Butterworths Medico-Legal Encyclopedia.* London: Butterworths.

_____. 1994. *Law and Medical Ethics.* London: Butterworths.

Reilly, Philip R. 1993. "Public Policy and Legal Issues Raised by Advances in Genetic Screening and Testing." *Suffolk University Law Review* (winter).

Smith, George P., II. 1981. *Genetics, Ethics, and the Law.* Gaithersburg, Md.: Associated Faculty Press.

_____. 1993. *Bioethics and the Law.* Lanham, Md.; New York; and London: Univ. Press of America.

Stever, Pamela S. 1989. "*Haymon v. Wilkerson:* The Wrongful Birth Cause of Action Emerges in the District of Columbia." *Contemporary Health Law and Policy* 51.

Vukowich, William T. 1971. "The Dawning of the Brave New World: Legal, Ethical, and Social Issues of Eugenics. *University of Illinois Law Review.*

Waltz and Thigpen. "Genetic Screening and Counseling: The Legal and Ethical Issues." *Northwest University Law Review* 68.

GENOCIDE

Chrisopoulos, Paul. J. 1995. "Giving Meaning to the Term 'Genocide' As It Applies to U.S. Immigration Policy." *Loyola of Los Angeles International and Comparative Law Journal* 17 (October).

GERRYMANDER

Clarkowski, Andrew J. 1995. "*Shaw v. Reno* and Formal Districting Criteria: A Short History of a Jurisprudence That Failed in Wisconsin." *Wisconsin Law Review.*

Hamilton, Jeffrey G. 1994. "Deeper into the Political Thicket: Racial and Political Gerrymandering and the Supreme Court." *Emory Law Journal* 43.

Harvard Law Review Association. 1995. "Voting Rights and Race-based Districting." *Harvard Law Review* 109.

Lewis, Terrence M. 1996. "Standard of Review under the Fifth Amendment Equal Protection Component: Adarand Expands the Application of Strict Scrutiny." *Duquesne Law Review* 34.

Stockman, Eric J. 1993. "Constitutional Gerrymandering: *Fonfara v. Reapportionment Commission.*" *Connecticut Law Review* 25.

GI BILL

Evans, Philip G., II. 1989. "The New GI Bill: The Trojan Horse of the 1900s?" *Army Law* 17 (October).

U.S. House Veterans' Affairs Committee Subcommittee on Education, Training, Employment, and Housing on the Montgomery GI Bill. 1996. *Federal News Service Congressional Hearing Testimonies: Prepared Statement of Samuel E. Ebbesen, Lieutenant General, Deputy Assistant Secretary of Defense for Military Personnel Policy, before the House Veterans' Affairs Committee Subcommittee on Education, Training, Employment, and Housing on the Montgomery GI Bill.* WL 5509489 (March 7).

GILBERT, CASS

Irish, Sharon. "A Machine That Makes the Land Pay: The West Street Building in New York." *Technology and Culture.*

Bluestone, Daniel M. 1988. "Detroit's City Beautiful and the Problem of Commerce." *Journal of the Society of Architectural Historians.*

Blodgett, Geoffrey. *Cass Gilbert, Architect, Conservatives at Bay.*

Irish, Sharon Lu. "Cass Gilbert's Career in New York, 1899–1905." (Ph.D. diss.).

McGurn, Barrett. 1982. "Slogans to Fit the Occasion." *Supreme Court Historical Society.*

Tunick, Susan, and Jonathan Walters. *The Wonderful World of Terra Cotta.*

Vyzralek, Frank E., and Neil B. Thompson. *Minnesota's State Capitol: The Art and Politics of a Public Building.*

Myers, Rex C. *The Montana Club: Symbol of Elegance.*

Jones, Robert Allan. *Cass Gilbert, Midwestern Architect in New York.*

Jones, Robert A. 1973. "Mr. Woolworth's Tower: The Skyscraper as Popular Icon." *Journal of Popular Culture.*

Cass Gilbert: Minnesota Master Architect. Catalog of an exhibition organized by the Touring Exhibitions Program at the University of Minnesota.

Lord, Margaret P. "Supreme Courthouse." *Connoisseur.*

Gaskie, Margaret F. "The Woolworth Tower." *Architectural Record.*

Murphy, P. 1981. "Minnesota's Architectural Favorite Son." *American Institute of Architects Journal.*

GILPIN, HENRY DILWORTH

Gerdts, William H. 1983. " 'The American "Discourses" ': A Survey of Lectures and Writings on American Art, 1770–1858." *American Journal of Art.*

Gray, Ralph D., ed. 1965. *Washington in 1825: Observations by Henry D. Gilpin.* Delaware Historical Society.

Gray, Ralph D. 1968. "A Tour of Virginia in 1827. Letters of Henry D. Gilpin to his Father." *Virginia Magazine of History and Biography.*

Rimini, Robert V. 1967. *Andrew Jackson and the Bank War.*

Tobias, Clifford I. 1975. *Henry D. Gilpin and Bank War, A Study in Reform Politics.* Cleveland, Ohio: Case Western Reserve Univ.

_____. 1975. "Henry D. Gilpin: Governor in and over the Territory of Michigan." *Michigan History.*

GINGRICH, NEWTON LEROY

Gingrich, Newt, with David Drake and Marianne Gingrich. 1984. *Window of Opportunity.* Tom Doherty Associates.

_____. *To Renew America.* 1995. New York: HarperCollins.

1995–1996 Official Congressional Directory, 104th Congress. 1995. Washington, D.C.: U.S. Government Printing Office.

Wilkins, David. 1991. "Newt Gingrich." In *Newsmakers 1991.* Edited by Louise Mooney. Detroit: Gale Research.

GLANVILL, RANULF

Glanvill, Ranulf. 1996. *Tractatus de legibus et consuetudinibus regni Angliae.* English translation available at http://vi.uh.edu/pages/bob/elhone/glanvill.html; Internet.

GLASS, CARTER

Brostoff, Steven. 1995. "Bank Bill May Limit Comptroller Power." *National Underwriter Property and Casualty—Risk and Benefits Management* (June 12).

"Insurers Back the Right Man, Still Lost Glass-Steagall Fight." 1996. *Best's Review, Life-Health Insurance Edition* (August).

McConnell, Bill. 1996. "Glass-Steagall Repeal, Wider Powers Depend on Push by Congress' Leaders." *American Banker* (October 22).

_____. 1996. "GOP Congressional Victories Seen as Boost for Glass-Steagall Repeal." *American Banker* (November 7).

Palmer, James E., 1938. *Carter Glass: Unreconstructed Rebel.* Roanoke, Va.: Southeastern Press.

GLASS-STEAGALL ACT

Cintron, Ivan. 1995. "Bankers Hope Reform Helps Shatter Glass." *Nashville Business Journal* (September 4).

Class, Edgar. 1995. "The Precarious Position of the Federal Deposit Insurance Corporation after *O'Melveny and Myers v. FDIC.*" *Administrative Law Journal of the American University* (summer).

Eaton, David M. 1995. "The Commercial Banking-related Activities of Investment Banks and Other Nonbanks." *Emory Law Journal* (summer).

Feibelman, Adam. 1996. "The Dukes of Moral Hazard." *Memphis Business Journal* 18 (July 1).

Smoot, James R. 1996. "Financial Institutions Reform in the Wake of Valic." *Creighton Law Review* (February).

Sullivan, Edward D. 1995. "Glass-Steagall Update: Proposals to Modernize the Structure of the Financial Services Industry." *Banking Law Journal* 112 (November–December).

Woeful, Charles J., 1994. *Encyclopedia of Banking and Finance.* 10th ed. Chicago: Dearborn.

GOING CONCERN VALUE

Bernstein, Donald S., and Nancy L. Sanborn. 1993. *The Going Concern in Chapter 11.* New York: Practising Law Institute.

Oswald, Lynda J. 1991. "Goodwill and Going-concern Value: Emerging Factors in the Just Compensation Equation." *Boston College Law Review* 32 (March).

GOLDBERG, ARTHUR JOSEPH

Stephens, Otis H., Jr., and John M. Scheb II. 1993. *American Constitutional Law.* St. Paul: West.

GOLDEN PARACHUTE

"New Powers: FDIC Cuts Down Golden Parachutes." 1995. *The Banking Attorney.* 5:12.

Mogavero, Damian J., and Michael F. Toyne. 1995. "The Impact of Golden Parachutes on Fortune 500 Stock Returns: A Reexamination of the Evidence." *Quarterly Journal of Business and Economics* 34: 4.

GOLDMAN, EMMA

Forster, Margaret. 1985. *Significant Sisters: The Grassroots of Active Feminism 1839–1939.* New York: Knopf.

Goldman, Emma. 1982. *Living My Life.* Salt Lake City: Peregrine Smith Books.

Wexler, Alice. 1984. *Emma Goldman: An Intimate Life.* New York: Pantheon Books.

GOLDWATER, BARRY MORRIS

Goldwater, Barry M. 1979. *With No Apologies.* New York: Morrow.

Goldwater, Barry M., with Jack Casserly. 1988. *Goldwater.* New York: Doubleday.

GOOD SAMARITAN DOCTRINE

Crawley, Annette T. 1993. "Environmental Auditing and the 'Good Samaritan' Doctrine: Implications for Parent Corporations." *Georgia Law Review* 28.

GOVERNMENT NATIONAL MORTGAGE ASSOCIATION

Benson, John D. 1991. "Ending the Turf Wars: Support for a CFTC/SEC Consolidation." *Villanova Law Review* 36.

Hadaway, Beverly L. and Paula C. Murray. 1986. "Mortgage Backed Securities: An Investigation of Legal and Financial Issues." *Journal of Corporation Law* 11.

Malloy, Robin P. 1986. "The Secondary Mortgage Market: A Catalyst for Change in Real Estate Transactions." *Southwestern Law Journal* 39.

GOVERNMENT PRINTING OFFICE

United States Government Manual, 1994–1995. Washington, D.C.: U.S. Government Printing Office.

GRAND JURY

Abramson, Jeffrey. 1994. *We, the Jury: The Jury System and the Ideal of Democracy.* New York: Basic Books.

Brenner, Susan W. 1995. "The Voice of the Community: A Case for Grand Jury Independence." *Virginia Journal of Social Policy and the Law* 3.

Frankel, Marvin E., and Gary P. Naftalis. 1977. *The Grand Jury: An Institution on Trial.* New York: Hill and Wang.

"Hillary Testifies." 1996. *MacLean's* (February 5).

Justice Department. National Institute of Justice. Office of Development, Testing, and Dissemination. 1983. *Grand Jury Reform: A Review of Key Issues.* Washington, D.C.: U.S. Government Printing Office.

Leipold, Andrew D. "Why Grand Juries Do Not (and Cannot) Protect the Accused." *Cornell Law Review* 80.

GRAY, HORACE

Friedman, Leon, and Fred L. Israel, eds. 1995. *The Justices of the United States Supreme Court, 1789–1969: Their Lives and Major Opinions.* New York: Chelsea House.

"Horace Gray." 1992. In *The Supreme Court of the United States: Its Beginnings and Its Justices, 1790–1991.* Washington, D.C.: Commission of the Bicentennial of the U.S. Constitution, Library of Congress.

Library of Congress. 1981. *Memorials of the Justices of the Supreme Court of the United States.* Vol. 2. Littleton, Colo.: Rothman.

GRAY PANTHERS

Hom, Sharon. 1984. "Does Real Estate Syndication Provide a Viable Financing Strategy for Low Income Housing?" *Brooklyn Law Review* (summer).

Hemp, Susan J., and Cheryl Rae Nyberg. 1995. "Elder Law: A Guide to Key Resources." *Elder Law Journal* (spring).

1995. *Gray Panthers Supports Generic Drug Campaign.* Press release, July 19.

McKenzie, Paula, communications director, 1995. Telephone conversation, January 19.

GREENBERG, JACK

Greenberg, Jack. 1994. *Crusaders in the Courts: How a Dedicated Band of Lawyers Fought for the Civil Rights Revolution.* New York: Basic Books.

GREENMAIL

Bayne, David C. 1995. "Traffic in Corporate Control—Greenmail: The Definition of the Reverse Premium-Bribe." *University of Dayton Law Review* 20 (spring).

Crain, Mark E. 1991. "Disgorgement of Greenmail Profits: Examining a New Weapon in State Anti-Takeover Arsenals." *Houston Law Review* 28 (July).

"Securities and Exchanges: Greenmail." 1991. *United States Law Week* 60 (November 5).

GREEN PARTY

Feinstein, Mike, member of Santa Monica City Council and of the Green party. 1996. Telephone interview, November 25.

Green Party Clearinghouse, Blodgett Mills, N.Y. 1996. Telephone interview, November 19.

Leavitt, Jonathan, co-coordinator, Massachusetts Green party, Cambridge, Mass. Telephone interview, November 6 and 7.

Schinella, Tony, Massachusetts Green party, Cambridge, Mass. 1996. Telephone interview, November 19.

GREGORY, THOMAS WATT

Anders, Ivan. 1989. "Thomas Watt Gregory and the Survival of His Progressive Faith." *Southwestern Historical Quarterly* 93.

Gregory, Thomas Watt. Papers. Southwest Collection. Texas Tech University.

GRIER, ROBERT COOPER

Hall, Kermit L. 1989. *The Magic Mirror.* New York: Oxford Univ. Press.

Stephens, Otis H., Jr., and John M. Scheb II. 1993. *American Constitutional Law.* St. Paul: West.

GRIGGS, JOHN WILLIAM

Kramer, Irwin R. 1990. "The Impoundment Control Act of 1974: An Unconstitutional Solution to a Constitutional Problem." *University of Missouri–Kansas City Law Review* 58 (winter).

Raymond, John M., and Barbara J. Frischholtz. 1982. "Lawyers Who Established International Law in the United States, 1776–1914." *American Journal of International Law* 76 (October).

GROESBECK, WILLIAM

Bowers, Claude G. 1929. *The Tragic Era.* New York: Blue Ribbon Books.

Castel, Albert. 1980. *The Presidency of Andrew Johnson.* Lawrence, Kan.: Regents Press of Kansas.

Dewitt, David M. 1903. *The Impeachment and Trial of Andrew Johnson.* New York: Macmillan.

Milton, George F. 1930. *The Age of Hate: Andrew Johnson and the Radicals.* New York: Coward-McCann.

Stryker, Lloyd P. 1936. *Andrew Johnson: A Study in Courage.* New York: Macmillan.

GROUP LEGAL SERVICES

Costich, Julia Field. 1993–94. "Joint State-Federal Regulation of Lawyers: The Case of Group Legal Services under ERISA." *Kentucky Law Journal* (winter).

Schwartz, Alec M. 1989. "Lawyer's Guide to Prepaid Legal Services." *Legal Economics* July/August.

GUARDIAN AD LITEM

Goldenberg, Renee, and Nancy Palmer. 1995. "Guardian Ad Litem Programs: Where They Have Gone and Where They Are Going." *Florida Bar Journal* 1994 (December).

Lorenson, Rick. 1994. "Court Defines Role of Guardian Ad Litem in Abuse and Neglect Cases." *West Virginia Lawyer* (November).

Prescott, Dana. 1995. "Family Law Guardian Ad Litem: Defenses to Tort Claims." *Fairshare* (January).

Wright, Charles Alan, Arthur R. Miller, and Mary Kay Kane. 1990. *Federal Practice and Procedure: Federal Rules of Civil Procedure.* St. Paul: West.

GUEST STATUTES

Appendix E: Letter from Friedrich K. Juenger to Harry C. Sigman, Esq., September 16, 1994. 1995. *Vanderbilt Journal of Transnational Law* (May).

GUN CONTROL

American Civil Liberties Union. 1991. *ACLU Answers: Gun Control.* ACLU Dept. of Public Education.

Cook, Philip J., Stephanie Molliconi, and Thomas B. Cole. 1995. "Regulating Gun Markets." *Journal of Criminal Law and Criminology* 86.

Cozzolino, Marc Christopher. 1992. "Gun Control: The Brady Handgun Violence Prevention Act." *Seton Hall Legislative Journal* 16.

Dolan, Edward F., and Margaret M. Scariano. 1994. *Guns in the United States.* New York: Watts.

Dunlap, Colonel Charles J., Jr. 1995. "Revolt of the Masses: Armed Civilians and the Insurrectionary Theory of the Second Amendment." *Tennessee Law Review* 62.

Gottfried, Ted. 1993. *Gun Control: Public Safety and the Right to Bear Arms.* Millbrook Press.

Hook, Donald D. 1993. *Gun Control: The Continuing Debate.* Second Amendment Foundation.

LaPierre, Wayne. 1995. Address to the Annual Meeting of National Rifle Organization, May 20, 1995.

National Public Radio. November 19, 1993. "Morning Edition." Transcript via National Rifle Association site. World Wide Web.

National Rifle Association. 1994. *Anti-gun "Study" on Women and Guns: All Sputter, No Science.* Press release, July 19.

Udulutch, Mark. 1989. "The Constitutional Implication of Gun Control and Several Realistic Gun Control Proposals." *American Journal of Criminal Law* 17.

HABEAS CORPUS

Bright, Steven B. 1996. "Does the Bill of Rights Apply Here Anymore?" *Champion* (November).

Harrington, James C. and Anne More Burnham. 1995. "Texas's New Habeas Corpus Procedure for Death-Row Inmates: Kafkaesque—and Probably Unconstitutional." *St. Mary's Law Journal* 27.

Jones, Andrew A. 1994. "*Keeney v. Tamayo-Reyes* and Federal Habeas Corpus Evidentiary Hearings: Has the Court Deliberately Bypassed Section 2254(D)?" *Wisconsin Law Review.*

Morse, Charles R. 1993."Habeas Corpus and 'Actual Innocence': *Herrera v. Collins*, 113 S. Ct. 853 (1993)." *Harvard Journal of Law and Public Policy* 16.

HAMER, FANNIE LOU TOWNSEND

Colman, Penny. 1993. *Fannie Lou Hamer and the Fight for the Vote.* Conn.: Millbrook Press.

Mills, Kay. 1993. *This Little Light of Mine.* New York: Penguin Press.

Rubel, David. 1990. *Fannie Lou Hamer: From Sharecropping to Politics.* N.J.: Silver Burdett Press.

HAMILTON, ALEXANDER

Alexander Hamilton: To Provide for the Common Defense. CMH Pub 71-16. Washington, D.C.: U.S. Government Printing Office.

Christman, Margaret C. S. 1992. *The Spirit of Party: Hamilton and Jefferson at Odds.* Washington, D.C.: National Portrait Gallery.

Cooke, Jacob Ernest. 1982. *Alexander Hamilton.* New York: Scribner.

Emery, Noemie. 1982. *Alexander Hamilton, An Intimate Portrait.* New York: Punam.

Epstein, David F. 1984. *The Political Theory of the Federalist.* Chicago: Univ. of Chicago Press.

Flaumenhaft, Harvey. 1992. *The Effective Republic, Administration and Constitution in the Thought of Alexander Hamilton.* Durham, N.C.: Duke Univ. Press.

Hendrickson, Robert A. 1981. *The Rise and Fall of Alexander Hamilton.* New York: Van Nostrand Reinhold.

HAND, BILLINGS LEARNED

Griffith, Kathryn P. 1983. *Judge Learned Hand and the Role of the Federal Judiciary.* Norman, Okla.: Univ. of Oklahoma Press.

Gunther, Gerald. 1994. *Learned Hand: The Man and the Judge.* New York: Knopf.

Schick, Marvin. 1970. *Learned Hand's Court.* Baltimore: Johns Hopkins Press.

HARDING, WARREN GAMALIEL

Watkins, T. H. 1990. *Righteous Pilgrim: The Life and Times of Harold Ickes, 1874–1952.* New York: Holt.

HARLAN, JOHN MARSHALL

Hall, Kermit L. 1989. *The Magic Mirror.* New York: Oxford Univ. Press.

Stephens, Otis H., Jr., and John M. Scheb II. 1993. *American Constitutional Law.* St. Paul: West.

HARLAN, JOHN MARSHALL II

Hall, Kermit L. 1989. *The Magic Mirror.* New York: Oxford Univ. Press.

Stephens, Otis H., Jr., and John M. Scheb II. 1993. *American Constitutional Law.* St. Paul: West.

HARMLESS ERROR

Kimble, Raymond A. 1995. "Casenote: Harmless Error." *Seton Hall Constitutional Law Journal* (spring).

Mitchell, Gregory. 1994. "Against 'Overwhelming' Appellate Activism: Constraining Harmless Error Review." *California Law Review* (October).

HARMON, JUDSON

Burke, James L. 1973. "Judson Harmon: The Dilemma of a Constructive Conservative." *Cincinnati Historical Society Bulletin* 31.

Cohen, Jonathan E. "International Law and the Water Politics of the Euphrates." 1991. *New York University of International Law and Politics* (fall).

Harmon, Judson. Papers. Cincinnati Historical Society.

HARRISON, BENJAMIN

Socolofsky, Homer E., and Allan B. Spetter. 1987. *The Presidency of Benjamin Harrison.* Lawrence, Kan.: Univ. Press of Kansas.

HARRISON, ROBERT HANSON

Degregorio, William A. 1984. *The Complete Book of U.S. Presidents.* New York: Dembner Books.

Elliott, Stephen P., ed. 1986. *A Reference Guide to the United States Supreme Court.* New York: Facts on File.

Witt, Elder, ed. 1990. *Guide to the U.S. Supreme Court.* 2d ed. Washington D.C.: Congressional Quarterly.

HARRISON, WILLIAM HENRY

DeGregorio, William A. 1984. *The Complete Book of U.S. Presidents.* New York: Dembner Books.

HASTIE, WILLIAM HENRY

Cohen, Mark S. 1986. Review of *William Hastie: Grace under Pressure*, by Gilbert Ware. *Michigan Law Review* 84 (February–April).

Tushnet, Mark V. 1985. "Being First." Review of *William Hastie: Grace under Pressure*, by Gilbert Ware. *Stanford Law Review* 37 (April).

Ware, Gilbert. 1984. *William Hastie: Grace under Pressure.* New York: Oxford Univ. Press.

HATCH ACT

Bridges, Michael. 1993. "Release the Gags: The Hatch Act and Current Legislative Reform." *Capital University Law Review* (winter).

Feinstein, Andrew A., and Douglas K. Nelson. 1988. "Hatch Act Reform." *Federal Bar News and Journal* (July/August).

Polley, James D. 1994. "Hatch Act Reform Amendments of 1993." *Prosecutor* (September/October).

TABLE OF
CASES CITED

435

INDEX

INDEX

BY SUBJECT

References that include photos or exhibits are printed in italic type.